PLATO'S CRETAN CITY

A HISTORICAL INTERPRETATION
OF THE *LAWS*

PLATO'S CRETAN CITY

A Historical Interpretation
of the LAWS

❧❧

BY GLENN R. MORROW

PRINCETON, NEW JERSEY

PRINCETON UNIVERSITY PRESS

1960

❖

Publication of this book has been aided
by the Ford Foundation program
to support publication, through university presses,
of works in the humanities
and social sciences

❖

The frontispiece is a reproduction
of an unrestored Roman copy (the best of sixteen copies extant)
of a fourth-century portrait bust of Plato,
in all probability the one made by the sculptor Silanion
and erected in the Academy by "Mithridates the Persian"
(Diog. III, 25).
It is reproduced here, by generous permission of the author,
from Robert Boehringer, *Platon: Bildnisse und Nachweise,*
Breslau, Verlag Ferdinand Hirt, 1935, Tafel 78/XVI.
The original is privately owned.

❖

Printed in the United States of America
by Princeton University Press, Princeton, New Jersey

TO GEORGE HOLLAND SABINE

ἡγεμόσυνα

PREFACE

No work of Plato's is more intimately connected with its time and with the world in which it was written than the *Laws*. The other dialogues deal with themes magnificently independent of time and place, and Plato's treatment of them has been recognized as important wherever human beings have thought about the problems of knowledge, or conduct, or human destiny. But the *Laws* is concerned with the portrayal of a fourth-century Greek city—a city that existed, it is true, only in Plato's imagination, but one whose establishment he could well imagine as taking place in his day. The materials of which it is composed are the political and social institutions characteristic of a small but talented people living more than two thousand years ago in the eastern Mediterranean; and it is pervaded throughout by the concepts and incentives that guided their actions and gave meaning to their lives. With the passing away of this people for whom it was intended, and the substitution of other horizons for those within which they lived, the *Laws* has tended to become a closed book, formidable in its contents, and at first sight offering little reward for the effort involved in mastering them.

But the interpreter of Plato cannot afford to leave the *Laws* out of account. There are many aspects of Plato's thought, to be sure, that may well be understood without it; but we cannot really understand Plato the philosopher without recognizing the central position he assigned to the guidance of life and the molding of the institutions in which life is lived; political philosophy was for him not an appendage, but the crown and goal of philosophic thought. Nor can we be content to rely upon the *Republic* alone for understanding his political philosophy. The very bulk of the *Laws* is evidence of the importance Plato himself attached to this later statement of his political aims. Whether it is a repudiation of his earlier principles, or a development and exemplification of them, can be determined only after a careful analysis of the later work. Compared with the *Republic*, the *Laws* has the special value of presenting its principles not in the abstract, but in their concrete reality, as Plato imagined they might be embodied in an actual Greek city.

But these details of constitution making and legislation cannot themselves be rightly understood apart from their setting, the life of fourth-century Greece from which they are drawn or adapted. The significance of some casual phrase, some detail of election procedure, for example, or some prescription regarding sacrifices and dances, can escape us if we do not know—as Plato's readers did—the practices to which he is referring or which he is modifying. Still less can we grasp the larger features of his construction without knowing the common institutions of the Greek city-state and the motives that actuated the citizen—a knowledge that Plato takes for granted. Unfortunately even the best-informed reader of today is unable to do more than approach the understanding that Plato could assume without question in his readers. This means that the *Laws* will always remain in some respects obscure to us, just as many passages in Thucydides or Herodotus defy understanding; but no Platonist should rest content until he has diminished the obscurity as much as he can. And anyone who attempts to do so will be rewarded by discovering that much in the *Laws* which has hitherto been condemned as confused, or contradictory to something Plato has said elsewhere, turns out upon examination in its historical context to be lucid and in order.

This book, then, attempts to set forth in some detail the main institutions of the state described in Plato's *Laws*, and to interpret them by comparing or contrasting them with the historical laws and social institutions of Plato's Greece, and in the light of the concepts and traditions current in his day. Part One examines the nature and extent of the major historical influences upon Plato's design, following the clue provided by the dramatic structure of the dialogue; in Part Three I venture an interpretation of his political principles in terms of the concrete legislation that embodies them; and Part Two provides the confirmation of my interpretation of the influences and the basis for my interpretation of the principles.

It was my former teacher and lifelong friend, George Holland Sabine, who first suggested to me, more than thirty years ago, the value of such a comparison of Plato's *Laws* and the historical institutions with which Plato and his readers were familiar; and the inquiry proved to be so fascinating that it has been the center of my scholarly interests and publications during almost all the intervening years. This book is therefore fittingly, and affectionately, dedicated to him; though it must be added that he would probably, nay certainly, dissent strongly from some of my interpretations. He cannot, therefore, be held responsible for anything here expounded; but only for the ideal of sober and dispassionate inquiry which has guided me, and to which I hope I have been faithful.

In a study that ranges as widely as this over almost all aspects of Greek life I cannot hope to have avoided errors. But the mistakes of fact or emphasis that I have unwittingly made can be—and I hope will be—corrected. It will be gratifying if this effort at synthesis acts as a challenge to others to set the picture right where my hand has gone astray.

My indebtedness is great, as my footnotes show, to the many scholars before me who have dealt with portions of this task, and without whose individual labors this undertaking would have been impossible. I acknowledge also the help of the many friends who have read parts of this work in manuscript and have given me the benefit of their advice—my colleagues at the University of Pennsylvania, Lloyd W. Daly, Paul Schrecker, and Francis P. Clarke; A. E. Raubitschek of Princeton University; L. A. Post of Haverford College; and Sir David Ross, Richard Robinson, and A. Andrewes of Oxford University. None of these men can be held responsible for the work as it stands, or for any part of it; but it is certainly less imperfect than it would have been without their counsel, and for their interest, their corrections, and their suggestions I record my sincere gratitude. I am grateful also to my former secretary, Mrs. Richard Parker, for valuable aid during the early stages of this work. But above all I am indebted to my wife, who has been my constant ally and aid from the beginning, in editing, in criticizing, in typing and retyping my numerous drafts, and in keeping a watchful eye on all the other humdrum details involved in a work of this sort.

To the Guggenheim Foundation I express my sincere thanks for the interest shown in this project from its beginning, and for the financial assistance without which it could not have been undertaken nor carried through; and also to the Fulbright Commission, on both sides of the Atlantic, who made it possible for me to spend a year at Oxford among colleagues especially sympathetic toward my study. Finally, I acknowledge with deep appreciation the hospitality and facilities afforded me by the American School of Classical Studies at Athens, where this book was begun, and by Oriel College, of Oxford University, where it was brought to completion.

GLENN R. MORROW

Philadelphia, Pennsylvania
July 1959

ADDITIONAL ACKNOWLEDGMENTS

I acknowledge with thanks the courtesy of Dr. Robert Boehringer in allowing me to use as frontispiece one of the reproductions published in his *Platon: Bildnisse und Nachweise*, Breslau, 1935; and the permission of the University of Illinois Press to reprint in Chapter IV several pages of my earlier monograph on *Plato's Law of Slavery*. I am indebted also to James L. Celarier, who rendered valuable help in checking references and in the preparation of the indices; to the anonymous readers of the Princeton University Press for important suggestions and corrections contained in their reports; to the officers and staff of the Press for their work in designing and producing this book; and to Miss Miriam Brokaw, in particular, for her warm interest, her sage advice, and her competent superintendence of the progress of the work through the press.

CONTENTS

CONTENTS

ANALYTICAL TABLE OF CONTENTS

Distinction between magisterial and court proceedings, 241.

Justice Before the Magistrates. Judicial powers of the minor officers, 242. Collegial action assumed with, however, some departures in other respects from Attic law, 244. Plato's remedy for magisterial injustice a civil suit against the magistrate, 246; this a novel provision, but with analogies and prototypes in Greek law, 247. The judicial powers of the euthynoi, 248; and of the guardians, 249. All magistrates responsible without exception, 250.

The Courts. The supremacy of the popular courts in Athenian justice, 251. Plato's criticism, 253; yet acceptance of them as expressing one of the prerogatives of citizenship, 254. His system a mixture of popular and select courts, 255. The courts of first instance: neighbors and arbitrators, 256. The courts of second instance: tribal courts, analogous to the Athenian popular courts, 257. The court of third instance: the court of select judges, 261. The court of the demos, 264; its analogy with the Athenian ecclesia, 265. The court for capital offenses, 267; its uncertain relation to the court of the demos, 269. Military and family courts, 270. General estimate of Plato's system of courts, 271.

Procedure. Private prosecutors the chief agency for bringing offenders to account, 274; but the distinction between private and public suits clearly marked, 276. The filing of suits, 279. The preliminary examination by the magistrate, 279. Trial procedure: (a) the presiding magistrate to have greater control over proceedings, 280; (b) an inquisitorial examination of charges and evidence to be made at some stage of every case, 281; (c) the party oath, the challenge to the oath, and the challenge to the torture prohibited, 283. Witnesses, 285; the suit for false testimony, 286. Open voting, 288. Discretion of judges in fixing penalties, 289. A judge's decision to be rendered under oath, 290. The responsibility of the state in the execution of judgments, 291. Devices for discouraging excessive litigation, 292. General estimate of Plato's procedural law, 295.

The following abbreviations have been used in the footnotes, and occasionally in the text, for authors and works frequently cited.

AJP. *American Journal of Philology.*

Apelt. Otto Apelt, *Platons Gesetze.* 2 vols. Leipzig, 1916.

Barker. Ernest Barker, *Greek Political Theory: Plato and his Predecessors.* London, 1918.

Bonner and Smith. Robert J. Bonner and Gertrude Smith, *The Administration of Justice from Homer to Aristotle.* 2 vols. University of Chicago Press, 1930, 1938.

Burnet. John Burnet, *Platonis Opera.* Oxford, 1901-1906.

Bury. R. G. Bury, *Plato: Laws.* Loeb Classical Library. 2 vols. London and Cambridge (Mass.), 1942.

Busolt-Swoboda. Georg Busolt, *Griechische Staatskunde*, Pt. I, Munich, 1920; Pt. II edited by Heinrich Swoboda, Munich, 1926.

Cassarà. Antonino Cassarà, *Platone: Le Legge.* Padua, 1947.

CQ. *Classical Quarterly.*

Des Places. Edouard des Places, *Platon: Les Lois,* Bks. I-VI. Vol. XI of the Budé edition of Plato, Paris, 1951.

Diels-Kranz. Hermann Diels, *Die Fragmente der Vorsokratiker.* 6th edn. by Walther Kranz. 3 vols. Berlin, 1951-1952.

Diès. Auguste Diès, *Platon: Les Lois*, Bks. VII-XII. Vol. XII of the Budé edition of Plato. Paris, 1956.

DS. Charles Daremberg and E. Saglio, *Dictionnaire des antiquités grecques et romaines.* 10 vols. Paris, 1877-1919.

England. E. B. England, *The Laws of Plato.* 2 vols. Manchester University Press, 1921.

FGH. Felix Jacoby, *Die Fragmente der Griechischen Historiker*, Berlin and Leiden, 1923-1958.

FHG. Karl and Theodor Müller, *Fragmenta Historicorum Graecorum.* 4 vols. Paris, 1841-1851.

Gernet. Louis Gernet, "Les *Lois* et le droit positif," in the Introduction to Vol. XI of the Budé edition of Plato. Paris, 1951.

Gilbert. Gustav Gilbert, *Handbuch der Griechischen Staatsalterthümer.* Vol. I, 2nd edn., Leipzig, 1893; Vol. II, Leipzig, 1885.

Hignett. C. Hignett, *A History of the Athenian Constitution to the End of the Fifth Century B. C.* Oxford, 1952.

IG. *Inscriptiones Graecae.*

JHS. *Journal of Hellenic Studies.*

Jowett. Benjamin Jowett, *The Dialogues of Plato.* 3rd edn. 5 vols. Oxford, 1892.

Lipsius. Justus Hermann Lipsius, *Das Attische Recht und Rechtsver-fahren.* Leipzig, 1915.

LSJ. Liddell and Scott, *Greek-English Lexicon.* New edn. by H. S. Jones, Oxford, 1925-1940.

Marrou. Henri-Irénée Marrou, *Histoire de l'éducation dans l'antiquité,* 2nd. edn. Paris, 1950.

Nilsson. Martin P. Nilsson, *Geschichte der Griechischen Religion.* 2 vols. Munich, 1941, 1950.

PR. *Philosophical Review.*

RE. Pauly-Wissowa-Kroll, *Realencyclopädie der Classischen Altertums-wissenschaft.*

REG. *Revue des Etudes Grecques.*

Reverdin. O. Reverdin, *La Religion de la cité platonicienne.* Paris, 1945.

Ritter. Constantin Ritter, *Platons Gesetze: Darstellung des Inhalts und Kommentar.* 2 vols. Leipzig, 1896.

Robin. Léon Robin, *Platon: Oeuvres Complètes.* 2 vols. Paris, 1950.

Stallbaum. Gottfried Stallbaum, *Platonis Leges et Epinomis.* 3 vols. Gotha, 1859-1860.

Stengel. Paul Stengel, *Die Griechischen Kultusaltertümer.* 8th edn. Munich, 1920.

Syll. W. Dittenberger, *Sylloge Inscriptionum Graecarum.* 3rd edn. 4 vols. Leipzig, 1915-1923.

TAPA. *Transactions of the American Philological Association.*

Taylor. A. E. Taylor, *The Laws of Plato,* London, 1934.

Tod. Marcus Tod, *A Selection of Greek Historical Inscriptions.* Vol. I, 2nd edn. Oxford, 1946; Vol. II, 1948.

Wilamowitz. Ulrich von Wilamowitz-Moellendorff.

Abbreviations of the names of ancient authors will in most cases be clear, but the following should perhaps be mentioned to avoid confusion.

Aesch. Aeschines or Aeschylus, the former when followed by a Roman numeral, the latter when followed by the title of a play.

Diod. Diodorus Siculus.

Diog. Diogenes Laertius.

Aristotle is cited by the pages and lines of Bekker's (the Berlin) edition, except for the *Constitution of Athens* and the Fragments, and Plato by the pages of Stephanus' and the line numbers of Burnet's edition.

PLATO'S CRETAN CITY

A HISTORICAL INTERPRETATION
OF THE *LAWS*

INTRODUCTION

THE SCENE is Crete, and the characters in the dialogue are three old men—Cleinias, a Cretan; Megillus, a Spartan; and an unnamed Athenian—who have started out from Cnossos on a pilgrimage to the cave and sanctuary of Zeus. The distance is considerable, and the Athenian suggests that it would be a pleasant pastime during their tedious walk to discourse about government and laws (περὶ πολιτείας τε καὶ νόμων), and the others readily agree. The conversation begins with an inquiry by the Athenian regarding the purpose of the common meals and the gymnastic and military exercises prescribed by the Spartan and Cretan legislators; and from there it proceeds to more general considerations concerning the purpose of law, the importance of education, and the secret of stability in a constitution. The conclusions they reach turn out to be peculiarly timely; for at this point (the end of the third book) Cleinias reveals that he is a member of a commission charged with making laws for a new Cretan city that is to be established under the sponsorship of Cnossos and other cities in the island. He therefore urges that they pursue their inquiry by imagining themselves as legislating for a city of which they are the founders; in this way their theoretical interest will be satisfied, and he will perhaps be able to use their results in the colony with which he is concerned. The remainder of the *Laws* is an exposition, in sometimes elaborate detail, of the institutions and laws that it would be appropriate to establish in this new city.

The establishment of colonies was a habit of long standing among the Greeks, less evident in Plato's century than it had been in earlier days, but still regarded as the best way to deal with a surplus of population (707e)[1] or with a discordant faction in a city (708bc). The great age of colonization during which the Greeks had spread themselves and their culture all over the Mediterranean area, from the northern shore of the Black Sea to the western coast of Spain, was a thing of the past; but the tradition was kept alive by the Athenian cleruchies and other more pretentious establishments in the fifth and fourth centuries, and another era of colonization was to begin soon after Plato's time with the conquests of Alexander.[2] Such new cities

---

[1] References unaccompanied by the name of a dialogue are to the *Laws*.
[2] H. Bengtson, *Griechische Geschichte*, Munich, 1940, 338.

always started their political life with a set of laws especially designed for them, and a competent legislator was often called upon to advise the founder, or the sponsoring city, in the task of legislation. The great Protagoras was asked to draw up the laws for Pericles' ambitious colony of Thurii in southern Italy; and Plato himself, according to one tradition, was invited to legislate for the new city of Megalopolis in Arcadia set up after the defeat of Sparta at Leuctra.[3] We see, therefore, that the Athenian Stranger is in a historically familiar situation, and the conversation he carries on with his companions is but an idealized version of the discussions that must have taken place on countless occasions among persons responsible for establishing a new colony.

Furthermore, it was a situation that might confront Plato or a member of the Academy at any time. Plato's deep and lifelong interest in politics, in the broadest sense of the term, is evident from the large place that the problems of political and social philosophy occupy in his writings. His theories of education, of law, and of social justice are inquiries carried on not merely for their speculative interest, but for the purpose of finding solutions to the problems of the statesman and the educator. It may well be affirmed, when we view Plato's work as a whole, that he was more concerned with practice than with theory.[4] In the autobiographical passage of the *Seventh Epistle* he tells us that in his youth it was his intention to enter public life, a career that seemed the obvious one to a young man of his high connections and great abilities (324b). But he was disillusioned by the excesses of the Thirty, a revolutionary movement for which he had at first had considerable hope, and later by the unjust action of the restored democracy in condemning Socrates on a charge of impiety, "which he of all men least deserved." The disillusionment with contemporary politics increased as he came to know better the men active in public life and saw more clearly the instability of the laws and customs of his own and other cities; and although he did

---

[3] For Protagoras and Thurii see Diog. ix, 50. For Megalopolis see below, Note 11.

[4] "Platon est en effet, contrairement à ce qu'on croit souvent, beaucoup plus préoccupé de pratique que de théorie." Robin, *Platon*, Paris, 1935, 254. Similarly Diès, in the Introduction to the Budé edn. of the *Republic*, v: "Platon n'est venu en fait à la philosophie que par la politique . . . La philosophie ne fut originellement, chez Platon, que de l'action entravée." But we must not suppose that for Plato theory was a substitute for action. Indeed the scientific statesman, he says in *Polit.* 260ab, cannot be content with theoretical principles alone, but must supplement them with directions for action—the ἐπιτακτικὸν μέρος of the statesman's science. Cf. also *Phil.* 62ab.

not give up the hope of taking an active part in affairs, he devoted his chief attention to considering how a reform of lasting character could be brought about. He soon saw, he says, that it would be impossible to accomplish anything unless one had like-minded fellow citizens and faithful comrades upon whom he could rely; and eventually he came to the conclusion that there was no hope for improvement until men "of truly philosophic nature" came into office, or alternatively, until the men holding political power became philosophers.

From these statements we must infer that one purpose of the Academy which Plato founded and directed during these years, perhaps at times its chief purpose in his eyes, was the training of statesmen, or legislative advisers, imbued with the insights of philosophy. How did the Academy prepare its members for the practical work of legislation and constitution making? By the study of mathematics and dialectic, of course, for the statesman must first of all be a philosopher; but also, it seems clear, by the study of Greek law and politics. It must not be forgotten that in the *Republic* the education of the philosopher-guardians includes more than the abstract sciences. The fifteen years of mathematics and dialectic are to be followed by fifteen years of service in subordinate administrative posts before the candidate for guardianship is completely trained. The Academy was not a polis and it could not offer its students the advantages of actual experience in office; but it could encourage them to gain a wide knowledge of the history and characters of actual states. This it certainly did, attracting students from all parts of the Greek world, and therefore possessing within its own membership considerable resources for a comparative study of laws and customs. Plato himself had traveled —certainly to the Pythagorean cities in southern Italy, to Sicily, probably to Egypt and Cyrene, perhaps also to Crete, a convenient stopping place on one of these other voyages. Whether he ever visited Sparta we do not know; but he could have learned much about it from reports that were widely current in the fourth century, and from conversations with persons who had been there and seen the famous Lycurgan laws in operation.

However Plato's knowledge of Greek laws and political institutions was acquired, the *Laws* shows clearly that his knowledge was accurate and extensive. He had made a special study of the Spartan constitution, with its anomalous dual "monarchy," its γερουσία or council of elders, and its ephors; and he had a historical conception of the steps by which that constitution had come to be what it was in the fourth century. He seems also to have known a great deal about the constitution and laws of Cretan cities. The traditions about Athens and the reforms of Solon he knew, and of course the Athens of his own lifetime, with its division into tribes and demes, its assembly, council, prytanies, its courts of law, its multitude of officers and the laws they were responsible for enforcing. He knew Athenian law not merely as an intelligent citizen might come to know it through personal experience, but as it would be known by a student bent on attaining systematic and accurate comprehension. The extent and accuracy of his knowledge is apparent, not only from a multitude of casual and passing references whose significance is clear only when we understand the political and legal practices of his time, but also in his own code of laws. Here we find him using not merely the classifications and principles, but also the legal terminology of positive law—such terms and phrases as we find in the inscriptions, or in the orators when they cite the law. Plato's interest extended beyond the cities mentioned, certainly to the Ceians and the Locrians—both of them well-governed peoples, he says (638b)—to the Egyptians and Carthaginians (637d, 674a, 656d, 747c, 819b), to Heraclea Pontica and Thessaly (776cd), to the Scythians, Celts, Iberians and Thracians (637d), to the Syracusans (638b) and Persians (637d, 694a), to the Milesians, Boeotians and Thurians (636b), and probably also to many others to whom he does not refer by name. Rostovtzeff has even declared, with some exaggeration but with essential insight, that Plato's *Laws* is a collection and codification of the whole of Greek law.[5] His interests would certainly establish a norm for the other members of the Academy. Aristotle, the greatest, was himself a master of empirical inquiry in politics; the foundations of this mastery must have been laid, and the impulse to attain it acquired, during his twenty-year residence in the Academy.[6]

[5] *A History of the Ancient World*, Oxford, 1929, I, 337-338. Cf. similar statements by Ludwig Mitteis, *Reichsrecht und Volksrecht in den östlichen Provinzen des römischen Kaiserreichs*, Leipzig, 1891, 237; Bruno Keil, *Griechische Staatsaltertümer*, in Gercke and Norden, *Einleitung in die Altertumswissenschaft*, Leipzig, 1910-1912, III, 382; Wilamowitz, *Staat und Gesellschaft der Griechen*, Leipzig and Berlin, 1910, 207. For a detailed and balanced appraisal, see Gernet cciii-ccvi.

[6] The second book of the *Politics* was probably written when Aristotle was still at the Academy and while Plato was working on the *Laws*; cf. Werner Jaeger, *Aristoteles: Grundlegung einer Geschichte seiner Entwicklung*, Berlin, 1923, 300-301n.

On one occasion that we know of Plato had himself taken a hand in politics, when the death of the elder Dionysius of Syracuse in 367 had brought his young and promising son to the throne. Dion, the uncle of the young tyrant, had become Plato's devoted follower during the latter's earlier visit to Syracuse, and he now saw an opportunity of bringing about a political reform. He persuaded the young tyrant to invite Plato to Syracuse, and himself sent an urgent request that Plato should come and take the young man's education in hand. Plato acceded, but with some reluctance, he tells us, because he feared the young Dionysius was not sufficiently stable in character to make promising material for a philosophical ruler; but his doubts were outweighed by his friendship for Dion, and by his feeling that he should make an effort, at least, when there was an opportunity of putting into effect his ideas of law and government.[7] This mission at first seemed likely to succeed, and Plato may have collaborated with Dionysius on legislation for the resettlement of the Sicilian cities of Phoebia and Tauromenium.[8] But the court at Syracuse was filled with supporters of the tyranny, opposed to reforms of the sort Plato and Dion had in mind. They succeeded in poisoning the young tyrant's mind with suspicions, and within four months Dion was banished. Plato returned shortly afterwards to Athens. But the Sicilian venture did not end here. Some years later Dionysius again sent for Plato, this time with the threat that unless he came to Syracuse all hope of Dion's being recalled would disappear. It was even less possible for Plato to refuse this time than on the earlier occasion; and the result was a second journey to the young tyrant's court (Plato's third journey to Syracuse), from which Plato barely escaped with his life. This history, unhappy though its outcome, shows that Plato's principles were meant to be applied to the actualities of fourth-century politics. Some prominent members of the Academy later took part (though Plato refrained) in Dion's later expedition against Syracuse and were associated with him in

---

In this book Aristotle deals with the institutions of Crete and Sparta, and examines the accounts of various ideal states, including two by Plato.

[7] The *Seventh Epistle* portrays dramatically Plato's difficulty in coming to this decision. See my *Studies in the Platonic Epistles*, University of Illinois Press, 1935, 146ff.

[8] *Ep. III* 316a, 319a; E. Meyer, *Geschichte des Altertums*, Stuttgart, 1902, v, 510. But the authenticity of the *Third Epistle* is not so generally admitted as is that of the *Seventh* and the *Eighth*.

his brief period of power after the overthrow of Dionysius.[9] These later events would only confirm the reputation that the Academy had as a center of political influence.

There are other evidences of the influence of Plato and his Academic colleagues on fourth-century states and statesmen. There is a tradition that Plato was invited by the Cyrenians to legislate for them;[10] and another, which I have referred to above, that he was asked to draw up the laws for the Arcadian city of Megalopolis. Both these invitations Plato declined; but in the second case he seems to have sent Aristonymus to act in his stead.[11] Plutarch names several members of the Academy who were influential as legislators or advisers to statesmen and rulers.[12] Aristonymus was sent to the Arcadians, Menedemus to the Pyrrhaeans; Phormio gave laws to Elis, Eudoxus to the Cnidians, and Aristotle to the Stagirites. Xenocrates was a counsellor to Alexander; and Delius of Ephesus, another Academic, was chosen by the Greeks in Asia to urge upon Alexander the project of an expedition against the Persians. Thrace, he says, was liberated by Pytho and Heraclides, two Academics; they killed the tyrant Cotys, and on their return to Athens were feted as "benefactors" and made citizens.[13] Athenaeus tells us, on the authority of Carystius of Pergamum, that Plato sent Euphraeus of Oreus as adviser to King Perdiccas of Macedon; later Euphraeus seems to have become the champion of the independence of his native city, and was slain when

[9] Among them were Timonides of Leucas, and Eudemus of Cyprus, whose death in the fighting was later commemorated by Aristotle in one of his lost dialogues. Others of less savory memory were Callippus and his brother Philostratus. The former eventually assassinated Dion, ostensibly because he thought that Dion was betraying the principles for which they had fought.

[10] Plut. *Ad Princ. Inerud.* 1; cf. Aelian *Var. Hist.* xii, 30.

[11] Diog. iii, 23; Plut. *Adv. Colot.* 32; Aelian, *Var. Hist.* ii, 42. The founding of Megalopolis took place shortly before Plato's second visit to Syracuse. It attracted great attention throughout the Greek world, and may have suggested to Plato the project fulfilled in the *Laws*. The number of its οἰκισταί was ten (Hiller von Gaertringen in re s.v. Arkadia, 1128), as it is for the colony Cleinias is concerned with (cf. ἐμοί τε καὶ ἄλλοις ἐννέα, 702c).

The *Eleventh Epistle* reflects a tradition that Plato was asked by a certain Leodamus of Thasos to assist in some project of legislation or reform. But the letter is probably spurious, and it is impossible to see what the situation is which it implies. See my *Studies*, 220n.

[12] *Adv. Colot. loc.cit.* Cf. also P.-M. Schuhl, "Platon et l'activité politique de l'Académie," reg lix, 1946, 46-53. Aristotle's *Protrepticus*, addressed to King Themison of Cyprus, is another indication of the far-flung attempts of the Academy to exert influence of a philosophic sort upon kings and statesmen.

[13] Cf. *Academicorum Index Herculaneum* (ed. Mekler) vi, 15ff.; *Pol.* 1311b 20; Dem. xxiii, 119.

the city was reduced by Philip.[14] Hermeias, the tyrant of Atarneus and friend of Aristotle, may have studied in the Academy; and the *Sixth Epistle* is a letter supposedly written by Plato commending to him two students of the Academy who are coming to live near Atarneus. Finally, at Athens there must have been many persons prominent in public life, like the generals Chabrias and Phocion, who were former students of Plato.[15] We know that the orator and statesman Lycurgus, who came into power after Chaeronea, was such a former student;[16] and the legislation of Demetrius of Phalerum, at the end of the century, shows clear traces of Plato's influence, through Aristotle and Theophrastus.[17]

Some of this evidence is of questionable value, but its cumulative effect is to show that the Academy was widely recognized as a place where men were trained in legislation, and from which advisers could be called upon when desired.[18] It is easy therefore to understand why Plato should have devoted the closing years of his life to the composition of such a painstaking piece of hypothetical legislation as the *Laws*. It expresses one of the main interests of his philosophical mind; and it may also have been intended as a kind of model for use by other members of the Academy.[19] Plato had indeed set forth in the *Republic* the principles that should guide a legislator, but they are expounded in very general terms, with little specific legis-

[14] Athen. 506e, 508d. The *Fifth Epistle* purports to be a letter written by Plato or some member of the Academy introducing him to King Perdiccas.

[15] Plutarch's language suggests that these two are merely instances of many: Ἀθηναίων δὲ Χάβριαι στρατηγοὶ καὶ Φωκίωνες ἐξ Ἀκαδημίας ἀνέβαινον. *Adv. Colot. loc.cit*; cf. *Phoc.* 4. On Hermeias see my *Studies*, 190 n. 4.

[16] Diog. III, 46; Olympiodorus on *Gorgias* 515d; Ps. Plut. *Lives of the Ten Orators* VII, 2. There was a tradition that Demosthenes also had been a student with Plato; Cicero, *De Orat.* I, 89; Plut. *Dem.* 5; cf. *Lives of the Ten Orators* VIII, 3, and Olympiodorus, *loc.cit*.

[17] See W. S. Ferguson, *Hellenistic Athens*, London, 1911, 42ff. The role of philosophical advisers to monarchs and statesmen was taken up later by the Stoics in the generation of the Diadochi.

[18] Plato's willingness to respond to such requests is clearly implied in *Ep. VII* 329a. In the reproach he imagines that Dion might address to him if he refused to come to Syracuse, it is the length and difficulty of the voyage that is presented as the cause of his refusal. "If I had lived in Megara," Dion is imagined as saying, "you would have come to help me." On the other hand, Plato has just said (328c) that one reason for his acceding to Dion's request was that he did not like to think of himself as merely a theorist, one who had never laid his hand to a practical task— which suggests that at that date, at least, Plato's ventures into practical statesmanship had been few, if any.

[19] As Taylor suggested (xiv); cf. *Plato: the Man and his Work*, New York, 1927, 464.

lation. In the *Laws*, however, the author descends into the arena of practical difficulties, and we can see why he thought it necessary to do so. For if the ideal, or any worthy imitation of it, is to be realized, it has to be exemplified concretely—among a people living in a specific setting in time and place, possessing such-and-such qualities and traditions. This translation of his political ideal into the terms of fourth-century Greek politics was, as he says, "an old man's sober pastime" (685a, 712b), but it was a form of amusement that he must have thought would give guidance to actual statesmen.

Plato's conception of the legislator's task in bringing his ideal into existence becomes clearer if we consider the analogous work of the demiurge in ordering the cosmos as described in the *Timaeus*. In both cases the craftsman must be attentive not only to the design he wishes to realize, but also to the materials in which it is brought about. It may seem to some persons unworthy of the divine Plato to occupy himself with such things as the laws of inheritance, the registers of property, the procedures of election, the regulation of funeral expenses; or with the organization of songs, dances and athletic contests; or with questions of drainage and water supply. A large part of the *Laws* consists of just such materials—materials on a par, certainly, with the discussion of respiration, the mechanism of vision, or the functioning of the liver and spleen that we find in the *Timaeus*. For the cosmic demiurge such attention to his materials was necessary, if he was to operate on the world of Becoming and remold it in the likeness of the Ideas. Similarly the political demiurge cannot neglect the understanding of his social and human materials if he is going to construct a state that resembles the ideal. Just as the world craftsman in the *Timaeus* has to use the stuff that is available, with its determinate but unorganized and irregularly co-operating powers, so Plato has to use the Greeks of his day, with their traditions of freedom and respect for law, and their fallible human temperaments. They are not always the best adapted to his purpose, but as a good craftsman he selects them carefully and handles them with skill, so as to create a likeness as close as possible to the ideal.

It is in this emphasis upon the concrete that the *Laws* presents the greatest contrast with the *Republic*. In the *Republic* the portrayal of the ideal is independent of geography and history. The state Socrates describes might be in the Peloponnesus, or in one of the islands, in Plato's native Attica, or in heaven only, as Socrates himself once suggests. But the state described in the *Laws* is a Cretan colony, located in the plain of the Messara in the south central portion of the island, about eighty stadia from the sea, possessing a usable harbor or harbors on the coast, with a terrain containing a mixture of forest, mountain, and plain, generally productive, but a little lacking in lumber for shipbuilding (704b-705c). Again it is a colony made up of emigrants from other Cretan cities and from the Peloponnesus under the leadership of Cnossos (702c, 708a) and its future citizens bring with them the Dorian traditions of their native cities. Plato, like a good craftsman, deliberately chooses these physical and cultural features from the rich variety of physical settings and cultural types that the Greece of his day offered. The sea is "a right briny and bitter neighbor," Plato says, quoting Alcman (705a); hence the site he selects is one that will not tempt his state to commercial or naval enterprise. He had an admiration for the Dorian way of life—for its solidity, its simplicity, its orderliness. But the Dorian way was exacting, and most Ionians, though they admired it, would have found it uncomfortable and difficult. So again, as a good craftsman, he selects for his citizens men who have already been habituated to Dorian rhythms in song and dance and in the larger patterns of living. But this material has defects as well as advantages. The Dorians were little acquainted with the higher learning and were inept in theory. Plato's spokesman, the Athenian Stranger, finds his Spartan and Cretan companions unacquainted with the idea of incommensurable magnitudes (819d-820c), and although they are prompt to affirm their belief in the existence of the gods, when it comes to the important proof of this dogma they do not venture into the depths of the argument but, as Plato puts it, listen in safety on the shore (892e).

The state that Plato describes in the *Laws* is therefore not a Utopia. It has a definite location in Greek space and time, with all the disadvantages as well as the advantages that the choice of a specific location involves. To accept the disadvantages is the mark of the demiurge in Plato. If he had started with materials perfectly fitted in every respect for realizing his purposes, instead of the materials actually available in fourth-century Greece, he would have been assuming as already solved precisely the problem to be solved. A part of his purpose as a demiurge is the eventual improvement of these elements with which he starts; but the most he can do at the outset is to select his materials as sagaciously as possible, taking into account not only their now manifest qualities, but also the possibilities that he has reason to think are latent in them. Nor is the state described in the *Laws* an ideal state, in the strict sense of the word. It is what Plato calls an "imitation" of the ideal, in the sense in which any particular thing imitates the Idea whose name it carries. The most that Plato would say of it, I think, is that it was as good an imitation as he thought was possible in fourth-century Greece (739e). But Plato's construction does not preclude the possibility of other constructions, for the ideal can be imitated in many ways and under varying conditions. One of these other constructions might be, under its determinate conditions, the best that a competent demiurge could do (739e, 745e-746c). We hardly need to be reminded that this is the philosophy underlying Aristotle's *Politics*. Aristotle thinks it important to discuss not only what is the best constitution, but also what is best under certain conditions, and finally, how any constitution can be best preserved from corruption.[20] These are alternatives that spring out of the concept of political craftsmanship that he had learned from Plato.[21]

To understand the *Laws*, then, we need to get as full an idea as possible of the historical materials with which Plato worked, the practices and customs current in the Greece of his day. We shall need to understand not only the institutions themselves, of which in some cases we have fairly adequate information, and about which in almost all cases we are steadily learning more from the philologist, the epigraphist, and the archaeologist, but also the ideas about their origin and purpose which were accepted in Plato's day. The conceptions of Plato and his contemporaries may be less accurate as judged by the historian than ours are, but these are the conceptions with which he worked, and it is these that we must try to understand if we would see Plato's building stones as they appeared to him. His craftsmanship consisted in the way in which he selected, placed in new combinations, and otherwise adapted these given materials to his purpose; and it is obvious that we can form no true opinion of his craftsmanship until we know how much in his law is received practice and how much is Platonic invention. Finally, since Plato was

---

[20] *Pol.* 1288b 22ff., 1289b 23ff.

[21] The three preceding paragraphs and some portions of earlier ones have been adapted from an address published in *Proceedings and Addresses of the American Philosophical Association* XXVII, 1954, 1-23.

a philosopher, his craftsmanship was guided by principles; and at the end of our study we shall find it useful to examine these principles, not merely for the light they may throw upon the details of his legislation, but also for the better understanding of these principles themselves. Political principles, like all general principles, can be fully understood only in their concrete applications. The rule of law, the mixed constitution, the rule of philosophy—these are ambiguous formulas until we see what particular institutions of law and government they imply for the man who holds them. It is our good fortune that Plato has given us the means of understanding his principles in this way, and they are means of which in the past we have too little availed ourselves.

PART ONE

THREE HISTORICAL STATES

CHAPTER I

CRETE

THE CHOICE of Crete as the setting of the *Laws* is at first sight surprising. During the closing years of his life Plato had been much occupied with affairs in Sicily, and we know that one of the projects he urged upon the young Dionysius was to re-establish some of the old Greek cities that had been sacked by barbarians during his father's reign and still lay desolate.[1] We should then have expected that Plato would select Sicily as the setting for his imaginary colony, especially since this island in the two preceding centuries had played an important part, sometimes a decisive one, in Greek affairs. Crete, on the other hand, had exerted little influence upon the rest of Greece during this period. Its cities had given almost no help against the Persians. In the Peloponnesian War it stood aloof, its sympathies divided and its effect upon the fortunes of the two leading contestants negligible. It had contributed very little to the development of Greek culture, and seems to have been relatively unaffected by cultural movements elsewhere. In the long roll of philosophers from Thales to Aristotle not a single one (unless, with Diels, we count Epimenides among the philosophers) comes from Crete. There was no Cretan school of sculpture or ceramics or painting or medicine. "We have not much use for foreign poems," says Cleinias in the *Laws*, explaining his countrymen's ignorance of Homer (680c). There were Cretan poets, but they were almost unknown elsewhere and have passed into oblivion. What was there in the island to commend it to Plato's attention as the setting for this dialogue and the site of his imaginary city?

In spite of its lack of political and cultural importance in the classical period, Plato as well as his countrymen had a lively memory of the island's former glories, of the vast power that Minos, the ancient king, once exerted over the Hellenic Sea,[2] and of the many respects in which Crete had contributed to Greek culture in the archaic pe-

[1] *Ep. VII* 332e; cf. 331e. It is possible that the early books of the *Laws* were composed during his stay in Syracuse with the young Dionysius. See L. A. Post, "The Preludes to Plato's *Laws*," TAPA LX, 1929, 5-24.

[2] Thuc. I, 4 and 8; Herod. III, 122; Arist. *Pol.* 1271b 37; *Laws* 706ab; cf. Diod. IV, 60, 3.

riod.[3] The legendary figure of Daedalus—associated with Crete, as well as with Athens and Sicily—expresses the high level of the arts and crafts attributed to Crete in earlier days. It had been one of the early centers of choral music and the dance; Cretic rhythms, Cretan paeans to Apollo, and the armed dances—familiar both at Athens and Sparta, and supposedly introduced in imitation of the dances of the Cretan Curetes—are evidences of the mainland's indebtedness.[4] It was the legendary birthplace of Zeus, and the source of a large part of the myths and practices that formed the lower stratum of Greek religion underlying the worship of the Olympians.[5] From Crete Apollo was believed to have brought to Delphi his rites of purification, later written into the homicide law of Athens and of Greece in general.[6] Of Cretan origin is the story of the "golden age" of Kronos and the associated myth of the Islands of the Blessed;[7] and from Crete also came many of the mystics and wonder-workers, the specialists in purification and prophecy, of the archaic period. Of these the best known was Epimenides of Cnossos, beloved of the Pythagoreans, whose legendary services to Athens are mentioned in the *Laws* (642d; cf. 677d). Whether facts or fancies—and we are now beginning to realize that there is usually a basis of fact beneath the fancies—these stories and beliefs indicate the hold that the great island held on the imagination of the Greeks of historical times.[8]

[3] On the importance of Crete as a center of influence in the archaic period see P. Demargne, *La Crète dédalique*, Paris, 1947.

[4] Plut. *De Mus.* 9-10, 42; Strabo x, iv, 16; cf. Vetter in RE s.v. Thaletas.

[5] Nilsson I, 281ff.; Bengtson, *Gr. Gesch.* 45.

[6] See the Homeric *Hymn to Pythian Apollo*, 388ff. and L. R. Farnell, "Cretan Influence in Greek Religion," in S. Casson, ed. *Essays in Aegean Archaeology*, Oxford, 1927, 26. Apollo himself was said to have been purified by Caramanor of Crete after he had slain the python; Paus. II, xxx, 3; x, vii, 2. On the Cretan origin of certain Delphic rites, see J. Defradas, *Les Thèmes de la propagande delphique*, Paris, 1954, 22, 72ff.: e.g. the tripod, 77ff.; the paean, 81ff.

[7] Nilsson I, 302ff.; Diod. v, 66; cf. Hesiod *Works and Days* 111ff. The cult of Eleusis may be of Cretan origin (W. K. C. Guthrie, *The Greeks and their Gods*, Boston, 1951, 282f.); but for a contrary view see Wilamowitz, *Der Glaube der Hellenen*, Berlin, 1931, I, 99, 124.

[8] It has been plausibly suggested by Frost, "The *Critias* and Minoan Crete," in JHS XXXIII, 1913, 189-206, that in the legend of Atlantis the glories of the ancient Cretan empire of the sea exerted their spell over Plato without his knowing the source of the enchantment. Plato says in the *Timaeus* that Solon got this story from the priests of Egypt and planned to write an epic on the theme. Now it is possible that Plato was stating a fact, not a fiction, and that this uncompleted work was known to him and was the basis of his famous legend. Except for the location of Atlantis beyond the pillars of Hercules, the details in the Atlantis story fit perfectly the

But however hallowed by ancient memories, the Crete that figures in Plato's *Laws* is the Crete of his own day, with its archaic institutions and its famed "lawfulness" (εὐνομία). "The laws of Crete are held in exceptionally high repute among all the Hellenes," says the Athenian in the opening book (631b). This statement is confirmed by what fragments of evidence we have. The proud Spartans of Herodotus' day believed that their own Lycurgan legislation was derived from Crete.[9] Aristotle mentions an attempt to make not only Lycurgus but also Zaleucus and Charondas dependent upon a certain Thaletas of Gortyn;[10] he rejects this tradition on chronological grounds, but agrees with the tribute to Crete that it implies. "The true statesman," he says, "wishes to make his citizens good and obedient to the laws; we have an example of it in the Cretan and Lacedaemonian legislators."[11] Even Solon was alleged by some enthusiasts to have been helped in lawmaking by the Cretan Epimenides[12]—for this strange genius, besides being a specialist in religious law, was credited with having written a poem on the Cretan constitution.[13] These fourth-century traditions indicate what was believed, not necessarily what was true; but the admiration they express for Cretan legislators is amply justified by the inscriptions that have come to light during the past century. The great inscription at Gortyn and a number of other fragments from the same area give us considerable information about a part of the laws of this Cretan city in the fifth and fourth centuries. They show that the Gortynians were no amateurs in legis-

---

geographical position of Crete and the power of Cnossos over the adjacent islands. The story preserved in the Egyptian records would of course be an account from the Egyptian point of view. What the nonseafaring Egyptians of that period would describe as an attack from the far west or from the ends of the world would hardly seem so to the Greeks of Solon's day, to whom Crete was nearer the southern than the western extremity of their world; hence the displacement of the mythical islands beyond the pillars of Hercules. The sudden and complete destruction of the Minoan power, a fact now attested by the archaeologists, and its disappearance henceforth from Egyptian knowledge might well have seemed like a physical catastrophe, the subsidence of the island into the sea, as it is described in the tale told by Solon. See also W. Brandenstein, *Atlantis*, Vienna, 1951, for a similar hypothesis.

[9] Herod. i, 65.

[10] *Pol.* 1274a 25-31. This Thaletas is the melic poet who was reputed to have established the naked-boy dances (γυμνοπαιδίαι) at Sparta. Cf. *Rep.* 452c and Note 4 above.

[11] *Nic. Eth.* 1102a 8-11.

[12] Plut. *Solon* 12. Plutarch's source was probably an ancient one, possibly Theopompus; cf. Diog. i, 109.

[13] Diog. i, 112. See Note 22 below.

lation, but rather the inheritors of a long tradition.[14] And Ehrenberg has found in a recently discovered inscription from Dreros—"probably not later than 600 B.C."—an early source of the polis type of constitution which became a common feature of the Greek states in the classical period.[15]

The high regard that Plato expresses for Crete was no late development in his thinking. In the *Protagoras*, a dialogue written many years before the *Laws*, Socrates professes to believe that the love of knowledge was more ancient and more earnestly cultivated in Crete and in Sparta than in any other part of Greece (342a-343b). There are humor and paradox in this passage, to be sure, but there is also a serious tribute which should not be overlooked, a tribute to the deeper wisdom that the Cretans and Spartans had artfully concealed. Socrates surely recognized this deeper wisdom, for Plato represents him as praising Crete and Lacedaemon on various occasions, and in the *Republic* he cites "the Cretan and Spartan constitution" as an example of the best of the imperfect forms of government.[16]

From this interest in Crete manifested in Plato's dialogues from an early period, it is obvious that Cretan institutions would be an important part of the studies in law and politics carried on in the Academy. We know that Aristotle wrote a *Constitution of the Cretans* which has been lost, except for the fragments preserved by Heraclides.[17] To what part of Aristotle's literary career this work belongs we cannot say, but his interest in the subject must have been acquired during Plato's lifetime. The second book of the *Politics* contains a long account of Crete, with a careful comparison of Cretan and Spartan institutions and a discussion of their historical relationship; and Jaeger has expressed the opinion that the materials used by Aristotle in this portion of the *Politics* were assembled during the period of his residence in the Academy, "when Plato was working on the *Laws* and Spartan and Cretan institutions were a favorite subject of discussion."[18] And to the same period, or a little later, belongs the Platonic *Minos*, which is of Academic origin, if it was not written by

[14] Cf. Guarducci, *Insc. Cret.* IV, Pref. 32: "quorum plurimi [i.e. Gortyniorum tituli] iidemque gravissimi Gortynios in iure exercendo ab antiquis temporibus studiose versatos esse indicant." The attention paid to rules of procedure shows that the law of Gortyn had reached maturity; cf. A. S. Diamond, *Primitive Law*, London and New York, 1935, 340ff.; and Headlam, "The Procedure of the Gortynian Inscription," JHS XIII, 1892-93, 48-69.

[15] CQ XXXVII, 1943, 14-18.

[16] *Crito*, 52e; *Rep.* 544c.

[17] Arist. Fr. 611, 14, Rose.

[18] Jaeger, *Aristoteles*, 300-301 n. 1.

Plato himself—a dialogue in which the character of the legendary Cretan king is defended against the current misrepresentation of him by the Athenian dramatists.

The interest of Plato and the Academy in Cretan institutions is only one phase of what has been called "the discovery of Crete"[19] that took place about the middle of the fourth century. Another contributor to this work of "discovery" was Ephorus, who in the fourth book of his *Histories* gave an account of Crete and its constitution, the "chief points" of which have been preserved by Strabo.[20] There is another more shadowy figure, Dosiades (or Dosiadas), probably a Cretan himself, who wrote a work about Crete at some time during this period.[21] Again Strabo's summary of Ephorus' account shows that someone of a theoretical turn of mind had formulated what he thought was the philosophy underlying the Cretan laws. "The lawgiver," he says, "seems to assume that liberty is a city's greatest good, for this alone makes property belong to those who have acquired it; under slavery everything belongs to the rulers, not the subjects." This is the doctrine put forward by Cleinias, the Cretan participant in Plato's dialogue, in his opening statement about the intent of the Cretan lawgiver: "Nothing else is of any value, neither possessions nor institutions, if a people is not victorious in war, but all the goods of the vanquished fall into the hands of the victors" (626b). It is probably useless to try to determine the identity of this unknown interpreter of Cretan law who is echoed by Cleinias and whose doctrine Plato criticizes (it is evident from reasons given later that it cannot be Ephorus himself); but if one wishes to make the shadowy figure of Dosiades a little less indistinct, there is nothing in the evidence to forbid our ascribing this further bit of substance to him.[22]

---

[19] The phrase is not altogether an apt one, as Henri van Effenterre points out (*La Crète et le monde grec de Platon à Polybe*, Paris, 1948, 84): "La Crète resta trop connue de la Grèce classique pour avoir jamais eu besoin d'être découverte."

[20] Strabo x, iv, 16-22.   [21] FGH 3B, 394-396.

[22] Athenaeus (143a-d) contains a long excerpt from Dosiades describing the Cretan system of contributions to the common meals, and elsewhere (264a) indicates that his account contained something about slaves and perioikoi. Besides Dosiades, Diodorus names as his sources for Cretan history Ephorus (v, 64, 4), Epimenides, Sosicrates, and Laosthenidas (v, 80, 4). If the Sosicrates who wrote the Κρητικά is the same as the author of the Διαδοχαί mentioned in Athen. 422cd, he is clearly too late to be the object of Plato's criticism. Laosthenidas is known only from this reference in Diodorus. The Κρητικά of Epimenides used by Diodorus is now regarded as a later falsification (Kern in RE s.v. Epimenides, 176; and Bethe in *Hermes* xxiv, 1899, 402ff.). Plato may have known a genuine work of Epimenides, but one gets the impression that his controversy in the *Laws* is with someone nearer his own time.

The relation of these various accounts to one another (and to the unknown *Forschungsreisender* postulated by Wilamowitz[23]) has been the subject of much inconclusive speculation. Miss Chrimes thinks that Dosiades is the source (perhaps through Ephorus) of all the detailed information that has come down to us about Cretan social institutions.[24] Wilamowitz takes Ephorus to be the source of Aristotle's information, but Jaeger seems to think the question is still open whether Ephorus was the source of Aristotle or Aristotle of Ephorus.[25] But the truth is, neither supposition fits the facts that we have. A comparison of the chief points of Ephorus' account, as preserved by Strabo, with Aristotle's account in the *Politics* reveals such considerable divergences that it is impossible to conclude that either was dependent entirely upon the other.[26] Both seem to have had access to some common source of material. Shall we follow Miss Chrimes and identify this common source with Dosiades? There is at least another alternative that has never been considered, so far as I know. It is possible that both were relying upon Plato, not necessarily upon the *Laws*, but upon material that he had collected and made avail-

---

[23] *Aristoteles und Athen*, Berlin, 1893, II, 25-26.

[24] K. M. T. Chrimes, *Ancient Sparta*, Manchester University Press, 1949, 234.

[25] Wilamowitz, *op.cit.* I, 305f.; Jaeger, *op.cit.* 301 n. 1.

[26] There are of course many points of agreement. Both mention the fact that the common meals are called φιδίτια by the Spartans but ἀνδρεῖα in Crete, and that the Cretan tables are supported by the public treasury, not by private contributions, as at Sparta. Both allege a similarity in function between the Cretan kosmoi and the Spartan ephors, and both point out that the former are ten in number, whereas the latter are five. Both point out that there are "elders" in both constitutions, elected in one case from previous kosmoi, in the other from former ephors, and note that this body is called the council (βουλή) among the Cretans. Both also believe the Cretan customs to be the older and in many cases the archetype of the Spartan. But Aristotle refers to the perioikoi of Crete and explains why they are not a source of danger as are the Helots at Sparta, a point passed over without mention by Ephorus. Furthermore, Aristotle's account of the powers of the Cretan kosmoi, council, and assembly (not even mentioned by Ephorus) is much fuller and more critical, and culminates in a severe judgment on the irresponsible power of the kosmoi. On the other hand, Ephorus pays much more attention to the education of the young, a subject completely omitted by Aristotle, and describes at length the peculiar Cretan customs of love, again a topic that Aristotle passes over.

Van Effenterre (*op.cit.* 77-78) seems to me to overstate the similarity between Ephorus' and Aristotle's account, but he comes to much the same conclusion as I do. "It looks as if the major outlines of Cretan studies had already been laid down in previous literature, or as if the principal themes for discussion had already become fixed, constituting so many conventional topics to which one would be expected to make at least some reference, more or less forced, in passing. Aristotle and Ephorus are independent of one another only in the sense that it is impossible to trace all the information one of them gives to what is found in the other. But there is no doubt that both made use of previous works."

able in the Academy to others interested in the subject. And indeed there are features of both Ephorus' and Aristotle's accounts that make Plato's influence upon them more than a bare possibility.[27]

On at least one point the dependence of Aristotle and Ephorus, not merely on the Academy, but specifically on Plato's teaching, can be definitely established. Strabo tells us that there was a sharp difference of opinion between Ephorus and "the ancients" regarding the character of Minos. The ancient writers pictured him as a tyrannical and violent collector of tribute, and they constructed tragedies based on the stories of the Minotaur and the labyrinth and the adventures of Theseus and Daedalus.[28] None of these fifth-century tragedies dealing with Minos has been preserved, but their number was considerable, to judge from the titles that have come down to us.[29] The early Attic historians, Pherecydes and Hellanicus, also emphasized, it appears, the role of Minos as an enemy of ancient Athens.[30] But the reputation of Minos underwent a complete change in the fourth century; henceforth he is the great and wise legislator instructed by Zeus, and this is the opinion that Ephorus held, according to Strabo. This is also the view that Plato, and presumably many others,[31] espoused in the fourth century as a result of the new interest in Cretan customs and the belief in their great antiquity. But what is striking in Ephorus' position is that he uses a curious argument identical with one we find in the Platonic writings. Strabo tells us that he quoted Homer's lines

$$\text{ἔνθα τε Μίνως}$$
$$\text{ἐννέωρος βασίλευε Διὸς μεγάλου ὀαριστής.}$$

[27] Plato attaches great importance to the common meals, the first point about which the Athenian Stranger enquires (625c). These are mentioned early in both Aristotle's and Ephorus' accounts and are treated as a fundamental institution. Aristotle is interested in the division of powers among the organs of government, the very point of constitutional theory to which Plato gives special attention in the third book of the *Laws*, and Aristotle's criticism of the Cretan constitution because the "elders" (γέροντες) are irresponsible seems an echo of Plato's repeated warning that no officials should be ἀνυπεύθυνοι. Ephorus, on the other hand, treats other matters that engaged Plato's attention: the gymnastic and military exercises of the youth, the use of the pyrrhic dance and Cretic rhythms, and the customs of boy love.

[28] Strabo x, iv, 8.

[29] Sophocles wrote a *Theseus*, a *Daedalus* and a *Camicii*, which must have dealt with the death of Minos at Camicus in his vain attempt to recapture Daedalus after his flight from Crete (Herod. VII, 170). These works may have constituted a trilogy. Euripides wrote a *Cretans*, and one of the dramas of the politician-poet, Plato's cousin Critias, was entitled *Rhadamanthys*. For these and other titles of lost works, see Poland in RE s.v. Minos, 1891.

[30] For Pherecydes see FGH Pt. I, 3, F148-F150; for Hellanicus Pt. I, 4, F164.

[31] Isocrates, for example (XII, 205).

This appeal to Homer is exactly the defense we find in the pseudo-Platonic *Minos*. The lines quoted are highly obscure. Not only was ὀαριστής an unfamiliar word to the Greeks of the fourth century, but the meaning of ἐννέωρος is ambiguous; and whatever it means, it is uncertain whether it is to be taken with βασίλευε, with Μίνως, or with ὀαριστής. The Socrates in the *Minos* explains that ὀαριστής is to be taken as meaning "associate in discourse" (συνουσιαστὴς ἐν λόγοις), i.e. a pupil; and that ἐννέωρος means "every ninth year." The meaning of the passage, therefore, is that Minos went every ninth year to be tutored of Zeus, the great master of wisdom (319b-e). This is obviously not the only possible interpretation of this passage, nor even the most plausible. It is a good specimen of ingenious Socratic exegesis.[32] For our purpose it is not necessary to decide whether or not the *Minos* is a genuine Platonic dialogue, for the gist of the interpretation is contained in the Athenian's question on the opening page of the *Laws*: "And do you, Cleinias, say, as Homer does, that Minos used to go every ninth year and converse with his father Zeus and that he was guided by his oracles in making laws for your cities?" The agreement of Ephorus with Plato in this strained Homeric exegesis is too much to be a coincidence. If Ephorus' history began to appear, as is now generally believed, about 350 or a little later,[33] the fourth book, in which he dealt with Crete, could hardly have appeared before Plato's death; so that Plato could not have been influenced by it, even if we assume that he was willing to make such an undisguised borrowing from another author. Ephorus' interpretation of Homer points definitely, therefore, to his acquaintance with this picturesque bit of Platonic teaching and possibly also to a reading of the *Laws* and the *Minos*.[34]

The evidence is therefore considerable that the Academy, and Plato in particular, played an important part in the revival of interest in Crete that took place in the fourth century. Plato's discussion of the island in the *Laws* is the earliest of the fourth-century accounts about

[32] *Odyss.* XIX, 178-179. For the four interpretations of this passage in later antiquity see Poland, *loc.cit.* 1902-1903. The effrontery of Socrates is evident elsewhere in this defense of Minos. He cites Hesiod's characterization of Minos as the "kingliest of kings," and *Odyss.* XI, 569, where Minos, not Rhadamanthys, is said to wield the scepter over the dead. But he refrains from mentioning the Μίνως ὀλοόφρονος of *Odyss.* XI, 322—a distinctly unflattering epithet, in spite of the attempts in ancient times to interpret it favorably (see Poland *loc.cit.* 1891).

[33] FGH 2C, 25.

[34] On the *Minos* see Excursus A.

which we know anything. At the very least it is contemporary with Aristotle's account in the *Politics*, and it is certainly earlier than Ephorus' fourth book. Whether or not Plato was preceded by Dosiades or some completely unknown traveler or writer, his influence seems to have been paramount in molding the later tradition. With the *Laws* he made himself the coryphaeus of the pro-Cretan group, and is always quoted by later writers who speak of the alleged merits of Cretan laws.[35]

But how much of Plato's admiration for the Crete of his day was based on accurate knowledge, and how much was the result of imagination working upon fragments of information about a mysterious and legendary country? Among the numerous traditions regarding Plato's travels there is none that reports a visit to Crete. He is said to have gone to Cyrene and Egypt during his *Wanderjahre* after the death of Socrates, and if this is true he might well have stopped at Crete *en route,* as Ritter supposes.[36] He visited southern Italy and Syracuse about 387 and later in 367 and 361. Since the sea route from Athens to Sicily led around the Peloponnesus it is possible that he stopped at Crete on one or more of these passages. But we have no evidence that he did so, and until recently it has been assumed that he had no firsthand knowledge of Crete; and furthermore that because of the relative isolation of the island in classical times he could have had very little accurate knowledge of it at second hand. This view was stated with great vigor by Wilamowitz,[37] but van Effenterre has re-examined the evidence and come to a different conclusion.

In the first place, it is certainly not correct to assume that Plato could have known little about the island if he had not visited it. In spite of its relative isolation in classical times, Crete had not been forgotten or ignored by the rest of Greece, nor had the Cretans lost their sense of membership in the Greek community. The hope entertained by the Greek allies in 480 that Crete would send help against the Persians shows that it was regarded as part of the Hellenic world, and the explanation given later for their failure to respond shows that the Cretans were uncomfortable about it. They consulted Delphi, so Herodotus says, and on the basis of the oracle's response

---

[35] E.g. Polyb. vi, 45; Strabo x, iv. 9; Clem. Alex. *Strom.* i, 170, 3.

[36] *Platon*, Munich, 1910-1923, i, 87-88; cf. also Albert Rivaud, *Hist. de la philosophie*, Paris, 1948, i, 163, 204.

[37] Wilamowitz, *Platon*, 2nd edn., Berlin, 1920, i, 661.

thought it wise to stand aloof.[38] But the story of this oracle, as well as another story of Cretan archers sent to the battle of Salamis, appear to be inventions after the event, and somewhat contradictory inventions at that. During the Peloponnesian War there was sympathy at Gortyn for Athens and at Cydonia for Sparta; and the strategic geographical situation of the island along the maritime routes—from Athens to Sicily and from the Peloponnesus to Egypt and the eastern islands—made it a tempting area of operations for both the Athenians and the Spartans.[39] There are many evidences of commercial and cultural relations between Crete and the other parts of Greece in the fifth and fourth centuries.[40] Thucydides mentions a Nicias of Gortyn who was a proxenus of the Athenians.[41] In the Attic inscriptions of the fourth century are several which make reference to Crete or the Cretans; one of them mentions a crown received by the Athenians from the Cnossians.[42] The wood of the famous cypress trees of Crete was much prized for naval construction and for woodwork in the temples; Cretan wool was employed in making a garment known in Athens in Aristophanes' time; and Cretan archers were a familiar contingent in almost all the battles of the late fifth and early fourth centuries.[43] There is little doubt that Plato could have got abundant information—from traveling merchants, from Cretan mercenaries, from reports of other members of the Academy who had traveled to Crete, or from philosophical visitors to the Academy who had come from there, and possibly even from earlier written accounts about the island.[44]

---

[38] Herod. VII, 169-170; cf. van Effenterre, *op.cit.* 35-36.

[39] Thuc. II, 85. Against the earlier view that the attack of the Athenian fleet on Cydonia is evidence of the stupidity of the Athenians and their blind hatred of Aegina, van Effenterre (*op.cit.* 37) has put this incident in its proper perspective as part of a well-considered policy of occupying strategic points along the trade routes. Cf. Thuc. IV, 53, and G. B. Grundy, *Thucydides and the History of His Age*, London, 1911, 326-327.

[40] Van Effenterre, *op.cit.* 40-44, 109-115.

[41] Thuc. II, 85, 5.

[42] IG II² 1443, lines 120-121. The date of this decree is earlier than 344-343 (van Effenterre, *op.cit.* 111).

[43] On the export of cypress wood, see van Effenterre, *loc.cit.*; Plut. *Quaest. Conv.* I, ii, 5, 4; Hermippus apud Athen. 27f. On Cretan wool see Aristoph. *Thesm.* 730. A small contingent of eighty bowmen formed a part of the Athenian expedition against Syracuse (Thuc. VI, 43; cf. VII, 57, 9). Clearchus the Spartan had two hundred Cretan bowmen in the force he brought to the aid of Cyrus the Younger (Xen. *Anab.* I, ii, 9), and Xenophon's *Hellenica* contains several references to Cretan mercenaries (IV, ii, 16; VII, 6; VII, v, 10).

[44] An Arabic manuscript containing a quotation from a lost dialogue of Aristotle

A realistic Cretan setting is provided on the very first page of the *Laws*. The three old men have started to walk from Cnossos to "the cave and sanctuary of Zeus." Now there are at least three caves and sanctuaries once sacred to Zeus in the vicinity of Cnossos. There is the Dictaean Cave, a short distance above the modern village of Psychro in the Plain of Lassithi, lying to the southeast of Cnossos, where Zeus was born, according to the ancient legend. There is also the Idaean Cave, lying just above the Plain of Nida on Mount Ida, to the southwest of Cnossos, where Zeus was said to have been taken and brought up after his birth. Lastly there is Mount Juktas to the south of Cnossos, known even to this day as the μνῆμα Διός, the burial place of Zeus; here also there is an ancient sanctuary on the summit, and on the south slope a cave which has revealed evidences of ancient worship. This last cave is hardly far enough from Cnossos to justify the description of the walk as a "sufficiently long" (ἱκανή) one. Of the other two, the Dictaean Cave seems at first sight the more likely destination, for it can be reached in nine or ten hours of walking, as compared with a probable twelve or thirteen hours for the other.[45] But the archaeological finds seem to show that the Dictaean Cave had fallen into disuse as a place of worship in the eighth century,[46] whereas the Idaean Cave was a center of worship and a place of pilgrimage throughout the classical period and on into Hellenistic

seems to show that there was a Cretan member of the late Platonic Academy. See Richard Walzer, "Fragmenta Graeca in litteris arabicis," *Journal of the Royal Asiatic Society*, 1939, 416-417.

[45] J. D. S. Pendlebury, *The Archaeology of Crete*, London, 1939, 10, gives the distance to the Dictaean Cave as nine hours. Mr. Karousos, the guide at the Museum in Heracleion, estimates it as ten hours. As to the Idaean Cave I have verified from actual experience that it can be reached in four and a half hours from Anogeia, a modern village to the north of the Plain of Nida. The distance to Anogeia by the auto road from Heracleion is forty kilometers, a walk of at least eight hours, which would make a total of twelve and a half hours by this route. But it is probable that the ancients used a more direct route into the Plain of Nida from the east. The topographical maps show that there is such a route along the north slope of the mountain called Koudhouni, taking off from the valley not far from the present village of Korfais, and I have ascertained from inquiries at this village that this route is used by shepherds today and takes about five hours. These same informants told me that it was about five hours from Korfais to Cnossos. Making due allowance for the fact that shepherds do not carry watches and that these estimates are only approximate, it seems clear that this route from Cnossos would be considerably shorter than the other. Whether the ancients actually used it cannot be affirmed in the absence of archaeological traces of ancient usage. I have not explored it, and since it may have been nothing more than a path in ancient times, it is not likely that any clear traces of it remain.

[46] D. G. Hogarth, *Annual of the British School at Athens*, 6, 1899-1900, 114.

times.[47] It seems very likely, therefore, that Plato is referring to the Idaean Cave,[48] and the description of the walk given by Cleinias supports this conjecture. "As we go along we shall come to cypresses of wonderful height and beauty, and there are moist grassy places where we can rest and talk" (625b). Theophrastus remarks that the cypresses on Mount Ida were of unusual size, even for Crete, where the cypress in ancient times grew in great abundance.[49] And whoever has walked over this rugged region will recall the numerous upland meadows that afford relief from the toil of the rocky ascent; and above all the great grassy Plain of Nida, lying just below the summit, where the pilgrim is tempted to rest and talk with the shepherds who live there in the summer. The cave lies some three hundred feet above this plain, and when I visited it—in May, 1953—the entrance was almost blocked by an immense heap of snow. Hence a pilgrimage would ordinarily not be made until June or later; and Plato describes this walk of the three old men as taking place in midsummer (683c). One gets the impression that Plato knew this pilgrim's way, if not from personal experience, at least from a vivid account given by someone who had made the pilgrimage. The failure to denote the cave more specifically indicates that there was no need in his time to say that the Cnossians worshipped Zeus on Mount Ida—a point which, as we have seen, is confirmed by the archaeological evidence.

It is difficult to judge the accuracy of Plato's numerous references to Cretan life and customs, but some of them indicate more than ordinary knowledge about the island. The common meals of the Cretans (625c and elsewhere), their preference for archers and light-armed soldiers rather than cavalry and hoplites (625d, 834b), their devotion to liberty (711a), their boy love (636bc, 836b),[50] their attention to gymnastic exercises (673b),[51] the military bent of their education

[47] Nilsson I, 242, 285.

[48] There is epigraphical evidence that the cave above the Plain of Nida was the sanctuary of Idaean Zeus; see Fabricius, *Mittheilungen des Deutschen Archäologischen Institutes in Athen* x, 1885, 280; and "Die Idäische Zeusgrotte," *ibid.* 59-72. A. B. Cook (*Zeus*, Cambridge, 1914-1925, II, 933f.) even infers from Plato's text that Cnossos and the Idaean Cave "were connected by a tolerable road and pilgrims could rest in the shade of trees by the wayside." According to Fabricius (*op.cit.* 71) Plato's text shows us "dass die heilige Grotte des Zeus auf dem Ida ein Wallfahrtsort war, den auch Fremde im Sommer von Knossos aus häufig besuchten."

[49] *Hist. Plant.* IV, i, 3; cf. Pind. *Paeans* IV, 50-51.

[50] It is not without significance that whereas Megillus assents readily to the Athenian's strict law against paederasty, Cleinias withholds his opinion (842a).

[51] Thucydides (I, 6, 5) says that the Spartans were the first to adopt the custom

(626ab), perhaps even their reference to their country as their "father-and motherland"[52]—these features of Cretan life were commonly known and presuppose no special knowledge. Plato also refers to the Cretans' ignorance of Homer and of foreign poets generally, except Tyrtaeus (680c, 629b),[53] and to their lack of acquaintance with mathematics (818e). The Athenian congratulates Cleinias on the fact that the writings of the Ionian physiologers are not current in his country (886b-e). He speaks with approval of a Cretan law that forbids discussion of the merits of the laws among the young (634de) and he is well aware of the differences between the Cretan and the Spartan institution of common meals.[54] He mentions the Cretan law on the use of wine (639d; cf. 674ab) and regulations regarding poetry and the dance (660b). He is aware of the fact that tyranny—the lawless rule of a single man—is unknown in Crete (711a) and regards the Cretan constitution, like the Spartan, as being a mixed one, difficult to classify (712e). What Plato says about the part played by the Argives in colonizing Crete is well attested, as well as his mention of Aeginetans and "other Greeks" who had settled in the island.[55] There is a very significant omission of Crete from the list of places where the institution of slavery has led to disturbances (776cd); and Aristotle also, in comparing Cretan and Lacedaemonian laws, points out that Crete, unlike Sparta, was not troubled by revolts among the subject population.[56] Cleinias reflects appropriately the Cretan version of the Persian wars: "We Cretans regard the battle of Salamis as having saved Greece"; whereas the Athenian and the Spartan regard the land battles of Marathon and Plataea as the decisive engagements (707bc).

---

of exercising naked; Plato, however, says it was the Cretans (*Rep.* 452c), relying perhaps on the tradition concerning Thaletas of Gortyn. See Notes 4 and 10 above.

[52] *Rep.* 575d: "φιλὴ μητρὶς καὶ πατρίς, as the Cretans say." Cf. Plut. *An Seni Sit Ger. Resp.* 17, 2. For the thought see *Menex.* 239a.

[53] Van Effenterre (*op.cit.* 53) gives references to inscriptions of the second century showing the Cretans still attached to their native poets.

[54] 842b, 847e. Wilamowitz, who thought Plato knew very little about Crete, explains this as merely an administrative rule of which Plato might have heard; "in einem Gesetzbuch hat es nicht gestanden" (*Platon* 1, 661n.). But it is hard to see how this makes it less indicative of special knowledge about the island; and in any case 847e refers to a Κρητικὸς νόμος. That the Cretan system was different from the Lacedaemonian is asserted by Aristotle (*Pol.* 1271a 28, 1272a 13).

[55] 707e, 708a; Beloch, *Gr. Gesch.* 1, i, 128ff. Van Effenterre (*op.cit.* 29 n. 4) calls attention to the epigraphical evidence regarding Cretan-Argive relations in the fifth century.

[56] *Pol.* 1269a 39.

The political relation of the various Cretan cities to one another at this time is difficult to make out. Plato speaks of these cities as "many," and implies that they are independent, with Cnossos exercising a hegemony over most of them (702c, 752e) and Gortyn holding a position of greatest moral prestige (708a). This is fragmentary, indeed, but it is more than we could derive from any of Plato's contemporaries. It is a puzzling fact that all the writers of this period speak of Crete as if it were in some sense a unified political entity. Both Ephorus and Aristotle describe the "constitution of the Cretans," not that of Gortyn, Cnossos, or any other individual city. Either they were unaware of any differences between them, or they chose to describe the government of the leading city only; but if the latter is the case, they give no hint which they consider the leading city.[57] Plato's statements do something (though unfortunately only a little) to dispel the haze that covers the actual situation. Strabo, writing more than three hundred years later, says that Cnossos and Gortyn were the leading cities, and when they cooperated with one another they held in subjection all the others, but when they fell out there was dissension throughout the island.[58] Plato's words show that he was writing in one of those periods when Cnossos and Gortyn were on good terms with each other.

The description that Cleinias gives of the site of the new colony he is charged with establishing (704b-705c) suggests that Plato has in mind a definite place in southern Crete. This site is described as about eighty stadia (nine or ten miles) from the sea; it has a good harbor; its terrain contains a mixture of forest, plain, and mountain; on it there are plane trees and pines, with some cypress and fir, though not enough for extensive shipbuilding. It was formerly occupied, but the inhabitants moved away long ago, and it has been deserted for a great many years. Later the citizens of Plato's new colony are called Magnesians, and they are specifically enjoined to give due

---

[57] It is possible (see R. F. Willetts, *Aristocratic Society in Ancient Crete*, London, 1953, 225ff.) that the Cretan federation (the κοινόν) of which we learn from inscriptions after the fourth century, was really a revival of a much older confederation of the Dorian communities in Crete, similar to that which had formerly existed among the Dorian conquerors of the Peloponnesus. It would have been a loose federation indeed, but sufficiently strong in earlier centuries, considering the common language and social traditions of its members, to give them the appearance of unity to the outside world, in spite of the independence of its member cities and the considerable ascendancy which some of them acquired over the others. Cf. van Effenterre, *op.cit.* 26ff.

[58] x, iv, 11.

honor to any local divinities of the earlier Magnesians whose memory
is still preserved.[59] All this indicates that Plato remembers—or imagines—an ancient Cretan city named Magnesia. Now we have a third-
century inscription from Magnesia-on-the-Maeander in Asia Minor
which records a tradition that the Asiatic city was settled by emigrants from a Cretan Magnesia.[60] The Asiatic Magnesia really lay
on the Lethaeus, which flowed into the Maeander just below the city.
There was also a Lethaeus in Crete, now called the Hieropotamos,
flowing through the plain of the Messara past Gortyn and Phaestos.
The third-century tradition from Asiatic Magnesia put the Cretan
mother city in the valley of this stream, and more specifically between
Gortyn and Phaestos. This location at the western end of the Messara,
about ten miles from the sea, with small but usable harbors on the
coast beyond the Asterousian mountains, fits quite well the physical
location of the site that Plato describes. Unfortunately there is no
archaeological confirmation of this ancient tradition, for none of the
sites that have been examined in this region can be clearly identified
as ancient Magnesia, though the exploration of the area is far from
complete. Scanty as the evidence is for the existence of this Cretan
Magnesia, it is enough to make it unlikely that the third-century
tradition is a pure invention of the Asiatic Magnesians. Even if it is,
the *Laws* shows that it was in circulation a century before the inscription in which it has been preserved to us; and Plato, having heard
of it,[61] must have informed himself about the geographical features
of this region. On the other hand, if there is truth in the ancient
tradition—and this may at any time be confirmed by further exploration in the Messara—Plato may have got his information from someone who had been in this part of Crete and learned of, or seen, the
site of an abandoned city known as Magnesia. Only the spade of the
archaeologist can decide between these two alternatives. But in either
case we have additional evidence that for Plato Crete was a region
about whose physical character and social institutions he had taken
pains to inform himself.

[59] Μάγνητες first appears as a designation for the citizens of the proposed colony
in 848d; but it occurs four times thereafter: 860e, 919d, 946b, 969a.
[60] O. Kern, *Inschriften von Magnesia am Maeander*, Berlin, 1900, 17, lines 7ff.
This inscription is discussed by Wilamowitz, *Hermes* xxx, 1895, 177-198. For another
ancient reference to this tradition see Strabo xiv, i, 11. The Palatine Anthology (vii,
304) preserves an inscription from the gravestone of a man from Cretan Magnesia.
[61] The mathematician Theudius of Magnesia is said by Proclus (*Com. on Euclid*,
67, Friedlein) to have been a member of the Academy in Plato's time.

Crete and Sparta were generally associated in Plato's time, not only as law-abiding states (εὐνομουμέναι), but also as having markedly similar laws. They had been linked in Plato's thought from the earliest period of his literary activity,[62] and in the *Laws* the kinship between their institutions is emphasized. The Athenian once mentions their ἀδελφοὶ νόμοι (683a), and it is generally assumed throughout the discussion that Megillus and Cleinias will see alike or stand together on most questions.[63] Plato nowhere gives a systematic statement of the resemblances he sees between the two bodies of law, but Aristotle—in that part of the *Politics* which seems to have been written while he was in the Academy with Plato—does draw up a table of similarities and differences.[64] Miss Chrimes has recently subjected this passage in Aristotle to a searching examination and has shown very convincingly that his view of the similarities in governmental structure is superficial and erroneous; on the other hand, the parallels in social organization she finds to be even more numerous and significant than Aristotle appears to have realized.[65] Plato never refers to any specific Cretan office or agency of government, though he once praises Crete for following, like Sparta, a middle way between the extremes of despotism and liberty (693e), and shortly after brings out the fact that the constitution of Crete, like that of Sparta, is difficult to classify (712e)—which is his way of implying that it is "mixed."[66] In the several other passages in which Plato refers to the similarity of the two constitutions he is thinking of social and educational institutions—their common meals, their use of gymnastics, their prohibition of wine, their boy love, their regulation of the poets, their use of song, and their practice of war dances. These are the points emphasized in Ephorus' account of the Cretan constitution, as reported by Strabo; they are also the main themes of Xenophon's description of Sparta; and it is fair to say that they are

[62] *Crito*, 52e, *Prot.* 342a,d, *Rep.* 544c.

[63] E.g. on the regulation of the poets (660b), the importance of gymnastics (673b), the common meals (780b, 842b; 633a); the discipline of pleasures (635b), and the regulations regarding the use of wine (674a).

[64] *Pol.* 1271b 40ff.

[65] *Ancient Sparta*, 209ff. On one point Miss Chrimes seems to have missed the real object of Aristotle's comparison. She is doubtless right in pointing out that the Cretan περίοικοι, as Aristotle erroneously calls them, have a legal status quite different from the Spartan Helots, to whom he compares them. But for Aristotle, as as for Plato, the important likeness is the freeing of the citizens from labor through the existence of a special class of agricultural workers; see especially 1272a 1.

[66] See the Index s.v. Mixed Constitution.

the similarities that Plato regards as making the two systems "brothers."

How does Plato account for this kinship? The most common explanation among his contemporaries was that one of the two peoples had imitated the other; but whether the Spartans had imitated the Cretans, or the Cretans the Spartans, was a matter of some doubt.[67] The Lacedaemonians themselves in Herodotus' day asserted that their Lycurgan legislation was derived from Crete;[68] and a century later Aristotle records a tradition, which he thinks is probably true, that the Laconian constitution is an imitation, in most respects, of the Cretan.[69] Aristotle adds another tradition, which again he does not dispute, that Lycurgus had spent a considerable time in Crete before enacting his laws. Most other writers of his own and later times agree with Aristotle in thinking that Lycurgus visited Crete; this appears to have become, in fact, the accepted and almost unquestioned view.[70] On the other hand, the Delphic origin of the Spartan constitution was also asserted in Herodotus' day and later. No writer of the fourth century could fail to recognize that the basic document in this constitution, the Big Rhetra, was allegedly based on an oracle from Delphi. Aristotle knew this rhetra and went to some pains to clarify the meaning of its archaic terms.[71] These two beliefs are not irreconcilable; for the role of the oracle was, as Xenophon interprets it, to sanction the legislation that Lycurgus had previously drawn up.[72] This is the way Aristotle also reconciled the two traditions, as is shown by the early chapters of Plutarch's *Lycurgus*, where Plutarch seems to have drawn heavily upon Aristotle; and this reconciliation of the traditions is found also in Ephorus.[73] Thus the prevailing interpretation in Plato's day, put forward by those who had given most

[67] Arist. *Pol.* 1271b 20ff., 1272a 2f.; Strabo x, iv, 17.

[68] Herod. 1, 65.

[69] See Note 67. Both Socrates and his interlocutor in the *Minos* accept this view (318d, 320b).

[70] For Ephorus see Strabo x, iv, 19. Plutarch's account of this visit (*Lyc.* 4) makes Lycurgus meet Thaletas, as does Ephorus'; but Aristotle declares this to be an impossibility (*Pol.* 1274a 29). Plutarch must therefore be relying here, directly or indirectly, upon Ephorus. It is evident from this chapter of Plutarch that there were many previous accounts of Lycurgus' travels, quite diverse in some respects, but all agreeing on the voyage to Crete. For later times see Lucian *Anacharsis* 39.

[71] Herod. 1, 65; Plut. *Lyc.* 6. For a discussion of this rhetra and its relation to the Spartan constitution see Busolt-Swoboda, *op.cit.* 42-52; and H. T. Wade-Gery in CQ XXXVIII, 1944, 115-126.

[72] *Const. Lac.* VIII, 5.

[73] Strabo x, iv, 19.

thought to the matter, was that the Spartan constitution, though sanctioned by Delphi, was copied after institutions that Lycurgus had observed in Crete.

Plato's indifference to this explanation is noticeable. There is nowhere in the *Laws* any suggestion that the Spartans had imitated the admirable Cretan laws,[74] although the setting would certainly seem to invite it. Both the Athenian Stranger and his two companions always say that the Lacedaemonian laws come from Apollo, whereas those of the Cretans come from Zeus (624a, 632d, 634a, 662c, 686a). Minos and Lycurgus are kept distinct (632d); and in the passage in which the work of Lycurgus is mentioned (691e) not only is there no hint that he had gone to Crete, but his reform is pictured as a modification within a pattern of life that the Lacedaemonians had brought with them when—"calling themselves now Dorians instead of Achaeans"—they had come down into the Peloponnesus (682e-685e, 691d-692a). How then would Plato account for the similarities between the Cretan and the Lacedaemonian ways of life? A modern historian would, like Plato, ignore the facile explanation that one was an imitation of the other; the true explanation, he would say, is the common Dorian stock to which these two peoples belonged.[75] Of all the Greeks, the Cretans of Plato's day and the Lacedaemonians represented the traditions of this stock in their purest form. Many Dorian communities had fallen away from the customs of their ancestors; but Crete, its major cities colonized in post-Minoan times by Dorians from the mainland, and protected from outside influence by its geographical situation and the distaste of its people for the sea, naturally exhibited a pattern of life and society similar to that found in Lacedaemon, which had protected itself from the outside world by deliberate policy. Plato never gives this explanation, but he may well have divined it. Like Aristotle, he was aware of the Dorian colonization of Crete in post-Minoan times.[76] When, therefore, he

---

[74] Despite Strabo x, iv, 9, which implies that Plato pictured the Spartans as emulators (ζηλωταί) of Cretan laws. Plato says only that Crete is generally recognized, like Sparta, as εὐνομουμένη and implies that the two systems of law are similar in aim and in many details. It may be that this misinterpretation of Plato comes from Ephorus, who is cited by Strabo in the same sentence.

[75] "There is no question of Crete copying Sparta or Sparta Crete. Both inherited these institutions from an earlier phase in the development of the Dorian race, before that race split up into the separate Dorian states of Greek history. The peculiarity of Sparta and Crete is that they kept these institutions up for so long after others had discarded them." A. Andrewes, *The Greek Tyrants*, London, 1956, 69.

[76] 707e-708a; Arist. *Pol.* 1271b 27.

refers to Minos as the legislator of Crete, he cannot be taken literally as implying that all Cretan laws are derived from that ancient source before the coming of the Dorians; and like Aristotle he must have perceived the difference between the laws of the περίοικοι—reputed to be the original laws of Minos, Aristotle says—and the laws of the later dominant settlements.[77] In his imaginary colony the Dorian pattern is to be continued, for its members are to come mainly from Crete and the Peloponnesus (708a). These glimpses of Plato's thought suggest that he was close to the correct explanation, if he did not clearly see it.

In any case, the kinship between the institutions of the two communities represented by Cleinias and Megillus is a fundamental feature in the design of the *Laws*; and it appears to be Plato's purpose to confront these Dorian traditions, as found in the states where they were best preserved, with those of his fellow Athenians and their Ionian kinsmen. But the exploration of this suggestion must be deferred until we have examined Plato's attitude toward Sparta, that other and in Plato's time more important representative of Dorian traditions.

EXCURSUS A. THE *MINOS*

THE composition of the *Minos* has been assigned to various dates within the century and a half after Plato's death; but the evidence presented above indicates that it was already in existence before Ephorus composed the fourth book of his *Histories*, i.e. by 350 or a few years later. The similarity between its interpretation of Homer's lines and that found at the opening of the *Laws* suggests that it was already in existence when Plato wrote these opening pages. And if that is true, there is a strong presumption that it is from Plato's own hand, as the ancients evidently thought. But few modern critics (except Grote) have been willing to accept this inference. The case against it was stated long ago by August Boeckh (*Commentaria in Platonis qui vulgo fertur Minoem*, Halle, 1806), and later by W. A. Heidel (*Pseudo-Platonica*, Baltimore, 1896, 39-43), Josef Pavlu (*Die Pseudoplatonischen Zwillingsdialoge Minos und Hipparch*, Vienna, 1910), and most recently by Joseph Souilhé (in the Budé edition, Paris, 1930, 81-85). Besides alleging "imitations" of genuine Platonic writings, the critics find that it lacks the grace and subtlety of the

---

[77] *Pol.* 1271b 30-32.

early Socratic dialogues to which in form it seems related; that it contains fallacies in reasoning; and that its various statements about law—as a "discovery of reality," ἐξεύρεσις τοῦ ὄντος; as "right opinion," ἀληθὴς δόξα; and as being everywhere the same—are far too simple to express the complexity of Plato's thought.

The question deserves to be examined afresh, though I can here make only two suggestions. It has not hitherto been sufficiently noticed, I believe, that the *Minos* is not finished; it breaks off abruptly at a point of transition to another part of the inquiry. Thus it has the appearance of a fragment, like the *Cleitophon*; perhaps it is something which Plato had begun, had become dissatisfied with and laid aside, and which was therefore never "published," but found among his "papers" after his death. Again no one has seriously explored the kinship between it and the *Laws*. The similarities are indeed pronounced. Besides (1) its eulogy of Minos as the confidant of Zeus, (2) the mention of the Cretans and the Lacedaemonians as the only peoples who refrain from symposia (ἀπέχονται συμποσίων) and make no use of the "sport of wine" (ταύτης τῆς παιδιᾶς, οὗ ἔστιν οἶνος, 320a), and (3) the metaphor of the herdsman (νομεύς) and his human flock (ἀνθρώπεια ἀγέλη, 318a)—a favorite of Plato's in both the *Politicus* and the *Laws*—there is (4) a clearly Platonic touch in the play on the double meaning of νέμειν—"distribute" and "govern" —and its derivative νόμος (318a, 321cd). What Lamb (in the introduction to his translation in the Loeb edition) calls the "absurd forcing of the primitive notion of 'distribution' or 'apportionment' from the word νόμος" is authentically Plato's; it occurs in the *Laws* in the famous definition of νόμος as τοῦ νοῦ διανομή, the "distribution of Reason" (714a). These similarities, plus the fundamental theme of the inquiry—the search for a definition of law and the insistence on a distinction between law, in the absolute sense, and the decrees of a city (δόγματα πόλεως)—show that the writer of this fragment was concerned with the very questions that occupied Plato during his later years. The *Minos* reflects the common view that the Lacedaemonian laws were derived from Crete (318d), whereas the *Laws* refrains from giving this explanation of their similarity. But the author of the *Minos* is obviously as much interested as is Plato in the peculiar stability that has characterized the laws of these two peoples. If it is a Platonic composition it clearly belongs to the period of the *Laws*, and this destroys one of the premises taken for granted in all previous discussions. Its difference from the early Socratic dialogues is then easily explained; and its attempt to develop in the Socratic manner the complex conception of law that is found in Plato's later thought may indeed have been misguided (and the author himself apparently gave it up) but it need not arouse our suspicions.

But what motive could Plato have had for writing it? Possibly it was a preliminary attempt to construct an introduction to the *Laws*. Very probably Plato first thought of Socrates as the logical choice to lead the discussion in a work that was to be a companion piece or a supplement to the *Republic*. Aristotle, it should be remembered, refers to the *Laws* as a "Socratic discourse" (*Pol.* 1265a 11)—a sheer error, but one whose excuse might be a change of plan on Plato's part. If Plato did experiment with this as his introduction, no doubt he saw very soon that it was not adequate, as his design for a fourth-century Cretan colony took shape in his mind. Yet some of its contents survive in the text of the *Laws*—in the eulogy of Minos, in the discussion of symposia and the use of wine, in the recognition of the Cretan and Lacedaemonian laws as akin. The doctrine with which it breaks off—that right law should be directed above all toward the improvement of the soul (321d)—forms the major theme of the present introductory book. Apparently Plato (like less gifted authors) had difficulty in providing an appropriate introduction to his work; the first two books of the text as he left it are not altogether satisfactory; they are joined to Book III by the most formal of transitions (ταῦτα μὲν οὖν δὴ ταύτῃ), and give the appearance of having been prefixed to the rest of the work when it was in the main complete (see below, Excursus F). If the *Minos* was written for the reason I have suggested, it is a tentative draft only and should therefore not be judged by the criteria that we apply to a finished composition.

However unworthy of Plato the first half of this fragment may seem, "it is hard to conceive who else could have written the last five pages" (Shorey, *What Plato Said*, University of Chicago Press, 1933, 425). Socrates' exegesis of the Homeric lines is so ingenious, so sophistic, yet presented with such assurance and made so persuasive in its context that one can only compare it with his equally strained exegesis of the poem of Simonides in the *Protagoras*. The hand of the same master seems to be at work in both passages.

This little fragment had great influence upon later writers. Having shown that Cretan laws are the oldest in Greece, and having taken stability as a mark of excellence, Socrates points to Minos and Rhadamanthys as the best of all legislators. His companion remarks that Rhadamanthys is indeed said to have been a just man, but Minos is supposed to have been savage and unjust. That, replies Socrates, is what the Attic tragedians say; but Homer and Hesiod speak differently. Then follow the citation and exegesis of the Homeric passage discussed above which constitutes, says Socrates, the highest encomium Homer ever bestowed upon anyone. Minos' pre-eminence even over Rhadamanthys is supported by another passage from Homer (*Odyss.* xi, 569), which shows Minos, not Rhadamanthys, holding the scepter in the realms of the dead, and by Hesiod's reference to him as "the kingliest of kings."[1] If this is true, asks Socrates' companion, how has the report got abroad that Minos was uncivilized and cruel? Because, replies Socrates, he made the mistake of antagonizing the poets—that is, he made war on Athens, where poetry has flourished from very ancient times, and the poets have been punishing him ever since for exacting tribute of ancient Athens.

This defense of Minos is echoed again and again in later writers. Ephorus, as we have seen, accepts the exegesis of Homer and the pre-eminence of Minos that it implies; but to reconcile it with an earlier tradition which made Rhadamanthys the first Cretan legislator, he distinguishes two men by that name, one before Minos' time and imitated by him, the other his brother over whom he had the supremacy (Strabo x, iv, 8 and 19). In his lost *Constitution of the Cretans* Aristotle, apparently recording only what he takes to be the fact behind the Homeric lines, describes Minos as an important legislator who made a revision of his laws every ninth year (Fr. 611, 14, Rose). One of Diodorus' sources (that followed in v, 78 and 79) says that Minos was a "most law-abiding king" ($\beta\epsilon\beta\alpha\sigma\iota\lambda\epsilon\upsilon\kappa\grave{\omega}\varsigma\ \nu\omega\mu\iota\mu\acute{\omega}$-$\tau\alpha\tau\alpha$) who claimed to get his laws from association in a cave with his father Zeus; another (iv, 60) distinguishes between an earlier and a later Minos, the latter being the enemy of ancient Athens. Nicolaus of Damascus (FGH, 2A, 387) cites the Homeric lines and gives the full interpretation that we find in the *Minos*; and this interpretation is found in both Plutarch (*Thes.* 16) and Pausanias (iii, ii, 4). Even the

---

[1] Minos' pre-eminence over Rhadamanthys is asserted in the myth of the *Gorgias* (523e, 526cd). Both are named at the opening of the *Laws*, Minos as the legislator and confidant of Zeus, and his brother Rhadamanthys as the just judge, or the author of legal procedure. The former's function is described in $\theta\acute{\epsilon}\nu\tau\sigma\varsigma\ \tau\omicron\grave{\upsilon}\varsigma\ \nu\acute{\omicron}\mu\omicron\upsilon\varsigma$, the latter's in $\delta\iota\alpha\nu\acute{\epsilon}\mu\epsilon\iota\nu\ \tau\grave{\alpha}\ \pi\epsilon\rho\grave{\iota}\ \tau\grave{\alpha}\varsigma\ \delta\acute{\iota}\kappa\alpha\varsigma$ (624b, 625a).

peculiarly Platonic explanation of Minos' unpopularity among the Athenians had its effect. We see evidence of it in the mention by Strabo (x, iv, 8) of the dramatists (τραγῳδοῦντες),[2] and even more notably in Plutarch's *Theseus* (16). After giving Philochorus' and Aristotle's rationalized versions of the Minotaur story—which seem to satisfy him—Plutarch goes on to moralize about the danger a man runs in being at enmity with a city which has a language and a literature. "For Minos was always abused and reviled in the Attic theaters, and it did not avail him either that Hesiod called him 'most royal,' or that Homer styled him 'a confidant of Zeus,' but the tragic poets prevailed, and from platform and stage showered obloquy down upon him, as a man of cruelty and violence. And yet they say that Minos was a king and a lawgiver, and that Rhada-manthys was a judge under him" (Perrin's translation). By this time the defense of Minos, with the explanation of his evil reputation, had become as much a part of the tradition as the praise of Cretan laws which it was intended to enforce. It is probable that Plato (if this is his work) would have been surprised at the seriousness with which following generations took this little *jeu d'esprit.*

[2] If this expression is taken from Ephorus, as is most of the material in this part of Strabo, it affords further evidence of the influence of the *Minos.*

CHAPTER II

SPARTA

THE LITERARY and artistic remains from ancient Sparta are so meager in comparison with the rich legacy that has come down to us from Athens, Corinth, Sicily, and the Ionian cities in Asia Minor that we find it hard to realize how important Sparta was in the eyes of all Greeks, even the Athenians, throughout the classical period. From the end of the seventh century to the middle of the fourth there were very few intervals when she was not regarded as the most powerful state in Greece. After the conquest of Messenia she controlled a territory that was vast in comparison with even the largest of the other Greek cities; and with the establishment of the Peloponnesian League she had almost undisputed control over the whole of the Peloponnesus. When Croesus in the sixth century was instructed by the oracle to make an alliance with the most powerful of the Greek cities, he turned to Sparta; and sixty years later it was Sparta who was naturally assumed to be the leader of the Greeks in the resistance to the Persians. Even after the battle of Marathon, when the Athenians almost alone had met and defeated the enemy, the Spartan contingent not arriving until the day after the battle, Spartan leadership was still unquestioned; and when the menace again appeared, with the news of Xerxes' preparations for a second invasion of Greece, it was still Sparta who took the lead, nominally at least, in the deliberations of the allied states and in the command of the armed forces. After Salamis the situation was different. The Athenians had demonstrated the importance of sea power, and for half a century they shared the lead with the Spartans. But when these two leaders turned from friends and allies into enemies and tested their strength against each other in war, it was Sparta that eventually dictated the terms of peace; and from the Athenian surrender in 404 to the battle of Leuctra, thirty-three years later, the Spartan hegemony, though sometimes challenged, was never broken. Thus Sparta had for three hundred years been regarded by the Greeks as their leader, and for only half a century or so had she even shared that leadership with another state. It was axiomatic that anyone interested in politics or legislation should give first attention to Sparta, whose success in maintaining her commanding position in Greece seemed to be evidence of peculiar excellence in her laws.

Yet it has sometimes been assumed that Plato's interest in Sparta was due primarily to his aristocratic connections. Some of his friends and relatives in the upper circles of Athenian life did have pro-Spartan leanings at the end of the Peloponnesian War; and their attitude may have influenced him in his youth. Critias, the leader of the oligarchical revolution at the end of the war, was his mother's cousin. This Critias was not only a politician but also a literary man of extraordinary versatility. Among his varied compositions was a eulogistic account of the constitution of Sparta.[1] He apparently believed that everything was done better there; even the Lacedaemonian drinking cups and furniture were superior to those of other peoples. Plato's youthful attitude toward his brilliant cousin in those days is a matter for speculation. Years later, in the *Charmides*, he portrays Critias as an admirer of Socrates, with whom he had associated for many years, and as a wise man ($\sigma o \phi ό s$) in his own right, the author of a definition of temperance ("doing one's own business") which Plato himself uses in his theory of political justice. It is tempting to suppose that the attitude of the young Charmides toward his elder cousin in this dialogue—respect and admiration, mingled with a mischievous pleasure in seeing his guardian taken down a peg—represents Plato's own early attitude toward this important kinsman. It is probable that Critias looked upon the gifted young Plato as his protégé, as Charmides is in the dialogue. Plato tells us in the *Seventh Epistle* (324d) that when the government of the Thirty was set up his "relatives and acquaintances" in the group urged him to join them in an undertaking with which they thought he should be concerned ($ώs \ επ ì \ προσ-ήκοντα \ πράγματα$). These acquaintances included Critias, and possibly also Theramenes, the leader of the moderate party, whose memory continued to be held in great respect by Aristotle and others in later days, and who was later to come to his death at the hands of the extremists with whom he had collaborated.[2] Plato confesses that

---

[1] Diels-Kranz, II, 378-380, 391-394; Wilamowitz, *Platon* I, 116f., 122.
[2] They may also have included Socrates. Diod. XIV, 5, 1-3 reports that he was present at the meeting (presumably a meeting of the council; cf. Xen. *Hell.* II, iii, 50) when Theramenes was condemned to death, and endeavored to save him. The illegal arrest that he was ordered to carry out under the Thirty (Plato, *Apol.* 32c; *Ep. VII.* 324e) may have been a commission assigned to him as a councillor; we know that he had been a member of the council under the democracy a year or

in his youthful enthusiasm for reform he at first entertained high hopes for this change of government, though he seems not to have taken any part in it; but that in a short time he was shocked and disillusioned by its excesses. Evidently he could not stomach, any more than could Socrates and the majority of his fellow citizens, the high handed and violent actions of his cousin.

Besides Critias there were other Laconizing influences on Plato's youth. He probably served in the cavalry; only rich young men could afford the equipment for this branch of the armed forces. There is evidence that these young cavaliers affected Spartan manners and a decided preference for the Spartan "aristocratic" constitution.[3] Such associations have their effect undoubtedly; but how much they affected Plato, and in what way, we do not know. There are humorous remarks in the dialogues about the affectations of these Laconizers, an indication that Plato did not take them very seriously.[4] One notorious member of the older generation in this group was Alcibiades, who was, at some periods at least, pro-Spartan; but this sentiment probably sat as tightly to his self-interest as did his occasional loyalty to Athens, and Plato, though fascinated by him, shows no great respect for his memory.[5] Was Socrates also a Laconizer? We can hardly assume that he belonged to the group of shallow admirers whom Plato satirizes, but the evidence of both Xenophon and Plato shows that he had a high admiration of the Spartans' obedience to their magistrates and the laws.[6] But such praise of Sparta had become commonplace by this time. The only other witness we can summon is Aristophanes, and his testimony is ambiguous.

> There was a Spartan mania, and people went
> Stalking about the streets, with Spartan staves,

---

two before (*Apol.* 32b). It is probably true that Critias in power "hated" him, as Xenophon reports (*Mem.* I, ii, 31ff.), but if Theramenes had studied philosophy with him, as Diodorus says, he might well have been selected by Theramenes during the early period of the regime.

The alternative reading "Isocrates" in Diodorus' text does not seem plausible; for Isocrates was a young man of thirty at this time, whereas Theramenes was in his fifties.

[3] See Albert Martin, *Les Cavaliers Athéniens*, Paris, 1886, 519ff.

[4] *Prot.* 342bc; *Gorg.* 515e.

[5] The purpose of *Alcibiades I* (whoever is its author) cannot have been to honor Alcibiades; he appears in a very unpleasing garb of egoism and pretence. In the *Symposium* the picture of the drunken Alcibiades is brilliant, but certainly not flattering.

[6] Xen. *Mem.* III, v, 15; IV, iv, 15; Plato *Crito* 52e.

With their long hair, unwashed and slovenly,
Like so many Socrates's.[7]

Is this more than a comparison of Socrates' well-known appearance with the affected austerity of the Laconizers? We cannot say. In the *Clouds* Aristophanes attacks Socrates as a scientific disturber of the old order and an unscrupulous teacher of rhetoric, but there is no hint of pro-Spartan leanings. Such a charge would hardly jibe with Aristophanes' main indictment; for of all the Greeks the Spartans were the most devoted to the existing order and least likely to take up with the new science and rhetoric.[8]

It is evident that these inquiries into the personal influences that may have molded Plato's thought do not carry us very far, nor to any sure result. Plato's interest in Sparta can easily be explained on other grounds. Eunomia had been so often asserted of the Lacedae-monians that the term had become a popular synonym for the Spartan way.[9] Both Herodotus and Thucydides record that at one time the Lacedaemonians had been almost the most lawless of all the Greeks, but at some ancient date (Thucydides puts it in the ninth century) had undergone a drastic reorganization of their lives which had brought about εὐνομία.[10] Almost a century later Aristotle echoes this judgment: as the aim of the physician is to cure, and of the orator to persuade, so the genuine statesman tries to bring about εὐνομία, and of this the Lacedaemonian "legislator" is an example.[11] He puts the Lacedaemonian constitution at the head of his list of historical states that he thinks worth examination.[12] Xenophon, whose personal experiences and intellectual qualities were so different from Plato's and Aristotle's, shares their admiration of Sparta;[13] so did Plato's rival Isocrates, and the orator Lysias, not a man of Athenian birth but certainly a loyal Athenian metic.[14] Aristotle's pupil Dicaearchus

[7] *Birds* 1281-1283, Frere's trans.

[8] Socrates' association, if it be a fact, with Theramenes and the Thirty might indicate only that he advocated a return to the "ancestral constitution," the professed purpose of this group. Cf. Arist. *Const. Ath.* xxxiv, 3; Xen. *Mem.* iii, v, 14.

[9] The literature on eunomia is extensive. See especially Andrewes, in CQ xxxii, 1938, 89-102; Victor Ehrenberg, "Eunomia," in *Aspects of the Ancient World*, Oxford, 1946, 70-95; Wade-Gery, CQ xxxviii, 1944, 1-9, 115-126; A. W. Gomme, *Historical Commentary on Thucydides*, Oxford, 1945, i, 128-131.

[10] Herod. i, 65: μετέβαλον εἰς εὐνομίην; Thuc. i, 18, 1: ηὐνομήθη.

[11] *Nic. Eth.* 1102a 9, 1112b 14.

[12] *Pol.* 1269a 29ff.; cf. 1272b 24-29, 1273b 24-26.

[13] *Const. Lac.* i and passim.

[14] Isoc. vii, 61; viii, 95; xii, 41, 109, 210ff.; Lysias xxxiii, 7.

wrote a treatise on Spartan laws which so pleased the Spartans themselves that they provided for annual public readings of it.[15] Ephorus regarded the Spartan constitution as one of the sources from which Zaleucus drew his famed legislation for the Locrians.[16] Of all the eminent men of the fourth century, Demosthenes seems to be the only one who had nothing good to say of Sparta. But the chorus of praise is continued in later times. Polybius praised Lycurgus for being the first to draw up a mixed constitution, thus anticipating the Roman state, which was to him the acme of political wisdom;[17] the Romans themselves, according to Strabo, held the Spartan constitution in high honor.[18] And Plutarch, that echo of ancient thought, dramatized the virtues of its men and the excellence of its laws for generations of later readers.

This is an impressive chorus.[19] If this picture of Sparta is a "mirage," as Ollier thinks, it is an illusion to which a great variety of ancient observers, philosophers and nonphilosophers alike, were subject. But to make the record complete we should add that this universal acclaim was by no means uncritical, at least not in the early period. The writers of the fifth and fourth centuries, in a better position than the later ones to see the reverse of the medallion, are unsparing in their condemnation of certain traits of the Spartans. Herodotus notes their susceptibility to bribes.[20] Thucydides points out their secrecy and dissimulation, their lack of initiative, their harshness to foreigners, their brutality in combat, and their lack of culture.[21] Aristotle's pages fairly bristle with critical comments on the unwholesome influence of the Spartan women, the great inequality of property among the Lacedaemonians, the corruptibility of the ephors, the irresponsibility of the gerontes, and the warlike tendency of their educational system.[22] Even Xenophon sorrowfully mentions the respects in which the Spartan harmosts failed to live up to the traditions he had so grandly presented.[23] It is only in later times that the "idealization"

---

[15] Suidas, s.v. Dicaearchus = Fr. 1, Fritz Wehrli, *Die Schule des Aristoteles* I, Basel, 1944.

[16] Strabo, VI, i, 8.   [17] Polyb. VI, 3; cf. Cic. *De Rep.* II, 41-42.

[18] Strabo IX, ii, 39.

[19] For further details see F. Ollier, *Le Mirage Spartiate*, Paris, 1933.

[20] Herod. III, 148; Cf. Aristoph. *Peace* 623-624, and the Delphic oracle reported in Arist. Fr. 544, Rose.

[21] Secrecy and dissimulation: I, 90, 1-2; V, 68, 2; 74, 3; lack of initiative: I, 118, 2; VIII, 96, 5; injustice to foreigners: III, 93; brutality in combat: II, 67, 4; III, 32, 68; lack of culture: I, 10, 2; 84, 3.

[22] *Pol.* 1269b 12-1271b 19.   [23] Xen. *Const. Lac.* XIV, 1-5.

of Sparta occurs which modern critics rightly find it difficult to understand. The admiration of Plato's contemporaries was neither blind nor uncritical.

Plato's attitude was equally a mixture of admiration and criticism. The dialogues contain many echoes of the conventional praise of Sparta for the excellence of her laws and the character of her citizens. These commonplaces of popular thought are used to good effect in the *Hippias Major*. Spartan concern for the right education of their young men is used to discredit Hippias' claims as a teacher, since he admits that the Spartans refused to put their sons under his tutelage (283c-e). Again Hippias' claim to be able to improve Spartan education is shown to imply that the Spartans are "lawless" (παρά-νομοι, 285b)—an obvious *reductio ad absurdum*—otherwise, since education produces εὐνομία, they would have wanted to become εὐνομώτεροι through his teaching. Similarly in the *First Alcibiades* the Spartans are described as possessing the full panoply of virtues (122c); but these virtues are paraded as excellences which the young Alcibiades can as yet make no claim to possess, and the situation suggests that Plato (if Plato is the author) is here merely using a popular opinion for dramatic effect.

But there seems to be a serious tribute in the *Symposium* (209d). "Who would not prefer," asks Diotima, "to leave behind him, rather than any children of his flesh, the offspring that Lycurgus left in Sparta, to be the saviors of Lacedaemon and, we can even say, of all Greece?" There is also a subtle tribute in the *Protagoras*, in a passage in which the underlying seriousness is veiled, as so often in Plato, by satire. Socrates contends that of all the Greeks, the Spartans and the Cretans have cultivated philosophy the most seriously and for the longest time (342a-343c). The irony is obvious; the Spartans were generally regarded as uncultivated (they were even proud of this) and as interested only in gymnastics and in military exercises. But this pretense is part of their cleverness, says Socrates. It misleads the Laconizers into thinking that if they practise boxing and other forms of gymnastics, and wear short cloaks in the Spartan fashion, they can conquer the rest of the Greeks, like the Spartans. But the truth is, the Spartans' superiority is due to their wisdom (σοφία)—not a wisdom that shows itself in fluent and eloquent discourse, but such as comes out unexpectedly in some pithy saying, like the "Nothing in excess" attributed to Chilon, the Lacedaemonian member of the Seven Sages.[24] The wisdom meant here is of course not the dialectical or intellectual σοφία which Plato regards as the crowning achievement of education; it is rather a sturdy moral sense, unpolished by superficial accomplishments, and unaffected by reflective doubts. The choice of the maxims that illustrate this wisdom ("Know Thyself"; "Nothing in Excess"; "Excellence is Hard") shows clearly the serious undertone beneath Socrates' irony. One can even take this passage as an attempt to correct the current misconception about the Spartans which, in exalting their military prowess and the efficiency of their military training, overlooks a deeper source of Spartan strength.[25]

But Plato's references to the Spartans are by no means all laudatory. The passage in the *Protagoras* shows that he was not blind to their lack of intellectual interests.[26] A more telling criticism occurs in the eighth book of the *Republic*, the very book in which he gives Sparta the place of honor in his survey of historical states. Here his criticism bears on precisely those qualities of the Lacedaemonians that were most admired, viz. their moral integrity and respect for law. This best of the imperfect states, which is said on two occasions to be exemplified by the Laconian constitution (544c, 545a), is called timocracy, and is characterized by the supremacy of the θυμός, the ambitious, combative, and passionate elements in human nature. Having thrown off the control of reason and intelligence, such a state is in an unstable position between aristocracy and oligarchy. It has some of the institutions of the former, e.g. respect for law and for public officials, common meals, military and gymnastic exercises. But its citizens distrust intelligence and are inclined to war rather than peace (547de). They are covetous of money, and since they cannot indulge their desire openly, they acquire their treasures secretly and hide them away from the law, as children evade their fathers (548ab). Even if Plato had not explicitly mentioned Sparta, it would be clear enough what state he had in mind; the avarice of the Spartans and the great wealth of gold and silver accumulated by some of them, in spite of the prohibition in the law, made one of

---

[24] Critias makes a point of attributing this saying to Chilon. Diels-Kranz II, 380.

[25] It is an anticipation of the *Laws* (630d), where the Athenian Stranger endeavors to show his Cretan and Lacedaemonian friends that they do not truly understand the intent of their legislators if they regard their laws as designed solely for success in war.

[26] Cf. *Hipp. Mj.* 285cd.

the juiciest scandals of Plato's time. Plato's readers would also be likely to see a reference to Sparta in the description of oligarchy that immediately follows. Socrates describes the inequality of wealth in an oligarchy, the restriction of the rights of citizenship to those having a property qualification, and the consequent division of the city into two classes, the rich and the poor—traits that duplicate those which Aristotle explicitly mentions as grave defects in the Lacedaemonian constitution.[27]

This critical attitude is especially marked in the *Laws*, particularly in the early books, where the principles are being laid down for the detailed legislation to follow. The Athenian Stranger is obviously bent on improving the opportunity presented by his casual encounter with the two Dorians to examine their laws and probe his companions' opinions about them. Although the conversation remains always at the level of Attic urbanity, the Athenian's questions are searching and critical, and he does not hesitate to pronounce judgment against his companions and indirectly upon the laws that they are defending. "There is no young man present," he remarks, "hence we can criticize the laws freely; and no one of us should take offense if we find fault" (634c, 635a). At the very outset of the discussion Cleinias' interpretation of the Cretan and Spartan laws as designed primarily for success in war is deftly refuted. You must have misunderstood your legislators, says the Athenian, if you think this was their aim (630d). Peace is the good and healthy condition of a state; war is sometimes necessary, but only that peace may result (628c). And a worse evil than defeat in battle is the weakness that results from internal faction. Your poet Tyrtaeus, who sang the virtues of the warrior citizen, overlooked the more serious malady against which a state should protect itself (629a-630c). In fact the virtue of courage, which he extolled, is only a part of virtue, and the lowest part at that (630c); if he concentrated his attention upon this virtue, as you say, he neglected the greater part of his task (631a). And your interpretation of him may be correct; for although you can easily name your institutions that develop courage—the common meals, gymnastic exercises, the practice of hunting, the secret service, the contests in endurance of pain—you have difficulty, and no wonder, in naming any customs designed to promote temperance (633a-

[27] *Pol.* 1270a 15ff., 29ff.; 1307a 35-38.

634b).[28] The prohibition of wine, which is the only thing you put forward as your contribution here, does not really promote temperance, but is likely to lead to the opposite extreme of drunkenness when restraints are removed (637ab). You are shocked by the disorderly behavior of Athenian citizens at the rural Dionysia, but one of us could equally well criticize the looseness of the Spartan women (637c). Your common meals and gymnastic exercises have brought great benefit to your state, but they also have disadvantages; they are a source of faction and they lead to unnatural love (636bc). To say that your institutions are better because you can rout your enemies in battle is stupid; it is the bigger states, not always the better ones, that win victories and subdue their enemies (638ab). In fact your state has the constitution of an armed camp; you have never learned the highest music (666de).

This is not blind admiration. Obviously Crete and Sparta figure in this dialogue not because Plato thought their constitutions to be above criticism, but because he considered that they were worth criticizing. For Plato seems never to have abandoned the common judgment of his countrymen that Sparta was "well-governed" (εὐνο-μουμένη) as compared with other states.[29] Then what was it in the Lacedaemonian laws and in the conduct of the Spartans that Plato and his countrymen held in such high esteem? Thucydides gives us a part of the answer, perhaps the most important part. "Sparta has never had a tyrant (αἰεὶ ἀτυράννευτος ἦν)," he says; "for it is a little more than four centuries, counting to the end of the present war, that the Lacedaemonians have had the same constitution."[30] This long record of stability would be especially impressive to the conservatives among Plato's countrymen, conscious as they were of the changes that their own constitution had undergone during the same period, and all would be impressed by the record of freedom from faction and tyranny, the twin evils to which the small city-state was by its nature exposed. Factional strife could often be terminated only by the advent of a tyrant to reduce the warring parties, and tyranny in turn bred new enemies and new divisions in the citizenry. If Sparta was one of the few Greek states that had been exempt from this recurrent cycle of disorder during the previous centuries, she

---

[28] For a similar criticism of Spartan education see *Rep.* 546d, 548b.

[29] Cf. 635e, 696a, and the tradition, which Plato accepts, that Spartan laws came from Apollo.

[30] Thuc. I, 18, 1.

could not but seem to the other Greeks an outstanding example of a well-ordered commonwealth, all the more remarkable in the fifth and fourth centuries because she still retained her hereditary kings, when kingship had disappeared everywhere else, and kings who were commonly believed to be direct descendants of the two kings who had held power at the time of the Dorian conquest.[31] How had the sovereignty of law been upheld in Sparta through all these years, when it had been lost at some time or other, for longer or shorter intervals, in almost all other cities? Thucydides had probably meditated on this question, but he ventured no opinion in his history. Plato also gave much thought to it, and his reflections led him to one of his most striking discoveries, which we shall come to later.

The complement to this constitutional stability at Sparta was a peculiarly stubborn devotion of the Spartans to their laws. Herodotus, writing of Xerxes' expedition against Greece in 480, describes the Spartan Demaratus, then in exile from his native land, as speaking frankly to the Great King about the quality of his opponents whom he was about to meet at Thermopylae. "They are free men," he says, "but not free in all things. For the master set over them is the law, and this they fear ($\dot{v}\pi\epsilon\rho\delta\epsilon\iota\mu\alpha\acute{\iota}\nu o\nu\sigma\iota$) far more than your subjects fear you."[32] This profound fear and respect that the Spartans felt for their law is the sentiment immortalized by Simonides in the famous epigram composed for these same Spartans who died at Thermopylae.[33] The Spartans did not always die at their posts; one of the things that shocked the Greeks during the Peloponnesian War was the surrender of the beleaguered Spartan garrison at Pylos.[34] But the surprise and shock that this caused is testimony to the ideal the Spartans represented and to their reputation for living up to it. This ideal had been memorably expressed for all Spartans by their poet Tyrtaeus, whose songs had stiffened their determination during the long war with the Messenians and were ever afterward cherished and sung as the best expression of their conception of civic virtue. One of Tyrtaeus' elegies actually bore the title "Eunomia," and Plato's reference to these songs (629a,e) shows that he is aware of their importance in

[31] See Andrewes, *The Greek Tyrants*, 66ff.; Busolt-Swoboda, 672.
[32] Herod. VII, 104.
[33] Herod. VII, 228: "Go, stranger, tell the Lacedaemonians that we lie here obedient to their commands."
[34] Thuc. IV, 40.

molding the Spartan character.[35] The ideal Tyrtaeus describes is not that of the Homeric hero, set above the undistinguished mass of his followers and engaged in single combat with an enemy king or chieftain; Tyrtaeus sang the praises of the citizen soldier who stands in the forefront of the battle, in serried disciplined ranks, his feet firmly planted apart, determined to conquer or to die for his sires, his children, and his fatherland.[36] This ideal of the warrior citizen emerged in various parts of the Greek world with the rise of hoplite warfare in the seventh century—we find it in a fragment of Callinus of Ephesus—but it was the Spartans who took it most seriously and adapted their other institutions to it. Henceforth, as Jaeger says, Spartan education no longer had as its aim the selecting of heroes, but the formation of an entire city of heroes.[37]

The impression that such well-disciplined heroes made upon their fellow Greeks is reflected in another passage in Thucydides. After describing the disposition of the opposing forces before the battle of Mantinea, he mentions briefly the exhortations made by the Mantinean, Argive, and Athenian generals to their respective troops, reminding them of the issues at stake and the prizes to be won by victory. But the Lacedaemonians, he says, reminded themselves individually of the rules of war which they had mastered, secure in the knowledge that long practice in doing things is more conducive to safety than an eloquent speech just before the battle. And in the engagement which follows he describes the Lacedaemonian troops advancing slowly to the sound of flutes "not for reasons of religion, but in order that they might march more evenly, and not break their ranks, as so often happens when large armies are advancing."[38] In short, the Spartans were not amateurs in battle; by long and strenuous discipline the individual hoplite had become a conscious and intelligent part of the fighting unit at the disposal of his commander.

This military discipline which Thucydides here describes with such manifest admiration, and which made the Spartan hoplites invincible on the battlefield, is but an illustration of the lifelong discipline required of the Spartan citizen. He was a member of a small dominant

---

[35] For an analysis of Plato's use of Tyrtaeus see des Places, "Platon et Tyrtée," in REG LV, 1942, 14-24.

[36] Frs. 11 and 12, Edmonds.

[37] Jaeger, *Paideia* I, 125ff. (Eng. trans. 84ff.).

[38] Thuc. v, 69-70. Plutarch (*Lyc.* 22) gives a similar description (doubtless taken from one of his ancient sources) of the Spartans marching into battle in close formation to the music of the flute.

group in the midst of a subject and hostile population many times larger. Surrounded by enemies who might rise and attack them at any time, the Spartans knew that they could survive only by standing together and by ruthlessly subordinating individual interests and ambitions to the good of all. These were the hard facts of life as the Spartans confronted them. It is true that the predicament was of their own making. Few conquerors in history have been as ruthless as they were toward the peoples whose lands they took over in Laconia and Messenia.[39] We can even argue, from the perspective of today, that it would have been far better for the Greeks as a whole if the Spartans had not met their difficult situation with such undeserved success. But the fact is, they did meet it successfully. At some period in their history they imposed upon themselves a discipline of the most rigorous sort, involving a virtual militarization of all their life from the cradle to the grave. This discipline was their "laws." It cost them much that other Greeks enjoyed. It required the cultivation of physical endurance to an incredible degree; it meant living more frugally than was customary even in Greek states whose soil was much less fertile; it demanded the renunciation of wealth and the acceptance of a certain equality of poverty and hardship. They turned their backs upon the enjoyment of the poetry, science, and art that were flowering throughout the rest of the Greek world at this time. They even stopped taking part in the contests at Olympia; athletic prowess was incompatible with the training of the soldier, and perhaps also a dangerous incentive to individual ambition.[40] All this their "Lycurgan" laws cost them; and it is no little tribute to their hard social sense and their tenacity of purpose that they maintained their discipline over themselves for at least four centuries, so Thucydides believed.

The supremacy of law, the courage and political concord of the citizens—these are what the thoughtful Greeks of Plato's time evidently had in mind when they praised Spartan eunomia. The success of the Spartans in battle was one of its striking results; but admiration

[39] That is, according to the common account. We must admit, however, that reliable evidence regarding what actually happened at the conquest, about the origin of helotage, and even about the status of the Helot in historical times is woefully scanty.

[40] Guy Dickins, in JHS XXXII, 1912, 18-19; E. N. Gardiner, *Greek Athletic Sports and Festivals*, London, 1910, 56-59; Andrewes, *op.cit.* 69-70. For the archaeological evidence, see R. M. Dawkins, ed. *The Sanctuary of Artemis Orthia at Sparta*, JHS *Suppl. Papers* 5, 1929.

of the Spartans was not dependent on their military success, for this admiration survived the defeat at Leuctra in 371, and most of the contributors to the chorus of praise cited earlier come after that date. A constitution that could maintain the supremacy of law for so long a period, and could mold its citizens so efficiently into conformity with the law's demands, certainly had some secrets of wisdom to reveal to the earnest inquirer into politics, as Plato was. What were the causes of this eunomia so manifest among the Lacedaemonians, so frequently lacking elsewhere? To understand Plato we must try to find his answer to this question.

One of these causes, so Plato undoubtedly thought, was the strict educational system at Sparta. His attention is directed from the very first to this fundamental feature of Spartan life; the discussion of education in the first two books of the *Laws* takes its departure from the Athenian's inquiry regarding the common meals, the gymnastic exercises, and the other familiar elements of the Spartan system. Lacedaemon was one of the few Greek states (perhaps the only one, with the exception of Crete), that dealt seriously and systematically with the task of educating its youth. Education was made a primary concern of the state and placed under the supervision and control of the ephors. This was strikingly different from the custom of other cities of Plato's time, where the father alone was responsible for the kind and amount of education that his sons received.[41] Furthermore, the Spartan system appeared to be peculiarly efficient in producing the type of character that the Spartans thought the constitution required. However limited might be the Spartan conception of excellence—and the discussion in the opening book of the *Laws* reveals that in Plato's opinion it was decidedly limited—it showed what finished results can be obtained when the state has a definite idea of what it wants its citizens to be and pursues this end with vigor and consistency.

The Spartan system—the ἀγωγή, as it came to be called—was indeed single-minded in its aim and unremitting in its demands, if we can believe the accounts of it given by the ancient authorities.[42] At the age of eight the Spartan boy was taken from his home and placed

---

[41] Xen. *Const. Lac.* II, 1-2; *Educ. of Cyrus*, I, ii, 2; Arist. *Pol.* 1337a 31f.

[42] The most familiar ancient accounts are those in Xenophon's *Constitution of the Lacedaemonians* and Plutarch's lives of *Lycurgus* and *Agesilaus*. For a critical account based on these and other ancient testimonia see Busolt-Swoboda, 694-702.

with others of his own age in a band or "herd" (ἀγέλη),[43] whose members exercised, played, ate, and slept together, under the constant supervision of an older youth, himself under the supervision of his elders. They went barefoot, their clothing was scanty, their allowance of food was kept to a minimum, they made long marches, they slept on beds of rushes, they studied some "letters," but not much, they had athletic and military contests, they danced and sang together. Breaches of discipline were heavily punished; there is no disciplinarian more rigorous than an older boy who has gone through the drill himself. But bodily strength and endurance were not the sole purpose of this training. They were taught to be grave in their demeanor, sparing of words, respectful to their elders. They were encouraged to supplement their meager rations by stealing food from the barns and homesteads in the country. This was presumably to cultivate ingenuity and dexterity, for one who was caught in the act, Plutarch tells us, was severely punished. Above all the boys learned to live not as individuals, but as members of a herd. Year after year this training continued, until at the age of twenty the youth was eligible for military service and received the rights of citizenship. At this age also the law prescribed that he should marry, but for ten years longer he continued to live with the young men of his own age, seeing his wife only by stealth at night when no duties were demanded of him. He was not allowed to go abroad, nor was any foreign teacher of the youth allowed at Sparta. Only at the age of thirty was he free to live in his own house, and even then he continued to be a member of a "mess" (φιδίτιον) consisting of about fifteen other Spartan citizens with whom he was obligated to take his meals. Absence from the mess without legitimate reason (such as a family sacrifice) was severely punished. Thus the common meals, with their frugal fare and their strictly regulated conversation and singing, carried on into the mature life of the citizen that discipline by the community begun in early years and designed to make the individual first of all a Spartan.

Such was the Spartan agoge, a system likened by Simonides to the process of breaking horses to the rider and the bridle. Sparta, he says, was "man-mastering" (δαμασίμβροτος).[44] It would be difficult, in

---

[43] This word is ordinarily used in Greek prose for sheep, goats, or cows. There is possibly a reflection of the peculiar Spartan usage in *Laws* 666e, 680e; but cf. *Polit.* 295e.

[44] Plut. *Ages.* 1.

fact, to cite a better historical example of success in imposing group standards on the thought and emotions of the individual. The stern demands of Spartan citizenship became the heart and core of the citizen's nature; his way of life was thought of not as a hard necessity, but as something desirable for its own sake, and as distinguishing him from his weaker fellow Greeks. The effectiveness of this educational system is shown by its survival into later times, after the need for it had disappeared. Long after the Spartans had ceased to be a power in Greece, long after the menace of revolt in their midst had vanished under the Romans, they continued to adhere to their agoge with an affectionate and pathetic pedantry.[45]

There was certainly much in this system of which Plato does not approve. We have already noticed his mention of certain disadvantages of common meals and gymnastic exercises—their encouragement of faction and of unnatural sexual relations. In his own program of education for the young we shall see that he ignores, if he does not explicitly reject, the most extreme features of the agoge—the grouping of the young men into bands, or herds, the brutal and brutalizing ordeals in endurance of pain, and the systematized pugnacity of their games and contests. On the other hand, he introduces mathematics and letters, which the Spartans of his time disdained, and makes a place for an advanced level of higher education altogether unknown at Sparta. The common meals that he proposes are in fact to be more akin in grace and liveliness to Athenian symposia than to the abstemious and gravely dull gatherings of the Spartans. But he clearly follows Spartan precedent in making the state responsible for the education of the young, and he sees that it must use unremittingly all possible means of persuasion, in all areas of the citizen's life, if the principles of the law are to form the character and become the inner motives of a man's actions. Something like this, he thinks, is necessary if a state hopes to assure its own continuance by creating among its citizens the kind of men that the constitution requires.

A second source of strength in the Spartan constitution, as Plato evidently saw it, was the peculiar and distinctive way in which the organs of government in the Spartan state were separated and balanced against one another, so that Sparta was able to avoid both

---

[45] Busolt-Swoboda 694 n. 5.

despotism and license, the two extremes that he thought destructive of wisdom, freedom, and friendship in a society. This point is developed at considerable length in the third book of the *Laws,* where the Athenian Stranger traces the political history of Sparta from the entry of the Dorian invaders into the Peloponnesus and the establishment of the three original Dorian kingdoms (683b-693d). The history of these three kingdoms Plato finds to be full of instruction. Two of them—Argos and Messenia—very early lost their constitution and laws, while Lacedaemon alone remained (685a). Where else, he asks, could we more clearly discern the difference between laws that preserve a kingdom and those that bring about its downfall (683a-c) than in the contrasting fortunes of these three states—states which, if they had all remained stable and united, would have provided ample security to the Peloponnesus and to all Greece against the barbarians (685bc)? When the need arose to resist the Persians, the Spartans were the only one of these peoples who came to aid the Athenians in the defense of Greece—the Argives having refused to help, and the Messenians actually hindering the Spartans by warring against them at the time (692de).[46] What is the secret of the stability of the Spartan constitution? Plato finds the answer in a series of factors that he introduces into his picture one by one.

All three of these Dorian kingdoms apparently began in a promising way by establishing laws prescribing the rights of kings and peoples respectively. Each king took oath not to extend his powers, and his people likewise took oath not to try to overthrow their king; and each of the kings and peoples swore to come to the aid of either of the other two kingdoms if it should be threatened with disorder (684a). But obviously this was not enough. Plato asserts, almost as vigorously as Thomas Hobbes did two thousand years later, that oaths will be only a weak restraint for a powerful and ambitious king (691a, 692b). Other curbs were necessary if these kings were to be saved from that worst of all forms of ignorance, the discrepancy between their principles and their ambitions (689a). What these further restraints should be is easy enough for us to see now, the Athenian Stranger says, though probably impossible for any legislator of that time to foresee (691b). The Spartans were saved, in the

---

[46] Plato's attitude toward Argos and Messenia and his judgment as to the causes of their downfall are somewhat puzzling. For a discussion of these matters see below, Excursus B.

first instance at least, not by an act of human wisdom but by an accident—or as Plato puts it, by an act of divine providence—viz. the birth of twins in the royal family (691d). The Spartan kingdom, as we know it in history, was a curious dual arrangement. Procles and Eurysthenes, the twin sons of Aristodemus, had ruled jointly at the beginning, the Spartans thought; and ever afterward the successive descendants of these first kings had held the royal power together. Obviously a dual kingship cannot be as absolute as a monarchy; the two kings must act together in most respects if they are to preserve their position. This provided the first limitation on the royal power.

The second check was set up with the establishment of the gerousia, or council of elders, a reform which Plato, like most of his contemporaries, attributes to Lycurgus, a man "in whose human nature there was an admixture of divine power" (φύσις τις ἀνθρωπίνη μεμειγμένη θείᾳ τινὶ δυνάμει, 691e).[47] Its purpose was to correct the "swollen authority" (ἀρχὴ φλεγμαίνουσα) of the kings by setting up a body which would have an equal weight with them on important matters (ἰσόψηφον εἰς τὰ μέγιστα τῇ τῶν βασιλέων δυνάμει). The gerousia consisted of twenty-eight members (with the two kings added ex officiis), all over sixty years of age, and selected by popular acclaim on the basis of their "virtue."[48] The division of powers that

---

[47] This is an oracular but unambiguous reference to Lycurgus and would have been so understood by Plato's contemporaries. Herodotus (1, 65) tells us that when Lycurgus went to Delphi the oracle professed to be uncertain whether to address him as a god or as a man. The reported words of the oracle, perhaps taken from the Spartan archives, are given in Herodotus and were undoubtedly common knowledge in the fourth century. Xenophon refers to them in his *Apology of Socrates* (15), and according to Plutarch (*Lyc.* 5, 3) this response of the oracle was famous.

Plato's reference to Lycurgus at this point in his story indicates that he regarded him not as the author of the entire Spartan constitution (as was commonly said by his admirers; cf. Herod. 1, 65; Xen. *Const. Lac.* 1 and passim); but only as one who made an important change at a particular time in its development (see below, Excursus B). This is evidently the view that Aristotle also took, to judge from the fragments of his lost account of the Spartan constitution (Fr. 611, 10, Rose). But at other times Plato uses "Lycurgus" in a more popular and less critical sense. He is named as the author of the Lacedaemonian laws, as Minos is of the Cretan (630d, 632d); and when later the noncommittal phrase "the legislator" occurs in connection with Lacedaemonian usages it can only be taken as referring to Lycurgus. There are similar references in other dialogues (*Symp.* 209d, *Phaedr.* 258bc, *Rep.* 599de). Thus Plato sometimes speaks (and perhaps thinks) with the vulgar, despite his awareness that the historical Lycurgus built on institutions established before his time and that his own work was in turn added to by others.

[48] Busolt-Swoboda, 679-680; on virtue as the sole relevant qualification except age see 680 n. 1.

resulted, as we see it in historical times, was real indeed. The kings, as descendants of the legendary Procles and Eurysthenes by whom their dynasties were founded, enjoyed the prestige that belonged to their ancient houses; they received handsome emoluments and preferments; in command of armies outside the borders of Lacedaemon their authority was unrestricted. But at home in times of peace their functions, apart from the conduct of the sacrifices, were restricted to their role as members of the gerousia, and to certain minor responsibilities in the administration of justice.[49] The rivalry between the two kingly houses even made it difficult at times for them to present a united front against an adverse opinion in the gerousia. Thus the institution of the gerousia did in fact, as Plato says, provide a counterpoise to the hereditary power of the kings ($\tau\hat{\eta}$ κατὰ γένος ῥώμῃ), which was likely to be stubborn or willful (αὐθάδης), and which in consequence became "mixed" (σύμμεικτος) and "moderate" (μέτρον ἔχουσα).

The Spartan constitution in historic times contained another body of powerful officials, the ephors, five in number, selected annually from the people and invested with very great powers over policy and administration. In Plato's account the institution of the ephorate (ἡ τῶν ἐφόρων δύναμις) is said to have been the work of a "third savior" (τρίτος σωτήρ) who saw that the government was still bursting with energy and self-assertion (σπαργῶσα καὶ θυμουμένη) and who set up this new body to be a bridle (οἷον ψάλιον) upon it (692a). The establishment of this office, Plato evidently thinks, occurred after the time of Lycurgus.[50] In historical times the ephors were in

---

[49] Busolt-Swoboda, 673ff.

[50] This was one of the most controverted points in the Lycurgan tradition. Herodotus (1, 65), Xenophon (*Const. Lac.* VIII, 3), and Ephorus (Strabo x, iv, 18) regarded the ephorate as the work of Lycurgus. But Aristotle agrees with Plato in giving it a later origin; in the *Politics* (1313a 26) he says it was established in the reign of King Theopompus, i.e. two generations after Lycurgus' time, as he conceived it. This view may have arisen as a result of the publication of a pamphlet by the exiled King Pausanias in the early fourth century setting forth the Great Rhetra on which the Lycurgan legislation was based (Strabo VIII, v, 5). Pausanias wanted to have the ephors abolished (Arist. *Pol.* 1301b 20); hence his publication of the rhetra, which makes no mention of them and which may have been relatively unknown before outside the circle of Spartan officials who had access to the archives (cf. Herod. VI, 57; Plut. *Adv. Colot.* 17, 2). Plutarch's account of it is dependent upon Aristotle, and shows that Aristotle had made a careful study of its archaic language (*Lyc.* 6; see also Chapter I, Note 71). We can hardly believe that Plato was ignorant of it. When therefore he describes the establishment of the ephors

fact a very effective curb upon the powers of kings and gerousia. They had the right to convoke the assembly; they had control of foreign relations; they had oversight over internal affairs, with power to punish; they supervised the agoge; they could—and sometimes did—bring a king to trial and see him heavily punished, sometimes even deposed. In short, their powers were such as to make their office something like a tyranny.[51] But there were also definite checks on their power. They were limited to one year in office, they could not act as individuals but only as a group, and they were subject to an accounting before their successors at the end of their year.

As a result of the separation of these three powerful organs of government the Spartan kingship, as Plato sees it, "having become properly mixed and moderated, has been preserved" (692a). It was a graphic illustration of one aspect of the mixed constitution that Plato thinks a legislator should aim at, and he proposes something similar for his state. This mixture was very old (the first of the ephors, according to Spartan records, belong to the middle of the eighth century by our reckoning) and it had shown its toughness by its survival unchanged—so Plato's contemporaries thought—through the four succeeding centuries. Thus the study of Spartan history gave Plato the explanation of the anomalous survival of kingship at Sparta when it had disappeared everywhere else in Greece; and it also illustrated, if it did not suggest to him, the conception of a government controlling itself by a balancing of powerful forces checking one another. The discovery of this principle counts as one of the great events in the history of political science, for this idea was to have a considerable future in the political theory of the western world. Polybius and Cicero adopted it, and from them it passed down to Montesquieu and the thinkers of modern times.[52]

In discussing Plato's choice of Crete as the setting for this dialogue, and of a Cretan and a Spartan as the two companions of the Athenian Stranger, we noted his apparent insight into the reason for the simi-

---

as a later addition to the work of Lycurgus, he was not expressing an arbitrary fancy, but the view of his critical contemporaries (see below, Excursus B).

When in *Ep. VIII* 354b he attributes to "Lycurgus" both the gerousia and the ephorate, we have only another instance of his speaking with the vulgar (see above, Note 47).

[51] Busolt-Swoboda, 687ff.; Xen. *Const. Lac.* VIII, 4; Arist. *Pol.* 1270b 14; cf. *Laws* 712d.

[52] See below, Chapter X ad fin.

larity between Cretan and Spartan laws—i.e. the Dorian stock to which the two peoples belonged; and when we see that most of the non-Cretan colonists for the new city are to be drawn from Dorian regions like Aegina and the Peloponnesus, it becomes evident that Plato considers the Dorian peoples peculiarly adapted to his purposes. We have, then, a third source of strength in the Spartan constitution that Plato thought a competent legislator would take into account, viz. the peculiar virtues of the Dorian character.

The Dorians were relative newcomers in Greece. The tradition of their coming from the north after the Trojan War was well established. But they were not thought of as an alien people; they were really Achaeans, Plato seems to say (682e), who had been expelled from their lands and simply returned to regain their ancient possessions; and this was the generally accepted tradition.[53] Yet the disciplined severity of their social organization, the simplicity of their motives and ambitions—whether genuine survivals from the period of the conquest or the results of a deliberate revival in the seventh century—set them apart from their kinsmen who had preceded them into Greece and who had become, particularly the Ionians in Asia Minor, somewhat softened by their contacts with Minoan and Oriental culture. The special qualities of the Dorians had been a subject of admiration since at least the time of Pindar. The distinctness between these two branches of the Greek people—between the "soft-living Ionians" ($\dot{\alpha}\beta\rho\acute{o}\beta\iota o\iota$ Ἴωνες)[54] and the "man-mastering" ($\delta\alpha\mu\alpha$-$\sigma\acute{\iota}\mu\beta\rho o\tau o\varsigma$) code of the Dorians—underlies all Greek history and culture. It was evident in the difference between the dialects spoken by the two stocks; it was canonized in the orders of architecture and the modes of music; and though it was submerged during the years of the Persian threat, it led later to the fratricidal strife of the Peloponnesian War. For both Herodotus and Thucydides the distinction between Ionian and Dorian is never far below the surface of the events they describe. Herodotus, a Dorian himself (by birth, though not in mentality), regards the Dorians as the only true Hellenes; and in spite of his admiration for Athens very clearly looks down upon the Ionians as lacking in manly qualities, and suspects that the Athenians were reluctant to call themselves Ionians.[55] This contempt was of course common among the Dorians, who looked

[53] See Excursus B.   [54] Bacchylides 13, 2, Edmonds.
[55] Herod. I, 56, 143; IV, 142; V, 69; VI, 12-13.

upon the Ionians as their "eternal enemies."[56] On the other hand, the Ionians were puzzled and annoyed that the Spartan rules of life, their νόμιμα, were incompatible (ἄμεικτα) with those of the Greeks elsewhere, and noted with bitterness that a Spartan away from home not only failed to observe his own laws, but also flouted those that were generally recognized elsewhere in Greece.[57]

The Athenians occupied a kind of middle ground. In intellectual curiosity and versatility they were the finest representatives of these strains in the Ionian character; and they recognized their kinship with the Ionians, often exploited it for political and imperial purposes, and on occasion made themselves their avowed champions. Yet they also seem to have felt some contempt for the softness of the Ionian character, and obviously took advantage of it in transforming the Delian League into an Athenian empire.[58] In Pericles' eulogy of Athens that Thucydides records, there is no mention of Ionian ancestry; on the contrary there is an evident effort to differentiate Athens from her Ionian kinsmen. "We cultivate refinement without extravagance, and knowledge without effeminacy," Pericles boasts.[59] On the other hand, he makes an even more marked differentiation between Athens and Sparta, noting the freedom from official surveillance which Athenians enjoy in their daily life, the openness of their city, the absence of alien purges, and the contrast between the painful discipline imposed by the Spartans upon their youth and the Athenian way of promoting manliness.[60] The classic comparison of the Athenian and the Lacedaemonian characters is contained in the speech that Thucydides puts into the mouth of the Corinthian envoys to the meeting of the confederacy at Sparta. He emphasizes the contrast between the conservative self-satisfaction of the Spartans, their slowness to comprehend a threat to their interests, their reluctance to act, their despondency when their belated and insufficient efforts are unsuccessful—and the Athenians' love of innovation, their brilliance and quickness in conceiving and executing their designs, their ungrudging expenditure of both physical and intellectual energy in their country's service, their resilience in adversity. The Athenians, in short, "were born into the world to take no rest themselves and to give none to others."[61]

---

[56] Thuc. vi, 80, 3; 82, 2. [57] Thuc. i, 77, 6.
[58] Herod. ix, 106, 3; Thuc. i, 75, 99; iii, 86, 3; vi, 76, 2-3.
[59] Thuc. ii, 40, 1. [60] Thuc. ii, 38-39.
[61] Thuc. i, 70, 9.

The Peloponnesian War, as Thucydides records it, takes on the character of a contest between these two ways of life.[62] Its outcome certainly shook the confidence of the Athenians; and in the bitter self-examination that took place among them at the close of the fifth century we know that many of Plato's fellow countrymen came to the conclusion that the Dorian way—with its "taste for what is solid, for work well done, for the love of order"[63]—was definitely better. The restless Athenians, with their boundless curiosity and their desire to make further improvements on what had already been well done, did not feel quite at home in the more stolid Dorian cities, so tenacious of the old ways; but they had come to respect, and even to envy, that very stability and conservatism. And this sentiment was widespread in the fourth century, as the eulogies of Spartan eunomia show. "The ordinary Greek," says Bury, "looked upon the Spartan constitution as a structure of severe and simple beauty, a Dorian city stately as a Dorian temple, far nobler than his own abode, but not so comfortable to dwell in."[64] To us, Sparta and Crete seem clearly cases of arrested development; but in the disillusionment that followed the Peloponnesian War many Athenians found it good to look upon these survivals of a simpler and nobler age.

Plato was of course acutely aware of this conflict of ideals. Megillus remarks on one occasion that the mode of life Homer describes is always Ionian rather than Laconian (680c). The true "Hellenic harmony," as Laches puts it in the dialogue named after him (188d), is not Ionian but Dorian, a harmony between noble words and deeds. This is not merely dramatic characterization, for in the *Republic* Socrates rejects the Ionian mode in music as "relaxed," but retains the stern Dorian mode, the mode of manly resolve in the hour of danger (399a). When Plato is writing to his friends in Syracuse about their prospects for reform, he issues the stern advice: "If anyone of you prefers the Sicilian way and is unable to live in Dorian fashion (Δωριστὶ ζῆν) according to the customs of your ancestors, don't count

[62] Note particularly the list of contingents in the two contending forces at Syracuse, VII, 57.

[63] Gustave Glotz, *Hist. grecque*, Paris, 1925, I, 304. On the special qualities of the Dorian peoples K. O. Müller's *Die Dorier* (Breslau, 1824; 2nd ed. 1844), in spite of its exaggeration and idealization, is still the classic treatment. Müller's insight into these special qualities need not be discredited because of his assumption of an inherent racial superiority in the Dorians, though this feature of his work has given rise to much controversy. See Marrou, 474 n. 4, for a bibliography of this controversy.

[64] *Hist. of Greece*, 134.

on him, for he will be of no use to you in your undertaking."[65] We need not then be surprised that in planning the model city described in the *Laws* he selects, as the most promising foundation for his purpose, colonists of Dorian stock, already habituated to the simpler and more austere life that he thinks necessary, and places them among Dorian surroundings relatively isolated from the currents of the fast-moving Greek world around him.

But how could Plato, who is almost the finest embodiment of Attic culture, take so seriously a people so manifestly lacking, in the fourth century, in the elements that we most prize in the Athenians and their Ionian kinsmen? Plato saw well the cultural deficiencies of the two Dorian states he makes prominent in the *Laws*. There is more than one sly reference to the ignorance of Cleinias and Megillus on certain matters with which the Athenian is quite familiar (e.g. 820a, 886b, 892e), and the reference to their neglect, or lack of appreciation, of Homer was certainly not intended as a compliment (680c). But it was not purely through qualities of character that the Dorians had made their impress upon Greek life. It is easy for us to underestimate the intellectual and artistic creativeness of the Dorians, dazzled as we are by the fuller splendor of the Ionians. But Plato would remember, and we should not forget, the contributions to philosophy, mathematics, and medicine made by the Pythagoreans and the school of Hippocrates;[66] the magnificent sculpture produced in the school of Polyclitus at Argos; the fine Corinthian vases that held the Mediterranean market until they were supplanted by the even better ones of Attica. There was a brilliant school of painting at Sicyon, but its products, having perished, can be judged only by the high reputation that they enjoyed in antiquity. The first trireme was made at Corinth. The first system of standard weights and measures was introduced by Pheidon at Argos. Corinthian and Sicyonian dithyrambs were the source of Attic tragedy, and the choral passages in the drama continued to be written and performed in a conventional Doric dialect. The first Greek coinage appeared at Aegina.

---

[65] *Ep. VII* 336cd. The Syracusans were Dorians, but both Syracuse and Tarentum, another Dorian colony, had discarded the simplicity and severity of their mother countries.

[66] Pythagoras, of course, was an Ionian from Samos. But Plato's friend Archytas of Tarentum was a Dorian; Tarentum was a Dorian city and Archytas even wrote in the Doric dialect. The Hippocratic writings, however, are in Ionic, like the *Histories* of that other Dorian from Asia Minor, Herodotus.

Attic comedy came from the Megarians, another Dorian people. Plato would remember especially the great school of choral music and dancing that flourished in the seventh and sixth centuries at Sparta, where such artists as Terpander, Alcman, and Tyrtaeus were happy to live and work. His own incomparable dialogues were a development of the suggestions afforded him by the mimes of another Dorian, Sophron of Syracuse, whom he greatly admired. Above all, we should remember that simple but powerful style of architecture which was originated by the Dorians and to which their name has ever since been attached. The Doric temple, with its apparent poverty but profound inner logic, is the creation of that hidden sophist in the Dorian nature, so nicely divined by Socrates in the *Protagoras*.

But though the Dorians initiated, it was nearly always the Ionians who brought their inventions to perfection. It was Athens that developed the dithyrambs into tragic drama; it was Athenian sculptors who transformed the athletes of Polyclitus into ideal forms in which humanity is scarcely distinguishable from divinity; and it was at Athens that the greatest of all Doric temples, the Parthenon, was built. In its combination of strength and grace, this structure seems a perfect symbol of that fruitful mixture of Dorian and Ionian qualities which distinguished Athens in her greatest period.[67] Why should not the same mixture take place in political creation? Plato at least was following a tradition well established when he took the Spartan polis as his point of departure. If this solid Dorian structure could be redesigned to accommodate the moral and intellectual graces of Ionian life, would that not be a worthy creation?

EXCURSUS B. PLATO'S VERSION OF PELOPONNESIAN HISTORY

PLATO's account of the three Dorian kingdoms deserves attention, not merely for the nuggets of historical truth it may contain, but also for the information it gives us of Plato's attitude toward the conflicting traditions that we know were current in his day regarding these even then distant events. Plato's declared intention is to use history for the principles it may reveal for the guidance of the legislator (676a, 683b). But when history is used for didactic purposes,

[67] Emile Boutmy, *La Philosophie de l'architecture en Grèce*, Paris, 1870, 30f.

fact (or what is believed to be fact) is often distorted, consciously or unconsciously, in order to support a theory already arrived at. For this reason, because Plato's historical references (here and elsewhere) are nearly always tied up with a theory which they reveal or illustrate, his reliability as a historian has usually been questioned, and the "facts" he recites have been ignored by both philosophers and historians.

It is by no means a simple matter to determine how faithfully Plato adheres to historical facts. Clearly it will not do simply to compare his statements with what present-day historians say about the same events: for historical facts are themselves interpretations of traditions, documents, and physical evidence of past events—interpretations that have been critically arrived at, to be sure, but nevertheless not simply given and incorrigible. To determine how reliable Plato is as a historian one must compare his statements with the judgments of his contemporaries about the traditions current in the fourth century. Furthermore, some parts of fourth-century belief and tradition have undoubtedly been lost with the passage of time; and if on occasion he seems to depart from those traditions as we see them, there is always the possibility that he is relying upon evidence that has since disappeared but that he thought worthy of credence. I shall not attempt an answer to the larger question of Plato's historical reliability; that would require a wider-ranging inquiry than is possible here. But it will be relevant to that larger question if we can partially reconstruct the background of tradition—and conflict of traditions—by which his statements about early Peloponnesian history are to be judged. Furthermore, since the mist that envelops those distant events that he speaks of is almost impenetrable, the attempt to identify the sources of his information may afford some welcome gleams of light.

Plato describes the Dorian invasion as a return of the Achaeans previously expelled from their cities during the turmoils following the Trojan War; they now call themselves Dorians, after their leader Dorieus (682e). He mentions the division of their forces into three parts and the founding of three cities, Temenus becoming the king of Argos, Cresphontes the king of Messenia, and Procles and Eurysthenes joint kings of Lacedaemon (683d). Later these kings are said to be brothers, and children of Heracles (685d). These are all parts of the μυθολογία which he says the Lacedaemonians enthusiastically cultivated (682e; 683d; cf. *Hipp. Mj.* 285d) and which we know of from other sources. How much of this Plato regards as reliable it is hard to say; but it is worth remarking that in some details he departs from the fifth-century Lacedaemonian tradition. He considers that it was the twin sons of Aristodemus, rather than Aristodemus himself, who led the Spartans into their land, though the Spartan tradition, as reported to Herodotus (vi, 52), was that these sons were born after the settlement. Plato evidently accepts the alternative and more generally accepted account—the tradition of "the poets," Herodotus calls it—that Aristodemus died and was succeeded by his two sons before the conquest. Yet there is a slight inconsistency in Plato's calling these first kings brothers—which is not literally true if it was the sons of Aristodemus who established Lacedaemon; and later, ignoring the sons, he speaks of Lacedaemon as "the portion of Aristodemus" (692b). Again of these twin sons he gives the pre-eminence to Procles, though the Spartan story was that it was Eurysthenes, and after him the kings in the Agid line, who were regarded as having precedence (Herod. vi, 52). It is possible that Plato's reversal of the usual order of these names reflects the greater prestige of the Eurypontid kings of the fourth century (i.e. Archidamus, Agesilaus, Agis) in comparison with their Agid colleagues, and if so the Lacedaemonian tradition itself may have undergone change since the time of Herodotus. In any case the tradition appears to have been still plastic in Plato's day (Ephorus himself seems uncertain whether it was Procles, or Eurysthenes and Procles, who established Sparta; compare x, iv, 18 with viii, v, 4-5) so that no particular significance is to be attached to Plato's departures from the fifth-century Spartan version.

The most striking feature of the Spartan constitution, the dual kingship, is taken for granted at this part of Plato's history. It is only later that it is emphasized as the first of the three saving characteristics that checked at Sparta the natural tendency of monarchy to excessive power. When it is mentioned later (691d) it is said to have come about by divine providence (θεὸς . . . κηδόμενος ὑμῶν τις, ὃς τὰ μέλλοντα προορῶν κτλ), through the birth of twins in the royal family. This is the Spartan explanation as given by Herodotus (vi, 52) and followed by Xenophon *Ages.* viii, 7). Modern historians have suggested different explanations of this anomalous form of kingship —e.g. that it was the result of a compromise, or division of power, between the Dorian conquerors and the native kingdom (cf. J. G.

Frazer, *Pausanias*, London, 1913, III, 312); but none of Plato's contemporaries seems to have doubted the official Spartan tradition.

The establishment of cities obviously requires laws; and Plato proceeds at once to what we may call the first stage of legislation in Spartan history (684ab). He apparently regards these early laws as a kind of constitution specifying the powers of kings and peoples respectively (νόμους οὓς ἔθεντο τοῦ τε ἄρχειν καὶ ἄρχεσθαι κοινούς). Furthermore, he thinks of these laws as constituting a kind of confederation, sanctioned by solemn oaths and aimed at the preservation not merely of the alliance, but of internal order in each state. The kings swore not to extend the powers assigned to them, and the peoples not to try to overthrow their kings; and peoples and kings also promised aid to any member of the confederacy which was threatened with internal dissension. This confederation was intended not merely as a safeguard of order within each state, but also as defense against possible attack from without (685cd). Plato mentions here the Assyrian empire which had a grievance against the Greeks for the sack of Troy and might be expected to attack, just as the Greeks of more recent history feared an attack from "the Great King," i.e. Persia. This reference to Troy as a part of the Assyrian empire has caused surprise. England quotes Stallbaum's note: "hoc unde Plato hauserit, incertum." But Eusebius (*Chron. Arm.* p. 28, Kaerst) quotes Cephalion as saying: "I begin my history at the same point at which others begin, viz. Hellanicus, Ctesias and Herodotus: the Assyrians in ancient times ruled over Asia." Plato is therefore following the current conceptions of the historians (cf. Herod. I, 95).

The oath of allegiance and mutual assistance between the three cities in Plato's description has been questioned by Busolt and Glotz. But it seems unlikely that Plato invented it; much of the force of his later argument would be lost if the promising beginning he has described were regarded by his readers as nothing but a Platonic fiction. He is probably drawing from some writer now lost, possibly Hellanicus, who we know dealt with the settlement of the Dorians in the Peloponnesus (FGH I, 4, F115-F116). Meyer (*Gesch. des Altertums* II, 267) remarks that Plato's mention of the oath taken by these three kings rests on a correct perception of the close relationship that must have once existed between the early Dorian states. The evidence of similar institutions in these regions—such as the observance of an armistice during the month Karneios, for the Dorians a sacred month —and other similarities of social structure (Chrimes, *Ancient Sparta*, 272ff.) show that Plato's reference to this oath of mutual assistance is something more than an empty embellishment of the tradition. The oath between kings and peoples is accepted by Busolt, so far as Sparta is concerned (*Gr. Gesch.* I, 227). Xenophon mentions the monthly exchange of oaths between the kings and ephors at Sparta, the king swearing that he would reign according to the established laws of the state, and the ephors, on behalf of the state, swearing that they would keep the kingship "unshaken" (*Const. Lac.* xv, 7). This Spartan custom may very well go back to ancient times. Isocrates (vi, 21ff.), like Plato, conceives the oath between kings and peoples to have been taken in each of the three kingdoms at the time of the original settlement, and blames the downfall of Messenia on the faithlessness of the people toward their king. But this may be a part of the Spartan propaganda after Leuctra, devised to counter the effect of traditions invented—or reasserted—by the liberated Messenians. It may be that Plato himself lost his way among these competing traditions.

Closely connected with—perhaps a part of—this original legislation was the division of the land into equal allotments (684de; cf. 736c). One of the fundamental Lacedaemonian institutions, in the opinion of Plato's contemporaries, was the unalienable κλᾶρος of the Spartan citizen. Despite the current tendency to attribute all the excellences of the Spartan constitution to "Lycurgus," Plato clearly regards this distribution as coeval with the establishment of the Lacedaemonian kingdom, several generations before Lycurgus' time, as his contemporaries reckoned. He remarks that the invaders were in a favorable situation to establish equality, since there were no large properties as yet and no vested interests to overcome. Is this merely a projection into the past of an arrangement that Plato, to judge from his own laws, regards as a wise one? Or is it an inference from the practice of his own time at the establishment of a colony? (The settlement of the Heraclidae is actually called an ἀποικία in 736c.) Or is it the reflection of an oral tradition? The allotment was generally regarded as old in Plato's time. Aristotle says that at Sparta it was forbidden to sell the ἀρχαία μοῖρα (Fr. 611, 12, Rose); and the poems of Tyrtaeus contained evidence, he thought, that in the seventh century there were demands for a redistribution of the land (*Pol.*

1307a 2), which seems to imply an earlier distribution that was no longer satisfactory (cf. Plut. *Inst. Lac.* 22: τῆς ἀρχῆθεν διατεταγμένης μοίρας). Plato is not indulging in free invention here; he is following traditions which he may have misinterpreted, but which gave him some guidance. This part of his account has been treated with respect; Busolt defends it vigorously, as resting on "historical memory" (Busolt-Swoboda 633 n. 6).

Who were the legislators responsible for this early constitution and social organization? Plato does not say; indeed he seems deliberately to avoid committing himself on this point. He refers vaguely to "the legislators of that time, whoever they were" (692b), "whether it was the kings who legislated or some other persons" (εἴτε οἱ βασιλῆς ἐνομοθέτουν εἴτ᾽ ἄλλοι τινές, 684b). From this early legislation he distinguishes two later stages, the first marked by the establishment of the gerousia, and the second by the establishment of the ephorate (692a), both of which were designed to provide checks upon the royal power, and which had the result of producing that beneficent "mixture" in the Spartan executive that Plato found so instructive. In distinguishing these stages in the development of the Spartan constitution he abandons the conventional view that looked upon all Spartan laws in their entirety as the work of Lycurgus, an opinion held by Herodotus (1, 65), by Xenophon (*Const. Lac.* 1 and passim), and probably also by Ephorus (Strabo VIII, v, 4-5). It is likely that this view was sedulously fostered by the Spartans as a part of the legend of immutability attaching to their laws. Isocrates (XII, 153) appears to accept it, but gives a curious twist to the legend when he professes to believe that Lycurgus was imitating ancient Athens in his legislation. It is probably to refute this current but erroneous opinion that Aristotle begins his *Constitution of the Lacedaemonians* by remarking that "some persons attribute to Lycurgus the whole of the Lacedaemonian constitution" (Fr. 611, 9, Rose); for in the *Politics* (1313a 26) he asserts that the ephorate was established in the reign of King Theopompus, two generations after Lycurgus' time, as he conceived it. Now the name of Lycurgus does not appear in Plato's account of the development of the Lacedaemonian constitution, but there is a quite unambiguous reference to him in the description of the second "savior"—the human being in whose nature there was an admixture of divinity (691e)—who established the gerousia (see Chapter II, Note 47). This appears to be Plato's considered judgment as to the part played by the historical Lycurgus. Although both he and Aristotle often speak of Lycurgus in the conventional manner as "the legislator" of Sparta, both had converted the mythical and legendary hero into a historical person who made an important reform in a constitution that was already existing when he appeared and that underwent other changes after his death.

How much else besides the institution of the gerousia Plato would attribute to the historical Lycurgus it is impossible to say. His silence in this passage with regard to other elements of the Lycurgan tradition shows only that his purpose here is to describe the way in which the power of the kings became "mixed," or moderated. The part assigned to Lycurgus in the political development was an important one (the third "savior" who established the ephorate may be regarded as completing his work of devising checks on the executive power) and might well be coupled in Plato's mind with changes in the system of education, or even with the drastic reorganization of Spartan life referred to by Thucydides (1, 18, 1). But what is important in Plato's insight here is the recognition that the laws of the Spartans expressed a mode of life and a type of character which antedated Lycurgus and which provided the foundation on which he could build.

But if Lycurgus was a historical person, to what date was he to be assigned? The account we have been considering gives him only a vaguely determined position after the settlement and before the establishment of the ephorate. This vagueness may be deliberate. "About Lycurgus," says Plutarch, "nothing can be said that is not disputed, and there is least agreement as to the times in which the man lived" (*Lyc.* 1). There is evidence that the disagreements were as pronounced in Plato's day as in Plutarch's. Xenophon places him with the Heraclidae, i.e. at the time of the conquest (*Const. Lac.* x, 8). Herodotus (1, 65) says the reform of Lycurgus occurred during the reign of Leobates, who was third after Eurysthenes in the Agid line, twelve or thirteen generations (or about 433 years, counting three generations to a century) before the expedition of Xerxes, which would put him at the end of the tenth century. Thucydides (1, 18) reckons that the Spartans have enjoyed the same constitution a little more than four hundred years, counting to the end of "the present war"; this would put the reorganization toward the end of the ninth century. But in the fourth century Lycurgus is connected with the

Eurypontid rather than with the Agid line of kings; both Aristotle and Ephorus regard him as the uncle and older contemporary of King Charillus in the Eurypontid line (Strabo x, iv, 19; Arist. *Pol.* 1271b 25), i.e. ten generations before the battle of Thermopylae. Plutarch reports that Aristotle believed Lycurgus had helped establish the Olympic truce, alleging as evidence a discus at Olympia on which the name of Lycurgus was inscribed; this would put him in the first quarter of the eighth century. (The authenticity of this discus is quite properly doubted by modern scholars; it may have been evidence manufactured at a later time to add to the repute of Lycurgus and Sparta.) There is only one passage in any of the Platonic writings that suggests a date for Lycurgus, and this occurs in the possibly spurious *Minos* (318c). Socrates in this dialogue says that the legislation of Lycurgus is perhaps a little more than three hundred years old. If we assume that the writer is reckoning from the time of Socrates, we get a date for Lycurgus around the third quarter of the eighth century. Since the writer is emphasizing the relative newness of even the oldest Greek laws as compared with those of Crete, we must make allowance for dramatic emphasis. This statement, therefore, accords very well with Aristotle's dating—which is what we might expect, for the dialogue, even if not written by Plato, comes from the Platonic circle and was written before the middle of the fourth century (see Excursus A).

The central purpose of Plato's history is to explain why, of the three Dorian kingdoms that were founded together under such favorable auspices, only the Lacedaemonian has been preserved; "the other two very soon destroyed their constitution and laws" (685a). Plato is thinking of very early events, i.e. of the degeneration that took place in Messenia before its conquest by the Spartans in the eighth century, and of the parallel decline in the power of the kings at Argos, leading to the deposition of the last of the Temenidae (for these events see Paus. II, xix, 2 and Diod. VII, Fr. 13, 2). The source of both Pausanias and Diodorus seems to be Ephorus (Andrewes, CQ XLV, 1951, 39-40) who devoted his first book, according to Andrewes' brilliant reconstruction of it, to the same theme as that which occupies Plato in the third book of the *Laws*. Ephorus' thesis apparently was that in both Argos and Messenia the kings failed to maintain themselves against the demos. Plato seems to blame the kings rather than the demos; Sparta was saved because the royal power was checked, whereas in the other kingdoms the possessors of power did not know how to use it with restraint. Despite this possible difference in attitude, apparently both Plato and Ephorus saw the decline as a failure to retain the original division of powers between kings and peoples (684a). Plato ignores more easily than we like the later conquest of Messenia by the Spartans, and the efforts of the Spartans to extend their conquests into the territory of Argos. But the lesson of the prior events seems to him clear, and it is apparently the same moral that Ephorus drew, as Andrewes states it: "In all three states kings and peoples quarrelled. But whereas in Argos and Messenia the quarrel ended only with the downfall of the king or state, in Sparta a solution was found" (*op.cit.* 41).

The fact that both Ephorus and Plato treat an identical theme and draw markedly similar conclusions can hardly be explained as a coincidence. Yet it is hard to see how either could have been influenced by the published work of the other. If Ephorus' *Histories* began to appear about 350 (see FGH 2C, 25), and Plato's *Laws* was published only after his death in 347, then Ephorus' first book could not have been influenced by the *Laws*. On the other hand it seems unlikely that Plato's third book—which is so fundamental in the whole design of the *Laws* and so closely knitted to the succeeding books—could have been written after 350. We must assume either (1) that there was some close association between the two men during the closing years of Plato's life, or (2) that a part of the *Laws* containing the present Book III was in circulation some years before Plato's death and had become known to Ephorus. (I have called attention in Excursus A to the similarity of Ephorus' views about Minos' relation to Zeus with those expressed by Plato in Book I.) Whether it was Plato or Ephorus who first proposed this interpretation of Peloponnesian history is of little relevance to our immediate purpose; what is important is that Plato's ideas are in such close accord with those of the most eminent historian among his contemporaries.

In two passages of this book Plato refers to a Messenian War of which historians have usually taken no account. One of the deplorable consequences of the decline of Messenia, he says, is that when the Persian menace appeared she actually hindered Sparta from sending help to the defenders of Hellas by warring against her at the time (692d; cf. 698de). This is clearly a reference to the battle of Marathon in 490. Historians usually recognize only three Messenian wars—the war of conquest in the late eighth century, the revolt in the middle of the seventh, and a second revolt after the earthquake in 464 (Bengtson, *Gr. Gesch.* 74f., 183). Plato's references to still another war have recently been interpreted as an instance of his succumbing to Spartan propaganda[1] (the Spartans were a day late in arriving at Marathon, as is well known). But Strabo (VIII, iv, 10) reckons that there were four Messenian wars, and Pausanias (IV, xxiii, 5-10) mentions a war between the Spartans and Messenians "when Miltiades was archon at Athens." Quite recently Miss L. H. Jeffery (JHS LXIX, 1950, 26-30) has found archaeological evidence confirming Pausanias' reference to an early fifth-century rising among the Messenians. Evidently Plato knew what he was writing about.

Our survey has failed to show any important instances in which Plato has distorted facts in the interests of theory. In most cases he relies on traditions generally accepted, or accepted by the most competent of his contemporaries; and when he departs from these generally accepted traditions he is moved by critical considerations that were decisive also for Aristotle. It is possible that his belief in the original oath of confederation between the three Dorian kingdoms and in the oaths in each kingdom between king and people was influenced by spurious traditions stimulated by the liberation of Messenia after Leuctra, or by Spartan counter propaganda; but even here a considerable part of his belief has found support among modern historians. More important evidence of Plato's loyalty to history is his deliberate portrayal of the Spartan constitution as having come about through a series of changes. It would have served his philosophical purpose equally well to describe all of the checks on the royal prerogative as having been set up together at one time by a wise legislator, as most of his contemporaries thought. In looking at the Spartan constitution in this historical fashion he set a pattern which Aristotle seems to have followed, to judge from passages in the *Politics* and the fragments of his lost *Constitution of the Lacedaemonians*. Both men see that if Lycurgus was a historical figure

---

[1] W. den Boer, "Political Propaganda in Greek Chronology," *Historia* v, 1956, 162-177. The explanation given by Plato of the Spartans' failure to arrive at Marathon until the day after the battle originated "in all probability . . . after the liberation of Messenia by the Thebans. . . . Not only the glorification of Sparta but also the defamation of Messenia became its object. . . . The philosopher has preserved for us a version of the Messenian wars which appealed to his anti-Athenian inclination. . . . His admiration for Sparta made him accept with alacrity the Spartan version of the events in 490" (169-170, 177).

who brought about an important reform in the constitution, then the constitution as it existed prior to his time was obviously not of his making. The kingship in its dual form, the division of the land, and other features of the social and military organization were therefore older than Lycurgus. Likewise Lycurgus had successors, and some parts of the constitution, particularly the ephorate, came into being after his time. Whether it was Plato or Aristotle who was the originator and chief investigator in these historical inquiries we cannot well decide. Plato's account is the earlier; but we do not know how much he was indebted to his younger colleague in the Academy who must already have begun those inquiries into Greek constitutions that are one of his most notable achievements.

CHAPTER III

ATHENS

Plato's choice of an Athenian Stranger to be the interlocutor with the two Dorians undoubtedly was deliberate, and it indicates clearly his intention to confront the Dorian way with the traditions of his native city. The rivalry between Sparta and Athens to set the pattern of life for the Greeks was of long standing. It had engaged Plato's attention in earlier dialogues, and it is most natural that it should be the center of attention in this his latest one. But who is this anonymous representative of Athenian traditions? Is he a spokesman for Plato, a fourth-century Socrates, as Aristotle evidently interprets him?[1] Or is he to be taken as some learned member of the Academy, or perhaps merely as a thoughtful and cultivated Athenian whose opinions Plato would think worth presenting but may not altogether agree with?

The first alternative is the one usually adopted. In no other dialogue do we feel less of a dramatic screen between ourselves and Plato. The anonymity of the Athenian means that there is no independent character to be sustained, as is true of the Socratic dialogues, even the *Republic*; and Plato is free as nowhere else to put forward his own doctrines. And yet the same caution is required of us here that we observe in dealing with the Eleatic Stranger in the *Sophist* and the *Politicus*, with the Timaeus in the dialogue named after him, and even with the Socrates of the *Republic*. The dramatic form is always something of a mask, and seems deliberately chosen by Plato as a way of presenting ideas and conclusions in process of formation, as distinct from dogmas and final opinions that he holds. The dogmatic tone and the note of finality are more evident here than in some of Plato's other dialogues; but there are many points in the proposed legislation that are recognized as tentative, and what is more relevant, the Athenian sometimes says things about himself that are hardly appropriate to Plato and suggest rather some less learned fellow countryman. On the other hand, there are some passages which can be understood only if we take the Athenian to be speaking as Plato, with a consciousness of what he had previously said in his dialogues and of what his readers would know about his

[1] *Pol.* 1265a 11.

work in the Academy.[2] In any case, the problems discussed and the solutions proposed in this latest and longest work of Plato's are certainly intended to be taken seriously; and we can properly substitute Plato for the Athenian Stranger on most occasions, if we remember that the real Plato, more than most authors, remains inscrutable.

In the conversation between the three old men the leading part belongs to the Athenian. It is he who suggests that they talk about laws and government during their walk to the sanctuary of Zeus, and it is he who starts the discussion by inquiring about the purpose of Cretan and Spartan laws. His critical examination of the answer given by his two companions evokes a burst of admiration from Cleinias for leading the argument back to first principles (626d). But these first principles prove none too favorable to the conventional Dorian views of the purpose of law and the place of warlike courage among the virtues; and when the discussion turns into a controversy over the value of Athenian symposia, the Athenian's role becomes more openly didactic. Cleinias presses him to show them that his view of symposia is correct, and assures him that they will try to understand what he says. "Very well," replies the Athenian, "this is the way we must proceed, you making every effort to understand and I trying in some way or other to make my statement clear. But first let me say this. All the Greeks consider my city to be fond of words and as always having much to say; whereas Lacedaemon and Crete they regard as short in speech, cultivating richness of thought rather than loquacity. Now I am eager not to seem to be drawing out a long discourse on a trivial matter. But the truth is, the right treatment of this question—the use of wine, which is a trivial matter—can never be clearly and adequately handled apart from a correct theory of music; nor music, in turn, apart from a consideration of education in general. This will mean a lot of words" (641e-642a).

Megillus responds by revealing that his family have long been proxenoi of Athens and that from his youth up he has been trained to take pride in praises of the Athenian city and to resent criticisms of her; and he quotes with approval the "common saying" that when Athenians are good they are incomparably good, for they alone are

[2] The Athenian is an old man (657d et al.); he has traveled widely (639d); he has given much attention to laws and legislation (968b), and he knows where to find others equally skilled. Yet if he has only recently learned of incommensurable magnitudes (819d, 820ab) he can hardly be Plato (see Chapter VII, Note 171).

good not by compulsion but by inner disposition. Cleinias in turn recalls that an ancestor of his, the famous Epimenides, had once rendered great services to Athens, and that his family have ever since been united to Athens by ties of hospitality and feelings of goodwill. The Athenian is thus placed in the position of a teacher to whom the Spartan and the Cretan listen with respect; and this is the role he maintains throughout the rest of the dialogue. We are frequently reminded of it by comments of his two companions (cf. 676c, 688d, 694a,c, 700a); on one occasion they are explicitly called μαθηταί (770c); and sometimes the dialogue disappears completely and becomes, particularly in the later books, a continuous exposition by the Athenian.[3]

The respective positions thus assigned the Athenian and his two companions is a historically convincing one. It was the Ionians, and among the Ionians the Athenians, who produced practically all the theories about law and government that have come down to us from the Greeks. From them we have the political discussions in Herodotus, the speeches in Thucydides, the reflections of the Attic dramatists, as well as the explicit philosophical arguments of Heraclitus and Democritus, of Xenophon and Plato; and nothing like them was produced by Crete or Sparta or any other Dorian state. But the description of the Lacedaemonians and Cretans as rich in thought, though sparing of words, shows that they have an important contribution to make; it recalls Socrates' statement in the *Protagoras* (342de) that the Spartans and Cretans have a secret wisdom disguised under the mask of taciturnity. Plato's purpose seems to be clear. As the Ionians had so often in Greek history taken over and developed the discoveries of the Dorians, so the role of the Athenian in this dialogue is to elicit and put into philosophical terms the implicit wisdom in the institutions of the Lacedaemonians and Cretans.

But to appreciate fully the Athenian's right to lead the discussion we must recall that Athens had more to contribute than the spirit of inquiry and the gift of expression. Athenian laws were famous and respected. "Solon the Athenian," as Herodotus often calls him, had a reputation that antedated by far the fame of Lycurgus; his name appears in all the lists of the Seven Sages. Livy reports that the Law of the Twelve Tables, the first great monument of Roman law, was

---

[3] The Athenian's superiority is frequently acknowledged by his two companions (639e, 818e, 769ab) and asserted by himself (641e, 711a, 886ab, 892de, 897d, 900c).

the work of a commission that had been explicitly instructed to study "the laws of Solon and of other Greek states."[4] Ephorus records that the famous Zaleucus had drawn up his laws for the Locrians by borrowing from the Cretans, the Lacedaemonians, and the Areopagites.[5] Whether or not these statements are historically reliable, they indicate the prestige of Athenian law in the fourth and later centuries. Isocrates even contends that the famous legislation of Lycurgus was not original with him, but an imitation of the ancient institutions of Athens.[6]

But Athenian democracy, as it had developed in the late fifth and early fourth centuries, was the subject of violent controversy in Plato's time. It would enormously facilitate our understanding of Plato and Aristotle if we had more of the extensive literature that this controversy seems to have provoked. Practically all of it that has come down to us is highly critical of Athens, and from the reading of it one is likely to get the impression that for the serious fourth-century thinker Athenian democracy was, as Alcibiades had put it much earlier, "an admitted folly."[7] But a more careful reading of the literary sources and a study of the other evidence available show that to be critical of Athens in Plato's day did not necessarily mean abandonment of the Athenian way. It is true that in the closing years of the Peloponnesian War there were many persons, at Athens and elsewhere, who thought of oligarchy as a tempting substitute for democracy, and the Spartan way of life as preferable to the Athenian. Plato's cousin Critias was one of this number. But in the fourth century Athenian thinkers were more circumspect. Since the time of Alcibiades' remark the Athenians had experienced the rule of the Thirty Tyrants, an explicit and avowed oligarchy of their own; and all the Greeks had had a taste of imperialism as practised by Sparta during her brief period of supremacy after the conclusion of the great war, and had observed the discrepancy between Spartan principles and the behavior of the Spartan harmosts abroad.[8] The disillusioned Athenian of this period might still look to an idealized Sparta as

---

[4] Livy III, 31.

[5] Strabo VI, i, 8. So far as I know, this is the first mention, outside the *Laws*, of this trio of Greek states famous for their legislation, though it became a commonplace in later times. On Ephorus' relation to Plato, see Chapter I and Excursus B.

[6] Isoc. XII, 153-154; IV, 39.

[7] Thuc. VI, 89, 6.

[8] Xen. *Const. Lac.* XIV; Isoc. VIII, 67-68; IV, 122-128; Lys. II, 67-69; Plato *Menex.* 244c; cf. Thuc. I, 77, 6.

an answer to the problems of his city, but if he had any sense of political realities he was far more likely to look for guidance to his own city's past, to the earlier democracy—or aristocracy, as one might prefer to call it—that existed before the days of Pericles. The demand for the restoration of the "ancestral constitution"—the πάτριος πολιτεία—was first raised, so far as our evidence indicates, in the closing years of the Peloponnesian War, and it seems soon to have become the slogan alike of the democrats and the moderate conservatives, and perhaps also of the extreme oligarchs as well— each of these parties, of course, attaching its own interpretation to the slogan.[9] For all these parties the appeal to the ancestral constitution meant not an appeal to something alien to the Athenian tradition, but a return to the very heart of that tradition, as the critics saw it—a return to the principles under which Athens had developed from a backward unimportant state to her position of leadership during the Persian Wars.

Who was the lawgiver responsible for this ancestral constitution? It was generally regarded in the fourth century as the "constitution of Solon and Cleisthenes." The appearance of Solon alongside Cleisthenes seems to have been a result of the controversies just mentioned. During the fifth century Cleisthenes was generally regarded as the founder of Athenian democracy; so at least he appears in Herodotus.[10] Solon's name seems to have been first invoked in party politics by the moderate conservatives,[11] who argued that the "democracy" of Cleisthenes, when examined closely, would be found not to be democratic in the sense of that term common in the late fifth century,

[9] A fragment of Thrasymachus (Diels-Kranz II, 321-324) shows that there was bitter controversy over the meaning of πάτριος πολιτεία. According to Hignett (5, 273) it was the slogan of the extreme and moderate oligarchs. Alexander Fuks (*The Ancestral Constitution*, passim) takes it to have been invoked by the moderate conservatives and the democrats. Aristotle reports that a clause in the peace terms imposed by Sparta prescribed that Athens should be governed by its ancestral constitution (Arist. *Const. Ath.* xxxiv, 3). This is now generally regarded as a fabrication devised by "later writers who sought to excuse the part played by Theramenes in the subsequent events." Hignett 285; cf. Fuks, *op.cit.* 52ff.

[10] Herod. vi, 131; cf. also v, 66. See J. A. O. Larsen, "Cleisthenes and the Development of the Theory of Democracy," in *Essays in Political Theory Presented to George H. Sabine*, eds. Konvitz and Murphy, Cornell University Press, 1948, 1-16.

[11] In Cleitophon's "rider" to the motion of Pythodorus in 411 (Arist. *Const. Ath.* xxix, 3; Fuks, *op.cit.* 4ff.). The reference to Solon was probably not a part of Cleitophon's amendment, but may be taken as valid evidence of the motive behind it, particularly since it contradicts Aristotle's own view of the relation of Cleisthenes' constitution to Solon.

but quite similar to the constitution of Solon. This was a clever move, for the radical democrats could hardly deny that Cleisthenes had done little to decrease the power of the Areopagus; that had been the work of Ephialtes and Pericles, a generation later. Furthermore, the democrats honored Solon as a legislator; and the revision of the laws, undertaken after the restoration of the democracy in 410 and completed after the second restoration in 403, was explicitly a restatement of the "laws of Solon." In general his was too honored a name to be relinquished to their opponents. On the other hand, the conservatives had to establish the fact that Solon could be credited with a constitution. There was living evidence of his laws, engraved on stone pillars in the Stoa Basileios and on the wooden axones in the Prytaneum, where citizens and officials could consult them at any time. But these laws did not make a constitution; they were simply instructions to the city's officials as to the laws they were to enforce.[12] Had Solon also set up the system of officials and allotted to them and to the people their respective powers and responsibilities? On this point there was no similarly reliable evidence. And if he was responsible for the establishment of the popular courts, as came to be generally believed, it was he who had opened the way for the demos to become, as Aristotle puts it, the ruling power (δ $\kappa\rho\alpha\tau\hat{\omega}\nu$) in the state.[13] Thus the controversies over the democracy, and the ancestral constitution which it had replaced, came to involve the nature and purpose of Solon's famous reforms. The extreme conservatives, the diehards, would have none of him; they looked to Draco as the author of the ancestral constitution. But Solon was accepted by the other two parties: by the democrats as the author of the laws, and by the moderates as the author of both the constitution and the laws of the ancestral democracy.[14]

[12] On this difference between laws ($\nu\acute{o}\mu o\iota$) and constitution ($\pi o\lambda\iota\tau\epsilon\acute{\iota}\alpha$) see Note 19.

[13] *Const. Ath.* XLI, 2. Hence the temptation to go behind Solon and find in Draco the founder of the ancestral constitution. Draco's laws on homicide had been incorporated with Solon's in the legislative revision at the end of the fifth century. Some unknown partisan of this persuasion actually drew up an account of this alleged constitution of Draco, and it seems to have deceived even Aristotle—if indeed the fourth chapter of the *Constitution of the Athenians* is his and not a later insertion.

[14] Gomme (*Hist. Com. on Thucydides* I, 47) says that in the fourth century the moderate democrat praised Cleisthenes and Aristides; the moderate oligarch repudiated Cleisthenes but accepted Solon; and Solon himself was discountenanced by the extreme oligarchs.

Plato must have followed this controversy with the keenest interest. His maternal ancestor, Dropides, had been a kinsman of Solon, and there is evidence that he was proud of the connection between his family and the great legislator. In the charming picture of the young Charmides, Plato's uncle, at the beginning of the dialogue named after him, Plato takes pains to bring out the young man's illustrious family and its connection with Solon (155a, 157e). It is Solon to whom Plato attributes one of his most genial creations, the story of the empire of Atlantis and of the heroic defense put up against it by the citizens of ancient Athens.[15] It is quite possible, as I have said, that this story is in fact not a free creation, but a tradition about Solon preserved in Plato's family which he accepted and used without being fully aware of the historical truth that underlay it. There are numerous other references in the dialogues to Solon—as a wise man, as a legislator, and as a poet;[16] and for his qualities as a poet Plato has the highest praise. "If Solon had been able," says the aged Critias in the *Timaeus*, "to cultivate poetry without the distraction of the civic quarrels that he tried to settle, he would have been more highly esteemed than even Hesiod and Homer."

But what was Plato's opinion of Solon's legislation? The explicit references in the dialogues help us very little. Except for the passage just quoted, referring to his efforts to settle the civic quarrels of his time, and another that refers to his archonship, they contain no specific information about Solon's work nor judgment upon it. There is a passage in the *Symposium* (209d) where, after mentioning the "immortality" that Lycurgus achieved by leaving behind him his laws to be the saviors of Lacedaemon and of all Greece, Plato adds that "among us" Solon also is revered as the father of the laws (διὰ τὴν τῶν νόμων γέννησιν). But is this merely a report of common opinion, or an avowal of personal admiration? If it is the latter, we still do not know the reasons for this admiration. But it is possible, I think, to get a good idea of Plato's opinions by examining the account of Solon contained in the second book of Aristotle's *Politics*, which certainly was written soon after Plato's *Laws* and is probably contem-

---

[15] *Tim.* 20e-25d. See Chapter I, Note 8.
[16] A wise man: *Prot.* 343a; *Tim.* 20d, 21bc; *Ep. II* 311a; a legislator: *Rep.* 599e; *Symp.* 209d; *Phaedr.* 258c, 278c; *Laws* 858e; *Tim.* 27b; a poet: *Charm.* 155a; *Tim.* 21bc; *Crit.* 113a; cf. *Erast.* 133c; *Rep.* 536d; *Laches* 188b, 189a; and archon: *Hipp. Mj.* 285e.

porary with it.[17] Like Plato, Aristotle knew and admired the poems of Solon and regarded them as peculiarly authoritative evidence regarding the principles and intentions of his reforms.[18] This passage is the earliest and probably the most authoritative of all the ancient accounts of Solon's work that have come down to us, and it contains, as we shall see, a highly individual interpretation of his legislation.

Aristotle begins by asserting that Solon was the author, not only of laws, but of a constitution as well[19]—at once taking a position with the moderates on the issue which we have seen was a matter of controversy. There are "some persons," he says, who regard him as an excellent (σπουδαῖος) legislator, in that he did away with the oligarchy, which was "too unmixed," ended the servitude of the demos, and established the "ancestral democracy," by judiciously "mixing" the constitution; the oligarchic element was represented in Solon's mixture by the council of the Areopagus, the aristocratic element in the provision that officers should be elected, and the democratic element in the establishment of the popular courts. Aristotle proceeds to correct what he conceives to be a certain exaggeration in this account of Solon's work, but his correction proves to be rather a minor one. The fact seems to be, he says, that Solon did not establish the Areopagus, nor the system of filling offices by election; he found them in existence and his contribution was that he left them as they were. (This was indeed no little service, since Solon, according to the tradition, was given authority to make whatever changes he thought necessary.) Solon's great innovation, as Aristotle sees it, was his establishment of the popular courts and his making service on them open to all citizens. Thus it seems to be true that he established the democracy. As if to confirm this interpretation, Aristotle cites the critics who say that Solon really destroyed the "other elements" in the state by making the popular court sovereign in all matters, thus

[17] *Pol.* 1273b 34 - 1274a 21; Jaeger, *Aristoteles*, 300-301n.
[18] Aristotle's use of these poems is most marked in the *Const. Ath.* v and xII; but there is a citation from one of them in *Pol.* 1256b 33, and another reference to them as authoritative in 1296a 20. These poems are in fact our only contemporary evidence of Solon's work. They seem to have been somewhat neglected, perhaps even forgotten, during the fifth century (cf. *Tim.* 21b); and one suspects that their revival, and their use by Aristotle, were due to Plato's interest in them.
[19] The distinction used by Aristotle here and elsewhere (*Pol.* 1289a 10-20; cf. 1290a 8) is that made by Plato in *Laws* 735a (and reaffirmed in 751a; cf. 768e). See Chapter V, Notes 100 and 101.

preparing the way for "the democracy now established." But Aristotle defends Solon against these critics. The later developments of democracy were due to special circumstances that could not have been foreseen and were not part of his intentions. He gave the people, Aristotle thinks, only such power as was necessary to prevent their subjection and alienation from the polity, viz. the power of electing officials and of holding them to account for their actions,[20] at the same time safeguarding the other elements by requiring that all officials be chosen from the three upper classes, the members of the lowest class, the Thetes, not being eligible to any office.

The interesting feature of this interpretation of Solon's work is that it makes him the author of a mixed constitution. Unfortunately Aristotle does not name the persons whose views these are. Could they be Plato and his fellows in the Academy?[21] Aristotle often refers to Plato's views with the phrase, "some people say."[22] The suggestion is made at least plausible by the fact that in the *Laws* Plato points out the danger of having "unmixed" offices, and insists throughout on the necessity of a moderate—or "mixed"—constitution; this encomium of Solon's work sounds as if it came from the same thinker. It should be noticed that Aristotle does not dispute the theory of the mixed constitution of Solonian Athens, but only corrects what he thinks are misapprehensions regarding the part played by Solon in bringing about this mixture. It is therefore a view of the ancient constitution with which we may presume he agrees.

Apart from Plato and Aristotle there is no thinker we know of at this date who could be the author of such views. Isocrates in the *Panathenaicus* refers to the mixture of democracy and aristocracy that Lycurgus set up at Sparta, in imitation, he says, of the constitution "of our ancestors."[23] But the *Panathenaicus* was written some

---

[20] Aristotle refers elsewhere (1281b 33) to Solon's wisdom in assigning to the people only ἀρχαιρεσία and εὔθυναι.

[21] Wilamowitz (*Aristoteles und Athen* I, 74 n. 49) considered this possibility and rejected it, on the ground that Plato's political thought [which regarded ἀρετή as the sole aim] was too simple for such complications as these. "Purity will permit of no mixture." (Plato's advocacy of a mixed constitution seems to have completely escaped Wilamowitz.) But he apparently admired the man who made this interpretation, considering him superior in historical knowledge and political judgment to most of his theoretical or practical contemporaries. "Who he was I do not know; Aristotle knew, but underestimated him." But *did* Aristotle underestimate him?

[22] There are many instances in Aristotle's text where τινές clearly refers to Plato (and his followers, of course); see H. Bonitz, *Index Aristotelicus*, s.v. Πλάτων.

[23] *Isoc.* XII, 153.

years after Plato's death and certainly well after the passage in Aristotle's *Politics*.[24] Another possible candidate is Androtion, whose history, it is now generally thought, was extensively used by Aristotle in his *Constitution of the Athenians*. But there is no surviving fragment of Androtion that indicates any such conception of Solon's work, and no hint of this conception in the passages of the *Constitution* that deal with Solon.[25] So far as our knowledge goes, it is only Plato and his like-minded disciples who can be plausibly identified as those meant in Aristotle's passage.

We can reinforce this tentative interpretation of Plato's views about Solon by citing certain clear references to Solonian institutions in the third book of the *Laws*. Immediately after the Athenian Stranger has expounded the "mixture" which brought moderation and with it stability to the Lacedaemonian constitution, he proceeds to give what looks like a negative demonstration of his thesis, using the examples of Persia and Athens to show how a state may degenerate through loss of wisdom and moderation (693e-701d). The consequence for Persia was an excess of despotism, for Athens an excess of freedom. What was the character of the Athenian constitution in the good old days before the decline set in, that is, when it was still characterized by the moderation that it has since lost?

At the time when the Persians attacked the Greeks, our constitution was an ancient one. Our officers were drawn from four property classes (τιμή-ματα), and there was in the city a mistress whose name was Modesty (αἰδώς) and because of her we were willing to live in servitude to the laws then established. 698b

There are three points of constitutional importance in this brief

---

[24] Besides, the theory Aristotle refers to implies a mixture of three forms—aristocracy, oligarchy, and democracy—whereas Isocrates mentions only democracy and aristocracy, though in an earlier passage of the same work (132ff.) he has distinguished three ("the only three") forms of constitution, viz. monarchy, oligarchy, and democracy. Aristocracy, he says, is not really a separate form, but can be realized in any of the others when the ablest citizens are selected for office. Thus on Isocrates' principles the aristocratic democracy which he champions is hardly a mixture of fundamental forms at all, still less a mingling of the three forms mentioned by Aristotle. Isocrates and his school may have worked out a different interpretation which Aristotle knew from oral discussion, but if so it is strange that we have no hint of it in any of Isocrates' numerous references to the ancient constitution of Solon and Cleisthenes.

[25] Furthermore, if Androtion's work appeared only after 344, as is now believed (Felix Jacoby, *Atthis*, Oxford, 1949, 74; Hignett 11-12) we have again a chronological difficulty, for it is extremely unlikely that this part of the *Politics* was written at such a late date.

passage. The first is the mention of the four property classes. The division of the citizens into four τιμήματα was a well-known feature of Solon's constitution. Whether it was instituted by Solon, or was merely taken over by him and adapted to his purposes, seems to have been a matter of controversy in Plato's day, as it still is.[26] In either case, these four classes were a memorable part of the constitution as Solon left it and had been retained in form down to Plato's time, though the change in the value of money had made them in fact obsolete. Their importance for Plato can be judged from the fact that he proposes, for his Cretan colony, a similar division of the citizens into four timemata.

In the second place, Plato indicates that these four timemata in some way determined the eligibility of citizens for office, though his language is too vague to show how he thought the officials were selected from them. Aristotle tells us that they were elected (i.e. not simply drawn by lot; the procedure is αἵρεσις)[27] and says that this was the aristocratic feature of the "mixed constitution" as conceived by the persons whose views he cites. Furthermore, he says they were elected by the people (δῆμος). It is significant that in Plato's legislation the procedure almost invariably prescribed for the selection of officials is election (the lot alone is rarely employed), and for almost all offices it is election by the full body of citizens, with eligibility to office in some cases dependent upon membership in one of the higher property classes, as in Solon's law.

The third feature of that ancient constitution mentioned by Plato is the respect accorded to the laws. Why should this be mentioned as a feature of the constitution? Again Aristotle's text gives us the clue. The Areopagus was one of the institutions explicitly credited to Solon by persons whose views he is citing. Now the function most generally attributed by later writers to the Areopagus of the sixth century was the "guardianship of the laws" (νομοφυλακία).[28] In Plato's proposed commonwealth the chief officials are actually named "guardians of the laws" (νομοφύλακες); hence his reference to the authority of the laws in the ancient constitution may properly be taken as a reference to the Areopagus and to the important role it

[26] See Hignett 99-100; and Busolt-Swoboda 820 n. 2.
[27] On the meaning of αἵρεσις in Aristotle, see Chapter V, Note 24, and Excursus C, below.
[28] Cf. Isoc. VII, 37-49; Arist. *Const. Ath.* VIII, 4.

was believed to have had in supervising the actions of officials and the conduct of private citizens. Thus Plato could regard the habit of law observance that distinguished the ancient Athenians as a direct result of the character of the constitution, and he endeavors to embody something similar in his own.

If, as Aristotle says, the officials of that ancient time were elected by the people, the author of the views he is citing must have considered the demos sovereign in certain important respects. This is confirmed as Plato's view by a sentence two pages later in the *Laws*.

Under the ancient laws there were certain matters over which the demos was not sovereign (οὐκ ἦν ὁ δῆμός τινων κύριος) but, so to speak, the willing servant of the laws. 700a

This sentence does not say, as some translators have been tempted to render it, that the people was not sovereign over anything. The emphasis is in fact quite the opposite; the demos was sovereign, but not over certain things, viz. the laws. What would this sovereignty include? Aristotle says it included the power of electing officials and the right to call them to account for their conduct in office. In defending Solon against his critics he asserts that such a right was necessary to prevent the people's subjection and alienation from the polity. "For if this also was not in the power of the demos, it would be a slave and an enemy."[29] This calling of officials to account (the εὐθύνειν of Aristotle's text) is inseparable from the establishment of the popular court mentioned a few lines earlier, so that participation in the administration of justice through the popular courts, as well as the election of officials, may well be implied by the limited sovereignty that Plato attributes to the people under the ancient constitution. Here again it is significant that Plato's legislation for his imaginary colony includes provisions for the use of popular courts in the Athenian style, and for a court of the πλῆθος, the full body of citizens, to judge offenses against the state; and there are procedures for calling officials to account before these two kinds of popular courts. He supports both these institutions by saying that participation in the administration of justice, and particularly the right to share in deciding cases of alleged injury to the public, are regarded as inseparable from citizenship, thus affirming his (or the Athenian

[29] *Pol.* 1274a 18.

Stranger's) complete agreement with common Athenian opinion on the principle involved.[30]

  There are still other features of Solon's reforms, as they were understood in the fourth century, that have their parallels in Plato's legislation, but these will come to our attention later. The central motive of these reforms, as Solon himself says in the fragments of his poems that Aristotle quotes, was to find a middle way between the claims of "those who had power and wealth" and the demands of the demos, who had risen in revolt. He was himself a man of the upper classes, though only moderately wealthy;[31] and both parties apparently expected him to become their champion. But he disappointed the expectations of his aristocratic friends, and refused to accede to the demands of the poor for a redivision of the land. Instead he set up a "boundary" between the warring parties, according "straight justice" to each. "I did not care to give an equal share of the fertile land to noble and base alike." Solon's decision did not satisfy everybody; faction continued for some time afterwards; but the settlement was never reversed, and it is fair to say, as Aristotle does, that he "set free the demos, not only for his own time, but for the future,"[32] and thus laid the foundation for the greatness of the Athens that Plato knew. His policy of moderation had proved itself by its fruits, and it was a policy with which Plato was wholly in accord. It finds its echo in Plato's continued emphasis upon the μέτριον as the secret of health in a city, and in his description of his own projected constitution as a mean between monarchy and democracy.[33] Evidently Plato thought that the older Athens embodied, in its own fashion, the excellences that he attributes to the Spartan and Cretan constitutions.

  But the *Laws* shows that Plato thought the Athenians of his own day had departed from the moderation that characterized their ancestors. In the *Gorgias* Socrates refuses to accord the name of statesman to the great leaders of the age following the Persian Wars (515c-519a). It is true that they provided the city with walls, docks, shipyards, and all the attributes of wealth and power, but they failed

[30] 767e, 768a. For these courts see Chapter VI below.
[31] Arist. *Const. Ath.* v, 3; *Pol.* 1296a 19.
[32] Arist. *Const. Ath.* VI, 1.
[33] When we come to examine Plato's doctrine of the mixed constitution more fully it will be evident, I think, that Solon was one of its chief sources. See Chapter X.

to make the citizens better; in fact they made them worse, and this shows that they lacked the fundamental requirement of the political art. In the *Republic* Plato pictures democracy as close to the lower limit in the scale of political value, and it has been assumed, probably with justice, that the faults he finds with it—its abuse of the principle of equality; its excess of freedom, even to the disregard of law; its absence of wisdom and moderation—are those he saw in the democracy he knew best, that of fourth-century Athens. But there is another view of Athens sometimes presented in the dialogues. In the *Crito* Socrates is portrayed as a loyal subject of Athenian laws, and as having chosen to live at Athens in preference to any other city (52b); he dies a victim, not of the laws, but of men (54c). Again in the *Meno* (93e, 94b,d) and *Protagoras* (319e) the great statesmen described in the *Gorgias*—Themistocles, Pericles, Thucydides, Aristides —are cited as examples of wisdom and civic virtue. How they acquired their excellences seems to be a mystery, and it is clear they did not know how to teach them to their sons, but their own eminence is unquestioned. Evidently a city able to produce such men has not altogether lost the virtue that distinguished its past.

The *Menexenus*, if we read it with caution, may afford a clue to the way in which Plato looked upon the Athens of his own time in relation to her more glorious past. This is one of the most puzzling of Plato's dialogues, and I shall not attempt a full interpretation of it here. But it cannot be ignored, for it contains a statement about the ancient constitution, and this is clearly relevant if we can take it seriously. The body of the composition is a funeral oration, allegedly prepared for delivery shortly after the Peace of Antalcidas, at one of the big state funerals for the war dead which were a custom at Athens.[34] It begins, as was customary in compositions of this genre, with a eulogy of the forefathers of the dead and of the land which gave them birth. This eulogy of the land and of its people parallels the praises of legendary Athens in the *Timaeus* and *Critias*.[35] Socrates then says that it is appropriate to speak briefly of the constitution "our ancestors devised," for a constitution is a nurse of men. The ancient constitution was the same "for the most part," he says, as that under which we are now governed, an aristocracy.

[34] The dramatic date is clear from the fact that the account of Athenian history is carried down to the Peace in 387.
[35] *Tim.* 24cd; cf. 23c; *Crit.* 109cd, 112e.

Some call it democracy, others apply other names to it; but it is in truth an aristocracy with the approval of the people (μετ' εὐδοξίας πλήθους ἀριστοκρατία). 238d

Socrates goes on to explain that it could be called a democracy because the people is sovereign, by virtue of its right to elect its officials. Again it had and still has a king (in Solon's time, as in Plato's day, the second archon was officially "the king") and this suggests a monarchy. It can also be called an aristocracy, because it provides that the best (or those thought to be best) should hold office.[36] The hidden meaning of this description is clear from a parallel passage in the *Laws* (712de). When Megillus is asked to say what kind of constitution the Lacedaemonians have, he confesses that he can give no answer in the usual terms. At times it seems to be the most democratic of all states; it is apparently a monarchy because of its kings; but on the other hand it would be strange not to call it an aristocracy, and the power of the ephors at times resembles a tyranny. The discussion that follows shows that this uncertainty is just what we should expect to find in a mixed constitution, where no element is so prominent as to dominate the others. Aristotle uses precisely this criterion for distinguishing a constitution that is well mixed.[37] Since this has been said to be the constitution "under which we are now, and have always been, governed for the most part," Plato here presents the ancient polity as having the excellence of a mixed constitution, and fourth-century Athens as preserving at least some traces of this ancient mixture.

How seriously are we to take this judgment? This funeral oration is an example of a type of composition that we do not find elsewhere in Plato, though it has its parallels in similar compositions ascribed to Lysias, Demosthenes, and Hyperides, and in the famous funeral oration of Pericles that is referred to in the introductory section of the dialogue. It conforms perfectly to the rules of this genre; it has its exordium, followed by a eulogy of Athens and her glorious sons, and a concluding section of consolation for the survivors of the dead; and it displays in profusion the figures of speech and the sophisticated

[36] Thucydides (ii, 65, 9) says the Athenian "democracy" in Pericles' time was really an ἀρχὴ ὑπὸ τοῦ πρώτου ἀνδρός. The scholiast on Pericles' funeral oration interprets it as insisting that Athens is a democracy in name but actually an aristocracy; see Larsen, *op.cit.* (Note 10), 14.

[37] *Pol.* 1294b 15.

devices cultivated by the professional rhetoricians of Plato's day.[38] It is notoriously difficult to divine Plato's purpose in writing it.[39] Was he simply trying to show that he could do as well as the professional rhetoricians if he tried? Or is it a satire directed at the art of rhetoric and the Athenian public which is so readily enchanted by it? Or is it a serious encomium of Athens, cast in an unfamiliar and for Plato a somewhat artificial form?[40] The answers to these questions have been almost as varied as the commentators who have discussed them, and I shall not venture to pass judgment here, for we have not time to examine the encomium as a whole, which would be a prerequisite. But on the passage I have cited an opinion may be permitted. We can see that the description of the ancient constitution as a mixed one accords with the evidence previously adduced regarding Plato's attitude toward the older Athens, so that this part at least can be taken as Plato's real opinion. Could he also seriously maintain that the Athenians of his day had retained enough features of that older constitution to justify the claim that they were still living under it "for the most part"? An ardently patriotic Athenian could do so, feeling that the virtues that remained were more truly expressive of his Athens than the evidence of decline, that the relics of the ancient mixture represent the authentic spirit of his city through the ages. This would be an idealization of Athens, but so also was Pericles' famous oration, to which this is dramatically attached in the introductory dialogue. Some such idealization would seem not only possible, but necessary for those who, like Plato and many of his contemporaries, dreamed fondly of a restoration of that ancestral constitution.

Plato has not usually been regarded as an ardent patriot; in fact he has sometimes been presented as hating everything that Athens stood for.[41] The evidence I have already presented shows that this is an exaggeration, to say the least. What his private feelings were

[38] See Louis Méridier's careful analysis of these features in his introduction to the Budé edition of this dialogue.

[39] But its authenticity can scarcely be doubted. It is referred to twice by Aristotle (*Rhet.* 1367b 8, 1415b 30), no objection can be taken to it on stylistic grounds, and the ancient critics, with no known exception, seem to have regarded it as genuine.

[40] The Athenians of later days apparently took it seriously. Cicero tells us that they liked it so much that it was appointed to be read each year at the ceremony in honor of the dead. *Orator* XLIV, 151.

[41] Most vigorously by K. R. Popper, *The Open Society and Its Enemies*, 2 vols, London, 1945, Part I, especially Chapter 10.

toward his native city it is obviously impossible for us to discern with any certainty. But his Athens had a history extending far back beyond Solon's time, and he evidently takes pleasure in recounting the legends of its ancient glories. In the *Timaeus* and the *Critias*, as in the *Menexenus*, he lets his imagination play upon the traditions of the heroic age and pictures Athens as embodying the best of all constitutions, as the historic replica of the ideal that Socrates had portrayed in the *Republic*. It is ancient Athens that he casts in the role of the victorious defender of Europe and Asia against the invaders from the island of Atlantis. Of all the Greeks, the Athenians claimed to be the only ones who were autochthonous, native to the soil, not immigrants from some other part of the world. Plato accepts this claim: "We are not stepchildren of our motherland, as other races are."[42] At a time when other lands were bringing forth all sorts of animals, wild and tame, this country of ours chose to produce man, who surpasses all other animals in intelligence and is the only one who considers justice and the gods.[43] The climate of this land is nicely blended, capable of producing men of superior wisdom (φρονι-μωτάτους ἄνδρας).[44] This is why Hephaestus and Athena, both lovers of wisdom and of artistry, chose this land as their portion; and here they planted the stock that now inhabits it.[45] The men of this land, so happily endowed, so augustly sponsored and tended, were the first to discover the order of the cosmos and to develop the arts and sciences. And they were the first to live under laws, laws older even than those of Egypt, in which human life was properly ordered. "At one time . . . what is now the Athenian state was the bravest in war and supremely well organized also in all other respects. It is said that it possessed the most splendid works of art and the noblest polity of any nation under heaven of which we have heard tell."[46] This is the nation to which, we must recall once more, Plato assigns the heroic role of turning back an invasion from the island of Atlantis and thus preventing the enslavement of all Europe and Asia.

These statements about the land, the institutions, and the heroic deeds of that antediluvian era are obviously the product of imagination, but it is imagination inspired by affection and respect for the Athens that Plato knew. For he insists always on the continuity of

[42] *Menex.* 237b.
[43] *Ibid.* 237d.
[44] *Tim.* 24c.
[45] *Crit.* 109c; cf. *Tim.* 24d.
[46] *Tim.* 23c, Bury's trans. Cf. *Tim.* 24d, *Crit.* 109c, *Menex.* 238b.

the stock that has inhabited Attica;[47] and the climax of the ancient tale, the repulse of Atlantis, is obviously but a prehistorical replica of the Athenian victory over the Persians, a matter of vivid historical memory. The Athenian state, "acting partly as leader of the Greeks, and partly standing alone by itself when deserted by all others, . . . after encountering the deadliest perils . . . defeated the invaders and reared a trophy."[48] Thus he describes the victory over the forces of Atlantis in words which, without their context, would be taken as referring to Marathon. In similar terms Plato does in fact, on two separate occasions, celebrate the valor and intelligence of the "men of Marathon"—accepting apparently without reservation the thesis of Herodotus that it was Athens whose resolution preserved the liberty of Greece and of the whole Hellenic race.[49]

After all, this is the city that had produced Plato's beloved teacher Socrates; it not only gave him birth but also, as Plato himself expresses it in the *Crito*, formed his mind and character (50de). It was the city Socrates loved so much that he had seldom left it, except on military campaigns. This was the city in which Plato also chose to live. The alternative that he describes as open to Socrates—of leaving Athens if he disliked its laws—was equally open to him. He had traveled and seen other communities. He had congenial friends in Tarentum who would have welcomed him to their city and their Pythagorean brotherhood. But it is to Athens that he returned to set up his Academy, and it is in Athens that he lived and worked for forty years thereafter. This is the city he chooses as the setting for all his dialogues except the *Laws*, the only city in Greece in which such conversations could be pictured as taking place, the city that Hippias in the *Protagoras* calls the prytaneum of wisdom (337d). This city had provided the atmosphere congenial to Plato's labors, and from its traditions he had derived some of his fundamental political principles. Instead of calling him a renegade, we can best explain the severity of the criticism he directs against the Athens of his day as the reverse side of his deep-seated loyalty and patriotism.[50]

But however this may be, obviously the Athenian Stranger does not

---

[47] *Tim.* 23b,c, *Crit.* 109d, *Menex.* 238c.
[48] *Tim.* 25c, Bury's trans.
[49] *Laws* 699a-d; cf. 692e; *Menex.* 239d-240e; Herod. VII, 139.
[50] In *Rep.* 607e Plato speaks of the "noble polities" (καλαὶ πολιτεῖαι) under which "we" have acquired our love of poetry. Need we take this as ironical, as Shorey and Adam do?

think that Athens has ceased to be a leader and a teacher of the Greeks. He guides the inquiry carried on in the *Laws* and he alone formulates the legislation set forth. He finds in the ancestral constitution of Athens an example of the moderation which he regards as essential to a healthy state; and we shall see, as we study the details of the legislation for the Cretan city, that he often follows an Athenian prototype, even adopting or imitating institutions characteristic of fourth-century Athens, and sometimes in preference to the Spartan or Cretan alternatives. There must be a return to the vigor and simplicity of the Dorian way if any lasting improvement is to be made in the life of the Greek city—that Plato certainly believes. But some of this simplicity is also evident in the institutions of early Athens; and in any case the Dorian ways, if they are to serve the highest purpose, must take on some of the grace and intelligence manifested in the later developments of Ionian life. It is to Athens that Plato apparently looks to provide this necessary supplement.

PART TWO
PLATO'S CITY

CHAPTER IV

PROPERTY AND THE FAMILY

PLATO'S COLONY has a definite location. It is to be established at the site of an ancient city (later called Magnesia) whose inhabitants emigrated from the area a long time ago, and which now lies desolate (704c). This makes it highly probable that Plato is thinking of a definite region in south central Crete, the plain now called the Messara, where, according to the tradition we examined earlier,[1] the ancient Cretan Magnesia was located. The Messara is a broad valley, extending some fifty miles parallel to the coast from the mouth of the Hieropotamos (ancient Lethaeus) on the west to the foot of Mount Lassithi (the ancient Dicte?) on the east. On the north it is bounded by the tremendous massif that extends like a backbone through the center of the island, with Mount Ida (now called Psiloriti) looking down upon the western end of the Messara, and on the south by the much lower Asterousian range, which separates it from the sea. As one approaches the Messara from the north, through the pass in the mountain range between Mount Ida and the Dictaean mass—the route followed from time immemorial by travelers from Cnossos to the south—the sudden sight of this long fertile valley is unforgettably imposing. Archaeologists have not yet found any evidence that would identify more exactly the site of Cretan Magnesia, or even confirm the tradition that such a city once existed. Whether this tradition was founded on fact, or was merely a fiction invented by the Magnesians on the Maeander, there can be no doubt that Plato knew of it and knew the region in which it located the ancient city. It provides a concrete setting for his colony, which is to be an inland city, but possessing good harbors on the coast, with a terrain containing a mixture of forest, mountain, and plain, and generally productive (704a-d).

These physical features of the site have obvious advantages. Like a good craftsman, Plato deliberately chooses, from the rich variety of physical settings that the Greece of his day afforded, a site that will provide the most favorable conditions for the establishment of his model colony. Its inland location means that it will be less exposed to the contagion of foreign manners and customs; and the fact that

[1] In Chapter I.

95

it is productive—but not too productive—means that its inhabitants will not be tempted to engage in commerce to import needed products from abroad or sell their own surplus in foreign markets. The sea is "a sweet companion for daily life" (how could any Greek think otherwise?), but at the same time it is a "right briny and bitter neighbor"; for it fills the city with foreign and retail trade, engendering tricky habits in its citizens and making them an object of dislike to one another and the rest of mankind (704d-705b). Of the effects of trade upon the character of the trader Plato speaks even more harshly later; and since some buying and selling in his city is a necessity, we shall see that he takes special measures to counteract the dangers involved. By setting his new colony in a location without temptations to commercial enterprise, Plato is avoiding what he and many of his contemporaries regarded as a serious threat to good government. Aristotle records that the question was much debated.[2] He clearly agrees with Plato as to the corrupting influence of foreign traders; but he recognizes the advantages, both for security and for the supply of the city's needs, in having access to the sea, and thinks the disadvantages can be to a great extent avoided by segregating the traders and their operations at the seaport from the city proper, but "not too far away." This was the common Greek practice, though the segregation was seldom as strict as Aristotle would have it, and the influence of the Piraeus upon the politics of Athens was particularly strong. Plato evidently would not approve of Aristotle's compromise. He imposes strict limitations not only on foreign commerce, but on all intercourse with other lands, and seems to be strangely indifferent to the fact that without the expansion of commerce and craftsmanship that took place in the sixth and fifth centuries the Athens that he praises as the "prytaneum of wisdom" would have been impossible.

A second advantage that Plato sees in an inland location is that the inhabitants will not be tempted to become a naval power. When the people live near the sea and are harassed by raiders, they will be inclined to imitate their enemies' methods of warfare, and this will make a profound difference in their character. Instead of standing his ground like the unyielding hoplite when the enemy approaches, the naval soldier, whose ships are drawn up behind him on the beach, learns to run to them and withdraw from the conflict, even throwing away his arms (the ultimate disgrace for a Greek

[2] *Pol.* 1327a 11-41.

soldier) in order to save himself and his precious vessels (706a-e). Quite clearly Plato has his native city in mind here, for he refers to the ancient days when the fleets of Minos forced the Athenians to pay him tribute. "They had no ships of war then as they have now." But his description of the naval soldier does less than justice to the valor of the Athenian fleets in genuinely naval battles, at Artemisium, at Salamis, at Arginusae, and on other memorable occasions which Plato himself eulogizes in the *Menexenus.* It is so obviously an unfair picture of naval warfare in the fifth and fourth centuries that one can only take it as a disguised criticism (inspired by the text of Homer that is cited in this passage) of the military strategy dictated by sea power which had guided Athens since the days of Themistocles. This strategy, as seen clearly and stated by Pericles on more than one occasion, was to refrain from engaging the enemy on land, even if it meant abandoning the Attic countryside to devastation by the Spartan invaders. This unwillingness to defend the sacred soil of Attica must have seemed to the old-fashioned Athenians an exhibition of rank cowardice, prudent indeed, but dishonorable to the memory of the men who had fought at Marathon. While Plato admits that the sea battles of Salamis and Artemisium "helped to save us," it was the land battles of Marathon and Plataea, he says, that really brought about the salvation of Greece (707c). Moreover, these battles "made the Greeks better," whereas the sea fights made them worse, i.e. they initiated a policy which eventually proved disastrous not only for Athens but for all other states that aspired to naval supremacy.

Plato was by no means alone in condemning Athenian naval policy. Doubts about the legitimacy of maritime empire and its eventual advantage to a state were first stirred by the events of Periclean days;[3] and they were revived in the following century by the resurgence of Athenian power in the second naval confederation of 377. The Athenians of the fourth century seem to have profited little from the experience of their grandfathers, for they again converted a league of nominally autonomous allies into an empire exploited for their own ends. The result was the revolt of Chios, Cos, and Byzantium, whose independence the Athenians were forced to recognize, fol-

[3] The first critic we know of was Stesimbrotus of Thasos (Plut. *Them.* 4) who attacked Athenian policy and Themistocles as a corrupter of the Athenian people. See Arnaldo Momigliano, "Sea Power in Greek Thought," *Class. Rev.* LVIII, 1944, 1-7.

lowed by the secession of many other allies. At the end of the Social War in 355—at the time when Plato was writing the *Laws*—the second maritime league had collapsed, the Athenian treasury had been exhausted, and Athenian power and dignity fatally impaired. The events of this decade, with the dramatic fall of Athens a second time from a position of supremacy to one of poverty and humiliation, could hardly have failed to confirm Plato in his distrust of sea power. He had expressed this distrust earlier in the *Gorgias*. One of his main charges against the statesmen of the fifth century is that they provided the state with ships, docks, and arsenals without regard to their effects upon the citizens' characters—which shows that they had no conception of the statesman's function.[4] And now the imperialism involved in the Athenian naval enterprises must have appeared to him to be as bankrupt as the imperial policy of Persia (697d). The story begun in the unfinished *Critias* is evidently to be an account of the heroic victory of a healthy land power, ancient Athens, over the presumptuous maritime empire of Atlantis. But as a patriotic Athenian he may often have taken pride in the valor and skill of his countrymen, and may even, like Isocrates, have occasionally thought of Athenian naval power as a benefit to all the Greeks. In the *Menexenus*, written before the rise of the second naval confederation, he was able to ignore the imperialistic aspect of Athenian successes and portray them as campaigns in defense of their own liberty and that of all Greece. But his later utterances express unambiguously the old Hellenic ideal of free and autonomous communities, bound together, however, by friendly alliances between cities of like constitution against their common enemies.[5]

---

[4] *Gorg.* 515bc, 519a; *Alc. I* implies a similar criticism of Athenian statesmanship; cf. 118-124, 134b.

[5] See the account of the original alliance between Argos, Messene, and Lacedaemon in 683d; his advice to Dion and Dion's friends and his defense of Dion against the charge of imperialistic aims in *Epp. VII* 332e, 336a, 351b and *VIII* 357ab. Aristotle's similar attitude toward Athenian imperialism is evident in a fragment of his περὶ δικαιοσύνης (Fr. 82, Rose); Paul Moraux, *Le Dialogue "Sur la Justice,"* Paris and Louvain, 1957, 60. The disastrous end of the Social War evidently caused a fundamental change in Isocrates' views. At the time of the *Panegyricus* (about 380) he had looked upon Athenian sea power as a benefit to all the Greeks and the loss of it at Aegospotami the "beginning of evils" (119); and he had expressed the wish that Athens might recover her naval supremacy—as in fact she did in the following years. In the *Areopagiticus* (written, as I think Jaeger has successfully shown, not at the end of the Social War but at its beginning—see *Paideia* III, 109ff.) he still looks upon Athenian naval power as a blessing to the Greeks and the world, but he sees the jealousy and antagonism it has aroused. But in the *Peace*, written at the

But the foundations of imperialism are moral, Plato thinks. Hence in this last treatment of the subject he condemns primarily the effects of naval policy upon the character of the citizens and upon the leaders whom it brings into power. In cities whose power and safety are dependent upon their navies, the honors are accorded to "that element of the fighting forces which is not the best" (707a). Plato is obviously referring to the fact that the Athenian fleet, as well as the pilots and carpenters required to direct and maintain it, consisted mainly of poorer citizens and metics, those who were unable to provide the equipment of a hoplite or cavalryman. The dependence of Athens during the Peloponnesian War upon this group of citizens was a major factor in the development of the later democracy. This was clearly recognized in the earliest political pamphlet we have, the account of the Athenian constitution included in the works of Xenophon but now generally taken to be the composition of an otherwise unknown oligarch toward the beginning of the Peloponnesian War.[6] The "Old Oligarch" was indeed a shrewd observer of political realities. The attitude of the fleet was something that no politician in the late fifth century could safely ignore, for upon its loyalty depended not merely the hope of winning the war, but even the provisioning of the city, which had to rely upon the sea lanes for its food supply. The "honors" to which Plato refers in this passage are obviously the political power and influence that the "navy men" (ναυτικοί) acquired.[7] Neither the extreme conservatives nor the moderates were happy about this. One of the proposals of the constitution devised by the oligarchs in the abortive revolution of 411 was to restrict citizenship to those capable of providing hoplite equipment; and the power of the fleet was most strikingly shown on this very occasion by its thwarting the schemes of the extremists and eventually restoring the democracy. Aristotle, like Plato and the

---

end of the Social War in 355, he advises the Athenians to renounce their naval ambitions and concentrate upon putting their own house in order. The assumption of naval supremacy had been a catastrophe for both Athens and Sparta in turn (*Peace*, 101-103; cf. *Philip*, 61). Sea power is nothing but tyranny, he says in the *Antidosis* (64), written the following year. Finally, in the *Panathenaicus*, finished in 338 at the end of his long life, he declares that sea power is disruptive of the internal order of the state and of its relations to other states (115-116). But this passage probably contains his wisest utterance: naval power is something that Athens could not have avoided without becoming a prey to her enemies.

[6] Ps. Xen. *Const. Ath.*

[7] Cf. τιμάς τε καὶ ἀρχάς, 744c; and Arist. *Pol.* 1281a 31: τιμὰς γὰρ λέγομεν εἶναι τὰς ἀρχάς.

Old Oligarch, connects the rise of the "more democratic" constitution of Periclean days with the expansion of Athenian naval power. But Aristotle is unwilling to renounce all naval power for his ideal state. A state must be formidable, able to protect itself and its neighbors by sea as well as by land; and if it expects to play the role of leader (live the ἡγεμονικὸν βίον) it must have naval as well as land forces proportionate to its activities. For his own ideal state such a naval force is assumed, and he proposes that the rowers be drawn from the noncitizen part of the population to prevent their having a detrimental influence on the polity.[8] But this compromise was apparently as unacceptable to Plato as was the similar compromise regarding commercial enterprise. There are no naval forces in his state; and he deliberately selects a site that will assist the legislator in restraining the citizens from taking the course which had proved so disastrous for Athens.[9]

Another matter which has been to a great extent settled in advance by Plato's choice of Crete as the setting for his colony is the quality of his citizens. Just as an expert shepherd or cowherd will not take great pains with inferior animals, but will eliminate them from his flock, so the serious legislator will want to know that his citizens are of good stock and worth his efforts (735b-736c).[10] There is an initial presumption that this will be the case for the present colony, since it is to draw its members from Crete and the Peloponnesus (708a-d), those Dorian lands so noted for their εὐνομία. There are some interesting observations upon the relative advantages and disadvantages of homogeneity of traditions among the settlers of a new colony. Similarity of language and laws makes for friendliness, but a homogeneous group is likely to be especially intolerant of legislation differing from that of their homelands, so that the faults of the ancestral tradition are merely preserved in the new settlement. On the other hand, a colony made up of elements from diverse traditions will be more ready to submit to new laws, but will be difficult to

---

[8] *Const. Ath.* xxvii, 1; *Pol.* 1304a 22; 1327b 8-13. In 1329a 26 we learn that the γεωργοί are to be δοῦλοι or περίοικοι.
[9] Was Plato's condemnation of sea power later used by the Romans to justify the destruction of Carthage? "So much is certain, that the Roman offer that the Carthaginians should settle at least eighty stades from the sea corresponds exactly to the suggestion of the *Laws*." Momigliano, *op.cit.* 6. The influence of Plato upon Cicero (*De Rep.* ii, 5-9) seems probable.
[10] Aristotle likewise at the beginning of his sketch of an ideal constitution takes pains to declare what he thinks should be the "natural character" (φύσις) of the citizens. *Pol.* 1327b 18ff.

organize into a team animated by a common spirit. We can assume that Plato believes there will be enough elements in common among these Dorian settlers and enough variety in their respective Dorian traditions to avoid the extremes of disadvantage just mentioned. Even so the individual applicants must be carefully tested to prevent the admission of vicious elements that may corrupt the whole group.

Finally, we come to another important matter that will be easier to settle satisfactorily at the founding of a colony than in a state already existing. Plato asserts that the establishment of a right attitude toward property is the foundation (κρηπίς) of all legislation, the secret of the security of a state (736e). The best commentary on this statement is his own picture in the *Republic* of the course of political degeneration, where each successive stage is explained as having its origin in economic causes. Plato is evidently one of those persons who think, as Aristotle reports, that "property is the universal source of faction."[11] Aristotle himself is not far from this opinion, for property plays a large part in his analysis of constitutions and his explanation of historical changes. Phaleas of Chalcedon, a political theorist and planner about whom we know only what Aristotle tells us, made the equalization of property fundamental in his ideal constitution.[12] In fact, the effects of economic discontent are clearly evident in the life of the Greek cities, both in the revolutions it brought about, and in the measures taken by the wiser statesmen to allay this discontent. We hear frequently of a demand for a "redistribution of the land" (ἀναδασμὸς τῆς γῆς), a slogan which was likely to send cold chills down the spines of solid citizens and statesmen. Athens in the fifth and fourth centuries was happily spared the more extreme forms of party strife. This was the result partly of the willingness of wealthy citizens to assume the burdens of extraordinary state expenses (the λειτουργίαι), and partly of the exceptional opportunities at Athens for making a livelihood, whether in commercial enterprise and craftsmanship, or in the employ of the state, or as a settler in a cleruchy; and it is to the credit of the democracy that it consistently followed policies that would foster such public spirit in the wealthy and provide such opportunities for the poor. But there were factions even in Athens, and other states were far less fortunate in keeping the tension between oligarchs and demos under control.

[11] *Pol.* 1266a 37. Cf. Plato *Rep.* VIII.
[12] *Pol.* 1266a 39.

To illustrate how indispensable the spirit of moderation is, Plato points to the problem faced by a legislator in an established state who considers it necessary to make changes in the laws of property (736c-e). He cannot leave things as they are, yet any proposal for change is met by the cry μὴ κινεῖν τὰ ἀκίνητα.[13] The most that any reformer can do is to make a cautious move in the desired direction; and to do even this it is essential that he should be supported by a few large landholders with many debtors who are willing to deal equitably (δι' ἐπιείκειαν κοινωνεῖν) with their less fortunate fellow citizens by remitting some of their claims and distributing some of their land. Only through such persons can a legislator "move the immovables." It is tempting to think that Plato has his great ancestor Solon in mind here.[14] Solon himself was a man of moderate property,

---

[13] "Don't move the immovables!" or "Don't change what should be left alone!" This slogan appears elsewhere in the *Laws*; in 684e it has the same sense as here, and appears as a principle obstructing the legislator's purposes; in 843a the legislator invokes it as a sanction against the shifting of boundary stones; and in 913b against appropriating buried treasure. In the last passage it is said to have a variety of proper applications. In later Greek law the term ἀκίνητα (like French *immeubles*) meant real property; and it is quite likely that the potency of this slogan in Plato's day lay in its expressing the peculiarly close relation thought to hold between a family and its landed property. We shall see later that at Athens custom, if not law, forbade the alienation of the family land. The slogan then is more than an expression of the interests of a small conservative group of landholders; in this respect most Athenian citizens, even in the fourth century, were conservatives. In any case it is property in land and houses (γῇ τε καὶ οἰκήσεις, 737b) that Plato is concerned with here.

[14] If so, this passage has some relevance to the determination of the exact nature of Solon's reforms. For Plato twice distinguishes two procedures, a cancellation of debts and a distribution of land (γῆς καὶ χρεῶν ἀποκοπὴ καὶ νομή, 736c; τὰ μὲν ἀφιέντας, τὰ δὲ νεμομένους, 736e). Aristotle says that Solon abolished debts (χρεῶν ἀποκοπὰς ἐποίησε, *Const. Ath.* VI, 1), but says nothing about a distribution of land; indeed one of the poems of Solon cited by Aristotle (XII, 3) shows that he never contemplated making an "equal division," though this may have been one of the things the demos hoped for. On the other hand, Aristotle mentions as one of the evils of pre-Solonian days that the whole land was controlled by a few (ἡ πᾶσα γῆ δι' ὀλίγων ἦν, II, 2). If the debts were mortgages, then their cancellation would mean the freeing of the land, which was one of the accomplishments that Solon claimed for himself (*Const. Ath.* XII, 4, line 7). Yet apparently the source of the evil as described by Aristotle was that loans were made on the security of the debtors' persons. Furthermore, if land was not alienable in Solon's days, as seems now to be most generally believed, then it could not be used as security for loans, and the debts of that time could not have been mortgages. For radically different interpretations of Solon's reforms and their consequences see the works of Woodhouse and Lewis cited in Note 39 below; and A. French, "The Economic Background to Solon's Reforms," CQ L, 1956, 11-25. With the present passage one should compare the earlier account of the settlement of the Heraclidae in the Peloponnesus, where also it is said that the legislators were happily free from the difficulties that would

but a member of the upper class, so Aristotle says;[15] and he must have had the confidence and support of this class to have been selected as arbitrator. The effect of his example and that of other like-minded moderates (τῆς μετριότητος ἐχόμενοι, 736e 2) must have been important in gaining acceptance for the settlement he imposed. And just as Solon, Plato seems to imply, thought it necessary to relieve long-standing economic grievances before proceeding to further reforms,[16] so any legislator "with a grain of intelligence" who is laying down laws for a new colony, where such grievances have not yet arisen, will make it his first business to establish such conditions of land ownership as will prevent the later rise of jealousy and strife (737b).

THE ALLOTMENT OF THE LAND

Plato proposes that the land be divided at the outset into equal portions and distributed by lot, one portion to each head of a family (737e). This embodies a very ancient procedure. The first act of an invading host, according to tradition, was to allot the conquered land among the men who had conquered it; and in Plato's day the first act in the history of a new colony was the distribution of the lots.[17] In one of the few inscriptions we have pertaining to the founding of a colony (this was a colony from Athens) it is explicitly provided in the decree that ten "land dividers" (γεωνόμοι) be elected, one from each tribe.[18] The numerous Athenian cleruchies established in the sixth and fifth centuries followed the same practice.[19] Distribution by lot was thought to be particularly equitable, and the plot of ground allotted carried the name of the process (κλῆρος) by which

---

beset a reformer in an established city (684d). Here likewise debts and ownership of land are connected together (γῆς τε κτῆσις καὶ χρεῶν διάλυσις).

[15] *Const. Ath.* v, 3.

[16] On the order of Solon's reforms Aristotle (*op.cit.* x) is quite definite.

[17] Paul Vinogradoff, *Historical Jurisprudence*, Oxford, 1922, ii, 202f.; Paul Guiraud, *La Propriété foncière en Grèce*, Paris, 1890, ii. *Odyss.* vi, 9-10; Diod. v, 81, 83, 84; Athen. 167d; Herod. iv, 159; v, 77.

[18] Tod i, No. 44. The colony is to be established at Brea in Thrace, and the decree belongs to about the year 445. Another colonial inscription refers to the establishment of a Locrian colony at Naupactus (Tod i, No. 24). Though there is no mention of γεωνόμοι, the distribution is implied in other provisions of the inscription. See Vinogradoff, *loc.cit.*

[19] Schultess on κληροῦχοι in RE. In Aristoph. *Clouds* 202ff. when Strepsiades is told that geometry is for the purpose of measuring land, he asks, "What? In cleruchies?"

it was assigned.[20] In general we may assume that in these distributions there was an effort to make the lots as equal as possible. In Plato's colony the land to be occupied is said to be varied, like Crete in general—some mountainous, some forested, and some flat plain; and these inequalities of productive capacity must be taken into account (745cd). Plato's only innovation seems to be the proposal that each lot be divided into two portions, one nearer the city and one farther away—a provision that Aristotle also includes in his own sketch of an ideal polity.[21]

This establishment of something like private property in land involves a departure from the principles laid down in the *Republic* where, for the guardians at least, there will be no privately owned land or houses.[22] Plato remarks that this "move" in his legislation will at first hearing arouse surprise,[23] and indeed it has always been cited as a striking difference between Plato's later and his earlier state. But he then points out that experience and reason show that no state we can establish could be anything but second best as compared with the ideal. The first in point of excellence is that which observes in all its parts the Pythagorean principle, "Friends have all things in common." Whether or not such a state ever existed or will exist we cannot say; it seems that its inhabitants would have to be either gods or sons of gods. The best we can do is to take it as our model and try to establish something as nearly like it as possible. This is what we are doing in the present instance, he adds; the constitution we are now framing will be quite close to the first in "immortality" ($\dot{a}\theta a\nu a\sigma i a s$ $\dot{\epsilon}\gamma\gamma\acute{v}\tau a\tau a$).[24]

---

[20] "Überall in Griechenland wird das in erblichem Privateigentum befindliche Grundstück als Los ($\kappa\lambda\hat{\eta}\rho o s$) bezeichnet." Meyer, *Gesch. des Altertums*, Stuttgart, 1893, II, 297.

[21] *Pol.* 1330a 14.

[22] *Rep.* 416d-417b.

[23] "Because it is unusual ($\dot{a}\acute{\eta}\theta\eta s$ $o\dot{v}\sigma a$)" he adds (739a). This is the really surprising part of Plato's text and is difficult to explain satisfactorily. With the establishment of private ownership of land Plato also sets up the private family, abandoning his earlier proposal for common wives and children. But surely a legislator who proposed to recognize the private family and private property could hardly be regarded as proceeding in an unusual fashion, certainly not by a Cretan nor a Spartan, nor by the ordinary reader. It seems that Plato has forgotten the dramatic setting and thinks of himself as addressing here only the members of the Academy, or others of like mind, who would be surprised by his departure from the "sacred line" he had previously adhered to.

[24] 739e. The reading $\dot{\eta}$ $\mu i a$ (e4) is hard to make sense of and is probably corrupt (see England's note); but fortunately the sense of the whole passage is clear enough.

We must therefore divide up the land and the houses; for common ownership and cultivation is more than we can demand of our citizens with the nature and education we can presume them to have (740a). Private ownership in land, however, is coupled with important conditions and reservations. The recipient of the lot is to regard it as belonging in a sense to the whole state (740a, 877d, 923ab). The land is to be regarded as sacred to all the gods, a goddess herself, and to be cherished more faithfully than children cherish their mother. The acceptance of a lot is confirmed by a solemn religious ceremony with threefold sacrifices and prayers (741c). There is to be no buying or selling of the lot in whole or in part (741b). Nor is the state to touch the allotment. If a citizen has committed an offense punishable by a fine, this shall be collected only from the surplus the offender has over and above the lot and its equipment (855ab). The lot is to remain forever in the possession of the citizen to whom it is first assigned, and to his heirs, natural or adopted. The holder of a lot is to bequeath it at death to one of his sons, whichever he may choose (745b, 923c). If he has only daughters, he may select the son of some other citizen who is not already a designated heir to be the husband of one of his daughters and his own successor (923e); and if he has neither sons nor daughters, he chooses the son of another citizen as his heir (740c; cf. 929c, 924a). If a childless man has committed an offense punishable by exile, his relatives on both sides shall meet and—in consultation with the nomophylakes and the priests—appoint an heir to the lot left vacant (877cd). When three successive generations in a family have committed crimes punishable by death, the remaining children are to be deported and the heir named by lot, with the aid of Delphi, from the sons of other citizens (856de).

There are also restrictions on the use of the land. Some—such as the laws designed to prevent damage to neighboring properties, and to assure access to water, or to market, for all landholders (e.g. 843c-844d, 845d-846a)—fall within the police power and would hardly be considered as limitations on the rights of private property. But there is no right of abuse, for the land must be preserved as the source of livelihood for the people (740a, 923ab). There are laws regarding the distribution of the annual produce (847e-848c) and some of them—e.g. that one third of the produce is subject to compulsory sale to alien residents and foreign visitors—involve definite restrictions on the rights of use and enjoyment. Finally, since there are no legally enforceable claims to repayment of loans (742c) there can be no mortgaging of the land; a record of the assignment of lots is to be set up in the temples, and one of the magistrates is particularly charged with the duty of seeing that these regulations are observed (741cd).[25]

The Platonic institution of land ownership is thus not easy to classify and has been variously interpreted. It is certainly not private property in the usual sense, for it does not include the right of disposal. Pöhlmann thought that Plato reserved ownership to the state, only the right of use being conferred on the lot holder.[26] The text occasionally seems to imply this conception. "You and this your property do not belong to yourself but to the whole of your family (γένος), past and present, and still more do both your entire family and its property belong to the state" (923a). But Gernet has pointed out that this formula, and other similar texts, have no juridical content; and there is no mention anywhere of a reversion to the state, even when a lot has become vacant through any of the circumstances mentioned above. In fact confiscation by the state is expressly forbidden (855a).[27] The officials sometimes step in to oversee the succession (856de, 877d), but the state has no right of free disposal; the succession is determined in the one case by lot and the aid of Delphi, in the other by a family council. Again Plato's institution is very much like family ownership, which in fact Guiraud declared it to be.[28] Certainly one of its functions is to preserve the continuity of the family and its worship (740bc), but there is no mention of a right of subsistence from the lot in the case of children who do not inherit, though the father may freely give them any portion of his property apart from the lot and its equip-

[25] In insisting upon a public registry of landed property and also (see below) of movable property, Plato was well in advance of his time. "Public record-keeping in Greece was generally spasmodic, impermanent and unreliable. . . . Of a roster of landed properties [in Athens] there is not a trace. The eisphorai and the liturgies were paid on the basis of the individual's own declaration." M. I. Finley, *Studies in Land and Credit in Ancient Athens, 500-200 B.C.: The Horos-Inscriptions*, Rutgers University Press, 1951, 14.

[26] Robert Pöhlmann, *Geschichte des Antiken Kommunismus und Sozialismus*, Munich, 1893, I, 502-503.

[27] Gernet, cliv-clv.; cf. also Josef Bisinger, *Der Agrarstaat in Platons Gesetzen (Klio, Beiheft XVII, 1925)*, 64.

[28] Guiraud, *op.cit.* 583. Cf. also Walter G. Becker, *Platons Gesetze und das Griechische Familienrecht*, Munich, 1932, 135: "Das Grundprinzip ist ein gentilizisches." Becker asserts (131) that Plato's various statements are contradictory. In reply see Gernet cliv.

ment (923d). When the successor of a childless exile is chosen by a family council (877d), its choice is not limited to the members of the family—an omission which is certainly intentional. Plato's institution does not fit any of our familiar conceptions, but it can best be described as private ownership, subject to very special controls that Plato thinks necessary in the interests of the family and the state. These latter interests take precedence in a moral sense over those of the individual, but the legal responsibility for the proper use, maintenance, and control of the land lies with the persons who at any given time are recognized as lot holders.[29]

For this form of landed property there were plenty of precedents in Greece. Sparta indeed was (or had been) a living example of the most important of Plato's proposals. At Sparta the "city land" (πο- λιτικὴ χώρα), as distinct from the land in the possession of the περίοικοι, was divided into lots theoretically equal in yield. These lots could not be bought or sold, either wholly or in part, nor—at least until the early fourth century—given away during life or by bequest. They were intended to pass at death from the father to one of his sons, or if sons were lacking, to a daughter, for whom the father had the right to choose a husband from among the other Spartans, the lot thus passing to the adopted son.[30] But the older law against alienation of the lot seems to have been relaxed in the fourth century. Aristotle criticizes the great inequality of possessions at Sparta, the concentration of ownership in the hands of a few, and the consequent decline in the number of persons who were able to pay their contributions to the common meals. "Though the land is capable of supporting fifteen hundred knights and thirty thousand hoplites, the number has fallen to less than a thousand."[31] This startling decline in the number of full-fledged Spartans in the fourth century is attested by other sources. In the time of King Agis we are told that Sparta could muster only seven hundred Spartiates, whereas in the previous century she had been able to put over five thousand in

---

[29] Gernet clvi: De propriétaire, il n'y en a qu'un de concevable, c'est le détenteur du κλῆρος. . . . Le droit de propriété, c'est celui d'un administrateur exclusif."

[30] On the equality of the κλῆροι, Plut. *Lyc.* 8; Polyb. vi, 45; Busolt-Swoboda 660. On unalienability, Arist. Frag. 611, 12, Rose; Plut. *Inst. Lac.* 22. On inheritance, Plut. *Agis* 5; Busolt-Swoboda, 634. There is a hint also of Spartan institutions in Plato's proposal that the land, and consequently each of the lots, must be sufficient to provide a modest subsistence, but no more (737d).

[31] Arist. *Pol.* 1270a 29-31.

the field.[32] How had this condition come about? Plutarch mentions a change introduced by the ephor Epitadeus (in the early fourth century) that permitted disposal of the lot by bequest or by gift.[33] Some such change as this would partly explain the inequality of possessions in Aristotle's time, for under such a law a transfer that was really a sale could take place disguised as a gift or a bequest. It is likely that many Spartans in the fourth century, pressed between the fixed yield prescribed for them from their allotments and the ever increasing cost of living brought about by the influx of wealth after the Peloponnesian War, resorted to the expedient of borrowing money on the promise of the gift or bequest of their lots. If Plato has taken Sparta as a model here, it is the Sparta of the older time; and it is no doubt to avoid the disastrous results evident in fourth-century Sparta that he lays down his strict law against the alienation of the lot in any fashion.

But Sparta was not the only state that could furnish precedents for this restricted kind of ownership. In Crete also the land—except for that held by the περίοικοι and the considerable portions regarded as common or public land—was divided into κλᾶροι, which were allotted to the various tribes; and within each tribe each household had its allotment, which was inalienable.[34] Elsewhere in Greece restrictions on landed property were somewhat rare in the classical period, though certainly more common in earlier days. Aristotle asserts that in ancient times it was legally forbidden in many cities to sell the original lots, and he gives several examples of such legislation from former days.[35] But apart from Lacedaemon, the only example he gives of comparable legislation in his own time is the law of Locri, probably the Locri in southern Italy whose legislation Plato so much admired.[36] From this we get the impression that restrictions on alienation by sale or bequest were once rather common, but had disappeared for the most part by Aristotle's day. Yet we have a fourth-century inscription from Melaena Corcyra recording an agreement among the colonists of that island that the original lot was to be unalienable.[37]

As for Athens and Attica, we know of no written law at any pe-

---

[32] Plut. *Agis* 5; Herod. ix, 10, 28, 29.   [33] Plut. *Agis* 5; cf. Arist. *Pol.* 1270a 21.
[34] Busolt-Swoboda 742.
[35] *Pol.* 1319a 10-13; cf. 1266b 18-23, 1274b 2-5.
[36] 638b; *Tim.* 20a.   [37] *Syll.* No. 141.

riod that forbade the alienation of land, while for the fourth century we have abundant evidence of the mortgaging and sale of land, and some even for the late fifth.[38] Yet it would be wrong to conclude that there were no restrictions in the earlier days. Unwritten law and ancestral custom may well have produced much the same result as explicit legal prohibition. The question of land tenure in early Attica has long been a subject of controversy. The view now most accepted is that land was unalienable in early Attica, that in fact the system in effect up to Solon's time was quite similar to that proposed by Plato in the *Laws*.[39] A man's land was regarded as belonging to him as head, for the time being, of a larger group, his family; it was not his to sell or give or bequeath as he pleased. It can be plausibly argued that it was this unalienability of land that accounts for the distress of the poorer citizens in Solon's day. To borrow the money needed to convert their fields from wheat to olives and vineyards they could offer only the security of their persons, since the land, being inalienable, could not be mortgaged. If they defaulted on their loans, they were liable to sale into slavery at the pleasure of their creditors, who however often preferred to retain their debtors on their lands, thus controlling both their debtors and the land of which they were the legal owners. This older system of tenure also enables us to understand the elaborate rules of intestate succession and the restrictions on testamentary rights that still prevailed in later Attic law; they were obviously intended to keep the land in the family. In Aristotle's day the archon was charged with the responsibility of protecting orphans and their estates, and more generally with the responsibility of seeing that no household died out or lost its estate.[40] But evidently in Aristotle's day these were only relics of the older system.

When was this older system of land tenure abandoned? Solon has sometimes been credited with its destruction by his legislation granting a childless man the right to select any one he pleased as his heir.

---

[38] See Finley, *op.cit.* and J. V. A. Fine, *Horoi* (*Hesperia Suppl.* IX, 1951, 167ff.).
[39] W. J. Woodhouse, *Solon the Liberator: A Study of the Agrarian Problem in Attika in the Seventh Century*, Oxford, 1938, 74ff.; Naphtali Lewis, "Solon's Agrarian Legislation," AJP LXII, 1941, 144-156; Fine, *op.cit.* 179ff.; and Glotz, *La Solidarité de la famille dans le droit criminel en Grèce*, Paris, 1904, 325ff. For the view that private property in land existed in Solon's day, see H. Swoboda, "Beiträge zur griechischen Rechtsgeschichte," *Zeitschrift der Savigny-Stiftung* XXVI, 1905, 241; J. H. Thiel, "Solon's System of Property Classes," *Mnemosyne* IV, Ser. III, 1950, 1-11.
[40] Arist. *Const. Ath.* LVI, 6; Busolt-Swoboda 1082.

But what Solon did was merely to give a man without natural heirs the right to adopt whomever he pleased, i.e. he was not required to follow any prescribed line of kinship, nor even to select a kinsman. This adopted heir, however, served the function of carrying on the family and did not himself possess any rights of alienation.[41] When did the right of free disposal come to Athens? Fine stresses the fact that we have no evidence of mortgages on land until the last quarter of the fifth century, and has convincingly argued that it was the disruption caused by the Peloponnesian War—the deaths in battle and from the plague and the devastation of the Attic countryside—that brought about the removal, or the ignoring, of the older restrictions on the sale of land.[42] Yet custom and ancestral morality, if not law, discouraged the alienation of the family land, even after mortgaging and sale had become legally possible.[43] If this interpretation is correct, we can see that Plato's proposal is in effect to establish in his imaginary colony something like the conditions of land tenure that prevailed in his native Attica down to the time of his childhood, and which formed the basis of the social organization of that earlier Athens. We can also better understand the reasons for his passionate denunciation in the *Gorgias* of the statesmen of the Periclean age whose policies had brought about—unintentionally of course—the disruption of the older order.

Since in Plato's state the number of lots and households is to remain constant and since only one son, or daughter, can inherit, ways must be found of providing for the other sons and daughters. Some of them will be taken care of by the provisions already mentioned—the daughters by marriage to the sons of other citizens, the sons by

---

[41] See Gernet, "La Loi de Solon sur le 'testament,' " REG XXXII, 1920, reprinted in *Droit et société dans la Grèce ancienne*, Paris, 1956, 121-149; Kathleen Freeman, *The Work and Life of Solon*, 115-118. For the law itself see Ps. Dem. XLIV, 63, 67-68; XLVI, 14.

[42] Fine, *op.cit.* 177ff.

[43] Aesch. I, 30-31, 96; Isaeus VII, 31; cf. Leopold Schmidt, *Die Ethik der Alten Griechen*, Berlin, 1882, II, 392; Vinogradoff, *op.cit.* II, 206ff. In the Athenian cleruchies established in the fifth century it was expected that the cleruch would live on his allotment and cultivate it himself. Special action of the assembly was required for a cleruch even to move to Athens and live on the rent of his allotment, and a fortiori he would hardly be allowed to sell it without permission (Guiraud, *op.cit.* 448; Glotz, *Ancient Greece at Work*, London, 1926, 152). An almost illegible decree of the late sixth century, as restored by Luria, contains a clause prohibiting any cleruchs on Salamis from leasing their holdings except in a case of clearly established financial or physical incapacity, and we can infer that sale would also be prohibited (Tod I, No. 11).

adoption by other citizens who lack sons to succeed them. But since these measures may not provide for all, Plato mentions various devices the officials can employ, from the discouragement of births to the sending out of colonies. In the opposite case of a shortage of citizens, there are devices for encouraging births—such as fines for failure to marry by a certain age, distinctions for fathers of large families —and, in extremity, the calling in of new colonists to fill the gaps in the ranks (740de). In any case, it must be one of the primary concerns of the officials to keep the population constant; Plato's state will not work if that is not done.[44]

One important implication of Plato's legislation is that only citizens may own land in the state. In this respect he adheres closely to the spirit and practice of most Greek states, including Athens. The Spartans, as we have seen, permitted their περίοικοι to occupy—and so far as we know, legally own—large areas of Lacedaemonian territory. Their legal status is not easy to make out from the scanty evidence we have, but they were probably regarded as owners of their lands, just as they were permitted to govern their own cities with considerable independence, though always subject to Spartan control.[45] But this situation in Lacedaemon was anomalous. It was a principle valid elsewhere that the right to own land (ἔγκτησις γῆς καὶ οἰκίας) was essentially a prerogative of the citizen; a foreigner could only acquire it, as he could only acquire citizenship, through an explicit act of the sovereign power.[46] The earliest grant of ἔγκτησις we know of at Athens occurred in the late fifth century, and there are others attested for later times. Such grants were usually made in recognition of special services and accompanied by the grant of other rights.[47] It is obvious that nothing of this sort could take place in Plato's state, except when a dearth of citizens as a result of war or pestilence required the admission of new members to the colony. In this respect, therefore, Plato's law is less lenient than the practice of

---

[44] In view of Plato's lengthy discussion of this problem it is hard to understand why Aristotle should criticize him for not taking it into account (*Pol.* 1265a 38). This and other discrepancies between Aristotle's criticisms and the *Laws* as we have it suggests that Aristotle's comments are based upon an earlier version which was corrected and added to after this part of the *Politics* was written. See my article, "Aristotle's Comments on Plato's *Laws*," in *Aristotle and Plato in the Mid-fourth Century*, edited by Ingemar Düring and G. E. L. Owen, Oxford, 1960.

[45] Busolt-Swoboda 663ff.

[46] Emil Szanto, *Das Griechische Bürgerrecht*, Freiburg, 1892, 7.

[47] See Thalheim in RE s.v. ἔγκτησις.

his countrymen. But it is a safe inference that among Greeks generally the ownership of land by others than citizens was regarded with jealousy and sometimes suspicion.[48] In the constitution of the second Athenian confederation the Athenians explicitly renounce all right to ἔγκτησις in the territory of their confederates; and Isocrates, commenting on this action, says they wished to make the alliance as strong as possible.[49] Aristotle appears to follow Plato here in restricting landownership to citizens in his ideal state.[50]

CITIZENSHIP AND THE FAMILY

It is evident that the lot holders and their families are the important members of Plato's state and the chief object of his legislation. I have designated them as citizens, since this is the language of Plato's text, in which the distinction between citizens and other residents is clearly marked by familiar terms of Greek law;[51] and Plato's institutions are in turn but a reflection of the common theory and practice of the Greek city. "The city is a collection of citizens," says Aristotle; the other elements in the state, however necessary for its functioning, are not truly parts of it.[52] But the legal and political

[48] Vinogradoff, op.cit. II, 200ff.

[49] Tod II, No. 123; Isoc. XIV, 44; cf. Vinogradoff, op.cit. II, 159.

[50] Arist. Pol. 1329a 25, b 35.

[51] In the texts of Plato's laws the citizen is commonly designated ἀστός or πολίτης (e.g. 849a-d, 854de, 866c, 869d, 872a, 882a, 938c). There is no perceptible difference in meaning between these terms (contrary to LSJ, s.v. ἀστός) and they are indeed sometimes used interchangeably (e.g. 869d). The citizen, whether designated ἀστός or πολίτης, is distinguished from the foreigner (ξένος) whether resident (μέτοικος) or transient, and from the slave (δοῦλος or οἰκέτης). Sometimes ἐπιχώριος, "native," is used as a synonym of πολίτης (e.g. 764b, 846d, 847a, 879de, 881c). Since in Plato's Cretan city no noncitizen can ordinarily be a permanent resident of the state, the two terms tend to be identical in denotation; but it may be doubted whether ἐπιχώριος ordinarily carried any connotation of political rights, and Plato's use of it probably reflects conditions peculiar to his state. In one passage (871a) ἐμφύλιος clearly denotes "fellow citizen." This usage is not peculiar to Plato. At Athens the admission of a foreigner to citizenship involved also admission to one of the tribes, and conversely. Thus Aristotle (Pol. 1275b 37) says that Cleisthenes ἐφυλέτευσε ξένους καὶ δούλους, where the context clearly shows that he made them citizens. In Polybius and Plutarch πόλεμος ἐμφύλιος and στάσις ἐμφύλιος mean "civil war"; so does ἐμφύλιος πόλεμος in the Epidamnian decree of 207-206 (Syll. No. 560, line 13). And 871a must be taken as referring to the murder of a fellow citizen, not kinsman, otherwise the further provisions in 872a (τὰ αὐτὰ δὲ ἔστω ταῦτα ξένοισι κτλ) would have no point. Most striking is Plato's use of ἐλεύθεροι to denote citizens, or those by birth eligible for citizenship (848a, 816e; cf. 794a, 807d). Here again Plato's usage has its parallels in other writers of the fourth century. See Chapter VII, Note 88.

[52] Pol. 1274b 41, 1328a 23ff.

implications of this distinction must be made more precise. What are the qualifications entitling a man to this status, and what are the functions the citizen performs in the state as compared with other residents?

At first sight it may seem that one of the qualifications for citizenship is ownership of land. But although there will be exactly 5,040 lots, it does not follow that there will be only 5,040 citizens, as is sometimes hastily assumed. For we must not forget the sons and heirs of lot holders; these will be liable to military service upon reaching the age of twenty (785b) and thereafter qualified, as we shall see, to take part in the elections;[53] and at the age of thirty they can hold office (785b). But none of these will count as the owner of an allotment until his father dies and he has succeeded to the property.[54] There will also be those sons who have not been designated heirs, either to their fathers' or to other citizens' lots. They are presumably subject to military service until they have been sent abroad, and are likewise eligible to vote in the assembly. Finally, there are the wives and grown daughters, none of whom can ever succeed to the ownership of land, though Plato in one passage speaks of "citizens and citizenesses" (πολῖται καὶ πολίτιδες).[55]

If with these points in mind we look again at Plato's description of the division of the land and the provisions for succession to a lot, we shall see that it is the maintenance of the original number of families—variously designated as "hearths" (ἑστίαι) or "households" (οἶκοι, οἰκήσεις)—that he insists upon. He often refers to the 5,040 households, and much of his legislation—e.g. regarding marriage, divorce, adoption, testamentary rights, the filling of a vacant lot— is inspired by his plan to maintain this number unchanged.[56] The original recipients are called γεωμόροι (i.e. landholders, not citizens),

[53] See Chapter V, The Assembly and the Council.

[54] Gernet (cxvi) would call theirs a "citoyenneté virtuelle." But Plato thinks of them as citizens, for in one passage he mentions the possibility of a surplus of citizens (740e).

[55] 814c. Szanto (op.cit. 60) says that to call a woman a citizen merely means that she is the daughter of a citizen, and that beyond this the term is useless as a legal concept. This may be true of Greek law generally, but it is certainly Plato's expressed intention (though not fully carried out) to give women a more equal status under the law. See 804d-805d.

[56] The texts are numerous: 737e; 740b,d,e; 771c; 877d,e; 919d,e; 923a; 929a. For ἑστία = "household" see Herod. ɪ, 176; v, 40; vɪ, 86; and the fifth-century inscription from Locris (Tod ɪ, No. 24).

and "guardians of the distribution" (737e).[57] Nowhere, I believe, does Plato speak of 5,040 citizens. Indeed in one passage he refers to the possibility of a surplus of citizens (740e), a situation which will call for the sending out of a colony. This shows that he is concerned to keep the number of citizens fairly constant, but this number will necessarily be greater than the 5,040 lots, since there must always be grown sons in reserve to succeed to the headship of the various households on the death of their elders.

Hence we cannot say that ownership of land is a qualification for citizenship;[58] to be a citizen, however, one must be a member of one of the households of which the city is composed. These households are all landowning, in the sense that the head in each case is the owner of one of the original allotments, and all draw their subsistence from the land. This ideal of an agrarian citizenry was deeply imbedded in Greek tradition, and was followed to some extent in all the cities we know of. We have seen that the division of the land into allotments was a procedure taken for granted in the establishment of colonies. The Dorian settlements on the mainland began with this principle and adhered to it consistently. It was apparently the condition for citizenship that prevailed in early Attica; and even after the encouragement offered by Solon, the Pisistratids, and perhaps Cleisthenes to alien artisans to settle in Athens,[59] and after the admission of many of them to citizenship, the citizens of Athens continued, in the main, to be landowners, or members of landowning families in the sense above defined. Thucydides tells us that at the beginning of the Peloponnesian War most Athenians lived in the country; and even at the end of the war, after the destruction it had brought to the countryside and to the old customs, it appears that three fourths of the Athenian citizens were landowners.[60] Perhaps

[57] Cf. also 919d. This word apparently does not occur elsewhere in Plato. The γεωμόροι in Syracuse and Samos were the old land-possessing families whose holdings went back to the original settlement of the colonies (see Boerner in RE s.v.), an association of the word which makes its use particularly appropriate in these two passages of the Laws.

[58] As does Bisinger, op.cit. 13, 19, 20, 33. It is likewise false to affirm this principle for Sparta, as does Becker (op.cit. 129 n. 2) who seems to confuse it with another, that only citizens can be landowners.

[59] Plut. Solon 24; Arist. Pol. 1275b 34ff.

[60] Thuc. II, 14, 2, 16, 1. Lys. xxxiv (Arg.) says that the proposal of Phormisius in 404 to restrict citizenship to landowners would have meant the disfranchisement of 5,000 citizens, and it has been estimated (Finley, op.cit. 56ff.) that this would be about one fourth of the citizen body.

the main motive for the establishment of the numerous cleruchies by Athens in the sixth and fifth centuries was to provide land for her landless citizens. The restriction imposed on the sale of land in these cleruchies, and the disapproval that continued to be felt at Athens for the sale of one's patrimony, are sufficient evidence of the vitality of this agrarian ideal even down to Plato's time. "The laws prescribe," says Dinarchus, writing in the late fourth century, "that any general or any speaker who wishes to receive a hearing from the people must own land within our borders."[61]

Other thinkers besides Plato took this ideal of an agrarian citizenry as their guide. Phaleas of Chalcedon, whose sketch of an ideal polity Aristotle discusses at some length, was clearly thinking of an agricultural citizenry, with equal amounts of landed property.[62] Aristotle judges that the best sort of democracy is that in which the sovereignty lies with the farmer class possessing moderate property, his own ideal constitution providing that the land is to be owned by the citizens, though tilled by slaves or barbarians.[63] But even closer in spirit to Plato is Xenophon's *Economics*, a treatise on the management of property, i.e. landed estates. Here Xenophon (speaking through his dramatic spokesman Socrates) declares that of all the arts of peace, agriculture is that which is most appropriate to a gentleman. It increases one's estate, it gives strength to the body and alertness to the mind, it arouses interest in national defense and trains men who are able to defend their country.[64] He notes with approval that the Great King himself regards the overseeing of agriculture in his empire as of equal importance with the practice of arms. Xenophon is not thinking only of gentleman farming, but also of actual labor on the land; for he quotes with evident pleasure a remark of Cyrus, the young prince whom he served and admired, that "he never sat down to dinner when in sound health without having first worked hard at some task of war or agriculture," and that he had with his own hands planted many of the trees in his park in Sardis.[65]

Since one must be a member of one of the 5,040 households before one can be a citizen, it follows that one of the qualifications for citi-

[61] Din. I, 71; for other evidence, see Vinogradoff, *op.cit.* II, 91ff.
[62] Arist. *Pol.* 1267b 15.
[63] Arist. *Pol.* 1292b 25; 1318b 6 - 1319a 18; 1329a 26.
[64] *Econ.* IV-V.
[65] *Econ.* IV, 24.

zenship is descent from citizen parents. There is no provision for
the adoption of aliens. If a lot holder without sons of his body wishes
to adopt a son, he is required to select another citizen's son who has
not been designated heir to his father's lot. Similarly a lot holder
without sons but with an heiress daughter must (or if he dies intestate,
his kinsmen must) select as her husband the son of another citizen,
if there is no relative to claim her and the lot (923e, 924d, 925ab).
This privilege extends so far as to permit her, with the consent of
her guardians, to select as her husband one of the colonists whom
the city has sent out (925bc). But further than this the privilege does
not extend. Nor is there any provision for the naturalization of aliens
by the state, except in a case of dire necessity, such as the depletion
of the population by war or pestilence (740e), for "not even the gods
can force necessity." It is a little less certain whether Plato intends
to forbid the marriage of a citizen with an alien woman. There is no
provision explicitly requiring the male heir to a lot to select a wife
from among the daughters of citizens; in fact the solemn statement
of the marriage law seems to give the young man the right to choose
a bride at his own discretion.[66] In the counsel which follows, however, it is obvious that Plato is considering marriage as a union be-
tween families as well as between individuals, and the use of $\dot{\epsilon}\sigma\tau\dot{\iota}\alpha$
seems to show that he is thinking of the 5,040 households in his state.
Furthermore, surplus daughters as well as surplus sons would be a
problem in such a state as Plato's, and the presumption is that a
citizen will restrict his choice to the eligible daughters of his fellow
citizens. If this is the intent of his legislation, then its effect is to
make citizenship depend upon descent from a citizen mother as well
as from a citizen father.

Such a requirement accords with Aristotle's implication about the
common Greek practice of his day.[67] It is certainly an exact reflection
of Athenian law in the fourth century and for a long time previous
to it. For Aristotle informs us definitely that at Athens "those per-
sons are citizens ($\mu\epsilon\tau\dot{\epsilon}\chi o\upsilon\sigma\iota$ $\tau\hat{\eta}s$ $\pi o\lambda\iota\tau\epsilon\dot{\iota}\alpha s$) who are born of two

[66] 772d; $\kappa\alpha\tau\dot{\alpha}$ $\nu o\hat{\upsilon}\nu$ $\dot{\epsilon}\alpha\upsilon\tau\hat{\omega}$. This impression is strengthened if we accept, as England
does, Aldus' plausible alteration of the MS. $\dot{o}\pi\dot{o}\tau\epsilon$ to $\dot{o}\pi\dot{o}\theta\epsilon\nu$ in d5.
[67] Pol. 1275b 21. We know that this requirement of descent from citizens on both
sides prevailed at Byzantium (Ps. Arist. Econ. 1346b 26), at Rhodes (IG XII, I, No.
766), at Halicarnassus (Syll. No. 1015, lines 6ff.), and probably also at Oreus (Dem.
XXIII, 213). Some states went so far as to require descent from citizen grandparents
or great grandparents, according to Arist. Pol. 1275b 23.

citizen parents."[68] This is confirmed by the references of the orators to the oath taken by a father when he presented his child for registry in his phratry; the father had to swear that the child was "a citizen of a duly wedded citizen mother."[69] This law goes back to the early days of Pericles' leadership,[70] and remained in force until the loss of citizens in the Peloponnesian War caused it to be ignored, if not actually repealed. With the restoration of the democracy in 403-2 it was again enacted in the archonship of Euclides, but with the express provision that no one who was in de facto possession of citizenship should be deprived of it. Any child born after the passage of this law, however, would have citizen status only if both parents were citizens.[71] In this form the law was in effect in Aristotle's time.

But what the law was prior to the time of Pericles cannot be discerned with any clarity. It is evident that the requirement of a citizen mother was not in force in the period immediately before the passage of the famous law of 451, for we know that some of the most prominent Athenians of that era—Themistocles, Miltiades, Cimon, and Cleisthenes—were sons of non-Athenian mothers. On this evidence Kahrstedt asserts that "in earlier times there was clearly no precondition of citizenship other than that the father must be an Athenian; the status of the mother was immaterial, exactly as at Sparta."[72] Gomme, however, contends that the Periclean law was an attempt to restore what was regarded as normal. "The idea of kinship as the basis of membership in the state was fundamental throughout Greece, and in this respect the nationality of the mother was as important as that of the father. . . . There had been, inevitably, some intermarriage; but the law of 451 was . . . in accordance with average sentiment."[73] Unfortunately we have no good evidence of

---

[68] *Const. Ath.* XLII, I.

[69] Dem. LVII, 54: ἀστὸς ἐξ ἀστῆς ἐγγυητῆς γεγενημένος; Isaeus VII, 16 and VIII, 19: ἦ μὴν ἐξ ἀστῆς καὶ ἐγγυητῆς γυναικὸς εἰσάγειν. For evidence of the careful scrutiny employed to establish citizenship in disputed cases, see Arist. *Const. Ath.* XLII, I; LV; and Dem. LVII, 67-68.

[70] Arist. *Const. Ath.* XXVI, 3; Plut. *Per.* 37; Aelian, *Var. Hist.* VI, 10; XIII, 24; cf. Eur. *Ion* 671ff.

[71] Schol. to Aesch. I, 39; Dem. LVII, 30; Isaeus VIII, 43.

[72] Ulrich Kahrstedt, *Staatsgebiet und Staatsangehörige in Athen*, Stuttgart-Berlin, 1934, 60-61. So also O. Müller, "Untersuchungen zur Geschichte des attischen Bürger- und Eherechts" in *Jahrbuch für Klass. Phil. Suppl.* XXV, 1899, 858ff.; and Artur Ledl, "Das Attische Bürgerrecht und die Frauen," in *Wiener Studien* XXIX, 1907.

[73] *Essays in Greek History and Literature*, Oxford, 1937, 86-87. See also Adolf Philippi, *Beiträge zu einer Geschichte des attischen Bürgerrechts*, Berlin, 1870, 31ff.

what "average sentiment" was; moreover we know too little of the circumstances surrounding the act of 451 to be able to understand clearly why it was introduced. Aristotle says the law was passed "because of the multitude of citizens."[74] If this means that its purpose was to decrease the number of citizens then on the rolls, Aristotle is clearly in error; for Thucydides and Cimon were not deprived of citizen rights, which shows that the law was not retroactive. On the other hand, if its purpose was prospective, it would produce no considerable effect unless the taking of a non-Athenian wife was not unusual before this time and could be expected to continue.[75] Perhaps its motive, as Gomme suggests, was to encourage the choice of Athenian citizens as wives; unmarried daughters must have been a problem in Athens as they would have been in Plato's state. If this is so, the Periclean legislation was intended to accomplish by explicit prescription what Plato's tightly knit family organization almost inevitably involves. The very absence of an explicit prescription in Plato's law may support the contention that in early Athens—which Plato's family state follows so closely—there was no legal or moral objection to the admission of an alien woman into the family; it was only the force of circumstances that ordinarily made such marriages undesirable.[76]

For Plato, then, the state is a union of households or families, not a collection of detached citizens. This clearly emerges from his account of the origin of the state in the third book. The first organization of human beings formed among the survivors of the great deluge was the family, living in peaceful isolation under the rule of the father, who gave laws to his wife and children (680a-e). From the smaller family developed the γένος, or clan; and out of this came the union (συνοικία) of various families and clans into a larger group, the πόλις (681a-d). Quite similar is Aristotle's account of the origin of the πόλις in the *Politics*: first the family (οἶκος); then the village (κώμη), which is an extension of the household, composed of kins-

[74] *Const. Ath.* xxvi, 3.
[75] See Gomme, *op.cit.* 87n.; and Hignett 345-346.
[76] Gomme rightly questions the common interpretation of the Periclean law as an expression of the selfish exclusiveness of the Athenian democracy (see Tod, Walker, and Adcock in *Cambridge Ancient History* v, 4-5, 102-103, 167-168). Grants of citizenship by the assembly are frequent in this period and even more numerous in the following century. Oligarchic Sparta was much less generous. Aristotle's reference (*Pol.* 1270a 34) to the tradition that under the early kings the Spartans conferred citizenship rather freely implies that the Sparta of the fourth century did not.

men; and finally the society (κοινωνία) formed of several villages, which is the πόλις. Aristotle evidently had Plato's discourse in mind when he wrote.[77] But the similarity of their views is not due only to a common Academic tradition. Aristotle and Plato agree on the main outlines of this story because both are writing what they understand to be history; this is the way they think the polis actually came to be. Aristotle explicitly says that the best way to study the state is to look at it in its process of development from the beginning; and Plato's account is also derived explicitly from ancient tales and from probable speculation.[78] Both Plato and Aristotle find in the household ruled by its head the explanation of the kingship they regard as characteristic of early societies and still to be found, as Plato remarks, in many places among the Greeks and the barbarians (680b). The picture that they give of the polis as emerging comparatively late through a union of families, clans, tribes, and villages, and retaining as vital parts in its later structure these elements of which it was put together—this we see is eminently correct, in the main, for the Greek world in which they were most interested; and especially true of Athens, the city we know best.[79]

The vitality of the family in Plato's state is evident at many points in his legislation. There are to be family shrines, in which the ancestral gods (πατρῷοι θεοί) are worshipped and "service" (θεραπεία) rendered to the dead members of the family. The lot holder, as head of the family, passes on his lot at death to the son whom he has chosen to succeed him, and this son is the minister (θεραπευτής) not merely of the gods of the city, but also of the gods of the family (γένος) and all its members, living and dead (740bc, 923a).[80] The rules we have already noted regarding inheritance, bequest, adoption, the marriage of an heiress, and the attention paid to the guardianship of orphans (922a, 924a-c, 926d-928d) and to funeral rites and me-

[77] *Pol.* 1252b 12ff. Not only are the main outlines of the development the same, but Aristotle even quotes as evidence of earlier practices the same passage from Homer. *Odyss.* IX, 112ff.

[78] *Pol.* 1252a 24; *Laws* 676a,c, 677a.

[79] The importance of the family in the structure of the Greek city has been expounded in several of the most imposing works of modern scholarship. For an extreme and over-schematic view, see Foustel de Coulanges, *La Cité antique*, Paris, 1864; for a more sober presentation, Glotz, *La Cité grecque*, Paris, 1928. Cf. also Glotz, *op.cit.* (Note 39 above), 3-18; and A. E. Zimmern, *The Greek Commonwealth*, Oxford, 1911, 65-78.

[80] These family rites are dealt with in Chapter VIII, The Gods and their Worship.

morials (717de), are all clearly intended (sometimes it is explicitly said so) to assure the continuance of the family as an important part of the state. There are family courts that adjudge certain acts of violence within the family (878d) and similar family assemblies to authorize disinheritance (929ab). Marriage is regarded as a union of families; the individual should choose his mate not for pleasure only, but with the interests of the families and of the state in mind (773ab). Furthermore the family is the source and nurse of the ancestral customs, or unwritten laws, which are much older than any written legislation (680a). These ancient ancestral customs, says the Athenian Stranger, are the bonds of the whole constitution. If they are properly established they support all other legislation; but if not, like imperfect mortises in a carpenter's work, they give way and let the whole structure come tumbling down (793bc).

The most striking evidence of the vitality of the family is the law of homicide. Plato's law puts the responsibility of bringing a murderer to justice upon the nearest kinsman of the slain man.[81] It is only when the kinsman has failed to act and has thus allowed the murderer to bring pollution upon the city by frequenting the assemblies and the sacred places, that anyone else can act; and even here the prosecutor proceeds, not necessarily with an action for homicide against the slayer, but with an action for impiety against the delinquent kinsman (866b, 868b, 871b).[82] This was in full accord with Attic law in Plato's day, and nothing could be better evidence of the autonomous and self-protecting clans out of which the Athenian state had developed. The idea that homicide involved not merely an injury to the family of the slain but also a breach of public order found expression only in the idea that the shedding of blood brought pollution upon the community. This concept of pollution is itself a later development—we do not find it in Homer—and is undoubtedly the result of an effort by the larger community, under the guidance of the Delphic oracle, to prevent bloodshed and maintain public order.

In most details of his family law Plato simply follows the principles of Attic law. Sometimes he departs from them for reasons peculiar to his state, as when he prescribes integral transmission of the κλῆρος to the son designated as heir, limits the right of free bequest to mov-

---

[81] For the provisions of the homicide law see 865a-874d; esp. 866ab, 868bc, 871b.
[82] On this part of Plato's law see Gernet, *Platon, Lois, Livre IX, Traduction et Commentaire*, 1917.

able property over and above the equipment of the lot, and limits it here in favor of the other sons and daughters of the testator (922b-924a). He accentuates parental authority by withdrawing from the son the right of self-defense against his father (879c), and by apparently conferring upon the father the right to "give" one of his sons to another citizen for adoption (923c). More notable departures, because not motivated by conditions peculiar to his state, are to be found in certain provisions regarding the status of women. In the law governing betrothal, the relatives on the mother's side are given the right of betrothal, if there is no one in the paternal line competent to assume this function (774c). The prohibition of dowries (742c) seems to have the effect of severing the wife's connection with her former family; and this has the further consequence that a widowed or divorced woman has no κύριος, and can bring action in the courts in her own right (937a). Plato gives an unmarried heiress who has no kinsman to claim her, the right to choose her own spouse as she pleases, subject to the approval of her guardians (925a-c); and his law of divorce (784b, 929e-930c) shows a systematic development and a recognition of the personality of the wife far in advance of Greek law generally.[83]

Between the family and the state comes the tribe. The land is to be divided into twelve parts as nearly equal as possible in fertility, if not in extent (745bc, 958e), and the colonists likewise divided into twelve groups equal in number and as equal as possible in the amount of movable property possessed by their members (745d). Each of these groups of colonists (presumably inhabiting one of the twelve divisions of the land) constitutes a tribe, and is to be dedicated to one of the twelve gods and called by the name of its patron deity (745de).[84] Ideally the city (ἄστυ) should be situated at

---

[83] For a fuller examination of Plato's "droit de famille" see Gernet cli-clxix. On Plato's law of divorce see Becker (*op.cit.* 137ff.), whose estimate of it, and whose belief that it shows the influence of the law of Gortyn are, however, questioned by Gernet.

[84] It is not explicitly said that each of the twelve μέρη into which the colonists are divided is to be assigned to one of the twelve μέρη into which the land is divided, but this is a natural inference. If this is not Plato's intention, then the twelve parts of the land are administrative divisions distinct from the twelve tribes, as England interprets them (see Chapter V, Note 82). But the other is the usual interpretation and I adopt it, though with some hesitation. For nowhere are the geographical divisions called tribes, not even in the account of the duties of the rural police (760ff.) and of their counterparts in the city (763c). The provisions for policing the country make it especially evident that these geographical divisions have no local autonomy;

the middle of the land, and the boundaries marking the divisions should radiate outward from the center of it; in this way each division will be a continuous area from the acropolis of the city to the borders of the state, including land within the city proper and in the country outside. Plato does not say how the equality of wealth between the tribes is to be preserved; but it is clear that he does not want any tribe to secure an undue measure of power or influence because of its wealthy members. The same demand for equality is expressed in the provision that each lot is to be divided into two portions, one relatively near the city and the other relatively near the border. By adjusting these distances the legislator can bring about an approximate equality of location among the various lot holders. It seems also to be implied that each lot holder will also possess houses within the city, again two in number and so situated as to equalize the advantages and disadvantages of location (745e). This is highly schematic; and the Athenian Stranger at once reminds himself and his companions that the conditions for realizing these and other provisions he has just discussed are not likely to be realized, and the founder of a city may have to be content with something less than the ideal; nevertheless, he continues, he should permit the legislator to develop his model (παράδειγμα) in detail, and afterwards consult with him concerning what parts may be embodied, and what will have to be omitted, in legislation for his particular state (745e-746d).

These divisions are obviously important for administrative purposes; and we shall see that they underlie the organization of the rural police (the agronomoi) and to a less extent the duties of the city magistrates (the astynomoi).[85] The citizen's legal designation includes the name of his tribe (753c); and tribal distinctions also play a part in military organization and levies (746de, 755c-e). But their political importance is surprisingly small, when we think of the part played by tribal distinctions in the government of Athens. With the exception of the agronomoi (760b) and the women superintendents of children's play (794b), they are never considered in filling the offices of Plato's state; and they are openly disregarded in the election of the council, in which the distinction between the four property classes plays the decisive part. They figure, however, in the adminis-

---

if they are tribes, each will be policed for eleven twelfths of the year by agronomoi chosen from other tribes. See Chapter V, The Magistrates.

[85] See Chapter V, The Magistrates.

tration of justice, in that Plato's courts of second instance are to be constituted κατὰ φυλάς, as were the heliastic courts at Athens.[86] In religious life their importance is much greater. Each tribe is, as we have seen, dedicated to one of the twelve gods and called by the name of the patron deity; and two annual festivals are prescribed for each of the gods, one to be held in the city and the other in the country (828c). The country festivals would certainly take place in the territories of the appropriate tribes, and it is likely that in both the city and the country festivals the tribe concerned would have special responsibilities, though of what these are Plato gives us no hint. These festivals, like those arranged in the smaller divisions of the state, will give opportunity for the citizens to learn to know one another and will promote the spirit of friendliness and the sense of common purpose that Plato regards as so important for the well-being of a state (771d). Finally, in the selection of the exegetes, the expounders of religious law, the tribes are divided into three groups of four tribes each—an indication indeed of their importance in this area of law, but without the supporting details that would enable us to see precisely how these groups are formed or how they function.[87]

Despite the political unimportance of Plato's tribes as compared with those at Athens, there are features of his scheme that definitely recall the system of Athenian tribes as it existed after the reorganization of Cleisthenes.[88] Plato is obviously concerned to make impossible the rise of powerful clans related by blood, the situation at Athens which Cleisthenes endeavored to correct by his drastic new grouping. Henceforth the Athenian tribes no longer stood for any real relation of kinship, and the same is true of Plato's tribes. Cleisthenes' device of giving each tribe a share of land in the city, the shore and the interior is reflected in Plato's geometrical scheme of tribal boundaries radiating from the center. As Cleisthenes provided a sentimental basis of unity for each tribe by naming each of them after a hero, so Plato selects the twelve gods as divine patrons and fictional ancestors for his tribes. Again, the ten tribes of Cleisthenes were an unusually large number as compared with the traditional three tribes into which the Dorians were divided and the four tribes

---

[86] See Chapter VI, The Courts; and Index, s.v. Tribal Courts.
[87] See Chapter VIII, Religious Officials; and Index s.v. Exegetes.
[88] On Cleisthenes' changes see Arist. *Const. Ath.* xxi; *Pol.* 1319b 20ff.; Fr. 385, Rose.

found in early Attica and some other Ionian states.[89] But Plato goes further and makes twelve instead of ten, thus bringing the number of tribes into agreement with the number of months in the year (771b). No student of the Athenian constitution can fail to be surprised that Cleisthenes did not do likewise. It would have made the prytanies coincide with the twelve months, and would have obviated the awkwardness of making another division of the year into ten parts, in order that each tribe might have its equal share in the presidency of the council.[90] Aristotle no doubt gives the correct explanation of Cleisthenes' failure to do this: each of the four older tribes was divided into three trittyes, so that if Cleisthenes had used the number twelve he would not have accomplished his purpose of making fresh combinations. However compelling Aristotle considered this consideration to be, it is obvious that twelve seemed to him a better number. Plato's colony does not face the problem of long-standing interests entrenched in hereditary groups, and he is free to follow the simpler principle that Cleisthenes may also have preferred.[91]

Plato also provides for other subdivisions of his citizen body, such as phratries, demes, and villages (746d); but his references to these other groupings are so few and so casual that it is impossible to discern his intentions clearly. It would appear to be a sound principle of interpretation that when Plato mentions an institution without explanatory details he assumes it to have the constitution and powers that his readers would understand without explanation. Following this principle here, we can take the demes as subdivisions of the

[89] Busolt-Swoboda 130ff., 256ff. But according to Paus. v, ix, 5, Elis was divided into twelve tribes in 368. Miletus also had twelve tribes after the Samian War (Kathleen Freeman, *Greek City-States*, 161; cf. Latte, RE. s.v. Phyle, 1002). There were also twelve tribes in Ankyra (Latte, *loc.cit.*). But these instances seem to have been unusual.

[90] This change was actually made at Athens at the end of the fourth century with the creation of two new tribes. Busolt-Swoboda 931.

[91] James H. Oliver (*Athenian Expounders of the Sacred and Ancestral Law*, Johns Hopkins University Press, 1950, 55f.) has advanced the interesting theory that Plato's model here is actually the twelve old Attic trittyes that Cleisthenes deliberately ignored. They seem to have persisted into the fourth century (Oliver, *Hesperia* IV, 1935, 5-32; Ferguson, *Classical Studies Presented to Edward Capps*, Princeton University Press, 1936, 151-158). What evidence we have of them in the fourth century shows them exercising certain functions in religious law, which would accord with the position of the tribes in Plato's law (see Index, s.v. Trittyes). For the tradition in the fourth century about the old Attic trittyes see Arist. Fr. 385, Rose.

tribes. In Attica the deme possessed a considerable measure of autonomy over its local affairs, which it managed through a deme assembly and an annually selected demarch;[92] these terms do not appear in Plato's text, but there would be no contradiction in assuming that he took this organization for granted. Something like it would in any case be necessary for the management of local affairs, though one may suppose that deme autonomy would be somewhat less than it was at Athens; this seems to be implied in the account of the powers of the rural police (agronomoi) which we shall consider later.[93] The only other passage explicitly referring to the demes is the prescription that a citizen shall be designated by his patronymic, his tribe, and his deme (753c). The young Athenian was presented to his father's deme on the completion of his eighteenth year; and upon acceptance he became a demesman (δημότης), and his deme designation (δημοτικόν) was henceforth attached to his name in all official acts concerning him.[94] There is no mention in Plato's text of such a ceremony of presentation and enrollment in the deme registry; but Plato's readers would certainly assume it, and we can safely do so also.[95] Again at Athens the fifty members from each tribe in the council were composed of members from each deme;[96] but since the tribes are ignored in the constitution of Plato's council, so also will be the demes.

A more difficult matter is to determine the number of demes that Plato assumes. The suggested subdivision of each of the tribes into twelve parts (771b) would, if we take these parts to be demes, give us one hundred forty-four, which corresponds fairly closely to the

[92] Busolt-Swoboda 964ff.

[93] See Index, s.v. Agronomoi.

[94] It was the reforms of Cleisthenes that seem to have given the deme its importance in the Athenian constitution. Cleisthenes' intention was to displace the patronymic in the designation of the citizen, but the evidence of the inscriptions and the ostraca shows that the Athenians accepted the newer form reluctantly and clung tenaciously to their patronymics; in the late fifth and fourth centuries the common usage was to combine the two. Kahrstedt, op.cit. (Note 72), 199-206; A. E. Raubitschek, Dedications from the Athenian Acropolis, Cambridge (Mass.), 1949, 472-476, and Actes du IIᵉ Congrès Int. d'Epigraphie, 1953, 67-69. Plato, as we see, would add the tribal designation to the others.

[95] Plato provides that a man becomes liable to military service at the age of twenty (785b). This need not imply a departure from Athenian practice, since the young Athenian, after enrollment in the deme register, spent two years in ephebic training within the borders of Attica; only after reaching the age of twenty would he be called upon for war service.

[96] Busolt-Swoboda 1022.

number of Attic demes.[97] But Plato's state would be considerably smaller than Athens, and probably not many demes in Attica had as few as thirty-five households, which on this supposition would be the normal number in Plato's state. Another difficult question is the relation of the demes to the villages. In one passage (848cd) Plato seems to think of twelve villages in all, one situated at the center of each tribal district. But if the demes are subdivisions of the tribe, then most of the demes would be without any village center, which seems improbable; and some of the details given elsewhere (761cd) imply something like communities scattered over the countryside, with sacred areas and gymnasia and warm baths for the health and comfort of the local laborers. It seems most probable that in 848cd Plato is thinking of the chief village in the district, with its temples, market place, and facilities for festivals, and taking for granted that there would exist other smaller hamlets dispersed over the countryside. There is a lack of clarity here, however, which suggests that these details had not been worked out fully in Plato's mind.[98]

The phratry is another subdivision of the citizen body mentioned in 746d. This is a very old institution; but our guiding principle for interpreting Plato's intentions is of little use here, for our notions about the constitution and functions of the Attic phratries are exceedingly uncertain.[99] They were apparently groups of clans associated for religious and other purposes. Cleisthenes allowed the citizens to retain their phratries, with their clans and hereditary priesthoods; but it appears that he created other new phratries, and probably limited somewhat the prerogatives of the old ones.[100] Their designation by a term derived from the old Indo-Germanic word for "brother" implies kinship; but this was only a fiction, at least in historical times. They had their cults, and officials, and regulated their affairs at meetings of the members. To be admitted to a phratry was a matter of considerable importance, for it was regarded as good proof of citizen-

[97] See J. E. Sandys, *Aristotle's Constitution of Athens*, 2nd edn., London, 1912, 84.
[98] Bisinger (*op.cit.* 25) suggests that in his references to the deme Plato has simply assumed an Athenian institution that is without meaning in his state, and that if the *Laws* had received final revision these references would have been eliminated. But local subdivisions of some sort would be necessary in Plato's state.
[99] On the phratry see Hignett, 55-66; Wade-Gery, CQ XXV, 1931, 1-2, 129-143; Busolt-Swoboda 958ff.; and Latte, RE s.v. Phratrie.
[100] *Const. Ath.* XXI, 6. In *Pol.* 1319b 20ff. Aristotle seems to say that Cleisthenes introduced not merely new tribes but also new φρατρίαι. See W. L. Newman's note on this passage (*Politics of Aristotle*, Oxford, 1887-1902, IV, 522f.) and Sandys, *op.cit.* 82, 87.

ship. But whether all Athenian citizens were members of phratries, how many phratries there were, and what their relation was to the other subdivisions of the citizen body—the answers to these questions are enveloped in the mist that conceals so much of Greek religious law, and unfortunately Plato's text contains little, if anything, to increase our knowledge. The single reference to phratries, other than the mention of them in 746d as subdivisions of the citizenry, concerns the registration of members (785ab). Plato's law here prescribes that in every phratry there shall be a list on a whitened wall of all the living members, the name of each to be inscribed (presumably at birth, with the name, or number, of the archon eponymous for the year) and erased at death.[101] Gernet points out that this is a kind of *acte de naissance*, rendering unnecessary the litigation about personal status which was so common at Athens. Such litigation is nowhere provided for in Plato's law, and this passage shows us why. In this respect, then, Plato seems to be simplifying Attic law by substituting a single uniform procedure of admission for the variety of methods apparently used by the Attic phratries,[102] and also, by prescribing that it shall take place in the first year of the child's life, making it something like incontestable evidence of age and of citizenship. A consequence of this law is, as Gernet remarks, that the phratry becomes an organ of public law and a subdivision of the tribe, instead of being a private corporation as it was under Attic law. Evidently all citizens in Plato's state are to be members of phratries; and it is par-

[101] I assume with Gernet (cxiv-cxv) that the "family shrines" (ἱερὰ πατρῷα, 785 a5) are distinct from the phratry mentioned in the next sentence. Plato assumes two registrations, and it is natural to infer that the phratry registration, like that in the family shrine, is to take place during the first year of life. The grammatical peculiarities in this passage (for which see England) fortunately do not obscure the sense.

The contrast between the full and finished discussion of marriage that immediately precedes and the uncouth brevity of this passage (and of the two immediately following ones concerning the age of marriage and of military service) suggests that these were loose memoranda which the editor of the *Laws* placed here in default of a more explicit designation in the fragments themselves. The implication that the years are officially designated by their eponymous archons contradicts 947a, where the euthynos chosen as high priest gives his name to the year. The term ἄρχων is used very loosely in Plato's text, but usually refers to one of the nomophylakes when it is unqualified. I suspect that we have in 785 a8 an unconscious reflection of the Athenian method of marking the year, a lapse which would be quite natural if Plato is thinking of a reform of Athenian law. Again the requirement of marriage between thirty and thirty-five is at variance with 772d, where we have "twenty-five to thirty-five," but identical with that stated in 721ab.

[102] Busolt-Swoboda 960ff.; Latte, *loc.cit.* 749ff.

ticularly stated that the names of girls as well as boys shall be inscribed upon the whitened wall.

In discussing the meaning of citizenship in the states of his day, Aristotle says that "citizen," in the "unqualified" meaning of the term—that is, the citizen who is old enough to have come into the full enjoyment of his rights and who is not under atimia for any cause—is to be defined in no other way than by the right of access to deliberative and judicial office.[103] There is no similar passage in Plato dealing thus summarily with this question, but the details of his legislation show that he is in essential agreement with Aristotle as to what citizenship should mean in a properly ordered state. The offices in his state are of course to be filled by citizens, and access to office is in principle open to all; for only a few offices, and those minor ones, are there any property qualifications. Age is more frequently a requirement. A man must be at least thirty years old to be eligible for any office, and for election as a guardian of the laws or a euthynos he must be fifty; but these are hardly violations of Aristotle's principle. For election to the council ($\beta o \nu \lambda \acute{\eta}$)—an office to which Aristotle may be specifically referring in the mention of "deliberative office" ($\mathring{a} \rho \chi \mathring{\eta} \ \beta o \nu \lambda \epsilon \nu \tau \iota \kappa \acute{\eta}$)—there is no special requirement. Aristotle's $\mathring{a} \rho \chi \mathring{\eta} \ \kappa \rho \iota \tau \iota \kappa \acute{\eta}$ probably refers to judicial office, and Plato explicitly defends the right of the citizen to sit on courts of justice. "He who does not have the right of sitting with his fellows on courts of law thinks he is without a share in the city" (768b). This language suggests that the principle enunciated by Aristotle and implicitly followed by Plato had its foundations in common Greek conceptions of right. It is the citizens, and the citizens alone, who are responsible for filling the offices, administering the business of government, and determining violations of the laws; and the right (and in some cases the duty) of sharing these responsibilities belongs to all, by virtue of their status as citizens.

Assuming 5,040 heads of families, plus an equal or slightly larger number of grown men to serve as replacements and successors, we can estimate that Plato's state would have a body of male citizens numbering, at a rough estimate, between ten and twelve thousand. It would be considerably smaller than the Athens of the fourth century—less than half its size, on Gomme's estimate of Athenian popu-

---

[103] $\tau \mathring{\omega} \ \mu \epsilon \tau \acute{\epsilon} \chi \epsilon \iota \nu \ \kappa \rho \acute{\iota} \sigma \epsilon \omega s \ \kappa a \grave{\iota} \ \mathring{a} \rho \chi \mathring{\eta} s$, 1275a 22; $\mathring{\omega} \ \mathring{\epsilon} \xi o \nu \sigma \acute{\iota} a \ \kappa o \iota \nu \omega \nu \epsilon \mathring{\iota} \nu \ \mathring{a} \rho \chi \mathring{\eta} s \ \beta o \nu \lambda \epsilon \nu -$
$\tau \iota \kappa \mathring{\eta} s \ \kappa a \grave{\iota} \ \kappa \rho \iota \tau \iota \kappa \mathring{\eta} s$, 1275b 18.

lation—and even smaller as compared with the Athens of the Persian wars.[104] Its effective military force would be greater than that of Sparta in Plato's time, but Sparta was then suffering from a shortage of men; as compared with the Spartan power of the preceding century Plato's state again appears modest. Yet it would not be a small state by Greek standards.[105] The roll of cities in which the number of citizens was between five and ten thousand is not long, and it includes some important ones, such as Megara, Sicyon, Mytilene; and many well known states—e.g. Aegina, Mantinea, Tegea—were well below this size.[106] Plato does not give his reasons for this choice of something like a mean between the extremes to be found in his day. A state should have enough men, he says, to be able to defend itself against injury and to send help to its neighbors if they should be attacked (737d). On the other hand, what Aristotle later says—that the state should be small enough so that its citizens may know each other well—would be especially important for Plato's state, since the selection of officers rests mainly in the hands of the citizens. This consideration also seems to be presupposed in certain details of Plato's electoral procedures, and in the various institutions he sets up for promoting the friendliness and fellow feeling that are fundamental criteria of a good society.[107]

The number 5,040 may strike us as unnecessarily, perhaps childishly, precise. But granted that it is desirable to maintain a fixed number of households in the state, the mention of a specific number only adds emphasis to the principle; and if a number is to be selected

[104] Gomme, *The Population of Athens in the Fifth and Fourth Centuries*, 26, Table I. Gomme estimates the male citizen population at 35,000 in 480, 22,000 in 400, and 28,000 in 323.

[105] Aristotle (*Pol.* 1265a 13ff.) indeed says it would require a territory as large as Babylon or some other area "of unlimited extent." This is obviously an exaggeration. Aristotle assumes that the "five thousand men" are to be "supported in idleness." Even so Sparta supported more idle warriors than this in the fifth century. But Plato's state is more comparable to Attica, as I have shown. If we multiply the number of male citizens by four to get the total citizen population (for a justification of this method of calculation, see Gomme, *op.cit.* 75ff.), we reach a figure of forty to forty-eight thousand. Assuming in Plato's state the same proportion of metics and slaves as lived in Athens in 431, we would add seven or eight thousand metics and twenty-seven to thirty-two thousand slaves. These estimates of the slave and metic population are probably too high for Plato's state. Even so they would give us a maximum population of 80,000, slightly more than one fourth of the estimated population of Athens in 431, surely not an impossible figure.

[106] Glotz, *La Cité grecque*, 27-28.

[107] For electoral procedures, see especially 751cd, 753cd, 763d, 946a; for the need of φιλία 693d, 743c, 771d ff.

for this emphasis, it is well to have one that can be used conveniently. The number 5,040 has, as Plato says, the most numerous and most consecutive divisors (738a). This is not number mysticism, but practical convenience. If we are to have twelve tribes, each with twelve subdivisions, and further subdivisions of these, and an indeterminate number of other divisions for purposes of war, taxation, religious festivals, and all the other enterprises that filled the life of a Greek city, there is no point in having a number that will divide only with awkward remainders.[108]

Thus far we have found only one presupposition of citizenship in Plato's state, and that is membership in one of the 5,040 families. We have also seen that, as respects the social organization of which these families are the units, the influence of Athenian institutions seems the dominant one. Plato is thinking of the Attica of an older time, no doubt, the Attica whose families guarded their ancestral seats and hereditary dignities more carefully than in his day, the Attica in which the ancestral customs still controlled the conduct of the citizen. But Plato is legislating for a time in which these ancestral customs no longer have their ancient authority. He may also have thought that the decline of the older Athenian constitution might have been prevented by more deliberate effort to maintain and direct these ancestral traditions. In any case, there appears in his state another requirement for citizenship, a requirement that shows unmistakably the influence of Sparta. Each of his citizens must undergo in his youth a course of training controlled by public officials and as persistent in its purposes as the Spartan agoge. In Plato's city, as at Sparta, the state takes over from the family, in order to create the type of mind and character that it thinks its citizens should have.[109] The educational system that Plato proposes can best be understood after we have surveyed the political institutions which these citizens will have to work. Here we can only point out that Plato takes away from the family one of its most important functions. In requiring the child to be educated by the state, in relieving the father not only of

---

[108] The fourth-century chroniclers upon whom Aristotle relied for details of early Attic tribal organization (Fr. 385, Rose) seem to have taken arithmetical symmetry for granted in the tribal structure: the twelve trittyes (three in each tribe) were said to have contained thirty γένη each, and each γένος had thirty men.

[109] 751c. Similarly those who attempt to enter the colony at the beginning are to be tested thoroughly, in order to exclude the unfit or vicious (736bc). It is assumed in 708a that the colonists will be Greeks, mostly from Crete and the Peloponnesus.

the responsibility but also of the right to give his sons and daughters the education he thinks they should have, Plato's law marks a great departure from the law of his native city and from Greek customs generally. This is perhaps Plato's greatest innovation.

PROPERTY CLASSES

Plato next turns to the regulation of movable property. "It would have been well if every man entered the colony with an equal amount of other goods; but since that is not possible, and one man will come with more and another with fewer possessions, it is necessary . . . to have unequal property classes" (744b). The basic evaluation ($\tau \acute{\iota} \mu \eta \mu \alpha$)[110] on which these classes depend is the value of the lot (744de). From other references we infer that the equipment of the lot, i.e. the tools and animals necessary for its cultivation, are also included in the basic $\tau \acute{\iota} \mu \eta \mu \alpha$ (855ab, 856d, 923d, 958ab). This is the "limit of poverty" ($\pi \epsilon \nu \acute{\iota} \alpha \varsigma$ $\acute{o} \rho o \varsigma$); no man's goods shall be allowed to fall below this level. Taking this as a measure, "the lawgiver will allow a man," Plato says, "to acquire twice or three times or four times this amount" (744e).[111] This gives four classes, the richest (or as Plato calls it, the first) class consisting of persons whose acquisitions, over and above the lot and its equipment, have a value between three and four times the value of the lot.[112] If any man acquires more than this fourfold amount, whether from money-making, or a gift,

---

[110] The word $\tau \acute{\iota} \mu \eta \mu \alpha$ is sometimes used by Plato in its strict and primary sense to denote the evaluation of a man's property (see Busolt-Swoboda 821 n. 2) and sometimes to denote the class of persons whose property has a certain evaluation. Aristotle generally uses $\tau \acute{\iota} \mu \eta \mu \alpha$ in the strict sense, and $\tau \acute{\epsilon} \lambda o \varsigma$ to denote the property class; but $\tau \acute{\epsilon} \lambda o \varsigma$ does not seem to be used by Plato in this sense. When Aristotle mentions Plato's property classes (*Pol.* 1266a 15ff.) he uses $\tau \acute{\iota} \mu \eta \mu \alpha$.

[111] In an economy in which land is never exchanged for other property, it will be necessary to determine somewhat arbitrarily the value of the lot in terms of other goods. Perhaps there is a reference to this problem in the phrase $\mu \acute{\epsilon} \tau \rho o \nu$ $\alpha \acute{\upsilon} \tau \grave{o} \nu$ $\theta \acute{\epsilon} \mu \epsilon \nu o \varsigma$ (744e).

[112] This means, as Aristotle states it twice in the *Politics* (1265b 22, 1266b 7), that the upper limit of "total property" permitted is five times the value of the minimum. E. Bornemann (*Philologus* LXXIX, 1923, 249) objects that $\kappa \tau \hat{\alpha} \sigma \theta \alpha \iota$ in Plato's text can hardly be taken in the sense of $\epsilon \pi \iota \kappa \tau \hat{\alpha} \sigma \theta \alpha \iota$. But that Aristotle's interpretation is correct is shown by other features of Plato's law. As we shall see later, there is a scale of fines prescribed for various offenses, graduated according to the $\tau \acute{\iota} \mu \eta \mu \alpha$ of the offender. If citizens of the lowest class owned no property except the inalienable lot and its equipment, it would not make sense to prescribe fines for this class. The same observation applies to the scales of expenditure permitted for weddings, funerals, and the like, similarly graduated according to the class to which the citizen belonged.

or a lucky find, or any other source, the surplus above the maximum permitted shall be given to the city and "to the gods that have the city in their keeping" (745a).[113] Any violation of this law is punishable with forfeiture not only of the undeclared surplus, but also of an additional equivalent amount, half of which is to be dedicated to the gods. As in the case of land, a public register of all movable property is to be kept by the officials to facilitate the administration of the law and the settlement of suits arising under it.[114]

What purpose does this division into property classes serve? Plato's statement on this point occurs in a passage which, if it has not been corrupted by later interpolations and alterations, was left by him in a syntactically confused state and is very difficult to translate faithfully.[115] But this much seems fairly clear: the purpose of these unequal classes (ἄνισα τιμήματα) is to prevent dissension among the citizens (ἵνα ... μὴ διαφέρωνται) by distributing honors and offices (τιμαί τε καὶ ἀρχαί) as equitably as possible (ὡς ἰσαίτατα) by the

[113] On the θεοὶ πολιοῦχοι see Chapter VIII, Note 124.

[114] See 745a, 754e, 850a, 855b. The δίκαι referred to in the first passage are not only legal actions brought by magistrates, but also suits brought by citizens, since Plato's law provides that anyone who is aware of such a violation shall make a φάσις, i.e. lodge information with the magistrates, and if the offense is established he is entitled to half the amount forfeited. The second passage cited shows that it is the responsibility of the citizen to keep the officials informed of increases in his property, since he is liable to financial penalty and disgrace if it should be established that he actually owns more than the official records show.

[115] 744b4-c4: δεῖ δὴ πολλῶν ἕνεκα, τῶν τε κατὰ πόλιν καιρῶν ἰσότητος ἕνεκα, τιμήματα ἄνισα γενέσθαι, ἵνα ἀρχαί τε καὶ εἰσφοραὶ καὶ διανομαί, τὴν τῆς ἀξίας ἑκάστοις τιμὴν μὴ κατ' ἀρετὴν μόνον τήν τε προγόνων καὶ τὴν αὑτοῦ, μηδὲ κατὰ σωμάτων ἰσχὺς καὶ εὐμορφίας, ἀλλὰ καὶ κατὰ πλούτου χρῆσιν καὶ πενίαν, τὰς τιμάς τε καὶ ἀρχὰς ὡς ἰσαίτατα τῷ ἀνίσῳ συμμέτρῳ δὲ ἀπολαμβάνοντες μὴ διαφέρωνται. For an introduction to the difficulties of this passage and suggested amendments, see England's notes on b 4ff. and b 5ff. The syntactical confusion is in the long clause ἵνα ... διαφέρωνται. Obviously the subject of this verb is not the nouns immediately after ἵνα, but a word understood (such as πολῖται) agreeing with ἀπολαμβάνοντες. None of the suggested modifications and excisions solves the difficulties; I prefer to keep Burnet's text and explain this final clause, with England, "as containing a rather gross zeugma," surely understandable on account of the length of the period. Furthermore, the preceding τῶν τε ... ἕνεκα is ambiguous in the extreme, as is shown by the variety of translations that have been suggested for it. Does this phrase furnish the grounds for the classification (as Ritter argues), or its purpose, as the majority of translators have assumed? Again, does καιρῶν ἰσότης mean "equality of opportunity" (England, des Places, Taylor), or "equality in special contingencies" (Apelt, Cassarà, Jowett, Bury, Stallbaum)? Robin reverses the dependence of the two nouns and translates them "chances d'égalité." My own preference would be to take the phrase as purposive, parallel to the ἵνα clause which follows and explains it, and to translate: "in order to preserve equality in special contingencies." But this is a case in which the author's intention has to be gathered from elsewhere rather than from the words of the passage.

criterion of proportionate inequality (τῷ ἀνίσῳ συμμέτρῳ δέ). Plato explains later the important but difficult distinction between true equality, the equality of ratios, and the undiscerning equality of measure, weight, and number (757a-e). True equality makes its awards proportional to the nature of the recipients, giving more to the deserving and less to those who are deficient in virtue and training. This alone fits the proverb, "Equality produces friendship"; since arithmetical equality is often the cause of serious inequality and the source of political discontent and faction. The institution of these classes serves therefore, Plato thinks, to reduce political friction and bring about that friendship which is one of the chief aims of all legislation.

The objects whose equitable distribution is to be effected by this principle of proportionate inequality are offices (ἀρχαί), honors (τιμαί), contributions (εἰσφοραί), and distributions (διανομαί). It is surprising to find wealth included as one of the criteria of desert for offices and honors, for in an earlier passage Plato has said that office will be assigned to a man not because he is rich, or strong, or wellborn, but because of his loyalty to the laws (715bc). We can easily exaggerate, however, the discrepancy between these two passages. Plato is not speaking of office and honors alone in this later passage, but of various things, burdens as well as benefits, that have to be distributed; and he says only that in many of these cases the amount of a man's property must be taken into consideration if we are to make an equitable distribution. Before we insist that there is a real contradiction here, let us determine just how these property classes are actually concerned in the distribution of the various honors, responsibilities, and burdens in the state.

In the filling of offices these property classes play a very minor part. They are disregarded completely in the selection of the most important officers of the state, viz. the guardians, the euthynoi, the educator, and the members of the court of select judges.[116] They are also disregarded in the selection of generals and other military officers. All citizens are admitted to the assembly and to the popular law courts without consideration of property. Some of the less important offices, however, are open only to members of the upper property classes. Temple treasurers and astynomoi are to be chosen from the highest class, the agoranomoi from the first and second

[116] For references to matters referred to in this paragraph, see Index.

classes, and the supervisors of athletic contests from the second and third classes. In the case of the astynomoi, it is said that these officers must have leisure to devote themselves to public duties, and this is presumably the reason for having them chosen from the wealthiest class. We may infer that the same reason underlies the other provisions. Since there will be no salary for public office, it would be more of a burden to the poor than to the rich.

The only important election in which the property classes play any part is that of the council (756b-e). This body is to consist of three hundred and sixty members, ninety from each of the four classes. Since the wealthier classes are presumably smaller in absolute numbers, this means they are proportionally better represented in the council than the poorer classes. Furthermore, in the preliminary (or nominating) stage of the election voting is compulsory for the members of the first and second classes, whereas the members of the third and fourth classes are excused, the former from one day's proceedings, the latter from two. The hardship of neglecting their business for the whole of the five days required for this election must be one explanation of Plato's provision. But the consequence is that the electors in the nominating stage may be (though they need not be) predominantly members of the wealthier classes. This will not result, however, in producing an oligarchic council; all four property classes will have an equal number of members in it. It is one of Plato's striking departures from Athenian law to constitute his council by property classes instead of by tribes; and when we come to examine this part of the government we shall see, I think, that Plato had good reasons for proposing this kind of deliberative body for his state.

Another use made of the property registers is to determine the amount of a man's taxes (εἰσφοραί). Plato provides that the authorities (τὸ δημόσιον) are to determine each year whether to require a certain proportion of the whole registered property of a citizen, or a proportion of his current yearly income (955de). In either case the tax levied will be proportionate to the citizen's property; but since there will presumably be finer gradations of liability than the four that define the property classes, these classes are naturally kept in the background. But they appear explicitly in the determination of fines imposed for violations of the law. An unmarried man past the age of thirty-five pays a tax or fine of a hundred drachmae a year if he is of the highest property class; if of the second, seventy drachmae; if of the third, sixty; and if of the fourth, thirty (774a). One section of Plato's law of assault prescribes a fine of one mina for a man of the first class, fifty, thirty, and twenty drachmae respectively for members of the second, third, and fourth classes (880d). There are other similar cases in Plato's legislation.[117] Finally there are certain laws regulating expenditures, and these usually take account of property classes. One law prescribes that funeral expenses are to be limited to five, three, two, and one mina, according to the class to which the deceased's family belongs (959d), and there is a similar scale of expenditures permitted for a bride's trousseau (774d), and for a banquet or marriage feast (775a).

The distributions which Plato mentions in his enumeration of contingencies occur only once in the later legislation. It is provided that a man proved guilty of having failed to declare surplus property and to turn it over to the state shall have no share of the public goods; "whenever the state makes a distribution he shall go portionless" (755a). Plato was probably thinking of such occasions as the gifts of grain that were sometimes made to Athens by foreign friends and which were distributed to the citizens. On what principle the distribution was made at Athens we do not know, except that it was limited to citizens. (In 445 some 6,000 persons came to grief when they claimed shares in a big gift of grain from King Psammeticus of Egypt and could not prove their citizenship.) Plato's mention of property classes in connection with distribution suggests that some account would be taken of relative needs; and this suggestion would be in accord with other measures he takes to prevent the increase of inequality. But this supposition is nowhere confirmed explicitly in Plato's text.

These classes have an obvious resemblance to the four classes of the Solonian constitution, and it is plausible to suppose that this is another instance in which Plato is following the example of his great ancestor.[118] One purpose of these classes as Solon employed them was

[117] Cf. 756de, penalties for failure to vote; 934d, for allowing an insane member of the family to be at large; 945a, for cowardice in battle, and for negligence by military officers in entrusting responsibilities to persons convicted of cowardice; 948a, for failing to gain one fifth of the jurors' votes in a prosecution.

[118] In 698b Plato refers to the four classes in the ancient Athenian constitution, but no reference to this feature is made in the *Menexenus*. Solon may have found these classes already existing, as is now generally believed, and merely utilized them for his purposes (see Chapter III, Note 26). They were in any case a part of the constitution he left behind him. Bisinger (*op.cit.* 36; cf. also Gernet, cxi n. 5) has

to determine fitness for office; Solon prescribed that officials should be chosen only from the three upper classes, and gave to the Thetes only the right of sitting in the assembly and on the popular law court.[119] At some later date, perhaps soon after Solon's time, the equivalence between one medimnus and one drachma was recognized, probably so that persons whose income did not come from landed property could be fitted into this classification.[120] These classes, with the privileges and disabilities they involved, continued to be recognized, formally at least, down to the fourth century, though the decline in the value of the drachma after Solon's time meant that the restriction of offices to the first three classes had ceased to have any meaning. There were probably few citizens who could not qualify for the archonship in terms of Solon's archaic standard.[121]

But though these property classes had ceased to have any political significance at Athens, they seem to have been of importance elsewhere. Aristotle refers to such τιμήματα no less than twenty times in the *Politics*, usually without any reference to specific cities, which is

---

warned against accepting too readily the view that Plato is following Solon here, pointing out that Solon's classes were differentiated according to annual income, whereas the citizens in Plato's state are classified according to the amount of property owned. This suggests to Bisinger that Plato's model is really the so-called constitution of Draco decribed in *Const. Ath.* IV. But the difference between these two methods of rating is not clearly evident in Aristotle's text. The details of IV, 2 suggest that "Draco" used the value of the person's estate (οὐσία) as a criterion, yet the following section mentions the class of Pentacosiomedimni, which obviously refers to annual income. Nor is the distinction one that could easily be adhered to in ancient times. It is likely that Solon's income criterion would be translated into landholdings for practical purposes, as is usually done by modern students attempting to ascertain its concrete significance. Plato's text therefore does not suggest that he knew of and accepted the account in *Const. Ath.* IV which is now regarded as spurious. A more legitimate basis of doubt whether Plato is following Solon here is his failure to use these property distinctions in determining qualifications for high office. Plato's division of the land into equal lots is definitely not Solonian; Solon was unwilling, as he said, "to see the rich soil of the fatherland divided equally among good and bad" (Arist. *op.cit.* XII, 3, line 9).

[119] Arist. *op.cit.* VII, 3; *Pol.* 1274a 15.
[120] On the date of this innovation there is no agreement. Busolt-Swoboda (837) assigns it to Cleisthenes; Beloch (*Griech. Gesch.* II,² 89 n. 2) "spätestens um die Zeit der Perserkriege"; Hignett (143) is inclined to doubt this "alleged innovation," but if it is a fact he thinks it is more likely to have been introduced by Pericles than by Cleisthenes. But from *Const. Ath.* XIII, 2 it appears that soon after Solon's archonship δημιουργοί were eligible to this office, which implies an evaluation of property in terms of money, not agricultural products.
[121] Arist. *Const. Ath.* VII, 4; XLVII, 1. See the interesting figures in Glotz, *Ancient Greece at Work*, 169, showing how the class of Thetes emptied itself imperceptibly into the Zeugitae, and the Zeugitae into the two classes above.

probably an indication that the institution was widespread.[122] In practically all these references these classes are cited as a means of defining political rights, in particular as defining access to office, to the assembly, and to the law courts. The use made of this institution became for Aristotle an important criterion for distinguishing oligarchies and democracies and their various subtypes. Oligarchies set up a high property qualification for admission to office, democracies a low one or none at all. There is no doubt that Aristotle considers that the main purpose of such property classes is to determine access to office, and that he regards property as a reasonable qualification for office in a well-ordered state.[123] All the more striking therefore is Plato's failure in general to use his property classes for any except the minor offices in the state. The one exception is the council, and even here it is not used to deny the poorer classes access to this body, but merely to provide equal representation to all property classes. The council in Plato's state, moreover, will be less powerful than the corresponding body at Athens. Above it are the guardians of the laws, in whose selection property qualifications play no part.

Plato's prescriptions are therefore formally in accord with his intention of making property subordinate to character and intelligence as a qualification for office. Their effects in operation, however, might be quite contrary to this intention. The reason Plato gives for excusing the poorer classes from certain minor offices—that they must have time to devote to their private affairs—would apply a fortiori to the higher offices. The duties of the guardians will certainly give them little time for other occupations, and only those who are relatively prosperous, or have prosperous and generous friends, could assume these duties. Was this result seen by Plato and a part of his intentions, though not expressed in his law? Aristotle evidently thought so; it is an oligarchical trait of Plato's constitution, he says, that it endeavors to assure that most of the officers will be chosen from the well-to-do, and the highest officers from the richest classes.[124] One would hesitate to follow Aristotle in attributing to Plato a deliberate intention so contrary to what he openly expresses. The more likely explanation is that Plato sometimes thinks of all his citizens as having sufficient means and leisure for the "craft of citizenship," as he calls

[122] See especially *Pol.* 1278a 23, 1291b 39ff., 1292a 39ff., 1294b 3-10, 1298a 35-39, and *Nic. Eth.* 1160a 33.
[123] *Pol.* 1283a 16-18.
[124] *Pol.* 1266a 11-15.

it—living, like the Spartans, on the labor of slaves who till the soil for them (806de). In such a city, property qualifications for office could be ignored altogether. But he more often regards his state as comparable to the Attica of older days, with its small proprietors living on their land and most of them compelled to give attention and labor to its cultivation.[125] Under these conditions the law should properly recognize differences of economic ability, as Plato's law sometimes does, in distributing the burdens of citizenship. But to provide equal access to the honors and responsibilities of high office some positive provision is necessary, such as payment for public service, of which there is no hint in Plato's law. The Athenian policy in this regard was apparently as unacceptable to him as it was to Aristotle.

INDUSTRY AND TRADE

Thus every head of a household in Plato's state is to own a plot of land which in normal years and when tended diligently will yield a return sufficient for himself and his family. Beyond this Plato gives no thought to the problem of assuring production.[126] What he is more concerned with is to prevent the desire for unlimited acquisition from taking root (736e, 741e). The law setting an upper limit of property is supported by other laws regulating the economic life of his citizens. Their only gainful activity is to be farming (743d; cf. 842cd, 949e). No citizen is to engage in handicraft or trade; these occupations are to be left to resident aliens and their slaves (919de, 920a, 846d, 849b-d). All foreign commerce is to be strictly controlled; there is to be no import of luxuries nor export of necessities; the foreign trade that is necessary for military purposes will be carried on by the hipparchs and generals (847b-d).[127] Thus Plato has closed to his citizens three of the main sources of wealth, other than land, in his day. Moneylending, however, was even more important than craftsmanship, retail trade, and foreign commerce. This too is excluded from Plato's state (not merely for his citizens, but also for the

---

[125] On these two conceptions in Plato's law, see Slaves ad fin.

[126] Bisinger (op.cit. 69) calls this "unverständlich." But it is no more unintelligible than the procedure of Athens on numerous occasions when she planned to provide for her poorer citizens by giving them plots of land in the cleruchies established abroad.

[127] The unqualified prohibition of gainful trading in 847d is, however, not consistent with the provisions of 849de, 918ff., and other incidental references to trade carried on by metics.

resident aliens) by the device of refusing redress in the courts to any depositor or creditor who claims repayment. Even the lending involved in sales on credit or contracts with deferred delivery is excluded; all exchange must be for cash or barter, and no suit will lie for enforcing payment or delivery later.[128] The only exception to this principle is the contract for work to be done at a prescribed time on the promise of payment at a prescribed time. In this case failure of either party to perform will make him liable to a suit in the courts, and to severe penalties if he loses (921a-d).

As a further safeguard against unwholesome accumulation Plato forbids the possession of gold or silver by private persons (742ab). Whatever currency is needed in the state as a standard of value or for purposes of exchange or payment of wages shall be a local currency that is not legal tender abroad. The state must of course have a supply of common Hellenic currency for its necessary foreign purchases, and for embassies and other trips that its officials and citizens will have to make abroad. But every citizen or official on his return must turn over to the state any foreign currency he has left and receive its equivalent in local currency.[129] Transactions within the state are to be entirely in this local currency. But the number of the transactions implied, the highly developed market practices referred to, and the numerous references to payments in coin show clearly that Plato's economy is not a simple system of barter. It is a money economy, but insulated, so far as possible, from the corrupting influences of foreign trade and international "capital."

[128] 742c, 849e, 915de. The law that most contracts are at the contractor's risk, not enforceable by legal process, is said in *Rep.* 556ab to be second best. The best apparently would be the abolition of private property; see 739bc. Aristotle refers to Plato's denunciation of δίκαι περὶ συμβολαίων in *Pol.* 1263b 21.

[129] Has Plato forgotten this regulation when he prescribes fines in drachmae, as he does on numerous occasions? There is no contradiction here, as has been alleged (Maurice Vanhoutte, *La Philosophie politique de Platon dans les "Lois,"* Louvain, 1954, 238). The common Hellenic currency in Plato's day was undoubtedly the Attic; but the mina, drachma and obol were by no means peculiar to Athens. There were drachmae struck at Syracuse and other Sicilian cities, in the Peloponnesus, at Delphi and in northern Greece, in Rhodes and the Ionian cities of Asia Minor. Drachmae (δάρκναυς) even appear in the law of Gortyn (e.g. II, 10) though penalties are often stated in terms of staters, "cauldrons" (λέβητες), or "tripods" (τρίποδες). But these terms would have been less familiar to most of Plato's readers, and he is writing for a common Hellenic public. His purpose is served if the drachmae in his state, like the silver-plated copper pieces issued at Athens during the Peloponnesian War, are usable locally but of less value elsewhere. But there does seem to be a contradiction between 742b and 916b, where private transactions in currency are assumed, but regulated. See Gernet, cii n. 1.

It is tempting to suppose that Sparta is the model from which most of these anticapitalistic proposals are borrowed. This is certainly suggested by the prohibition of gold and silver, and by the provision for a local coinage without exchange value abroad. Whether the archaic iron currency used at Sparta was merely a survival of usages that had been superseded elsewhere, or the cunning enactment of a Lycurgus, it was notorious in Greece and effectively checked the accumulation of private fortunes at Sparta in the older days.[130] Though Plato's text says nothing about the metal to be used in his local currency, the variety of transactions implied in his state makes it unlikely that he was thinking of the bulky iron currency of Sparta.[131] Any currency whose metallic content was considerably less valuable than the value stamped on its face, as measured by the common Hellenic coinage, or any currency which was not widely used and therefore less acceptable abroad, would serve his purpose. The truth is that Plato's requirement could be met by most of the states of his day, except Athens and Corinth. "In most cities," says Xenophon, "when the foreign trader has sold his cargo he has to take on a new cargo in exchange, for he cannot use their currency to advantage elsewhere; but at Athens . . . if a man does not want to take on another cargo, he can do a good business merely carrying away the silver coin."[132] Plato's proposal, then, is not so much an imitation of Sparta as a protest against the policies of Athens. Because of the intrinsic value of Athenian currency, the strategic location of the city, and the excellence of the facilities afforded foreign traders at the Piraeus, the port of Athens played a predominant part in all Mediterranean commerce, and the city drew a considerable revenue from the tax imposed on all transactions in the harbor. But Plato will have none of this; foreign trade is to serve merely the purpose of furnishing the state with necessities that it cannot provide from its own resources, and fortunately the site proposed for his colony produces most of the things a city needs (704c). But because trade does serve a useful purpose it is tolerated, and no import or export duties are to be imposed, nor any tax on buying and selling, nor even the usual residence tax for metics (847b, 850bc). Plato could not have shown more sharply his disapproval of

---

[130] Xen. *Const. Lac.* VII, 5-6; cf. Plut. *Lyc.* 9; Diod. XIV, 10, 2; Polyb. VI, 49.
[131] See Gernet cii.
[132] Xen. *Ways and Means* III, 2. See Glotz, *op.cit.* 234-236.

Athenian policy.[133] But Athens was an exceptional city. The policy that Plato recommends was essentially that followed by most Greek cities, whose commercial contacts with the outside world were on a much smaller scale than those of Athens, and who were by no means so hospitable as Athens to the foreign trader and the moneylender upon whom his operations depended.

Likewise in prohibiting his citizens from engaging in trade and handicraft, Plato is merely closing a door which, the facts seem to show, the citizens of all Greek cities, except possibly Athens and Corinth, were increasingly reluctant to enter. His proposal is extreme in that it makes legally punishable many activities that in most Greek cities were merely regarded with disdain. Only Sparta and perhaps two or three other cities went so far as to prohibit these occupations to citizens.[134] At Thebes, an aristocratic stronghold, there was a law that disqualified for office any man who had followed a trade at any time during the previous ten years.[135] At the warlike little city of Thespiae, a neighbor of Thebes, it was regarded as disgraceful for citizens to engage in any gainful labor, even agriculture.[136] Some Cretans had similar ideas; we have a fragment of a poem written by one Hybrios, of Crete, who boasts that his wealth consists of "a big spear and a sword and a thick shield for my body. With these I plow and reap and tread the sweet wine from the grapes."[137] Xenophon speaks vaguely of "certain cities, especially those reputed warlike," in which it was not lawful for the citizen to work at banausic occupations, but he fails to mention any by name.[138]

Outright prohibition is therefore not very common, but the attitude that underlay it was widespread.[139] Athens was, at least in her official policy, a striking exception. Solon had been a trader, and we have already noticed the tradition that he encouraged foreign artisans to settle in Athens with a promise of citizenship. Another of his laws, still cited in later centuries, provided that every father should teach his son a trade, if he expected to be supported by him in his old age.[140] One motive of Pericles' great program of public works, so

---

[133] Nor, we may add, his disapproval of Xenophon's proposals in *Ways and Means*. Xenophon would encourage commerce in the port of Athens by all possible means, as a source of revenue for the state.

[134] Xen. *Const. Lac.* VII, 1-2; Isoc. XII, 46.

[135] Arist. *Pol.* 1278a 25, 1321a 28.   [136] Arist. Fr. 611, 76, Rose.

[137] Bergk, *Lyrici Graeci,*² 1024.   [138] Xen. *Econ.* IV, 3.

[139] Did the Greeks learn this from the Egyptians? asks Herodotus (II, 166-167).

[140] Plut. *Solon* 22.

Plutarch tells us, was to provide employment to the various classes of artisans in the city;[141] we can infer that many of these were citizens, and the Erechtheum building inscriptions confirm the inference. Socrates, as quoted by Xenophon (evidently with rhetorical exaggeration), says that the Athenian assembly is made up ($\sigma \upsilon \nu \acute{\iota} \sigma \tau \alpha \tau \alpha \iota$) of fullers, cobblers, carpenters, coppersmiths, farmers, and traders.[142] Some of the leaders of the people after Pericles, such as Cleon and Hyperbolus, either were, or had been, traders or artisans. Nevertheless the proportion of Athenian citizens engaged in such occupations remained small and seems to have declined steadily. Of the stonemasons, contractors, carpenters, and other workmen employed in the building of the Erechtheum only twenty-eight per cent, according to Glotz's calculation, are Athenian citizens. The accounts of Eleusis in the following century show an even smaller proportion.[143] As for foreign trade and banking, it is significant that of the merchants and shipowners whom we hear of from the speeches of the Athenian orators only a few are Athenian citizens.

It has been inferred from these facts, and from various disdainful remarks about banausic occupations in the ancient writers, that the Greeks generally felt a contempt for trade and handicraft.[144] This inference is difficult to accept. It would be hard indeed to explain the high level of technical excellence attained in the building trades and the mechanical arts at Athens and other great centers of culture if these activities were generally despised. These metics who work with Athenian citizens on the Erechtheum and the buildings at Eleusis are often themselves Greek; they are Greeks from other cities who have been attracted to Athens because of the encouragement that city offered to the practice of their crafts. On the other hand, there was undoubtedly a strong current of disdain among the aristocrats of the fifth and fourth centuries for the artisan, the disdain of a "free man" for persons whose occupations bind them closely to a fixed routine and whose bodies and minds are often deformed by the habits of their trades. This disdain seems to have been felt

141 Plut. *Per.* 12.

142 *Mem.* III, vii, 6. Cf. also Plato *Prot.* 319cd.

143 Glotz, *op.cit.* 172-174.

144 A. Büchsenschütz, *Besitz und Erwerb im griechischen Alterthum*, Halle, 1869, 259ff. Johannes Hasebroek, *Staat und Handel im alten Griechenland*, Tübingen, 1928, 22ff., esp. 36, 39, 40. Hasebroek's thesis has been widely challenged; see Ure's review in *Gnomon* v, 1929, 220-226, and Hommel in RE s.v. Metoikoi, 1449-1450.

even more strongly for merchants and moneylenders. But there was a law at Athens which made it an offense to cast reproach upon a citizen for the trade he followed. We learn of it from Demosthenes, who calls it a law of Solon, but it is more likely a product of the Solonian revival at the end of the fifth century and a deliberate effort to counteract the aristocratic attitude we have mentioned.[145]

Plato's legislation on this point and the reasons he gives in support of his proposals may afford us some clue to understanding this puzzling feature of Greek life, as well as some insight into his own personal and philosophical convictions. There is in his text a clear echo of that aristocratic disdain above mentioned. In one passage he speaks of "servile forms of money-making" (ἀνελεύθεροι χρηματισμοί), and again of "performing services for persons who are not one's equals," where the retail merchant (κάπηλος) and the foreign trader (ἔμπορος) are given as examples of what he means.[146] But more important are the reasons he gives elsewhere. The citizen's craft (τέχνη) is one that demands long practice, much study, and continuous attention; it cannot be made secondary to other interests (846d). What Plato means we shall appreciate more clearly when we have considered the institutions of government, education, and religion that he sets up and can realize the demands that they make on the citizen's time and energy. Citizenship is by itself a profession in Plato's state. So it was also in Sparta, and even more so in Plato's democratic Athens. A mere reading of Aristotle's account of the Athenian constitution in his day is likely to oppress a modern reader, with its multitude of annually selected officers, its meetings of assembly, council, boards of magistrates, its law courts, its scrutinies and audits, its public festivals—all of which the citizens had to man and manage, year in and year out, besides training for war and serving in the military forces. This is certainly one reason why at Athens so few citizens are found in the trades and crafts, especially after compensation for public office became the rule. Plato's state, as we shall see, makes equally great demands upon its citizens. No man can practise two professions thoroughly; handicraft and trading must therefore be left to those who do not carry the burdens of citizenship.

There is another reason why Plato regards trading in particular as

[145] Dem. LVII, 30.

[146] 741e; 919d. I have given the usual translation to κάπηλος and ἔμπορος; but the Athenian usage was by no means fixed. See Finkelstein, *Class. Phil.* xxx, 1935, 320-336.

unsuitable for his citizens. The profession of citizenship is to be a discipline in excellence, and there is something inimical to virtue in the tradesman's activities and the motives that actuate him. The natural function of trading is a laudable one, viz. the proper distribution of goods in the community, and whoever engages in it is a benefactor (918ab). This is why it is tolerated at all in Plato's state. But it is the field in which moderation is particularly difficult for human beings. "When most men want, they want without limit, and when they can make a moderate profit, they prefer to make an inordinate one; and this is why all the classes concerned with retail or foreign trade or innkeeping are abused and despised" (918d). If, he suggests, we could compel the best men everywhere to keep the inns and run the shops, we should learn that these callings are really "friendly and acceptable." As it is, however, a man sets up an inn in some remote place to receive travelers at the end of a long day's journey; but "instead of receiving them as comrades, and providing friendly hospitality, he treats them as captive enemies in his hands, demanding his unholy and monstrous and unjust price before he will let them go" (919a). Plato does not condemn the desire of gain; it is indeed at the bottom of the scale of desires, nonetheless it is legitimate, and his citizens in the management of their farms will presumably be influenced by it (743d). But farming seldom presents an opportunity for unlimited or excessive gains, whereas trading frequently does.

Because trading contains these moral hazards, Plato not only leaves it to metics and foreigners ("the class whose corruption would be least harmful to the state"), but also provides that it shall be carefully regulated in order to prevent this corruption as far as possible (919c, 920a). The guardians shall consult with men "experienced in the various trades" (who could these be but the traders themselves?) and establish a scale of fair prices, to be enforced in all the markets in the city and the villages throughout the country (917e, 920bc). There is to be no haggling over prices (an unusual requirement indeed for an eastern market), and all transactions are to be for cash. There will also be rules to prevent adulteration and misrepresentation. All these regulations are to be posted in front of the office of the agoranomoi, who have the responsibility of enforcing them and generally supervising conduct in the market.[147]

[147] 919d-920c; 917e; 849e. Most of these provisions parallel regulations we know of at Athens. On adulteration and fraud see Hasebroek, *op.cit.* 186-188; Arist. *Const. Ath.* LI, 1-3. On cash transactions see Finley, *op.cit.* (Note 25), 81-82.

Artisans are clearly a more respectable class than traders. "Sacred to Hephaestus and Athena is the class of craftsmen, who have furnished our life with the arts."[148] The numerous references to the arts and crafts in the dialogues, often with a considerable exactness of detail, show that Plato was always interested, and sometimes fascinated, by the procedure of the artisan; and in the *Timaeus* he chooses the δημιουργός as a symbol of the creative activity of divine reason. This respect for the craftsman may have been learned from Socrates, himself a sculptor at one time in his career; at least it must have been strengthened and confirmed by this association with Socrates, who habitually used the arts to illustrate moral questions, and who made virtue itself an art. Nevertheless we have seen that no citizen in Plato's state is to be numbered among the artisans, nor any slave of a citizen. Perhaps in this case it is Plato's very respect for the arts that motivates his prohibition, and his consciousness of the exacting demands they make on those who would do them well, for it is just here that he emphasizes the citizen's craft and asserts that no man can do two crafts well. He is so much in earnest with this principle that he forbids even the noncitizen artisan to practice more than one craft under penalty of imprisonment, fines, or expulsion from the state.[149] Artisans are particularly enjoined not to disgrace their ancestors—i.e. their patron deities[150]—by misrepresenting the quality of their work. On the other hand, the artisan is given special protection against injustice by the drastic law (921cd) which prescribes severe penalties for the citizen or other resident who fails to pay an artisan the money due him. The craftsmen are to be divided into thirteen groups, one to be settled in the city and the others in the twelve country villages, where they will be near the farmers who need their services (848e).[151] The numbers of artisans needed in the

---

[148] 920d, Bury's trans. This is no merely rhetorical flourish, but an expression of genuine Hellenic feeling. Cf. *Critias* 109c. "Greek religion takes more serious cognizance of science and art than any other religion of the world has ever done. . . . The artistic interest enters as a divine attribute into the characters of certain Hellenic deities and establishes a fellowship between the human craftsman and the divine." Farnell, *Higher Aspects of Greek Religion*, New York, 1912, 117.

[149] 846e-847a. The same prohibition against practising more than one trade is found in *Rep.* 374b, and the reason given is that the work may be well done.

[150] 920e. Farnell, *op.cit.* 60-61.

[151] Bisinger (*op.cit.* 88) and Willetts (*Aristocratic Society in Ancient Crete*, 40, 153) suggest that Plato may have been influenced by Gortyn in these regulations. But the idea of a special quarter for the metics and artisans cannot be derived from Plato's text without an arbitrary interpretation of συνοικοῦντες in 848a; it is more naturally taken as a synonym of μετοικοῦντες used in the same passage.

various localities and the residences to be assigned them are left to be determined by the local officials.

The activities performed by the resident aliens are indispensable, and a modern reader is likely to wonder how Plato could be sure that such persons would be available and willing to accept a kind of second-class status in the community. Apparently this problem does not greatly concern him. The institution of μετοικία, whereby a foreigner was granted access to the city's courts and the protection of the city's law and—in Athens, at least—allowed to share fully in the life of the city, except for participation in the responsibilities of citizenship—this institution was so widespread in Greece that a city without metics would have been regarded as most exceptional. We think wrongly of the Greeks if we picture them all as living each in his little city earning his livelihood and at the same time helping to run its government. A large proportion of the residents of any Greek city—it may be as much as one half—were emigrants from other cities, or the descendants of such emigrants, who had been attracted at first either by the economic opportunities the new city afforded them, or by the quality of its laws, or the richness of its culture, or perhaps by mere love of adventure; and who had been content to remain and work in their adopted city, many of them making considerable contributions not only to its wealth but also to its cultural life. The number of famous metics whom we meet in the history of Athens is amazing. It includes sculptors and painters, such as Zeuxis of Heraclea and Parrhasius of Ephesus; architects like Hippodamus of Miletus, who laid out the Piraeus on a new and strikingly modern plan; potters and vase painters, such as Amasis and Duris; metalworkers of all sorts; doctors and bankers; writers of speeches (λογογράφοι), including three—Isaeus, Lysias and Dinarchus—who found a place in the canon of the ten Attic orators; philosophers like Anaxagoras, Aristotle, Theophrastus, Antisthenes, Zeno; and in the fourth century even dramatists, such as Alexis and Philemon.[152] This was the fruit of the policy of Solon, which Athens seems to have followed consistently after his time; and the example of Athens' success may have been responsible for the popularity of this institution in the Greek world. The existence of metics, or a class of semicitizens analogous to them, is attested for some seventy dif-

[152] See Glotz, op.cit. 182ff.

ferent cities. But Sparta was not one of them; even in ancient times she was known as the city without metics.[153]

Plato may well have thought, therefore, that the problem a legislator faced was not how to attract metics to his city, but rather how to provide against their exerting too much influence on local affairs and customs (949e-950a, 952d-953e). His regulations concerning metics follow in many respects the pattern set by Athens. Admission to metic status is open to anyone from abroad who can show that he is master of a craft (850a). He cannot own land or houses, yet he is definitely regarded as a part of the city and an object of the legislator's care; and his life is given the same protection as that afforded the citizen.[154] He may be honored by the city for special services (881b). But Plato departs from Athenian policy in certain respects. At Athens there was no limitation on the metic's term of residence; but in Plato's state it is limited to twenty years, unless an extension is granted (which may be for life) because of special services performed for the state (850b; cf. 915b). The children of a metic, if they are artisans, may remain as metics for twenty years past their fifteenth birthday, with the same privilege of obtaining an extension for special services (850c). This is obviously an orderly procedure for enabling the state to get rid of undesirable metics, and Plato may have consciously designed it as a more civilized alternative to the "alien purges" (ξενη-λασίαι) practised at Sparta.[155] Again, the metic in Plato's state cannot acquire more than the amount of property possessed by a citizen of the third property class (915bc). On the other hand, the metic is exempt from all taxes and apparently also from military service; his only obligation to the state is good behavior (850b).

What would be the effect of these modifications? Certainly the restriction of the metic's term of residence would tend to discourage foreigners from emigrating to Plato's state, though this would depend eventually upon the liberality which the city came to show in granting extensions of residence. Plato evidently does not think there will be many such aliens permanently residing in the state (cf. 949bc).

[153] Hommel in RE s.v. Metoikoi, 1454-1455, and Busolt-Swoboda 293.
[154] 866cd, 867c, 869d, 872ab, 882ab. In this respect Plato's law is in advance of Attic law. For further details concerning the rights of metics, see the author's article, "The Status of the Alien in Plato's *Laws*," *Scientia* xxxv, 1941, 38-43.
[155] These uncivil ξενηλασίαι are mentioned in 950b and 953e, without any reference to Sparta, though κηρύγματα ἄγρια and τρόποι αὐθάδεις would suggest it to any Greek reader. Cf. Aristoph. *Birds* 1012ff.

The limitation on the amount of property that a metic could acquire would also tend to make residence in Plato's state much less attractive economically than it was at Athens. Against this must be set the abolition of taxes and possibly of military service. The demands made upon the metic at Athens were certainly not light, for the metic tax (μετοίκιον) of twelve drachmae annually was considerably more than a nominal tax, as is sometimes asserted. Tod estimates the cost of living for a married couple at Athens at the end of the fifth century at about one hundred and eighty drachmae annually;[156] thus the metic tax would represent twenty-four days' living expenses. There were numerous other taxes and special levies to which the Athenian metic was liable; and military service would require not merely an expenditure of time, but also in some cases a considerable financial outlay. On the whole, it is fair to say that the metic in Plato's state, though denied the greater economic rewards, would find it easier to attain a modest degree of prosperity than the Athenian metic. This form of the institution clearly reflects Plato's intention to preserve the integrity, as he conceives it, of the citizen body, and his recognition of the danger of having in the city a large class of permanent residents possessing wealth but lacking political power.

SLAVES

A Greek city without slaves was almost unknown in Plato's day, hence we should not be surprised that they are taken for granted in the *Laws* and figure constantly in the details of Plato's scheme.[157] Some slaves, it is assumed, will be owned by the state, as at Athens (794b). Of those privately owned some will belong to citizens and some to metics. The distinction between the slaves of citizens and the slaves of foreigners was apparently of no consequence in positive Greek law, but it appears in Plato's legislation because of the distinction he draws between the occupations suitable for citizens and those that are left to foreigners. Plato applies the prohibition on trade and handicraft not merely to his citizens but to their slaves as well, evidently believing that if the citizen is to be protected from the

[156] *Cambridge Ancient History* v, 22.
[157] How completely slavery was taken for granted by the Greeks generally is shown by Finley, "Was Greek Civilization Based on Slave Labor?" *Historia* VIII, 1959, 145-164. For a fuller discussion of the material in my text, see my *Plato's Law of Slavery in its Relation to Greek Law*, University of Illinois Press, 1939, from which some parts of the following section are reprinted with permission.

corrupting influences of industry and trade, he must be prohibited from employing his slaves in them.[158] The citizen's slaves will work on their master's land (805e, 806d), or in the house (808ab), or in personal attendance upon their master and their master's children (808e; cf. 763a). When not needed by their masters they may also be employed on public works, such as the building of fortifications, highways, canals, dams, aqueducts, fountainhouses, and baths (760e, 763a). Mention is made of slave actors who perform comic parts beneath the dignity of citizens (816e); but whether these are slaves of the state, slaves of citizens, or slaves of metics or visiting foreigners is not clear.

What is the status of the agricultural slave in Plato's state? The similarity of Plato's land tenure to the institutions of Sparta suggests at once that he intended the slaves in his state to have a position analogous to that of the Spartan Helots.[159] The Helots in Lacedaemon were bound to the soil, i.e. they could not change their residence within the country, nor emigrate, nor be sold beyond it; but they were relatively free to carry on the cultivation of their lands as they pleased, subject to the obligation to pay a fixed annual rental to their masters.[160] We find analogous forms of servitude in other Doric lands, particularly Crete and Argos, and something like it seems to have existed in Thessaly, Boeotia, Sicyon, and other parts of Greece.[161] Plato's references to the equipment of the lot as being unalienable suggests this form of land tenure; and in another passage he seems to have such an arrangement definitely in mind. "The cultivation of the fields is committed to slaves," says this passage, "who deliver to their masters the first fruits of their labors, an amount sufficient for men who live temperately" (806de).

But whatever he may have had in mind when he wrote this passage, the other provisions of Plato's law and the general intentions manifest in his institutions make it certain that he did not contemplate the

---

[158] 846d. This passage mentions only handicraft (δημιουργικὰ τεχνήματα); but if Plato's intention is to protect his citizens from degrading influences, trading (except for the purpose mentioned in 849b) would a fortiori be forbidden.

[159] So Büchsenschütz, *op.cit.* 195; Siegfried Lauffer, in *Vierteljahrschrift für Sozial- und Wirtschaftsgeschichte* XXIX, 1936, 247ff.; and Barker, 323 n. 2.

[160] Busolt-Swoboda, 284f.; Ehrenberg, "Spartiaten und Lakedämonier" in *Hermes* LIX, 1924, 40ff. Kahrstedt's contention (*Griechisches Staatsrecht: Sparta und seine Symmachie*, Göttingen, 1922, 58ff.) that the Helots were not bound to the soil is answered by Ehrenberg, *loc.cit.*

[161] Henri Wallon, *Histoire de l'esclavage dans l'antiquité*, Paris, 1879, 93-94, 121ff.; Guiraud, *op.cit.* (Note 17) 407ff.; Poll. III, 83.

establishment of a class of serfs. The passage above quoted must be interpreted in the light of the later law governing the distribution of the annual produce (847e-848a). The whole shall be divided into three portions, one part for the citizens (here called freemen), one part for the slaves, and a third part for the craftsmen and other foreigners. The farmer is obligated to put the third portion on the market; but the other two portions are at his disposal to divide as he thinks fit among the free and slave members of his household (848c). This regulation obviously puts the slave in an entirely different position from that of the Helot in Lacedaemon, where the amount of his annual payment was fixed, apparently beyond the master's power to alter it, and without regard to the yield in any given year. Under favorable circumstances, and with appropriate diligence, it was possible for a Helot to acquire a modest property, since he was entitled to all the surplus above the fixed annual rental;[162] whereas the slave in Plato's state must be content with the amount allotted him by his master. When we recall that Plato rigidly limits the amount of wealth that a metic can acquire, we can readily understand that the relatively independent status of the Lacedaemonian Helot would not accord with his purpose.

Again, it is clear that Plato did not intend his agricultural workers to be bound to the soil.[163] The ancestral lot and its equipment are unalienable, but there is no prohibition on the sale of slaves in Platonic law, though the law takes notice of traffic in slaves and attempts to provide remedies against fraud (916a-c). If it had been his intention to prevent the sale of agricultural slaves, it could hardly have escaped mention here. Again, the master in Plato's state has the power of emancipation, which in Sparta rested only in the state.[164] Furthermore, Plato would have his slaves of different nationalities and speaking different languages (777c). He was opposed to any form of slavery which would involve the presence within the city's boundaries of a large homogeneous subject population. He expressly mentions the Helots in Lacedaemon, the Mariandyni in Heraclea, and the Penestae in Thessaly as types of slavery open to grave criticism (776cd), and it is significant that these are all instances of

---

162 Busolt-Swoboda, 669. Plut. *Cleom.* 23 tells that in the third century 2,000 Spartan Helots purchased their freedom.
163 See Bisinger, *op.cit.* 20.
164 Busolt-Swoboda, 667; Arist. *Pol.* 1263a 35; Ephorus apud Strabo VIII, v, 4; Thuc. IV, 26, 80; Xen. *Hell.* VI, v, 28.

homogeneous peoples, once free, who had been reduced to servitude by conquest. If the slaves in Plato's state, even though of various alien stocks, were attached to the soil from generation to generation, they would inevitably become assimilated to one another and constitute the kind of element which Plato thinks a danger to the state.

Lastly, the distinction between the agricultural slave and the personal or domestic slave does not appear in Platonic law. There is no distinctive terminology for the agricultural slave, as there was in Crete, Sparta, Thessaly, and in other places where serfdom existed.[165] Nor in the many provisions of Plato's law touching slaves is there any separate provision for a class of slaves that most certainly would have required it if they had existed. Although there seems to be a reference to the Spartan κρυπτεία, or secret police, in Plato's instructions regarding the functions of the agronomoi, there is no suggestion that they will have to be on the lookout to anticipate revolts among a subject population, as at Sparta.[166] We can only conclude that Plato does not intend his agricultural slaves to constitute a class of serfs analogous to the Helots. This was a notoriously weak part of the Spartan system and Plato wisely takes pains to avoid it.

If we are to seek historical parallels to Plato's agricultural economy, we must look rather to Attica than to Lacedaemon. Nothing like the institution of serfdom existed in Attica, at least after the time of Solon. Attic law did not recognize the distinction between agricultural slaves and others. The small proprietor in Attica could not afford to maintain a number of slaves for the exclusive cultivation of his small holding. The poorest owned no slaves at all, and the average proprietor had only one or two slaves whom he employed in the household or in personal service when there was no work in the fields.[167] A few wealthy citizens maintained elaborate estates on which large numbers of slaves were employed, and sometimes their management was entrusted to slave overseers;[168] but absentee landlords were the exception at Athens in the fifth century, though they became more common in later times and their life was even looked upon in some quarters as the ideal for the freeman. Nevertheless Xenophon's praise

[165] The terms most commonly used to denote slaves are δοῦλος and οἰκέτης, and they often seem to be used interchangeably; e.g. 763a, 776bc, 777d. The criminal law, however, regularly employs δοῦλος. See my *Plato's Law of Slavery* 17 n. 1.
[166] See Chapter V, The Magistrates.
[167] Busolt-Swoboda, 273-274; Glotz, *op.cit.* 202.
[168] Glotz, *op.cit.* 201.

of country life in his *Economics* shows that the older ideal of an agrarian aristocracy was still strong in the fourth century.

This seems closer to what Plato intends in the *Laws*. Though he sometimes asserts that the work of a citizen is enough to absorb all a man's time (807a-d; 835e), yet his legislation is full of indications that he realized such a life would be impossible for large numbers of his citizens. The poorer classes are excused from certain public services that may be demanded of the rich, on the ground that they have less leisure to devote to public affairs (763d; 764a). His citizens will be tillers of the soil, shepherds, beekeepers (842d), and he gives prescriptions regarding boundaries, pasturage, water supply, and other rural matters on which disputes are likely to arise (842e-846c). That these "agricultural laws" (νόμοι γεωργικοί) are intended to regulate the relations of citizens, not slaves only, is clear from the fact that the penalties for violations are fines and damages, not stripes; and the distinction is in one case drawn between a slave and a free offender (845ab). He provides for the location of villages outside the central city, each of them to have its festivals in honor of local deities. He takes particular pains to advocate the beautification of the countryside, and its equipment with fountain houses, surrounded by trees, where the traveler and the local resident alike can find shade and refreshment. There are to be neighborhood courts to settle litigation between the persons, obviously freemen, living in their area.[169] Thus Plato clearly intends that his citizens shall give personal attention to their lots, and recognizes that they will be compelled, in greater or less degree, to engage in manual labor. It is not Lacedaemon but Attica—doubtless the Attica of an older and more fragrant time—that most clearly parallels the life described in the *Laws*.

[169] See Chapter VI, The Courts.

CHAPTER V

GOVERNMENT

"Tell us more clearly," demands Cleinias (712c), "what kind of constitution you have in mind to set up. Will it be a democracy, an oligarchy, an aristocracy, or a kingship?"

These were alternatives that had long been current in Greek political discussions, although by the middle of the fourth century the terms had lost much of their original meaning and importance. Kingship was practically extinct in Greece in Plato's day, but tyranny, its counterfeit, was well known from Syracuse, Thessaly, and Cyprus; and some serious minds even advocated it as a remedy for the factional strife so prevalent in fourth-century cities. Aristocracy, the rule of "the best," was an honorable appellation that could be invoked by the adherent of any form of government. But in its older sense, as the rule of a generally recognized elite, such as the Eupatrid families of older Athens, it also was extinct beyond hope of revival; the older families themselves had died out, or had lost their quality or the wealth on which in former days their power depended. In practical politics aristocracy was indistinguishable from oligarchy, which in spite of its neutral designation as the rule of the few invariably meant the rule of the wealthy few. In contrast, democracy was claimed by its adherents to be the rule of the sovereign demos, rich and poor alike being equal before the law; but since the rich were necessarily a minority, they thought of it as the rule of "the many" (οἱ πολλοί) and its paramount concern the interests of the poor. Thus in practical politics the only live alternatives in the fourth century were oligarchy, democracy, and tyranny; and the last of these three was so abhorrent to common Greek feeling that it was contemplated, by those who looked to it at all, only as a necessary transition from the current disorder to something better.

In Plato's thought these alternatives of practical politics seem always to have been of secondary importance. The *Republic* portrays as his ideal a state in which political power rests in the hands of philosophically trained rulers. It is taken for granted that "the multitude cannot become a philosopher,"[1] hence a government worthy of the sovereignty it exercises will necessarily be a government of one

[1] *Rep.* 494a; cf. *Polit.* 292e, 297b, 300e.

or a few men, a monarchy or an aristocracy. Which of these alternatives is realized seems to be a matter of little importance in the *Republic*; and the philosophical wisdom Plato requires as the qualification for rule is a quality entirely apart from good birth, manly virtue, wealth, or freedom—the criteria used in popular controversies. He employs the same criterion in his description and evaluation of the existing states of his time. These imperfect states are ranked by the degree to which the quality of their rulers, and through them the tone of the society, approaches or falls short of the rational self-control of the philosopher-ruler. At the top is what he calls timarchy, a state which, as he describes it, closely resembles the popular conception of aristocracy, followed by oligarchy, democracy, and tyranny. These are all defections, progressively more extreme, from the rule of philosophy. But even this scale of value is not always adhered to; for tyranny, which is at the bottom of the scale, is the form which Plato thinks sometimes affords the best opportunity for bringing about that drastic reorganization under the guidance of philosophy that he regards as necessary. Obviously it is the rule of philosophy and the conditions necessary to bring it about that occupy the center of Plato's political thought.

In the *Politicus*, evidently written much later than the *Republic*, Plato comes to closer grips with current controversies, and here another principle appears in the foreground. He begins by classifying constitutions according to the familiar distinction between the rule of one, a few, or "the many"; but this threefold classification is immediately cut across by another distinction based on the presence or absence of law. This cross classification yields "five" (really six) forms: monarchy and tyranny, the one the lawful and the other the lawless rule of a single man; aristocracy and oligarchy, the former again distinguished by the presence of law and the latter by its absence; and democracy which, though one in name, also exists in a lawful and a lawless form. Plato (or his spokesman, the Eleatic Stranger) insists on the superiority, in each case, of the government that adheres to a basic law by which rulers as well as subjects are bound. But the best of all states will be, he says, a monarchy whose king possesses the "royal science," or whose laws imitate the laws of an ideal polity. This stands over and above the six forms presented in his classification. Evidently Plato still adheres to the ideal of the rule of philosophy, here described as the authority of the royal science; but the myth which precedes this discussion indicates that he thinks it is unrealistic to expect such an ideal polity in states ruled by men with human frailties, and that under the conditions of "the present age" the rule of law must be taken as its surrogate. At the same time these various imitation states that embody the rule of law are ranked by the extent to which their laws imitate the laws of the ideal polity.[2]

In the *Laws* the sovereignty of law is reaffirmed; but here a third principle comes into view, the idea of a mixed constitution, embodying a mean between monarchy and democracy, authority and liberty, so blended as to preserve the stability of the whole in a fashion impossible in any of the unmixed forms. This idea is first presented indirectly, in the search for the cause that had preserved the constitution of Sparta for so many generations when her sister Dorian states had collapsed. This secret Plato finds, as we have seen, in the fact that the executive powers of the state were divided among a number of powerful organs: the dual kingship, itself an example of division of power; the aristocratic gerousia; and the popularly elected board of ephors. The lesson to be derived from Spartan history is confirmed by the picture, drawn immediately afterward, of the decline of the Athenian state through excess of freedom, and the degeneration of the Persian monarchy through excess of despotism, each of these states illustrating, in its own way, the necessity of maintaining a balance between the forces of freedom and authority. It is implied in numerous scattered passages that these warnings are to be heeded in the construction of the Cretan colony, and it is explicitly affirmed in the statement that our constitution is to be a mixture of monarchy and democracy (756e). The mixed constitution is the only kind that deserves the name, Plato says; each of the unmixed forms is a faction state (στασιωτεία), getting its popular designation from the dominance of one part of itself over the rest (713a, 832c). Not even the rule of law, Plato here thinks, is a proper safeguard against such tyranny of one class over others; for law itself, as employed by politicians and as defined by certain sophists, expresses the interest of the ruling power in the state (890a); there can be oligarchic law and democratic law, and where this happens the rule of law simply sanctifies the special interest it represents. Genuine law, the expression of that Nous which Plato takes as the ultimate sovereign in the state,

---

[2] On the *Politicus*, see Chapter XII ad fin.

is law that aims at the common good, not the special interest of any class (714b-715b).

Now one peculiarity of a mixed constitution is that it is difficult to characterize in the usual terms of political controversy. Hence the Athenian's answer to the question of Cleinias quoted at the beginning of this section is to ask each of his companions to identify the type to which his own constitution belongs. Megillus, who as the elder replies first, confesses that he cannot say with certainty; in some respects Sparta resembles a tyranny, yet sometimes it seems the most democratic of all constitutions; again it is absurd not to call it aristocratic, and its kings make it appear to be the oldest kingship in Greece. Cleinias admits being equally uncertain how to describe the constitution of Cnossos. "No wonder," replies the Athenian. "Your states have constitutions; those that have been named are not constitutions (πολιτεῖαι), but merely cities of residence in which one part is master and the rest slaves, and each is named after its ruling power. If our city had to be named in such a way, we should give it the name of that god who is truly the ruler of all right-minded men" (712e-713a). Who this god is, the Athenian leaves us to infer from the sequel. There follows a brief repetition of the picture given in the *Politicus* of the blessed life during the age of Kronos, when men lived under the rule of higher beings in peace and justice with one another. The states of this present age, being ruled by men, can do no better than imitate, in every way possible, that life of the earlier age, by installing law, the ordinance (or distribution) of Reason (τὴν τοῦ νοῦ διανομήν), as their sovereign. "A state in which the law is subject and without authority I consider ripe for destruction; but where the law is master over the rulers and they are its subjects, there, as I see it, the state will be safe and will have all the other benefits that the gods bestow" (715d).

The rule of philosophy, the rule of law, the mixed constitution—these, then, are the three principles to which Plato has successively committed himself. The commitment seems to be cumulative. It is evident that in the *Laws* the idea of the mixed constitution supplements, but by no means displaces, the rule of law. Whether Plato's adoption of these two principles means the abandonment of the rule of philosophy as a guiding principle for the statesmen of his time is a question of more difficulty which we shall have to consider later; but it will then be evident, I believe, that the rule of philosophy is still present, though in a form somewhat different from the doctrine usually attributed to Plato by those who take only the *Republic* into account.[3] We should therefore keep these three principles in mind during the examination of the numerous provisions that follow; for they will frequently make clear some detail of Platonic law that would otherwise be obscure, and their meaning will in turn be more evident when we see what they imply in the concrete detail of Plato's institutions.

Assembly, council, and annually elected magistrates—these were the usual organs of government in the Greek cities of Plato's time, even in those that had not followed, like Athens, the path toward democracy. The differences between the various types of democracy, and between democracies and oligarchies and tyrannies, was evident not so much in the presence or absence of these organs, as in the manner in which they were constituted, the powers they enjoyed, and the presence or absence of other officials of a higher order limiting their powers or controlling their use. Let us begin by examining the form which these three familiar Greek institutions take in Plato's state.

THE ASSEMBLY AND THE COUNCIL

The assembly of the citizens is taken so much for granted in Plato's law that its existence as an organ of government is nowhere explicitly stated; it is only mentioned, and almost casually, in connection with certain important functions that it discharges or with duties that it imposes.[4] Admission to it is the privilege of all citizens (764a), or—as it is stated in another passage—of all those who are or have been members of the armed forces (753b). Since military service is compulsory in Plato's state for all men who have reached the age of twenty (785b), the assembly of the armed forces is indistinguishable from the assembly of the people.[5] Plato's provision that women also should share in the duties of the state, even in military service against the enemy (785b, 805a,c), would mean that they attend the assembly as well; but there is no hint that Plato has this point in mind in any

---

[3] See Chapter XII.

[4] It is called σύλλογος in 755e, 764a, and 765a; κοινὸς σύλλογος in 764a; cf. 871a, 935b; ἐκκλησία in 764a. Πλῆθος and δῆμος in 768a clearly refer to the assembly, as is shown below, Chapter VI, Note 45.

[5] The reference to the council and its prytanies in 755e shows that the assembly of the armed forces mentioned in 753b is a meeting of the political assembly.

of the references that follow in this section. This conception of the assembly as consisting of the citizen soldiers recalls vividly the conditions of earlier times out of which the political assemblies in all Greek cities developed; and it reflects faithfully what was thought, even in Plato's time, to be the relation between the citizen body and the military forces. Nevertheless Plato's assembly, like his military forces, will differ markedly from their Athenian prototype. In the first place, there will be no naval forces in his state, only cavalry, hoplites, and light-armed infantry; in the later fifth century the navy men—that is, the poorer citizens who were serving as rowers in the fleet—formed a preponderant and, as many of the conservatives thought, a pernicious element in the Athenian ἐκκλησία. Again, his forces will contain none but citizens; the Athenians on occasion made use of their metics and slaves and, in the fourth century, of foreign mercenaries as well. Plato's purpose seems to be to restore the equivalence between citizens and soldiers which was breaking down in the cities of his time.

Plato's assembly is to have regular meetings fixed by law, and it may be called into special session by the prytanies of the council (758d). This is in accord with Athenian custom. Attendance is compulsory in Plato's state for citizens of the first and second property classes, with a fine of ten drachmae for absence, but optional for the two lower classes, except when the magistrates have called for a full assembly (764a). There was no such compulsion at Athens; the Athenians adopted the device of paying citizens for attendance at the ecclesia—at first one, later two, three, and finally six obols a day.[6] This rate of pay was probably sufficient to attract the poorer citizens, but it could not have been a great inducement to the well-to-do; its effect therefore was democratic, in that it tended to assure the presence of the demos rather than the wealthier classes. Aristotle records that it was characteristic of democracies to pay for attendance at the assembly, and of oligarchies to compel the attendance of the wealthier and excuse the poorer citizens.[7] Plato's intentions may be oligarchical, as Aristotle suggests, but another motive that is certainly present in

---

[6] Arist. *Const. Ath.* XLI, 3, LXII, 2. See Note 89.
[7] *Pol.* 1297a 17-19, 35-38; cf. 1266a 10-12. The constitution of the Four Hundred in 411 imposed a fine for not attending the council (Arist. *Const. Ath.* XXX, 6), the only instance of this sort that we know of in Athenian history, except the similar provision in the alleged constitution of Draco (Arist. *op.cit.* IV, 3). See Bonner and Smith I, 145.

his thought—we shall see it appearing in other features later—is that attendance at the assembly would be more of a burden for the poorer citizens than for the richer ones.

The function of the assembly that is most often referred to in Plato's text is the election of officers.[8] Elections are surrounded by religious sanctions. Sometimes it is explicitly prescribed that they are to be held in a sacred area (753b, 755e, 945e, 949a), and we can certainly infer it in other cases. An oath is required when a nomination is challenged (755d), votes are deposited "on the altar of the god" (753c), and sometimes the voters "pass between slain victims" (753d), a peculiarly solemn ceremony of oath taking.[9] The names of persons to be voted on are proposed by members of the assembly, except in the election of military officers; here generals and hipparchs are selected by vote from lists presented by the nomophylakes (the "guardians of the laws"), and taxiarchs from lists presented by the newly elected generals. But there is a provision that anyone who thinks that someone not on the list should be substituted for one of the officially proposed candidates may present the name of his candidate, and a vote of the assembly shall decide which is to be retained (755cd). At the election of the nomophylakes there is likewise a provision that permits a citizen to challenge the name of a candidate (753c). The challenged nomination (i.e. the tablet on which it is made) is to be posted in the agora "within thirty days."[10] How the

---

[8] In Plato's law the duty of attending the assembly carries with it the obligation of voting. The principle is stated in 763e-764a, χειροτονείτω δὲ πᾶς πάντα· ὁ δὲ μὴ 'θέλων . . . ζημιούσθω. (The use of χειροτονεῖν here to signify voting in general is probably due to the fact that the elections discussed in the immediately preceding passage have been cases of χειροτονία.) Since the duty of attendance is graduated according to property, so also is the duty of voting; from some elections the poorer classes are excused (e.g. 756cd, 765c), and for failure to vote there are fines graduated according to property classes (756de). In view of this clear statement of principle and the specific applications of it, we must take as mandatory, not permissive, the imperatives that occur in certain other passages dealing with elections (e.g. 753b: πάντες κοινωνούντων τῆς . . . αἱρέσεως; 755c: αἱρείσθων . . . πάντες; 763d: προβαλλέσθω πᾶς ἀνήρ). The obligation to vote seems not to have been a part of Attic law, but Plato's provision here recalls a memorable feature of Solon's legislation requiring every citizen in time of civil strife to take sides with one or the other party (Arist. Const. Ath. VIII, 5).

[9] Cf. Arist. Const. Ath. LV, 5. Dem. XXIII, 68. Paus. V, xxiv, 9.

[10] Ἀνελόντα εἰς ἀγορὰν θεῖναι μὴ ἔλαττον τριάκοντα ἡμερῶν (753c). Does the last phrase go with ἀνελόντα (i.e., as England interprets it, the challenge must be made "within thirty days") or with θεῖναι (i.e. it must be deposited "for a period of not less than thirty days")? Most translators give the second interpretation, but I believe England's is the more probable. On either interpretation a period of at least thirty days is to elapse between the two stages of this election.

challenge is disposed of Plato does not say; but by analogy with the previous case we infer that here also the issue is decided by vote of the assembly. Voting is sometimes by ballot ($\psi\eta\phi\circ\phi\circ\rho\iota\alpha$) and sometimes by show of hands ($\chi\epsilon\iota\rho\circ\tau\circ\nu\iota\alpha$). The former method is explicitly prescribed for the election of the nomophylakes; the citizen writes on a tablet the name of his candidate with patronymic, tribe, and deme, and also his own name with patronymic, tribe, and deme (753c). We may assume that the same procedure is followed in the election of the council (756c-e), the exegetes of religious law (759d) and the auditors of official accounts, the euthynoi (946ab).[11] Voting by $\chi\epsilon\iota\rho\circ\tau\circ\nu\iota\alpha$ is used for the election of generals and other military officers (755d-756b) and for the election of astynomoi (city wardens), agoranomoi (market wardens), and supervisors of musical and athletic contests (763de, 765bc). Since in each of these cases there are several persons to be elected, a careful counting of the hands would be necessary to determine which candidate received the most votes,[12] and disputes might easily arise as to the accuracy of a count. At the election of military officers Plato permits a challenge and a second challenge of any count; if at this point the challenger is still unsatisfied, the issue is apparently settled by a ballot taken among the officials who are in charge of the election (756b).

We know practically nothing from other sources about election procedures at Athens or elsewhere, hence these details of Plato's text are of peculiar interest. Unfortunately this very ignorance makes it impossible for us to compare with any confidence his procedure with that of Athens or any other Greek city. It seems, however, that voting by written ballot was, if not unknown at Athens, at least so rare that no evidence of its use in the election of officers has come down to us. We know that writing was used in voting on a proposal for ostracism, and hundreds of ostraca have been recovered from the Athenian agora. It also seems that writing was employed in voting for awards of merit ($\dot{\alpha}\rho\iota\sigma\tau\epsilon\hat{\iota}\alpha$).[13] But the offices at Athens were distinguished only as $\chi\epsilon\iota\rho\circ\tau\circ\nu\eta\tau\alpha\iota$, those filled by show of hands, and $\kappa\lambda\eta\rho\omega\tau\alpha\iota$,

---

[11] The verb $\phi\acute{\epsilon}\rho\epsilon\iota\nu$, which is used in all these cases, is short for $\psi\hat{\eta}\phi\circ\varsigma$ $\phi\acute{\epsilon}\rho\epsilon\iota\nu$ ("to cast a ballot"), which appears in 766b. Since Plato's elections sometimes involve one or more preliminary votes to establish the final list of candidates, $\phi\acute{\epsilon}\rho\epsilon\iota\nu$ often has to be translated "nominate"; but where, as in 756c 2 it refers to the final result of a series of ballots, it means "elect."

[12] Cf. $\dot{\eta}$ $\pi\lambda\epsilon\acute{\iota}\sigma\tau\eta$ $\chi\epsilon\iota\rho\circ\tau\circ\nu\iota\alpha$ of 755d, 756b and 763e (where $\chi\epsilon\iota\rho\circ\tau\circ\nu\iota\alpha\iota$ is obviously understood after $\pi\lambda\epsilon\hat{\iota}\sigma\tau\alpha\iota$).

[13] Cf. Plut. *Them.* 17.

those filled by lot.[14] Plato prescribes not only written ballots, but also signed ballots. Even when writing was used in procedures analogous to elections at Athens, it is probable that the voting citizen kept his identity secret; the ostraca that have been found in the Agora contain only the name of the person to be ostracized, not the name of the voter. What Plato's motive was it is difficult to judge. When citizens are secure against political reprisals, the signing of a ballot becomes a manifestation of confidence in one's choice, and when the voter is required to sign, he will probably be more careful in making up his mind. But it also provides a means whereby an authoritarian government can supervise the citizens and exert a subtle pressure on their decisions.

On another point of procedure a more confident comparison is possible between Platonic law and that of fourth-century Athens; in fact such comparison is invited by Plato himself. Whereas at Athens voting ($\chi\epsilon\iota\rho\sigma\tau\sigma\nu\iota\alpha$) was used only exceptionally, the lot being normally employed, in Plato's state the relations are reversed: the lot is exceptional, voting (either $\chi\epsilon\iota\rho\sigma\tau\sigma\nu\iota\alpha$ or $\psi\eta\phi\sigma\phi\sigma\rho\iota\alpha$) is the usual procedure. And when Plato uses the lot it is seldom the simple $\kappa\lambda\eta\rho\omega\sigma\iota\varsigma$ that was so common in fourth-century Athens, but nearly always $\kappa\lambda\eta\rho\omega\sigma\iota\varsigma$ $\dot{\epsilon}\kappa$ $\pi\rho\sigma\kappa\rho\iota\tau\omega\nu$, a process of using the lot on a list of previously selected candidates.[15] Thus the nomophylakes are chosen by elaborate procedures of nomination followed by voting in the full assembly, and generals and other military officers are chosen by the same procedure. In the election of the council the lot is used at the end to effect a choice from a panel of double the number to be elected, this panel itself being the result of previous voting; and in the election of euthynoi the lot is used to break a tie and to determine the order of seniority among those elected. Of the minor officials, the astynomoi and the agoranomoi are chosen by a combination of voting and the lot, and the same is true of the ath-

---

[14] Arist. *Const. Ath.* XLIII-LXII: Aesch. I, 19, 106; III, 13. On methods of voting in Greece, see Busolt-Swoboda 454; and Koch in RE s.v. $\chi\epsilon\iota\rho\sigma\tau\sigma\nu\iota\alpha$.

[15] In fourth-century Athens almost all the regular offices were filled by lot ($\kappa\lambda\eta\rho\omega\tau\alpha\iota$) including the archonship; the only important exceptions were the military offices (Arist. *Const. Ath.* XLIII, 1; LV; LXI). There is no hint of a preliminary selection ($\pi\rho\sigma\kappa\rho\iota\sigma\iota\varsigma$) preceding the lot, though in earlier chapters Aristotle records that the archons had formerly been selected by a $\kappa\lambda\eta\rho\omega\sigma\iota\varsigma$ $\dot{\epsilon}\kappa$ $\pi\rho\sigma\kappa\rho\iota\tau\omega\nu$. The precise nature of this method, the date at which it was introduced, and the still earlier method of selection which it supplanted, are difficult to determine. For possible help to be gained from the *Laws*, see Excursus C.

lothetai (the supervisors of musical and athletic contests). It is only for the selection of priests that the lot alone is employed (759b).[16] This almost unvarying departure from Athenian practice is obviously the result of deliberate policy.

It is not difficult to divine Plato's reasons for refusing to follow Athenian precedent here. The officials of a state, Plato says, should be distinguished from the other citizens by their greater strength of character and their superior loyalty to the laws (734e-735a; 715cd). The democratic assumption that any citizen was competent to fill almost any office was a clear violation of this fundamental principle; as well choose our physicians or our pilots by chance as entrust to the lot the designation of these persons who are to constitute the warp of the social fabric. A wise state will then choose its best men, or those who are thought to be its best, to fill its offices. To the modern mind Plato's willingness to leave the choice of these "best men" to the full body of citizens seems truly democratic; and the words he uses in another context may be cited to show that it was not a desperate expedient, but the result of reflection: "Ordinary men, though they may be incapable of any excellence themselves, have a kind of inspired shrewdness in distinguishing it in others" (950b). But the Greeks of Plato's time would probably have looked upon this procedure as an aristocratic or oligarchic feature of Plato's mixed constitution.[17]

The question to be raised with regard to Plato's proposals is not why he makes so little use of the lot, but rather why he retains it at all. He regards it as a particularly stupid and unjust application of the demand for equality; it is one of the aspects of democracy that he satirizes with peculiar bitterness in the *Republic*.[18] We have already noted the distinction he draws between the genuine principle of equality which apportions honor and authority to merit, and the spurious equality of the lot (757b-e); a legislator whose purpose is justice, he says, and not the preservation of oligarchy, or tyranny, or the power of the demos, should aim at the former sort of equality.

---

[16] This does not mean that there are no qualifications for holding a priesthood; on the contrary (see 759c). Whether a candidate selected by lot possesses these qualifications is determined at the δοκιμασία which follows the κλήρωσις. Note 759c 2: δοκιμάζειν τὸν ἀεὶ λαγχάνοντα. Obviously a person who did not think he could pass the dokimasia would be foolish to put himself forward as a candidate.

[17] Arist. *Pol.* 1294b 8.

[18] *Rep.* 557a, 561ab; cf. *Polit.* 298e.

Nevertheless Plato admits that a state must sometimes depart from strict justice and make use of the other sort of equality if it wishes to avoid dissension, i.e. the "discontent of the many."[19] Apparently the power of democratic sentiment, and of the lot as a symbol of political equality, was too strong to be ignored even in Plato's Cretan colony. Another consideration also enters in to justify the use of the lot in certain cases. It was an ancient belief, some relics of which certainly persisted into Plato's time, that the lot was a method of receiving divine guidance; and priesthoods (when not hereditary) were usually filled in this way.[20] Plato follows religious tradition here, entrusting the selection of priests to the "divine chance" of the lot, so that what is pleasing to God himself may come to pass (759bc). But these are the only offices that he fills by the use of the lot alone; and in other cases, where the lot is used as a supplement to election, it is not for religious reasons but "for the sake of friendship" that he advocates a "mixture of democratic and nondemocratic" procedures (μειγνύντας πρὸς φιλίαν ἀλλήλοις δῆμον καὶ μὴ δῆμον).[21] The method of election, like the constitution as a whole, is to be a "mixture."

In substituting election for the lot, so far as the need for social harmony permits, Plato is not indulging in free invention, but returning to what he and many others in his day considered the procedure of early times. It is a return to the constitution of Athens described in the *Menexenus* (238d), under which "offices and authority are given to those who from time to time are thought to be the best," a constitution which some call democracy, but Plato thinks can best be called "an aristocracy with the approval of the people." Aristotle on two occasions refers to the "ancestral democracy" (πάτριος δημοκρατία) in which offices were elective.[22] If we are correct in assuming, as was argued above,[23] that Plato is one of the persons to whose views

[19] 757d: εἰ μέλλει στάσεων ἑαυτῇ μὴ προσκοινωνήσειν; 757e: δυσκολίας τῶν πολλῶν ἕνεκα; 759b: ὅπως ἂν μάλιστα ὁμονοῶν εἴη.

[20] 757e; cf. 690c. On the earlier belief that the lot was a method of receiving divine guidance, see Ehrenberg in RE s.v. Losung, 1461ff. See also England's note ad loc. and P.-M. Schuhl, *Essai sur la formation de la pensée grecque*, Paris, 1949, 64 n. 5.

[21] 759b. England is clearly right (see his note on b6) in asserting against Stallbaum, Ritter, and others, that δῆμος here means "democracy," just as in 714d δῆμος and τύραννος indicate types of πολιτεία. In Herod. III, 82 the three constitutions discussed are δῆμος ἄριστος, ὀλιγαρχίη, and μόναρχος. Overthrow of the democracy is called κατάλυσις τοῦ δήμου (Arist. *Const. Ath.* VIII, 4; Xen. *Hell.* II, iii, 28); and in Arist. *Pol.* 1277b 3 δῆμος ἔσχατος obviously means "extreme democracy."

[22] *Pol.* 1273b 38ff., 1305a 29.   [23] See Chapter III.

Aristotle is referring in the earlier of these two passages, it may be that this phrase comes from Plato himself; although, as Aristotle goes on to say, the thinkers he is referring to conceive the constitution as a mixture in which the method of electing magistrates is the aristocratic element. In any case, both Plato and Aristotle evidently consider that the older constitution of the Athenians, whether they would call it a democracy, or an aristocracy, or a mixed constitution with both aristocratic and democratic features, was one in which the offices were filled by election.[24] Others besides Plato and Aristotle held the same opinion in the fourth century. Isocrates draws a sharp contrast between the democracy established by Solon and Cleisthenes and the democracy of his day; and one of the great differences, as he sees it, is that they did not select officers by lot from the whole body of citizens, but elected the best and ablest for each function.[25] And when the ancestral constitution was forcibly established by Antipater at Athens in 321 after her defeat in the Lamian War, the practice of filling offices by lot seems to have been restricted, if not abolished.[26]

Plato assigns another function of considerable importance to his popular assembly. "In accusations of offenses against the public it is necessary to give the multitude ($\tau\hat{\omega}$ $\pi\lambda\acute{\eta}\theta\epsilon\iota$) a share in the decision; for all are wronged when anyone wrongs the city, and would rightly take it ill if they did not share in such judgments" (767e-768a). The words $\pi\lambda\hat{\eta}\theta\circ\varsigma$ and $\pi\acute{\alpha}\nu\tau\epsilon\varsigma$ in this text, as well as the use of $\delta\hat{\eta}\mu\circ\varsigma$ in the immediately following sentence describing the procedure in such trials, show clearly that Plato is thinking of the full assembly of the people.[27] In the fourth century such cases were often tried by the popular courts rather than the assembly; but it was the assembly that on recommendation of the council determined the handling of

[24] But whether by pure election or by $\kappa\lambda\acute{\eta}\rho\omega\sigma\iota\varsigma$ $\grave{\epsilon}\kappa$ $\pi\rho\circ\kappa\rho\acute{\iota}\tau\omega\nu$ it is impossible to say, since in Aristotle (and in Plato also) $\alpha\acute{\iota}\rho\epsilon\sigma\iota\varsigma$ may denote either of these procedures. See Excursus C.

[25] Isoc. VII, 16, 22; XII, 145; cf. 130 and 148. In the latter oration he puts the origin of this ancestral constitution even further back to the time of Theseus (126ff.); and in both his language suggests that it is the $\kappa\lambda\acute{\eta}\rho\omega\sigma\iota\varsigma$ $\grave{\epsilon}\kappa$ $\pi\rho\circ\kappa\rho\acute{\iota}\tau\omega\nu$ that he regards as characteristic of this ancestral constitution. "Probably Isocrates . . . merely invented an origin in the remote past for an institution which seemed to him essential to an ideal democracy" (Hignett 323).

[26] Ferguson (*Hellenistic Athens*, 22-23) says "abolished," but for the evidence see Busolt-Swoboda 926ff.

[27] $\Delta\hat{\eta}\mu\circ\varsigma$ $\pi\lambda\eta\theta\acute{\upsilon}\omega\nu$ was a technical term in Attic law designating a full or sovereign assembly. See Chapter VI, Note 45.

each case, and it could and occasionally did decide to judge the case itself.[28] Plato evidently prefers to adhere to the older procedure, for there is no provision in his law that these cases shall be referred to his equivalent of the Athenian popular courts. He does, however, place certain restrictions on the judicial competence of the demos in such cases, restrictions which were not recognized at Athens. But these and other details of this court we can best consider later in connection with the administration of justice.

There are three other passages in the *Laws* where action by the assembly is mentioned or implied. It seems that the assembly is the body that makes awards of merit,[29] and any proposal for changes in the law regarding sacrifices and dances must apparently be referred to the demos before it can go into effect (772cd). Of most significance is the casual provision that a foreign resident who has performed noteworthy service to the city may appear before "the boule and ecclesia" and appeal for an extension of his term of residence (850b). What these isolated references imply as to the range of competence Plato would assign to the assembly is difficult to determine; and we can best defer the consideration of the question until we have examined the structure and functions of the council.

In every Greek city, whatever the final competence of the assembly might be, there was alongside it, or above it, a smaller body, the council, with prerogatives that varied widely from state to state according to the degree of oligarchic or democratic feeling that underlay the constitution. At Athens there were in fact two councils. The earlier in time was the council of the Areopagus, composed of ex-archons; since the archons in early days were selected on the basis of birth or wealth, the Areopagus was definitely an aristocratic council. Aristotle tells us that before Solon it controlled the most important affairs of the state, administering justice and appointing officers at its discretion.[30] One of Solon's innovations was to set up a new council of four hundred members, one hundred from each tribe. We know nothing of the functions Solon assigned to it, and very little concerning the effect its creation had upon the prerogatives of the older council, though Aristotle's language implies that these pre-

---

[28] Busolt-Swoboda 1007-1009; Bonner and Smith I, 197ff., 294ff.
[29] On ἀριστεῖα, see Chapter VI, Note 65.
[30] *Const. Ath.* III, 6; VIII, 2.

rogatives were somewhat diminished.[31] Cleisthenes replaced the Solonian council by a council of five hundred, consisting of fifty
members from each of his ten new tribes, and in this form the council remained, with brief interruptions toward the close of the Peloponnesian War, down to Aristotle's time. By then the council of
the Areopagus had lost almost all its earlier powers and retained only
its jurisdiction over cases of willful homicide and various other offenses against religion. The word βουλή in the Athens of the fourth
century meant always the council of five hundred, or what we may
fairly call the "democratic council."[32]

This Athenian institution is clearly the model of Plato's βουλή,
though he departs from his model in several respects. It is to consist of
"thirty twelves," i.e. of three hundred and sixty members; thus in size
it is more like Solon's than Cleisthenes' council. It is likely that Plato's
chief reason for the choice of three hundred and sixty (rather than
four hundred and eighty, for example, also divisible by twelve) was
its approximation to the number of days in the year; each member
will be able to serve as chairman of his prytany once during his year
of office. A more startling innovation is that the council is constituted,
not by tribes, as at Athens, but by property classes, ninety from each.
In the discussion of these property classes in the preceding chapter
there was a brief account of the election of the council; but the procedure contains many interesting and some puzzling features, and it is
well for us now to examine Plato's text in more detail.

Ninety members[33] shall be elected from each property class. On the first

---

[31] *Const. Ath.* VIII, 4; Busolt-Swoboda 845f. Hignett (92ff.) doubts this part of
the tradition about Solon's reforms; but it has received confirmation by the recent
excavations in the Athenian agora. In the area occupied by the so-called Old Bouleuterion in the fifth century the foundations have been uncovered of a still older
building erected in the time of Solon or immediately after his reforms (see Homer
Thompson, *Hesperia Suppl.* IV, 1940, 8-15, 43-44). Hignett remains unconvinced by
this evidence (393).

[32] Βουλὴ δημοσίη occurs in a constitutional inscription from Chios of about
575-550 (Tod I, No. 1; for the dating see L. H. Jeffery, *Annual of the British
School at Athens*, 51, 1956, 157ff.) which suggests that in Chios both a newer βουλή
and an older aristocratic one were in existence about Solon's time. Since an assembly
needs a probouleutic body to prepare proposals for its consideration (cf. Arist. *Pol.*
1299b 32ff.) the creation of a "democratic council" corresponds to the enlarged
power that the assembly came to exercise in Athenian affairs as a result of Solon's
reforms.

[33] N. G. L. Hammond (CQ XLVI, 1952, 7) proposes to bracket ἐνενήκοντα βουλευτάς
as a marginal comment that has erroneously got into the text. This allows φέρειν
to mean "nominate" here as elsewhere in this passage. But I see no objection to

day all citizens shall be required to make nominations ($\phi\epsilon\rho\epsilon\iota\nu$) for councillors from the highest property class, and whoever refrains shall be fined the approved fine ($\tau\hat{\eta}\ \delta o\xi\acute{a}\sigma\eta\ \zeta\eta\mu\acute{\iota}\alpha$). When the nominations are complete, the names of those nominated shall be publicly recorded ($\kappa\alpha\tau\alpha\sigma\eta\mu\acute{\eta}\nu\alpha\sigma\theta\alpha\iota$). On the next day they shall nominate ($\phi\epsilon\rho\epsilon\iota\nu$) councillors from the second property class in the same way as on the preceding day. On the third day, for councillors from the third property class anyone who wishes may vote ($\phi\epsilon\rho\epsilon\iota\nu$), but voting is obligatory for the first three classes, while anyone in the fourth class who does not wish to vote shall be free of penalty. On the fourth day likewise all may vote for councillors from the fourth or lowest class, but anyone in the third or fourth class who does not wish to vote may abstain without penalty, while any member of the second or first class who does not vote shall be fined, the former triple and the latter quadruple the basic fine ($\tau\hat{\eta}s\ \pi\rho\acute{\omega}\tau\eta s\ \zeta\eta\mu\acute{\iota}\alpha s$). On the fifth day the officials shall exhibit all the names recorded for all citizens to see, and everybody shall vote for councillors from these lists or be fined the primary fine; and when they have selected one hundred and eighty from each of the property-classes, half of these shall be chosen by lot and these shall be councillors for the year. 756c-e

Probably nothing like an election of this kind has ever been held in all history. Seven hundred and twenty persons, one hundred and eighty from each of the property classes, have to be selected by ballot before the final choice is made by drawing lots. Gernet has expressed doubt whether this number of candidates could be obtained annually from a state the size of Plato's, particularly the quota from the first class, which presumably will be the smallest in the state.[34] The list of those eligible, however, will include not only the 5,040 lot-holders, but also their designated heirs who are thirty years old or older;[35] and it

---

taking it as meaning "cast a ballot," and therefore capable of referring either to a nominating or to an electing ballot according to the context. See above, Note 11.

[34] Introd. to Budé ed. cx n.: "360 bouleutes annuels, c'est déjà beaucoup pour 5040 citoyens, même en admittant l'itération comme à Athènes, ce que Platon ne précise pas. Si l'on ajoute que la première classe, où s'en recrute le quart, est par hypothèse la moins nombreuse, que les 360 sont tirés au sort parmi 720 désignés à l'élection, que l'élection se fait entre des noms antérieurement proposés, on se demande où tous ces noms pourront être trouvés."

[35] It has been shown above that persons other than lot holders are counted as citizens in Plato's state. It might still seem that to membership in the council only lot holders are eligible, since they alone seem to be owners of property and members of the property classes. But Plato's penal law, which imposes fines for certain delinquencies graduated according to the property class of the offender, shows that membership in a property class is attributed to others than lot holders, for certainly lot holders will not be the only free offenders. Apparently all the members of a household would be counted as belonging to the property class of the head

must be remembered also that women above the age of forty can hold office in Plato's state (785b). Thus the number from which these candidates will be drawn is considerably larger than the 5,040 that first comes to mind. Again, there seems to be no bar to re-election to Plato's council, hence we need not suppose that seven hundred and twenty *new* candidates must be found each year. It may well have been Plato's intention that some members of his council, particularly those from the first and second classes, should serve the state repeatedly in this office. Aristotle devotes critical attention to this election but does not bring up any of the difficulties just mentioned.[36] Plato's proposals are certain to appear stranger to us than to his contemporaries, for the elections that we know are carried on in an entirely different climate of expectation. In a modern state the number of persons who have held office, or have even thought of doing so, is a very small proportion of the citizen body, and it is difficult for us to imagine a state in which, as at Athens, every citizen could expect at some time or other to be a public official. However cumbersome the procedure may seem to us, and however great the demands it makes upon the citizenry, let us assume that Plato's scheme was a feasible one and try to picture to ourselves what it would involve.

This election is an example of κλήρωσις ἐκ προκρίτων, but the κλήρωσις is a rather mild affair, since every man on the final list has one chance in two of being designated councillor.[37] The preliminary selection, or πρόκρισις, which precedes the final decision by lot, is clearly the more important part of the proceedings. It is divided into two stages of voting—what we may call the nominating stage, which occupies the first four days, and the electing stage, which occurs on the fifth day. We may assume that on the first day there will be posted a list of all the citizens who belong to the first (or highest) property class, in accordance with the official registers of property kept by the nomophylakes, and similar lists for each of the

---

of the family. I think, therefore, that Gernet (cxvi) is hardly justified in taking this passage as evidence that Plato alternates between the notion of a military class, and the custom of oligarchical cities where only the heads of families participated in government.

[36] *Pol.* 1266a 14ff.

[37] If Plato's state is to follow the custom of Athens, it will select an alternate for each person chosen (Busolt-Swoboda 1022); in this case every man on the final list will be either a councillor designate or an alternate.

other classes, one on each of the three succeeding days.[38] On the first day the full body of citizens assembles. For how many persons from the first property class does each man vote? Plato does not say, but a little reflection shows us, I think, that he thought of each citizen as voting for one, that is as making one nomination. If each was expected to put in nomination a slate of ninety candidates, the burden of tabulating the results would be insuperable, not to mention the difficulty of seeing that each citizen had done his duty and voted for ninety persons. The use of φέρειν shows that the voting is by written ballot, and we may assume that the vote was prepared as in the election of the nomophylakes, each man writing on a tablet the legal name of his nominee and his own legal name (753c). When the tablets are in, the recorders will make a list of all the persons who have been nominated. The same procedure we may imagine as taking place the second day to provide a list of nominees from the second class. On the third day the number of voters will probably be less, since the fourth class is excused from taking part; and on the fourth day still less, since both the third and fourth classes—presumably the largest—are excused. On the final day all four classes vote. Lists are posted of the names of the nominees in each of the four classes, and from each of these lists the voters are to "select" (ἐκλέξαντες) one hundred and eighty. Here again it is probable that Plato intends each voter to vote for only one candidate in each class. How the number is to be reduced to one hundred and eighty Plato does not say. Perhaps each candidate's name will carry beside it the number of nominating ballots cast for him; this would tend to prevent a mere duplication of the previous balloting by showing some voters that their nominees had little chance and that it would be wiser to use their votes for more favored candidates. The procedure described elsewhere for the election of the nomophylakes (753cd) would suggest a series of ballots on the candidates from each property class, the list being reduced for each vote by eliminating a certain number of those who ran lowest in the previous ballot. No provision is made for filling up the list in case there are fewer than one hundred and eighty nominees in any class. Apparently

---

[38] There was a place in the Athenian Agora where such public notices were posted, viz. the monument of the Eponymous Heroes. Andoc. 1, 83; Aristoph. *Peace* 1183. The recent excavations in the Agora have revealed the foundations of this monument and of the fence that surrounded it. Thompson, in *Hesperia* xxi, 1952, Pl. 16; cf. 58 and 92.

Plato did not think this contingency would be likely to arise, or was willing to give the assembly *carte blanche* to deal with it if it should arise.[39]

What advantage does Plato hope to gain for his state by setting up a council organized by property classes instead of by tribes? This is no conventional oligarchical scheme. Oligarchies usually set a property qualification, low or high according to circumstances, for membership in the council, and those who could not meet this qualification were simply excluded; whereas Plato provides for equal representation from all economic classes. But what is the use of recognizing property qualifications if they play no part in determining admission?[40] The answer is that just as the lot must sometimes be used if a legislator wishes to avoid faction in his state (757de), so also must differences of property be recognized; they are a divisive force of which Plato is always acutely aware. His council therefore recognizes these different interests, and even gives them equality of representation in this deliberative body, producing thereby a certain "democracy" of interests meeting in council.[41] This is a novel—and far-sighted—device for attempting to resolve by deliberation conflicts of interest that might lead to civil strife. The traditional procedure of constituting the council by equal contingents from all the tribes had long ceased to have any but a sentimental basis, for tribal differences were not a source of faction in historical times; representation by economic interests was an appropriate substitute in a day when the strife between oligarchs and democrats—the rich and the

[39] Such discretion was enjoyed by the Athenian assembly. Aristotle (*Const. Ath.* XLIV, 4) says, for example, that the election of generals and other military officers was carried out by the ecclesia "in whatever manner the people think best."

[40] This point is overlooked by those who find Plato here taking property as an index of merit. Membership in the council is not dependent upon the amount of a man's property; rather it is determined by the choice of his fellow citizens, those admittedly fallible judges (757b) whom Plato, *faute de mieux*, makes responsible for the decision. It is then the elaborate procedure of voting, involving reflective judgment rather than the accident of the lot, that embodies Plato's effort at the true principle of justice expounded in this passage; distinction by property classes, on the other hand, is an example of the easy equalitarian principle, based on measuring, weighing, and counting (τὴν μέτρῳ ἴσην καὶ σταθμῷ καὶ ἀριθμῷ, 757b). It would be hard to explain the words in the passage just cited if Plato were not thinking of property classes as well as of the lot.

[41] It might seem inequitable that all four classes, despite possible difference in their numbers, should have equal representation in the council. But this is the way in which the upper chambers of modern legislative bodies are often constituted; e.g. in the United States Senate the state of Alaska and the much more populous state of New York have each two Senators to represent them.

poor[42]—was particularly acute. When Aristotle in the *Politics* is discussing ways in which the quality of the deliberative branch of government might be improved, he suggests that it would be expedient to have the parts of the state—by which he means the rich and the poor—represented in the deliberative body by an equal number of members. "The results of deliberation are better when the people (δῆμος) are mixed with the notables (γνώριμοι) and they in turn with the people."[43] Plato's proposal seems only a more detailed exemplification of this suggestion afterward advanced by Aristotle; and the fact that we know of no historical Greek state that followed this principle leads one to think that the idea was born in political discussions in the Academy. In a council so organized the extremes of wealth and poverty would each be powerless to impose its will; only by combining could they equal the voting strength of the two middle classes, which would ordinarily, therefore, be the stabilizing force in the constitution. This is what Aristotle elsewhere says is the best attainable constitution for most states; and for Plato it would embody the supremacy of the mean, the "middle way" characteristic of the mixed constitution.[44] The clue to Plato's thought in this paragraph is therefore found in the opening declaration, that a council so chosen would be a mean (μέσον) between a monarchical and a democratic constitution (756c).

The members of the council, though chosen *from* property classes, are chosen *by* the whole body of citizens, or by all those whose attendance can properly be required. Such attendance is in fact required of all citizens on three of the five days—the first, second, and fifth; Plato's reason for excusing the third class from one day's proceedings, and the fourth class from two, is probably—despite Aristotle's suggestion of oligarchical intent[45]—that some of the poorer citizens could not neglect their affairs for the whole period. The penalty for failure to vote is a fine, a fine that is particularly heavy for members of the first or second class who absent themselves from

[42] A. H. M. Jones "Athenian Democracy and its Critics," *Cambridge Historical Journal* XI, 1953, 1-26, makes some judicious observations on the relations between the rich and the poor at Athens and notes the lack of evidence that the rich were exploited by the demos. Other democracies probably did not show as much self-restraint as the Athenians.

[43] *Pol.* 1298b 13-22; cf. 1318a 7-17. Ernest Barker (*The Politics of Aristotle*, Oxford, 1946, 192n) even asserts that Aristotle here suggests a *representative* organ of deliberation.

[44] *Pol.* 1295b 1ff.   [45] *Pol.* 1266a 14ff.

the proceedings on the fourth day, when members from the poorest class are being nominated.[46] Plato's concern to assure general participation in the nomination and election of these officers shows that they have a double function: they are not merely representatives of the special interests of their respective classes, but also councillors deliberating for the common good.

Following common Greek precedent, Plato gives his council the duty of summoning and dissolving the assemblies, both the regular ones appointed by law, and the special ones that may be called if need arises; and also of "guarding" the state during the intervals between such meetings. But the council as a whole is too large a body to exercise responsibly the constant watchfulness, day and night, that a state, like a ship at sea, needs if it is to escape disaster (758a). Hence it is to be divided into twelve parts—or prytanies[47]—each to serve for one month as guardian of the city.

The majority of the councillors must be allowed to remain for most of the time at their private business, ordering their own households. We must assign a twelfth part of them in turn to each month of the year, making them our guards for that period, to be ready to receive one of our own citizens or someone coming from abroad who wishes to lay information before us, or to make an inquiry of the sort that it is proper for cities to make of one another and to reply to, and also to receive a reply from another city when we have made such an inquiry; and especially, since revolutions of various sorts are wont to occur in cities from time to time, to be able to take measures to prevent their occurrence, or if they have occurred, to assure that the city perceives them and cures the evil as quickly as possible. For these reasons this presiding part of the city must be competent to summon and dissolve assemblies (συλλογῶν), both those fixed by law and those needed in an emergency. Thus a twelfth part of the council will be the body that looks after all these matters, [itself] resting [in turn] for eleven twelfths of the year; and each such part in succession shall, in conjunction with the other officers, constitute these guards that guard the city. 758b-d

This division of the councillors into smaller groups, each exercising in turn the executive functions of the council, was a familiar feature

[46] The amount of the basic fine is not stated; but if the provision of 764a is taken as governing the present election, it would be fifty drachmae—a fine stiff enough to make the duty of voting a compelling one for at least the poorer classes. The ten-drachma fine mentioned in the next sentence of 764a is a fine for not attending an assembly.
[47] These μέρη are not called prytanies here, but see 755e.

of the Athenian constitution; and under the influence of Athens it appears to have been widely adopted elsewhere.[48] At Athens each of the ten tribes held the presidency (πρυτανεία) in turn, in an order determined by lot; its members took their meals together in the Tholos, next to the Bouleuterion, and one of their number was chosen by lot each day as ἐπιστάτης, or chairman. Together with other members of the prytany selected by himself he was required to remain constantly in the Tholos, with the keys of the archives and temples and the public seal in his possession.[49] It is evidently the customs of his native city that Plato is imitating here. Similarly the specific duties he assigns to his prytanies are all reminiscent of Athens. Like their Athenian counterparts they receive heralds and ambassadors (cf. 953b) and in general act as head of the state in relation to other states; they listen to petitions and information from private citizens; together with the other magistrates they act as guardians of the peace; and they summon and dissolve assemblies (σύλλογαί)—i.e. meetings of the council as well as of the assembly (the σύλλογος). It is likely also that they supervise the elections that are held in the assembly (except for the very first; see 755e), and that the officials (ἄρχοντες) so frequently mentioned in the descriptions of these elections are the members of the prytanies designated for this function.[50]

But there were many duties performed by the council at Athens that Plato fails to include. The Athenian boule established agenda for the meetings of the ecclesia and prepared recommendations (προβουλεύματα) on matters that were to come before it;[51] it assisted the other officers in their duties and exercised supervision over them, espe-

---

[48] Busolt-Swoboda 476.

[49] On the prytanies in the Athenian constitution, see Arist. Const. Ath. XLIII-XLIV.

[50] Plato does not say how these prytanies are to be constituted. At Athens they were set up by tribes, each of the ten tribes in turn taking over the presidency of the boule. Since Plato's council is constituted not by tribes but by property classes, analogy would suggest that these classes should take turns in the presidency. But to get twelve prytanies, each of the property classes would have to be divided into three parts; and of this there is no hint. Furthermore Plato's concern that rich and poor should be equally represented on the council makes it certain that he would want the same mixture of elements in any section of the council which exercised its powers. Unfortunately a prytany of thirty members cannot be divided into four equal parts. This difficulty is surprising, for Plato's numbers in all other cases are perfectly adapted to their functions in the state. Ritter (Kommentar, 160) thinks Plato probably intends that there should be eight members from each of two classes and seven from each of the others. This is possible, but it is equally likely that this is a detail that escaped Plato's attention.

[51] For these details, see Const. Ath. XLV-XLIX, and Busolt-Swoboda 1025ff.

cially over those concerned with the finances of the city, auditing their accounts each month and at the end of their terms; it supervised the construction and repair of triremes, their equipment, and the dockyards where they were kept; it inspected the cavalry troops and their horses; it kept watch over public buildings and prosecuted persons thought to have damaged them; and at the end of the year it conducted the scrutiny (δοκιμασία) of the incoming councillors and the newly elected archons. In addition it had various duties in connection with festivals and games, with the relief of the poor, and with the audit (εὔθυνα) of outgoing officials. Finally, the Athenian council of Plato's day had certain remnants of the more extensive judicial powers it had once enjoyed; it frequently heard charges against magistrates, though its decisions were subject to appeal to the assembly; and it gave a preliminary hearing to a denunciation (εἰσαγγελία) for injuring the people, and referred it to the assembly with a recommendation. None of these items appears in Plato's statement of the duties of his council. Most of these omissions can be readily understood in the light of Plato's later legislation. Some of the matters that occupied the attention of the boule at Athens will not have to be looked after at all in Plato's state; the supervision of the triremes, for example, will be unnecessary, since there is to be no navy. Other matters mentioned by Aristotle are, as we shall see, entrusted to other officers distinct from the council: the audit to the euthynoi, and the general supervision over the magistrates to the nomophylakes. Finally, the council never functions as a court in Plato's state, though it appears, in a much diminished role, in Plato's equivalent of the Attic εἰσαγγελία: if the accuser and the defendant in such an action cannot agree upon the selection of the magistrates (supposed to be chosen "from the highest officers") who are to make an examination of the charge before it is referred to the popular assembly for trial, the council shall make the selection for them (768a). This is but a pale reflection of the function of the council as described above under Attic law.

What is difficult to interpret is Plato's omission of what was considered a primary function of the Athenian boule—viz. the laying of recommendations before the ecclesia. Any large assembly requires that the matters upon which it has to decide be given previous consideration by a smaller body, so that the issues involved may be presented in the form of specific proposals to be accepted, rejected, or modified.[52] There was a nice division of powers between assembly and council at Athens. The assembly could not act upon any matter that had not been previously considered by the council and presented in writing; any action in defiance of this rule was null and void, and its proposer was liable to indictment for illegality, through the γραφὴ παρανόμων.[53] On the other hand, the Athenians were ever alert to curb independent action by the council; the limits of its authority were not sharply defined, and for that very reason the validity of any particular action could always be called in question. Plato's bare statement that the prytanies have power to summon and dissolve assemblies leaves some room for doubt as to his intentions. Does his silence indicate that he intends to give his council power to act without the approval of the assembly? Or that recommendations for action by the assembly are to be presented by some other board of officers? For the former supposition there is no positive evidence. The power given the prytanies to make replies to foreign envoys (758c) might suggest it (in democratic Athens all such matters had to be laid before the people and the proposed reply approved by them); yet this may be one of those occasions mentioned immediately after (758d) which will require the summoning of the assembly. Most oligarchical-minded reformers of Plato's day thought it important to strengthen the council at the expense of the assembly's powers; but if Plato shares their views he gives no evidence of it. On the contrary, the evidence suggests that he follows a different path; the most important deliberative body in his state, as we shall see later, appears to be the nomophylakes, a body of superior officials with a tenure of office that lasts from their election (some time after their fiftieth year) until they reach the age of seventy. Whether this "superior council," as it may properly be called, is intended to present its proposals directly to the assembly or through the democratic council is left uncertain in Plato's text. Aristotle—who is aware of this kind of constitution as a possibility and apparently had some historical examples of it in mind—says that these πρόβουλοι are set over the councillors (καθιστᾶσι ἐπὶ τοῖς βουλευταῖς);[54] and this implies that the council still functions, though in a subordinate role. In the absence of an explicit statement, we can most probably infer that

[52] See Arist. *Pol.* 1299b 32ff. and Note 32 above. Plutarch (*Solon* 19) emphasizes the probouleutic function of the council as part of Solon's intention.
[53] Arist. *Const. Ath.* XLIII, 3-6; XLV, 4; Lipsius 390.
[54] *Pol.* 1299b 36f.

Plato does not intend to abandon the accepted procedure, especially since, in one of the few references to action by the assembly, βουλή and ἐκκλησία are explicitly joined (850bc).[55]

The creation of a body of superior magistrates undoubtedly gives the council in Plato's state considerably less importance than it had in Athens or other contemporary states. We cannot infer, however, that its role becomes unnecessary or unimportant. Though subordinate, it need not be merely a rubber stamp for the proposals of the nomophylakes; for as we shall see the powers of these high officers are legally limited, and their only recourse against what they conceive to be abuse of power by lower magistrates is to bring charges against them before the courts. Furthermore, the elaborate procedure of selection Plato devises for the council shows that he thinks it will be an important organ of deliberation. It is indeed seldom mentioned after the sixth book of the *Laws*; but this feature of Plato's text, like the rarity of references to the assembly, may be taken as evidence that the assembly and council are everywhere presupposed as functioning in the familiar Greek manner. Nevertheless there is an important gap in Plato's constitutional law which it is regrettable he did not attempt to fill by defining more clearly the range of initiative left respectively to the council and assembly and the procedures through which recommendations are prepared and presented to the assembly.

Another important question is the range of matters that are within the competence of the assembly and council. Together they constitute what Aristotle designates the "deliberative" (τὸ βουλευόμενον), as distinct from the executive (τὸ περὶ τὰς ἀρχάς) and the judicial (τὸ δικάζον) parts of a constitution.[56] Aristotle further enumerates the matters over which the "deliberative" is sovereign (κύριον), namely (1) war and peace and the formation and dissolution of alliances; (2) legislation and questions affecting the constitution; (3) sentences of death, exile, or confiscation of property; and (4) the election of magistrates and the audit of their accounts. It is interesting to see which of these appear as functions of the deliberative in Plato's state. The election of officers is a function of the assembly acting, as we have seen, under the prytanies of the council. Some (possibly all) proposals for changes in the laws have to be accepted, or ratified, by

---

[55] The constitution that Plato proposes to the warring factions at Syracuse provides that questions of war and peace shall be decided by the five-and-thirty nomophylakes μετά τε δήμου καὶ βουλῆς (*Ep. VIII* 356d).

[56] *Pol.* 1297b 37ff.

the demos. Questions of war and peace and political alliances were universally within the province of the deliberative in Greek states, and Plato's acceptance of this precedent is indicated in the constitution he proposes for the warring factions at Syracuse.[57] The audit, however, he assigns to a special board of magistrates; this is in fact a judicial function not properly belonging to the deliberative, and Plato's judgment in this matter commends itself to modern ways of thinking. Yet the purpose that had led Solon to entrust this function to the people—i.e. that they might call their magistrates to account —is explicitly asserted and its realization provided for in other parts of Plato's legislation. Likewise the imposition of the death sentence is properly a judicial rather than a deliberative function, and this also Plato assigns elsewhere, to his court for capital offenses; though it appears to be his intention that the preliminary stages of some such cases, especially if they involve allegations of "injury to the people," shall take place before the court of the demos. Thus the people's voice will be heard, but the final decision will rest with a select court of experienced officials.

These limitations that Plato places upon the traditional functions of the assembly and council suggest that he had a clear conception of the distinctive part the deliberative branch should play in a constitution—a clearer conception, in fact, than is evident in Aristotle's discussion of the question. Though Aristotle was the first to formulate this distinction between the three "powers," he seems not to question the traditional functions assigned to them; his recommendations are concerned only with ways in which their organization could best be adapted to the needs of various types of constitution. But Plato's insight into the distinctive function of the deliberative is clearly a consequence of his endeavor to prevent what both he and Aristotle regarded as the unbridled and illegitimate sovereignty of the people. This sovereignty of the demos at Athens came about, as Aristotle points out,[58] by its control of judicial functions (i.e. in the popular courts), and through its disposition to regard the decrees of the assembly as supreme even over standing laws with which they might be in conflict. Plato would prevent these excesses by a specially devised and highly original system of courts, and an elaborate set of devices for maintaining the supremacy of law. The reduction of the

[57] See Note 55 above.
[58] E.g. *Const. Ath.* IX, 1-2; XLI, 2.

powers of assembly and council are a necessary consequence of these other fundamental reforms.

THE MAGISTRATES

The nomophylakes are by far the most important officials in Plato's constitution; but since one of the chief functions of these "guardians of the laws" is supervision of the other magistrates, it will be better to defer the study of their office until we have gained a general view of the areas of law and administration over which they are to preside. In this section, therefore, we shall be concerned with the ordinary civil and military magistrates of Plato's state—the ἐγκύκλιοι ἀρχαί, as Aristotle calls their counterparts in the Athenian constitution[59]—whose tenure of office was short and whose duties were more or less routine.

Of these magistrates the first to be considered in Plato's text are the generals (στρατηγοί) and other military officers. They are to be elected in an assembly of all the citizens, i.e. of all those who are or have been members of the armed forces.[60] For this election the citizens are grouped according to the branch of the military service to which they belong, the hoplites sitting in one place, the cavalry in another, and the light-armed troops in a third. All voting is by show of hands, χειροτονία. The generals are elected by the whole assembly from a list of nominees presented by the nomophylakes; but if anyone in the voting body wishes to substitute another name for one of those officially proposed and is willing to take oath that he thinks his nominee a better man, the assembly decides, by majority vote, which candidate is to remain on the list. The three candidates on

---

[59] *Const. Ath.* XXVI, 2, XLIII, 1.

[60] For the details that follow in this paragraph, see 755b-756b. That this is a meeting of the assembly is put beyond question by the reference (755e) to the prytanies as the officials whose duty it would normally be to summon it. Several commentators have remarked that the description of this assembly is reminiscent of the oligarchical proposal of the late fifth century to restrict citizenship to the ὅπλα παρεχόμενοι (Gernet, cxi-cxii; Wilamowitz, *Aristoteles und Athen* I, 78; Bisinger, *Der Agrarstaat in Platons Gesetzen*, 23). If this is intended to imply that Plato's is a belated version of the fifth-century proposal, the suggestion seems unwarranted. We have seen that for Plato the fundamental requirement for citizenship is membership in a lot-holding family. Nor is the similarity between Plato's proposals and the former ones at all close. The ὅπλα παρεχόμενοι (a phrase that does not occur in Plato's text) of the fifth-century program included only the hoplites and the cavalry; whereas in Plato's text it is clear that the armed forces participating in the election include the light-armed contingents as well—that is, the units to which the poorer citizens would belong.

the final list who receive the highest number of votes in the election are declared generals. Next the hoplites elect as their commanders twelve taxiarchs, one from each tribe. Nominations for these posts are made by the newly elected generals, though there is the same privilege of counter nomination (ἀντιπροβολή) as in the election of the generals. In command of the cavalry will be two hipparchs, and under them phylarchs, presumably one for each tribe, as at Athens. These are elected by the cavalry[61]—"in the presence of the foot soldiers," Plato reminds us—from nominations made by the generals, the list of nomines again being subject to amendment in the fashion already described. The officers of the bowmen and other light-armed forces are not elected, but appointed by the generals.

This table of military officers parallels that at Athens, and the electoral procedures are likewise based upon Athenian practice, though with considerable modification. Aristotle tells us that all military officers were elected by show of hands in the ecclesia, "in whatever manner seems good to the people."[62] These words are broad enough to cover election of taxiarchs by the hoplite portion of the assembly, and of hipparchs and phylarchs by the cavalry; but if this procedure was ever followed at Athens we have, I believe, no evidence of it.[63] It is probable that the Athenian boule presented nominations, in the form of προβουλεύματα, to the ecclesia;[64] and Plato's words (755e) suggest that the nomophylakes in the election described are performing functions that would later fall to the council. The provision for nomination from the floor may be a reflection of Athenian procedure, though Plato's additional clause that such a nomination could only be considered as replacing an official nominee seems, from the care taken to describe it, something unfamiliar to his readers. Plato provides for only three generals, in place of the ten annually elected at

---

[61] There is a contradiction in Plato's text on this point. In 755e he says that the hipparchs, like the generals, are to be elected by the whole assembly; but he returns to the subject a few lines later and prescribes that the cavalry are to elect them. Wilamowitz (Hermes XLV, 1910, 402-404) thinks that there is a double version in the text, reflecting Plato's first and second thoughts on the subject, and suggests that the later version was induced by memories of Plato's youth, when the cavalry were suspected of oligarchical tendencies by the people and were not given the officers they liked. Stallbaum simply brackets καὶ ἱππάρχους in e9.

[62] Const. Ath. XLIV, 4, LXI, I.

[63] See the references in Kahrstedt, Untersuchungen zur Magistratur in Athen, Stuttgart, 1936, 42 n. 2; for taxiarchs elected by the demos, Ps. Dem. XL, 34; for phylarchs, Hyp. I, 17; for hipparchs, Lys. XVI, 8; XXVI, 20.

[64] Const. Ath. XLIV, 4; Busolt-Swoboda 469 n. 3.

Athens.[65] After the decline of Athenian naval power it seems there was no longer any real need for ten generals, though the offices continued to be filled each year. Plato does not say that the term of office in all these cases is one year, but this was the law at Athens, and it is safe to presume it in Plato's law whenever a longer term is not explicitly prescribed.

The generalship was an office of great political importance at Athens. Here the Athenians ignored their fondness for the lot and recognized the necessity of experience and competence.[66] The generals sat ex officiis with the council to advise it and to make proposals for the public welfare; for the proper management of military affairs naturally involved not only the levying and training of soldiers, but also the conduct of foreign affairs and of domestic matters relevant to them. There seems in fact to have been no restriction upon the competence of the generals; their powers were limited only by their ability to persuade the council and the assembly to accept their advice. Under these circumstances an able general would be recognized not only as the leader of his colleagues but also as the head of the city; and since there was no bar to re-election, such a man could retain this headship as long as he had an adequate following in the assembly. This was the only office that Pericles held during the long period of his ascendancy over Athenian affairs.

It is extremely unlikely that Plato expected the generalship in his state to carry such prerogatives and exert so much influence,[67] but there is no bar to re-election, and the function of guarding the city (760a) which the generals exercise is capable of a broad interpretation. The duty explicitly laid upon them at their election is the supervision of military affairs (755d). This would certainly involve training the armed forces as well as leading them in combat; and since the main purpose of gymnastics in Plato's state is to prepare the citizens to defend their country in war, we should expect the military officers to play an important part in education. Presumably they are the "archontes" in charge of the monthly field days, with their military exercises and games in imitation of actual combat (829b). The generals and their subordinate military officers are to have con-

[65] *Const. Ath.* LXI, I.
[66] Evidence of the intelligence of the demos, says the Old Oligarch; Ps. Xen. *Const. Ath.* I, 3.
[67] 908d shows Plato's awareness that the generalship in a Greek city was often the tool of the demagogue and a stepping stone to tyranny.

trol of the imports necessary for military purposes (847d); and in conjunction with the prytanies they receive and entertain persons coming from abroad on public business (953b). Naturally they preside over military courts that try cases of desertion and cowardice in battle, and also over the assemblies that decree awards of valor (943a-945b). We even find the military officers in one passage constituting a court for trying cases of assault (880d).[68] These details show that Plato interprets very broadly their function of guarding the city; but no doubt he think the control assigned to the nomophylakes would be a sufficient check upon abuse of this elective office by a popular leader.

But the detailed policing and protection of the various parts of the city and countryside are the responsibility of various other magistrates: astynomoi for the city proper (ἄστυ, 779c) and its suburbs (προάστειον); agoranomoi for the civic center, the agora; agronomoi for the country; and finally, priests and priestesses in charge of the temples and sacred areas (758e-759a). The priests can best be discussed in connection with Plato's religious law, and we shall therefore defer consideration of their qualifications and functions to a later chapter.

The astynomoi are to be three in number, the agoranomoi five, each group to be selected by lot from a list of twice their number previously established by voting (763de). At Athens they were simply selected by lot, presumably from a list of declared candidates.[69] These are two of the rare offices in Plato's state for which a property qualification is imposed; an astynomos must belong to the first (or highest) property class, an agoranomos to the first or the second. The reason Plato gives for this provision is that these men must have both the ability and the leisure (δυνατούς τε εἶναι καὶ σχολάζοντας) to look after public affairs. Most of their duties, as we shall see, are matters of public housekeeping; and it is not strange if Plato thinks that citizens who have managed well their own estates would be particularly competent to look after the city's property. There was, however, no such qualification for the parallel offices at Athens. Nominations for these offices are made by the members of the assembly, presumably from an official list of the members of the two property

---

[68] Apparently cases involving aliens or metics. This may be an echo of the jurisdiction of the polemarch at Athens over lawsuits involving metics (Arist. *Const. Ath.* LVIII, 2).

[69] Arist. *Const. Ath.* L, 2; LI, 1; Kahrstedt, *op.cit.* 39f.

classes. It seems to be taken for granted that a man has no right to refuse an office for which he has been selected,[70] unless—as Athenian law provided—he declares upon oath that he has not the time, or has some other disability that would prevent him from discharging it.[71]

In order to picture as vividly as possible the duties assigned to these officers, let us try to envisage the physical structure and appearance of Plato's city. It is to be centered around an acropolis, an agora, or public square, and the temples adjoining it (745b, 778c). Around the agora and beside the temples will be the houses of the magistrates and the law courts (778cd). Elsewhere there is mention of a public prison (908a) and offices for the astynomoi (an ἀστυνόμιον) and the agoranomoi (an ἀγορανόμιον) near the market (917e, 918a). Plato also mentions gymnasia, schools, theatres (779d, 804c), and other temples or shrines in the country around the city (761c, 833b). Greek cities were built on much the same plan everywhere, but these details fit so perfectly the Athens and the Athenian Agora of Plato's time that Plato might well be describing his native city. It is significant that he makes no mention of the men's houses (ἀνδρεῖα) or eating clubs (φιδίτια) that in Crete and in Sparta must have been a prominent feature of the central city.[72] Plato would prefer that there be no city walls (here he looks to Sparta, rather than Athens), since they are of no advantage either to health or valor, inducing the citizens to think of them rather than their borders as the line of defense against the enemy (778d-779b). Nevertheless if there must be a wall, it would be better to build the private houses from the start so that they will form a continuous wall along the outer circuit of the city—a plan which Plato thinks is both pleasing to the eye and useful for defense. Outside the city there are to be markets, harbors, and public buildings for the accommodation of transient foreign traders and their wares (952e)—an arrangement which reminds us of the Piraeus at Athens, but which also had its parallel in most Greek cities that were situated at some distance from their harbor towns. It seems clear that there is to be a fairly rigorous building code; and it is one of the duties of the astynomoi to see that it is observed, that property

---

[70] This is at least how Aristotle interprets Plato (Pol. 1266a 10f.).
[71] Only compelling reasons, sworn to by the petitioner, were sufficient to excuse a man; Busolt-Swoboda 470.
[72] On the imperfect adaptation of the common meals to the other provision of Plato's law, see Chapter VII ad fin.

lines are respected, and that the inhabitants keep their property in repair (763c, 779c).

From he center of the city radiate the boundary lines separating the twelve divisions of the territory occupied by the twelve tribes. The authority of the agoranomoi covers the agora and its temples and fountains (764b), while each of the three astynomoi takes care of four of the twelve sections into which the city is divided (763c). Their responsibilities are to see that the streets are kept clean and that no one damages the buildings and fountains, or that whatever damage occurs is repaired (759a, 764b). They are also to look after the supply of water, a precious commodity in ancient as in modern Greece. There will be aqueducts or conduits to bring in water from the mountains around, and the astynomoi are to see that the supply is kept pure and sufficient to feed the fountains set in the agora and elsewhere to adorn and serve the city (763d, 764b). The problem of handling rainwater was something that the builders of ancient cities had mastered, by constructing drains to guide the flow of water and cisterns to conserve it, and there are allusions to these matters as part of the duties of the astynomoi (779c). Public slaves are mentioned elsewhere (794b; cf. 882b), so it is evident that Plato takes this familiar feature of Athenian life for granted. These officers would certainly employ such slaves, and would probably also have the right to requisition the slaves of private citizens (as is authorized in the case of the rural police) for public works under their jurisdiction.

They are responsible also for maintaining order (κόσμος) in the streets and public buildings, i.e. for seeing that "no injury is done by men or other animals" (759a). This means that they have authority not only to fine persons who violate the building and sanitary ordinances or damage public property (764c), but also to deport beggars (936c) and to administer summary punishment for various offenses, such as slander in public places (935b), acts of violence in the streets, and failure to aid a victim of such violence (879e, 881c). They help the women officers in charge of children to maintain order on the playgrounds (794b); they hear denunciations for the appropriation of buried treasure (913d), and they assist in a search for stolen property (954b). They may even hear and judge claims for damages by one person against another and impose a settlement (844c, 845e). The agoranomoi are responsible in addition for enforcing rather intricate market regulations; they are to allot places for the various wares (849e), and see that citizens bring to the market that portion of their products that they are required to sell to non-citizens (849a-c); they prevent the sale of adulterated or spurious goods (917d), and the naming of more than one price by a seller for a single article on a single day (917bc).[73] With the nomophylakes they are to draw up regulations as to what constitutes fair practice and post them on a pillar in front of the ἀγορανόμιον (917e); among other things, these rules would fix the amount of profit allowed a dealer in his trading (920bc). Apparently any violation may be punished on the spot by the magistrate cognizant of it. In one case it is prescribed that punishment shall be inflicted after the herald has proclaimed to those present what the offense is which is being punished (917e)—presumably a salutary warning to other dealers in the market. Similarly the astynomoi, in consultation with the nomophylakes, are to post on the ἀστυνόμιον a similar list of the regulations they are responsible for enforcing (918a).

One duty particularly laid upon the astynomoi is to supervise the alien craftsmen in the city and see that they observe the Platonic principle of "one man, one craft" (847a). They also may adjudge disputes regarding wages or workmanship, or any other claims made by artisans against them, to the amount of fifty drachmae (847b), and disputes for even larger sums in which a foreign visitor is involved (953b). They and the agoranomoi are evidently the archontes who meet the casual trader from abroad and guard against the bringing in of "innovations";[74] thus in addition to their other duties these officials function somewhat like immigration officers, and they would certainly be involved in any request made by an immigrant for the metic status recognized in Platonic law (850b; cf. 915b).

These two offices and their duties in Plato's state are in the main a reflection of the common practices of his day. Aristotle lists the superintendency of the market and the supervision of streets and

---

[73] One must assume that they oversee the markets at the harbor mentioned in 952e, as the corresponding magistrates at Athens did for the Piraeus. Whether ἀγοραὶ τῶν ξένων in 849d 1 refers only to these harbor markets or also to separate markets in the city adjacent to the "common market" of 849e 3 cannot be clearly determined, but the latter seems the more plausible. There is a hint in these provisions of Aristotle's proposal (*Pol.* 1331a 30ff.) for two agoras in his "best city"—a free agora devoted to public business, worship, and recreation, and the traders' agora separated from it.

[74] 953a. Νεωτερίζειν meant for the Greek "subvert" as well as "innovate." Cf. νεωτερισμοί, 758c; νεωτερίζοντες, 798c.

public and private buildings as two of the indispensable functions of government.[75] Agoranomoi are found in Athens—ten in number, five for the city and five for the Piraeus; and their existence elsewhere is attested in inscriptions from more than a hundred different cities, including Sparta. The strictness of control exercised over the market seems to have varied, but it was seldom a free market, as we understand the term. Inspection of wares, supervision of weights and measures, and regulation of prices are common features and attested particularly for Athens. Misrepresentation and false statements by sellers and buyers alike were forbidden by Athenian law; and as in Plato's state the agoranomoi at Athens were empowered to punish infractions of the rules by fines (within limits), or by stripes in the case of slaves.[76] Peculiar to Plato is his regulation requiring the sale to foreign residents of a certain proportion of the annual product of the soil (848a), a provision that follows from the special character of his economy. But the secondary status of aliens is not peculiar to Plato, though at Athens the foreign trader had to pay a special tax,[77] a feature which does not occur in Plato's law. Astynomoi also are frequently found in fourth-century cities,[78] though if the city was a populous one they were sometimes replaced or supplemented by more specialized officials, such as "inspectors of walls," "superintendents of wells," "harbor wardens," "repairers of temples" and the like.[79] Plato seems to have interpreted the control over public decorum ($\epsilon \dot{v} \kappa o \sigma \mu \acute{\iota} a$), which was generally recognized as a function of the astynomoi, to include matters of behavior that were left unregulated at Athens, though even here there are Athenian analogies to his proposals; and other critical Athenians of his day, such as Isocrates, were inclined to look

---

[75] *Pol.* 1321b 12ff. Arist. *Const. Ath.* LI, 1; Busolt-Swoboda 491ff., 1116ff.

[76] Theophrastus apud Harpocration κατὰ τὴν ἀγορὰν ἀψευδεῖν. Cf. also the reference to this law in Dem. xx, 9 and Hyp. III, 14; and Lipsius 91f., 95.

[77] Lipsius 94.

[78] Busolt-Swoboda 492. Aristotle's description of the duties of the astynomoi at Athens provides a good commentary on this part of Plato's laws. "Five of them are officials in the city, and five in the Piraeus. They watch over flute girls, harpists, and players on the lyre to see that they do not hire themselves out for more than two drachmae; and if there are several persons who want to hire the same girl, they cast lots and hire her to the winner. And they see that no collector of ordure deposits his stuff within ten stadia of the city wall; and they prevent the construction of buildings that encroach on the streets, or balconies that overhang them, or roof drains that empty on them, or doors that open outward; and they take up the bodies of persons who have died in the streets, having public slaves to assist them" (*Const. Ath.* L, 2).

[79] Arist. *Pol.* 1321b 23; *Const. Ath.* L, 1; cf. *Pol.* 1322b 23.

185

back to the good old days when strict control was thought to have been the rule. Plato's greatest innovation is that he gives to these magistrates much more judicial competence for settling private suits than they possessed at Athens; but this is a matter that can be discussed more appropriately later.

The policing and protecting of the country outside the city is entrusted to a third set of officers, called agronomoi. The space Plato devotes to the description of these officers, their selection and their duties, is disproportionally long (760b-763c). When this happens in Plato's text it is usually an indication that the proposal under discussion involves something more or less unfamiliar to his readers, and we shall find that this is true here. There was no such office as this at Athens, and officials with this name are not referred to in any of the inscriptions; but Aristotle's mention of them in one passage shows that the title was not unknown.[80] Their recruitment is as follows. Each of the twelve tribes selects five men, and each of these groups in turn selects twelve others from its own tribe between the ages of twenty-five and thirty.[81] This body of phrourarchs (as the primary "fives" seem to be denoted in the later portions of the text)

[80] "Officials of this sort [i.e. with responsibility for looking after the χώρα and τὰ ἔξω τοῦ ἄστεως] are called by some ἀγρονόμοι and by others ὑλωροί." *Pol.* 1321b 28-30. But agronomoi do not occur at all in the inscriptions, and hyloroi only in those from Thessaly. Busolt-Swoboda 493.

[81] Translators and commentators have generally interpreted Plato as intending that each of the five phrourarchs shall select twelve others from his own tribe, thus making each "watch" consist of sixty-five instead of seventeen men. This would mean a total enrollment in the rural police of seven hundred and eighty men, seven hundred and twenty of them between the ages of twenty-five and thirty. Mr. Paul H. Jacobson, Vital Statistics Analyst for the Metropolitan Life Insurance Company, has informed me that a population of 40,000 would be necessary—according to the present age distribution in the population of the United States—to supply every second year a fresh group of seven hundred and twenty males aged between twenty-five and thirty. Thus to furnish a biennial quota of this size would probably be difficult if not impossible in Plato's state. More decisive is the fact that other texts (760e, 761e and 762e) imply that a watch is to consist of twelve men and five. What has misled the translators and commentators is the ambiguity of ἑκάστῳ τῶν πέντε (760b 7) and τοὺς ἑξήκοντα ἑκάστους (761d 6). The first can be—and in the light of 761e and 762e should be—taken as meaning "each of the fives," not "each man in the group or groups of five." The second phrase is more naturally taken as "each (group of) sixty" (i.e. the "men" as distinct from the "officers" of each watch); but it seems we are compelled to take it as meaning "each (group of) five among the sixty phrourarchs." This is awkward but not impossible syntactically; τοὺς ἑξήκοντα is written as the subject of φυλάττειν to follow, then immediately specified by the addition ἑκάστους [sc. τῶν πέντε] τὸν αὐτῶν τόπον, this phrase then being thought of as in apposition to τοὺς ἑξήκοντα. This interpretation is confirmed by 763c, where the three astynomoi are said to correspond (in the city) to the *sixty* agronomoi, i.e. to the sixty phrourarchs of the rural police.

and their fellow agronomoi are to serve for a term of two years. At the beginning each of the twelve groups, or watches, is assigned by lot to one of the twelve divisions of the country and they occupy these stations for one month; then all move under the leadership of their respective phrourarchs to the next territorial division "on the right" (that is, moving clockwise around the city as a center). At the beginning of the second year they are again assigned to their first month's stations by lot,[82] and the order of their successive monthly movements is reversed. This provides an opportunity for these officers to acquire knowledge of each part of the country, and at different seasons of the year for most of them.

Plato pictures his colony as having a village in each of its twelve districts, with its temples, its market place, and barracks (οἰκήσεις) for the guards on a spot of high ground that can easily be fortified (848de). The duty of these rural guards is, first of all, to assure the safety of the inhabitants by digging moats and building fortifications to prevent invasion of the territory from the outside (760e). Next they are to look after the roads, to make communication within the land as easy as possible (761a). Then they take measures to control the flow of rainwater down the mountain sides, providing channels to prevent damage to the crops, and damming the outlets of the valleys to provide reservoirs (761ab). There is a suggestion that irrigation ditches are to be dug to supply the drier areas with water from these reservoirs (cf. 844a). At springs, or at suitable sites along the borders of streams, fountain houses are to be built and trees planted around them. Underground conduits are to connect these pools with one another; and if there is any sacred grove (ἄλσος) or enclosure (τέμενος) nearby, water is to be directed into its shrines. Gymnasia are to be constructed, with facilities for warm baths for the older men and a plentiful supply of dry wood for the use of visitors (761c). Plato obviously has a loving vision of what the Greek

---

[82] 760b: φυλὴ δὲ μία τῷ ἑκάστῳ μορίῳ ἐπικληρωθεῖσα κατ᾽ ἐνιαυτόν. England (in loc.) is correct: the assignment by lot in this passage is an ad hoc arrangement for organizing the rural police; though if the usual interpretation of these land divisions as identical with the tribes is correct, some similar procedure must be presupposed at the beginning for assigning the tribes to their respective areas. See Chapter IV, Note 84.

There is no inconsistency (as maintained by Vanhoutte, *La Philosophie politique de Platon dans les Lois*, 28) between ἐπικληρωθεῖσα κατ᾽ ἐνιαυτόν, 760b, and the provision that these guards are to serve for two years. The assignment by lot each year is merely to determine their initial stations for that year.

countryside becomes when properly attended to. The remains that have been discovered of the fountain houses and rural shrines in Greece show that these proposals are little more than translations into his law of practices quite familiar to his countrymen. In the *Critias* he deplores the destructive effects of past erosion in carrying away the valuable soil of Attica and the disappearance of the forests that once covered its mountains (111a-d). If he had included reforestation among the duties of these rural magistrates, and some control of the goats—whose destructiveness he mentions earlier (639a)—there would be little to add to this picture of what such officers should look after in safeguarding the resources of an agricultural community. The labor required for carrying out these constructions is to be obtained by requisitioning the slaves and animals of the local inhabitants, but they are to be used, so far as possible, only when they are not needed by their owners (761a; cf. 762a).

These guards are also responsible for maintaining order in their districts; as Plato says, they guard the city not only from its enemies without, but also against its professed friends within (761d). They take over in the villages and countryside the functions performed in the city by the astynomoi and the agoranomoi, together with other matters peculiar to their stations, such as the enforcement of the agricultural laws (νόμοι γεωργικοί).[83] They receive reports of annual harvests from the citizens in their area and transmit them to the government for guidance in levying taxes (955d). They supervise the noncitizen craftsmen and have authority to determine how many artisans are needed, what skills are required, and where these craftsmen are to live so as best to serve the local inhabitants (848e). Like the astynomoi and agoranomoi they have, besides these administrative duties, considerable judicial power as well. They can adjudge claims for damages up to three minae (761e). In the ensuing passage they are called judges (δικασταί), and their liability to a suit for damages for unjust exercise of their powers, administrative or judicial, is explicitly affirmed and provided for.

Plato takes a special interest in the mode of life to be followed by the agronomoi during their two-year term of service—an indication of what he thinks to be the peculiarly novel element in this office.

[83] Cf. 842e, 843d-846b, 847e-850a. It is also their duty to apprehend an exile who returns without authorization (881de). Such a person would try to slip over the border, rather than return by the city's harbor.

The men in each of the twelve watches are to live and take their
meals together; absence without authorization or compelling reason,
either by day or night, is a grave offense and is severely punished—
the case of a younger man being judged by the five phrourarchs of
his watch, that of a phrourarch by the sixty phrourarchs of all the
watches (762cd). Their rations are humble and uncooked. They have
no servants for their personal use, but are to rely on their own and
one another's services for their needs; thus they will learn that no
man can command worthily who has not learned how to serve
(762e). They are to engage in hunting, for recreation and even more
to develop familiarity with their country. This life, Plato suggests,
should become for the agronomoi a kind of play, "a not undignified
sport" (761d).[84] All this suggests that one important purpose of this
institution is to provide a course of training for the younger men,
perhaps a period of service through which every promising young
citizen would normally pass before reaching the age of thirty, when
he would become eligible for office.[85]

At the end of his account Plato emphasizes the novelty as well as
the importance of this corps of officials. "Call them 'secret police'
(κρυπτοί), or agronomoi, or whatever you please; their way of life
is what every man should strenuously live who intends to be an able
defender of his country" (763bc). The use of the term κρυπτοί is
doubtless a reminiscence of the Spartan κρυπτεία. Plutarch tells us,
apparently on the authority of Aristotle, that every year the Spartan
officials selected the brightest of their young men and sent them into
the country with food and weapons; by day they concealed themselves, but at night they went out on the roads and killed any Helot
whom they encountered.[86] The parallel Plato suggests is unfortunate;
for although there is a similarity between the two institutions in the
simplicity of life and the strict discipline that governed them—
and this is doubtless what Plato wishes to point out—the essential
purpose of the Spartan corps, as Plutarch sees it, was determined by

[84] We shall see later that Plato believes education (παιδεία) is most effective when
it is play (παιδιά).
[85] There is a slight inconsistency here between the requirement set in 785b and
the fact that these agronomoi are regarded as officers, yet are most of them under
thirty. We can remove the inconsistency by assuming that only the older men, the
twelve "fives," or phrourarchs, are counted as officers. Yet this interpretation is hard
to reconcile with the judicial functions explicitly assigned, in some cases, to both
the younger and the older agronomoi (761e).
[86] *Lyc.* 28; for other evidence see Busolt-Swoboda 670 n. 1.

the existence of helotage and the necessity of preventing uprisings; whereas there is no hint of such a subject class in Plato's state, as we have seen in the preceding chapter. Plato's association of ideas has led both to unwarranted attempts to gloss over the cruelty of the Spartan corps and to suspicions of the purpose of his own. There is a closer parallel between Plato's program for the agronomoi and the two-year term of ephebic training introduced at Athens, or drastically reformed after the battle of Chaeronea, and it is not unlikely that his proposals had some influence upon at least the later form of this institution.[87]

This by no means completes the cycle of annually or biennially elected magistrates in Plato's state. There are some quite important officers, particularly those concerned with religion and education, whose status and duties can best be considered later. There are also numerous scattered phrases (such as "superintendents of emigration," ἐπιμεληταὶ τῶν εἰς τὴν ἀποικίαν, in 929d) that may indicate special offices. It is possible that some of these, like the numerous occurrences of the term archontes, are intended to refer to officials whose manner of selection and whose duties are elsewhere described under other titles. It is more likely, however, that Plato does not profess to anticipate all the magistrates that would be needed and is willing to leave to "later legislators" the supplying of these and other deficiencies. Some of these gaps, however, are so noticeable and so important that they require our attention.

---

[87] Few scholars now believe that the ephebia was first established in 335, as Wilamowitz confidently declared (*Platon* I, 701; cf. *Arist. und Athen* I, 193). Aesch. II, 167 shows that something like a two-year ephebic training existed as early as 370; and the ephebic status is implied in the oaths referred to by Lycurgus (I, 76), Demosthenes (XIX, 303) and Plutarch (*Alc.* 15) as taken by the young men when they were enrolled in the ληξιαρχικὸν γραμματεῖον and became ἔφηβοι. It is generally agreed that there was a reorganization about 335, and it is possible that the *Laws* left its mark upon it. The account Aristotle gives of ephebic training in his day (*Const. Ath.* XLII, 3-4) contains some features that resemble Plato's program for the agronomoi, but it also exhibits some striking differences, and these have usually not been noted. The Athenian program was for youths just turned eighteen; Plato's is to take place somewhere between the ages of twenty-five and thirty. The former was obviously a preparation for citizenship and the military obligations that citizenship involved at Athens; whereas Plato's seems rather a preparation for office, of men whose full citizenship had been attained some years before. Of course ancient readers, like some modern ones, may have overlooked these differences in purpose and in details; but if the Athenian program reflects Plato's ideas, it does so dimly and with distortion. See Marrou 481 n. 1; K. O. Lofberg, "The Date of the Athenian Ephebia," *Class. Phil.* XX, 1925, 330-335; and Gomme, *The Population of Athens in the Fifth and Fourth Centuries*, 8 n. 3.

It is surprising that there is no mention in Plato's constitution of any financial officers, such as the vendors (πωλῆται), the receivers (ἀποδέκται), and the treasurers of various state funds which played a part in the government of Athens and most other Greek cities.[88] At Athens the boule exercised close supervision over the collection and expenditure of public moneys, but the multifarious duties in connection with these functions were assigned to special officers, their actions always being subject to approval by the boule and eventually by the ecclesia. Neither a general principle nor any details of its execution are made clear in Plato's law. Before we attempt to determine his intentions, let us first try to ascertain what expenditure of public money will be necessary in his state, and how the funds to cover these expenditures are to be obtained.

In the first place, there is no mention in Plato's law of any annual salary or daily pay for his officials. At Athens all servants of the state received some compensation, from at least the fifth century onward.[89] Plato seems to follow an opposite procedure; for example, instead of paying for attendance at the assembly, he imposes fines for nonattendance, except for members of the third and fourth property classes (764a). There are other cases of fines prescribed in Plato's law for the nonperformance of a civic function, but no instances of financial compensation for performance. It is clear that Plato would follow what Aristotle[90] calls the aristocratic or oligarchic (but what Plato would probably call the "ancestral") principle that prevailed in Athens before the introduction of pay for officeholders in the fifth century. Thus this item of public expenditure would be altogether lacking in his state.

Again the direct costs of the military forces would be much less in Plato's state than in the Athenian state of his time. It seems that every citizen soldier would provide his own equipment; this was customary at Athens, in the main, the richer citizens being thereby

[88] Arist. *Const. Ath.* XLIII-XLIX passim; Busolt-Swoboda 624-30.

[89] Even attendance at the ecclesia was compensated for in Aristotle's time, at the rate of one drachma (six obols) for ordinary meetings, a drachma and a half for the "sovereign" assemblies held ten times a year. Service on the jury courts was paid for at the rate of half a drachma a day. Members of the boule received five obols; when members of the prytany they got an extra obol. But their annual pay was much greater than that of the ecclesiasts, for the council met every day in the year. Each archon received four obols a day for food, but part of this was spent in the maintenance of a herald and a flute player (Arist. *Const. Ath.* LXII, 2; cf. XLI, 3).

[90] *Pol.* 1273a 17, 1317b 35.

eligible for the cavalry, the less well-to-do for the heavy infantry (hoplites), and the poorer for the light-armed and other contingents. Would they receive pay for active service? The introduction of pay for the armed forces was another innovation upon the older practices made at Athens in the fifth century—first for service in the marine, where large numbers of rowers began to be needed with the expansion of the Athenian navy and the introduction of triremes in place of the older pentekonters, then for hoplites on service abroad on military expeditions entailed by Athens' ambitious imperial policy, and finally to all those in service, domestic or foreign, in all branches.[91] The pay seems in most cases to have been little more than enough to cover subsistence, except for the mercenaries, whom Athens began to use in increasing numbers in the fourth century. Foreign mercenaries have no place in Plato's scheme, and the subsistence of his citizen troops during the period of service would presumably be a part of the program of "common meals," a military institution which he thinks of instituting for all his citizens and would certainly establish in the military forces. Plato seems to be guided by the earlier Greek conception, still cherished at Sparta, that the defense of one's country is a service which the city can demand of its citizens without pay;[92] the true reward of these "craftsmen of security," as Plato calls the military forces, is honor (921d-922a). Under these conditions the direct costs of the military establishment would be very little.

But its indirect costs to the public treasury might be considerable. Some military supplies—materials that the state does not itself produce—will have to be purchased abroad; and there are to be foreign teachers of music and gymnastics used in the training of the citizens (804cd). Both these items will require payment from the treasury, and possibly payment in "Hellenic currency," not the currency valid only in internal exchange. The state must always have a supply of Hellenic currency for various purposes—for military expeditions abroad, for foreign ambassadors and heralds, for the expense of the

---

[91] Arist. Const. Ath. xxiv.

[92] This interpretation is not contradicted by 945a, which says that the soldier who has been found guilty of throwing away his arms in battle, besides being debarred from further military service, shall pay a personal penalty (not, as Bury translates, "shall pay back his wages"). The sum mentioned as the penalty imposed, being differentiated according to property classes, is clearly a fine, not a repayment of wages. Μισθός here is used as in 650a, in the sense of "serious consequences," or "penalty."

delegations sent to the games at Delphi, at Olympia, at Nemea and the Isthmus, where Plato expects his state to make a good showing, of course, and also for the officially authorized "visitors" (θεωροί) who go abroad from time to time to survey and report on the outside world (742ab, 950e, 951a). Some of these items will be wholly, others perhaps only partially, covered by public funds. For internal affairs other sums will be required. The temples, houses of public officials, the gymnasia, schools, theatres, and prisons mentioned at various times in Plato's text suggest a program of public building reminiscent of Pisistratus or Pericles. Money will also be necessary for the construction and repair of streets, aqueducts, cisterns, fountains, and sewers. The publication of state documents was a considerable item in the Athenian budget and it would certainly not be less in Plato's state, for he is more insistent than his native Athens on publicity for all laws and decrees, on registration of property, and on public records in general. And the numerous festivals he prescribes would constitute another considerable demand on public funds.

From what sources would Plato's state derive the income to cover these demands? Some of the usual methods of financing employed in Greek states are ruled out. There are to be no import or export duties (847b). The Greek cities derived a considerable income from such sources and from the harbor tax on goods coming through their ports.[93] There are apparently to be no public lands for rent nor mines to be leased, as there were at Athens. There is, however, one novel source of revenue for Plato's state: when a citizen's property increases beyond the maximum allowed, the surplus goes to the state (754e; cf. 850a). Besides this, the only sources Plato mentions are familiar ones. There is the income from fines imposed by the courts, which at Athens was devoted to the payment of the dicasteries but in Plato's state would presumably be used for other public purposes; and there are direct levies (εἰσφοραί) on property or income. Both these forms of direct levy were known at Athens and elsewhere. The income tax on agricultural products was the oldest of all general taxes in Greece; in later days the levy upon capital, rather than income, seems to have been the more common.[94] Plato mentions both of these types of direct tax, but leaves it to his officials (τὸ δημόσιον) to choose each year which kind of levy they will impose (955de). The determination of

[93] Busolt-Swoboda 612-614.
[94] Busolt-Swoboda 610-612, 1223-1226.

this tax would be facilitated in Plato's state by his provision for registers of all property, both landed and movable property (741c, 745a, 754d, 850a, 855b); and by the requirement that the citizens must render each year a report to the agronomoi on the amount of the year's produce (955d). These levies bear only on the citizen; the resident alien is exempt from all taxes (850b).

One of the passages just referred to (955de) implies that the officials of the government each year would consult (cf. βουλευόμενον) regarding the needs of the treasury and the best way of meeting these needs. There is at least the suggestion of a schedule of estimates, without which no competent financial policy is possible. But such a schedule seems to have been unknown at Athens, at least until the middle of the fourth century.[95] Plato probably wrote these lines after the end of the Social War, when the finances of his native city were going through a grave crisis. It was at this time that Eubulus, as treasurer of the theoric fund, exerted his ascendancy over the Athenian government, and by his energetic measures brought about a considerable improvement in the administration of finances. He was succeeded in this path in 338-7 by an even greater financial wizard, the "incorruptible" Lycurgus, one of Plato's own pupils, who for four years held the specially created office of ταμίας τῆς διοικήσεως, a kind of ministry of public finance, and who in the twelve years of his public activity put the finances of Athens in a sounder condition than they had known since the days of Pericles.[96] It is fair to suppose that something of Lycurgus' ideas, as well as his integrity and public spirit, are due not merely to his aristocratic descent but also to his studies with Plato.

Plato leaves us completely in the dark as to the identity of these agencies of government that are responsible for financial policy and its execution. The nomophylakes are to be the guardians of the registers of property; we can also assume that they have supervision over the determination and execution of financial policy in general, though it is possible that Plato intended the primary responsibility to lie, as it did at Athens, with the council. Whether, as at Athens, the decisions of these officials would have to be accepted and ratified by the assembly we can only speculate.

There is an even graver gap in Plato's scheme when we compare

[95] Busolt-Swoboda 1215ff.
[96] Busolt-Swoboda 1147-1149; cf. Felix Durrbach's introduction to the Budé edition of Lycurgus, Paris, 1932.

it with the constitution of Athens, viz. the lack of any officials corresponding to the king, the polemarch, and the archon. These were the most ancient offices at Athens. Even after the creation (probably in the seventh century) of a board of nine archons, with the addition of the six thesmothetae, the original three archons retained their official individuality, the king as religious head of the state, the polemarch as protector of the legal rights of metics and aliens, and the archon as the special guardian of property and the family.[97] It was from the last of the three that the year took its name in official records. These functions would be as important in Plato's state as at Athens, so it is obvious that he expects them to be performed by officials other than these familiar Athenian ones, and we shall see that this is in fact the case. For the interpretation of Plato's abandonment of these offices it may be significant that they had ceased to be of any political importance at Athens after they began to be selected by lot in 487;[98] before this time the office had been held by some of the foremost Athenian statesmen, including Solon. But even so, Plato might have chosen to rehabilitate the office his great ancestor had held by restoring the earlier method of election. Why he did not choose to do so I see no way of determining. There are numerous respects in which the changes proposed by Plato anticipate changes that were actually introduced after his death. But this is an exception. The office of archon was retained at Athens and continued to be a position of dignity at least down to the very end of the Hellenistic period.

THE GUARDIANS OF THE LAWS

In interpreting the nature and function of the nomophylakes in Plato's constitution we encounter peculiar difficulties. There is no evidence of officers bearing this title at Athens until toward the end of the fourth century;[99] and of the few states in which we know that

---

[97] Arist. *Const. Ath.* LV-LVIII.

[98] Arist. *Const. Ath.* XXII, 5. Though this procedure was a κλήρωσις ἐκ προκρίτων, the number of the προκριθέντες (five hundred if we accept the unamended text, one hundred if it is amended as has been proposed) meant that there was no real πρόκρισις of the candidates. See Ehrenberg in RE s.v. Losung; Hignett 173-174, 322; and Excursus C.

[99] The fragment of Philochorus (Fr. 141b, FHG; Fr. 64, FGH 3B, 117) cannot really be taken as evidence to the contrary, despite Jacoby (FGH Pt. III, Vol. I, 338f., Vol. II, 241ff.). The fragment comes from Philochorus' seventh book (as quoted by Harpocration s.v. νομοφύλακες), in which he is describing the constitution of Demetrius of Phalerum. If the nomophylakes there described are fifth-century Athenian of-

such officers existed in Plato's lifetime, our information is so fragmentary as to be of little help. There are references in Aristotle and
Xenophon to nomophylakes as existing in some particularly well-
governed cities; but unfortunately they do not name these cities, and
what they say of the functions of these magistrates is in Xenophon's
case too general, and in Aristotle's too specific, to afford us a guiding
principle. We are left, therefore, with almost no resource except the
Laws for interpreting the relation of these important officials to the
assembly, council, and annually elected magistrates; and Plato's text,
unfortunately, fails at critical points to show us his precise intentions.

These "guardians of the laws," or "guardians"—as we shall frequently call them—are a board of thirty-seven members, chosen from
citizens fifty years old or older, each to hold office from the time of
his election until he reaches the age of seventy (755a). The first
statement of their duties is at first sight puzzling. These officers, Plato
says, are to be guardians—first, of the laws, and next of the registers
of property; and they are to act as a court to try persons accused of
having more than the amount of property reported (754de). This is
clearly a general statement of their responsibilities followed by its
application to one particular law, the law requiring registration of
property. Since this is the only law that has yet been formulated, the
statement here made—containing the "three injunctions" referred to
immediately afterward—is not to be taken as a full account of their
duties. "As our legislation proceeds, each new law will involve additional matters over which these men are to have supervision" (755b).
The promise contained in this sentence is amply fulfilled. We meet
the guardians sixty or seventy times in the ensuing books and in connection with the most diverse parts of Plato's legislation; but nowhere
is there any statement of principle for understanding this variety of
functions other than that laid down at the very beginning. It is for
us to try to interpret what this function of "guarding the laws"
(νομοφυλακία) means for Plato.

The Athenians since at least the time of Solon had thought of laws

---

ficials taken up "and made important" in the reforms after Chaeronea, they must
have been incredibly unimportant before that time to have left no evidence in the
inscriptions, and to have escaped mention by any historian, orator, dramatist, or
philosopher. The attribution of their institution to Ephialtes in this fragment is
probably due to the lexicographer's misunderstanding of some reference made to
Ephialtes in Philochorus' account of Demetrius' reforms. See Gilbert I, 172; Busolt-
Swoboda 895 n. 1, 925 n. 4; and Hignett 209.

as instructions to magistrates, indicating the rules they were responsible for enforcing, the actions they could take, and the penalties they could impose. This principle seems to have been followed in the publication of the laws, the various items of the code being grouped together according to the different officers whose responsibility it was to enforce them.[100] Plato follows this tradition of his native city almost as a matter of course. "There are two aspects (εἴδη) of a constitution," he remarks; "one is the establishment of offices (ἀρχαί), the other is the laws that are apportioned to each of them."[101] A body responsible for the guardianship of the laws would obviously be expected to see that the officers of the state followed the instructions laid down for them. The Athenians of Plato's time had the same concern; all magistrates took an oath at the beginning of their year of office that they would abide by the laws, i.e. by their instructions. At the end of their term of office they had to undergo an audit of their accounts and defend themselves against any charges of malfeasance that any citizen cared to bring—the procedure known as εὔθυνα. During the year their official conduct was under the supervision of the boule and ecclesia and a vote (ἐπιχειροτονία) was taken once during every prytany on their conduct of their office. If the vote on any official was adverse, the case was referred to a popular court for trial.[102] Plato does not mention the oath nor the monthly ἐπιχειροτονίαι, though he emphasizes the εὔθυνα, and we have seen that his council would also exercise certain powers of supervision (758d). But he apparently thinks that more continuous and competent supervision is required than could be provided by the assembly and the council, and establishes this higher board of officers—in effect a kind of superior council—to keep the magistrates within the law.

---

[100] See Wilamowitz, *Hermes* XLV, 1910, 398; Busolt-Swoboda 303 n. 3; Dem. XXIV, 20.

[101] 735a. The distinction is expressed by Aristotle in *Pol.* 1289a 15ff., and it is the basis of his comment (1265a 1) that Plato's *Laws* consists for the most part of νόμοι, with only a few prescriptions regarding the constitution (πολιτεία). Cf. also Aristotle's interpretation of Draco's laws (*Pol.* 1274b 15f.) as distinct from a previously existing constitution. Plato expresses the idea more fully in a later passage. "There are two aspects of constitution making: first the determination of offices, how many there are to be, and how they are to be filled; and then the assigning of laws to them, determining what they are to be, and how many and what sort would be appropriate for each office" (751ab; cf. 763e, 768e).
It seems clear, from comparison of 735a with 751a, that ἑκάστοις in the former has lost its original position and gender; clearly it must go with ἀρχαῖς.

[102] Arist. *Const. Ath.* XLIII, 4; LXI, 2.

For this function the guardians would be peculiarly fitted because of their age and their long tenure of office.

The mention of the guardians appears like a recurrent refrain (μετὰ τῶν νομοφυλάκων) in the laws of the later books. They are associated with the generals and hipparchs in regulating imports for military purposes (847d); with the astynomoi, agoranomoi and agronomoi in policing the markets (849e, 917e, 918a, 920a-c) and overseeing the construction and care of buildings in the city (779cd); with the phrourarchs in enforcing the strict mode of life required of the agronomoi (762d). They collaborate with the women supervisors of marriage (784bc, 794b, 929e, 932b), with the directors of music and athletics (772a,c, 835a), with the priests (799b) and exegetes (828b). It is from their number that the director of education is to be chosen (766b) and they frequently advise with him in the discharge of his duties (801d, 829d, 835a). Their cooperation in enforcing the laws takes various forms. Sometimes they are a higher authority to whom a magistrate can resort, in difficult cases, to secure obedience to his orders (e.g. 799b, 800a); sometimes they act as a court of arbitration between magistrates and citizens (784b); sometimes they join with a body of magistrates to draw up the rules these magistrates are to enforce (917e, 918a); sometimes they formulate the laws themselves, the magistrates being responsible (κύριοι) for enforcing them (847d); and always, we may assume, they are supervisors (ἐπίσκοποι), charged with seeing that the magistrates commit no breach of law, or if they do, that the offense receives its proper punishment (e.g. 762d).[103] But Plato's law appears to give them no disciplinary powers; it is clearly not within their competence to depose a magistrate, or to fine or otherwise punish him. What they can do is bring a charge against him before the courts, or report a magistrate's misconduct to the euthynoi for consideration and judgment. But probably most important will be the moral authority they command because of their age, prestige, and experience; their judgment of a man's conduct in office would certainly affect his chances of future office and honors in the state. In short they seem to possess the unlimited inquisitive functions of a military officer, but without the arbitrary power usually associated with military command.

[103] Under certain circumstances they may impose fines or other punishment on private citizens; but this, as we shall see later, is one of the general prerogatives of magistrates in Plato's state (as it was in Greek states generally), so that in this respect they are not set apart from the annually elected officials.

It is clear that Plato conceives his guardians as a superior body of officers in close touch with all areas of administration. There is, however, one rather striking omission. It might naturally be supposed that one problem the creation of this board of officers would be intended to solve is that of preventing action by the assembly and council in contravention of the laws. The distinction between laws (νόμοι) and decrees (ψηφίσματα) was firmly imbedded in Athenian practice of the fourth century; no decree of the assembly was valid if it ran counter to the standing laws.[104] At Athens, at least after the middle of the fifth century, the only procedure available for giving effect to this principle was the "indictment for illegal proposal" (γραφὴ παρανόμων) which could be brought by any citizen against the proponent of a decree alleged to be contrary to the laws. The case came to trial before a popular court, which had power to determine the penalty to be imposed—fines, loss of civic rights, or even death— if the accusation was sustained.[105] This procedure seems to have been frequently abused, nevertheless is praised by the orators as the bulwark of democracy. Its effect was obviously to make the people, through the popular courts, the final judges of legality. This is that excess of freedom which Plato says has been the corruption of Athens, when the people is sovereign, not the laws (698ab, 699e-701c). It is what Aristotle even refuses to call a constitution, because the decrees of the assembly override the law.[106] Whether or not Plato and Aristotle were justified in their condemnation, there can be no doubt that they regarded the Athenian constitution as lacking an adequate check against illegal action by the demos. It is almost certain, therefore, that Plato's guardians are intended to furnish such a check,[107] though the way in which they will do this is not clear. Perhaps Plato intends that they should act as a superior council to prepare προβουλεύματα for the deliberations of the assembly, as Aristotle says was the function of nomophylakes in some states.[108] But one would expect an explicit statement of this function, if Plato intends them

[104] Andoc. I, 87. See Henri Francotte, "Loi et décret dans le droit public des Grecs," in *Mélange de droit public Grec*, Liège and Paris, 1910, 3-23.
[105] Busolt-Swoboda 896, 1014f.; Lipsius 383-395.
[106] *Pol.* 1292a 5-38.
[107] This kind of check was provided by the nomophylakes in the constitution of Demetrius of Phalerum, according to the fragment of Philochorus. See below, Note 146.
[108] *Pol.* 1298b 28ff. See Newman's note on this passage (*The Politics of Aristotle* IV, 251). Apart from Aristotle's assertion, we have no evidence of nomophylakes acting in a probouleutic capacity.

to have it. Even if he is content simply to give them general powers of supervision over the other officers—among whom the councillors would be included—one would expect the guardians to be mentioned in connection with the duties of the council, as they are with respect to all other magistrates.

A second function that Plato assigns to the guardians is to act as a kind of legislative commission to revise and supplement the laws formulated by the legislator at the beginning. There are many references to the inevitable deficiencies and imperfections in the legislation that is being laid down. On some points the legislator does no more than provide an outline to be filled in later; on other points he constructs a model which is to be imitated by later legislators in similar cases; and on still others experience may show the need of revision as well as addition. Who is to fill these gaps and correct these imperfections? The answer is given at the end of the account of the offices (768e-771a). The guardians whom we have chosen to be "the saviors of the laws" must themselves become legislators, Plato says, nomothetai as well as nomophylakes (770a). They are not merely to fill in the outline according to the principles that inspired the original legislators (770b), but also revise or reject whatever does not in practice actually serve the purpose for which the laws are intended, viz. to make good men (770de). Examples of the supplementation that Plato thinks may be necessary are regulations concerning choral dances (772a-c), religious festivals (828b) and contests (835a), civil disputes (843e), and certain details of legal procedure (846bc, 855cd, 957a)—all of which are knowingly left incomplete. To these examples we should add the numerous references (already given) to administrative regulations that the guardians must make—such as those covering imports and exports, retail trade, and the supervision of metic artisans and traders. Sometimes the original legislation will require to be replaced, rather than supplemented. A good example is the suggestion of a possible "second law" on sexual relations that may be found necessary if the law originally laid down proves to be too severe for human nature (840e). One famous piece of unfinished business is the regulation of the higher studies (818de) and of the Nocturnal Council which is concerned with them (968c). Though the guardians are not mentioned in these passages the laws required are obviously to be worked out in consultation with that very Nocturnal Council itself, of which the eldest guardians will form a part.

Here Plato departs notably from Athenian practice in vesting a single permanent board with a function which at Athens was ordinarily entrusted, when the need arose, to a special commission of νομοθέται. In the troubled times of the sixth century the Athenian people had chosen a single man, Solon, to revise their laws—an old procedure which had its parallels elsewhere in other legislation of the seventh and sixth centuries. After the overthrow of the Four Hundred in 410 the assembly set up a commission to prepare a new codification of the laws of Solon and Draco. Shortly after the beginning of the fourth century an elaborate plan was adopted providing for a vote each year on all sections of the laws, to ascertain whether it was the opinion of the assembly that revision should be undertaken. If on any law or group of laws the vote was unfavorable, a commission of nomothetai selected from the roll of dicasts was empowered to entertain suggestions and draw up proposals in conjunction with the council. The proceedings before this commission took the form of a trial, in which the advocates of change appeared as the plaintiffs against the existing law, defended by speakers chosen by the assembly.[109] We do not know how the nomothetai were chosen, but it is probable that they were selected by lot, as were the dicasts for the various courts. Plato would substitute a relatively permanent body of what he hoped would be carefully selected members in contrast to what must have seemed to him the casual and amateurish commissions that functioned at Athens.

Plato does not say whether all or any parts of this legislative work of the guardians have to be approved by the assembly before going into effect. In one passage—which certainly refers to modifications of the laws governing religious festivals and perhaps to all changes in the laws—Plato prescribes that a proposal for a change must be approved by all the officers, all the people ($\pi \acute{a} \nu \tau a \ \tau \grave{o} \nu \ \delta \hat{\eta} \mu o \nu$), and all the divine oracles (772cd). The mention of the demos in this passage shows that he thought a reference to the assembly was at least sometimes necessary, even of proposals upon which the guardians and their fellow officers were agreed; but what precisely the areas are in which the consent of the demos is required he never says. The relation of the guardians to the assembly in this respect, as in those mentioned above, are left in obscurity.

[109] Lipsius 385ff.; Busolt-Swoboda 1011-1012. Aristotle says nothing of this procedure, though it must have been in effect in the fourth century.

But the guardians are not only supervisors of the other officers, and a legislative commission for supplementing and revising the laws; they are also high officers on their own account and have special areas of administration. They are in charge of foreign trade, determining what products may be exported and imported (847cd), as Solon had regulated exports in his day.[110] They have rather intimate supervision over the actions of private citizens. Aristotle mentions νομοφυλακία as one of the functions of government peculiar to states that have more leisure and prosperity and take an interest in public decorum (εὐκοσμία).[111] This conception of νομοφυλακία is evident at many points in Plato's law. The guardians may fine a man for improper expenditure on a wedding feast or a funeral (775b, 959d). They are to know the citizens well enough to decide who shall be required to take part in the election of officers of musical contests (765a). It is they who determine whether a man's character and achievements justify giving him "freedom of song" (παρρησία ἐν Μούσαις), i.e., the right to sing at a public festival without prior approval of his composition (829d). And they alone have authority to grant permission for travel abroad, except on a public mission; and such permission they will grant only to a man who is held in high esteem for his civic and military qualities, and will serve as a kind of model (δεῖγμα) for exhibition to other cities (951a-d).

Other duties laid upon them are similar to those of the archons at Athens. The frequent references to their supervision of festivals and contests (772a, 828bc, 835a) recall the responsibilities of the Athenian king. Likewise their authority to bring suits before the courts (910c,e, 929e) is similar to the function of the six Athenian thesmothetae. But the most striking example is their responsibility in the sphere of family law, which at Athens was under the special supervision of the archon. Plato's guardians have the care of orphans (a point on which Attic law also was particularly insistent); they appoint guardians if no provision has been made in the parent's will (924bc), and lay down rules for the exercise of the trust (926e, 928a). They supervise accession to lots; this will involve the filling of a lot when its owner has died without heirs (877d), and enforcing the rules regarding the marriage of heiresses (926b-d). They hear charges of neglect or mistreatment of parents (932ab); they form a kind of court of domestic relations (784bc, 929e); they are guardians of fam-

---

[110] Plut. *Solon* 24.   [111] *Pol.* 1322b 38.

ily property, through the registers in their care (754d; cf. 855b); and they are especially concerned with maintaining modesty and propriety at funerals, one of the guardians being appointed by the relatives of a dead man to supervise the arrangements (959e). Most of these matters were the responsibility of the archon at Athens.[112] To them must be added other responsibilities based on legislation peculiar to Plato's state, such as the enforcement of the law limiting property (754de) and of the law banishing the child of mixed slave and free parentage (930e). All these closely touch the integrity of the family on which Plato's state is built; and it is probably the guardians who are expected to devise and apply procedures for maintaining the number of households unaltered (740d).

But Plato's guardians, unlike the archons at Athens, always act as a board—sometimes as a full board of thirty-seven members, sometimes in groups of three, five, ten, twelve, or fifteen members.[113] Even in the rare cases in which a guardian acts alone—as in making arrangements for a funeral—the penalty for disobedience is determined by the board. "He that disobeys one of the nomophylakes shall be penalized by them all with a penalty that they all have decided upon in common" (960ab). Thus Plato emphatically applies to his highest officers the principle of collegiality generally implied for all the other officers. This seems to have been a peculiarly Athenian principle; and Plato goes even further than Athens by making the archons (or their equivalent in his state) subject to it.

Finally, the guardians have important judicial functions. We have already seen that they constitute a court for the trial of a man alleged to have more than the amount of property registered (754e), a case that would come peculiarly under their jurisdiction because of their responsibility for the family and property. Again they are mentioned as a court for the trial of a litigant who has resisted a court judgment against him (958c), and together with the "select judges" they constitute a court for the trial of all cases involving the death penalty (855c). They are also the court before which charges against a select judge are tried (767e); and likewise they form a part of the high court set up to try charges against a euthynos (948a). These judicial

[112] Arist. *Const. Ath.* LVI, 6-7; Ps. Dem. XLIII, 75; cf. Lipsius 58ff.
[113] The three eldest (914d, 932b); the five youngest (916c); ten (784b, 929e); twelve (867e); the twelve junior to the five eldest (847c); fifteen (926c); the eldest (οἱ πρεσβύτατοι, 929e). The ten eldest are also ipso facto members of the Nocturnal Council (951d, 961a), but here they do not constitute a board.

functions will be discussed more fully later in connection with the administration of justice.

Officers as important as these should obviously be selected with the utmost care (752e), especially at the very beginning of the colony; yet Plato sees that this is just the time when a wise choice will be most difficult, since the citizens will not know each other well, and will not themselves have been trained as yet in the laws and in the discrimination of persons competent to administer them (751b-d). But what follows in Plato's text is at first sight most puzzling. After emphasizing the difficulties involved in starting the government of a new state, and the particular importance of the choice of the first magistrates, the Athenian Stranger suggests that the Cnossians come to the aid of the new colony by selecting these first officers— eighteen from themselves, and nineteen from the members of the new colony (752e). No further details are given as to the manner of their selection, but it is clear that they are to be regular officers of the new state, since the Cnossian members are to be a "gift" of the mother city to the daughter state (753a). Then, the Athenian Stranger proceeds, as time passes and the new constitution has become established, "their election is to be as follows," and a procedure is described in considerable detail for the election of thirty-seven nomophylakes (753b-d). In spite of the sentence that introduces this description, it is obvious that the election described is the *first* election, for only at the beginning will it be necessary to select the whole body of guardians at once; since each guardian holds office until he dies or reaches the age of seventy, later elections will be concerned only with filling vacancies in the group.

The puzzles in the text continue. The account of this election is immediately followed by a query which is unnecessary in the light of what has preceded: Who in our city is to preside over this election and conduct the scrutiny of the successful candidates (753e)? Then follows a discussion of the difficulties involved in first setting up a government—material which duplicates a similar discussion two pages earlier—concluding with the proposal that for the first election the Cnossians select one hundred of their citizens and an equal number from the colonists to act as a supervisory board and conduct the scrutiny (754c). Unlike the eighteen Cnossians mentioned earlier, the Cnossians who serve on this board do not become citizens of the new colony, but return home when these supervisory duties are ended. Thus we have in Plato's text not merely two discussions of the difficulty of getting started aright, but also two different proposals for aid from the Cnossians, and two different ways of choosing the first guardians.

This indicates clearly that we have two versions of Plato's thought.[114] The conclusion to which a comparison of the two texts leads us is that the earlier (in time) of these two versions contains the scheme of election that is described in detail and followed by the suggestion that a mixed advisory board of Cnossians and colonists supervise the election and conduct the scrutiny of the successful candidates.[115] The other version—which is most naturally explained as the result of further thought—discusses first and most fully the difficulty of assuring a wise selection at the start, and ends with the suggestion that the Cnossians themselves select these first officers by choosing eighteen of their own best citizens and selecting nineteen others from the new colonists. It seems that the earlier draft was not discarded, but was retained in the text just after the version which was intended to displace it—either by Plato himself, or by Philippus of Opus, who would naturally be reluctant to discard it, if he found it in situ, or among Plato's other papers. Whoever is responsible for the present text introduced this displaced version with an ill-advised sentence of transition (753b 1-4), evidently overlooking the fact (which most later readers also have overlooked) that the election described cannot be the later procedure, as this sentence promises, but must be the first election.

But neither of the versions deals explicitly with the procedure to be followed in normal elections to this office. These will obviously occur only when a member of the group of guardians has died or reached the age of seventy, and will be concerned with the selection of a single guardian, or, if such elections are held only once a year, with the filling of whatever positions have become vacant since the previous election. There is a provision elsewhere in the *Laws* covering the replacement of a guardian found guilty of malfeasance in office,

---

[114] On these two versions, see Excursus D, below.

[115] This would not have seemed a strange procedure to Plato's fellow Athenians. An inscription of about 450 relative to the establishment of a new regime at Erythrae, an important Ionian member of the Athenian League (Tod 1, No. 29) provides that the first βουλή of the new regime is to be installed by Athenian ἐπίσκοποι. On these officers see Busolt-Swoboda 1355.

but its import is ambiguous; in such cases, Plato says, "the government of the city" (τὸ κοινὸν τῆς πόλεως) shall select (καθιστάτω) another nomophylax in his place (928d).[116] This might mean election by the assembly, election by the council, or possibly even election by the remaining guardians. There are good reasons, however, for thinking that the first of the three is Plato's intention. Almost all other offices in the state are filled by election in the full assembly; Plato had actually proposed such a method in his earlier version for the *first* election of these officers, and one of the difficulties in carrying out the first election properly, Plato says in his later version, is that the citizens will not know each other well (751d), which implies that he still expects them normally to do the choosing. Let us then examine the election prescribed in this earlier version as being essentially what Plato intends to be the procedure in later elections.

All who are members of the armed forces, whether foot soldiers or mounted, or who have previously served in the military forces when their age permitted, shall participate in the election of officers. The election shall be held in the city's most venerable temple. Each citizen shall deposit on the altar of the god a tablet on which he has written the name of his candidate, with patronymic, tribe, and deme, and beside it his own name made out in the same fashion. It shall be permitted to anyone who objects to one of the names proposed to remove the tablet and post it in the agora. At the end of thirty days the officials shall exhibit publicly (δεῖξαι . . . ἰδεῖν πάσῃ τῇ πόλει) the three hundred names judged to come first (τὰ τῶν πινακίων κριθέντα ἐν πρώτοις μέχρι τριακοσίων) and the citizens shall vote again in like manner, each of them for that member of this group whom he prefers. The officials shall then make public a second list of one hundred preferred candidates (τοὺς . . . ἐξ αὐτῶν προκριθέντας ἑκατόν), and the city shall vote a third time, each man voting for whomever he pleases, passing through slain victims as he casts his ballot. The thirty-seven who have received the most votes, after undergoing the scrutiny, shall be declared archons.[117]

[116] Καθιστάναι, like αἱρεῖσθαι, is generally used to denote the filling of an office, as the passage on the κατάστασις ἀρχῶν (751-768) shows. It may therefore be used in connection with any method of selection; but in 756a, 764c, 766a,c,d the context shows that the procedure indicated involves voting. And in 948e voting is specifically mentioned in connection with it. See Excursus C, below.

[117] (753b-d). For the translation of μὴ ἔλαττον τριάκοντα ἡμερῶν (c7) see above, Note 10. Κρίναντες (d6) = δοκιμάσαντες; cf. δοκιμασθέντων καθάπερ οἱ νομοφύλακες (755d 6) and κρίσιν (755e 4). See below, Note 148. The subject of δεῖξαι (d3) and ἀποφηνάντων (d6) is understood from τοὺς ἄρχοντας (c8). Ὁ βουληθείς (d4) cannot mean "anyone who pleases [i.e. to vote]" (Jowett); that would be

It is obvious that with a slight modification in the last day's proceedings this method of election could be used at any later time, whatever the number of vacancies to be filled. The election procedure resembles that prescribed for the election of the council in providing for the selection of a slate of candidates by free and open nomination by the citizenry. Plato does not indicate how a challenged nomination is to be disposed of, whether by the officials in charge of the election, or by the assembly when it reconvenes after the thirty-day interval. The latter seems the more probable, since it gives point to the provision for publicizing the challenge. Nor does Plato indicate how the slate of three hundred names is to be selected from the total nominations presented, nor again how the later list of a hundred is to be made up. Of these one hundred candidates it is clearly said, however, that the thirty-seven receiving the most votes are to be declared elected; and this suggests that at every stage the selection is based on the number of votes cast for the various nominees. (The ambiguous ἐν πρώτοις in c8 may then be taken as "first in number of votes received," and thus as confirming this interpretation.) But Plato does not clearly say this, as he does in another similar case (the election of the euthynoi, 946a), and knowing the critical importance he attaches to the election of these important officers, we cannot be sure he does not intend that the supervisors of the election shall use their

---

inconsistent with Plato's requirement of compulsory voting (see above, Note 8), and besides, ὁ βουλόμενος would be the natural way of expressing this meaning. I think βουληθείς should be taken merely as strengthening the idea of reflective decision involved in the immediately following ὃν ἂν βούληται. Plato says that any citizen may challenge any nominating tablet ὅτιπερ ἂν φαίνηται μὴ κατὰ νοῦν αὐτῷ γεγραμμένον, but it is difficult to ascertain the precise meaning of this clause. Robin, Bury, Cassarà, and Jowett seem to think the objection is limited to matters of form (e.g. Bury: "any tablet which seems to him to have been improperly written"). But there is probably more than this intended, for an improperly executed tablet would be ipso facto invalidated. Des Places ("si quelqu'un ne trouve pas à son gré le nom inscrit") seems nearer the meaning. Remembering that νοῦς is for Plato the highest expression of reason in man, I am inclined to think that the idiom κατὰ νοῦν carries a hint of Plato's special meaning here, and thus implies that the objection should be based on principle, not on mere personal feeling or dislike. But this could be claimed for his objection by any challenger; hence it may be just as well to skirt the difficulty, as do other translators.

It is noticeable that the nomophylakes are referred to in this passage merely as ἄρχοντες. Indeed, except for νομοφύλακες in 752e, which occurs in the passage written later to replace the one we are examining, the first of the numerous uses of this term in the *Laws* appears in 754e. (Νομοφύλακες in 671d does not refer to state officials, but to the "rulers" of the symposia whose "laws" are under discussion at this point.) This is another indication that the present version is the earlier one, written perhaps before Plato had decided upon a name for these high officials.

judgment in making up these lists. For later elections the officials in charge will be the prytanies of the council, acting under the supervision of the guardians, not the ad hoc commission of Cnossians and colonists suggested in this discarded version (754c). If they conduct the scrutiny of the elected officers, as is suggested below, they will have an opportunity at this stage to exclude any persons clearly unfit for the office.

Considering the importance of these officers, one finds it surprising that Plato does not formulate any conditions of eligibility other than age. At the beginning of his description of the constitution he uses the distinction between the warp and the woof to illustrate the difference there must be between the officers and the citizens in the social fabric; the former must have a certain firmness of character to give body to the pliable reasonableness of the others (734e). Still earlier in the *Laws* he attributes the failure of the promising constitutions of Argos and Messene to the moral failure of those in power, an incapacity to desire and pursue the ends that reason declares to be proper, which in true Socratic fashion he calls "ignorance" (ἀμαθία, ἄνοια), and that of the gravest sort (688e); and no citizen in whom such a defect resides shall ever be entrusted with office, no matter how clever he may be (689cd). At the very end of the *Laws* Plato reverts to this theme, declaring that the guardians of our state must have a genuine superiority in virtue to their fellow citizens, a superiority that is firmly grounded in a prolonged study of things divine (964d-968a). These are evidences that he has not abandoned the idea that philosophical virtue alone fits a man for authority in a state; his problem is how to make this principle effective in the familiar institutions of the city-state which are his materials. For the moment he apparently provides no means for determining a man's moral fitness for office other than the judgment of his well-trained fellow citizens. "Those who rightly enter public office must have undergone an adequate testing—both themselves and their families—from childhood until the time of their election; and likewise those who are to be the electors must have been brought up and educated in lawful habits, so as to be able to accept or reject rightly those who deserve their favor or their dislike" (751cd). The burden obviously rests upon the scheme of education to be prescribed. If this produces the results Plato expects of it, a man who has reached the age of fifty will have shown whether or not he possesses the superior qualities that public office requires, and the electors will be able and willing to select those who manifest these qualities.

We have seen that Plato's guardians—with their long tenure of office and their panoply of legislative, executive, and judicial powers —have no counterpart in the Athens of his time. But it would be an error to look upon them as his political invention. For both Aristotle and Xenophon refer to the existence of such officers in certain well-governed states; and now that we have surveyed their functions in the *Laws*, what Aristotle and Xenophon say about the duties of these officers elsewhere will sound familiar. Critobulus, in Xenophon's *Economics*,[118] instructing his young wife in her responsibilities, tells her that in well-governed states the citizens do not think it enough to enact good laws; they go further and elect nomophylakes to act as overseers (ἐπισκοποῦντες), to praise him who observes the laws and punish anyone who acts contrary to them. "I bade her to consider herself the nomophylax in the house, to inspect the household equipment whenever she thought proper, as a commander inspects the persons of his watch, and signify her approval (δοκιμάζειν) if everything was in good condition, as the council approves the horses and cavalrymen, and like a queen to praise and reward the deserving, according to our means, and to rebuke and disgrace anyone who merited such treatment." Xenophon's military mind no doubt exaggerated the degree of order and supervision in even the best-governed cities of his time, just as Critobulus seeks an impossible degree of discipline in his household; nevertheless this passage shows that Xenophon knew of cities in which there were officers comparable to the nomophylakes that Plato describes. Aristotle's less imaginative references give us more precise information about such officers and their duties. There are three such references in the *Politics* and they tell us (1) that in some states there were officials called πρόβουλοι or νομοφύλακες who prepared προβουλεύματα for the deliberative body,[119] (2) that νομοφυλακία was a concern in states that had more leisure and prosperity and paid attention to public decorum,[120] and (3) that elections to the highest magistracies were sometimes supervised by νομοφύλακες, sometimes by πρόβουλοι, and sometimes

[118] Xen. *Econ.* IX, 14-15.   [119] *Pol.* 1298b 27ff.
[120] *Pol.* 1322b 38ff.

by the βουλή, the former method being aristocratic, the second oligarchic, and the third democratic.[121]

Unfortunately neither Xenophon nor Aristotle names the cities that had such officials; but one thinks immediately of the Spartan ephors, whose title (ἔφοροι, overseers) suggests the ἐπίσκοποι and the ἐπισκοποῦντες of Plato's and Xenophon's texts, and whose functions, as Xenophon describes them elsewhere,[122] include these that he ascribes to nomophylakes in the *Economics*. But Xenophon may have been thinking of the θεσμοφύλακες at Elis, in whose territory he was probably living when he wrote the *Economics*. The word θεσμός is the older term for νόμος, and the officers mentioned may have existed at Elis since its unification shortly after the Persian Wars.[123] They were certainly in existence in the later part of the fifth century, for in Thucydides' account of the treaty arranged in 420 between Athens, Argos, Mantinea, and Elis they are designated (in the official text of the treaty, which Thucydides evidently copies verbatim) to administer the oath to the other officials at Elis.[124] In this same document the officials at Mantinea who administer the oath are called θεωροί, another title suggesting duties of supervision and inspection. Again we hear of νομοδεῖκται ("expounders of the laws") in Arcadian Andania and of θεσμοφύλακες at Thespiae in Boeotia[125]—for the third century at least; and in these relatively unchanging parts of Greece we can assume that the offices, as the titles imply, are much older. Finally, nomophylakes are mentioned in inscriptions—some from the fourth century, more from the third and later centuries—from such widely separated cities as Abdera, Ceos, Corcyra, Mylasa Demetrias, Sparta, and Chalcedon.[126] Even if we assume that officials charged with "guarding the laws" were more numerous in Hellenistic times, nevertheless the diversity of the areas in which they are attested, the fact of their existence in some particularly conservative states in the fifth and fourth centuries, and the antiquity of the titles sometimes used to designate them suggest that the office is an ancient feature of Greek community life, in partial eclipse during the ascendancy of Athenian democracy, but destined

[121] *Pol.* 1323a 6ff.
[122] *Const. Lac.* VIII.
[123] Gilbert II, 102 and notes.
[124] Thuc. v, 47, 9.
[125] Gilbert II, 338.
[126] For references to the sources see Gilbert II, 102, 338; Busolt-Swoboda 490 n. 3. Francotte (*op.cit.* 1910, 26f.) adds Locris and Pergamum, though no references are given.

to be revived and made important in the centuries immediately after Plato.[127] The position and responsibilities of these officers, like their titles, must have been exceedingly varied; but guarding the texts of laws and decrees must have been one of their duties in the fourth century, perhaps the only one left to them in states of a democratic character. Hence the fourth-century inscriptions from Ceos and Priene, in which the nomophylakes appear as little more than clerks with a short tenure of office, are likely, when taken alone, to give us a wrong impression; the original substantive nature of the office is shown in the less progressive states, such as Sparta, Elis, and Mantinea.

But the archetype of Plato's board of guardians lay much nearer home than Elis or Sparta. For the Athenians of the fourth century remembered that they also had once had guardians of the laws—in the council of the Areopagus, as it existed in the days before Ephialtes. "He assigned the council of the Areopagus," says Aristotle, speaking of Solon, "to the duty of guarding the laws ($\epsilon\pi\grave{\iota}\ \tau\grave{o}\ \nu o\mu o$- $\phi\upsilon\lambda\alpha\kappa\epsilon\hat{\iota}\nu$), acting as before as the supervisor ($\epsilon\pi\acute{\iota}\sigma\kappa o\pi o\varsigma$) of the constitution." Ephialtes, Aristotle says later, stripped it of the powers which made it the guard ($\phi\upsilon\lambda\alpha\kappa\acute{\eta}$) of the constitution, assigning some of them to the council of five hundred and others to the demos and the popular courts.[128] Thus it is very likely that the Areopagus of pre-Periclean days was the inspiration and archetype of Plato's guardians.[129] Being made up of ex-archons who held office for life, it was a continuing body, like Plato's guardians, whose personnel changed very slowly as compared to the democratic council and the ordinary boards of magistrates. The average age of its members would be relatively high; it was a body of elders, as Plato's guardians would be.[130]

[127] Cicero (*De Leg.* III, 46) commends "the Greeks" for setting up officers called $\nu o\mu o\phi\acute{\upsilon}\lambda\alpha\kappa\epsilon\varsigma$, who not only guarded the text of the laws, but observed men's acts and recalled them to obedience.

[128] *Const. Ath.* VIII, 4; cf. Plut. *Solon* 19, 2. For the Areopagus before Solon's time, see *Const. Ath.* III, 6; and for the reference to Ephialtes, xxv, 2.

[129] As has been suggested by A. H. Chase, "The Influence of Athenian Institutions upon the *Laws* of Plato," *Harv. Stud. in Class. Phil.* XLIV, 1933, 135.

[130] Why are Plato's guardians to be thirty-seven in number? No reason is suggested in the *Laws*, so far as I can discover. That the precise number probably has no special significance is clear from a comparison of the *Laws* with *Ep. VIII* 356d, where Plato includes a board of *thirty-five* nomophylakes in the constitution he recommends to his friends in Syracuse. The gerousia at Sparta consisted of thirty members. We can only guess at the size of the Areopagus. S. B. Smith (TAPA LVI, 1925, 114n.) thinks its membership numbered near two hundred—i.e. nine ex-archons added yearly for a life expectancy of twenty years. But we do not know

But of more importance for understanding Plato's motives is the admiration universally felt in the fourth century for the way in which the Areopagus discharged its functions as a court,[131] and the persistent desire—especially among those who advocated a return to the ancestral constitution—to restore to it some of the other functions that it had once exercised. This seems to have been a part of the program of Theramenes in 411;[132] and after the overthrow of the Thirty in 403 the chastened democracy itself, in making provision for a codification of the laws, also decreed that the Areopagus should be charged with supervising them, to see that the magistrates followed the laws that had been ratified.[133] This may have been, as Hignett maintains, a provisional measure that was abrogated when conditions became normal;[134] nevertheless it indicates a vivid memory of the older powers of the Areopagus and at least a temporary willingness to have them restored. There is an expression of these sentiments in the encomium of the Areopagus that Xenophon attributes to Socrates in reply to a complaint about the degeneration of the Athenians.[135] "Do you know of any persons," he asks, "who give judgment and conduct all their other business with more dignity and honor, or with a more exact conformity to justice and the laws? We should not therefore despair, as if we thought the Athenians were without a love of order." One of Isocrates' most earnest discourses of advice to the Athenian people takes its central theme and its title from the role the Areopagus played in earlier days.[136] Aristotle's opinion of the Areopagus can be inferred from his association of νομοφυλακία with aristocratic constitutions.[137] Plato never mentions the Areopagus by name in any dialogue known to be genuine, but for his opinion of it we need only recall his admiration of Solon's mixed constitution,

---

that all nine archons were eligible for admission, and some of those eligible must have been excluded at their εὔθυνα (see Dem. XXII, *Hyp.* II, 2-3). There were probably other grounds for rejection (Athen. 566f) and Dem. LIV, 25 contains an account of an expulsion from the Areopagus.

[131] Cf. Lyc. I, 12; Xen. *Mem.* III, V, 20.
[132] Arist. *Const. Ath.* XXXV, 2 (cf. XXV, 1-2); Wilamowitz, *Arist. und Athen.* I, 68 n. 38; Jaeger, *Harv. Stud. in Class. Phil. Suppl.* I, 443; Fuks, *The Ancestral Constitution,* 22.
[133] This was the famous Decree of Tisamenus, cited in Andoc. I, 83-84. Despite the doubts of Francotte (*op.cit.* 15), this decree is now generally taken as authentic.
[134] Hignett 200, 300-301.   [135] *Mem.* III, V, 20.
[136] The *Areopagiticus,* written shortly after 355. For Demosthenes' attitude, see Din. I, 62.
[137] See Note 121 above.

in which the Areopagus was an important element, as he thought.[138]

Thus we can say with some certainty that the Areopagus of Solon's day is the model of Plato's board of guardians. But this still leaves us in the dark on many points. For there seems to have been much uncertainty among the ancients, and there certainly is no agreement among modern scholars, as to what was involved in the function of "guarding the laws" which Solon assigned to the Areopagus. Hignett thinks it was primarily the right to supervise the magistrates and see that they kept their oath to act in accordance with the laws, and the right to prosecute conspirators against the state.[139] It may have included, as Wade-Gery has asserted, a virtual right of vetoing actions of the assembly and the democratic council.[140] This is a right one would expect the nomophylakes in Plato's state to have, but Plato nowhere explicitly gives it to them; and we do not even know whether he believed it to have been a prerogative of the sixth-century Areopagus. Aristotle does not say as much, but only that "it supervised ($\delta\iota\epsilon\tau\dot{\eta}\rho\epsilon\iota$) the majority and the most important affairs of state."[141] He adds that it had the power to fine or punish without appeal ($\kappa\upsilon\rho\dot{\iota}\alpha$) offenders against the law ($\tau o\dot{\upsilon}\varsigma$ $\dot{\alpha}\mu\alpha\rho\tau\dot{\alpha}\nu o\nu\tau\alpha\varsigma$). This is a function that the nomophylakes in Plato's state do not have, except for the summary fines that are within the competence of any magistrate to impose.[142] Even the jurisdiction over premediated homicide

---

[138] There is some evidence that the Areopagus in the fourth century occasionally exerted considerable political influence. After Chaeronea it brought about the election of Phocion as general in place of Charidemus, who had been put forward by a clamorous group in the assembly (Plut. *Phoc.* 16); in another case it took cognizance of an accusation of treason and imposed the death penalty upon a certain Antiphon who had previously been acquitted by the assembly (Dem. XVIII, 133-134; Plut. *Dem.* 14; Din. I, 62-63); on another occasion it ordered the arrest and execution of certain citizens who had fled the city and thus endangered its defense (Lyc. I, 52; Aesch. III, 252). Perhaps it is these actions that account for the explicit mention of the Areopagus in the recently discovered inscription recording a law against tyranny in 337-6. The law, obviously intended to prevent "collaboration," prescribes that no official of the government shall continue to perform his functions in case the democracy is overthrown; and in particular, if any members of the council of the Areopagus "go up to the Areopagus or deliberate about anything," they shall be punished with atimia and confiscation of their property (Benjamin Meritt, in *Hesperia* XXI, 1952, 355-359). A similar law passed against tyranny in 410, and using language similar to that of this later law, contents itself with a general prohibition of the exercise of official powers (Andoc. I, 95-98). The explicit mention of the Areopagus in the later inscription is graphic evidence of the increased importance of this body in the late fourth century, and also of a certain feeling of distrust that it continued to arouse among ardent democrats.

[139] Hignett 91.

[140] CQ XXVII, 1933, 24 n. 3.

[141] *Const. Ath.* VIII, 4.

[142] See Note 103 above.

and treason which the Areopagus continued to exercise in the fourth century Plato entrusts not to his nomophylakes, but to a new court for capital offenses.[143] This shows that, however much Plato admired the Areopagus, his board of guardians is no mere duplicate of that ancient council. Besides withholding from them powers believed to have been exercised by the historic Areopagus, he assigns them other duties, some performed at Athens by the archons, others by legislative commissions. Plato's board of guardians is a new creation, involving a new grouping of political functions. But the inspiration of this creation was undoubtedly that ancient council that had guided Athens through her most glorious days and assured the victories of Marathon and Salamis, and whose judicial and moral prestige continued to be great throughout the fourth century.

How would these high officers be designated in Plato's state? Any reference to the Areopagus in their title would of course be inappropriate; the Areopagus was an Athenian hill. Plato had used the term φύλακες (guardians) to designate the highest officers in the state described in the *Republic*, and even called them "guardians of the laws" (421a, 484b,d, 504c), though the compound word does not occur in the *Republic*. The use of this compound in the *Laws* was but an adaptation of his earlier terminology, and also served as a reminder of the powers once exercised so beneficently, as many of Plato's contemporaries thought, by the Athenian Areopagus. But there is still another reason for this choice, a reason that comes to light at the end of Aristotle's discussion of the question whether it is better that good men or laws should be sovereign. "If it is better that certain men should rule, they should be appointed νομοφύλακες and servants of the laws."[144] This title expresses the twin conditions of political health, as both Plato and Aristotle saw them: government by superior men, but under the rule of law.

The fact that there were actually officials in Plato's time bearing this title, and that the function it implies was believed to have been a part of the ancestral constitution, made Plato's choice historically influential. Nomophylakes were in fact established at Athens within a generation after Plato's death—fewer in number indeed, but vested with powers and a dignity comparable to those of Plato's officials— as part of the reorganization of the government after Chaeronea, and

143 See Chapter VI, The Courts.
144 *Pol.* 1287a 21f.

perhaps under the leadership of Plato's former pupil, Lycurgus;[145] and they were re-established a decade later in the constitution drawn up by Aristotle's pupil, Demetrius of Phalerum.[146] After this time such officials, with coercive powers, are frequently mentioned in inscriptions from various parts of the Greek world.[147]

THE SCRUTINY AND THE AUDIT

Every official in Plato's state is required to undergo two public examinations, a δοκιμασία (scrutiny) immediately after his election and before he takes office, and a εὔθυνα (audit) at the end of his term.[148] The first, as its name implies, is a "testing" of his fitness for official duties; the second, a review of his conduct in office, is for the purpose of "correcting" (εὐθύνειν)—through fines or other penalties— any error or injustice of which he may be found guilty. Both of these are familiar institutions of Greek public law which Plato takes over, though with considerable modifications in the case of the audit. We shall proceed first to the scrutiny.

Only in rare instances does Plato's text give us any information about the particular kind of examination the δοκιμασία is to be, or about the officers who are to conduct it. This silence about the details of a procedure everywhere required shows that Plato intends to adopt with little or no change an institution already familiar to his readers. The requirement of dokimasia at Athens was sometimes attributed

[145] They are referred to (in the passage of Harpocration mentioned in Note 99) in two speeches of Dinarchus, one of them delivered certainly before 322. Lycurgus' public career began shortly after Chaeronea and lasted until his death in 324. See Durrbach's introduction to the Budé edition of Lycurgus, xvii, xxiiff. Distrust of the Areopagus among the ardent democrats (see Note 138 above) must have been the reason why the "reformers" created a new office instead of restoring this ancient function to the Areopagus.

[146] As Demetrius set them up the nomophylakes were seven in number; and the fragment of Philochorus mentioned above (Note 99) informs us that they compelled the magistrates to observe the laws, sitting with the presiding officers at meetings of the assembly and the council to prevent action detrimental to the city.

[147] See Cary, JHS XLVIII, 1928, 232.

[148] The δοκιμασία is prescribed for each of the officers mentioned in the account of the constitution in Book VI: for the guardians (753d,e), the generals and other military officers (755de), the council (756e), religious officers (759cd, 760a), the astynomoi and agoranomoi (763e), the supervisors of music and gymnastics (765bc), the director of education (766b), and the select judges (767d). The δοκιμασία is not mentioned at the election of the euthynoi in Book XII, but it seems to be implied in the κεκρίσθαι and κρίσις of 947e. (Κρίνειν and its derivatives are used of the δοκιμασία in 753d and 755e.) As for the εὔθυνα, 946cd states clearly that it is to be required of "all the officers."

by the orators to Solon;[149] but this may mean only that it was a practice of long standing. It is attested for the middle of the fifth century, and the law concerning it seems to have been revised at the
restoration of the democracy in 403. For the fourth century our information is abundant and clear.[150] Aristotle tells us that the scrutiny
of the nine archons and of members of the boule was conducted by
the outgoing boule, though an appeal to the dicastery was permitted
if the vote was adverse; formerly, he says, such an appeal was not
permitted, the vote of the boule being final. The dokimasia of all
other officers was conducted by the dicastery.[151] Its purpose was to
determine whether the candidate was fitted ($\epsilon\pi\iota\tau\eta\delta\epsilon\iota\sigma$) for the
office—which meant primarily whether he was a citizen, and in good
standing, i.e. not under atimia (loss of civic rights) for any cause.
At the scrutiny of the archons, Aristotle says, the questions asked
were whether the candidate was a citizen descended from citizen
parents and grandparents on both sides, and to what demes they
belonged; whether he had a shrine to Apollo Patroös and to Zeus
Herkeios; whether he maintained family shrines and a family burial
place; whether he had honored his parents, paid his taxes, and performed his military service. (Failures in these respects were the usual
causes of atimia at Athens.) Similar questions, we may presume, were
asked of candidates for other offices.[152] The answers of the candidate
had to be supported by witnesses. Then the presiding officer asked,
"Does anybody wish to bring a charge against this man?" Each member of the boule had not only the right but also the duty to speak,
if he knew of anything which in his opinion disqualified the candidate.[153] An accusation could bear upon any of the points previously
inquired into but it was not restricted to them; the dokimasia
orations of Lysias show that a man's whole life—private as well as

---

149 E.g. Dem. xx, 90.
150 For the fifth century, see Tod I. No. 29; for the fourth century, Arist. *Const.
Ath.* xlv, 3; lv, 2; Aesch. iii, 14-15. See also the introduction to the orations of
Lysias by Gernet and Bizos, Budé edn., ii, 3ff., 126ff., 131n.; Lipsius 271-276; Busolt-
Swoboda 1072-1073; and Kahrstedt *op.cit.* (Note 63), 59-63.
151 The members of the Areopagus constituted a special class; strictly speaking
they were not subject to dokimasia, yet in reality each candidate, having filled the
archonship, had passed both the dokimasia and the euthyna connected with that
office, and had furthermore to be approved by the council of the Areopagus before
being admitted. Dem. xxii, *Hyp.* ii, 3; Hyperides apud Athen. 566f.
152 Din. ii, 17-18; Xen. *Mem.* ii, ii, 13.
153 Lys. xxxi, 1-2.

public—was subject to examination.[154] It is surprising that no question was asked concerning other formal qualifications that we know were in force, such as age and property class; no doubt these were taken care of earlier, at some stage of the πρόκρισις which preceded the selection by lot.[155] It is significant also that no question was asked about the man's special qualifications for the office concerned; evidently the matter of chief importance was his moral and civic character.

On the four occasions on which Plato gives details of the tests to be applied at the dokimasia, what he says indicates an intention to use this procedure to establish also the special competence of the individuals for the office concerned. Thus at the selection of priests the dokimasia is to determine whether the person selected by lot is sound in body, of legitimate birth, and free of religious pollution and from families "as pure as possible" (759c). These requirements are closely parallel to those of Attic law—which in this case also showed its concern for special qualifications—but they carry an implication that something more than ritual cleanliness is required. Again at the dokimasia of officers of music, the main point to be determined (Plato actually says it is the only point, but this may be a dramatic exaggeration in the context) is whether the candidate is "experienced" (ἔμπειρος, 765b). The dokimasia of select judges is by implication equally emphatic; since the purpose of the election that precedes is to choose that magistrate in each of the offices who has the best reputation for justice and integrity, the dokimasia could hardly avoid concerning itself with the candidate's qualifications for the office. Since the dokimasia is conducted by the body that has just elected, Plato's law really provides for a preliminary choice, followed by collective deliberation on the qualifications of the candidates.[156] Like-

---

[154] Lys. XVI, 9; cf. XVI, 3ff. and XXXI passim. Thus it was charged against Mantitheos, a candidate for the council, that he had served in the cavalry during the rule of the Thirty; and against a certain Philo that he had not taken sides in the party strife but had fled to Oropos, where he had enriched himself by preying on the unfortunate victims of the disorder, and had besides been a bad son to his aged mother. Cf. also Lys. XIII, 10.

[155] Kahrstedt, *op.cit.* 55, 61. The point made in the text is not affected by our acceptance or rejection of Kahrstedt's view of the nature of πρόκρισις in Attic law. See Excursus C, below.

[156] It might be asked why a dokimasia would be necessary in this case, since each of the persons elected will already be an officer and will have passed a dokimasia before entering upon his present office. But one of the persons elected may have done something during his term of office which was known perhaps only to one or two of the electing body, and which would disqualify him, or suggest that

wise at the dokimasia of the director of education (766b), which is conducted by essentially the same body as that which has just elected him, his special fitness over all others could hardly be neglected.

Except for two of the offices just mentioned—those of educator and select judge—Plato does not say what body is to conduct the scrutiny. It may be assumed that he would not put this function in the hands of the popular courts, as at Athens. This is a priori plausible, and will become more so when we see that Plato takes the audit from the popular courts, where it resided at Athens, and entrusts it to a special body of selected officers. Of the religious officials it is said that the scrutiny shall be conducted "as for the generals" (760a); and of the generals that it is to be conducted "as for the guardians" (755d). Who conducts the scrutiny of the guardians? This is the question, it will be recalled, that gives Plato pause at the end of his first version of their election, and he suggests that the sponsoring cities—Cnossos and its associates—send a commission to oversee the elections and conduct the scrutiny (754c). In his later version, which prescribes that the guardians are to be selected by the Cnossians partly from their own citizens and partly from the colonists, no mention is made of a scrutiny (752e), but it would probably be conducted by the Cnossians. Nothing is said anywhere as to how the scrutiny is to be conducted at later elections after the state gets under way; but the earlier procedure at Athens may throw some light on Plato's intentions. Aristotle's text shows that the council's authority in this process was formerly much greater than it was in his day, and that before the reforms of Solon the Areopagus possessed unrestricted authority to examine candidates for office.[157] It seems likely then that Plato would entrust this function either to his council or, more probably, to the guardians, who would conduct the scrutiny of all other officers and of their own successors elected from time to time. The latter procedure would accord well with the spirit of his constitution

---

he was not the best person in his group for the new office. The second dokimasia would, then, be analogous to the euthyna which at Athens was required of a citizen before he could fill another office. Even apart from this, reflection shows that a second consideration would be appropriate. At the first voting each elector is voting *for* candidates of his own choosing, with no knowledge of the candidates to be proposed by others. The second session will give him a chance to bring in evidence *against* a person elected, perhaps by a majority which is not cognizant of facts that a minority of the electors may have against him. Thus the second session will not be a useless duplicate of the first.

[157] *Const. Ath.* III, 6; XLV, 1-2; LV, 1-2.

and with the admiration felt by many of his contemporaries (and certainly by Plato himself) for the ancestral constitution.

The εὔθυνα was another check upon official integrity provided in the public law of Athens which Plato adopts—nay, emphasizes—in his state. At Athens in the fourth century all officers without exception were ὑπεύθυνοι—which meant, for the annually elected officials, that they were required to pass the euthyna before being acquitted of their responsibilities; and something similar seems to have been provided for in all Greek states, except the most extreme oligarchies.[158] The euthyna was a feature even of the Spartan and Cretan constitutions,[159] though the members of the gerousia in neither case were subject to it (a defect in their constitutions, Aristotle thinks), and the kings at Sparta, as well as the holders of lifelong offices elsewhere, seem also to have been exempt. At Sparta the euthyna seems to have been conducted by the popularly elected ephors, who were themselves examined at the end of their terms by their successors. But we are otherwise almost completely in the dark as to Spartan procedure, whereas we are fortunate in being able to see with some clarity how the Athenians handled it.

The characteristic features of the euthyna as conducted at Athens in the fourth century were the elaborate procedures involved and the final competence of the popular courts. It was generally believed in this century that popular control over the euthyna was one of Solon's institutions,[160] but the elaborate procedure of the fourth century is certainly a later development.[161] As in other matters coming under the jurisdiction of the popular courts, Athenian law in Plato's time provided for a preliminary examination of the case before specially designated magistrates. Two groups of examiners were involved: λογισταί and εὔθυνοι. The former, a body of ten selected by lot in the council, had the function of examining the retiring magistrate's financial accounts, and could bring charges against him not only for embezzlement, but also for bribery or injustice; even if a magistrate passed their examination of his accounts, his case still had to be re-

---

[158] Arist. *Pol.* 1322b 8ff.; Börner in RE s.v. εὔθυνα; Busolt-Swoboda 472-473.

[159] *Pol.* 1271a 5ff., 1272a 37; Plut. *Agis* 12, 1; Kahrstedt, *Sparta und Seine Symmachie*, 157-158.

[160] Arist. *Pol.* 1281b 33; cf. 1274a 15ff.

[161] Hignett 203ff.; Bonner and Smith I, 164f. For the details of this procedure see Busolt-Swoboda 1076-1080; Lipsius 286-298; and Kahrstedt, *Untersuchungen*, 165-180.

ferred to a popular court, which alone could give him final clearance. The euthynoi were likewise a body of ten, also chosen by lot in the council, one man from each tribe. For a period of three days after a retiring magistrate's acquittal by the logistai, the euthynoi were authorized to receive charges that any citizen might wish to prefer against the officer in question; and if they received an accusation that they thought legitimate, they referred it to the proper officers for bringing it to trial. This entire procedure, both the λόγον διδόναι before the logistai, and the εὐθύνας ὑπέχειν before the euthynoi, was sometimes designated euthyna. It had to be completed within thirty days after the end of the magistrate's term, and within this period he was forbidden to leave the country or dispose of his property in any way.

The elaborateness of this procedure testifies to the importance the Athenians attached to the euthyna. In this respect Plato, too, was an Athenian; in fact he goes even beyond Athenian practice in insisting that judges, as well as magistrates, shall be held accountable (ὑπεύθυνοι) for their actions—as we shall see when we examine his provisions for the administration of justice.[162] But in the procedure of euthyna, and in the officials he designates to conduct it, his law diverges rather markedly from Athenian law. In the first place, the logistai do not appear; Plato provides only for a board of euthynoi. In this respect he seems to be adopting the simpler procedure of earlier Athenian law; for both the epigraphical evidence and the continued use of the term euthyna to denote the entire process make it likely that the procedure before the euthynoi was the earlier form, and the examination before the logistai a later stage superimposed upon it[163]—a consequence, probably, of the increased complexities of the finances of imperial Athens. In Plato's state, so he may have thought, the special circumstances that called for a separate board of accountants at Athens would not exist. He may also have been inclined to think, as do some modern critics of Athenian procedure, that it was inequitable to require an official who had once been cleared to submit himself a second time to the judgment of the courts

---

[162] Besides the euthyna in the strict sense, there are other procedures provided by Platonic law to hold officers to accountability, such as that provided for the euthynoi themselves, which will be examined below; and liability to these other procedures is part of what Plato means by calling his officials ὑπεύθυνοι.

[163] Hignett 203ff.

on the same official record—a requirement that comes close to violating the principle of *res judicata*.[164]

In the second place, Plato was more solicitous than was Athenian law regarding the qualifications of the euthynoi. The euthynos is not merely one officer among others; he is a "magistrate of magistrates" (ἄρχων ἀρχόντων, 945c), a "straightener" (εὐθυντής, 945b) of what has been done crookedly by the magistrates.[165] The euthynos himself must obviously be above crookedness if he is to be an adequate straightener. As is abundantly shown by Athenian history, a politician desirous to discredit a rival could often do so most effectively by bringing charges at his euthyna.[166] Pericles, so Aristotle records, made his reputation first by challenging the audit of Cimon on his generalship;[167] and the evidence suggests that the prestige of Ephialtes with the people and the apprehension he excited among the conservatives were due to his use of the procedure of euthyna.[168] The same procedure seems to have been used against Pericles himself in the difficult years before his death.[169] In the following century, Demosthenes' opening attack upon his rival Aeschines was a charge of maladministration in connection with the euthyna of the embassy to Philip of which Aeschines was a member.[170] Instances of the use of this powerful instrument for partisan purposes must have been in Plato's mind when he remarks that if the examination of the magistrates is not carried out properly it is an encouragement to faction (945d). The only control of this instrument provided by Athenian procedure lay in the euthynoi, who had the authority, if they chose to use it, to refuse to refer to the popular courts an accusation that they did not find properly substantiated. But since they were

[164] Lipsius 293. For a possible explanation of this anomaly, see Bonner and Smith II, 256ff., and Kahrstedt, *op.cit.* 170.

[165] The word εὐθυντής is poetic (cf. Theognis, 40), and is obviously used only to call attention to the metaphor underlying the function of the euthynos. It is a mistake to suggest, as Barker does (343), that this is Plato's legal designation of these magistrates. Their legal designation is εὔθυνοι, just as it was in Attic law; this term is used repeatedly in the following pages (945b-948b), whereas εὐθυντής occurs only in this introductory metaphor (945bc).

[166] See the evidence in Bonner and Smith II, 43ff.

[167] Arist. *Const. Ath.* XXVII, 1.

[168] Arist. *Const. Ath.* XXV, 2. Though not subject to εὔθυνα in the strict sense, since this implied that an office was being laid down, the Areopagites were certainly subject to accounting before the logistai for any public monies that had gone through their hands. Aesch. III, 20.

[169] Plut. *Per.* 35; Thuc. II, 65, 3.

[170] Dem. XIX.

themselves liable to the same procedure, their discretion must often have been tempered by a prudent regard to the state of public opinion. Plato, as we shall see, does not require his euthynoi to give an account of their actions before a popular court, and thus removes one of the factors that could lead, in times of crisis, to the perversion of the process. But there are other pressures to which they will be subject, so that this office will require a special degree of probity and public spirit: it is, in fact, one of the mainstays (945c) of the constitution.

How then are we to find examiners of the "divine quality" required? Plato proposes the following procedure:

Each year, after the time of the sun's turning from summer to winter, the whole city shall assemble in the common precinct of Helios and Apollo to present before the god three of its citizens. Each man shall vote for that person, not less than fifty years of age, who (besides himself) he considers is in every respect the best. Of the persons thus preferred (τῶν προκριθέντων) they shall select those who have received the most votes, down to the middle of the list, if it contains an even number, and drop the rest, as having been rejected by the count of the votes. If the number of candidates be odd, the man who receives the fewest votes shall be dropped; and if any candidates[171] receive an equal number of votes, thus making the [upper] half larger, they shall remove the inequality by rejecting the younger ones. They shall then consider and vote on the candidates remaining, until only three are left, ranked in the order of the votes for them. If all three have received the same number of votes, or if two of them be tied, they shall entrust the matter to good luck and

---

[171] I.e. at the middle of the list. If we think of a list of candidates (which is obviously what Plato is doing), not of a series of places on a scale one of which might be occupied by more than one candidate, the only point at which a tie could possibly hinder the division into two parts having the same number of candidates is at the middle. Thus a tie vote anywhere except the middle would be immaterial, though Plato's language is general and seems to have misled some translators (e.g. Taylor). The immediately following part of Plato's text also carries a meaning more precise than its expression. If we assume, for example, that there are twenty-four candidates arranged in order according to the number of votes each has received, and that candidates twelve and thirteen on the list have received the same number of votes; then if we keep them together we shall have two "halves" consisting of thirteen and eleven or of eleven and thirteen members respectively. To "take away the excess" (ἀφελεῖν τὸ πλέον) by "rejecting the younger" (ἀποκρίναντας νεότητι) means keeping the older in the upper half and putting the younger in the lower half, which consists of those rejected. The same procedure could be used if three or more persons are tied at the middle of the list, the upper half being filled from the tied candidates in the order of their age. No doubt it is an awareness of these various possibilities that leads Plato to express himself in such general terms.

chance, and determine by lot who is the victor and who are second and third. Then, having crowned them with wreaths and conferred the award of merit (ἀριστεῖα) upon them, they shall proclaim to the assembly that the city of the Magnesians, having by God's will been brought to life again, has presented its three best men to Helios, and offers them, according to the ancient law, as its first fruits to Apollo and Helios in common, for as long a time as they deserve this judgment of them. 945e-946c

This procedure would hardly be called democratic by Plato's contemporaries, since it relies upon election rather than the accident of the lot; but all citizens participate, and there are no qualifications other than age. The list of προκριθέντες from which the voting proceeds is constituted by the nominations of the citizens themselves, nor is there any device employed later for guiding the election other than the arithmetical halving of the list after each vote, and (in the case of a tie that would prevent halving) the selection of the older and the elimination of the younger candidate or candidates. When we consider the importance of these officers, it is significant that Plato chooses this popular method of selecting them.

The election just described is the regular procedure after the constitution has been established. Plato bethinks himself at once that more than three examiners will be needed at the outset, and prescribes that twelve shall be elected the first year and three each year thereafter (946c), without mentioning any modification of the procedure for the first election; we conclude therefore that the first election would terminate when the list of candidates has been reduced to twelve instead of three. Each of these officers is to serve until he has reached the age of seventy-five. This would give a normal maximum of seventy-five members on the board if all were elected at the age of fifty and lived and held office to the age of seventy-five. The actual number would probably be much smaller.[172]

It is tempting to assume that Plato intends the number of the board to be twelve, since this is the number elected the first year, and since later it is provided that the offices shall be divided into twelve parts for examination. This would make Plato's board more

---

[172] Ritter (*Darstellung* 363) assumes it would be about fifteen, i.e. the average tenure of office five years. Barker (344) thinks it would be a body of forty or less, with an average tenure of twelve years. All such guesses are futile, for even if we could estimate the life expectancy of a fourth-century Cretan at any given age, we have no way of determining the probability of his being elected at one age rather than another. It may be doubted whether Plato could have done so.

closely resemble the board of euthynoi at Athens, the change from ten to twelve corresponding to the fact that there are twelve tribes in Plato's state instead of the ten at Athens. But there is no provision in Plato's law that the first twelve shall be selected one from each tribe, nor any provision that in the later elections members shall be selected from the tribes left without representatives by death or retirement. On the contrary, the intent is clearly to select the best men, without regard to tribal distinctions. Furthermore, there is no rule of retirement other than the age limit of seventy-five.[173] It seems best to conclude, therefore, that the reference to the division of offices into twelve parts applies only to the first year, when there would be twelve members; in later years the board would normally be larger. But this portion of the text is singularly disjointed and shows clearly the lack of a final revision, which would probably have removed some of our uncertainties as to Plato's intentions.[174]

About the procedure of examination there are further uncertainties. The division of the offices into twelve parts is presumably to divide the labor and responsibilities among the members of the board. But Plato immediately adds that some acts (or some offices; the text is not clear) shall be handled by a single euthynos, others in conjunction with their colleagues; and the final judgment against an officer seems to be a collective decision, as one would expect from Plato's fondness for collegiality in official actions.[175] After the euthynoi

[173] England suggests (in his note on 946c 3) that the youngest would be the only ones "on the rota" at any given time. But this not only conflicts with Plato's pronounced preference for age, but introduces special complications. A newly elected euthynos might find that there were already on the board twelve members younger than himself and he would thus be retired from the rota without having served at all.

[174] Note the clause $\mu\acute{\epsilon}\chi\rho\iota\pi\epsilon\rho$ . . . $\gamma\epsilon\nu\acute{o}\mu\epsilon\nu\alpha$ (946c 3-4), which would follow more logically at the end of the previous sentence, and which interrupts the continuity between the two parts of the sentence in which it stands. Again $o\grave{\iota}\kappa o\acute{\upsilon}\nu\tau\omega\nu$ . . . $\grave{\epsilon}\kappa\rho\acute{\iota}\theta\eta\sigma\alpha\nu$ (c7-d1) interrupts the continuity between the passage just before it and the one immediately after it. These look like insertions made by Plato himself, who expected later to bring them into proper order. Again the proclamation referring to the rebirth of the city of the Magnesians (b6) seems to imply the first election of euthynoi, yet only three are presented to the god as the city's "first fruits," which would be true only of later elections. Finally, the sentence that seems to introduce an account of the euthyna of the euthynoi themselves (e 4-5) is followed by something quite different from what one would expect (see Note 178).

[175] In this examination Plato says that they may employ any tests ($\beta\acute{\alpha}\sigma\alpha\nu\sigma\iota$) that they think fit, provided that they are "appropriate to free men." The word $\beta\acute{\alpha}\sigma\alpha\nu\sigma\iota$ in Attic law was ordinarily used to denote testimony elicited from a slave under torture. Its conjunction with $\grave{\epsilon}\lambda\epsilon\upsilon\theta\epsilon\rho\acute{\iota}\alpha\iota$ shows that the word is not to be taken in its common legal sense. Plato uses it here and elsewhere to indicate the kind of

have completed their examination of the offices, they shall set up in the market place written statements of fines or other penalties that they think should be imposed on any of the retiring officials (946de; cf. 881e, 952d). This is presumably to be considered a legal verdict, the action constituting a judgment against the persons involved. If, however, any officer believes that he has been "judged unjustly" (μὴ κεκρίσθαι δικαίως) he may appeal his case to the court of select judges. Here he may be acquitted of the charges against him; but if he loses he is liable to double the penalty originally imposed. This is Plato's substitute for the appeal to the dicasteries provided in Athenian law.

Plato enhances the dignity and authority of the euthynoi by further provisions which are without precedent for these officers at Athens. Election is regarded not only as an award of civic excellence, but also as an appointment to the priesthood. The election takes place, as we have seen, in the precincts of Helios and Apollo, and is followed by a solemn act of dedication of these three best men as the city's "first fruits" (ἀκροθίνιον . . . ἀνατίθησι, 946bc); and during the period of their active service they reside in the sacred precincts (946c). They wear the olive wreath and the crown of laurel, a privilege reserved for them alone (946b, 947a). The euthynos who ranks first among the three elected in any year is to be called "high priest" (ἀρχιέρεως, 947a),[176] and his name is to be used to designate the year in the records of the city. So long as they live, they are to have first seats (προεδρίαι) at every festival—another prerogative of the important priests at Athens—and from their number are to be chosen the heads of sacred missions sent out to take part in joint sacrifices or congresses of Greek cities. The honors a euthynos has enjoyed during his life are crowned at his death by elaborate funeral ceremonies extending over two days, and by burial in a sacred grove in an underground vault with his departed colleagues. Every year afterward there are to be contests of music, gymnastics, and horse racing in his honor (947b-e).[177]

In a state in which every other official has to undergo the euthyna,

---

inquisitorial investigation, involving a thorough questioning of principals and witnesses, that he thinks necessary in a court of law if the facts are to be ascertained. See below, Chapter VI, Procedure. It is used in this sense also in 768a. Cf. 736c: διαβασανίσαντες; 961a: διαβασανισθέντες.

[176] For Plato's use of the Ionic form see Chapter VIII, Note 69.

[177] On these burial ceremonies see Chapter VIII, Note 218.

it would be anomalous if the euthynoi themselves were exempt, and no such exception is contemplated in Plato's law. On two occasions Plato speaks of the euthynai of the euthynoi themselves (946e, 947e). It is certain that he expects each of these officers, upon reaching the age of retirement, to undergo the audit in the regular fashion, either before the board he has just quitted, or before some other board; but he does not say who are to be the euthynoi of his euthynoi, and we must remain in doubt as to his intentions.[178] But Plato provides explicitly another means of calling these officers to account: a public suit (γραφή) which it is within the competence of any citizen to bring against a euthynos who he thinks is "unworthy of the office and its honors" (947e, 948a). The name of this graphe is not given, but the general nature of the offense which would substantiate it, and the earlier characterization of these officers as the mainstay of justice in the state, make it analogous at least to the γραφὴ ἀδικίου which could be brought under Athenian law against an officer for maladministration.[179] For the hearing of such a charge a court of very special dignity is provided, consisting of the guardians, the court of select judges, and the other "living members" (i.e. whether active or retired) of the board of euthynoi (948a). A euthynos convicted of the offense charged is stripped of his office and his honors, including the right of burial in the fashion described above. No mention is made of graver penalties, such as death, banishment, or fines, which we have seen the euthynoi are empowered to impose upon a delinquent magistrate. This is apparently merely an oversight, because Plato's attention is here concentrated upon the honors and dignity that a euthynos may forfeit by "crookedness" in office. To discourage irresponsible indictments, his law provides that a prosecutor who fails to receive one fifth of the votes shall be subjected to a fine.[180]

[178] I cannot agree with England (on 946e 4) that the description of the honors and dignity conferred on the euthynoi is intended by Plato as an account of their euthynai, in spite of the sentence with which this description is introduced. For later (947e) it is said that these are to be the rewards of those who have passed their euthynai. It would be a strange confusion for Plato to assert that the honors accorded an official of proved integrity are themselves the proof of his integrity. There is an inconsequence in Plato's text, but one easily explained. He asks what are to be the euthynai of the euthynoi, but before answering the question is diverted into the description of the honors they enjoy, perhaps because it is the loss of these honors that will constitute the chief penalty for maladministration.

[179] Arist. *Const. Ath.* LIV, 2; Lipsius 291, 381.

[180] As is usual in Plato's law, the fine is proportioned to the property class to which the person belongs. At Athens a prosecutor who failed to obtain a fifth of the votes in a public suit was fined a thousand drachmae; Lipsius 940; Bonner and

Plato's procedure of euthyna thus appears to be a modified version
—a considerably modified version—of a very familiar institution of
Athenian law. His chief innovations are the careful selection of the
euthynoi, their long tenure of office, and the substitution of his court
of select judges for the popular courts as the final tribunal in litigation involving euthyna. This demotion of the popular courts from
the juridically supreme position they occupied at Athens is in accord
with the proposals Plato makes elsewhere for the system of courts
and the administration of justice, and in this regard is decisively nondemocratic. But in the election of the euthynoi by popular vote, and
in the provisions for the prosecution and removal from office of a
faithless or incompetent euthynos, it gives the public a definite measure of control, though in a fashion that would in Plato's time be
called aristocratic rather than democratic. The manner of their election and the supervisory powers they exercise over the other officials
suggest the Spartan ephorate (regarded by some persons, so Aristotle
tells us, as the "democratic feature" of the Spartan constitution);[181]
but the ephors held office for only one year, and we know too little
about the details of Spartan law to make any closer comparison. In
general, Plato's use of the terminology and principles of Athenian
law makes it more plausible to assume that it is the Athenian institution which he is here remodeling; though the result of this remodeling is an institution different from anything that we know of
in any historical state.

A more puzzling question is the relation between this new body
and the other institutions already set up in Plato's state. Barker points
out that the relation of the euthynoi to the guardians is not clear:
"It is difficult to see how the guardians of the laws can be supervised
by the examiners; for they, like the examiners, are elected to their
office at the age of fifty or more, and they hold office for twenty
years."[182] But a similar difficulty confronts us in interpreting the relation of the members of the Areopagus to the euthynoi under Attic
law; the Areopagites held office for life, yet were required under

Smith II, 56. Twelve minae for a person of Plato's highest property class would be
somewhat more than this, whereas the two minae imposed for a member of the
poorest class would be only a fraction of it. This means less of a deterrent for persons of the poorer classes; on the other hand, the risk involved in irresponsible
charges would be much less, so Plato would think, with a court of the select quality he provides.
[181] *Pol.* 1265b 39.
[182] Barker 343 n. 3.

certain circumstances to undergo the euthyna.[183] If Plato's guardians are the counterparts of the Athenian Areopagus, we should expect something similar in his state. Even if he intends a guardian to be exempt from the audit during his period of office, he would still be required to undergo it when he reaches the age of retirement. A greater difficulty concerns the division of responsibility between these two bodies in supervising the other officers. It is quite possible that Plato thinks the euthynoi will in general function only at periodic intervals, as at Athens, while we have seen that the guardians exercise a continuing supervision; yet the provision that the euthynoi are to reside in the temple precincts suggests continuing duties for them also. A more plausible ground of distinction between the two bodies is that the euthynoi alone seem empowered to impose penalties for official misconduct. The judicial powers of the guardians—though considerable, as we shall see—do not include the power to fine or penalize another officeholder; if they cannot persuade him to act as they think the law requires, it appears that they can only report the circumstances to the euthynoi for their consideration and judgment. From a legal point of view such a distinction of function is sensible and appropriate; and although it is nowhere stated explicitly, it is implied in the detailed provisions of Plato's text.

It is hard, therefore, to agree with Barker's opinion that with the appearance of the board of euthynoi in Plato's constitution, and still more with the setting up of the Nocturnal Council, the "normal Greek institutions of assembly and council, officials and courts of law, ... begin to fade away."[184] If Barker means that there is less mention of them in this part of Plato's exposition, that may be admitted, and the reason is obviously that they have already been dealt with. Where they are needed, as is the assembly in the election of the euthynoi, or the guardians in the trial of an accused euthynos, they appear as before. But Barker's statement seems to imply that these later institutions supplant the earlier ones, or alter seriously the powers previously assigned them; and that inference, I think, is false. There was still much to be done to Plato's constitutional provisions before they could be regarded as complete. The lines of authority between these various officials have to be more precisely drawn than Plato was able or inclined to do here at the end. These are matters

[183] See Note 168.
[184] Barker 342.

which he thought could be left to the "younger legislators." But the evidence seems to show that the result would be a considerably modified and more strictly regulated but still recognizable Greek city, a city committed above all, as was the Athens of Plato's time, to the principle that all officers should be held legally accountable for their actions.

"ARISTOCRACY WITH THE APPROVAL OF THE PEOPLE"[185]

Plato's account of the offices in his state is at many points incomplete. We have noticed in the preceding sections that there are important functions of government not clearly assigned to a specific office or board of officers, and conversely that the powers of important officers are left vaguely defined with respect to other organs of the state. Thus there is clear provision for an assembly of the people, but no provision for a probouleutic body to prepare recommendations for the assembly's action. Is it Plato's intention that this function shall be exercised by the council, or by the guardians, or by both? And if the latter, how are their respective prerogatives related to one another? Can the assembly itself initiate proposals, or has it only the right to discuss recommendations laid before it by one of these higher bodies? If it may not initiate, may the assembly reject a recommendation laid before it, and if so, is its veto unrestricted or are there circumstances in which it may be overridden? Finally, to ask Aristotle's question,[186] what is the sovereign power (τὸ κύριον) in the state—the many, the rich, or the good? Plato would answer, we know, that none of these is sovereign; the sovereign is the law, i.e. the Nous in the law. But this raises other questions not answered in this part of Plato's work. Where does the legislative power reside? The guardians are authorized to make administrative rules and to revise and supplement the basic law laid down at the founding of the state. On some matters of law, as we have seen, the changes proposed must be referred to the assembly for ratification; but the procedure in such cases is not laid down; and we are left in doubt whether all rules and laws formulated by the guardians have to be ratified by the assembly. This is intrinsically improbable, yet no hint is given for distinguish-

[185] Μετ' εὐδοξίας πλήθους ἀριστοκρατία, i.e. the ancestral constitution of the Athenians as it is characterized in Menex. 238d.
[186] Pol. 1281a 11. For the other questions raised, see Pol. 1299b 30ff., 1298b 26ff.

ing the areas in which these officers are sovereign and those in which they have to gain the assent of the assembly.

But in spite of these unanswered questions, Plato's basic intentions are clear. The demos is to be sovereign in certain matters, but it is not to rule. It is sovereign over questions of war and peace; it has to give approval to some changes in the laws, perhaps to all changes in the basic law; and it has the right, with rare exceptions,[187] to choose its officials, subject to control by the procedure of dokimasia. As a body it does not have the function, as the Athenian demos had through the popular courts, of conducting the euthyna of officers; yet any citizen, as we shall see later, has the right to bring an accusation of official misconduct before the courts for judgment. Thus of the two functions which Solon was thought to have given to the people—ἀρχαιρεσία and εὔθυνα[188]—Plato adopts the former in what he thinks was its ancestral form, but provides a different procedure for accomplishing the purpose of the latter. Since there is in general no property qualification for office, any citizen who has the confidence of his fellows may participate in the work of government. On the other hand, the chief officers of the state will be persons of maturity and experience, equipped certainly with some measure of the higher education that Plato later describes, and persons who have earned the confidence of their fellow citizens for their handling of public affairs. These qualities, plus their long tenure of office, will make them the warp of the social fabric, to recall Plato's metaphor; and a government with this clear differentiation between rulers and ruled is evidently what Plato means by the mixture of monarchy and democracy, of authority and liberty, which he intends to establish.[189]

Commenting on Plato's constitution, Aristotle says that it contains no monarchical element at all, but consists rather of features taken from oligarchy and democracy.[190] By the monarchical element, however, Plato obviously does not mean a king, but a strong executive such as he provides for in his boards of magistrates. Aristotle adds that the constitution inclines more toward oligarchy than democracy. If we take oligarchy as a government in which power is in the hands of the few rather than the many, and these few the wealthier members of the community, his judgment has a certain plausibility; for we can expect that few of the poorer members of Plato's society could

---

[187] The select judges and the educator.
[189] See Chapter X.

[188] *Pol.* 1281b 32f.
[190] *Pol.* 1266a 5f.

assume the duties of the more important offices. This seems not to be Plato's intention, although the actual working of his scheme might be oligarchical in the sense defined, particularly if we assume that he would retain the Athenian procedure of ἐξωμοσία, the refusal of an office under oath that one is unable to discharge it. But if oligarchy is taken to mean, as Aristotle defines it later in the *Politics*,[191] the government of the rich in their own interests, he has surely not understood the significance of Plato's insistence on the rule of law, and of the devices Plato proposes for bringing it about and maintaining it. If these devices, supplemented by the rigid educational system to which all citizens and officials are subjected, have in any degree the effects they are intended to have, the power exercised by these authoritative officials will serve other than merely special interests. The rule of law, as the expression of the common interest, must be taken into account in appraising Plato's constitution; a good state, he believes, requires not merely a strong executive, but also an executive kept within the bounds of law. We shall see later how he thinks this purpose can be accomplished without giving power into the hands of "the many."

Of the many Platonic innovations that we have examined in the preceding pages, some deserve special mention here at the end because of their relevance to the fundamental guiding principles just discussed. Plato devotes an unusual amount of attention to elections and electoral procedures, and some of the details are probably his own invention—such as the use of written ballots, the procedure of ἀντιπροβολή for revising an official list of candidates for office, and the use of a series of elections for successively narrowing the choice among προκριθέντες.[192] The reliance upon election expresses what Plato says was characteristic of the ancestral constitution, under which "the men thought to be best" were selected for office; and his attention to electoral procedures indicates that this part of Athenian law was undeveloped as a result of the almost universal reliance upon the lot at Athens in his time. One election to which Plato devotes particular attention is that of the council, and here he introduces another notable innovation, in constituting it by property classes instead of by tribes. To Aristotle's criticism that this is an oligarchical proposal Plato is immune, as we have seen; it is really a far-sighted device for improving the quality of deliberation in this body by assuring equality of repre-

[191] *Pol.* 1279b 7.   [192] See Excursus C.

sentation for interests that are most likely to lead to factional strife. Again, the institution of the rural police, made up of contingents from all the tribes, with a two-year period of service during which they become acquainted with all parts of the country and learn "how to serve as well as to command," is an innovation peculiarly important for the realization of Plato's central purpose. For this two-year period in the young citizen's life becomes an educational as well as a military experience; and from the ranks of these agronomoi will certainly come many of the future archontes of the state.

It will be noted that these innovations are based on Athenian institutions and—so far as we can see at this distance in time—could readily have been adopted by the Athenians without altering seriously the foundations of the state. The replacement of the lot by election (in part, at least), and the establishment (or reorganization) of the ephebia did in fact take place at Athens in the generation after Plato's death. The later establishment of a board of nomophylakes with powers similar to those that it was believed the ancient Areopagus enjoyed was another partial realization of Plato's proposals, and so also was the curtailing of the powers of the popular courts that took place after Chaeronea. In short, despite the dramatic setting of the dialogue, Plato's attention seems to be directed primarily upon Athenian institutions; his aim is to see how they could be remolded into something like the ancestral constitution, enlightened—as we shall see in the next chapter—by the lessons of later experience with democratic courts and legal procedures.

This fact suggests a partial explanation of the incompleteness of Plato's constitutional provisions. Many matters which we should like to have clarified he probably takes for granted as being already familiar to his readers, or as details which they could easily suppose from their knowledge of Athenian procedures. Furthermore, we must remember that constitutional law, in the continental and the American sense of the term, was unknown at Athens. There was no document in the Athenian archives delimiting the powers of the respective boards of officials; these powers were set forth only in the laws that these officials were responsible for enforcing, and in isolated decrees of the assembly, or embodied in long-standing habits and traditions. Plato at first conceives of his legislative task as consisting of two parts: the establishment of offices ($\kappa\alpha\tau\alpha\sigma\tau\acute{\alpha}\sigma\epsilon\iota\varsigma\ \acute{\alpha}\rho\chi\hat{\omega}\nu$), i.e. to determine "how many there are and how each is to be filled" ($\acute{o}\sigma\alpha\varsigma\ \tau\epsilon\ \alpha\dot{\upsilon}\tau\grave{\alpha}\varsigma$

εἶναι δεῖ καὶ τρόπον ὄντινα καθισταμένας); and then to assign appropriate laws to each of the various offices (ἑκάσταις, 751a). This plan of legislation accords with Athenian ways of thinking;[193] if he had carried it out, his account of the offices would have been followed by laws pertaining to the council (νόμοι βουλευτικοί),[194] and similar laws for all the other offices; and here we should have found more definite provisions delimiting the powers of these various offices when they impinge upon each other. But Plato's juristic reason seems to have intervened to alter his plan; the laws that follow are arranged not according to offices, but according to interests that need to be regulated, or activities that are to be controlled. Thus the law of marriage comes next, then education, then agriculture, and so on through the various chapters of what is designed to be a systematic code; and the critical questions we have raised are never answered. One can say that Plato's qualities as a systematic legal thinker are, in part at least, responsible for these gaps in his account of the offices.

EXCURSUS C. Αἵρεσις, κλήρωσις, πρόκρισις

Voting, the lot, and the combination of the two are three clearly distinct procedures for the filling of offices, each of which was probably used at some period or other in Athenian history, and each having its examples in Plato's constitution. Thus the elections of the nomophylakes, the generals, the euthynoi, the select judges, and the educator are all instances of voting (presumably by written ballot in each case); in the selection of priests the lot alone is used; while the members of the council, the exegetes, the astynomoi, the agoranomoi, and the athlothetai are selected by the use of the lot on a list of candidates previously elected by some form of voting, either written ballot (for the council and perhaps the exegetes) or show of hands. It appears that the junior agronomoi also are selected, the twelve from each tribe being enrolled by their respective phrourarchs. Plato's text does not tell us how the five phrourarchs from each tribe are to be chosen; but the parallel between them and the two boards of "city" wardens (astynomoi and agoranomoi) appears so frequently that we can assume that they also will be selected by a combination of voting and the lot.

Thus a person with a tidy mind could divide the officers in Plato's

[193] See Kahrstedt, *Klio* xxxi, 1938, 11; and Notes 190 and 101 above.
[194] Cf. Dem. xxiv, 20.

state into three classes according to the method by which they are chosen or designated. Aristotle in one passage of the *Politics* (1298b 8ff.) does just this for the states that he knows: officers, he says, are αἱρετοί (elected) or κληρωτοί (designated by lot), and the latter are either κληρωτοὶ ἁπλῶς (designated by the lot alone) or κληρωτοὶ ἐκ προκρίτων (designated by a combination of the lot and some other procedure whose nature remains to be determined). But elsewhere in the *Politics* Aristotle ignores this threefold classification, and his usage in the *Constitution of Athens* seems actually at variance with it. This puzzling feature of Aristotle's text has given rise to much difference of opinion as to the meaning of his statements. A similar uncertainty infects the other ancient sources. (See Hignett, 321-326; Ehrenberg in RE s.v. Losung, 1468ff.; and Kahrstedt, *Untersuchungen zur Magistratur in Athen*, 39-58). Since Plato is the only fourth-century writer who gives sufficient details about election procedures to enable us to attach precise meanings to the terms he employs, an examination of his usage may help to elucidate the terms and distinctions found in Aristotle and elsewhere. Although isolated texts of the *Laws* have frequently been cited as evidence for or against certain interpretations of the ancient evidence, Plato's text as a whole has never been systematically examined from this point of view.

There are, I believe, only two passages in the *Laws* in which Plato hints at anything like the distinctions made in the passage of Aristotle cited above.

(1) In 759, having described the election of the nomophylakes, the military officers, and the council, Plato turns to a consideration of the minor magistrates that will be necessary for the policing of the state. These he divides into three groups (ἐλέσθαι δεῖ τρία μὲν ἀρχόν-των εἴδη), of which he immediately names two, the astynomoi and the agoranomoi. The third is not mentioned. One expects the agro-nomoi to be named, for they are generally treated as discharging in the country the functions assigned to the astynomoi and the agoranomoi in the city, and have been anticipated in τῆς ἄλλης χώρας in 758e 1 (cf. τὴν ἄλλην χώραν, 760b 3). But the agro-nomoi do not appear until the next page (760b); instead Plato brings in priests and priestesses, and the remainder of 759 is concerned with the method of filling priesthoods. Just before the account of this method comes the passage of special interest to us: τούτων δὴ πάντων τὰ μὲν αἱρετὰ χρή, τὰ δὲ κληρωτά (759b). The

antecedent of τούτων can only be the ἀρχόντων εἴδη mentioned earlier as three in number, but now tacitly increased by the inclusion of these religious officials, who are not strictly ἄρχοντες in the constitutional sense of the term (τρία μὲν ἀρχόντων in a7 being balanced by ἱερῶν δὲ ἱερέας in a9). Of the various officers mentioned in the immediate context the priests are clearly κληρωτοί (this point is emphasized in the following sentence), while astynomoi and agoranomoi (who are selected in an identical fashion by a procedure which the Athenians would call a κλήρωσις ἐκ προκρίτων) must be the officers designated as αἱρετοί. If we enlarge the context to include the agronomoi to be discussed later, the junior agronomoi will obviously have to be classed as αἱρετοί, and the phrourarchs probably so also, on our assumption that the method of their selection would be analogous to that of the astynomoi and the agoranomoi. Thus it appears that the κληρωτοὶ ἐκ προκρίτων are regarded by Plato as αἱρετοί.

(2) In 945b the officers of the state are distinguished into those selected (γενόμενοι) "by the chance of the lot and for one-year terms" (κατὰ τύχην κλήρου καὶ ἐπ᾽ ἐνιαυτόν) and others "for more than one year" (εἰς πλείονα ἔτη) and ἐκ προκρίτων. The last phrase I have not translated, since its meaning is yet to be determined. Πρόκρισις and πρόκριτοι are frequently mentioned in the sources, but there is no clear evidence of the procedure which they imply (see Kahrstedt, op.cit. 52-58). Was it designed to effect merely a preliminary selection, or a preferential selection as well? In Plato's electoral law πρόκρισις clearly means the latter. Thus in the election of the nomophylakes, after the nominating ballot has produced a list of three hundred candidates, the next stage of voting reduces this to a shorter list of one hundred προκριθέντες (753d), and it is from these names that the citizens by a final ballot select the thirty-seven persons to fill the office.[1] Similarly at the election of the euthynoi each citizen first nominates the three best of his fellow citizens, as he judges them, and it is from these προκριθέντες (946a) that the voters make a further selection. Clearly in both these cases πρόκρισις means a preferential selection from among persons qualified to fill the office

---

[1] To confirm the identity of πρόκριτοι and προκριθέντες, see *Rep.* 537b,d. There is indeed a striking parallel between the successive stages of πρόκρισις in the *Republic* for selecting the young men who are to advance to higher education, and the procedure in the *Laws* for selecting higher officers by successive stages of voting. This surely provides additional evidence of what πρόκρισις means for Plato in the *Laws*.

concerned; it is a preliminary stage of election. This point is further emphasized when, at the election of the educator, both the nominator (ὁ προκρίνων) and the nominee (ὁ προκριθείς) are urged to keep in mind that this office is the most important in the state and that the best man must be selected to fill it (765e, 766a). Similar procedures are prescribed for the election of generals, select judges, and members of the council, although προκρίνειν and its derivatives do not appear in these texts, their place being taken by προβάλλεσθαι and προβληθέντες in the case of the generals (755b-d), ἐκλέξαντες in the case of the council (756e), and the ambiguous αἱρεῖσθαι in the case of the select judges (767d). Nor does προκρίνειν appear in the description of the elections that would certainly be called κληρώσεις ἐκ προκρίτων in Attic law, such as those of astynomoi, agoranomoi, and athlothetai. But in all these cases there is provision for nomination and for preferential voting, and thus the substance of a prokrisis in Plato's sense, though not so searching in character as it is for more important offices. Finally the exegetes are selected by Delphi from a panel chosen by majority votes in tribal assemblies (a procedure called προαιρεῖσθαι in 759e), so that here also there is a prokrisis of the selective sort that Plato has prescribed for the other cases.

These texts show that the fundamental distinction for Plato is that between πρόκριτοι and κληρωτοὶ ἁπλῶς, and that πρόκρισις means for him some procedure of preferential selection, more or less rigorous according to the importance of the office, but always involving a judgment passed by the electors upon the competence of the nominees or candidates for the office in question. Since prokrisis is thus a kind of preliminary election, the fundamental distinction Plato recognizes between officers could be expressed, as it is in 759b, as that between αἱρετοί and κληρωτοί (i.e. Aristotle's κληρωτοὶ ἁπλῶς).

But this distinction, with the twofold classification that results from it, ignores Aristotle's first class, officers elected without any use of the lot. This class is not, however, empty in Plato's state, as we have seen; his most important offices are filled by a series of preferential ballots followed by a final deciding vote on the remaining candidates. Furthermore, there can be no doubt that he regards this as the proper way for a well-ordered state to fill its high offices, viz. by selecting for an office not merely one of a group of approved candidates, but that one who is thought to be the best of them all. This is the sense of the passage in the *Menexenus* (238d) asserting that in the ancestral constitution the important offices were αἱρεταί. And if the passage in Aristotle's *Politics* (1273b 35ff.) concerning Solon is, as I have argued above (see Chapter III), a report of Plato's views, then this is the sense in which he thought the ἀρχαί in Solon's constitution were αἱρεταί. But Plato often uses αἵρεσις and αἱρεῖσθαι in a quite general sense (like καθιστάναι) to denote any procedure in which an office is filled. The whole account of the offices from the beginning of Book VI to 768e is said to be concerned with the αἵρεσις ἀρχόντων (768e 1), and it deals with some, at least, that are not αἱρετοί in either Plato's or Aristotle's special sense. Thus, although αἵρεσις is sometimes applied to an election that in fact makes no use of the lot (e.g. 767d), we can never infer, from the use of this term alone without supporting details, whether this is the kind of αἵρεσις that Plato intends.

But Aristotle may well have thought his threefold classification was better adapted to bring out Plato's intentions. Indeed Plato's division does not fit his material at all closely, for his class of αἱρετοί includes all the officers in his state except the priests and priestesses. In any case Aristotle sometimes employs his own distinctions in discussing Plato's provisions. Thus in one passage (*Pol.* 1266a 26) he mentions and criticizes a method of election that Plato, he says, employs in the *Laws*—τὸ ἐξ αἱρετῶν αἱρετούς, which can only mean, as his criticism shows, election from a slate of candidates previously chosen by preferential voting. This method is dangerous, Aristotle says, because under it a moderately small group of persons, if they work together, can dominate the choice of candidates. Elsewhere (1305a 28) he observes that the "ancestral democracy" is subject to revolutions under this procedure. "When offices are filled by election (αἱρεταί), without a property qualification, and election is by the demos (αἱρεῖται δὲ ὁ δῆμος), those who are eager for office act as demagogues and bring it about that the people becomes sovereign over the law." This is apparently the reason why the Heraeans abandoned election for the lot (ἐξ αἱρετῶν ἐποίησαν κληρωτάς; no doubt Aristotle means they changed from pure election to the κλήρωσις ἐκ προκρίτων), because of the electoral intrigues (διὰ τὰς ἐριθείας) possible under the former system; "the people used to elect those who canvassed" (1303a 14ff.).[2]

---

[2] Aristotle distrusted electioneering, and the notorious corruption that occurred at elections in Rome during the days of the Republic is a striking confirmation of his fears. It is worth noting that we have no evidence at Athens of anything like bribery of voters; the evils involved there were of a more subtle sort—the

Our examination has provided some support for the theory of Wilamowitz and Ehrenberg (viewed with disfavor by Hignett, 323) that αἵρεσις in the *Politics* can be taken to include κλήρωσις ἐκ προκρίτων. Plato would certainly have taken it so, and it is plausible to suppose that Aristotle, despite his correction of Plato's classification, occasionally reverted to the usage of his master. In the second place, however, our examination has shown that Plato (and perhaps Aristotle also in the *Politics*) believed that offices were filled in early times by pure election. Hignett's theory of a "steady and logical development in the method of appointment to the archonship"—i.e. the aristocratic procedure of pure election, followed by the introduction of the κλήρωσις ἐκ προκρίτων, and that in turn by pure κλήρωσις, or the "double sortition" of the full-fledged democracy—this accords well with Plato's conception of his people's constitutional history. And finally, unless Plato's conception of prokrisis is utterly at variance with Athenian traditions, Kahrstedt's theory that prokrisis never meant more than a formal scrutiny of the qualifications of the candidates coming up for sortition—in earlier times to determine their membership in the required property class, in later days to ascertain their freedom from atimia—this theory is shown to be even less plausible than it appears from a scrutiny of the ancient sources that he cites (*op.cit.*, 52-58).[3]

EXCURSUS D. THE DOUBLE VERSION IN BOOK VI

Wilamowitz (in *Hermes* xlv, 1910, 398ff.) long ago called attention to the duplication in this part of Plato's text, which suggests that it is a conflation of an earlier and a later version. He regarded the later version as beginning with σμικρὸν δὲ (751b 2) and extending to ἀποφηνάντων ἄρχοντας (753d 6); whereas the passage beginning

---

making of extravagant promises to the electorate, the misrepresentation of the character and purposes of an opponent, and the organized activities of political clubs, or ἑταιρίαι (see Charles Baron, "La Candidature politique chez les Athéniens," in reg xiv, 1901, 372-399). Plato likewise looks with disapproval upon these political clubs (cf. *Theaet.* 173d, *Ep. VII* 333e), and provides the death penalty for an attempt to subvert the laws by such means (856b).

[3] Kahrstedt's theory also includes the assumption that the lot was always preceded by a prokrisis; "jede Losung ohne πρόκρισις ist ein Unding" (*op.cit.* 54). Undoubtedly the use of the lot presupposes some procedure of enrolling or certifying the candidates; but to say that this is all that the Athenians meant by prokrisis is to render meaningless both Aristotle's distinction of κλήρωσις ἁπλῶς and Plato's proposals.

with τίνες οὖν (753d 7) he took to be the original version, pointing out that it follows aptly the sentence just preceding the insertion beginning with σμικρὸν δὲ, and furthermore that its displacement to the position it now occupies interrupts the continuity between ἀποφηνάντων ἄρχοντας and οἱ δὲ δὴ γενόμενοι (754d 4). This hypothesis, however, does not solve all our difficulties and it creates new ones of its own. Wilamowitz apparently overlooked the fact that the election described in 753b-d, which is included by him in the later version, obviously cannot belong there, since all the candidates put forward in this election are citizens of the new colony, whereas this version has already prescribed (752e) that eighteen of the thirty-seven are to be Cnossians. Nor did he notice the strange inconsistency between the promise in 753b of a description of the later procedure (i.e. προελθόντος δὲ χρόνου . . . αἵρεσις αὐτῶν ἔστω τοιάδε τις) and the description which follows and which obviously applies to the first election.

To remove these difficulties it is only necessary to modify Wilamowitz' hypothesis to make the earlier version begin with πάντες μὲν κοινωνούντων (753b 4). This would then be what originally followed after ἂν ἑκάσταις εἴη (751b 1), or after ἔχει γὰρ οὖν οὕτω (751a 3), as I suggest below. The sequence of ideas in the original version would then be as follows. "We are ready now for the establishment of offices," says the Athenian, and proceeds immediately to the election (the *first* election, of course) of the "archontes." After this has been described, he raises the question how this election can be properly carried out in a community so new and so inexperienced, and suggests that a supervisory board (of one hundred Cnossians and an equal number from the colonists) be set up ad hoc and discharged when "the offices" are filled. Then he proceeds to the discussion of the duties of the archontes just elected (754d 4ff.). This makes a smooth sequence of ideas and is consonant with Plato's manner of writing.

The later version, extending down to λεγόμενα (753b 1), also gives a consistent and continuous text. The course of thought is as follows. We are ready for the establishment of offices, says the Athenian. But before we proceed to the elections, we must note how important it is to select good officers, for without them our laws, however good, will be useless or worse. And to make a wise selection will be difficult for our colonists, who will not know each other well, and will not have had the proper training for this task. Some time will have to elapse before they can be properly habituated to our laws. I suggest that the Cnossians make the first selection of nomophylakes—by far the most important of the officers—choosing eighteen of themselves and nineteen from the colonists. When these have been chosen, their duties (and those of their successors) shall be as follows (754d).

Wilamowitz' judgment that the version which comes first in our text is the later of the two seems to be even more plausible when his hypothesis is revised as I have suggested. The difficulty of getting started—which is introduced almost as an afterthought in the other version—is here placed at the head of the account and is treated with greater fullness. But there is no good reason for making this second version begin with σμικρὸν δὲ (751b) and the thought it develops is so closely dependent upon the distinction between the establishment of offices and the making of laws for these various offices (751a) that it would seem better to make this later version begin with δύο εἴδη (751a 4). Πάντες μὲν οὖν of the earlier version would come as naturally at this point as at ἂν ἑκάσταις εἴη.

Thus considered, the first part of this passage has every appearance of being a revision intended to replace what follows, and perhaps actually in its intended position in Plato's text when Philippus took over the task of putting the *Laws* into final shape. Now if the earlier version was actually found among Plato's materials, we can understand why Philippus would hesitate to discard it; and we are thankful that he did not do so, for it contains an important account of a mode of election which Plato had carefully considered and worked out in detail. But in order to use it in the text Philippus had to provide some sort of plausible transition. The sentence ὡς μὲν οὖν γένοιτ' ἂν . . . τοιάδε τις (753b) looks like such a device—a careless one, as it happens, because it promises to describe something (the *later* election of the nomophylakes) which is quite different from what actually follows. If this inconsistency escaped Wilamowitz' sharp scrutiny, it is not surprising that it was unnoticed by Philippus.

CHAPTER VI

THE ADMINISTRATION OF JUSTICE

PLATO presents his proposals for the administration of justice as part of the law establishing "the offices" (767a); and like the constitution we have just examined they bear the imprint of Athenian experience. The courts and procedures with which Plato was familiar in fourth-century Athens were the result of a long process of development. As in most archaic societies the function of giving justice is a prerogative of kings and nobles, so in early Athens the nine archons and the council of the Areopagus were the chief judicial as well as administrative officers of the state. But this aristocratic system of justice was gradually whittled away with the development of democracy. Solon provided for appeal to the people, thus setting up a novel institution, the popular court, distinct from the administrative organs of the state and competent to reverse a magistrate's decision.[1] This right was no doubt at first exercised in a very halting and rudimentary fashion, but Solon's innovation gives the clue to understanding almost all later judicial developments at Athens. The successive reforms of Cleisthenes, of Ephialtes, and of Pericles gradually reduced the powers of the magistrates until their function in the administration of justice had become mainly that of giving a preliminary hearing to, and bringing before the popular courts, cases involving violations of the law in their respective jurisdictions. But the transfer of judicial powers to the popular courts was never complete. The court of the Areopagus retained jurisdiction over homicide, and even the magistrates still possessed some independent judicial competence; they could impose small fines, and settle disputes between citizens out of court when the amount of money involved was relatively small.

This was the judicial system under which Plato lived and with which, as the *Laws* shows, he was expertly acquainted—a system in which most legal issues were settled in court, though the magistrates still preserved some relics of an earlier and much more extensive

---

[1] This is the unanimous opinion of the ancient authorities (Arist. *Const. Ath.* VII, 3; IX, 1; *Pol.* 1274a 3-5; Lys. x, 15-16; Plut. *Solon* 18,2). We may honor this tradition without believing that Solon was the author of the fourth-century δικαστήρια, except as they were developments of his right of appeal to the people. Aristotle uses fourth-century terminology, but he shows that he is well aware of the distinction between what Solon instituted and what came out of his institution later. See Bonner and Smith I, 252-253.

judicial competence. Judicial functions accordingly are exercised in his state partly by magistrates (ἀρχαί) and partly by courts (δικαστήρια, κριτήρια). This distinction, however, does not imply—as a modern reader might infer—two kinds of personnel, magisterial and nonmagisterial; for Plato's higher courts are themselves composed of magistrates and ex-magistrates. It is rather a distinction of procedure, and we can understand it if we distinguish the preliminary stage of a trial—i.e. the filing of a claim or accusation and the summoning of the defendant—from the later stage of finding a verdict. The characteristic of court procedure is that judgment is rendered by a body (it may be a group of administrative officials) distinct from the magistrates that first hear the charges and bring them into court. When the same magistrates have not merely the function of receiving charges or initiating action but also the function of giving judgment, the proceeding may be called magisterial. We shall examine this procedure first.

JUSTICE BEFORE THE MAGISTRATES

The primary duty of all magistrates is to guard the city,[2] a duty that carries with it the right to punish for violations of the law and for breaches of public order in the various areas under their control. In performing his duties, therefore, a magistrate is sometimes exercising judicial powers: "Every magistrate must also be a judge (καὶ δικαστής) in some matters" (767a). Of the penalties that magistrates may impose, fines are the most frequently mentioned in Plato's law —fines for damage to public buildings (764b, 779c), for premature harvesting of grapes (844e), for careless use of fire (843e), for not keeping an insane person under control (934d), for failure to vote (756de, 764a) or to marry by the prescribed age (774a), for giving excessive dowry (774d), and (upon an inferior magistrate) for failing to perform a duty the law places upon him (774b, 936a). The

[2] "Nothing, so far as possible, is to be left without a guard" (760a). The "guards" (φρουραί) mentioned immediately afterwards include the generals and other military officers, the prytanies, the astynomoi, the agoranomoi, and the agronomoi. In another passage (935b) we read of ἄρχοντες in the temples (i.e. priests), at public ceremonies and sacrifices (probably the educator and the supervisors of music and gymnastics), in the courts (the πρόεδροι of 949a) and in the assembly. Besides these there are supervisors of marriage (784a), of nurses and children (794b), of emigration (929d), and others (813c) whose ἐπιμέλεια gives them, to Plato's way of thinking, something of the character of archontes. We have seen in the preceding chapter that the guardians exercise oversight over these subordinate "guards" and assist them on occasion in enforcing the law.

magistrates may also sentence an offender to be flogged (764b, 845a, 879e), or imprisoned (764b), or banished (935e). These last-mentioned penalties are in the main, it seems, reserved for metics and slaves. It was a principle of Attic law that free men are exempt from bodily punishment; but Plato sometimes prescribes stripes for metics (879e), and even for citizens on occasion (762c, 845c, 932b).[3] These particulars are not an exhaustive inventory of Plato's law on this subject, and no doubt his law itself pretends to give only an illustrative sample from the multitude of circumstances in which the magistrates are expected to administer reproof, correction, and punishment to persons careless of their duties and of the rights of others.

Although the principle is nowhere explicitly stated, it is evident that this judicial capacity of the magistrates is limited, at least in the punishment of citizens. For example, the agoranomoi and the astynomoi, when acting separately, may not impose a fine of more than a hundred drachmae, but if the two boards of magistrates are acting together the maximum is two hundred (764b). Again the law itself determines the fines for various offenses, perhaps for the great majority of them; if the magistrates think a particular offender deserves a greater fine, they may impose it, but have to take the case to court to have the penalty confirmed (949de). In thus setting a limit to the discretion of his magistrates, Plato is following Attic precedent, though he is apparently inclined to set the limit considerably higher; the maximum fines mentioned in 764b are double and quadruple the fine of fifty drachmae that appears to have been the limit at Athens in the fourth century for magistrates comparable to Plato's astynomoi and agronomoi.[4]

In addition to these police powers, some of these boards of officers have competence to hear and settle private claims. Thus "the priests" are to judge claims by or against transient foreigners, to the extent of fifty drachmae (953b). Likewise disputes between citizens and metics about payment for work done, and other claims for damages up to the amount of fifty drachmae, are within the competence of the astynomoi to adjudicate (847b); it must be merely an oversight that the same authority is not explicitly conferred on the agronomoi, in the villages (848e), since there are so many passages in which these two groups of officers are assigned parallel powers in their respective

[3] Cf. Dem. xxxii, 55, and my *Plato's Law of Slavery*, 66ff.
[4] Lipsius 53; Busolt-Swoboda 1054-1055 and notes; Bonner and Smith i, 279; and Kahrstedt, *Untersuchungen zur Magistratur in Athen*, 213f.

areas (881c, 920c, 936c; cf. 764b, 844c). In disputes between citizens the magistrates' authority is much more extensive.

When a man has wronged another, whether a neighbor or some other citizen . . . the judges of the plaintiff's claim shall be the five,[5] if it be for a petty matter; but larger claims, up to the amount of three minae, shall be judged by the five and twelve together. 761de

From the agricultural law (842e-846c) we get a vivid picture of the sorts of disputes Plato has in mind: claims for damages arising from trespass, straying cattle, decoying of bees, planting crops too near the boundary line, or the careless use of fire, as well as differences over rights of way and the use of streams and springs.

In all such disputes the agronomoi shall be arbiters (ἐπιγνώμονες), judges (δικασταί), and assessors (τιμηταί)—for claims involving larger amounts, the whole of the tribal contingent, as was said in an earlier passage [i.e. 761de], and for smaller ones the phrourarchs. 843d

The law of 846a makes it clear that any claim of injury to person or property, whether done by violence or stealth, whether done by the defendant himself or by one of his slaves or animals, comes within the competence of these magistrates; and 873e makes them judges in a case of death caused by an animal. In these provisions Plato is again following the precedent of Attic law, which permitted magistrates to settle small claims; but whereas at Athens the maximum in such cases was ten drachmae,[6] Plato will permit his magistrates to judge cases involving many times that amount. One drachma was the normal day's wage in the fifth century, and though wages were somewhat higher in the fourth, for the cost of living had risen, even so three minae (three hundred drachmae) would represent a considerable part of a year's income for a wage earner. It is perhaps for this reason that Plato limits to fifty drachmae the competence of the magistrates in cases involving metics; any claim involving more than this will go before the courts (847b).

It is clearly intended that these magistrates shall exercise their judicial functions as a group, not individually. The texts, with only one apparent exception, use the plural in these cases, some of them clearly asserting, the others implying, collective action.[7] Even the apparent

[5] For the meaning of the reference to the "five" and the "twelve," see the account of the agronomoi in the preceding chapter.
[6] Bonner and Smith 1, 282; Lipsius 53.
[7] 761de, 764bc, 843de, 844cd, 845e, 846a, 847ab, 879e, 936c.

exception, when carefully examined, comes into accord with the rest. This concerns a dispute between neighbors regarding a dam or drainage ditch:

Either party may call in an astynomos, if it is in the city, or an agronomos if in the country, and get an order as to what each is to do; and if either does not abide by the order, he is liable to prosecution . . . and if he loses he shall pay double damages to the injured party for refusing to obey the magistrates. 844cd

Here we seem to have a single magistrate making a judicial declaration, but his powers are in fact limited. He can issue an order, but he cannot enforce it, a court decision being required for this. But the collegial character of the action is shown in the closing phrase, which implies that in the original order the single magistrate was acting as representative of the group. Here we should recall what was said in the preceding chapter regarding the collegial character of actions taken by the guardians, the highest magistrates in the state.

In adopting collegiality, Plato is following a principle firmly imbedded in Athenian practice.[8] From the time of Solon, at least, all Athenian magistrates acted as boards, or colleges. This was probably not an original feature of Greek law.[9] In early days the magistrates acted as individuals, a practice that continued among certain Greek states and among the magistrates in Roman law. The development of collegiality in Attica is closely connected with the development of democracy; it brought more citizens into official positions, and the absence of any hierarchy within the board of magistrates emphasized the fundamental equality of its members. At the same time it provided a measure of protection against arbitrary or malicious administration, a protection obviously necessary after these offices began to be filled by lot. Nowhere else, so far as we know, was collegiality so generally followed. The law of Gortyn never mentions a court or a board of magistrates; it is always "the judge" who punishes or fines. And at Sparta Aristotle tells us that the ephors judged, some one kind of case, some another.[10] It was only after the middle of the fourth century that Athenian practice began to diverge from this principle, with the creation of a series of special offices held by individuals, such as the treasurer of the military fund, and the assignment of generals to spe-

[8] Kahrstedt, *op.cit.* 148ff.; Busolt-Swoboda 481, 1059f.
[9] Wilamowitz, *Staat und Gesellschaft der Griechen*, Leipzig, 1910, 76.
[10] *Pol.* 1275b 9.

cific functions.[11] Plato is therefore following a practice of long standing, and one particularly associated with democratic Athens.

No appeal from a decision by the magistrates seems to be permitted
in Plato's law, nor was it permitted at Athens.[12] But Attic law provided
that at the audit ($\epsilon \check{v} \theta v v a$) which a magistrate had to undergo at
the end of his term claims of redress for alleged injustice could be
heard and judged. Plato's law includes this provision, as we have
seen. But it also provides an immediate remedy for a wrong done
by a magistrate in the exercise of his judicial powers, viz. a suit for
damages in the ordinary courts.

If any magistrate appears to have shown injustice in imposing penalties,
he shall be liable for double the amount to the injured party; moreover
an unjust decision by a magistrate with respect to any claim may be
brought before the public courts by anyone who wishes. 846b

This is such an unusual remedy for judicial injustice that we are
inclined at first to suppose that the language does not mean what it
seems to. But this suit for damages occurs in another law covering
the abuse of their powers by the agronomoi.

As for the rural magistrates, if they commit any act of insolence ($\dot{\epsilon} \grave{a} v$
$\dot{v} \beta \rho \acute{\iota} \zeta \omega \sigma \acute{\iota} \ \tau \iota$) in the matters over which they have supervision, by issuing
inequitable orders, or trying to seize and take away the property of the
farmers without their consent, or if they receive gifts from persons seeking
favors or render unjust judgments ... if the damage claimed is one mina
or less, let the case be submitted for judgment by the villagers and neighbors; if it is more, or if they [i.e. the defendant magistrates] refuse to
submit to judgment, let the injured party bring suit in the common
courts, and if he wins his case, let him receive double damages. 761e-762b

The court of "villagers and neighbors" and the "common courts"
are, as we shall see later, the ordinary courts for settling private suits;
the suit against a magistrate, therefore, comes before the regular
courts, not before a special tribunal. Such special tribunals were
known in Plato's day, for Aristotle mentions, as one of the eight
kinds of courts in a state, a court "for settling disputes between private persons and magistrates about penalties."[13] In making no place
for such a special court, Plato's law embodies a feature of the rule of
law as it is understood by Anglo-American jurists, viz. that public

11 Busolt-Swoboda 1060.
12 Bonner and Smith II, 245f.
13 *Pol.* 1300b 21.

officials may be called to account before the ordinary courts. A second point to note is that this liability of the magistrate is re-enforced by permitting a suit to be brought against him not merely by the injured party, but by someone else on behalf of the person injured.[14] The importance of this becomes clear when we reflect that a man against whom a magistrate has pronounced judgment might be prevented from bringing suit by this very judgment (e.g. in a case of imprisonment), so that if he is to get redress it must be through some third party.

Whether this particular remedy of Platonic law is Plato's own invention or is a reflection of actual Greek procedure cannot be determined with certainty. Kohler and Ziebarth affirm that it was a general principle of Greek law that no magistrate could be sued during his term of office; but the situation is more correctly expressed by Lipsius who merely says that we know of no such suits.[15] The absence of instances may indeed justify an inference with respect to Attic law, at least in the late fifth and fourth centuries, for which the literary remains are so abundant; for if such a remedy was available at that time, it is strange that no reference to it should have survived in the orators and historians. But it must be remembered that the Athenian magistrates of this period enjoyed very limited judicial powers, so that there would be relatively little need for such a remedy. In the earlier period, when magistrates had less restricted competence, it seems that some redress was provided for judicial wrongs committed by them. If what Aristotle tells us about the Areopagus in the Draconian reforms can be relied upon, Draco provided that anyone who thought he had been wronged by a magistrate could lay his grievance before the Areopagus.[16] Solon provided for appeal to the dicastery. In the fourth century a litigant who felt he had been wronged by an arbitrator (not through the verdict, for that was subject to appeal, but through some defect in legal procedure) could bring him to account before the whole board of arbitrators, who could impose the penalty of atimia if they saw fit.[17] Finally, Aristotle's men-

[14] ὁ βουλόμενος (846b) is the regular way of expressing this capacity to bring suit on behalf of another person.

[15] Josef Kohler and Erich Ziebarth, *Das Stadtrecht von Gortyn*, Göttingen, 1912, 127; Lipsius 802-803.

[16] *Const. Ath.* IV, 4. The reliability of this portion of the Draconian constitution is not subject to the doubts that attach to the other provisions; see Bonner and Smith I, 95, 145 n. 3.

[17] Arist. *Const. Ath.* LIII, 6; Bonner and Smith II, 238.

tion of a special court for such disputes shows that some such remedy as Plato proposes was available in at least some Greek states. It is therefore highly probable that Plato's proposals for the protection of the citizen against abuse of magisterial powers had its analogies and prototypes in positive Greek law.

It may seem that the individual liability of the magistrate under Plato's law is inconsistent with the collegial character of the magistrates' action. When liability is under consideration, Plato often uses the singular; whereas the plural regularly occurs, as we have seen, in connection with magisterial actions and decisions. It is evidently the intent of Plato's law that a magistrate be held liable for an unlawful act, even though it was done under the authority of the board of magistrates of which he was a member. But the same anomaly is manifest in Athenian law, which permitted a charge to be brought against an individual at his euthyna, though the duties of the office he had held had been discharged jointly with his colleagues.[18] Any inequity which this individual liability might seem to involve would doubtless tend to be corrected, in practice, by the difficulty of obtaining judgment unless there was a real as well as a formal connection between the defendant and the action complained of.

We have yet to consider the judicial powers of the higher officials, the euthynoi and the guardians of the laws. The euthynoi are almost alone among the magistrates in being exclusively a judicial body; their sole function is to examine the records and accounts of the various officers and impose penalties for maladministration or injustice. The range of their discretion in assessing penalties is wide, for they have the right to impose the death sentence. But like the other magistrates they are held responsible for their decisions. We have already seen that an official who believes he has been judged unjustly by the euthynoi may summon them before the select judges, where he may be acquitted of the charges against him (946d). This is not a suit for damages, like the remedy considered earlier, but an appeal, the result being merely to confirm or to reverse the decision against the appellant. But Plato's law goes further: if an appellant wins his case before the select judges, he then has the right to prosecute the euthynoi who charged him unjustly (946e). Thus these high

---

[18] Busolt-Swoboda 1061. There is more than an analogy here with the principle of Anglo-American law that no public official can escape liability for unlawful acts on the ground that they were done under orders from above. Cf. Vinogradoff, *Historical Jurisprudence* II, 114; and Lys. XXII, 5-6.

officials, like all others, are liable to punishment for the misuse of their judicial power. There is no parallel to this in Attic law.

As for the guardians of the laws, there are some cases in which it is clear that they exercise magisterial justice, as this term was defined above. Thus they may punish extravagance at marriage feasts (775b), possibly also at funerals (959de). The three eldest guardians, in conjunction with three of the supervisors of marriage, may punish for neglect of parents, if the offender is under thirty years of age (932ab). They may banish a child born of mixed slave and free parentage, together with its mother (930e). There are certain fines imposed for failing to attend the assembly or to take part in elections, and it seems that the guardians are responsible for assessing the penalty (756c-e, 764a, 765a). They may also fine, or otherwise punish, for the possession of unauthorized private shrines (910c). They constitute a court before which an accusation of "ignoble gain" (αἰσχροκέρδεια) is to be tried, but the procedure implied is a γραφή (754e) or a φάσις (745a), which suggests a preliminary hearing before another magistrate; and if so this would not constitute a case of magisterial justice. On the other hand, there is no provision for an appeal from the verdict of the guardians in such a case. There is a similar uncertainty in the provision that they are to see that punishment is inflicted for a breach of duty among the agronomoi (762d); it is not clear whether this means that they are empowered to judge and impose penalties, or merely that they bring cases to the attention of the "five" and the "sixty."

In almost all other cases in which judicial responsibilities are assigned to them, either they are agents in executing a judgment, or they initiate legal proceedings before another court, or if they themselves render judgment, it is subject to appeal and reversal. Thus they are empowered to imprison a homicide who returns before the period of his exile has expired (864e); this is simply enforcing a judgment that has already been rendered by a court. Similar to this is their action against a homicide who has been exiled on penalty of death if he returns; here they execute the death penalty if the guilty man returns (866c). Likewise they can pronounce sentence of death upon a man who resists a court judgment against him (958c). But the pardoning of a homicide who seeks admittance at the end of his term of exile involves a new legal judgment, and there is no mention of an appeal from their decision in this case, if they are the "judges" referred to

(867e). They have the responsibility of supervising the guardianship of orphans, and constitute a court for deciding disputes that arise in such relations (924c, 926cd). But their decisions are subject to appeal to another court, and if one of them has himself been named guardian of an orphan he is subject to legal prosecution if he is thought to have neglected his duty (928bc). They also constitute a kind of court of domestic relations, with power (in conjunction with the supervisors of marriage) to grant a divorce to a childless couple, and punish with atimia certain kinds of domestic folly and vice not further specified (784bc); but the sentence of atimia may be contested in the courts. Again, the eldest guardian shall act as adviser to a son who thinks his father is mentally incompetent; and if he thinks the charge well grounded, he is the son's advocate and witness at the court proceedings that follow (929e). Finally, with the select judges they constitute a court for capital offenses, which will be discussed more fully in the next section of this chapter. These passages show that the function of the guardians is mainly to see that legal procedures are employed for the settlement of disputes and the punishment of offenses; only rarely are they empowered to give judgment and impose penalties.

Thus it seems that Plato's assertion of responsibility holds for all officials without exception. Or does it?

No judge or magistrate shall be ἀνυπεύθυνος in the exercise of his authority as judge or magistrate, except those who, like kings, render final decision. 761e

What is the meaning of this exception? The guardians are the magistrates who are most like kings in Plato's state; but to regard them as giving final judgment would conflict with some of the provisions just reviewed which show that their decisions may be appealed and reversed. The difficult clause in the passage quoted may better be taken, I think, as a reminder that in any legal system there must be some judges whose decision is final. We shall see in the following section that Plato's law is far more generous in its provisions for appeal than was Attic law, or any other Greek law that we know of; but a case cannot be appealed indefinitely to higher tribunals, and even in Plato's state there must be, for every kind of dispute, a decision which puts an end to the case. To render a judge at the final stage at law subject to further legal action for his decision would obviously be a contradiction in procedure. The persons here designated as rendering the final decision would be different for different cases. In some it would be the court of select judges,[19] in others the court for capital offenses,[20] in others some special court like that set up to try a charge against a euthynos (948a); and in still others, where no appeal or other remedy is permitted, it would be the magistrate who imposes the penalty. Plato does not always indicate where this process of legal remedies comes to an end, but the trail seldom leads us to the guardians.

Nevertheless the details of magisterial justice in Plato's state show clearly that Plato would assign to his magistrates a far larger measure of judicial competence than they exercised at Athens. Their discretion in assigning punishments and in awarding damages is several times higher than the limit allowed the magistrates under Attic law. In this respect Plato leans toward the practices of the oligarchies of his time, where magistrates were much more "respected" than they were in democratic Athens.[21] But as a counterpoise to this increase in magisterial competence Plato's law provides various, and sometimes unusual, legal remedies. This insistence on the responsibility of magistrates is something he had learned primarily from Athenian democracy, and in his effort to protect the private citizen against abuse of official power he goes even further than his native city had gone, further perhaps than any other system of law, ancient or modern, has ever attempted to go.

THE COURTS

The distinctive feature of the administration of justice at Athens after the middle of the fifth century was the supremacy of the popular courts (δικαστήρια)—large bodies of judges (δικασταί), containing from two hundred to a thousand members each, selected by lot immediately before the opening of the cases which they were to hear. Any citizen over the age of thirty, who was not in debt to the state nor under atimia for any other reason, was eligible for inclusion in the annual panel from which the judges, or dicasts, were drawn by lot to form the courts needed on any given day. These courts were not only the highest tribunals in the state, from which there was no appeal; they were practically the only tribunals, their

[19] 767a: τέλος ἐπιθέτω τῇ δίκῃ; 768b: τὸ τέλος κρίνειν.
[20] 856a: τέλος ἐπιθεῖναι τῇ τοιαύτῃ δίκῃ.
[21] Cf. Busolt-Swoboda 368, and Kahrstedt, *op.cit.* 196ff.; and below, Note 67.

competence covering almost the whole range of civil and criminal litigation. Of the older courts of magistrates only the council of the Areopagus retained something of its former judicial powers, viz. its jurisdiction over premeditated homicide, poisoning, and arson. All other matters (except those of the most trivial sort) came, either immediately or on appeal from arbitrators, before the heliastic courts[22] for settlement, or before that other manifestation of the sovereign demos, the full assembly (δῆμος πληθύων).

The supremacy of these courts was but a logical development of the fundamental principle of Athenian democracy, the right of all citizens to take part in the government, and a reaction against the system of earlier days, when power (including the power of declaring the law and applying it) reposed in privileged families. This extension of the democratic principle placed a heavy burden upon it, a burden greater, many people have thought, than the principle can bear. The members of the dicastery were judges in the strict sense of the term, authorized to determine the law covering the case as well as the facts in the arguments of the litigants. This required a much wider knowledge of the law than we can presuppose in the average citizen today. But Attic law was much simpler than modern law and more accessible; inscribed on pillars and wooden tablets in the Agora, it could easily be consulted and could hardly fail to be noticed by the citizen as he went about his daily business. The other institutions of Athenian life provided him abundant opportunity and incentive for making his knowledge of the law more precise and thorough. Every citizen was a member of the assembly from about the age of twenty. The assembly often had to deal with legal as well as with executive matters, and its many meetings during the year, attended usually by some thousands of citizens, could hardly fail to give the average Athenian a technical familiarity with his laws that the citizen in a modern state inevitably lacks. Service on the dicasteries, to which a man became eligible at the age of thirty, and experience in other offices of government, to which in almost all cases any citizen was eligible, would be simply a continuation of this education. Moreover, the very size of these courts (it has been conserva-

---

22 Ἡλιαία was evidently the name of the popular court instituted by Solon (cf. Lys. x, 16), a name probably related to the Doric word for public assembly, ἀλία or ἀλιαία (see Bonner and Smith I, 157 n. 5). In later days the popular courts, the judges who sat in them, and the oath they took were often designated by derivatives of this ancient term.

tively estimated that in the fifth century from several hundreds to more than a thousand dicasts would be hearing trials on every day that was not a holiday or a day of assembly)[23] brought about a wide diffusion of the educational effects of this experience. The size of these courts had another consequence which is too often overlooked. They were almost immune to bribery and intimidation, and were able—something always difficult for any legal system to effect—to bring wealthy and powerful offenders to account. We must conclude that the popular courts could not have held their own for so long a time among a people as intelligent as the Athenians if they had not possessed definite merits.

But this does not mean that they were universally approved. Many Athenians of Plato's day seriously doubted whether courts of this size and constitution were a proper agency for the administration of justice. The lack of opportunity for deliberation amongst the judges, or for questioning of the witnesses and principals before the verdict was rendered; the susceptibility of the dicasts to flattery and other appeals to their emotions; their distrust of cleverness, and at the same time their vulnerability to misrepresentations of law and fact; the ease with which they could sometimes be manipulated by the leaders in party strife; and the anonymity of their voting, rendering the dicasts individually immune to attack or criticism—these faults were frequently alleged in antiquity.[24] In his earlier dialogues Plato had given memorable expression to some of these criticisms. The *Apology*, though primarily a defense of Socrates, may also be read as an indictment of the system under which Socrates was condemned to death—before a court unable to devote more than a single session to this capital charge, so disorderly at times that the defendant could scarcely make himself heard, and withal left to its own devices for distinguishing between what was relevant to the formal charge and irrelevant appeal to political or personal prejudice. The *Gorgias*, treating of the sham art of rhetoric, also treats of the sham art of justice which it serves; for the purpose of rhetorical skill, as Gorgias states it, is "persuasion in the dicasteries and other crowds" (454b). The *Republic* is sprinkled with caustic observations, such as the ref-

[23] George M. Calhoun, *Introduction to Greek Legal Science*, Oxford, 1944, 34; cf. the whole section (30-48) for a fuller treatment of the material of this paragraph.
[24] Aristoph. *Wasps* passim; Andoc. II, 19; Xen. *Apol.* 4; *Const. Ath.* I, 18; Thuc. III, 38; VIII, 68; Isoc. VII, 54; VIII, 129-130; XV, 142. See Bonner and Smith II, 293-306.

erence to the "sleepy dicast" nodding on his bench during the proceedings (405c), and the unforgettable picture of the "Great Creature" (μέγα θρέμμα), who shows his most stupid and brutal side when sitting in judgment on those who displease him (492ff.). The comments in the *Laws* are in the same vein, but more pointed. "A dicast who is without voice, and who does not have more to say in the examination than the contending parties . . . would not be adequate to decide questions of justice; therefore it is not easy for a multitude to judge well—nor for a small court either, if its members are ordinary" (φαῦλοι, 766d). "In a city where the dicasteries [i.e. the dicasts] are ordinary and without voice and conceal their opinions and decide cases secretly; or, what is even more dangerous, when they are not silent but full of tumult, like theatres, applauding and hooting in turn this or that orator—then there is a very serious evil that affects the whole state" (876b).

From these criticisms, and from Plato's general distrust of popular judgment on matters requiring scientific analysis and intellectually informed judgment (and the giving of justice is certainly one of them), we might expect that one of the first items in his program of reform would be the elimination of the popular courts, as the oligarchs of his time usually demanded, though for less disinterested reasons. Nevertheless Plato does not feel free to dispense with popular courts, for they expressed something essential to the conception of citizenship held by his fellow countrymen. "He who is without the right of sitting with his fellows in the courts of law thinks that he is without a share in the city" (768b). The sentiment expressed here is brought out more fully in the passage of the *Politics* in which Aristotle seeks to define the nature of citizenship and concludes that the citizen, in the most exact sense of the word, is one who participates in deliberation (ἀρχὴ βουλευτική) and in the administration of justice (ἀρχὴ κριτική).[25] Whether this was Plato's own conviction, or merely a current dogma that he thought a legislator had to accept, we find that in his Cretan city he insists upon popular participation in the administration of justice through courts set up in the Athenian fashion.

But this insistence upon popular participation runs contrary to other principles to which Plato is equally committed. One is the need of special competence for the performance of such an important

---

[25] *Pol.* 1275a 22-33; cf. b 17-21.

function as rendering justice. The *Republic* had laid it down that in a rightly ordered society functions are assigned according to capacity: "In our state a shoemaker will be a shoemaker and not a pilot also, and a farmer a farmer and not a judge also" (397e). This requirement is to some extent met in the *Laws* by the social and economic regulations that free his citizens, in the main, for "the craft of citizenship," but even among such a privileged and carefully educated group there will be differences of capacity that ought to be taken into account. "In a state where the courts have the best possible constitution," he says, "those who are to be judges will be well trained and tested" (εὖ τραφέντες and δοκιμασθέντες, 876c). The dicasts at Athens were not subject to the dokimasia, and a fortiori not to the particular kind of testing that would determine their fitness for the judicial task. A small court of tested judges also has the advantage of being able to exercise initiative and make its own examination of principals and witnesses, a procedure which Plato regarded as indispensable but was obviously impossible in the popular courts.

Plato's third principle is that the processes of justice must be leisurely enough to permit repeated examination of a case if necessary. "The respective contentions of the two parties must always be made clear, and lapse of time, leisureliness, and repeated examination are an advantage in clarifying the issue in dispute" (766e). The manner in which important cases were disposed of by the heliastic courts under the tyranny of the water clock, with a haste necessitated by the mass of litigation coming before them and by the impossibility of prolonging a case beyond a single day when large juries had to be assembled and paid, must have dismayed many a litigant and spectator. It is well to recall Socrates' dignified protest in the *Apology*: "If there were a law at Athens, as there is in other cities, that a capital cause should not be decided in one day, then I believe I should have convinced you" (37a). This principle would involve changes in procedure as well as in the organization of the courts, and we shall find some of Plato's most striking suggestions under this head.

To all these principles Plato is committed, and the result is a compromise, or as he would probably call it, a "mixture." He devises a system in which popular participation, selected competence, and repeated examination all find a place, by developing a procedure which was known but utilized only rarely at Athens, the procedure of appeal.[26] The result is three grades of courts, courts of first instance and two stages of appeal. The courts of first instance are variously called "villagers," "neighbors," or "arbitrators"; next above them stand the "tribal courts," which we shall see are constituted in all essential respects like the familiar Athenian dicasteries; and above them all is a court of select judges, as it is called, whose decision is final in all matters coming before it.[27]

For his courts of first instance, Plato has adapted to his purposes one of the most interesting and admirable features of the Athenian judicial sytsem. Every private suit at Athens was first assigned by lot to a public arbitrator (διαιτητής), a man in his sixtieth year or older, who endeavored to bring about an agreement between the contending parties. If this proved impossible, he was required to make a decision on the basis of the written claims and the evidence submitted. If his decision was accepted, the suit was ended; but either party could appeal to the dicastery, and in that case the documents were sealed and transmitted, together with a written statement of the arbitrator's finding, to the higher court.[28] Plato's system differs from the Athenian in that he prescribes not one arbitrator, but a panel, and he permits them to be selected by the parties to the litigation. Athenian law also permitted the alternative of privately selected arbitrators, but from their decision there was no appeal. Plato's system therefore combines elements of both private and public arbitration as practised at Athens. It is implied that these arbitrators will ordinarily be selected from among the neighbors and friends of the

[26] The use of the appeal in Attic law of the classical period has been denied; but see Bonner and Smith II, 232ff., and below, Note 29.

[27] The main references here are 766d-768e and 956b-957c; in both these passages the three stages are mentioned and described briefly. Other scattered references help us to fill in the details. The courts of first instance are called "villagers and neighbors" (κωμῆται καὶ γείτονες, 762a), "neighbors or chosen judges" (γείτονες ἢ αἱρετοὶ δικασταί, 915c), and "arbitrators or neighbors" (διαιτηταὶ ἢ γείτονες, 920d). (The "or" in each of the last two passages indicates alternative designations, not alternative referents.) For the "tribal courts," see below, Note 30.

[28] See the account in Lipsius 220-233; Arist. Const. Ath. LIII, 2-6. "The public arbitrators are one of the most interesting products of Athenian democracy. The design of the institution was excellent, to procure the settlement of private suits by experienced and impartial men whose first aim was to make peace. How far it was successful, and what amount of business was terminated without an appeal, cannot now be discovered. . . . But in appreciating the democracy it is important to remember that in a large number of disputes the constitution did not compel two quiet citizens to face the ordeal of a trial in court, but provided a cheap and simple and reasonable means of getting justice." Wyse, in Whibley, Companion to Greek Studies, Cambridge, 1931, 473-474.

litigants, for there are several passages connecting "neighbors and arbitrators" as if they were synonymous terms. In one case (the sale of a sick slave) where professional knowledge would be essential for the settling of the points at issue, it is prescribed that the arbitrators shall be physicians (916b). Presumably the hearing would be open, as were arbitral proceedings at Athens, "before neighbors and friends and those who know most about the matters in dispute" (766e). Since the arbitrator is a judge (δικαστής) and every judge is to give judgment under oath (948e), the arbitrator will give his verdict under oath, as was done at Athens.[29]

A litigant who is not satisfied with the decision rendered in the court of arbitrators has the privilege of appealing his case to the tribunals which we shall call "tribal courts," though this is only one

[29] In one passage (956c) Plato's language suggests that at Athens such a hearing before arbitrators was not ordinarily regarded as a trial before judges: διαιτηταὶ δικαστῶν τοὔνομα μᾶλλον πρέπον ἔχοντες. This has been universally construed by translators and commentators as meaning that "arbitrators" would be a more appropriate name for these officials than "judges." Stallbaum regarded the phrase as equivalent to διαιτηταὶ ἐπονομαζόμενοι—an opinion which is echoed by England, and followed implicitly by Jowett, Apelt, Bury, Taylor, Robin, Diès, and Cassarà. But if this is what Plato means, he has certainly chosen an awkward way of saying it. It would be far more natural to take δικαστῶν with τοὔνομα rather than as dependent on μᾶλλον πρέπον, thus making the phrase mean that δικασταί is the more appropriate name. Δικαστῶν τοὔνομα is a perfectly good Platonic idiom; cf. τὸ ὄνομα φθόνου, *Phil.* 48b; and τὸ τῶν ἀνθρώπων ὄνομα, *Crat.* 399b, followed immediately by its equivalent, τὸ ὄνομα ὁ ἄνθρωπος (399c). Thus Plato is protesting against current usage, not conforming to it. This interpretation accords better with the introduction of the court of arbitrators in the chapter on δικασταί (767ab). It also explains why this court is called a κυριώτατον δικαστήριον (767b)—another phrase that has caused perplexity to the commentators. Obviously Plato does not mean that it is final in authority, for its decisions are subject to appeal, as he proceeds to say, but that it is a court in the strictest sense of the term. If the arbitrators' judgment is accepted by both parties it closes the case legally, so as to bar any further action on the matter at a later date. Cf. Joseph Schulte, *Quomodo Plato in Legibus publica Atheniensium instituta respexerit*, Münster, 1907, 44-45: "Κυριώτατον non sic intellegendum est, quasi velet philosophus ab arbitris provocari, sed apte explicatur ita, ut ratam esse eorum sententiam Plato dicat, modo scilicet utraque pars in ea acquiescat."

In this insistence that the arbitrators are really a court with full powers, Plato is expressing the realities of the Athenian institution in the fourth century. The judicial status of the arbitrators at Athens is the main point at issue between those who assert and those who deny that the appeal is found in Attic law of the classical period. Bonner and Smith II, 235, 237 have shown satisfactorily, I think, that the Athenian arbitrator, if he failed to reconcile the parties and was forced to proceed to a verdict, was a judge in the full sense of the word. "The proceedings . . . are now practically the same as those of a regular court and include depositions, challenges, and laws. . . . If a witness properly summoned did not appear, the litigant could at once file a δίκη λιπομαρτυρίου against him before the arbitrator."

of various ways in which they are designated in Plato's text.[30] Of
the constitution of these tribal courts we are told explicitly very little. But it is clear enough that they are to be popular courts, selected
by lot. "It is necessary even in the settlement of private disputes
that all should have a part, as far as possible. . . . For this reason we
must set up courts according to tribes (κατὰ φυλάς), with judges
selected by lot (κλήρῳ), as occasion demands" (ἐκ τοῦ παραχρῆμα,
768b). Most translators and commentators have taken these texts
as indicating local courts established in the several tribes.[31] But there
is little evidence in favor of this interpretation, while there are
weighty arguments against it; and its general acceptance, until recently, has obscured from view one of the most significant parts of
Plato's judicial system.

The objections to the traditional interpretation can be stated
briefly.[32] In the first place, if it is Plato's intention to set up local
courts of this character, it would involve something quite different
from anything in the judicial system of Athens, or of any other Greek
city that we know; whereas it is mentioned in the *Laws* as something
familiar and not needing to be described in detail. Again, to regard
these tribal courts as local courts would be to ascribe a degree of importance to the tribe in judicial matters completely out of accord
with the insignificant role it plays in the political system. The tribe
has no local autonomy in Plato's state; the most that can be said is
that tribal distinctions are occasionally recognized in the selection of
officers, and this is all we need admit with regard to the constitution
of these courts. Furthermore, what would be the jurisdiction of one
of these tribal courts, interpreted in the traditional fashion? Each
court would presumably have jurisdiction over disputes between
members of its own tribe; but what of disputes between members
of different tribes? Although Plato's text abounds in references

---

[30] I.e. δικαστήρια κατὰ φυλάς, 768b, 921d; φυλετικὰ δικαστήρια, 768c; φυλετικαὶ δίκαι, 915c, 920d; κωμῆταί τε καὶ φυλέται, 956c; κοιναὶ δίκαι, 762b; κοινὰ δικαστήρια 846b, 847b.

[31] Barker's interpretation (337) is typical: "The court of second instance is the tribal court of each of the twelve territorial districts." Taylor translates: "courts for the several tribes"; Bury: "courts for each tribe"; des Places: "il doit y avoir, même dans les tribus, des cours ou les juges"; Robin: "des tribunaux dans chaque tribù"; Apelt: "für die einzelnen Phylen Gerichtshöfe." On the other hand, Cassarà's "costi-tui per tribù" seems to render it properly and Gernet's comment (cxxxiii) is very apt: "le second tribunal est à rapprocher de l'institution si caractéristique des héli-astes."

[32] For a fuller discussion, see my "On the Tribal Courts in Plato's *Laws*," AJP LXII, 1941, 314-321.

to particular circumstances and conditions affecting suits, there is nowhere any suggestion of a distinction between the court of the plaintiff's tribe and the court of the defendant's tribe, and of course no statement as to which of these courts would have jurisdiction. Finally, the designation of these courts as "common courts" (762b, 846b, 847b) certainly suggests central rather than local courts.[33]

If, then, these tribal courts are not local courts consisting of the fellow tribesmen of one or both the litigants, what are they? The obvious answer is that they are tribal courts in precisely the sense in which the Athenian dicasteries were, i.e. they were constituted by tribes. From Aristotle's account in the *Constitution of Athens* we know that in his time each dicastery contained an equal number of representatives from each of the ten tribes.[34] This method of selecting the dicasts goes back at least to the middle of the fifth century, for it seems to be established that the panel of six thousand dicasts, attested for the time of Pericles, consisted of an equal number from each tribe, chosen by lot.[35] Though changes were made in the system during the fourth century, the principle of selecting by tribes was never abandoned.[36] It was apparently felt that the body of dicasts, and each dicastery, represented the sovereign people; hence this method of selection would result in a court more representative of the demos and thus more competent to carry the sovereign judicial power. This procedure, therefore, with the theory underlying it, was old and familiar, and when Plato asserts that the people's share in the administration of justice must be recognized by setting up courts κατὰ φυλάς, he most certainly would be understood as meaning that these dicasteries are to consist of representatives from each of the tribes, especially since no alternative description of their organization is given. The expression he uses is exactly that employed by

[33] In 762b the identification of κοιναῖς δίκαις (reading δίκαις with Burnet and des Places instead of δίκας) as the tribal courts follows from the fact that they are courts of second instance, above the κωμῆται καὶ γείτονες; cf. 767a, 768c, 915c, 920d, 956c. In 846b either the stage of arbitration has been inadvertently omitted, or κοινὰ δικαστήρια refers to *all* the courts (arbitrators, tribal courts, court of select judges). In the light of 762b, where the κοιναὶ δίκαι are clearly distinguished from the arbitrators, the former seems the more likely alternative. The case mentioned in 847b is similar to the preceding and should be interpreted in the same fashion.

[34] *Const. Ath.* LIX, 7; LXIII, 1; cf. LXIII, 4; LXV, 4. H. Hommel, *Heliaia, Philologus Suppl.* XIX, 1927, 59ff.

[35] Bonner and Smith I, 230; Lipsius, 135f.

[36] For these changes, see Bonner and Smith I, 365ff., 372ff.; Lipsius, 139ff. and Hommel, *op.cit.* 109ff.

Aristotle to express the constitution of the Athenian dicasteries.[37] For Plato this method of selection distinguishes these courts both from his court of arbitrators, who are chosen by the parties to the suit, and from the select judges, chosen on a merit basis from the officeholders of the previous year; and hence they may properly be called δικαστήρια φυλετικά; and also, to indicate the popular character of their members, κωμῆται καὶ φυλέται.[38]

This interpretation gives an unexpectedly clear meaning to an otherwise cryptic statement in 956c. It is said that the κωμῆται καὶ φυλέται are to be divided by twelve, or into twelve parts (κατὰ τὸ δωδέκατον μέρος). England takes this clause as meaning that the members of each tribe are to be divided into twelve parts, each part serving as the tribal court for one month in the year. But this is inconsistent with the statement that the judges are to be selected "as occasion demands" (768b). Besides, a twelfth part of the tribe would be only thirty-five households, a number hardly large enough to furnish a popular court. The clue to understanding this text is provided by Athenian procedure. We know that in the fourth century, and perhaps earlier, the dicasts at Athens were divided into ten sections, as well as into ten tribes, these sections being denoted by the first ten letters of the alphabet, A to K.[39] Aristotle designates these sections as μέρη, the term used by Plato in 956c. This division into

[37] See particularly *Const. Ath.* LXIII, 1 and 4.

[38] Since there were none but popular courts at Athens, they were called simply δικαστήρια. But this terminology obviously would not do in Plato's state where there are other species of courts, and in the *Laws* δικαστήρια reverts to its general meaning. The lack of any current specific designation for the popular courts may explain the variety of designations for them in Plato's text. Δικαστήρια κατὰ φυλάς is the least ambiguous, and its meaning I think I have established. Φυλετικὰ δικαστήρια and φυλετικαὶ δίκαι are transparent paraphrases of it and cause no difficulty. Nor do κοιναὶ δίκαι and κοινὰ δικαστήρια; the inclusion of the "tribal courts" under these designations emphasizes their central, not local, character. But the phrase κωμῆταί τε καὶ φυλέται is at first sight rather puzzling. If φυλέται is given its usual meaning of "fellow tribesmen," this phrase suggests the court of arbitrators, rather than the popular courts; but the passage in which it occurs (956c) leaves no doubt that Plato is referring to the courts of second instance, above the διαιτηταί which he has just mentioned. Φυλέται then must be taken as meaning something like "countrymen," or "commoners," analogous to κωμῆται in Attic usage. This meaning of the term is not recorded in LSJ, but the word is obviously used in this sense in 955d; κωμῆται regularly has this meaning in Greek usage. The use of these two terms in conjunction therefore emphasizes the popular character of these courts.

[39] Lipsius 136, 139ff.; Arist. *Const. Ath.* LXIII, 4. These section divisions cut across the division into tribes. Selection by sections as well as by tribes would give a double cross section of the people. Perhaps it was felt that this method would give a court even more representative of the demos and hence more competent to discharge its judicial functions.

sections also was old and familiar in Plato's time, and he merely takes it for granted that this procedure would be employed in selecting the members of his tribal courts. Since in his state there are to be twelve tribes instead of ten, he would naturally divide his dicasts into twelve sections; and it is easily understood why he should make a passing reference to this particular detail, since it involves a departure from the familiar Athenian system, while refraining from giving further explanation which would be unnecessary for his readers.

It seems, therefore, that Plato's tribal courts are the familiar heliastic courts at Athens. Since the popular courts were regarded by both their friends and their foes as one of the most characteristic features of a democratic constitution, the inclusion of these courts in his system is clearly a concession to democracy and a recognition of the democratic principle. But Plato does not take over the popular courts without modification. He proposes certain reforms in procedure, which we shall examine later, intended to correct some of their more notorious defects; but more important than this, he permits appeal from their decisions to a higher court, if a litigant feels that he has not received justice. The effect of this innovation is to deny to his popular courts the judicial supremacy which was such an important factor in the power of the demos at Athens. But it would be a mistake to infer that the introduction of these courts is merely an empty gesture to democracy. Besides their educational value (which was emphasized at the beginning of this section), they would settle much, perhaps the greater part, of the litigation coming before them, since there is a penalty for unsuccessful appeal. We must also take into account the influence of the lower court on the higher one, differing in degree according to circumstances, but never altogether negligible.

"If anyone wishes to fight his case a third time in court, let him bring his suit before the select judges" (956cd; cf. 767a). This court of last instance is Plato's greatest innovation, and for this reason it receives first and fullest attention in the systematic account of the courts (767c-e). It is elected annually by the full body of all the officials.[40] They meet under solemn auspices in a temple and select

[40] If Plato's phrases (πάσας τὰς ἀρχάς, πάντας τοὺς ἄρχοντας) are taken literally, the electoral body would include the three hundred and sixty members of the council, the thirty-seven guardians, the three generals, the two hipparchs, the taxiarchs and phylarchs (ten of each), the three astynomoi, the five agoranomoi, an unspecified number of religious and educational officers, and the agronomoi (possibly only the sixty phrourarchs)—a sizable electoral body. Is it conceivable that Plato intends all

from each office in the state that magistrate whom they, under oath, consider to be the most competent in his group, and most likely to decide suits for his fellow citizens during the ensuing year "in the best and most pious manner" (ἄριστα καὶ ὁσιώτατα). The election is followed by a scrutiny of those who have just been chosen, conducted by the same body as those who have elected.[41] Any one found unsuitable as a result of this scrutiny is replaced by another elected in the same fashion. The size of the court is not stated, but if one member is to be chosen from each office mentioned previously in the sixth book, their total number will be fifteen or sixteen. The election is to be held on the last day of the year. This means that persons elected from annual offices will just be completing their terms, while those selected from offices with a longer term will during the ensuing year be both members of the high court and office holders. This situation is clearly anticipated in Plato's text. The election is to be held annually, but there is apparently no bar to re-election.

One would have to search long before finding any parallel or counterpart to this court in the institutions of Plato's countrymen, Athenian or other.[42] To certain isolated features of it there are indeed parallels. For the vesting of supreme judicial power in the magistrates there are numerous analogies—in the ephors of Sparta, the Areopagus of the older Athens, the cosmoi of Crete, and officials in numerous other oligarchically constituted states. The Spartan ephors and Cretan kosmoi were elected annually, as are Plato's judges. The Areopagus consisted of former archons, a provision also reflected in Plato's laws. But nowhere do we find a court composed of such a variety of officials, chosen in such a democratic fashion by their colleagues and peers on all levels of the administration. Or rather, since election was regarded as an aristocratic procedure, we should say that Plato's court expresses the idea of an aristocracy of officialdom. His proposal is not a passing fancy; a similar proposal for selecting such a high

---

these officers to leave their public duties for what would probably be a long electing session, followed by what might be an equally long session for the dokimasia of the persons elected? A similar difficulty is found in the prescription (767de) that when this court hears a case the officers that have elected it should attend. Some qualification is no doubt intended in both these cases, but the text gives us no hint what it is.

[41] This scrutiny would not be an unnecessary repetition of the election. See Chapter V, Note 156.

[42] Plato's proposal had in part been anticipated almost a century earlier by Hippodamus of Miletus, who proposed setting up a court "of elected elders" to act as a court of appeal for cases thought to have been improperly decided in the lower courts (Arist. Pol. 1267b 39). There is no evidence that this proposal was ever adopted.

court is set forth in one of his *Epistles* to the friends of Dion in Syracuse (356de).

This court of select judges is evidently the court that best embodies Plato's demand for special competence. It is easy to see why he should recruit it from the body of magistrates. In the absence of a professional class of lawyers or jurists, the only experts in the law would be persons experienced in its administration who were deemed by others in similar positions to have done their work with special competence. The members of Plato's court will always be in close touch with the problems of administration at all points in the government. Its membership will be subject to annual changes, likely to be rather sweeping, in spite of the possibility of re-election; this would prevent this court, or any group of its members, from attaining a position of entrenched power. These are advantages, and perhaps they are advantages that Plato deliberately seeks. A conspicuous disadvantage that cannot escape attention is that the short tenure of office and the frequent changes in membership would prevent the development of anything like judicial competence, as we understand the term, and would hinder the development of a judicial tradition. Again, one would expect that for service on this court Plato would require something like that philosophical competence, that insight into principles of reason from which right law derives its authority, which is a cardinal doctrine of the *Laws*. Perhaps it is intended that this court, either directly or indirectly, is to be linked to the Nocturnal Council, the body set up to explore just these fundamental principles of law and social policy. But if this is Plato's intention it is nowhere made explicit, and no formal mechanism is provided whereby it could be assured.

A court thus constituted, says Plato, should be as incorruptible as is humanly possible (768b); nevertheless its members are subject to prosecution if anyone thinks they have deliberately given false judgment in a case before them (767e). The charges are heard before the guardians, and if the defendant is found guilty he is liable for double damages to the injured person and for any additional penalties that the court may see fit to impose.[43] This is essentially the same remedy as that for redressing an unjust decision rendered by a magistrate, except that the charges against a select judge come before the guardi-

---

[43] Adopting Ritter's reading, followed by England, of διπλάσιον for the MS reading ἥμισυ in 767e 6. This change brings the law into agreement with that of 846b 3.

ans instead of before the common courts; since the select judges are a court of appeal from the common courts, charges against them must be brought before a different tribunal. The emphasis here, as before, is upon the individual responsibility of the judge, even though the decision rendered is a collective one. Voting is to be open —an obvious requirement if individual responsibility is insisted on. As a further check on the integrity of this court, it is prescribed that its proceedings shall be open to all who care to attend, and that the officials who have elected the court are required to attend (767de).

The courts we have been discussing thus far are those explicitly designed to deal with private litigation, i.e. with all those cases in which a private person accuses another person of injuring him and seeks justice in the courts. From these courts Plato explicitly distinguishes other courts (767bc) which function "when a citizen thinks that someone is injuring (ἀδικεῖ) the state (δημόσιον) and desires to aid the commonwealth" (τῷ κοινῷ). The line of separation that Plato draws between these two areas of litigation follows a familiar distinction in Attic law, but we shall misunderstand it if we take it as identical with our modern distinction between civil and criminal jurisdiction. For Plato's "private courts" will deal with many cases that under our procedure would be regarded as criminal in character.[44] It follows that these private courts often have the right to impose punishment as well as award compensation to the injured party. In this broad conception of what constitutes private wrong Plato is simply following Attic law. On the other hand, and again in con-

[44] Plato's language permits us to see clearly the full range of what he would regard as private wrong. The law of 846a prescribes that the magistrates and the courts are to have jurisdiction over all claims arising from any act whereby a person, either by his own hand or through his property or agents, does injury to the person or property of another, whether by violence or by deception. Thus their jurisdiction covers thefts and assaults, as well as torts. But in the law covering τραῦμα (876ff.) it appears that wounding in an attempt to kill comes before the court for capital offenses (877b). Whether τραῦμα committed in anger (878bc) comes before this court or before the "common courts" we cannot determine, though the concern with damages (βλάβος) suggests the latter. Certain exceptional kinds of personal injury (the wounding of kinsman, of parents, and unintentional injuries) are referred to special courts discussed below. Another passage shows that the private courts have jurisdiction over claims arising from breach of contract (920d-921d). This passage also specifies the conditions under which an action for breach of contract will lie: "Whenever a man has entered into an agreement and fails to perform, if it be not some act forbidden by law or decree, if the agreement was not forced from him by violence, and if he was not prevented by unforeseen accident, an action for breach of contract may be brought against him in the tribal courts, unless the case has previously been settled by neighbors and arbitrators" (920d).

sonance with Attic law, the offenses that come before Plato's public courts are but a small part of the offenses that would be classed as crimes in modern law. A modern criminal court will not only punish offenses against the community in its collective aspect, but also wrongs done to individuals which the community has an interest in punishing. In Plato's state the latter class of wrongs, by far the larger part of what are known as criminal offenses, will come before the courts for settling private disputes. Though in a sense this narrows the jurisdiction of public courts, it also—through the vagueness of the concept of injury to the people—leaves the door open to a host of suits that under our system would never be allowed to come into court. Plato's system testifies to the vividness with which the conception of a wrong done to the security and well-being of the community was present in his thought, as it was in the thought of his countrymen.

"In accusations of offenses against the public, it is necessary to give the multitude (τῷ πλήθει) a share in the decision; for when anyone wrongs the city, all are wronged and would rightly feel aggrieved if they had no part in passing judgment" (767e-768a). The sequel to this passage makes it clear that a popular court is intended, distinct in character from the tribal courts for settling private wrongs. This popular court for trying offenses against the state is nothing else than the full assembly of the people, as the use of the terms πλῆθος and δῆμος clearly shows.[45] This was not an innovation, but a recognition of the traditional right of a Greek community to punish offenses against its well-being, not only through the establishment of courts, but also through direct participation of citizens in the judicial process.[46] There were judicial powers enjoyed by the Athenian ecclesia precisely parallel to those indicated in Plato's text. It was before the assembly that the big state trials of the fifth century took place, such as those of Miltiades, Themistocles, Alcibiades, and the generals after the battle of Arginusae. It seems that the basis of the assembly's powers in these cases was the famous Decree of Cannonus, of uncertain date, which provided that anyone charged with having wronged the Athenian people should be bound and tried

[45] Δῆμος πληθύων was a technical term in Attic law designating a full or sovereign assembly. Cf. the repeated occurrence of πληθύοντος δήμου in the inscription (CIA I, 57 = IG I², 114) cited by Bonner and Smith I, 201; cf. 209ff., 299-300.
[46] Busolt-Swoboda 544.

before the people.⁴⁷ The case was introduced by a denunciation
(εἰσαγγελία) before the council and assembly, and the assembly had
authority either to try the case itself or to refer it to a heliastic court.⁴⁸
As in modern impeachment proceedings, the trial of such cases was
often as much political as judicial, and in the fully developed democracy the procedure of denunciation came to be used for comparatively trivial charges. Some time between the year 406 and the
middle of the fourth century the Athenians attempted to fix more
precisely the offenses which could be proceeded against by way of
εἰσαγγελία,⁴⁹ and after the middle of the century it seems that most
denunciations were referred to the dicasteries for trial.⁵⁰ But in spite
of this attempt at clarifying the law, it appears that the process continued to be a common remedy for wrongs, whether or not specified
in the law, which could be regarded as injuring the state.⁵¹

Plato's court of the demos for trying offenses against the state is
a clear reflection of the earlier Athenian εἰσαγγελία. Like the Decree of Cannonus, Plato's text makes an individual liable on the
general grounds of "wronging the people," and his assigning to the
demos the right to judge this vaguely worded charge accords with
the sentiments, and quite often the deliberate practices, of Athenian
democracy. If there is a fault here, it is one that Plato shares with
his countrymen. But here again Plato adopts this procedure only
with reservations. "While the beginning and also the end of such a
suit should be assigned to the people, the investigation (βάσανος)
must be conducted by three of the higher magistrates whom the
plaintiff and defendant shall agree on; if they cannot by themselves
come to an agreement, the council shall make the decision between

⁴⁷ Xen. *Hell.* I, vii, 20: τὸ Καννωνοῦ ψήφισμα . . . ὃ κελεύει ἐάν τις τὸν τῶν
'Αθηναίων δῆμον ἀδικεῖ δεδεμένον ἀποδικεῖν ἐν τῷ δήμῳ. Cf. Bonner and Smith I,
205ff.; Lipsius 43, 185ff. The generality of the charge, the archaic terminology of the
law (cf. ἀποδικεῖν) and the remnants of primitive procedure suggested (the offender
is to be bound or, as Aristophanes pictures it in *Eccles.* 1089-1090, to be held by his
accusers on either side during the proceedings) show that it was a very old law.
⁴⁸ Maine has shown that this procedure of εἰσαγγελία at Athens is a survival
of a very early conception of a *crimen*, or crime, as "an act involving such high
issues that the State, instead of leaving its cognisance to the civil tribunal or the
religious court, directed a special law or *privilegium* against the perpetrator. Every
indictment therefore took the form of a bill of pains and penalties, and the trial
of a *criminal* was a proceeding wholly extraordinary, wholly irregular, wholly independent of settled rules and fixed conditions." *Ancient Law*, 1861, 219-220, Everyman's Library edn.
⁴⁹ See the νόμος εἰσαγγελτικός cited in Hyp. IV, 7-8.
⁵⁰ Lipsius 191.
⁵¹ Cf. Hyp. IV, 1-3; Bonner and Smith 306ff.; Lipsius 194f.

their respective choices" (768a). This is another echo of Athenian procedure. The "beginning" of the case to which Plato refers corresponds to the laying of the denunciation before the assembly,[52] which then decided whether or not to proceed against the individual denounced. At Athens, if it was voted to proceed, the next action was the consideration of the charges by the council, which would report back to the assembly with a recommendation as to the method of trial and the penalties to be imposed if the accused was found guilty.[53] Plato prescribes that this stage of the inquiry shall be conducted, not by the council, but by a small group of three superior magistrates, the only function left to the council being to select these magistrates if the principals in the suit cannot agree. Plato calls this enquiry a βάσανος, here again using this term to denote an inquisitorial investigation—the kind of examination which he thinks only a small court is able to conduct. It would be as difficult for the council, with its three hundred and sixty members, as for the popular courts to conduct a real βάσανος, and Plato deliberately dispenses with its services. By doing so he introduces into this area of justice a compromise, similar to that we have noted in private litigation, in which popular participation, selected competence, and repeated examination all find a place.

We hear nothing more about the court of the demos after the sixth book. When, in the ninth book, Plato turns to the legislation covering wrongs against the state which this court would normally be expected to judge, we hear instead of another court, which we may call the court for capital offenses (855c), though it is given no name in Plato's text. It consists of the guardians of the laws sitting together with the select judges, obviously a court of the highest competence.[54] It has jurisdiction over temple robbing (854de),

---

[52] Arist. *Const. Ath.* XLIII, 4.

[53] Cf. the procedure at the trial of the eleven generals after Arginusae, as described by Xen. *Hell.* I, vii, 9ff. The aspects of this probouleuma which were immediately denounced as illegal by members of the assembly were, as Bonner and Smith point out (I, 265ff.), that it recommended an immediate vote on the guilt or innocence of the generals on the basis of the evidence presented at the previous meeting of the assembly, with no provision for a trial, as had been the intent of the assembly resolution; and secondly, that it recommended a vote on all the generals at once, whereas according to Athenian law every man was entitled to an individual trial.

[54] This would make a court with a membership of somewhat over fifty judges. England, in his note on 855c 7, suggests that not all the guardians will sit on this court, but only a number equivalent to that of the select judges. He advances no reason in support of this suggestion, and it is hard to imagine one. No procedure is given for selecting the guardians who are to sit on the court, as elsewhere when

sedition (856bc), treason (856e, 857a), premeditated homicide (871d), wounding in an attempt at homicide (877b), and probably also certain cases of impiety (910cd). The proposal for this court is no unconsidered idea; like the select judges, it is included in Plato's letter to the contending parties at Syracuse (356de).

Both in constitution and in function this court reminds us of the court of the Areopagus at Athens. The Areopagus consisted of former archons and thus, like Plato's court, was a body of experienced magistrates. It had exclusive jurisdiction over cases of murder, wounding, poisoning, and arson.[55] The Areopagus also exercised some jurisdiction over religious matters in the fourth century,[56] but in this sphere its powers were but a fraction of those it had once had. Solon gave it the power to punish treason and sedition, and in spite of the reforms of Ephialtes and Pericles, it seems to have retained some vestiges of this competence even in the fourth century.[57] In Plato's time the Areopagus appears to have enjoyed the esteem of all parties in the state;[58] no fault seems to have been found with its handling of the cases brought before it, whereas many of the capital cases tried by the popular courts became *causes célèbres*, notably the trial of the generals after Arginusae and the trial of Socrates. It is not surprising, therefore, that Plato should take this court as a model for the handling of capital cases. There are somewhat uncertain analogies between his court and the Spartan and Cretan courts of magistrates, and with what Aristotle indicates is the practice in oligarchic states generally.[59] But the members of Plato's court are responsible, for they

particular guardians are assigned judicial functions (see Chapter V, Note 113); and the question seems to receive a decisive answer from *Epist. VIII* 356de, where a similar court proposed for Syracuse consists of the thirty-five guardians plus the selected magistrates.

[55] Arist. *Const. Ath.* LVII, 3.
[56] Bonner and Smith I, 258ff.
[57] See Chapter V, Note 138.
[58] See the striking encomium in Lyc. I, 12: "You have in the Areopagus, my fellow citizens, the most perfect model in all Greece, so superior to all other tribunals that even those condemned by it proclaim the equity of its judgments."
[59] The Spartan gerousia had jurisdiction over homicide, says Aristotle (*Pol.* 1275b 10) and he equates the Cretan elders with the gerousia at Sparta (*Pol.* 1272a 8). But the ephors also seem to have had competence to deal with treason and impose the death penalty (cf. Xen. *Hell.* v, iv, 24); and at the trial of a king both these bodies plus the other king constituted the court (Paus. III, v, 2). Cf. Karl Otfried Müller's account of "the high court at Sparta" (*Die Dorier*, 1844, III, vii, 4) consisting of "the gerousia, the ephors, and probably several other magistrates." Aristotle remarks that it is characteristic of oligarchies to give to a few only the power of sentencing to death and exile (*Pol.* 1294b 33).

have to undergo the euthyna, like all other officials; whereas Aristotle severely criticizes the Cretan and Spartan officials because they exercise their power irresponsibly.[60]

Is the court for capital offenses intended to replace or to supplement the court of the demos? It is possible that Plato changed his mind between the sixth and the ninth book, and that the later proposal represents his more mature solution to the problem of dealing with grave offenses against the state. If this is true, the earlier passage must have been left in by oversight. But it would be strange if Plato had abandoned the principle of popular participation which he had previously asserted with such earnestness. The alternative is to assume that Plato intends both courts to function in his state. If this is his intention, then the court for capital offenses would be a court of appeal, or of compulsory reference, from the court of the demos, at least when the offense is a capital one. There is no explicit statement in Plato's text to justify such an interpretation, but it is tempting to assume that he intended to have three stages of litigation in both public and private suits—for private suits the arbitrators, the tribal courts, and the select judges; for public suits the "three superior magistrates" of 768a, the court of the demos, and the final court, in which the select judges again appear. The situation is complicated somewhat by the fact that the supreme tribunal in private cases consists only of the select judges, whereas in public cases (if this interpretation is correct) they join with the guardians of the laws to constitute the highest court.[61] It is further complicated by the fact that the court for capital offenses also has jurisdiction over homicide, and for such cases it acts as a court of first instance, not as a court of appeal—for Plato's homicide law, like that of Athens, stuck religiously to the older procedure. These complications would explain why, if these were Plato's intentions, they were not, and could not have been, clearly expressed in the summary account of his courts in the sixth book.

But tempting as this interpretation is, our final conclusion on the matter must be more cautious. In the second of Plato's two summary accounts of his judicial system, which occurs towards the very end of the *Laws*, he again distinguishes between private and public litigation (he calls them private and public courts, ἴδια and δημόσια δι-

---

[60] *Pol.* 1270b 39 - 1271a 6; 1272a 37ff.
[61] The select judges also appear in the special court that functions only at the trial of euthynoi (948a).

καστήρια), and after repeating the provisions for private courts essentially as they are stated in the passage in the sixth book, somewhat pointedly refrains from making similar provisions for the public courts, leaving this task for the guardians, who, he says, will find "not unseemly regulations" on this point in "many cities" where there are good men (957a). This is not, I take it, a withdrawal of his specific proposals for the court of the demos and the court for capital offenses, but simply a recognition that there are further details of their competence and their relationship to one another to be worked out. Plato's account of his courts is, as he said at the outset, merely an outline (περιγραφή), and much will necessarily have to be left to "younger legislators" (768c, 957a).

Besides the system of courts we have described, Plato sets up a number of minor courts for special purposes which we should notice in conclusion. For failure to take the field with the military forces when summoned to do so, a citizen is subject to trial before his comrades when they return—before the cavalry if he is a cavalryman, before the hoplites if a hoplite (943ab). We can infer that a charge of desertion, mentioned immediately afterward in Plato's text, would be judged in the same way. Both the suits mentioned—failure to report for service (γραφὴ ἀστρατείας) and desertion (γραφὴ λιπο-ταξίου)—are familiar suits in Attic law; and there is nothing either in the procedure or the constitution of these courts, so far as we can see, that departs from Athenian practice.[62]

A family court is required when a father desires to disinherit his son. Disinheritance in Plato's state had certain peculiar consequences, because citizenship is tied up with ownership, or prospective ownership, of a lot; a disinherited son will lose his citizenship, unless he is adopted by some childless lot-holder. These peculiar consequences are pointed out in Plato's text (928e) and given as the reason why the father cannot be allowed to exercise alone the power of disinheritance, as was permitted under Attic law. The court to pass on the case consists of the adult kinsmen of the father as far as cousins, and the kinsmen of the son through his mother to the same degree of relationship (929a-d). The father shall set forth the reasons why the son should be cast out of the family, and the son shall have an opportunity of replying. The issue is decided by a majority vote of

[62] Lipsius 143; Lys. XIV, 5.

the court, "not counting the father, the mother, and the defendant son." It is an indication of the importance of the family in Plato's social structure that a family court should have final jurisdiction in a matter that affects the state so closely.[63]

Something like a family court is also suggested to deal with cases of bodily injury (τραῦμα) inflicted by a brother or sister (878de); but here, if the case cannot be settled by the kinsmen, the guardians are called in to reach a verdict. Bodily attacks by children upon parents are to be judged by a court of citizens over sixty years of age who have children of their own (878e), and the same court judges cases of unintentional injury (879b). Other kinds of assault (αἰκία) are apparently judged either by the astynomoi (879de) or by the military officers (880d). Proceedings for divorce do not come before a family court, but before a group composed of ten guardians and ten of the women supervisors of marriage (929e-930a). For neglecting or dishonoring parents a person is haled, not before a family court, but before a magistrate's court consisting of the three eldest guardians and three of the supervisors of marriage (932ab), provided that the offender is under thirty, if a man, and under forty, if a woman. Older offenders are brought before a curious court consisting of the hundred and one oldest citizens (932c). A citizen who engages in retail trade or handicraft is subject to an indictment for "disgracing his family" (919e).[64] In name this is an offense against the family, but it is also a violation of the fundamental law that citizens shall not engage in trade or handicraft, hence it comes before a court of those who have won distinction (ἀριστεῖα) for civic excellence.[65]

The organization of the courts that Plato proposes is systematic, reasonably complete (an outline only is intended, as he himself says in 768c) and on the whole coherent. The scheme bears the marks of prolonged reflection and thorough knowledge of the institutions of his native city. The arbitrators, the "tribal courts," the popular

---

[63] A son who is disinherited does not necessarily lose his citizenship, however, for he may be adopted by another citizen who has no male heir (929c).

[64] A γραφὴ γένους αἰσχύνης, a suit not known in Attic law.

[65] This would include the euthynoi (cf. 946b). Awards of merit are mentioned frequently, but there is no systematic account of the way in which they are won or conferred. Two sorts of public distinction seem to be contemplated, political and military (921e-922a), or what are elsewhere called ἀριστεῖα and νικητήρια (829c). Both are conferred by the πλῆθος (921e), or what is essentially the same thing, the military assembly (943c). Certain delinquencies disqualify a man for this honor (935b, 943b, 952d, 966d). See also 730d, 953d, and 964b.

assembly, the special courts for homicide, the appeal and compulsory reference to a higher court—all these are taken over, with more or less modification, from Attic law. Even when he adapts his borrowings to fit the structure of his more authoritarian state, it is often by the use of a principle already recognized in Athenian law. An illustration of this is his insistence on the responsibility of judges; conceiving of them as "officers" (767d), he merely applies to them the principle of accountability that the Athenians had long insisted on for their other officers. His outstanding departure from the Athenian system of justice is his demotion of the popular courts to a subordinate position; and his most original creation is his supreme court of select judges. The significance of this new institution can hardly be exaggerated. Its result is to take away from the demos that judicial supremacy which was one of the most cherished powers of the Athenian democracy. In this respect Plato's judicial system would be called, in the language of his time, oligarchical. But it is an oligarchy decidedly tempered, or mixed, with democracy. Plato preserves the popular courts, and we hear but rarely of popular courts in the Greek states governed by oligarchies.[66] He accepts the democratic principle that access to office—including judicial office—is one of the essential privileges of citizenship, a principle which no ancient oligarchy would have tolerated. Again, the liability of magistrates to be called to account by a private citizen had abundant precedents in Athenian law, but none whatever in oligarchies.[67] Finally, the creation of regular methods and courts of appeal is not found in oligarchies, and in most democracies it was not attained.[68] Even Athens had gone only a short way along this road. In all these features of his law, even in his innovations, Plato is following paths that Athenian experience had indicated.

In its provisions for appeal, and for special competence in the highest courts, Plato's system has a distinctly juristic character. But

[66] Aristotle cites the revolution in Heraclea Pontica (*Pol.* 1305b 34) as showing that it is dangerous to the stability of an oligarchy to have popular courts composed of persons not eligible to office. The example of Chios, cited by Leonard Whibley (*Greek Oligarchies*, New York and London, 1896, 175-176) is hardly to the point, for Chios was an ally of Athens and had a long democratic tradition. See Chapter V, Note 32.

[67] "The oligarchic conception of official power required that the magistrate should not be liable to be called to account by the ordinary citizen." Whibley, *op.cit.* 150.

[68] Keil, in Gercke and Norden's *Einleitung in die Altertumswissenschaft*, Leipzig, 1910-1912, III, 363-364.

a modern reader is likely to be disturbed by the close connection between judicial and executive functions, and the lack of a separate and independent judiciary. "There is no liberty," says Montesquieu, "if the power of judging be not separated from the legislative and executive powers."[69] But when Plato looks for persons especially qualified to administer justice, he invariably turns to his officials, or to persons who have had official experience. Sometimes this brings about a situation highly prejudicial to the accused, as when he puts his guardians of the laws, the most powerful administrative officers in his state, on the court for capital offenses, with power to judge treason and sedition. Why Plato follows such a principle can be understood if we recall the development of the judicial process in Greece. In the earliest times judicial and administrative functions were uniformly exercised by the same persons, an aristocracy of birth or wealth. The later centuries brought about a double change: public offices became elective or subject to the lot, and the administration of justice was more and more taken from officials and put in the hands of the people. In time the wheel went full circle; in the advanced democracies the people in their courts began to exercise administrative as well as judicial powers, so that once again there was a union of the two functions in the same hands. Those who saw the dangers of such a situation naturally turned to the remedy suggested by the past; they sought to reinvest in the officials a portion of the judicial power that had been taken from them. The creation of a trained judiciary, separate in personnel from executive officials and relatively independent in tenure of office, was an expedient which did not occur, so far as we know, to any Greek thinker.[70] It could hardly have come about in fact before the rise of a separate legal profession, and this was contrary to the amateur spirit that pervaded practically all spheres of civil life in Greece. Plato was one of the first to challenge the competence of the amateur, and he was especially clear as to the need for special competence in the interpretation and application of the law. This is one of the main motives underlying his provisions for the establishment of the Nocturnal Council. But the implications of this principle in modifying the distribution of powers in the state he only faintly anticipated, as we shall see.

[69] *Esprit des Lois*, Bk. xi, Chap. vi.

[70] Aristotle's recognition of τὸ δικάζον (*Pol.* 1298a 3) as distinct from the deliberative and the executive "parts" of the state did not imply for him a separate and independent personnel for the discharge of this function.

PROCEDURE

No system of justice will work without persons who can be relied upon to bring offenders to account before the proper tribunals. There is usually no difficulty about the prosecuting of offenses against individuals. Most legal systems have left the redressing of private wrongs to the initiative of the injured person himself or, if he is without competence to bring action in the courts, to his guardian or legal representative. This principle was followed by Platonic law and by Greek law generally; we have seen that whoever is injured in person or property has the right to come before a magistrate (if the damages claimed are below three minae) or before the courts (when the claim is for a larger amount) and summon the offending person to account. Normally the magistrates will not take the initiative in redressing private wrongs, except in the exercise of their police power, nor is it within the competence of any other private person to bring suit against an offender, except in certain special cases which we shall examine later. These principles are not stated explicitly in the *Laws*, but they are presupposed by countless details of procedure, and they were so firmly embedded in Greek custom and law that there can be no doubt of Plato's acceptance of them.

The point that calls for comment is the range of offenses for which private prosecution is the chief and sometimes the only remedy.[71] Private wrongs include all injuries to property or person, including homicide. When the homicide is premeditated or committed in anger, then the next of kin has the duty, as well as the right, to prosecute (871b; cf. 868bc). If the killing was accidental and the slayer voluntarily submits to the exile which the law requires in such cases, then the next of kin shall forego prosecution, but if the slayer refuses to go into exile, the kinsman is under a strict obligation here also to proceed against him (866ab). In these provisions Plato is moving in the well-worn paths of Attic procedure.[72] Normally only the relatives of the victim (or the master, if the victim was a slave) were permitted to prosecute under Attic law, but for them it was a duty, unless the slain man, before dying, had given a formal release to the murderer.[73] There are two exceptions to this principle, however, in

---

[71] See Note 44.

[72] Bonner and Smith II, 209ff. For the details of Plato's law of homicide and a comparison of it with Attic law, see Gernet, *Platon, Lois, Livre IX*, Paris, 1917.

[73] For a reflection of this detail in Plato's law see 869a,de; cf. *Rep.* 451b, *Phaedo* 114a.

Platonic law. If the next of kin fails to prosecute, then it is open to anyone to bring suit, not only against the murderer, but also against the delinquent kinsman (866b, 868b, 871b). Attic law had analogous ways of getting around the rule that only the kinsman could prosecute;[74] they are obviously a compromise between the principle that murder is a private wrong and the need of cleansing the community from the pollution of bloodshed. The other exception is the murder of an alien, when it is open to anyone to prosecute the murderer (866bc), for the reason, probably, that a foreigner might often have no kinsman in the city to avenge his death.[75] The procedure employed at Athens in these cases we do not know, but that such prosecutions took place is clear.[76]

What of prosecution for offenses against the public? There is no public prosecutor in Platonic law, nor was there at Athens in Plato's day. In early Athens such prosecutions probably were initiated by the magistrates, and particularly by the council of the Areopagus, as part of its function of guarding the laws and punishing conspiracy. Solon introduced freedom of prosecution, so that any citizen, even when his own interests were not immediately affected, could bring an accusation against an offender; and in later centuries private prosecution became the rule, even for offenses against the public.[77] By contrast, Plato on several occasions emphasizes the responsibility of magistrates to prosecute an offender, acting either on their own initiative or upon information supplied by a private citizen;[78] and this responsibility is enforced by disgrace (952d), the threat of prosecution (907e), or the warning that any such neglect of duty would be brought up against an official at his euthyna (881e, 952d). Here Plato evidently desires to revive the practices of an earlier time. Yet

[74] One was prosecution of a kinsman for impiety by a γραφὴ ἀσεβείας (cf. H. J. Treston, *Poine, A Study in Ancient Greek Blood Vengeance*, New York, 1923, 146, 181); another was the summary process of ἀπαγωγή by a magistrate or any citizen (Bonner and Smith II, 212ff.). There is a hint of this latter procedure also in Plato's law (871e).
[75] Platonic law gives the life of the foreigner the same protection as that accorded a citizen. See Chapter IV, Note 154.
[76] Arist. *Const. Ath.* LVII, 3 mentions the court that dealt with them.
[77] Gernet cxxxvff.; Bonner and Smith *op.cit.* II, 25ff.
[78] See 881e, 907e, 910e, 937c, 949cd, 952d. In some of these texts εἰσάγειν εἰς τὸ δικαστήριον might refer merely to the magistrate's formal function of introducing suits, and this would not preclude a prosecutor distinct from the magistrate. Yet in 910e it is clearly the magistrates who decide whether the offense is to be prosecuted, and probably also in 907e; and ἂν μὴ ἐπάγῃ δίκην of 881e certainly implies prosecution.

it is also evident that he would retain the advantages of volunteer prosecution as it functioned in Athens in his day, and intends to foster this kind of civic responsibility. In many of the cases mentioned the role of the private informer, and sometimes that of the private citizen as prosecutor, are referred to explicitly. And in another passage Plato describes the prosecution of an offense against the public in familiar Athenian terms: it is an action instituted "when any citizen thinks that someone has done injury to the state and desires to aid the commonwealth" (767b; cf. 856c). Thus an action before the court of the demos has its prosecutor (ὁ διώκων) and its defendant (ὁ φεύγων) just as if it were a private suit (768a). The action expected of the citizen is well set forth in the moral prelude in the fifth book: to refrain from doing wrong is honorable; more worthy of honor is he who, in addition, hinders others from doing wrong by giving information to the magistrates; and most honorable of all is he who helps the magistrates in obtaining a conviction (730d). A similar scale of dishonor is hinted at in a later passage: the greatest enemy of the state is he who foments civil strife; only slightly less dangerous is he who, knowing of sedition, fails to inform the magistrates or to prosecute the plotters (856bc).

In spite of the almost universal use of private prosecutors, the distinction between private and public suits was well marked in Attic law. The former were δίκαι, and could be instituted in general only by one who had a personal interest to protect or a personal wrong to avenge; the latter were γραφαί;[79] they concerned, either directly or indirectly, the public interest, and could therefore be initiated by anyone. This distinction in terminology and thought is closely adhered to in Plato's law. Public suits are referred to as γραφαί, or introduced by a familiar phrase from Attic law indicating that the right of bringing such a suit is perfectly general.[80] Such are the suits for impiety (868de, 869a, 907e), for perverse litigation (κακοδικίας, 938b), for sedition (856c), for treason (856e), for engaging in a degrading occupation (919e), for failing to report for military duty (943a), for desertion (943d), for kidnaping (955a), for faithless em-

---

[79] More precisely, the former were ἴδιαι δίκαι, the latter δημοσίαι δίκαι, or γραφαί. A statement of the charges in writing was required in both private and public suits in the fourth century; the use of γραφαί for the latter probably indicates that the requirement was first instituted for this species of legal action. See Busolt-Swoboda 545, 1176 and n. 2; Bonner and Smith I, 170f.

[80] Such as γραφέσθω ὁ βουλόμενος or ὑπόδικος ἔστω τῷ ἐθέλοντι.

bassy (941a), and probably also the actions against temple robbery (854d) and theft (857a). Plato's law also includes two special kinds of public suits found in Attic law, ἔνδειξις and φάσις, the former against a witness already twice convicted of perjury (937c) and the latter against a citizen who possesses more property than the law allows (745a, 754e).[81] Here also belongs the εἰσαγγελία for "injuring the state" which any citizen may bring before the court of the demos. Numerous and varied as are the items in this list, all have their parallels or analogies, sometimes their precise equivalents, in the forms of public prosecution in Attic law.[82] In fact, if we are to judge merely by what is recorded in Plato's text, the law of his model city is far less liberal in this respect than the law of Athens, and one is tempted to think that it was his purpose to prune what would seem to be the excessive luxuriance of Attic procedure. Such an inference would be imprudent, however, since we are told that the guardians will have much to add to the chapter on procedure, and particularly that they can make good use of legislation already established—quite surely a reference to Attic law (957a). Certainly the spirit that animated the judicial system of Athens is presupposed in Plato's law, viz. the feeling that an injury to the community may rightly be prosecuted by anyone, coupled with the belief that public safety requires that all citizens be on the alert to detect offenders.[83]

[81] Ἔνδειξις was a special remedy against a man exercising forbidden rights; it differed from the ordinary γραφή in that the summoning of the defendant was dispensed with, presumably because he was apprehended at the time of committing the illegal act complained of (Lipsius, 317f.). Ἐνδεικνύτω in 856c has the more general sense of "indict." Φάσις differed from other public suits in that the accuser was entitled to one half the fine imposed on the defendant, or one half the value of the goods which he illegally possessed. It was ordinarily used at Athens for the protection of state property or finances (Lipsius 309ff.). Plato's use of it is strikingly analogous. A similar public suit is attested for many other Greek cities under Athenian influence; Busolt-Swoboda 546.

[82] Precise equivalents: the γραφὴ ἱεροσυλίας, 854d, the γραφὴ ἀστρατείας and λιποταξίου 943a,d; and the ἔνδειξις, φάσις and εἰσαγγελία. Parallels: Plato's γραφὴ κακοδικίας (938b) and the Attic γραφὴ συκοφαντίας; Plato's procedure against sedition (856c) and the γραφὴ καταλύσεως τοῦ δήμου and παρανόμων of Attic law. The suit for degrading occupation (γραφὴ γένους αἰσχύνης) has naturally no parallel in Attic law. In 909c (δίκας ἀσεβείας) and in other passages referring to this suit, Plato strangely lapses from the restricted to the more general meaning of δίκη, which again may be a reflection of Attic law. See Chapter VIII, Note 240.

[83] In Attic law, if a citizen did not wish to assume the risk of prosecution he was expected at least to inform the magistrates if he knew of any offense that was indictable by a public suit, so that some one else could prosecute. This obligation appears frequently in Platonic law; e.g. 742b (possession of foreign money), 907e and 910c (impiety), 913d (appropriating treasure-trove), 932b (neglect of parents).

We find traces of another kind of public suit in Platonic law, viz. a suit whose chief purpose was to redress a private wrong, its "public" character consisting in the fact that it could be brought by any qualified citizen. This kind of public suit was a celebrated, though inconsistent, procedure of Attic law in the classical period. Aristotle lists the institution of this procedure as one of the three most democratic features of Solon's reforms.[84] Its most famous example was the γραφὴ ὕβρεως which could be brought by any citizen to punish insult or injury to the person of another.[85] Plato does not mention this suit, nor is it suggested in any passage of the *Laws*. But public prosecution is provided on occasion for the protection of clearly private interests—e.g. to protect orphans against a faithless guardian (928b), and to protect parents against abuse (932d). Here also belong the action against a convicted perjurer, the action for kidnaping, and the suit against the murderer of an alien, mentioned above; and to this list should be added the suit against a judge for false judgment which may be brought by "whoever wishes" (ὁ βουλόμενος), not merely by the injured party (846b).

How are the citizens to be induced to assume the burdens and risks of prosecution? In only one of the cases listed above is there a reward for the successful prosecutor, viz. in the action against a citizen for possessing more than the legal amount of property; here the prosecutor receives one half of the surplus established by the court.[86] In all other cases Plato would apparently rely upon civic spirit and the desire for distinction in the public service. This is the way the problem was handled at Athens; except for a few types of cases analogous to Plato's suit just mentioned, there were no financial rewards for prosecutors. Undoubtedly it was good policy for a man who wished to count in public affairs to show his zeal in bringing to justice the enemies of the people.[87] In any case, there was no shortage of prosecutors; sometimes there would be several for the same suit, as in the prosecution of Socrates by Meletus, Anytos, and Lycon.

[84] *Const. Ath.* IX. 1: τὸ ἐξεῖναι τῷ βουλομένῳ τιμωρεῖν ὑπὲρ τῶν ἀδικουμένων. Plutarch (*Solon* 18) describes this innovation as intended to make the common people more secure in their rights, and "to accustom the citizens, like members of the same body, to resent and be sensible of one another's injuries." That city is best, Solon is quoted as saying, in which those who are not injured try to punish injustice as much as those who are.

[85] Lipsius 420-429; cf. the author's article, "The Murder of Slaves in Attic Law," *Class. Phil.* XXXII, 1937, 214ff.

[86] For the analogy with Attic law, see Notes 81 and 82.

[87] See Bonner and Smith II, 39ff. The orators frequently emphasize their patriotism and civic spirit; cf. Andoc. IV, 1; Aesch. I, 1-2; Lyc. I, 149.

As to the technicalities involved in initiating a suit, Plato professes to leave these details to be filled in by later legislators (846bc, 855d, 956e-957a), in one passage making what looks like a clear and complimentary reference to Attic law. In any case, Attic procedure seems to be generally presupposed. Thus there is to be a summons (πρόσ-κλησις) to the defendant, both in private and in public suits (846bc, 855d), and witnesses (κλητῆρες) to this summons, as was provided in Attic law.[88] The plaintiff or accuser has to file a written statement of his claims or charges before a magistrate, and the defendant likewise files a written statement or denial with the officials (948d), again a reflection of Attic procedure. Attic law often required the accuser to include in his filed statement an assessment of the damages to be paid or the penalty to be exacted if the accused was found guilty. This also is presupposed in Plato's law (845e, 928b, 941a, 956c). The technical designation in Attic law for the filing of a suit was δίκην λαγ-χάνειν or λῆξις, phrases which recur naturally in Plato's text (e.g. 948d, 937a, 938b, 956e). For homicide cases Attic law prescribed a special procedure. According to the ancient belief, a murderer had brought pollution on himself and could communicate this pollution to all persons whom he might encounter; hence an action for homicide was always preceded by a solemn proclamation (πρόρρησις) warning the accused to stay away from the agora and temples and to refrain from exercising his normal rights of citizenship (εἴργεται τῶν νομίμων).[89] This procedure and these terms appear likewise in Plato's law (871c, 873ab, 874ab). Plato seldom specifies the particular magistrates before whom a given suit is to be brought; but the distribution of suits among the various officials is clearly intended (cf. 956e, 957a), and we know that this was meticulously prescribed in Attic law.

After the suit had been filed, it was the responsibility of the magistrates at Athens to conduct a preliminary examination (ἀνάκρισις) to determine whether or not the suit would lie, in Attic terms whether or not it was εἰσαγώγιμος. At the opening of this examination, it was required that the litigants should each take oath as to the truth of the claims or denials included in his written statement—a procedure called ἀντωμοσία.[90] Plato forbids the use of the oath at this stage. It is a fearful thing to think, he says, when there are so many lawsuits going on, that almost half of those one meets in the city have foresworn themselves (948de). This suggests that he

[88] Lipsius, 804ff.   [89] Lipsius 810.   [90] Lipsius 829ff.

thought of this oath as a mode of proof (in fact, it had ceased by the fourth century to be anything but a formality in Attic procedure), and Plato has been accused of an excess of moral scruple. The reply is that if the oath is to be used at all in the judicial process (and Plato does use it) any practice which employs it as a mere formality tends to weaken its importance where it is really significant.[91] Plato gives no further details regarding the preliminary examination; he would evidently make it the responsibility of the magistrate to disallow a suit on grounds of illegality, for example if it violated the statute of limitations covering the particular claim involved (cf. 928c, 916b, 915d), perhaps also on other less specific grounds. No mention is made of the "exception" or "objection" (παραγραφή, διαμαρτυρία) available in Attic law to a defendant who wished to contest the magistrate's decision that a suit was εἰσαγώγιμος.[92] Perhaps Plato thought his provision of an independent suit for damages against a magistrate was sufficient remedy and preferable to the complicated procedure of Attic law.

Plato's departures from Attic law are most pronounced in trial procedures. The conduct of a trial at Athens, as Gernet aptly says, was like an athletic contest;[93] the function of the presiding officer was to referee the combat, to see that the rules were observed, and to announce the decision; the dicasts were spectators, taking no part either in the establishment of the facts or in the determination of the penalties. They listened to the speeches of the litigants and to the reading of the evidence on which they relied; and at the end, if they voted for conviction, they had merely the option of choosing between the penalty proposed by the prosecution and the alternative penalty proposed by the defendant. The conditions presupposed in the trial of Socrates, as described in Plato's *Apology*, give a fair picture of the proceedings before an Athenian dicastery. Some of the things that Plato decries in such proceedings—such as the inability of the judges to question witnesses or principals, and to consult with one another about the verdict or the penalty to be imposed—are inevitable in the institution of large

91 Gernet cxxxviii; cf. Bonner and Smith II, 161-162.
92 Lipsius 845ff.; Gernet cxxxix.
93 Gernet cxl. In ordinary language, even in the language of the law and the courts, a suit (δίκη) was called an ἀγών, and to bring or contest a suit was ἀγωνίζεσθαι. For a good illustration, see the opening of Demosthenes' *On the Crown*.

popular courts; and having introduced such courts into his state, he can only acquiesce in these faults. But he gives the presiding officers in these trials a greater control over the proceedings than was permitted at Athens. The speakers are required to stick to the "right" or "law" (τὸ δίκαιον) of the matter, and the presiding officials are authorized to call a speaker back to the argument (εἰς τὸν περὶ τοῦ πράγματος ἀεὶ λόγον) if he digresses (949b). There is to be no appeal to the sympathy of the audience by abject supplications or unmanly sobs,[94] nor any use of imprecations or oaths to obtain credence. In Aristotle's day the litigants in private suits took an oath to confine their pleading to the matter at issue,[95] but this regulation, if we can judge by the extant speeches of the orators, was either very recent or very ineffective. Elsewhere Aristotle tells us that in well-governed states there were rules of procedure that excluded irrelevant pleading, and he mentions the Areopagus as one court in which such rules were in effect. His silence as to the heliastic courts is eloquent.[96]

But a searching examination of a litigant's contentions can never be made by a large court, and that is why Plato provides that every case, before it is finally adjudicated, shall come before at least one small court of selected judges. In private suits the arbitrators will have sifted the issues and clarified the respective contentions before the matter comes before the tribal courts; and if an appeal is taken from the decision of a tribal court, the matter comes before the select judges. Likewise in public suits the first stage of the trial is the "examination" before three high officials selected by the two parties; only then does it go before the court of the demos. The type of examination that Plato has in mind is revealed by the procedure he describes explicitly for the court for capital offenses.

During the hearing our judges shall sit next to one another in order of age and directly before the defendant and the prosecutor; and all citizens who have the time shall attend and follow earnestly such trials. Each party shall make one speech, first the prosecutor and then the defendant. After these speeches the eldest of the judges shall begin the examination and make a thorough inquiry into the statements that have been made. After the eldest has concluded, all the others in turn shall go through the case,

[94] Cf. *Apol.* 34c.

[95] *Const. Ath.* LXVII, I.

[96] *Rhet.* 1354a 21ff. For this rule of procedure before the Areopagus, see also Lys. III, 46 and Lyc. I, 12-13: and for evidence of this continuing tradition about the Areopagus, Lucian *Anacharsis* 19.

PLATO'S CITY

addressing any questions they like to either party with regard to what they have said or failed to say. He who has no question to ask shall hand the examination over to his neighbor. Whatever has been said that the judges deem to be relevant shall be set down in writing, sealed by all the judges, and deposited on the altar of Hestia. On the next day they shall come together again and go through the examination of the case in the same manner and set their seals on what has been said. And when they have done this a third time, giving due weight to all the evidence and witnesses, each shall give his solemn vote, after promising by Hestia to decide truly and justly as best he can; and thus they shall put an end to such a suit.[97]

This proceeding illustrates so well Plato's requirement of "time, leisureliness, and repeated examination" that we can take it as a sample of the kind of procedure he would employ elsewhere in his select courts. His proposals are not without precedent in Greece. Tradition says that the trials for homicide before the Spartan gerousia extended over several days, and Thucydides records that it was a Spartan custom to be slow in taking irrevocable action against one of their own number without indisputable proof.[98] Trials before the Areopagus at Athens regularly extended over three days, and the trial itself was preceded by three separate preliminary hearings ($\delta\iota\alpha\delta\iota\kappa\alpha\sigma\iota\alpha\iota$), one month apart, before the king.[99] Antiphon's Tetralogies show that each party before the Areopagus was entitled to two speeches. Plato's text indicates that each party would speak on each of the three days of the trial. However that may be, one may assume that for Plato the important thing was not the speeches of the litigants, but their answers to the questions of the judges. Socrates' examination of Mele-

[97] 855d-856a. The decision is presumably by a majority vote (cf. 856c). This text presents two points, both rather minor, on which differences of opinion are evident among the translators. (1) Does ἀνακρίναντα (e3) mean "examine by questioning," as Apelt, Diès, and Gernet take it, or "make a survey of summing up," as Taylor, Bury, and England interpret it? The first interpretation would make the procedure analogous to that of the United States Supreme Court during the actual hearing of a case; the second suggests the procedure of this court after the hearing, when the judges have met for consultation. Since the prosecutor and defendant are presumably still present during this part of Plato's proceedings, I see little warrant for the second interpretation. Furthermore, the sense it forces upon the Greek verb is unnatural, and so far as I know not found elsewhere, certainly not in Plato (cf. the meaning of ἀνακρίνειν in 766e). (2) Does Plato intend that only the eldest judge shall question the litigants, the other members of the court confining themselves to a review of the various statements made? Such is Robin's interpretation. This is not a priori implausible, but it seems to be excluded, for those who take ἀνακρίνειν as meaning "examine," by the use of the cognate ἀνάκρισις in e6 with respect to the other judges.
[98] Gilbert I, 89; Thuc. I, 132, 5.
[99] Ant. VI, 42; Poll. VIII, 117; cf. Lipsius 840.

tus in the *Apology* shows how an inconsistent indictment or an insincere litigant can be exposed by shrewd questioning. For such interrogation there were also Attic precedents; Athenian law permitted a litigant to interrogate his opponent, and the law required him to answer.[100] This was a very old feature of Attic procedure;[101] but to judge from the speeches of the orators it was very little employed in the fourth century, and the specimens of such interrogation that have been preserved[102] are quite brief. Nor was it customary to examine witnesses in Athenian courts in Plato's day, though the practice had no doubt been more common in earlier times.[103] Testimony was ordinarily presented to the court in the form of a written deposition prepared in advance and read to the judges, the witness being at hand to affirm that the deposition read was his. But in Plato's procedure the questioning of witnesses is implied by the description of the examination as bearing upon "everything that has been said," and by the explicit mention of witnesses (856a 5). With his Socratic training Plato would be well aware of the value of oral examination in clarifying motives and conceptions and bringing hidden things to light. In these proposals we seem to be witnessing the marriage of the judicial process with the technique of ἐρώτησις, or questioning, as it was practised by the sophists; the offspring of this marriage was the art of cross examination, and Plato may be regarded as at least its godfather.[104]

Other proposals regarding trial procedure are found elsewhere in the *Laws*. We have seen that Plato prohibits the use of the "party oath" by litigants in filing their cases with the magistrates. This prohibition is immediately generalized in his text to forbid the use of the evidentiary oath in any form by the litigants or witnesses ."Whenever it is obvious that a man has much to gain by the use of an oath in affirmation or denial, the parties to the contention must always be judged by trials without oaths."[105] Plato is combating an ancient prac-

---

[100] *Apol.* 25d; Ps. Dem. xlvi, 10. This appears to be the meaning of ἀποκρίσεων ἀνάγκαι, 956e.

[101] Aeschylus employs it in the trial scene of the *Eumenides*, 586ff.; cf. Aristoph. *Acharn.* 687. For the fourth century see Isaeus xi, 5, Lys. xii, 25; xiii, 30, 32; xxii, 5.

[102] Lys. xii, 25; xxii, 5.

[103] See the burlesque of a trial in Aristoph. *Wasps* 962-965.

[104] Aristotle's chapter on ἐρώτησις, *Rhet.* 1418b 39ff., uses Socrates' questioning of Meletus as an example. On cross examination (or the lack of it) in Athenian courts, see Bonner and Smith ii, 122, 297.

[105] 949a. I suspect that the ἐξομοσαμένῳ in a6 has somehow replaced an original ἐπομοσαμένῳ, and have translated it accordingly. After all both parties, not merely the defendant, are to be heard without oath. Cf. Note 114 below.

tice here, sanctioned by religious tradition.[106] He himself refers to an
early period in history when it was believed that a case could best
be settled by requiring or permitting both the litigants to take oath
as to the truth of their contentions, thus committing the judgment to
the gods. A litigant who refused, or hesitated, to take the oath would
lose his case; or if he swore falsely he would be delivered to divine
vengeance. This antique procedure, really a species of trial by ordeal,
survived in Attic practice in the "challenge to the oath" (πρόκλησις
εἰς ὅρκον) which appears frequently in the texts of the orators. The
challenge was seldom, if ever, accepted and was in practice merely
a rhetorical maneuver, usually to distract attention from the evidence,
or the lack of it. In forbidding its use altogether, Plato is merely
recording the actual impotence of this procedure in the law of his
time. The same thing can be said of his prohibition of the "challenge
to the torture" (πρόκλησις εἰς βάσανον), another favorite rhetorical maneuver.[107] The only way in which the testimony of slaves
could ordinarily be admitted in Athenian courts was through the use
of torture; and a litigant might challenge his opponent to allow his
slaves to be put on the rack, or offer his own for the same test. Again
this challenge was seldom accepted. What the Greeks really thought
of this kind of "evidence" is difficult to say. A speaker will praise
the peculiar trustworthiness of such testimony if his opponent has
refused the challenge to the basanos; on the other hand, a litigant
who refuses will point out how utterly unreliable such evidence is.
Plato does not dignify this procedure by even a bare mention, his
prohibition being evident from his acceptance of the slave as a witness in the usual sense. His express reason for prohibiting the evidentiary oath is the weakness of the religious sanction; the "way of
Rhadamanthus" was admirable at a time when belief in the gods was
general; but it is not appropriate now when some men do not believe
in the gods at all, and others think either that the gods are not interested in punishing injustice or can be bought off by gifts and flattery (948bc). One suspects that another reason for the prohibition of
both these rhetorical challenges was their irrelevance, and their in-

---

[106] The use of the oath to support statements of witnesses and principals is peculiarly marked in the law of Gortyn, with considerable technical elaboration of procedure. See Willetts, *Aristocratic Society in Ancient Greece*, 212; and J. W. Headlam,
"The Procedure of the Gortynian Inscription," JHS XIII, 1892-1893, 48-69.

[107] For the prohibition of the βάσανος in Platonic law, see my *Plato's Law of
Slavery*, 80.

effectiveness in establishing or refuting the facts alleged. We shall see confirming evidence for this supposition in the sequel.

A litigant's right to use witnesses in establishing his contentions is presupposed in Plato's procedure, as it was at Athens.[108] Any free man who was not under atimia was competent to give evidence (μαρτυρεῖν) in Athenian courts; free women were allowed to testify only in murder cases.[109] Plato enlarges Attic procedure by allowing any free woman over forty to give evidence, and also by permitting slaves and children to be witnesses in murder cases; the evidence of slaves would be admitted without torture.[110] Plato also permits a free woman who is over forty to act as advocate (συνήγορος) in a suit; the same right is also accorded slaves and children in murder trials,[111] provided that bond is given to assure their being available for possible later action for perjury (937ab). These various proposals for reform indicate an evident intention to adapt Attic procedure to a clearer conception of the role of evidence in the judicial process.

In his provision for compelling a man to give testimony if a litigant requires it, Plato again is following the procedures of Attic law. The litigant's right to witnesses is one which the state will enforce, but it is the duty of the litigant, not of the court, to issue the summons to a witness (936e).[112] A witness who ignores the summons to testify is subject to a suit for damages, as in Attic law, i.e. he is liable to his summoner, not to the court (937a).[113] A witness summoned to court can still avoid testifying if he is willing to take an oath as to his ignorance (936e).[114] In Attic law this oath was apparently not subject to legal attack; but a witness with a regard to his reputation in the com-

---

[108] For the following details, see 936e-937a.

[109] Lipsius 874.

[110] This is evident from the terminology. Μαρτυρία, evidence, was sharply distinguished in Attic law from βάσανος, information elicited under torture. It is further shown that the slave in Plato's law is a witness in the legal sense of the term by his liability to a suit for perjury (δίκη ψευδομαρτυριῶν). See also Note 107 above.

[111] Plato also provides that a woman over forty, if she has no husband, may bring suit in her own right (937a). At Attic law a woman could bring suit only through her κύριος or legal guardian. This increase in the legal capacity of women accords with other provisions giving them a more responsible part in the city than they had at Athens. Cf. 785b, 802a, 804d-805d, 813c-814b, 829b, 878de.

[112] Bonner and Smith II, 137; Lipsius 881.

[113] Bonner and Smith II, 139; Lipsius 876.

[114] This is the ἐξωμοσία of Attic law. Plato uses the more solemn but less technical ἀπομνύναι, but the procedure is identical. Bonner and Smith II, 163.

munity would naturally hesitate to take a solemn oath that he was ignorant when it was generally known that he had knowledge of the case. Plato's law says nothing about the witness who appears in court and then refuses both to give evidence and to take the oath of disclaimer; under Attic law such a witness was subject to a summary fine, and a heavy one, imposed by the court.[115] For forcibly preventing an opponent or an opponent's witness from appearing in court, Plato provides as a remedy that the suit shall be dismissed without judgment, and furthermore, if the witness in question was a free man, that the offender shall be imprisoned for one year, and shall be liable to prosecution for kidnaping (ἀνδραποδισμοῦ) by anyone who cares to bring suit (954e).[116] There probably was a similar penalty under Attic law for detention of principals or witnesses, but we have no direct evidence of it.

The oath was not regularly required of witnesses in Athenian courts, except in murder trials, though any witness might take the oath on his own initiative to make his testimony more impressive, or he might be asked to take it by his principal, or as a result of a challenge by the other side.[117] All such oaths, as we have seen, are forbidden in Plato's law. But he follows Attic law in providing a suit (δίκη ψευδομαρτυριῶν) against a witness for giving false testimony. As in Attic law, the testimony has to be formally challenged before the termination of the trial proceedings; these challenges (ἐπισκή-ψεις) are recorded, sealed with the seal of both parties, and preserved by the officials for use at the trial to follow (937b).[118] Attic courts would award damages to the prosecutor in such a case if he won, and perhaps also impose other penalties upon the defendant, though Athenian practice in the matter is not clear.[119] According to Plato's law, when a man has been twice convicted of false testimony he can no longer be compelled, and after a third conviction he is no longer permitted, to be a witness in court (937c). These provisions parallel those of Attic law.[120]

[115] Bonner and Smith II, 139.
[116] The suit is a public one (note ὑπόδικος τῷ ἐθέλοντι) in order to make prosecution possible when the violence has been of such a sort as to render the injured party incapable of action, e.g. by forcible confinement. The penalty for ἀνδραποδισμός under Attic law was death.
[117] Bonner and Smith II, 173.
[118] Arist. *Const. Ath.* LXVIII, 4.
[119] Lipsius 782f.; Bonner and Smith II, 262ff.
[120] The curious consequence of a second conviction—i.e. to be a competent but not a compellable witness—hardly seems a penalty at all. In fact it is not; Plato is

Finally, Plato's law provides, as did Attic law, that the outcome of a suit for false testimony may lead to the annulling of the verdict given in the previous suit. If a majority of the witnesses, or a majority of the evidence (it is not certain which is the correct translation of Plato's text), are later discredited through a suit for false testimony, then the previous judgment becomes null and void (937cd). Attic law granted a new trial if the testimony of even one witness had been successfully discredited;[121] but good sense would prevent a man from reopening a case if he had not succeeded in overthrowing a considerable part of the evidence, so that Plato's law, though formally stricter than Athenian law, probably comes close to the realities of Athenian procedure. What is novel in Plato's law is the requirement of a special hearing to determine whether this discredited evidence had brought about the adverse verdict. In spite of the familiar legal terms (ἀμφισβήτησις, διαδικασία) employed to designate this special hearing, it is impossible to bring it into relation with any known procedures of Attic law.[122] Lipsius infers that the officials who presided over the trial (they would be the same as those for the main suit) would make the decision, or alternatively that they would get such a decision from the judges who condemned the witness.[123] Neither of these alternatives seems to accord with Attic law; but the first seems compatible with the enlarged judicial powers that Plato confers on his magistrates. The magistrates in this case could only attempt to determine whether the discredited evidence was in fact essential to the decision reached in the earlier trial. Whatever their decision on this point might be, its effect, as Plato's law concludes, would be to put an end to the main suit, either by confirming or setting aside the previous verdict.

---

stating merely the man's standing as a possible witness. The penalty for his conviction would certainly involve the payment of damages. The reason for this "curious state of disability," as England calls it, is stated in Hyp. II, 12; it is in order that the demos (through its power of compelling a man to give evidence) may not be contributory to his falling into atimia, the penalty provided by Attic law. Plato's law provides that if after three convictions a man dares to appear as a witness in court, anyone may prefer an ἔνδειξις against him for this illegitimate exercise of rights, and if convicted by the courts he shall be punished with death.

[121] So Bonner and Smith II, 267ff., relying on Isaeus XI, 45-46.

[122] Ἀμφισβήτησις and διαδικασία are procedures usually employed with respect to disputes regarding inheritances, liturgies, or priesthoods; but it is unlikely that Plato is thinking merely of such cases here. Evidently a more general use of the process is intended.

[123] Lipsius 959-960.

Returning to the main trial, let us assume that the principals and their witnesses have all been heard, the objections (ἐπισκήψεις) to the evidence have been presented and recorded, and the case is ready for decision. At this point Plato proposes another reform—viz. open voting (φανερὰ ψῆφος). In the heliastic courts it was a secret how any individual dicast had voted. This was not merely an incidental consequence of the large numbers involved, but the result of deliberate policy, as we see clearly from the ingenious voting procedure employed. In Aristotle's time each dicast, as he went into the courtroom, was given two bronze discs (ψῆφοι) each with a cylindrical axis through the center; in one the axis was hollow, in the other solid. At the front of the courtroom stood two large urns, one of bronze called the "sovereign" or "counting" urn (ὁ κύριος), the other of wood, called the "invalid urn" (ὁ ἄκυρος). The former was to receive the discs which were to be counted in the voting, the other was for the discarded discs. At the end of the pleading the herald called for the vote: "A hollow disc is a vote for the prosecution, a solid disc a vote for the defense."[124] As the dicasts filed forward to the voting urns, a disc in each hand, it was a simple matter to place the fingers over the ends of the cylindrical axes, so that no observer could detect which of the two discs was deposited through the slit in the lid of the "sovereign" urn. The reason for this procedure was undoubtedly to enable the dicast to vote fearlessly; the voter's freedom from liability was a condition, as Attic law saw it, of an honest verdict. But it is contrary to one of Plato's fundamental principles: "No judge or official is to be irresponsible" (761e). Whether Plato really intends that the voting in his popular courts shall be public (i.e. by show of hands instead of by ψῆφοι) we cannot be sure; but there can be no question of his intention with regard to the smaller and more select courts (767d, 855d). For this there is some precedent in Attic procedure of his time—e.g. the decisions of arbitrators, and perhaps also the voting in the Areopagus, both cases in which the judges seem to have been immune, in the main, to legal action for their decisions. There was also the precedent of the Thirty in 404, who required the council to vote openly on the cases of persons denounced by the government; but this, as Gernet remarks, was not a precedent that should have influenced Plato.[125] For more respectable precedents he would have

---

[124] Arist. *Const. Ath.* LXVIII, 4.
[125] Lys. XIII, 37; Xen. *Hell.* II, iv, 9; Gernet cxliv.

to look back to the earlier aristocratic period of the judiciary at Athens, and this is no doubt the true source of his inspiration here.

Plato's proposal for open voting is indeed aristocratic, in the best sense of that term; for in any society the aristocrats worthy of the name are likely to be surer of the grounds for their opinions and more fearless in expressing them than the common man. But it is also an oligarchical proposal, in the worst sense of the term; for one of the first steps taken by an oligarchy is to intimidate the courts, if they are not already filled with their own henchmen. And in Plato's state, where there is such a close connection between the judiciary and the administrative officials, what the legislator ought to look to, it would seem, is rather additional devices for protecting the independence of the judges. But the juridical intent underlying Plato's proposal is clearly to enforce his principle of judicial responsibility, and thereby to protect the citizen against the abuse of judicial power. Viewed in this light his proposal seems clearly democratic in purpose. In itself the demand for open declaration of opinions by the judges who pass on a case has nothing to shock a modern democrat; it is in fact what we normally expect of judges, and sometimes also from members of a jury. Plato's proposal, therefore, has the curious merit of being so far in advance of his time that, in its own context, without the support of other practices that grew up later to make the judicial function more genuinely independent, it could only be regarded as antidemocratic and reactionary.

Plato follows another aristocratic or oligarchical principle in increasing the responsibility of the judges in determining penalties. Attic law, speaking generally, left little discretion to the court in this regard. The penalty to be imposed was stated either in the law that covered the case, or by the prosecutor in the written claim filed with the magistrate. In the latter type of case the court, if it found for the prosecutor, would be required to choose between the penalty demanded by the prosecution and an alternative proposed by the defense. Plato commends this policy for a state "where the courts are ordinary and without voice in the proceedings." But in a state where the courts are better constituted and the judges better trained and tested, there it is right and proper to leave to the judges, for the most part, the determination of the penalties (876bc, 934b). This is a declaration of the principle Plato proposes to follow, and does follow in the main, at least in public suits. In civil suits, as Gernet points out, this principle is less marked, perhaps because the cases dealt with are less numerous; but even here it shows itself clearly on occasion.[126]

Finally, a judge is to render his decision under oath, the oath to be taken presumably just before voting (856a, 948e). The judicial oath in this form was well known in Greece; it is particularly marked in the law of Gortyn,[127] and was also a feature of Attic law. Arbitrators were sworn, so were members of the council; but most important was the oath of the heliasts, taken each year in a solemn ceremony on the hill of Ardettos.[128] There is no evidence that a heliastic court took an oath before voting on a particular case; but at the annual ceremony just mentioned the heliasts swore to vote according to the laws and decrees of the Athenian people and council, to consider only the matter of the charge, to hear both sides impartially, and where there was no law covering the case, to vote according to their most honest judgment (γνώμῃ τῇ δικαιοτάτῃ). The oath closed with an invocation to Zeus, Apollo, and Demeter to punish violators by the utter destruction of themselves and their families, and to reward richly those who kept their oaths.[129] Plato's oath is much simpler: to decide the case justly and truly (τὰ δίκαια καὶ ἀληθῆ κρίνειν) to the best of one's abilities, by Hestia, the goddess of the public hearth (856a).[130] Is Plato inconsistent in retaining the judicial oath, while strictly forbidding the use of the oath by litigants and witnesses? The judges, at least in the smaller courts, are select persons, upon whom the religious sanction will be more effective than upon the chance litigant or witness. Again, the judge is seldom under the temptation that a litigant is always exposed to, the temptation of gain by perjuring himself, or by inducing his witnesses to commit perjury. Finally, what is most important, the effect of the oath is to make acceptance easier for the statement it accompanies. In the consideration of testimony this is highly undesirable, because it relaxes critical attention; but the purpose of a judicial decision is to put an

[126] Gernet cxlii-cxliii.
[127] Cf. the recurrent formula: τὸν δικαστὰν ὀμνύντα κρίνειν.
[128] Bonner and Smith II, 151ff.
[129] This is the content of the oath as reconstructed by Lipsius, 152. The text of the oath in Dem. xxiv, 149ff. is rightly suspected. See Bonner and Smith II, 152ff.
[130] Plato prescribes the oath also in the analogous case of judges of athletic or musical contests (949a) and in the case of nominating (755d) or voting for certain important offices (e.g. 767cd, 948e). It is striking that he makes no mention of an oath to be taken by a magistrate when he enters on his year of office, as was customary at Athens.

end to disputes, hence in this case whatever increases the acceptability of a decision is desirable. The very absence of the oath in the other cases makes its use in judicial decisions the more effective.

The final stage of a judicial process is the execution of judgment. Here also Plato's law, while usually following Attic precedents, contains some important innovations. For the graver crimes, when the penalty is death or exile, it is clear that the execution, with rare exceptions, is in the hands of the public officials.[131] The method of inflicting the death penalty is never specified.[132] Bail is always required of a man accused of murder; if he cannot find persons to go bail for him, he is imprisoned until the trial (871e). All this is in accord with Attic procedure. When a man refuses to pay a fine or taxes or to perform some service required by the state, the officials will take a pledge, that is, seize some of his property. If within a prescribed time he still has not performed, the property is sold and the proceeds appropriated by the state. In case the sale is not sufficient to cover his indebtedness, the offender is imprisoned until he discharges his obligations in full (949d). Attic law made use of imprisonment for this purpose, but not so generally, it would seem, as Plato's regulation would imply for his state. At Athens state debtors lost some of their civic rights (i.e. they became ἄτιμοι) but they were not confined. It appears that Plato intends to substitute imprisonment for the atimia of Attic law.[133]

But Plato's more important innovation is in the execution of judgments in private suits (958a-e). In such cases at Athens the property of the person against whom judgment had been rendered was subject to seizure by the victorious prosecutor; but this seizure was a private act, and if it was resisted, additional litigation would be necessary before the creditor could get possession. For Plato, on the contrary, the execution is as much an affair of the state as of the private litigant. Immediately on the conclusion of the trial the court assigns to the

---

[131] There is mention of a public executioner (δήμιος) in 872b, and of ἄρχοντες in 871de and 873b; cf. also 866c. One exception is the slave who has committed murder and who is delivered over to the relatives of the dead man to be put to death (868b). Similarly the slave guilty of injuring a free man is delivered to the injured person for punishment (879a, 882b).

[132] A curious relic of stoning is prescribed in 873b, but this is done after the criminal has been officially put to death.

[133] The Athenian penalty was not very effective, if we can judge from the large number of ὀφείλοντες τῷ δήμῳ that seem to have existed at Athens. In a time of national emergency it was customary to relieve such persons of their disability.

victorious prosecutor all the goods of the defendant, except of course the lot and its equipment. This is done by proclamation of a herald in the hearing of all members of the court. If at the end of the month following the conclusion of the trial the defendant has not yet settled with his prosecutor, the officials of the court shall assist the "victor" in taking possession of the defendant's property. If the property is materially less than would be enough to satisfy the successful plaintiff's claim (here, though it is not stated, a sale is evidently implied, analogous to the sale mentioned in connection with debts to the public) the debtor shall forfeit the right to bring suit in the courts until he has paid his debt in full. This penalty is a species of atimia, "similar to that imposed at Athens on public debtors, and here transferred deliberately to the realm of private litigation."[134] If the defendant resists the seizure of his property, his act is regarded as rebellion against the state; he is delivered to judgment by the guardians sitting as a court, and if condemned shall be punished by death (958c). The severity of this penalty emphasizes the importance Plato attaches to his new conception of the responsibility of the state in the execution of judgments—a conception in advance of Attic law, and one destined to gain general acceptance at a later date in all western law.

Excessive litigation is injurious to any community; and in Athens, where the cost of litigation was low and where there was such freedom of prosecution in both public and private cases, the dangers from abuse of the courts would be particularly great. We may assume they would be even greater under Plato's law, with its liberal provisions for appeal. A considerable check on litigation is, however, provided in the enlarged judicial competence of the magistrates, who have power to settle private claims up to the value of three minae. Since there is no appeal from their decisions, except by way of suit against the magistrate, a great deal of potential litigation would thus be eliminated. But there are other measures also which Plato adopts to discourage litigation.

To discourage unjustified use of the appeal he adopts the device of increasing the penalties and the awards when a case is heard a second time (956cd). For a defendant who loses on appeal the penalties are increased by one fifth, and by one half on a second unsuccessful appeal. Similarly a prosecutor who takes his case to a higher court with-

[134] Gernet cl.

out success has to pay a penalty of one fifth the damages he claimed in his original suit, and if he loses on a second appeal he pays damages equal to one half of his original claim. There is a parallel provision for extra awards to the prosecutor who wins on appeal. Nevertheless the raising of the stakes at each successive stage in the litigation would act as a deterrent.[135] This scale of penalties for unsuccessful appeal is far more extensive than anything in Attic law; but the practice is not without precedent. In at least some private suits an Athenian litigant who appealed from the arbitrator's verdict to the Heliaea was liable to the ἐπωβελία if he lost, that is, he was required to pay to the defendant one sixth (one obol for every drachma) of the amount of damages he had sought to obtain by the suit.[136] Plato seems to have adapted to the scale of his courts a device which had been found effective at Athens.

Sometimes Plato provides a penalty for initiating litigation instead of settling out of court. Thus the seller of a diseased slave who refuses to give satisfaction to the buyer upon demand and forces the issue into court is liable, if he loses, for double the value of the slave (916b). There are many cases in Platonic law where "double damages" are to be paid by the person who loses (868b, 915a, 927d); but whether this is to be taken as a penalty for litigation or a penalty for fraud or violence is not easy to determine. It is obviously Plato's intention to encourage the settlement of private disputes out of court, and Partsch has pointed out the frequent occurrence of double damages as a penalty for litigation in later Greek law.[137] To prevent unwarranted instituting of public suits, Athenian law provided that the prosecutor of a γραφή who failed to receive one fifth of the votes of the judges was penalized by a fine of a thousand drachmae and partial atimia.[138] There is a reflection of this in the Platonic law that the bringer of a γραφή against a euthynos is subject to a fine if he does not receive one fifth of the votes of the court (948a); there is no mention of atimia. This seems to be the single instance of the use of this principle in Plato's law, and in view of the exceptional position of

[135] The general principle stated in 956cd for private suits is also applied to appeals from the decision of the euthynoi (946de). Cf. also 767e (see above, Note 43) where the suit against a magistrate necessarily involves a rehearing of the case.

[136] Bonner and Smith II, 58.

[137] *Archiv für Papyrusforschung* VI, 70.

[138] There were probably some exceptions to the rule that every γραφή involved this risk. See Bonner and Smith II, 59. A similar law is reported to have been in force in Erythrae; Busolt-Swoboda 547.

the euthynoi in his state it would be hazardous to infer that he intended it to be used for all public suits.

Finally, Plato provides for a public suit (γραφὴ κακοδικίας) against anyone guilty of unreasonable or excessive litigation (938bc). This law is prefaced by the grave reflection that most fair things in human life have a kind of defiling parasite attached to them. Justice has civilized all human affairs, and to go to law to get justice for oneself or others cannot but be a fair thing. But justice and litigation are brought into disrepute by a "foul technique calling itself an art," which maintains that there is a way of managing lawsuits so as to win the victory, whether or not one's cause is just, and by the practitioners of this "art," who offer its benefits for a compensation. Whether this skill is really an art, or an artless trick got by habit and practice, it must never be allowed to take root in the state. Hence the law that follows: "If anyone appears to be endeavoring to pervert the sentiment of justice in the minds of the judges, or to be wrongfully multiplying suits at law, or aiding others to do so, whoso wishes may indict him for wrongful prosecution or wrongful advocacy, as the case may be." If a man is found guilty, and the court decides that he has acted from avarice, he shall be punished with death, if a citizen, and exile, if a metic. On the other hand, if the court finds that the defendant has acted from contentiousness, the penalty is lighter. The punishment in the latter case is partial atimia, i.e. loss of the privileges of the courts for a prescribed period; but a second conviction carries the penalty of death. Apparently contentiousness, being a part of the spirited element in human nature, is not intrinsically bad and can be redirected, but avarice can neither be redirected nor cured.

There are several analogies to this action in Attic law. An oration ascribed to Demosthenes contains the text of a law, probably genuine, which Bonner and Smith connect with the democratic restoration at the end of the fifth century, allowing a γραφή to be brought against an advocate (συνήγορος) who accepted pay for his assistance.[139] Besides this, there were the various legal processes available against sycophancy; a γραφὴ συκοφαντίας could be preceded by a "presentation" (προβολή) before the assembly or a denunciation before the council, which would serve to gauge the temper of public

---

[139] Ps. Dem. XLVI, 26; Bonner and Smith II, 10-11. Lyc. I, 138 says that pleading for malefactors in court for pay deserves the people's utmost indignation; but this statement shows that such actions were not always punished.

opinion and indicate to the prosecutor whether it would be wise to proceed with his suit. But sycophancy, like Plato's "wrongful prosecution" or "wrongful advocacy" was not easy to define, since it included "all abuse of legal process for mischievous or fraudulent purposes."[140] The penalty was probably not fixed by law and could be determined by the court. In one case that we know of, conviction for sycophancy carried a fine of 10,000 drachmae.[141]

These Attic procedures are clear precedents for Plato's law; but there is something peculiar to Plato in the description of the kind of offenses which would make a man liable to prosecution. Certainly a man who made a business of prosecution for financial gain—the "sycophant" of Attic life—would be condemned, but that term occurs nowhere in the *Laws*. Presumably also a person with a long record of litigation would have to show that there were quite special circumstances that necessitated it in his case. But it is clear that Plato's law is directed not only against litigants, but also against σύνδικοι, i.e. those who aid or advise litigants in the strategy of prosecution or defense, or write speeches for them. The description of the parasitic "art," as well as the distinction in penalties between those who acted from avarice and those who were merely contentious, shows that Plato has chiefly in mind the unscrupulous teachers of rhetoric and their close disciples, the λογογράφοι of fourth-century Athens, who practised their art for pay. This specious art, this counterfeit of justice, Plato had denounced on many previous occasions; the present passage is the last shot fired in his life-long campaign against sophists and rhetoricians.

Looking back upon the numerous and varied proposals we have dealt with in this section, we can see that the law of procedure was far more than a mere appendage to Plato's system. In spite of the gesture made on one or two occasions to leave such details to the younger legislators, it is evidently too important a matter to be left to their discretion without explicit guidance in the principles and practices to be adopted. Plato's juristic conscience, or his observation of Athenian life, taught him that substantive law is likely to be ignored or perverted without appropriate procedures for enforcing the duties the law imposes and giving effect to the rights it confers. The pattern he lays down is in the main the procedure of Athenian

[140] Kennedy, quoted in Bonner and Smith II, 43.
[141] Lys. XIII, 67.

law, with its freedom of prosecution and its rich variety of actions and remedies; but it is Athenian law modified at many points in directions, we may say, that are suggested by that law itself. In giving to the presiding magistrates power to control the pleading and prevent the introduction of irrelevant and misleading matter, in introducing something like inquisition of witnesses and principals, in excluding the opportunities for rhetorical jousting afforded by the archaic challenge to the oath and the challenge to the torture, in enlarging the range of competent witnesses and enforcing a litigant's right to compel their assistance, in eliminating the oath of witnesses and principals, in relying at all stages upon written documents, and in invoking the power of the state to assist a litigant in enforcing a judgment obtained in court—in all these provisions Plato's law, while still essentially Attic in character, embodies a conception of the judicial process broader and more enlightened than ever characterized Athenian practice at its best.

CHAPTER VII

EDUCATION

EDUCATION (παιδεία), as Plato's argument defines it, is "that training in virtue from childhood which makes a man eager to become a full-fledged citizen, knowing both how to rule justly and how to obey" (643e). By contrast, "any training (τροφή) which aims at wealth or strength or any other accomplishment unattended by wisdom and justice is vulgar, illiberal, and utterly unworthy to be called παιδεία" (644a). Thus defined, education becomes a matter of prime importance for the legislator; for if it is properly conducted it is an invaluable means of bringing about εὐνομία, by weaving the substance of the laws into the very fabric of the citizens' character (659de).

Probably few of Plato's contemporaries would have questioned this definition of paideia. The education extolled by the poets and wise men of the Greek tradition as an "ornament to the fortunate, a refuge for the unfortunate,"[1] was conceived as a liberal training of mind and character, rather than as preparation for a trade or craft. The preference for liberal training undoubtedly had its source in the aristocracy, but the standards set by the aristocracy were accepted by the Greeks generally as expressing the correct scale of values.[2] Even the sophists professed to be teachers of virtue in the broadest sense; the special skills in which they claimed proficiency were subsidiary to the attainment of good citizenship and the wise management of one's private affairs. Plato is in the main stream of Greek tradition here, a tradition that flowed on into Hellenistic times and left upon the whole Graeco-Roman world the conviction that the aim of education is to develop in the child the qualities of mind and character that most fully express the ideal of human nature.

Nor would many of Plato's contemporaries have been disposed to deny the conclusion he draws concerning the responsibility of the state for educating its young. Yet in most Greek cities the guidance of education was provided by public opinion and informal social

---

[1] Attributed to Democritus (Diels-Kranz II, 181, Fr. 180), to Aristotle (Diog. v, 19), and to Diogenes the Cynic (Diog. vi, 68). On παιδεία as contrasted with other forms of διδασκαλία, see Plato Soph. 229d, Phil. 55d.

[2] Thus Prot. 326c suggests that all citizens who could afford it gave their sons the education in gymnastics and music described.

forces, rather than by explicit organs of the state. In his description of the education that the young Cyrus received, Xenophon points out that the laws of the Persians, unlike those of most states, did not allow the father to educate his sons as he pleased.[3] Sparta, in classical times, was an even better example of deliberate policy. Here the state took its young members in hand in infancy and molded them relentlessly into the form of the mature citizen that the state required; and for the older citizens it confirmed this fashioning by the common meals and the life-long military exercises that did not permit the individual to forget for a moment that he was a Spartan and what was expected of a Spartan. Something similar was probably to be found also in Crete.[4] But if we can believe Xenophon,[5] Sparta and Crete differed in this respect from most Greek states, certainly from Athens. Pericles even boasts of the contrast. "In education, too, our ways are different," he says; "they endeavor to reach manliness by a painful discipline from youth onward; but we live without restraint, and yet are no less ready to confront dangers."[6] After the defeat of Athens many of her friends must have wondered if Pericles' confidence in the quality of Athenian education had not been misplaced; and others besides Xenophon must have been inclined to find the secret of Spartan superiority in the discipline attributed to Lycurgus.[7] What impressed Xenophon was the military power of Sparta; but the prestige of Spartan education survived the defeat at Leuctra, as we can see from the chorus of praise cited above.[8] We know that Phocion, who was one of the wisest and ablest of Athenian statesmen during the second half of the fourth century, sent his son to Sparta to be educated.[9] It is not surprising, therefore, that Plato thought the Spartan system contained something worthy of being imitated in his model state.

But usually when the Ionians took over something from the Dorians they transformed it by their own questioning intelligence and restless desire for improvement; and we should expect this to happen when Plato takes in hand the Spartan and Cretan agoge, clarifies and enlarges its purpose, and diligently seeks the best means of accomplishing it. The extent of Plato's dependence can be seen only after

[3] *Educ. of Cyrus*, I, ii, 2-3.   [4] Cf. Strabo x, iv, 16.
[5] See Note 3 above, and *Const. Lac.* II, 1-2.   [6] Thuc. I, 39, 1.
[7] Xen. *Const. Lac.* I, 1-3.   [8] In Chapter II.
[9] Plut., *Phoc.* 20. So too did Xenophon (Plut. *Ages.* 20) but he was in exile from Athens at the time.

we have examined the details of his program. But it is appropriate to remind ourselves at the outset of one point on which he expresses emphatic disagreement with the Spartan system, at least as it was commonly understood. Education has for its aim the development of all the virtues, not merely the virtues of the soldier. The Spartan and Cretan parties to the dialogue in the *Laws* are inclined to take it for granted that the purpose of all their institutions is to assure victory in war;[10] but the Athenian leads them to see that if their laws are of divine origin, as they claim, the intent of their legislators cannot have been limited to such a partial and trivial aim as this. For the readiness to die fighting "with well-planted feet apart" is something that is found in the most ordinary mercenary soldiers, most of whom, the Athenian remarks with considerable feeling, are rash and violent and incredibly stupid. Even as courage this level of virtue ranks far below the courage of the citizen who can hold his own in civil strife. Sedition (στάσις), not war (πόλεμος), is the real threat to the stability of a state, Plato believes, and the overcoming of sedition requires the cultivation not of courage alone, but of courage coupled with moderation, wisdom, and justice (628c-630d).

These comments, made the more emphatic by the Athenian's desire to save the reputation of Lycurgus and Minos, are a severe indictment of Spartan and Cretan life. Plato had expressed the same criticism in the *Republic*, where the timocratic state, expressly exemplified by Crete and Sparta, is pictured as an uneasy union of discordant factions, exalting military stratagems and contrivances and waging everlasting wars (547b-e). "Their friends and maintainers, whom they had formerly protected in the condition of freemen"—Plato is not writing history here, but describing the timocratic state as if it had arisen by degeneration from the ideal form—"they made into perioikoi and slaves, and they themselves were engaged in war and in keeping a watch against them." This was an undisguised thrust at a peculiarly sensitive part of the Spartan system. There were other forms of stasis to which the Spartans in their history were subject, in consequence of the rivalry between the two kingly houses and the scheming of the ephors against one or both of the kings. A people disciplined only for war is likely to settle such issues by violence. The Cretans were even more subject to faction within the ruling

[10] On Spartan education as primarily preparation for war, see Arist. *Pol.* 1324b 8; Plut. *Lyc.* 16-17; *Inst. Lac.* 4. Xenophon would probably not agree; cf. *Const. Lac.* XI, 1.

body, says Aristotle in the *Politics*—so subject to dissension, in fact, that their polity would long ago have been dissolved, had Crete not been protected by its location from the machinations of outside powers.[11] These grim consequences of a predominantly military education were too obvious to permit either Plato or Aristotle to advocate a Spartan regime without amendment.

If in spite of this severe judgment on Spartan life Plato nevertheless looks to its system of education for guidance in his own legislation, it is because he feels that the results fall short of what the system might produce. The Spartan agoge shows how virtues in general can be taught, and this is why Plato's interest in the Spartan system has survived the defeat at Leuctra. Victory in war is never the test of the excellence of a state, nor defeat an evidence of its moral inferiority.[12] Undoubtedly Plato sees in the Spartan state the imperfect, and in some ways perverse, application of a principle and a set of methods that might really remove the causes of faction and bring about the freedom, wisdom, and good will that make a state secure and happy.

But Plato brings to this problem a profounder conception of what is involved in the training of character than any Spartan ever had. "Can virtue be taught?" is a question that must have concerned Plato as much as it did the Socrates whom he portrays in the early dialogues as almost obsessed by it. Plato's answer is that virtue can be taught, but not primarily by admonition, nor by the explanation and proof of principles, as one would teach a science. The analogy between the virtues and the arts, on which Socrates so often insists, shows the way, or at least the first part of the way. No virtue or technical skill can be acquired except by long practice, by a process of habituation. The value of such habituation Plato could see in the products of the Spartan discipline. But since feeling is the mainspring of action— at least for the majority of men—no habit is firmly fixed in a man's character unless it is supported by the appropriate sentiments of pleasure and pain. The discrepancy between a man's real sentiments and the habits he has been disciplined to adopt was often too clearly

[11] *Pol.* 1272b 1-17.
[12] Ollier (*Le Mirage spartiate*, 271-272) asserts that Plato seems not to have appreciated the import of Leuctra and Mantinea; for him the Spartans are still invincible on the battlefield. The truth is, Plato seems never to have admired Sparta for her military prowess; 638b, to which Ollier refers in support of his statement, contains the Athenian's rebuke of Megillus' boast that the superiority of Spartan customs can be demonstrated on the battlefield.

marked in the behavior of the fourth-century Spartan.[13] The real problem is to induce those sentiments in the youth that will make his acquired virtues a genuine expression of his inner disposition. Education, then, if properly conducted, will not only produce an accord between the citizen's opinions and what the law prescribes; it will also produce an accord between these opinions and the feelings of pleasure and pain, of love and dislike, which are the chief determinants of action (653a-c, 659d). The rightly educated man loves what he ought to love (i.e. what the law prescribes) and hates what he ought to hate (i.e. what the law forbids).

Now Plato sometimes describes this as a process of "molding" the soul into a pattern (cf. 666bc, 671c), and sometimes as a process of leading or guiding. The former is the more obvious metaphor, and readily suggests itself to anyone who thinks of education as involving the use of an art or τέχνη, as Plato certainly did. But the latter is the more subtle analogy, and far more appropriate to one who thinks of the soul as the intermediary between the ideal and the sense world, and as the source of all motion, whether for good or for evil. The proper mode of action upon a soul is by means of persuasion, not compulsion; and scientific persuasion, as is made clear in the *Phaedrus* (261a), is an art of leading souls (ψυχαγωγία). Consequently when Plato defines education as the drawing and leading (ὁλκή τε καὶ ἀγωγή) of the child's soul to the feelings of pleasure and pain that accord with the law (659d), though he uses in this definition the very term ἀγωγή traditionally employed as a designation of the Spartan discipline, it carries with it the whole weight of his philosophy, and thus possesses a subtler and deeper significance than we can fairly attribute to the Spartans of history.[14]

[13] For ancient criticisms of Spartan behavior, see Chapter II. Contrast the tribute to the Athenian character in 642cd: when Athenians are good they are incomparably good, for they alone are good spontaneously (αὐτοφυῶς) and genuinely (ἀληθῶς), not by compulsion (ἄνευ ἀνάγκης) nor by artifice (οὔ τι πλαστῶς).

[14] See my "Plato's Conception of Persuasion," *PR* LXII, 1953, 234-250. It is by no means certain that the Spartan training was called ἀγωγή in Plato's time. It is significant that the word does not occur in Xenophon's account, and he must have known the Spartans well; he speaks only of the Spartan παιδεία. But ἀγωγή is used at least four times in the *Laws* as a synonym for παιδεία, or in close connection with it: i.e. 645a, 659d, 673a, 819a (cf. also *Rep.* 604b). Aristotle also uses it in this Platonic sense in *Nic. Eth.* 1179b 31, *Eud. Eth.* 1215a 32, and *Pol.* 1292b 14, 16. The title is preserved of a probably spurious work of Plato's contemporary and friend, Archytas of Tarentum, Ὑπὲρ παίδων ἀγωγῆς (Diels-Kranz I, 439, 24). The older Stoics likewise used it as meaning education (J. von Arnim, *Stoicorum Veterum Fragmenta*, Leipzig, 1902-1924, Index s.v.). The earliest mention of the Spartan ἀγωγή

MUSIC AND THE DANCE

Despite the etymological connection of the word παιδεία with childhood, and despite Plato's deliberate restriction of it in one passage (653b) to the training of the sentiments in children, the word is often employed in a broader sense, implying institutions for the older members of the community as well (653cd; cf. 631de). And there is one common instrument that Plato thinks effective for all ages, viz. the practice of choral singing and dancing (χορεία). This forms part of the education of children from the age of six onwards; and in later life the refreshing and renewing of the sentiments acquired in childhood is brought about by the great public festivals, at which choirs or choruses of various ages dance and sing under the inspiration of the Muses and Apollo. The gods are companions at the festival (συνεορτασταί) and companions in the dance (συγχορευταί), so that these festivals are not only periods of relief from toil, but also opportunities for spiritual refreshment. Thus the pleasure of the festival renews and confirms the sentiments acquired in childhood, linking the citizens to one another in common loyalty to the ideas expressed in these dances and songs (654a). The importance of this instrument of education is such that Plato defines the educated man (ὁ καλῶς πεπαιδευμένος) as "he who has learned to sing and dance aright" (ᾄδειν τε καὶ ὀρχεῖσθαι δυνατὸς καλῶς), while the uneducated (ἀπαίδευτος) is ἀχόρευτος, untrained in choral discipline (654b), and to the philosophical exposition of its effects upon the character Plato devotes the whole of the second book of the *Laws*.

In giving choreia this position of honor, Plato is not expressing merely a personal preference, but is reflecting the common opinion of his fellow countrymen. Greek music and dancing have left no enduring monuments comparable to those of the poets, sculptors, and architects; but the indirect evidence of the primacy of the musical arts is overwhelming and indisputable. Music and the dance formed a part of all the great religious festivals, both local and Panhellenic; at most of them musical contests were featured side by side with the athletic ones, and victories in them were almost equally coveted and honored. They were an essential feature of marriage and funeral

---

is, I believe, in Sosibius apud Athen. 674ab, at least a half century after Plato's death. Polybius uses the phrase in 1, 32, 1. By Plutarch's time the term had apparently become limited, in this educational sense, to Sparta (*Ages.* 1: τὴν λεγομένην ἀγωγὴν ἐν Λακεδαίμονι). How much of this history of the word is due to the influence of the *Laws*?

ceremonies, and of the rites of seed time, harvest, and vintage. Every occupation seems to have had its distinctive songs.[15] At banquets and social gatherings the guests entertained one another by singing in turn, or they listened to a minstrel or a chorus, or watched an exhibition of dancing or tumbling. There were professionals, of course, but all Greeks were amateurs of these arts, and some degree of proficiency was regarded as the mark of a gentleman. Even the Homeric heroes did not disdain them. Achilles in his tent soothes his angry spirit by playing the lyre and singing songs of heroes, while Patroclus listens with rapt attention.[16] The sorrowful Odysseus at the palace of King Alcinoüs is made glad at heart as he watches the twinkling feet of the young men dancing on the broad floor and listens to the song of the sweet minstrel Demodocus.[17] In classical times training in singing and playing the lyre was a part of the education of all Athenians who could afford it.[18] "Evermore rejoicing in lyre and dance and song, and keeping my wit high in the company of the good"—thus Theognis sums up the higher life.[19] A century later, Aristophanes describes the citizens of the good old style as "trained in music, chorus, and palaestra."[20] To these pleasures of dance and song the gods of course were not indifferent. For Hesiod the Muses danced on Helicon;[21] and Plato's vision of the gods as fellow choristers with their worshippers was a commonplace to the poets and the sculptors.[22]

This love of music and the dance seems to have been common to all the Greek stocks; it is a form of activity in which the Hellenic spirit at play most naturally engaged. But the Lacedaemonians seem to have first attained a special excellence in music, or a special capacity for enjoying it, for Sparta became for a time almost the

---

[15] See the impressive list of songs in Athenaeus 618c-619c.
[16] *Iliad* IX, 186-191.   [17] *Odyss.* VIII, 256ff.
[18] *Prot.* 326a-c. Themistocles in later life defended himself, somewhat arrogantly, for not having learned to tune a lyre and use a harp like his fellows; "but I can take in hand a small and obscure city and make it great and glorious." Plut. *Them.* 2.
[19] Lines 790-792; Edmonds' trans. Cf. Xenophon's lively description of the dances performed at an entertainment given by Greek soldiers (*Anab.* VI, i, 5-13).
[20] *Frogs* 729.   [21] *Theog.* 1-4.
[22] Cf. the many representations of the gods, or a god, leading the dance in Maurice Emmanuel, *La Danse grecque antique*, 1895 (Eng. trans. by Harriet Beauly, 1916). Apollo with his lyre leads the dance of his Cretan followers to Delphi (*Hymn to Pythian Apollo* 514ff.; cf. Athen. 22b). A. Brinckmann ("Altgriechische Mädchenreigen," in *Bonner Jahrbücher* 130, 1925, 118-121) gives a graphic summary of the way in which dancing entered into every phase of Greek life.

musical capital of the Greek world.[23] Terpander of Lesbos, who established the canons, or "nomes," of songs accompanied by the lyre; Polymnestus of Colophon and Sacadas of Argos, who did the same for the aulos, or "flute"; Xenodamus of Cythera, Xenocritus of Locri —these are some of the famous musicians of the seventh and sixth centuries who took up their residence at Sparta, certainly because they found there a congenial environment and a public responsive to their art. But it is in choral music—less individualistic in character and more appropriate to religious and patriotic ceremonies—that the Lacedaemonians particularly excelled. Thaletas of Crete is reputed to have established this art at Sparta, with his paeans and hyporchemes executed by youthful choirs. He was followed by Alcman of Sardis, famed for his παρθένεια, intended (as the name implies) to be sung by choruses of maidens, and by Tyrtaeus, whose war songs heartened the spirit of the Spartans in the second Messenian War. A sixth-century poet of Phlius calls the Spartan "that cicada ready for a chorus."[24] This early distinction in choral art seems to have been shared by the other Dorian stocks as well. The Cretans were noted for their dancing, according to Aristoxenus;[25] the dithyramb was first developed at Corinth; tragic choruses are first heard of at Sicyon; and Pratinas, the first writer of satyr dramas, came from Phlius. The influence of this choral music on the development of the musical arts in Greece must have been considerable; and its importance in the history of Athenian tragedy seems now to be generally admitted.[26] With the reorganization of Spartan life that occurred shortly after this period of flowering, leadership in the musical arts passed to other lands; but the thought of this early bloom of choral art among the Dorians, and the charm of the archaic forms preserved in their purity at Sparta, must have been in Plato's mind when his Athenian praises choreia to his Cretan and Spartan companions.

The two parts of choreia are dance and song. Both of these have their roots deep in human nature, according to a "widespread theory" which the Athenian expounds at the beginning of the second book.[27]

---

[23] Plut. *De Mus.* 9-10; Marrou 44; Ollier, *op.cit.* 15.

[24] Pratinas, in Athen. 633a. On the cicada in chorus, see below, Note 28. There is a lively portrayal of a Lacedaemonian chorus at the close of Aristophanes' *Lysistrata*.

[25] Athen. 630b. Cf. *Iliad* xvi, 617 for Aeneas' taunt at the Cretan dancer Meriones; and Lucian *The Dance* 8.

[26] A. W. Pickard-Cambridge, *Dithyramb, Tragedy, and Comedy*, Oxford, 1927, 148.

[27] ὁρᾶν οὖν χρὴ πότερον ἀληθὴς ἡμῖν κατὰ φύσιν ὁ λόγος ὑμνεῖται τὰ νῦν, ἢ πῶς,

This theory maintains that every young creature finds it difficult to keep still and is always leaping and skipping about, frolicking with his companions (dancing, as it were, in his games with them) and uttering all sorts of sounds. This is the raw material which, when reduced to rhythm (ῥυθμός), or ordered movement (τῇ τῆς κινή-σεως τάξει, 665a), produces dance and song. Besides rhythm, song involves harmony (ἁρμονία), i.e. an ordering of musical sounds with respect to high and low tones. Again the rhythm of the dance is itself ordered into figures (σχήματα), and the succession of musical sounds into songs (μέλη, 654e, 672e). Finally, this theory maintains that of all creatures man is the only one who has a perception of order and disorder in these various movements of body and voice, the only one capable, therefore, of enjoying the movement of dance and song. This enjoyment is said to be the gift of the gods (654a). Apollo and the Muses, the authors of dance and song, are therefore the authors of education.[28]

When we today use the word dance, we think of folk dancing, the ballet, or the formal dances of the ballroom; we should hardly regard military drill, for example, or an academic procession, or a group of priests and acolytes celebrating the mass, as forms of the dance. But these (or their ancient equivalents) would certainly be regarded by Plato and his countrymen as examples of choreia, particularly when accompanied by the music which adds a special completeness to the exercise or the ceremony. The Panathenaic procession depicted by Phidias in the famous frieze on the Parthenon is an elaborate and stately chorus, each figure in the procession not only

---

653d. The λόγος mentioned here seems to include not merely the details of 653d-654a, but also the material about rhythm and harmony in 664e-665a. There are later references to the theory in 672cd and 673cd. Is this Plato's own teaching to which the Athenian Stranger is made to refer? Or a well-known doctrine propounded by some musical theorist, such as Damon (see Athen. 628c), referred to by both Plato (*Rep.* 400b,c; 424c) and Aristotle (*Pol.* 1341b 27ff., 1340b 5ff.)? It is difficult to say. In any case the Athenian Stranger, in spite of this opening query, seems to regard it as a firm basis for his exposition of the educational importance of dance and song. The same theory of human nature, without the mythology, seems to underlie Aristotle's doctrine of rhythm and harmony (*Pol.* 1340a 2ff.; cf. *Prob.* 920b 29ff.; *Poet.* 1448b 20ff.).

[28] This λόγος also seems to include the derivation of χορός from χαρά in 654a, which found its way into the *Etymologicum Magnum*, s.v. χορός. There is a minor variant of this doctrine in the lovely myth of the cicadas in *Phaedrus* 259bc: The cicadas were human beings in the age before the Muses; when the Muses came and song appeared, they were ravished with delight and, singing always, never thought of eating and drinking, until at last in their forgetfulness they died; and now they live again in the cicadas.

maintaining its ordered position in the whole, but exhibiting in the lightness of its movement, and in the rhythmic opposition of arm and leg, head and torso, all the characteristic graces of the dance.[29] In Plato's famous picture of Protagoras and his troupe of admirers in the house of Callias they are described as a "chorus," and Socrates says he particularly admired the precision of their movements.[30] This is, to be sure, a humorous application of the concept, but its effect comes precisely from the "processional" use of the term. Again, we usually associate dancing with movements of the legs; but for the Greeks a dance was not merely a rhythmic pattern of steps, but an ordered movement of the whole body—head, arms, hands, torso, as well as legs and feet. Even the movement might sometimes disappear; a posture, or an arrested gesture, if seen and understood as a phase of a larger pattern, formed a "figure" of the dance, such as the gesture of the veil, or the postures of mourning or farewell or adoration so beautifully preserved for us in Greek vase painting and sculpture.

Thus the dance is not merely an exercise of bodily agility, but the introduction of pleasing and significant form into all the movements of a man's body, and thence into all that he does.[31] It is only on state occasions that the form is emphasized; but frequent participation in these formal dances, with their prescribed patterns, gestures, and postures, cannot fail to have its influence on the gestures, postures, and movements of ordinary life. And through their effect upon the spectators these public ceremonies would have a subtle effect on the demeanor, gestures, and bearing of all the citizens of a community. "The life of man in every part has need of harmony and rhythm." Plato speaks here as an aristocrat, but it is the manners of aristocrats that have served in every society as patterns of behavior for all.[32]

But manners are not morals, and we must follow Plato's thought further before we can appreciate the importance he attaches to the dance as a means of education in virtue. The movements of the dance and the melodies that accompany them are expressive, or—as

---

[29] Emmanuel, op.cit. Eng. trans. xv.

[30] Prot. 315b. Cf. Euthyd. 276b,d; 303b; the χορός of the gods (Phaedr. 250b); the χορεία of the heavenly bodies (Tim. 40c). For other references to such uses of the word, see Brinckmann, op.cit. 119 n. 7.

[31] Socrates used to dance, in private at least (Xen. Symp. II, 19), and commended the practice not only as good exercise for every part of the body, but as conducing to rhythm, harmony, and grace of movement (Cf. Lucian The Dance 25).

[32] Prot. 326b; cf. Symp. 187cd: the right use of rhythm and harmony is what is called παιδεία.

the Greeks would put it—mimetic; they are imitations of acts, emotions, and characters (655a-d).[33] All primitive dancing seems to be a stylized imitation of action and passion; the dancer is also an actor. Some of the Greek dances of the classical period preserved this imitative feature in a very lively form. In the armed dances, for example, the participants clashed their shields against one another and brandished their spears in defiance; and at funerals the mourners' gestures of grief were obviously derived from the primitive custom of tearing the hair. The more refined dances were less obviously imitative, but still subtly expressive of emotion in formalized gestures and rhythms. Even more subtle was the mimetic quality of music. For the Greeks certain "modes" were expressive of resolution or defiance; others of serenity and relaxation; still others of grief or adoration. It is difficult for us to verify or even understand such assertions; for whatever musical scores were used in antiquity have almost completely disappeared, and we are unable to interpret with assurance the information we have regarding the differences between the various modes. It may be true, as certain students have maintained, that there is no natural or inevitable connection between a certain mood and a certain melody or scale;[34] in any case it had become second nature to the Greeks to attach distinctive moral significance to the different musical modes. Each mode had its ethos, so strongly marked that a practiced musician would find it impossible to compose in a mode whose character did not fit his subject.[35] On this ethical character of the musical modes not only are Plato and Aristotle agreed, but they profess to be following the common teaching of the musical experts of their day.[36]

This mimetic function of the dance and song is so much taken for granted by the Athenian that he does not even pause to demand the assent of his hearers, but proceeds at once to its implications for moral training.[37] The postures and utterances of a manly soul beset

[33] Cf. Arist. *Poet.* 1447a 26.

[34] J. Combarieu, *La Musique et la magie*, Paris, 1909, 228ff.

[35] Cf. Aristotle's story of Philoxenus, *Pol.* 1342b 8ff.

[36] Note Plato's reference to Damon, and Aristotle's mention of the theorists of the subject (Note 27). Even granting that there were originally magical and religious reasons for this belief in the ethos of the modes (Pierre Boyancé, *Le Culte des Muses chez les philosophes grecs*, Paris, 1937, 129f.), it does not preclude Damon's role in formulating the theory in the fifth century, as Boyancé seems to think. See H. Ryffel, "Eukosmia: Ein Beitrag zur Wiederherstellung des *Areopagitikos* des Damon," *Museum Helveticum* IV, 1947, 23-38; and Raubitschek, "Damon," *Classica et Mediaevalia* XVI, 1955, 78-83.

[37] 655a. The assent is, however, explicitly given in 665b; cf. also 668b.

by troubles will obviously differ from those of a coward; more generally, the movements of dance and song connected with goodness of soul and body are sharply distinguishable from those associated with weakness and vice. The definition of the educated man can now be stated more precisely. The educated man is one who knows how to dance and sing well, not merely as a skilled performer, but rather as one who knows how to dance and sing the representations of the good in character and conduct, and takes pleasure in such representations (654cd). The specifically Platonic contribution here is the emphasis on the pleasure of the performer as a measure of his real cultivation. Otherwise Plato is simply making explicit a standard of fitness that the Greeks implicitly felt, however often they may have violated it in practice. Herodotus' amusing story of Hippoclides who danced away his prospects of winning a bride when, carried away by his own virtuosity, he executed some unseemly figures before his prospective father-in-law, shows that in cultivated opinion virtuosity should be regulated by decorum.[38] Further evidence is afforded by the uneasiness that the Greeks seem to have experienced at the excesses of Dionysiac worship, in spite of their enjoyment as participants or spectators. Plato sees that a standard cannot be maintained unless it is supported by cultivated feelings of pleasure and pain. For the fact is that many persons also take pleasure—whether they admit it or not—in representations of the vices and the passions. This becomes a major obstacle to making the representations of the good the standard for all dramatic and choral performances. A legislator of Plato's time would be defying long-established customs and deep-seated desires if he attempted to prohibit, for example, the phallic processions and orgiastic rites of a Dionysiac festival.[39] A still more formidable obstacle is the current doctrine (λόγος) that the test of excellence in a dramatic or choral performance is the pleasure it gives to performers and spectators (657e).[40] Plato meets this by accepting it, but only in part; the test of a work of art is the pleasure it gives to the good man and competent critic, not to the multitude, nor

[38] Herod. vi, 126-129. For the strong sense of the distinction in dancing between εὐσχημοσύνη and κόσμος, on the one hand, and ἀταραξία and τὸ φορτικόν, on the other, see Athen. 628de.

[39] Plato does not mention this example here, but we shall find that such dances are in fact disapproved, if not prohibited, in his state. See below, Festivals.

[40] It is difficult to say whether Plato is here referring to an explicit philosophy of criticism or merely to an opinion implicit in what he says is the current practice of allowing an audience, through its applause, to determine the victor in a musical contest (cf. 700de).

to the chance performer or spectator. If this is true, competent judges of dramatic or choral performances have the responsibility of rendering judgment and awarding the prize in accordance with their own cultivated taste, uninfluenced by the plaudits of the audience (659ab).

But from the point of view of the legislator a society is imperfectly educated if there is too wide a discrepancy between the judgments of the experts and what the multitude enjoys. How can the pleasure of the experts be transferred to the mass of the citizenry, so that they also will take pleasure only in worthy representations? Plato assumes that the feelings of pleasure and pain can themselves be trained (653b, 656b). The child enjoys what he has been accustomed to enjoy and dislikes what he has been accustomed to dislike; the same is even more true of the mature man (802cd). It is in the training of these feelings that dancing and singing are peculiarly important. As forms of play, dancing and singing are spontaneous expressions of natural exuberance and are intrinsically pleasurable. The feelings of delight that accompany them tend to become attached to the objects they represent, and if the representation is frequently repeated the attachment becomes permanent.[41] Plato's favorite designation in the *Laws* for a device intended to produce this effect upon the soul is "enchantment" (ἐπῳδή). "That the soul of the child may not become accustomed to feel pleasure and pain in ways contrary to the law and to those who obey it, but may join their company and take pleasure and pain in the same things as the older men—to this end there have been devised what are called 'chants' (ᾠδαί) but in truth seem to be 'enchantments' (ἐπῳδαί), whose serious function is to produce in souls that harmony which I mentioned" (659de). It is the duty of the whole state—the Athenian says later—to charm itself unceasingly (ἐπᾴδουσαν μὴ παύεσθαί ποτε) with the chants that have been prescribed, constantly changing them by ingenious devices and introducing variety in every way, so that the singers may have an insatiable thirst for the hymns and pleasure in them (665c).

At this first appearance of the term "enchantment" in the *Laws* one is disposed to think that Plato is simply indulging in one of his plays on words. But the term ἐπῳδαί and its cognates appear with notable frequency in the later discussions of education, and one can only conclude that he is deliberately emphasizing a definite tech-

---

[41] This is not a new doctrine. Plato had already presented it in a briefer form in *Rep.* 424c-425a.

nique.[42] This is at first sight strange, for ἐπῳδαί are most commonly connected, elsewhere in Plato and in Greek writers generally, with magic and sorcery.[43] Boyancé has pointed out the close affiliation between the Platonic ἐπῳδαί and the Orphic and Pythagorean "incantations," and has found the source of Plato's conception in the practices of these religious sects, who conceived of their incantations as having a magical efficacy upon both men and gods.[44] But this interpretation overlooks other more important associations of the word in Plato's thought. The power of the rhetoricians sometimes presented itself to Plato as a kind of enchantment,[45] and rhetoric had no traditional connection with the supernatural. Likewise moral discourses are often referred to as charms effective against certain kinds of error, and Socrates is particularly described as able to produce such enchantment. His discourse on immortality is an outstanding example.[46] It is a mistake, therefore, to interpret Plato as thinking that his ἐπῳδαί are effective not through their content, but only by virtue of some extra-logical or magical character. If there is magic in them, it is the magic of meaningful words addressed to an intelligent soul, when accompanied by rhythm and melody and the other adornments of musical art; and they are designed to produce an effect, not upon the gods, but upon the souls of the citizens. They are peculiarly effective means of persuasion;[47] and we shall find as we proceed that Plato employs them with a quite realistic awareness of their natural efficacy in the societies with which he was acquainted.

For we note that the "chants" which Plato says in the passage quoted above should really be called "enchantments" are not imaginary songs still to be composed, still less the religious hymns of Orphic or Pythagorean worship; they are the songs performed and enjoyed in the Greek cities that he knew. The word ᾠδαί, as we later learn (700b), is intended to cover explicitly a variety of well known types. It includes hymns, or "prayers to the gods"; threnodies, or dirges; paeans—hymns of thanksgiving, usually addressed to Apollo;

[42] Besides the passages above noted, cf. 666c, 671a, 773d, 812c, 837e, 887d, 903b, 944b.
[43] They are the spells with which the sorcerer charms snakes, or drives away diseases, or averts divine wrath. *Euthyd.* 290a, *Rep.* 364b, 426b; cf. *Symp.* 202e.
[44] Boyancé, *op.cit.* 155ff., especially 161.
[45] *Euthyd.* 289e.
[46] *Charm.* 157ab, *Rep.* 608a; *Phaedo* 77e, 78a, 114d.
[47] See my article cited above (Note 14), 236ff.

the dithyramb, a choral song distinguished by its elaborate structure and associated with the worship of Dionysus; and the citharoedic songs, so called because they were accompanied by the lyre (κιθάρα).[48] All of these and others not mentioned (καὶ ἄλλων τινῶν) were classical forms of composition in Plato's day, each governed by its own special rules, and as current in Athens as in Sparta. His careful listing of these types of song, and his insistence upon the preservation of the traditional canons of composition, show that it is the enchantment of these familiar forms that he intends to use, not some new and esoteric magic.

The effect of these songs on the souls of the hearers is vividly brought out in a passage in which the Athenian Stranger describes what takes place "in our part of the world" (ἐν τοῖς παρ' ἡμῖν τόποις), i.e. in Athens. "Whenever a magistrate performs a public sacrifice, the ceremony is followed by choruses—not one, but a number of them—who come and take their stand not far from the altars, sometimes quite near them, and pour out a flood of ill-omened speech upon the sacred places, exciting the souls of their hearers with words, rhythms, and melodies most dolorous; and whoever causes the most weeping in the city that has just sacrificed carries off the prize" (800cd). This seems to refer to the dithyrambic contests that took place at some of the public festivals at Athens. The dramatic contests also exhibited what Plato would regard as a similar enchanting power (817c; cf. 838c). The chorus passages of the Athenian drama would certainly fall under the designation ᾠδαί; they were often the most moving parts of the performance and were clearly designed to influence the mood of the audience.

But we shall fail to appreciate fully the enchanting effect of these performances if we think merely of their influence upon auditors and spectators. The dithyrambic and dramatic choruses were not composed of professionals, but of citizens and residents of the city.[49] A dithyrambic chorus consisted traditionally of fifty members; a tragic chorus of twelve or fifteen; while a chorus in comedy might have as many as twenty-four members. How many plays and dithyrambic choruses were exhibited each year at Athens we can only roughly guess.

[48] Plato is impressed by the fact that the citharoedic songs were explicitly called "nomes" (νόμοι), which he seems to take as confirming his conception of the close connection between the laws of a people and the songs that it sings. Cf. 722de, 799e, 800a, and *Rep.* 424c.

[49] Arist. *Prob.* 918b 20; Plut. *Phoc.* 30.

The dithyrambic contests took place between ten choruses, five of men and five of boys, and were a part of at least four of the annual public festivals.[50] For tragedy, if we assume that three tetralogies were presented at each annual Lenaean festival, and a similar number at each Dionysia, a total of three hundred choristers might be required each year. When to this we add the choristers in the comedies and in other choral performances, we see that the number of Athenians who took part in these choral activities during the course of a year was an impressive one. During the weeks of preparation before the actual performances the words, the melodies, and the dance movements of these choruses must have become familiar not only to the choristers practicing them, but to members of their various households.[51] Thus directly or indirectly a large part of the population was exposed to the enchantment of these songs before the actual performance. If music has the power that Plato thinks it has (and the evidence as to its effect upon the Greeks is altogether in accord with Plato's estimate), the dithyrambic and dramatic performances at Athens were in fact an educational institution of great importance. It is natural that he should desire to direct their influence toward a philosophically approved end.

If this is to be done, the poets who write the songs must be brought to accept the philosopher's standard of what is properly to be represented. Plato refers twice to the older days at Athens when the applause of the audience was not allowed to influence the judges' decisions, as it did later.[52] But he evidently thinks that something more than a reinstatement of the earlier practice is necessary. It is not enough to refuse the prize to a play which does not meet the experts' standards of moral and artistic propriety; why should such a play even be presented? The magistrates must have had a certain amount of discretion in granting or refusing a poet's application for a chorus, though being chosen by lot they may often not have been

[50] Pickard-Cambridge, op.cit. 51.

[51] I owe this observation to an unpublished manuscript of A. E. Raubitschek.

[52] 700cd and 659ab (assuming that ἐξῆν γὰρ . . . νόμῳ are Plato's words and not a marginal gloss that has crept into the text; see England and des Places ad loc.). Athenian audiences were notably noisy in the fourth century (Rep. 492b; Dem. xxi, 226; Athen. 538f); but it is hard to believe that there was ever a time when applause was not permitted, as Plato seems to say. In any case what Plato is deploring is the influence of the audience on the judges' verdict. Aristophanes is conscious of it (Birds 444-445). This influence may have become more serious in the fourth century, as Plato's language suggests; the instances of corruption mentioned in the orators belong to that time. Pickard-Cambridge, The Dramatic Festivals of Athens, Oxford, 1953, 97ff.

experts in such matters. Even the manner of selecting the official judges in the early days probably did not provide the safeguards that Plato thinks necessary. Finally, even if competent judges and magistrates keep the poets from presenting imperfect works to the public, there is still the problem of educating the poet himself. Poetic talent—which Plato always respects, though he often fears its influence—must be won over, not alienated. The poets must be given a treatment of their own medicine; they must be enchanted, i.e. persuaded to accept the standard of the good in their representations (660a). Some of this enchantment they will have experienced as youths going through the usual course of education and participating in the authorized songs at the festivals; but a mature mind, especially one with the creative urge of the poet, stands in need of more than this.

The concern with this problem of enchanting the enchanters seems to underlie the institution of the chorus of elders, one of the quaintest of Plato's proposals. To carry out the process of enchantment, the Athenian Stranger remarks that there are to be three choruses (664b-d). The first, the chorus of the Muses, consists of youths and maidens; the second, the chorus of Apollo, includes those "under thirty years of age" (presumably all those between twenty and thirty); and the third, later called the chorus of Dionysus (665a),[53] is made up of those over thirty and under sixty years of age. "All the three choruses must enchant the souls of the children while they are still young and tender by reciting all the noble doctrines we have gone through or may go through hereafter" (664b). The youngest chorus comes forward and sings these doctrines lustily before the whole city; the second chorus invokes Apollo as witness to the truth of what has been sung and prays that he will graciously persuade the youth. What is the function of the third chorus? It turns out that the men of this group are not to be a chorus in the literal sense of the word. Cleinias says, and the Athenian agrees, that it would be ridiculous to expect men of that age, particularly those over fifty, to dance and sing in public. The most that one could expect is that they might be willing to sing before small groups of friends, at least when they have been enlivened by a little wine to remove the crabbedness of age (666b). But singing in the literal sense does not seem to be their

---

[53] The reference in 665a is possibly to 653d, though there has been no mention of the three choruses up to this point.

most important function. The music that they have mastered is "nobler than the music of the choruses and the theatres" (667ab). It appears that they, or a select group of them, are to be the arbiters of moral and artistic taste in the community, for they are charged with the responsibility of selecting the songs and dances that are suitable for representation by themselves and the younger choristers (670d). Through example, perhaps, but mainly by teaching and sympathetic counsel they are to be the "leaders" of the younger men in the practice of choristry. Some of the elders will be unable to "raise a song" at all (664d) but can still make a contribution by stories (μυθολόγοι) and wise saws (θεῖαι φῆμαι). Such is their part in the program of enchantment.

What is this music "nobler than the music of the choruses and the theatres" which these elderly choristers are supposed to have learned? Socrates in the *Phaedo* declares that philosophy is the highest music (μεγίστη μουσική);[54] and this seems to be the result of the Athenian Stranger's long discourse on the standards of criticism in the musical arts (667a-671a). This discourse leads to the conclusion that the judicious critic requires three sorts of knowledge. Since music is representative in character, he must first know what is being represented, i.e. what is the intention of the work of art; secondly, he must be able to judge the correctness (ὀρθότης) of the representation, i.e. the authenticity of the expression of the moods and characters; and in the third place, the critic must know whether the subjects portrayed are worth being presented.[55] All this presupposes not merely a knowledge of the techniques and conventions in dancing and singing and of the norms of composition (670d)—the Athenian refers with a certain acerbity to some of the innovations in music that

[54] *Phaedo* 61a; cf. *Tim.* 88c; and Timaeus of Locri, περὶ ψυχᾶς κόσμω, XVII.

[55] 669ab: τὸν μέλλοντα ἔμφρονα κριτὴν ἔσεσθαι δεῖ ταῦτα τρία ἔχειν, ὅ τέ ἐστι πρῶτον γιγνώσκειν, ἔπειτα ὡς ὀρθῶς, ἔπειθ' ὡς εὖ, τὸ τρίτον. There is a marked difference of opinion among translators regarding the third element of the expert's knowledge. Jowett and Taylor take it as referring to the execution of the artist's design: the expert must know whether a work of art "has been well executed" (Jowett), or "how well a given representation has been effected" (Taylor). So also Cassarà: "se essa e ben espressa," and presumably also Schuhl, *Platon et l'art de son temps*, Paris, 1952, xvii, 45-46. But for Apelt it is the "sittlicher Wert" of the composition; for des Places "quelle valeur ont toutes ces images reproduites," and for Robin "ce que lui vaut d'être bonne et utile." England thinks that εὖ in this passage, as at 668d 2, refers to "the higher aesthetic or moral judgment." It seems clear to me from the context that the second group of interpreters are far closer to the thought that Plato intends to express. This is one of the many instances in which the philosophical doctrine of the *Republic* is presupposed in the *Laws*.

he regards as morally corrupting (669b-670a)[56]—nor this plus the psychological and moral insight possessed by a great dramatist or composer. Plato's "higher music" goes beyond the sphere of art, as it is usually conceived, into the philosophy of morals and politics—into the realm of the Good, to use the terminology of the *Republic*, which seems to be echoed here. It is not merely a philosophy of art (though that is clearly included), but philosophy in its most comprehensive form. This higher knowledge puts these masters of music above not only the younger citizens, but even above the poets; for although a poet needs to know the technicalities of harmony and rhythm and the art of representation, he may not, as a poet, know "whether the representation is noble or ignoble" (670e). The perfect musician, then, is the philosopher, who knows how to harmonize temperaments in men, not strings of the lyre—as Plato had expressed it in earlier dialogues.[57]

To call this chorus of elders a chorus of Dionysus is a paradox. Dionysus, the giver of wine and the leader in frenzied dances, was a powerful god among the multitude, but scarcely the god one would choose as patron of an Academy of taste and morals. But the wild Thraco-Phrygian god had already been partly tamed by the Greeks, through being associated with Apollo at Delphi and celebrated in the great tragic art of the Athenian theatre. The Greeks did not expel this lawless foreign god (though the legends regarding his arrival in Greece indicate that their first reaction was to do so); instead they eventually harnessed the vital energy of his worshippers to the tempered ritual of Apollonian worship.[58] The same genius for taming excess and reducing frenzy to ordered exaltation is at work in Plato. The wild Dionysiac dances are perhaps to be excluded, but not the spirit of Dionysus. It seems that Plato still felt, as he did when he was writing the *Symposium*, that "enthusiasm," or intoxication with the divine, was the driving force underlying all insight and achievement. The popular tale that Dionysus gave wine to man in vengeance for having been deprived of his reason by Hera is an affront to his divinity (672b). There is, moreover, a special reason why the name of Dionysus should be attached to this chorus and why his gift of wine should be useful to the elders. The younger choristers

[56] Schuhl, *op.cit.* 12 n. 1, finds here allusions to such innovators as Phrynis, Timotheus and Philoxenus. See Note 155.
[57] *Rep.* 432a, 443de; *Polit.* 306-308.
[58] Guthrie, *The Greeks and their Gods*, 176ff.; Nilsson 1, 578ff.

already have enough natural exuberance and "joie de vivre." It would
be a mistake, in their case, to "pour fire on fire" (666a). But "we
older men need to renew our youth," and for this the gift of Dionysus is a powerful medicine (666b)—a medicine, we can readily see,
that would be almost indispensable to a group of elderly men charged
with compiling an anthology of songs and dances.[59]

This is not to be taken as merely a jest on Plato's part. He is seriously
proposing, as a means of education for the older men, something
like the institution of the symposium as it existed at Athens.[60] The
Dorians, among whom the use of wine was sternly prohibited, are
pictured as unacquainted with a properly regulated convivial gath-
ering, and the Athenian has already devoted considerable time to persuading them that such gatherings, when rightly conducted, are an
important factor in moral education (637a-641d). And now, after
the account of the higher music in which the elderly choristers must
be trained, the symposium again appears (671a-672a). We can only
assume that Plato thinks of this as one means, at least, through
which this higher knowledge is to be attained. But if the symposium
is to play its part in developing aesthetic taste and moral judgment, Plato thinks it must be pruned of the faults which are almost
invariably found in it (639de).[61] In the *Protagoras* (347c-348a) Socrates ridicules the "wine parties of common market folk" who, being
unable to amuse themselves with conversation like educated people,
have to bring in a flute girl, or a dancing girl, or a harpist; but when
the companions at the banquet are educated gentlemen, there you
will find them content with their own conversation, each speaking
and listening in turn in orderly fashion.[62] Such presumably are to
be the gatherings (σύλλογοι, 671a; συνουσίαι, 672a) of the chorus
of Dionysus, as Plato sees them—friendly parties chiefly occupied
with serious conversation on some prearranged theme, with occasional dancing and singing by the members (666c).[63] They are to

[59] Cf. Taylor's note (45): "This, I think, explains the use they are to make of
'the bottle.' Their natural tendency would be to make the standard and the anthology too 'elderly.' They are less likely to commit this fault if they come to the work
mellowed by a bottle of generous wine."

[60] Robin, Introduction to the *Symposium* in the Budé edition, xivff.

[61] Recall the drunken disorder that marks the conclusion of the banquet at
Agathon's house described in the *Symposium*.

[62] Other forms of diversion at Athenian symposia were the singing of scholia
(Plato *Gorg.* 451e; Aristoph. *Wasps* 1224ff.); making similitudes (*ibid.* 1308-1318;
Plato *Symp.* 215a-d, 216de, 221de; *Meno* 80a-c): and asking riddles (*Rep.* 479b).

[63] Athenaeus (134a) quotes Alexis, a comic poet of the late fourth century, as
saying that the Athenians begin to dance when they have had but a smell of wine.

be governed by rules (συμποτικοὶ νόμοι, 671c) under the presidency of "officers of Dionysus" (671de) to restrain excess and disorder and preserve good feeling. Such convivial gatherings played a part in the program of the Academy and the Lyceum,[64] and there can be no doubt that they are seriously proposed here. In them we find education (παιδεία) conjoined with play (παιδιά), a condition which Plato considers essential to all molding of the character.[65]

Plato's institution of the three choruses is often supposed to have been copied from a Spartan model. Plutarch, when describing the practice of singing at Sparta and the powerful influences such practices had in the making of the Spartan character, tells us that in the festivals at Sparta three choruses took part—one a chorus of elders, another of men in the prime of life, and a third composed of boys and youths.[66] It may indeed be that the suggestion of the three choruses came to Plato from this source, but his chorus of elders is quite different from the institution that Plutarch describes. The Spartan choruses, according to Plutarch, conducted a kind of three-part antiphony, the older men boasting of their former prowess in arms, the younger ones vaunting their strength, and the youngest expressing their determination "to be the strongest by-and-by." This glorification of military prowess is precisely what Plato most disapproved of in Spartan education. Doubtless it would seldom have occurred to a flesh-and-blood Spartan that elders could play any other part in such a ceremony than that of old soldiers, examples of faded heroism. So the Athenian's Dorian companions cannot conceive of any music for this third chorus other than that learned in their youthful choric practices (666d). The Athenian's response is a rare outburst of indignation. "Naturally; the fact is, the noblest singing (ἡ καλλίστη ᾠδή) is out of your reach. For your 'constitution' is that of an armed camp, not one of city dwellers" (666e). This passage immediately precedes the account of the nobler music which the chorus of Dionysus is to exemplify, and the puzzlement of the Dorians is dramatic evidence of the difference between Plato's chorus of elders,

[64] On symposia in the Academy, see Athen. 4e, 419d, 574f; Plut. De Tuend. San. 9; Quaest. Conv. vi, Prooemium. Συμποτικοὶ νόμοι in the Academy and the Lyceum are referred to in Athen. 186b.

[65] 671e; cf. 656c, 798bc, 803c-804b, 832d; Rep. 537a.

[66] Lyc. 21; cf. Inst. Lac. 15; Schol. to Laws 633a. These three choruses seem to have been a part of the festival of the Gymnopaediae, to be discussed later. See Athen. 678c, Xen. Hell. vi, iv, 16 and Poll. iv, 107.

with their philosophically trained insight, and anything that they knew of as existing at Sparta.

The chorus of elders almost disappears from the *Laws* after this discussion of their role in the second book.[67] It may be doubted, therefore, whether it is to be taken as more than a symbol for the supervisory role of the elders, particularly as critics and censors of dance and song.[68] A definite organ of the state it cannot be, for the various references to it are by no means consistent. It is first described as a chorus of men between the ages of thirty and sixty (664d; cf. 665b); later the age of forty is prescribed as a condition for admission to its convivial gatherings under the patronage of Dionysus (666b); in 670b it is "men over fifty" whose function it is to sing for us; and finally in 812bc they are referred to as the "sixty-year-old singers to Dionysus." These varieties of expression are evidence not of uncertainty or confusion in Plato's mind, but rather of the exploratory character of the inquiry. As the discussion proceeds and we see more and more clearly the need for a higher kind of training than music ordinarily denotes, the requirements for membership in this chorus become correspondingly restricted, and age and maturity of judgment are more and more emphasized. Since the higher officials of Plato's state are drawn universally from persons above the age of fifty, and since the description of the chorus hints clearly at a differentiation in the group of elders between those who are and those who are not competent to direct the "enchantment" of the citizenry, we see that this is merely a preparation for the rigid control over music and the dance that is to be proposed in the seventh and eighth books, and an anticipation of the education of the elderly officers concerned with it.

THE TRAINING OF THE YOUNG

Aristotle remarks that the education of the young was a private matter in most states of his time, each man teaching his sons, or having them taught, whatever branch of knowledge he thought fit.[69] This does not mean that all education took place in the home—far

---

[67] There is only one later reference, 812bc, where they are called "sixty-year-old choristers of Dionysus."

[68] James R. Parmenter has suggested in an unpublished paper that the chorus of elders is a rough anticipation of the Nocturnal Council. This suggestion is confirmed by the inclusion of music, and its connections with law and ethics, in the studies of this Council (967e).

[69] *Pol.* 1337a 5, 24-25; cf. *Nic. Eth.* 1180a 24; and Plato, *Alc. I* 122b.

from it. Schools (διδασκαλεῖα) for the teaching of reading and writing were common in Greece in the classical period. But these were private enterprises, conducted by citizens or resident aliens, and the masters (διδάσκαλοι) charged the parents a fee for instructing their sons. Besides these grammar schools, every city of importance had its gymnasia and one or more palastrae to which both young and old resorted, the young to receive instruction from the gymnastic masters (παιδοτρίβαι), the older men to engage in exercise or conversation with their fellow citizens. These institutions were public in the sense that they were open to all citizens, and the gymnasia were public also in the sense that they had been erected either by the city or through the generosity of some wealthy citizen.[70] The gymnastic masters in these establishments were not public officials, so far as we know; the instruction they gave was, like that of the grammar master, in return for a fee. But the state necessarily exercised some supervision over them. In fourth-century Athens there were strict laws for both the schools and the gymnasia, regulating the hours of opening and closing, the number of pupils to be accommodated, and the age at which the young were permitted to attend.[71] These laws were attributed to Solon, an indication that they were at least as old as the legislative reorganization at the end of the fifth century, and they were possibly much older.

Nor does Aristotle's remark mean that there was no pattern of common education—i.e. education generally regarded as desirable, even though the initiative rested with the parent for providing it. Letters (γράμματα), music (μουσική), and gymnastics (γυμναστική) formed the staple content of the training of the young, certainly in Athens, and apparently also in other Greek cities.[72] We have already noticed how large a part music had played since Homeric times in the training of the Greeks, and how firmly rooted was their opinion of its profound effects on character. Gymnastics had an equally ancient lineage and an even more honorable position as a means of developing manly qualities and physical beauty. The am-

[70] Of the three gymnasia at Athens, for example, the Academy seems to have been founded, or at least remodeled, by the Pisistratidae; the founding of the Lyceum may also be their work, but the Attic chroniclers attribute it to Pericles; and as for the Cynosarges, we know only that it existed in the sixth century. W. Judeich, *Topographie von Athen*, 2nd edn., Munich, 1931, 413, 415, 423. There were some public palaestrae, but others were privately owned.

[71] Aesch. 1, 6, 9-10.

[72] *Theag.* 122e; *Rep.* 376e; *Cleit.* 407bc.

bition to excel sometimes reached an almost pathological extreme among the Greeks, and it found an approved outlet in the athletic games and contests of the local communities, and above all in the great Panhellenic contests at Olympia, Nemea, Delphi, and the Isthmus. To the victors in these games was accorded an immortality of glory comparable to that of the Homeric heroes. At first a preserve of the rich and the well born, athletics gradually became democratized; and by the end of the fifth century all Athenians frequented the gymnasia, and all of them, so far as their means permitted, put their sons at training under gymnastic masters.[73] The study of letters was the latest of the three parts of the curriculum to develop, coming in only with the general use of writing, probably in the early sixth century.[74] The institution of ostracism at Athens, introduced at the end of the sixth century, presupposes a knowledge of writing among Athenian citizens by that date; and grammar schools are well attested for various parts of Greece for the early fifth century.[75] With the prosperity that came to Athens after the Persian wars, we can certainly assume a great increase in the demand for the instruction these schools gave.[76] From the middle of the fifth century, at the latest, there must have been a highly literate public at Athens, and the other states of any size or wealth probably kept pace with her.[77] By Plato's time grammar schools had become a common feature of the typical Greek city.[78] The study of letters, formerly a part of

[73] Marrou 71f.; Ps. Xen. *Const. Ath.* II, 10; Plato *Prot.* 326b.

[74] The inscription from Chios (Tod I, No. 1), for which Miss Jeffery (*Annual of the British School at Athens* 51, 1956, 157ff.) suggests a date c.575-550, is part of a stele containing constitutional provisions. The democratic features of this constitution, as well as the fact of this inscription, certainly suggest a literate citizenry. If what Diodorus tells us about the legislation of Charondas is to be trusted (see Note 81), we see that in Magna Graecia also instruction in γράμματα had become a common feature by the sixth century.

[75] For Chios in 496, see Herod. VI, 27; for Astypalaea in 492, *Paus.* VI, ix, 6; for Troezen in 480, Plut. *Them.* 10.

[76] Cf. Arist. *Pol.* 1341a 30.

[77] The wealth of inscriptions from the fifth century—laws, records, dedications, epitaphs—indicates a people in whom the ability to read was taken for granted. The works of Anaxagoras were available in a cheap edition (*Apol.* 26d). Aristophanes (*Birds* 1288) refers to bookshops at Athens, and in the *Frogs* describes Dionysus as reading Euripides' *Andromeda* when on a military expedition (52) and the whole audience as following his play with copies of the text in their hands (1113-1114). Plato's remarks on the deficiencies of books (*Phaedrus* 274f.) suggest, as Turner says, that he is "fighting a rear-guard action." E. G. Turner, Inaugural Lecture at University College, London, 1952, "Athenian Books in the Fifth and Fourth Centuries, B.C."

[78] In Poll. IX, 41ff. the πόλεως μέρη include γραμματεῖα, διδασκαλεῖα and παιδαγώγια as well as stoas, theatres and law courts.

"music," and still often so designated even in the fourth century, had come to include the study and exposition of the poetic texts and possibly also the texts of certain prose writers.[79]

Thus there was a large degree of public or common education provided for the young in the Greek cities of the fourth century, provided as a matter of course and to a large extent out of public funds or the gifts of wealthy citizens. This was the education which the better citizenry (οἱ καλοὶ κἀγαθοί) thought indispensable, and which poorer citizens provided for their sons to the extent which their means permitted. Aristotle also says, as something which he thinks no one will dispute, that the training of the young is an important matter of policy for the legislator.[80] It is usually thought that he is expressing the ideals rather than the practices of his time; yet such concern for education was generally attributed, whether rightly or wrongly, to the great legislators of the past—to Solon, to Charondas, and above all to Lycurgus.[81] There is also a reference in Plato's *Crito* (50d) to Athenian "laws" concerning education, which admonish (παραγγέλλουσι) the father to educate his son in music and gymnastics. Since there is no other evidence of such laws, nor any recorded cases of prosecution for violating them, it may be assumed that Plato is referring to custom rather than legislation. In any case, the Greek states frequently expressed in striking fashion their concern for the training of the young. When the Athenians evacuated Athens on the eve of Salamis and their wives and children took refuge in Troezen, the Troezenians voted not only an appropriation for their support but also money to pay teachers for the children.[82] The Mytilenaeans punished their revolting allies on one occasion by refusing to allow their children to be taught γράμματα, apparently thinking this the severest penalty they could inflict.[83] Finally, the indictment and condemnation of Socrates is ample evidence of the seriousness with which the Athenians regarded the training of the young, despite the lack of explicit legislation.

[79] Cf. *Prot.* 338c and the exegesis of Simonides that follows. On prose writers see Note 142 below.

[80] *Pol.* 1337a 11.

[81] On Solon, see Aesch. 1, 6, 9-10; and Plut. *Solon* 22. Charondas' legislation is said to have contained a provision requiring parents to have their children taught γράμματα, the state defraying the tuition charges of the teachers (Diod. XII, 5; XIII, 1). Max Mühl (in *Klio* XXII, 1928, 441) thinks this law ascribed to Charondas probably comes from Thurii and is the work of Protagoras.

[82] Plut. *Them.* 10.

[83] Aelian *Var. Hist.* VII, 15.

It is only against this background of opinion and practice in Plato's day that we can understand precisely the import of his proposals. There was already a general agreement as to what kind of training the young should have; there was a wide recognition of its importance, both for the individual and for the state; and there were fairly ample facilities available and techniques for imparting it. Plato introduces two innovations. First he would make this training compulsory; no father would have the right not to send his sons and daughters to school (804d). He rests this proposal, not on the rights of the children, but on the interests of the community. The children belong to the state more than to their parents, for they are its future citizens, and the welfare of the state depends upon what they become. Plato's state has no other end, we should add, than the virtue and happiness of its citizens; but in order to attain this end it must have citizens capable of maintaining its institutions, and for this "craft of citizenship," as Plato calls it (846d), they need to be trained as for any lesser art or craft. In the second place, he proposes that this common education be controlled by the state. He intends not merely that its practitioners should be supervised and order maintained at the schools and gymnasia, as was done at Athens and elsewhere; but that its organization and content should be explicitly designed and employed to accomplish the particular end of the state. Aristotle furnishes almost a perfect echo of Plato's thought. "The citizens must always be educated to suit the particular constitution of the state. For what guards a constitution is the type of character appropriate to it, i.e., the type of character which originally created it. . . . Moreover, with respect to any capacity or form of craftsmanship some preliminary education and habituation to its particular operations is required; hence there clearly must be training in the practice of virtue. And since the end is one end for the whole state, evidently education must be one and the same for all and the supervision of it must be a public function."[84] Plato's city, then, will not merely charge the citizens to educate their sons; it will provide educational facilities at public cost and require parents to make use of them.[85] This will mean equal opportunities for rich and poor; but the value of this equalitarianism for Plato is that it puts all talents at the disposal of the state, without regard to the property class in

[84] *Pol.* 1337a 14-24. Cf. *Polit.* 308e for another clear statement of Plato's view.
[85] *Rep.* 543a: παιδεία κοινή is necessary for a state that is to be ἄκρως οἰκοῦσα.

which they may be found, and thus enables the state to make the best use of these varied talents.

Plato's legislator has a larger end in view than the Spartans ever contemplated, but there can be little doubt that the success of the Spartans in achieving their more limited purpose was an important influence in shaping Plato's thought.[86] The Spartan agoge was compulsory for all Spartans, but it appears not to have been restricted to them. There is evidence that occasionally persons not of pure Spartan blood were admitted to the discipline, and upon completing it some at least were granted the full privileges of Spartan citizenship.[87] Whether or not this would be a possibility in Plato's state we cannot say. The education is said to be designed for the sons of free men (ἐλεύθεροι), a term sometimes used by Plato as a synonym for citizens.[88] Children of mixed unions of citizen and slave are to be sent out of the land (930de); but what of other slave children? At Athens slaves were not admitted to the schools and gymnasia,[89] and the general tenor of Plato's law of slavery does not encourage us to

[86] And Aristotle's as well. Immediately after the passage quoted in the text Aristotle adds: "In this respect the Spartans are to be praised, for they take with the utmost seriousness the education of their young and make it a public function" (*Pol.* 1337a 31).

[87] Plut. *Inst. Lac.* 22; Arist. *Pol.* 1270a 34. Cf. Henri Jeanmaire, *Couroi et Courètes*, Lille, 1939, 489-490; Kenneth J. Freeman, *Schools of Hellas*, London, 1912, 15-17.

[88] See Chapter IV, Note 51. Although ἐλεύθερος is often used in its more strictly legal sense to distinguish metics as well as citizens from slaves (as in 882a, 930d, and probably also in 869d and 879a), yet in occasional passages it clearly denotes citizens, or those by birth eligible for citizenship. In 848a we find the disjunction ἐλεύθεροι . . . οἰκέται . . . ξένοι; and similarly in 816e ἐλεύθεροι are distinguished from δοῦλοι and ξένοι. Hence in all probability ἐπ' ἐλευθέροισι of 794a, which is contrasted with the preceding ἐπὶ τῶν δούλων, refers to the children of citizens; and the διατριβή of 807d prescribed for ἐλεύθεροι refers to the citizens' way of life. Evidently the term has a social and moral connotation for Plato. The Magnesians are not to engage in trade nor do any service to any who are not ἐλεύθεροι, for to do so would be ἀνελεύθερον (919c). Here the term evidently means "gentleman," as England translates it. Again the institutions of the *Laws* are to be more suitable for free men (ἐλευθέροις ἀνθρώποις) than those of most Greek states, because here the citizens' income will be derived from the soil, rather than from commerce and money lending (842cd); the citizen's ἐλεύθερον ἦθος will not be corrupted (741e). The use of ἐλεύθερος as equivalent to πολίτης is found also in other fourth-century writers, notably Aristotle (*Const. Ath.* XLII, 1; *Pol.* 1291b 27, 1290b 10, 1292b 39), Xenophon (*Const. of Lac.* VII, 2), Demosthenes (LVII, 45, 69) and Aeschines (III, 169); see also Diog. VI, 4; Newman, *The Politics of Aristotle*, I, 248n; Wyse, *Isaeus*, 281; and Hommel in RE s.v. μέτοικος, 1415. In the inscriptions, however, the term ἐλεύθερος, when it refers to persons, seems always to be used in contrast with δοῦλος or οἰκέτης, never in distinction from μέτοικος or ξένος.

[89] Aesch. I, 138.

think he would be more liberal than Athens in this regard.⁹⁰ Sons
and daughters of resident aliens present a more difficult problem.
A particularly deserving foreigner may receive the privilege of life-
long residence (850cd), and his sons and daughters likewise; hence
it is possible that these children would be admitted to the schools
and gymnasia by special grant of the council and assembly. But this
is a matter on which Plato has not legislated, and it would be useless
to look for precision where it is not to be found.

On the other hand, Plato clearly intends to avoid an error in the
Spartan system all too evident to a fourth-century observer. A Spartan
who became too poor to pay his contribution to the common meals
was automatically excluded from the rights of citizenship. This
would mean also the exclusion of his sons from the agoge, since the
training of the youths involved their association with their fathers
in the eating clubs (φιδίτια).⁹¹ The number of Spartans thus excluded must have been small in the early days; but in the fourth
century, when alienation of the lot by bequest was permitted and the
ownership of land tended to be concentrated in fewer and fewer
hands, Sparta suffered from an increasing want of men.⁹² It is interesting to note that Xenophon's picture of Persian education in his
Education of Cyrus reflects this feature of Spartan life. The "common
schools" he describes are open to all Persians, but those fathers who
cannot afford to bring up their sons without working (ἀργοῦντας)
are unable to take advantage of them.⁹³ Plato's strict provisions
against alienation of the lot and its equipment are intended to prevent
this consequence, and would incidentally assure access to the schools
and gymnasia for all sons of citizens equally.

The chief officer in charge of education in Plato's state is variously
described as the "superintendent of education," as the "officer in
charge of children," as the "superintendent of children," as the
"archon of music," and finally as "the educator."⁹⁴ There is no indication which of these is to be his official title, but we shall henceforth call him by the last, which has the virtue of brevity. This offi-

⁹⁰ See the author's *Plato's Law of Slavery*, 124ff.
⁹¹ Freeman, *op.cit.* 14.
⁹² Arist. *Pol.* 1271a 26-37. See Chapter IV, The Allotment of the Land.
⁹³ I, ii, 15.
⁹⁴ ὁ τῆς παιδείας ἐπιμελητής (765d, 936a, 951e, 953d); ὁ ἐπὶ τὴν τῶν παίδων ἀρχήν
(809a); ὁ τῶν παίδων ἐπιμελητής (813c); ὁ περὶ τὴν Μοῦσαν ἄρχων (813a); ὁ παι-
δευτής (829d, 812e, 835a); and sometimes he is referred to simply as the νομοφύλαξ
(e.g. 809a, 811d, 816c), where the context makes the reference unambiguous.

cer, "the most important of all the high officers in the state," is elected from the guardians by all the officials, excepting the council and the prytanies. They assemble in the temple of Apollo to make their choice, and each votes secretly for that guardian whom he considers best qualified by character and intelligence to direct educational matters (765de). To be eligible a guardian must be the father of children born in wedlock, preferably of both sons and daughters.[95] Whoever receives the most votes is subjected to a scrutiny conducted by the same body that has elected, except that the guardians abstain.[96] The guardian elected to this office holds it for a term of five years, and then a successor is elected in the same fashion. Re-election is apparently not intended in Plato's state.

There was no office comparable to this in any Greek state of historical times, so far as we know, unless it is the παιδονόμος at Sparta, mentioned by Xenophon and Plutarch.[97] There seem to have been officials called paidonomoi in various Greek states, particularly in those of an aristocratic or oligarchic cast. Aristotle mentions such officers in four passages, usually in conjunction with "supervisors of women" (γυναικονόμοι), but his references indicate that they were concerned primarily with behavior in public places, rather than with matters of educational policy.[98] Only in one passage is there a hint of the latter, when he says that the tales told by nurses to children should be a matter of concern to "the officers called παιδονόμοι." How important the paidonomos was at Sparta and in Crete it is difficult to determine. Both Xenophon and Plutarch say that at Sparta he was elected from the highest class of citizens,[99] but his functions, as they describe them, seem to be limited to the organization of the "herds" (ἀγέλαι) and the supervision of the boys' behavior. Strabo

---

[95] The requirement that he should be not less than fifty years of age (765d) is automatically taken care of by the requirement that he must be one of the guardians (cf. 755a).

[96] The reason for this exclusion of the guardians is not given. One would suppose that a candidate's colleagues on this body would be in an exceptionally good position for judging his qualifications; but it may be, as England suggests, that Plato feared there would be jealousy among them, or at least suspicion among those outside the electors that jealousy had played a part, if the result of the scrutiny was negative.

[97] Xen. *Const. Lac.* II, 2; Plut. *Lyc.* 17.

[98] *Pol.* 1299a, 22, 1300a 4, 1322b 39, 1336a 32. Παιδονόμος does not occur in the inscriptions, I believe, until the third century. This surely indicates that the office was not an important one in Aristotle's time.

[99] Xen. *Const. Lac.* II, 2 (ἐξ ὧνπερ αἱ μέγισται ἀρχαί); Plut. *Lyc.* 17 (from the καλοὶ κἀγαθοί).

says that in Crete a paidonomos presided over each mess (ἀνδρεῖον), which implies a number of such officers, certainly not a single director of education and morals.[100] But the educator in Plato's state is unquestionably an important officer. He supervises the whole of education (765d, 936a), both music and gymnastics, with their contests and festivals for young and old (813c, 835a); he appoints and supervises numerous minor officials (813c); he issues instructions to teachers (811d), selects appropriate material for the lessons in literature (811e), and he censors poetic productions intended for public hearing (936ab). Besides this, he is a member of the Nocturnal Council, not only for his term of office as educator, but for the rest of his life (951e); and he acts as host to important visitors from abroad (953d). The paidonomos at Sparta may have been the germ of Plato's conception, but if so this germ has so developed as to make the Spartan title and its associations altogether inadequate.

The other educational officials are divided into two groups: superintendents (ἐπιμεληταί) of gymnasia and schools; and supervisors of contests (ἀθλοθέται) in gymnastics and music respectively (764cd).[101] The former are especially concerned with the training of the young. They look after the maintenance and embellishment of the buildings, and supervise the instruction and attendance of the boys and girls. These officials are presumably appointed by the educator from among the citizenry, male and female, as needed (813c). Their number is not specified, but they will be fairly numerous, as the following details will show. In addition to these officials, and under their supervision, will be the teachers of the various subjects: e.g. teachers of letters and of the lyre (γραμματισταί and κιθαρισταί, 812b), dancing masters and mistresses (ὀρχησταί and ὀρχηστρίδες, 813b), chorus masters (χοροδιδάσκαλοι, 812e), and teachers for the various kinds of physical exercises (813e). These however will not be citizens, but resident foreigners, paid a salary by the state (804d, 813e). In spite of his high regard for education, Plato shares the current Athenian opinion that the task of a schoolmaster is no job for a gentleman.[102] There are to be public schools (διδασκαλεῖα κοινά),

[100] Strabo x, iv, 20.

[101] The first group are concerned with "education proper" (παιδεία αὐτή), as distinguished from "education in its entirety" (παιδεία πᾶσα, 765d; παιδεία ὅλη, 936a), the latter including the games and festivals as well as the training of the young. England's decision to follow ʟ and read αὐτῆς in 764c 7 instead of αὐτῶν gives the meaning obviously intended here.

[102] Demosthenes makes capital of the fact that his political opponent, Aeschines,

gymnasia, and playing fields (εὐρυχώρια) at three places in the city, and gymnasia and playing fields in three different sections of the country (804c; cf. 764c, 779d).[103] There will be both men and women officials in charge, the men looking after the instruction, the women supervising the games of the younger children and their feeding and discipline (795d). This implies that the children spend their entire day at these establishments, in supervised games and lessons. But only the teachers reside there (804d); the children live at home with their parents, going to their teachers at dawn under the guidance of their tutors (παιδαγωγοί, 808cd).[104]

But the training of the child must begin before the years of schooling. In fact the preschool years are of particular importance, for growth is then most rapid (788d) and the "first shoot" is what determines for any creature whether it will attain a growth suitable to its nature (765e). The Athenian recommends much walking about for expectant mothers, in order to give the unborn child the passive exercise it needs if its young body is to assimilate properly the abundant nourishment it is taking in.[105] The same treatment is prescribed for the first three years after birth. The mother or nurse is to carry the child about constantly, partly to avoid distorting its

was the son of a schoolmaster, and in his youth helped his father sponge the benches and sweep out the παιδαγώγιον. Aeschines' father, however, seems to have been a citizen, albeit an impoverished one (Dem. xviii, 257). Contempt for γραμματο-διδάσκαλοι enables us to understand two incidents related of Alcibiades' early life (Plut. *Alc.* 7). Protagoras was reputed to have begun his career as a village school-teacher (Epicurus apud Athen. 354c). If this was not related to his discredit, it was at least intended to show from what a low estate he had risen. The enemies of Epicurus said of him in turn that his father had been a schoolmaster (Diog. x, 4).

[103] This looks like a reflection of Athens, with its three gymnasia—the Academy, the Lyceum, and the Cynosarges, situated in the immediate suburbs of the city, the Academy to the northwest, the other two to the northeast.

[104] The pictorial details that emerge from Plato's text are all suggestive of the Athens of classical times—such as the παιδαγωγοί, undoubtedly slaves in Plato's state, as was usually the case at Athens; the teachers resident in the schools, whence the phrases, εἰς διδασκάλου and ἐν διδασκάλῳ (Aristoph. *Clouds* 964, 973; *Prot.* 325d, 326bc; *Theaet.* 206a and Theoph. *Char.* xxii, 6). School began early in Greece, as did all other daily activities; cf. the opening passages in the *Crito* and the *Protagoras.* In Thucydides' account of the sack of Mycalessus (vii, 29) the Thracians fell upon the city at dawn and butchered all the inhabitants, including the children in a school who had just begun their day's lessons. A law cited in Aesch. i, 9-10 forbids schoolmasters to open their schools before sunrise.

[105] Plato cites as evidence of the value of this passive exercise the benefits obtained from horseback riding and riding in a boat, and above all the practice of Athenian "sportsmen" who carry their fighting cocks about with them on long walks (789b-d).

legs by allowing it to walk too early, but mainly for the benefit of the passive exercise. This constant movement is good for the child's soul as well as his body; for bodily motion helps to overcome the internal motions of fright and thus prevents the first growth of timidity and cowardice (791bc). A mother rocking her child in her arms and crooning to it is its first enchanter; she is literally casting a spell upon it by this action, which is a "combination of dance and song" (790e), and giving it the first lesson in the mastery of fear.[106] Another part of virtue that can be cultivated in infancy is cheerfulness. The child's wants, which he can only indicate by crying, must be satisfied, though without overindulgence. The three years of infancy are no small part of a man's life, Plato says, and if they are spent in fretfulness an indelible mark is left on the character (792a-c).[107] These proposals, however, are not strictly part of a legislator's task; they belong to the field of "unwritten laws" ($\check{\alpha}\gamma\rho\alpha\phi\alpha$ $\nu\acute{o}\mu\iota\mu\alpha$) or "ancestral customs" ($\pi\acute{\alpha}\tau\rho\iota o\iota$ $\nu\acute{o}\mu o\iota$, 793a). The legislator can only hope that the adult citizens, when properly trained, will adopt these principles and enforce them, each in his own household (790b).

At the age of three, however, the child begins to come under public control. The children of each village come together at the various village sanctuaries ($\tau\grave{\alpha}$ $\kappa\alpha\tau\grave{\alpha}$ $\kappa\acute{\omega}\mu\alpha\varsigma$ $\iota\epsilon\rho\acute{\alpha}$), boys and girls alike, where they play games of their own devising (793d-794c). Their nurses accompany them and supervise their behavior.[108] Over each group, children and nurses, is set a state supervisor—one of twelve women officials appointed by the supervisors of marriage[109] to oversee the play at these sacred places and to administer punishment for breaches of decorum. Punishment is necessary to prevent children from becoming spoiled, but it must not be of a degrading sort—at least for the freeborn. The distinction carefully made here between the punishment of slaves and the punishment of citizens implies that Plato thought of the play groups as including all the children in the village, slave as well as free.

---

[106] Again Plato finds empirical support for his advice in the curative effects of Corybantic rites on certain kinds of emotional disturbances (790d, 791a). For an exposition of this misunderstood passage, see I. M. Linforth, "Corybantic Rites in Plato," *Univ. of Cal. Publ. in Class. Philol.* XIII, 1944-1950, 121-162, esp. 129-134.

[107] Aristotle criticizes Plato's advice here, on the ground that crying is exercise and contributes to the child's growth (*Pol.* 1336a 35).

[108] The frequent mention of the child's nurse ($\tau\rho o\phi\acute{o}\varsigma$) is another detail drawn from Greek life, as every reader of the dramas can appreciate.

[109] For an account of the duties of these officials, see 784a-e.

The course of study begins at the age of six, when children start going to the schools and gymnasia for their lessons (μαθήματα). At this time the boys and girls are separated, although the curriculum is in the main the same for both sexes. Plato has by no means abandoned the revolutionary proposal of the *Republic* for the equal education of women and men. But it is interesting to observe the cautious way in which this revolutionary proposal is put forward in the *Laws*. It first appears with the suggestion that the girls, "if they do not object," shall have lessons in riding, archery, javelin throwing, slinging, and fighting in armor like the boys (794c). The hypothetical clause literally refers to the girls themselves, but obviously it is the consent of their parents and of public opinion generally that has to be obtained.[110] The text immediately following contains a surprising anacoluthon. "The customs now prevalent on these matters are the result of almost universal ignorance"; but instead of enlightening his companions on the necessity of training women as well as men, the Athenian argues instead for the equal training of the left and right hands. The analogy is so apt and obvious—i.e. a state that neglects the training of its women is like a man who trains only his right arm —that Plato evidently feels the discussion of the less controversial matter is the best way of preparing the reader for the acceptance of the more difficult proposal.[111] But the Athenian soon returns to the real issue and declares emphatically that women must have the same training as men; riding and gymnastics are as proper for the one sex as for the other.[112] He not only believes the old legends about the Amazons but he knows that even now there are nations around the Pontus where women learn the handling of bows and horses and

[110] The text seems to mean that public consent would at least be granted for the girls' getting some conception of the arts of war (μέχρι γε μαθήσεως, 794d 1), as distinct from the practice of them. Cf. Apelt's translation: "wenigstens so weit, dass sie einen Begriff von der Sache bekommen." Diès, Introd. Budé edn. lv: "elles en apprendront au moins la théorie."

[111] The real purpose of Plato's remarks on ambidexterity has usually been overlooked, and most commentators, beginning with Aristotle (*Pol.* 1274b 13), have taken his suggestion far too seriously. Undoubtedly it does express his conviction of the importance of using both hands, but his real interest is in the importance of using both sexes. Plato makes no further mention of this proposal for ambidexterity, not even in his account of the athletic contests. There is only one representation of a left-handed throw on the Greek vases; cf. E. N. Gardiner, *Greek Athletic Sports and Festivals*, London, 1910, 352.

[112] 804d: τὰ αὐτὰ δὴ . . . ἀσκεῖν δεῖν. Immediately afterward Plato's proposal is generalized: women must share with men, to the greatest extent possible, not only education but all else (805c; cf. 805a).

practise these skills equally with men.[113] Since, then, this equal education is possible, it is reasonable to propose its adoption; for thus we get a whole, not merely a half-state (805a, 806c). Later the Athenian brings up the subject a third time and points out the absurdity of so neglecting the training of women that they would be unable to put up a fight if it were necessary (814ab). Suppose the city were suddenly attacked while the men warriors were absent in full force elsewhere; it would be a disgrace if the women could not fight for their young, as females of other species do, but simply fled to the temples and shrines. Something like this actually happened at Sparta when, after the defeat at Leuctra, an enemy army invaded their territory for the first time in history and threatened the city.[114] The panic of the Spartan women in that crisis must have shocked Plato, as we know it did Aristotle, and convinced him that the training of women at Sparta, despite the fame of their female athletes, left much to be desired.

For the Spartan system, Plato thinks, had gone only half way toward the goal of making effective use of its women citizens. It was indeed better than the procedure of the Thracians and other nations that put their women to work in the fields like slaves, and better also than that of the Athenians, who secluded the women in the home, making them custodians of the family possessions and overseers of the household arts of spinning and weaving (805de). The Lycurgan legislation took special pains with the physical training of women, requiring them to exercise themselves in running, wrestling, throwing the discus and the javelin, and in athletic contests with one another, just like the men.[115] The purpose of this regimen, according to both the ancient reporters, was to promote their physical vigor so that they would produce more healthy offspring for the state. But the Spartans neglected, Plato thought, another equally important end of athletic training, i.e. the military effectiveness of the state.

[113] It is difficult to believe that Plato's information was based on personal observation, though Bury's translation suggests it. Herodotus (IV, 116-117) is the source that comes most readily to mind.

[114] Xen. *Hell.* VI, v, 28; Arist. *Pol.* 1269b 35ff. An example of the contrary is the action of the Argive poetess Telesilla who, when the men had been badly defeated by Cleomenes and the Spartans, summoned the women to man the walls of the city, to such effect that the Spartans withdrew; so Paus. II, xx, 8-9. But this story is probably an invention of a later date to explain the oracle cited by Herodotus (VI, 77) in his account of this battle; see How and Wells, *Commentary on Herodotus*, Oxford, 1912, II, 94f.

[115] Plut. *Lyc.* 14; Xen. *Const. Lac.* I, 4.

This, we shall see, is the guiding principle in his program of gymnastics, and if women are to share in this plan of physical training, they also must be trained to be soldiers if the need should arise. "Let him who likes praise the Spartan legislators," says the Athenian firmly; "but this is my opinion" (806c).

It is indeed strange that Plato, in his vision of the larger contribution that women might make to the life of the community, emphasized an area in which they seem least fitted, by temperament and physical strength, to make their natural contribution. I say "emphasized," for Plato was not unaware of the other areas. Women are to share with men, to the greatest extent possible, in all the activities and duties of the state.[116] Honors and dignities are open to them equally with men (802a). Nor was he unaware of the specific differences between the psychical nature of women and that of men. The masculine nature tends towards majesty (τὸ μεγαλοπρεπές) and valor (τὸ πρὸς τὴν ἀνδρείαν); the feminine towards orderliness (τὸ κόσμιον) and temperance (τὸ σῶφρον, 802e). These differences are of considerable moral import; for the feminine qualities, it should be noted, are precisely those which in an earlier passage (628ff.) he has said a state most needs, and precisely those qualities that were neglected in the ideal which Tyrtaeus represented in the Spartan tradition.

The lessons are divided, in the traditional Greek fashion, into music and gymnastics.[117] The musical part includes not merely the study of the lyre, but also letters, which had become equally traditional by Plato's time, and finally mathematics, a study which apparently had just made its entry into the common curriculum. Regarding the order in which these studies are to be taken up and the amount of attention given to each, it is impossible to get a precise

[116] See Note 112.

[117] Cf. *Rep.* 376e: "And now what will our education be? It is difficult to think of anything better than that which long experience has discovered—gymnastics for the body and music for the soul." Similarly, in *Laws* 795d Plato says that gymnastics is concerned with the body and music with the soul. But this is only superficially true: the *Republic* explicitly revises the statement later (see 410c) and the *Laws* does so implicitly. In the same passage (795d) he proceeds to divide gymnastics into dancing and wrestling. But obviously dancing comes in part under the head of music and is frequently treated so. And wrestling does not cover the whole of gymnastics apart from dancing; we see later that gymnastics includes all the exercises that contribute to military efficiency, and gymnasia are said to exist for the bodily exercises that pertain to war (813d). Hence the distinction in 804d between instruction in music and instruction in war.

picture from Plato's account, despite the apparent precision at certain
points. He designates the tenth to the twelfth years for the study of
letters, and the following three years for the study of the lyre (809e-
810a). But it would certainly be a mistake to interpret this as meaning that gymnastics is completely given up during these six years,
and it seems equally unlikely that the years prior to the tenth are to
be exclusively devoted to gymnastics. Choral music and dancing,
like gymnastics, would certainly be a continuing feature of the curriculum. Again, the study of mathematics, it is implied in one passage, will begin early (819ab), and so also, we may assume, would
the study of reading and writing, the three years from ten to twelve
being especially devoted to literature. The most plausible supposition
is that Plato did not intend to have these various studies segregated
each into a particular period of youth, but that there would be varying emphasis upon the different subjects at different times.[118]

In Plato's treatment of gymnastics there is a curious mixture of
emphasis upon physical exercise and disparagement of it. Most kinds
of strenuous bodily exercise, Plato says in one passage, are not worthy
of a gentleman (796d). This is more than the intellectual's contempt
for mere athletic prowess; it is distaste for the professionalism that
had overtaken classical Greek sports in the fourth century. Pindar's
idealization of the Olympic victor had been its own nemesis. The
Olympic victor of Plato's day was no longer the noble amateur—
like Odysseus, a worthy competitor in all the sports of the younger
men—but a specialist, and sometimes a venal one, who with the aid

[118] See the excellent discussion of this matter in Marrou 117-119, 488-490. The
order of Plato's exposition is most informal. In Book VII gymnastics receives first
attention (794c-796d); but it must be remembered that this is the part of education that has been omitted in the discourses in Book II, which are almost exclusively devoted to music, and this fact is explicitly recalled in 796d. Then follow
additional prescriptions regarding music (797a-804b), after which the Athenian
reverts to gymnastics, but immediately launches into a defense of his proposal for
the equal education of women (804e-806d). The education of the young is resumed
in 808d, and prescriptions regarding letters and lyre playing occupy us until 813a.
Gymnastics receives its turn again at this point, and the Athenian lays down further
prescriptions regarding athletics and dancing, with special reference to public games
and spectacles. Finally, beginning with 817e and extending to 822d, there is a
lengthy discussion of the branches of mathematics that the young must study. The
informality of this exposition confirms the supposition that Plato did not intend
these various studies to be segregated into hard and fast divisions of the youth's
life. There is a similar informality in the *Republic*, which treats letters and music
first, then gymnastics. In the *Republic* the only period of exclusive concentration
appears to be the age of compulsory gymnastics—the two or three years corresponding to the Athenian ephebia—when the strenuous physical exercises required of
young men will make study difficult (537b).

of a professional trainer had prepared himself for victory at all costs in the contest of his own choosing, to the uneven development of his body and the neglect of his mind and character.[119] This is the "sleepy athlete" of the *Republic*, overfed and brutal, even his body, because of the specialized training it has undergone, being unfit to endure the changes of climate and regimen which the activities of ordinary life involve (404a). Such criticisms of the athlete were common by the fourth century. Aristotle condemned the athlete's training as unsuited to the duties of ordinary life and detrimental to health and the procreation of children.[120] Euripides had called the "tribe of athletes" one of the worst of all the countless evils afflicting Greece; the crowns awarded them by their cities, he continues, might better go to the statesman or orator who has conferred real benefits upon his city and the Greeks[121]—an echo of the sentiments Xenophanes had expressed almost a century earlier. The sophistic movement of the fifth century, with its emphasis on the arts of speaking and disputation, had tended to lower the prestige of athletics, as of other features of the old-fashioned education. This is one of Aristophanes' main complaints against the new spirit;[122] and the Old Oligarch roundly blames the "demos" for the disrespect into which the practice of athletics had fallen.[123]

But Plato's disparagement of the professional athlete is only the negative aspect of a deeper purpose, viz. to restore the practice of athletics to what he regards as its original function, the preparation of the citizen for service in war.[124] Tyrtaeus is Plato's authentic predecessor here, the Tyrtaeus who had challenged the glory of the athlete on behalf of the ideal of the citizen soldier;[125] or the Socrates who is described by Xenophon as reproaching Epigenes for not

---

[119] On the overdevelopment of sports and the evils of professionalism, see Marrou 97-98; Bruno Schröder, *Der Sport im Altertum*, Berlin, 1927, 48ff.; E. N. Gardiner, *Athletics in the Ancient World*, Oxford, 1930, 99ff.; and A. H. Gilbert, "Olympic Decadence," in *Class. Jour.* xxi, 1925-1926, 587-598. The first known bribery of a contestant occurred in the early fourth century; Paus. v, xxi, 16. Plato is well aware of such practices (see 906e).

[120] *Pol.* 1335b 5-11; 1338b 9ff.   [121] Athen. 413c-f.

[122] Aristophanes regards Socrates and Euripides as the chief offenders. Socrates' pupils, for example, are expected to "give up gymnastics and other foolishness" (*Clouds* 417); and as for Euripides, he "taught the Athenians to babble and chatter, thus emptying the palaestrae and wearing away their rumps" (*Frogs* 1069-1070).

[123] Ps. Xen. *Const. Ath.* I, 13; but the writer's charges are not consistently maintained, for later he alleges that the "poor" insist on having their palaestrae (II, 10).

[124] *Rep.* 404ab.

[125] Fr. 12, Edmonds, Loeb Classical Library.

keeping himself in physical condition. "But I am not a professional athlete," replies Epigenes. "Yes, you are," says Socrates, "as much so as those who are going to contend at Olympia. Don't you think it an important contest (ἀγών) to fight for your life on the battlefield?"[126] The obligation to fight for one's city when called upon was a generally accepted part of citizenship for the Greeks. But the preparation of its citizens for effective service when need arose seems to have been taken rather lightly at Athens. We hear very little of explicit military education there; in fact Pericles, in his famous oration, seems to count it as one of his city's virtues that its citizens acquit themselves with courage in battle without undergoing the strenuous training that the Spartans require.[127] But the truth is that the Athenian forces seldom dared face the Spartans on land; it was their command of the sea that enabled them to contend against an antagonist so manifestly superior in land fighting. Plato's state is not to be a sea power; its safety will depend upon the skill and stamina of its land forces; and Plato sees that something more than amateur proficiency was required. But instead of relying on professional soldiers, as was coming to be the custom in the fourth century, he looks back to the good old days of the Persian wars when the Athenian hoplites at Marathon, so Herodotus tells us, ran an entire mile in heavy armor before engaging the Persians.[128] Plato will have the whole of his citizen body trained to something like professional proficiency in combat. A state must "exercise for war" (τὸν πόλεμον γυμναστέον), not when war has broken out, but while there is peace (829ab). Just as a professional boxer or pancratiast does not go into the contest without having previously trained himself in the skills he will need for victory, so our citizens, young and old, will practise themselves in times of peace in all those physical exercises connected with actual combat (830ab).

This states the principle, and the principle determines the program of training. It will aim at a kind of physical fitness and a set of skills quite different from those of the professional athlete.[129] The children in the gymnasia will learn the use of the bow and the sling, will prac-

---

[126] Xen. *Mem.* III, xii, 1. [127] Thuc. II. 39, 1.
[128] Herod. VI, 112.
[129] Cf. Plut. *Phil.* 3. The young Philopoemen consults his friends about his education and they tell him—what is a fact, says Plutarch—that the life of the professional athlete and that of the soldier are directly opposed to one another. A variant of this opinion is found in the passage from Euripides referred to in Note 121. Cf. Plut. *Quaest. Rom.* 40.

tise riding and javelin throwing, cavalry drill, light-armed skirmishing, and fighting in heavy armor; they will learn to perform tactical evolutions, to march in various formations, and to lay out camps (813de, 794c). In the palestra only "stand-up" wrestling (ὀρθὴ πάλη) is to be cultivated, for "of all forms of exercise this is most akin to military fighting"; but wrestling on the ground, the use of leg holds, boxing with leather straps or thongs—all these are useless for military encounters and are not worth honoring (796a, 814d).[130] There will be training in running also, with foot races between contestants of various ages (833a-d). Finally, it is taken for granted that Plato's Cretan and Lacedaemonian colonists will "follow the hounds."[131] Fishing, fowling, and hunting with nets or snares are discouraged, since these sports require no great effort or spirit; but the hunting of wild beasts with dogs and horses is approved, as developing stamina, resourcefulness, and courage (823b-824c).

This training in gymnastics begins at the age of six and apparently continues in one form or another throughout the whole period of youth and on into later life. Learning the management of horses and the use of arms comes early; for it is prescribed that in all religious processions the boys (and probably the girls also) from the age of six onward are to take part with arms and horses (796c). The program of athletic contests at the festivals, with its series of foot races carefully graded as to difficulty in accordance with the age of the competitors, shows that training in running also begins in the early years and continues into adult life. Girls cease to compete in such contests when they reach the marriage age of sixteen or eighteen (833d; cf. 785b). But women who have passed the age of childbearing are eligible for military service (785b), and this implies that during the intervening years they keep themselves in condition by some appropriate form of physical and military exercise. Finally, the whole state—men, women, and children—is required to take part in the monthly field days and their military exercises (829b).

[130] For a vivid and amusing picture of young men engaged in these exercises of which Plato disapproves, see Lucian *Anacharsis* 1-5. We must rely upon the scholium for the interpretation of the "arts" introduced by the mythical personages mentioned in 796a. Antaeus could wrestle only on the ground; Cercyon introduced the leg hold, and Amycus the ἱμάντες or leather thongs used in boxing. Epeius also was a boxer (*Iliad* xxiii, 665), but what his particular art was we do not know.

[131] Hunting (θῆρα) is mentioned by Megillus in 633b as one of the institutions at Sparta that develop courage. In *Rep.* 549a the timocratic man (of whom the Spartan is here taken as an example) is φιλόθηρος. Cf. also Xen. *Const. Lac.* iv, 7.

Dancing may appropriately be considered next, since in one passage it is described as a branch of gymnastics (795e; cf. 814e), though its usual associations in Plato's text are with music. Plato distinguishes two types of dancing in which instruction is to be given to the young.[132] The first is that dancing "which imitates the diction of the Muse and aims at impressiveness and dignity." This seems to indicate the formal choral dancing performed on public occasions, and it will be considered more fully in the following section. Since the young are to take part in these festival dances along with the older citizens, they must obviously receive instruction in them as part of their school lessons (796c). The second type of dancing is described as aiming more generally at physical fitness (εὐεξία), lightness (ἐλαφρότης), and beauty (κάλλος); it consists in exercising the limbs of the body in their appropriate flexures and extensions, so as to give to each its own particular grace of movement and to "the whole of dancing" the rhythmic grace that properly belongs to it. I interpret this as a kind of preparatory training for the more elaborate and stately festival dances. Preparatory exercises of this sort must have been an indispensable part of ancient choral discipline, though we have surprisingly few references to them. An Athenian boy would learn from his παιδοτρίβης in the palaestra some of the movements (φοραί) and figures (σχήματα) of dancing;[133] and there were also dancing masters in Athens to whom he could be sent for further instruction.[134] These elements of dancing are apparently what is sometimes referred to in our authorities as the art of "gesturing" (χειρονομία).[135] A special form of χειρονομία

---

[132] The text of 795e is exceedingly rough and in spots ungrammatical. For the proper interpretation of the thought we must take it in connection with another quite different classification of dancing in 814e. The latter is a classification of the festival dances and will be discussed later; the former is, as the context shows, a distinction of two sorts of dancing lessons, analogous—to use a modern parallel—to the distinction in music between the learning of "concert pieces" and the practising of exercises.

[133] Plut. *Quaest. Conv.* IX, 15, 1.

[134] Athen. 21e-22a. This passage shows that Aeschylus, and doubtless other dramatists, often invented their own σχήματα and taught them to their choruses. The choregic inscriptions always refer to the author of the successful work as the διδάσκαλος. But the members of such choruses would usually be mature citizens, not schoolboys. In the dithyrambic contests, however, there were choruses of boys as well as men, so that some Athenian youths would get dancing lessons in training for these contests. See Louis Séchan, *La Danse grecque antique*, Paris, 1930, 240.

[135] Xen. *Symp.* II, 19: Charmides had learned χειρονομία but had never learned to dance. Athen. 629b: the art of χειρονομία was carried over from the choruses to the palaestrae. On this topic see Freeman, *op.cit.* (in Note 87) 129f.

seems to have been the practising of the war dance, or πυρρίχη,[136] a lively dance imitating all the movements and postures of combat. Spartan and Cretan boys, we are told, practised this dance from a very early age; and it seems also to have been taught by the παιδο-τρίβαι in the Athenian palaestrae.[137] The context shows that Plato had this exercise also in mind (796bc); it would serve the double purpose of preparation for war and for the festivals, for the πυρρίχη was one of the chief ornaments of the festivals in Plato's state, as it was at Athens.[138] When we recall the importance Plato attaches to correct σχήματα as imitations of the good in action and posture, we can see that the purpose of this drill is not merely physical training, important as that is, but training also in aesthetic expression and moral taste.

With the account of letters a new motive comes into the Athenian's exposition. "How is the law itself to give proper education to this guardian of ours?" (809a). The reference is to the educator, who has hitherto been taken for granted as supervising the studies of the young citizens. But once the state has got under way, he and all his associates in the government will be persons who have been trained in this very curriculum. From this time on it is clear that the Athenian is thinking not merely of the average citizen but also of the training of the select few who will rise to positions of leadership in the state. The distinction between these two groups is only once clearly and explicitly made (818a), but if we realize it is present in Plato's mind we shall understand better some of the details that follow.

The study of letters begins at the age of ten and continues for three years (809e). The word γράμματα in Greek covers a wide range of meaning, from the elements of reading and writing to the study of literature; and both the primary and the secondary levels of instruction seem to be referred to in the brief account with which this passage opens (810b).[139] It is unlikely, however, that Plato intends that there shall be no practice in reading and writing until this stage, though in his colony, as in modern times, some ten-year-

[136] Athen. 631c: "Another name for the πυρρίχη is χειρονομία."
[137] Plut. *loc.cit.*; for the Spartans and Cretans, see Athen. 631a and Strabo x, iv, 16.
[138] There is more about the πυρρίχη below, under Festivals.
[139] Plato gives a graphic picture of instruction in the Athens of his youth in *Prot.* 325c-326e, and other glimpses of pedagogical techniques in *Polit.* 277e-278ab, *Rep.* 402ab and *Theaet.* 203a-e.

old boys and girls might still have difficulty with their letters. The
Athenian says that of such students "whose nature does not push
them on" superior speed or accuracy shall not be required; a working proficiency is enough. The chief concern of the Athenian at this
stage is the content of their text books—which seems to presuppose
that all or most of them have progressed beyond the elements.[140]
What works of literature shall we put into their hands for exercise
in reading and reciting?[141] The range of choice for the fourth-century
Greek was a wide one, embracing almost the whole of the rich poetic
tradition from Homer to Aristophanes, as well as a considerable
store of prose writings which had become classics by this time, such
as Aesop, and perhaps even Herodotus and Thucydides.[142] Plato
must also have thought of the mimes of Sophron, which he so much
admired; of the numerous "Socratic discourses," of which his own
dialogues are the outstanding examples; and perhaps also of the writings of the Ionian physicists, which he mentions in the tenth book
and which we can infer had a considerable circulation even as early
as Socrates' time.[143] The passion for rhetoric which came in with the
sophistic movement produced a new type of composition, the "epi-
deictic discourse," composed by a teacher for study and imitation by
his pupils. Socrates' enthusiasm for such λόγοι as portrayed in the
Phaedrus is little if any less than that of Phaedrus himself. The study
of rhetoric belonged rather to higher than to secondary education,
but it is possible that some of the most celebrated of these pieces,
such as Prodicus' *Choice of Heracles*,[144] would be thought suitable
for use by a γραμματιστής with his pupils.

The practice of Plato's countrymen was on the whole conservative
but undiscriminating, based on the conviction that young men should
drink widely and deeply of their rich poetic literature. "Countless
persons tell us that the young, if they are to be rightly educated,
must be thoroughly steeped in these poems through having heard

[140] This is also the interpretation of Marrou, 489-490. Plato's text here implies a
distinction between calligraphy and a form of writing in which speed was the
principal aim. See Turner, *op.cit.* (Note 77) 7-8.

[141] Μαθήματα ἄλυρα, literally "lessons unaccompanied by the lyre." Μαθήματα
should be understood also to include προμανθάνειν, recitation from memory, as
the sequel shows. Cf. Theophr. *Char.* VII, 5-6.

[142] See the interesting catalogue of a school library from the fourth-century comic
poet Alexis (in Athen. 164bc). It includes Orpheus, Hesiod, "tragedies," Choerilus,
Homer, Epicharmus, and "prose works of all sorts" (συγγράμματα παντοδαπά).

[143] See Note 77.

[144] Xen. *Mem.* II, i, 21ff.

them often and having committed to memory large sections of them, sometimes the whole of a poet's works."[145] The poets were traditionally regarded not merely as teachers of manners and morals, but also as the repository of historical and geographical lore, and even of all sorts of technical knowledge, from generalship to fishing and chariot racing.[146] Plato had contested the claim of the poets in his earlier dialogues; they are simply imitators, and their omniscience is merely a deceptive pretence. In the *Laws*, however, he barely hints at this previous polemic, content to sum the matter up in a judgment which he thinks will be generally assented to. "Every poet has said many things well and many things badly; and if this is so, a wide knowledge is dangerous for our children" (811b; cf. 810bc). It is tempting to think that what Plato fears is the specious pretence of wisdom, and that his main purpose is to substitute science for literary lore. But although his proposals for higher education undoubtedly range him among the champions of scientific as contrasted with literary education,[147] I think his chief motive here is concern for the molding of the child's character. The power of enchantment which the poet possesses is dangerous unless properly guided: just as the poets in the *Republic* are to be censored, so also in the *Laws* there will be close supervision over the content of the young pupils' reading.

The educator will therefore have the responsibility of deciding what literary works the children are permitted to study and what ones are forbidden. No rules are laid down for his guidance, except that he is to use as a pattern "these very discourses in which we have been engaged since dawn" (811cd). In other words, he will direct the teachers to use as a reading book the *Laws* and any other literature, prose or poetry, written or unwritten, that accords with it;[148] and no teacher is to be employed who cannot agree with and com-

---

[145] 810e. The sequel to this passage shows that some teachers used collections of selected passages, no doubt in order to handle in schoolmasterly fashion the vast treasury available. "C'est la première fois que l'histoire mentionne ce recours aux 'morceaux choisis' destinés à une si belle carrière" (Marrou 112).

On the practice of memorizing, note what Niceratus says in Xen. *Symp.* III, 5: "My father, wishing me to grow up to be a good man, compelled me to learn all of Homer; and even today I could recite the whole of the *Iliad* and the *Odyssey* by heart."

[146] Cf. *Ion* 531b, 537-542; Strabo I, ii, 3-4; Xen. *Symp.* IV, 6; Aristoph. *Frogs* 1035.

[147] See Marrou 112.

[148] The ἐχόμενα of 811e1 conveys the sense of "ensuing," and thus links the later discourses in the *Laws*, as well as similar compositions by other writers, to the previous λόγοι of the Athenian.

mend the teachings contained in these officially prescribed readings
(811de; cf. 858cd, 957c-e). This provision seems at first sight to express a very harsh and egotistical dogmatism, and some interpreters
have thought Plato's suggestion to be at least half playful. But in some
ancient states, Crete among others, the laws of the land were actually
set to music and sung in chorus in the schools and on public occasions.[149] Plato may have had something similar in mind for his
model colony. Certainly some parts of the preceding discussion might
well be committed to memory—for example, the "great preamble"
of the fifth book, and some of the later "persuasive discourses." These
are some of the finest passages in Plato, and to recommend that they
be memorized and recited would have been quite appropriate and
certainly not offensive to ancient taste. Isocrates used his own compositions as a basis of instruction in his school.[150] Plato does not explicitly recommend memorizing his didactic passages, though it is
suggested by the educational practices of his time;[151] it is the content,
rather than the letter, of these discourses that he will have the children learn. If they are to grow up to be loyal citizens they must surely
become imbued in youth with the spirit of their laws; and what better
source from which to imbibe this spirit than the writings of their
founder and legislator? But these writings are not the only source
from which they can draw. The Athenian suggests that there are other
similar works (ἐχόμενα καὶ ὅμοια) that the guardian educator can
prescribe for study by the young. As for the restriction upon the teachers, it must be remembered that they are (mainly, at least) foreigners;
and it speaks rather for the universality of Plato's moral and political
standard that he apparently thinks there will be no difficulty in finding
persons from other lands who are willing to accept and commend it.

Next after letters comes the study of the lyre (809e). Our evidence
shows that at Athens this was not so common a part of primary education as was the study of letters. Socrates apparently did not learn
to play the lyre in his early years, for in the *Euthydemus* he confesses
that he is attending the music school of Connus, learning to play the

[149] Strabo x, iv, 18; xii, ii, 9; Aelian *Var. Hist.* ii, 39; Polyb. iv, 20-21. Solon is
said to have contemplated putting his laws into verse, obviously for public recitation
(Plut. *Solon* 3). The laws of Charondas were sung at banquets in Athens, according to Hermippus (Athen. 619b).

[150] Cf. *Isoc* xii, 200.

[151] Huntington Cairns, *Legal Philosophy from Plato to Hegel*, The Johns Hopkins
Press, 1949, 53: "Bentham also suggested that the father of a family might teach
Bentham's code to his children."

lyre "with the boys."[152] But the ability to play and sing at banquets was regarded as one of the accomplishments of a liberally educated man, at least until the Peloponnesian War, when the practice came to be regarded as somewhat old-fashioned.[153] Whether this was more than a temporary whim of taste we cannot say. In any case Plato, like Aristophanes, looks with favor on the older custom, and apparently not merely because lyre playing was a gentlemanly accomplishment. Like all music, it is useful ($\chi\rho\acute{\eta}\sigma\iota\mu\nu$, 812e) in a profound moral sense. The child has already had practice in singing and dancing, and now he learns to accompany his songs and recitations and the movements of the dance with the notes of the lyre. Thus this period of study will refine and deepen his knowledge of rhythm and harmony and increase his susceptibility to the charms of artistic song, with all the effects upon the character that this implied for Plato and the Greeks.

Hence the peculiar appropriateness of this instrument. Because of the distinctness ($\sigma\alpha\phi\acute{\eta}\nu\epsilon\iota\alpha$) of its different strings and their characteristic notes, the lyre is admirably fitted to emphasize the rhythmic and melodic elements of the song and dance. This advantage is not to be compromised, Plato says, by introducing needless and distracting complexities at this stage. The melody on the lyre must be the same as that which is sung, not a separate "voice" ($\acute{\epsilon}\tau\epsilon\rho\phi\omega\nu\acute{\iota}\alpha$), nor even a variation upon the melody sung (812de).[154] All such refinements of musical art are too difficult for children of this age, with all the other things they are expected to learn; and Plato is always solicitous that the process of learning be made as enjoyable and as much like play as possible. There was also to Plato a definite violation of good taste in what he regarded as the barbaric and meaningless complexities of the musical innovators of his day.[155] He would stick to the older canons as being aesthetically more satisfying and as corresponding more aptly to the simpler type of character he desires his education to produce. Apparently the lyre is to be used only as an accompaniment to words and dancing, never as a solo instrument.

[152] *Euthyd.* 272c. Cf. Aristoph. *Wasps* 959, 989: Bdelycleon pleads for the defendant that he doesn't know how to play the lyre, and Philocleon, the juror, later confesses that he doesn't know how, either.
[153] Aristoph. *Clouds* 1355ff.
[154] See England's notes for a fuller explanation of this highly compressed passage.
[155] 669de; 700de; cf. *Rep.* 424b-425a. The conflict between conservatives and innovators in music is reflected in Aristoph. *Clouds* 968ff.; *Thesm.* 130ff.; *Birds* 1377ff.; *Acharn.* 15ff. See also Cratinus Frs. 69, 70, Kock; Pherecrates Fr. 145; and Eupolis Fr. 139.

He remarks elsewhere that the wordless rhythms and harmonies produced by solo instruments are merely a tasteless display of meaningless virtuosity (669e-670a). The songs the children sing are selected
from the officially approved reading books used in their study of letters, or from an official collection of songs for the various festivals
which, as we shall see, is the work of a specially appointed commission of older citizens (812e, 813a; cf. 799a, 802a). Thus the children,
in learning the canons of musical composition, are not only undergoing the enchantment of these songs, but also preparing themselves
for participation in the public celebrations.

No mention is made of instruction on the pipe (αὐλός), though
this instrument is apparently not prohibited in Plato's state.[156] Aristotle tells us that it became very popular at Athens and even at conservative Sparta in the years immediately after the Persian Wars—
and this is attested by the numerous representations on Attic vases
of the early fifth century, as well as by the frequent use of it as an
illustration in Plato's dialogues—but that later it was rejected, "after
experience of its effects on the character."[157] The "flute"—as the
word is usually translated—was the instrument associated with Dionysiac revels; it was calculated to produce frenzy and intoxication
rather than soberness and temperance, and thus was hardly a suitable
daily companion for impressionable youth. Again, unlike the player
on the lyre, the flute player cannot use his voice; and Plato is insistent on associating melody with meaningful words. "The study
of flute playing has nothing to do with the mind," agrees Aristotle.
This shows why it is not a part of Plato's regular course of instruction; yet it seems to be assumed that some persons will learn it on
their own initiative, for contests of flute players are listed as part
of the program of the festivals (764e).[158]

[156] Although it is excluded from the state described in the *Republic* (399d). The
αὐλός, usually translated "flute," was a woodwind more like the clarinet or oboe
of modern times, played *à bec*, not *traverso*.

[157] *Pol.* 1341a 17 - b 8; on the popularity of the αὐλός in the fifth century see also
Athen. 184d-f. Alcibiades refused to learn it, according to Plato *Alc. I*, 106e. But
Aristotle's statement that the flute was later rejected can hardly be accepted at
face value. Its use in the fourth century, both in warfare and at festivals, is particularly well attested.

[158] Plato's references to the flute and flute playing show a curious ambivalence.
They are among his favorite examples for illustrating a point, e.g. in craftsmanship,
or technical proficiency, or the process of learning. But the flute is excluded from
the *Republic* state, and playing it is viewed with disdain as a symbol of licentious-
ness and excess (399d, 561c). In the *Laws*, however, it is regarded as a therapeutic
device of great effectiveness (790e, 791a). The explanation may lie in the associa-

In the remarks prefatory to this part of Plato's prescriptions there is a backward reference to the chorus of Dionysus and to the exceptional acuteness these elderly choristers will need to have in distinguishing good and bad rhythms and harmonies, if they are to perform properly their function of enchanting the souls of the younger citizens (812c). This is another indication that in this part of his educational program Plato has definitely in mind training these future leaders, as well as the ordinary members of the state. They will reveal themselves, no doubt, by superior perceptiveness and technical proficiency; and we should probably understand that the higher education for the select few which is cryptically described later will include further study of the elements of musical harmony and its relation to characters and institutions (818d, 967e).

The education of the young also includes training in the elements of mathematics (817e), specifically numbers and ciphering (λογισμοί τε καὶ περὶ ἀριθμούς), mensuration (μετρητική), and elementary astronomy (ἡ τῶν ἄστρων περίοδος πρὸς ἄλληλα). What part did these subjects have in the Greek schools of Plato's time?[159] There is no mention of them in the sketch of traditional education given in the *Protagoras*, but other references in Plato's dialogues and in Xenophon show that elementary knowledge of numbers and of the use of arithmetical rules is taken for granted in the fourth century.[160] One reference in the *Republic* implies that they were particularly thought of in connection with the mechanical arts, and may have had a "banausic" connotation, as if considered unworthy of a free man.[161] In any case, the high development of the arts indicates that such knowledge was widespread, probably being communicated to the young in connection with their study of letters. This practice would be facilitated, if not necessitated, by the use of letters to denote numbers, a convention which was introduced not later than the fifth century and became the common arithmetical notation

---

tion of flute playing with orgiastic rites (see E. R. Dodds, *The Greeks and the Irrational*, University of California Press, 1951, 97 n. 95, 273), which repelled the rationalist in Plato and attracted the mystic. Other references in Plato to corybantiasm are found in *Symp.* 215e, *Crito* 54d, *Ion* 536c, *Euthyd.* 277f. Cf. Arist. *Pol.* 1324a 7ff.

[159] See Thomas Heath, *Greek Mathematics*, Oxford, 1921, I, 18-25.
[160] *Rep.* 337ab; Xen. *Mem.* IV, iv, 7; *Econ.* VIII, 14. See Freeman, *op.cit.* 100ff.
[161] *Rep.* 522bc; cf. *Laws*, 747b. But see the praise in *Phil.* 55ff. of the mathematical element in τέχναι.

in later times.[162] Geometry and astronomy were taught in secondary schools in the fourth century, and their introduction was sufficiently recent for Isocrates to characterize them as an innovation upon the traditional education.[163] Finally we must remember the influence of the Sophists, some of whom made mathematics a part of their program of higher study. Hippias of Elis, inventor of the quadratrix and a mathematician of real quality, required his students to study arithmetic, geometry, astronomy, and music[164]—the four sciences cultivated by the Pythagoreans which later became the mediaeval quadrivium.

Plato's account does not specify the age at which his mathematical studies are to be pursued. They are mentioned after the discussion of letters and the lyre, and one might infer that they are begun at the age of sixteen, after the completion of the three years on the lyre. But in the light of their importance for the development of the child's mind it is not likely that they would be deferred so long;[165] and the reference to the practice of the Egyptians, which Plato admires so much as to recommend the adoption of their methods, seems to indicate that the first stages will be undertaken along with the study of letters, as was the custom in Egypt. As in the *Republic*, he points out their indispensability for the everyday problems of household management, civic administration, and the conduct of war (809c, 819c). Even astronomy, which informs us about the courses of the heavenly bodies, has its practical use in the arranging of the calendar and the appointment of days for the monthly and annual festivals (809cd). These practical advantages of such elementary mathematical knowledge were almost a commonplace in the fourth century, and Plato does not dwell on them.[166]

Of far greater importance is the effect of mathematics upon the mental powers. It wakes up the man who is naturally sluggish and slow of wit, making him sharp and eager to learn, lifting him by a kind of "divine art" ($\theta\epsilon\acute{\iota}\alpha$ $\tau\acute{\epsilon}\chi\nu\eta$) above his natural disposition.[167]

[162] Heath, *op.cit.* I, 32ff.

[163] Ps. Plato *Erast.* 132ab, *Axioch.* 366e; Isoc. XII, 26.

[164] *Prot.* 318de.

[165] The *Republic* (536d) says these studies should be presented to the mind in childhood.

[166] They constitute the limit of profit in this study, according to the opinions ascribed to Socrates by Xenophon (*Mem.* IV, vii, 2-8).

[167] 747b, 819c. It is instructive to compare the corresponding passages in the *Republic*: mathematical studies invite the intellect to reflection (523d), quicken the mental powers (526b), and draw the mind to the apprehension of "being" (524e).

It introduces him to mathematical necessity, a necessity quite different from the necessities of practical life.[168] It looks as if Plato were simply indulging in a playful analogy; but the ensuing text indicates that he has in mind the preparation of some of these young men and women for positions of leadership in the state. For the necessity that belongs to mathematics—and to all science, in the strict sense of the term—is something that must be apprehended by anyone, "whether god, daemon, or hero," who expects to attain genuine competence to supervise human affairs (818bc). Thus in the discussion of mathematics the thought of the training needed by the future guardians comes clearly into the open, with a distinct reference to a "certain few" (τινὲς ὀλίγοι) who will labor at these sciences with systematic thoroughness and exactness (σύμπαντα ὡς ἀκριβείας ἐχόμενα διαπονεῖν). These select few are obviously to be the ones who show the greatest proficiency; but how they are to be selected and how their higher study is to be organized is left to be determined later.[169]

But all students in this curriculum, regardless of their ability, are to be introduced to the realm of mathematical necessity. Knowledge of numbers and their relationships is necessary, the *Republic* says, if a man is to be a man at all (522e); the *Laws* adds that such knowledge makes him "godlike" (818c). The program begins with simple problems in numbering and calculation, to be taught by games involving the distribution of a number of toy sheep or chaplets or cups filled with coins among a larger or smaller number of persons.[170] These are the methods by which the Egyptians, the Athenian says, instruct their children in the use of arithmetic rules along with their letters—which shows clearly that we are dealing with instruction at the elementary level. Such games arouse the reflective powers

---

[168] This is the necessity implied in the proverb, "Not even the gods war against necessity"; for it is fatuous to assert that the gods do not contend against the necessities that plague human life (818b). Cf. *Tim.* 48a.

[169] 818a,de. See Chapter IX for the Nocturnal Council and its younger associates.

[170] 819bc. The description of these games is somewhat cryptic, and one can draw freely on his imagination in interpreting it. An early attempt is found in Athenaeus 670f-671a; for other suggestions see England's and Robin's notes, Taylor's translation, and Heath, *op.cit.* I, 19-20. The Academic tradition is probably seen in the scholium to Plato's *Charmides* 165e, where the specific character of λογιστική is said to be the fact that it deals with numbered things (ἀριθμητά), not numbers in abstraction; and the scholiast gives as illustrations "sheep numbers" (μηλῖται ἀριθμοί) and "cup numbers" (φιαλῖται ἀριθμοί) as if he had the present text before him. Most translators of our text take μῆλα as meaning "apples," but the *Charmides* scholium shows the correct rendering; cf. Heron *Deff.* 135, 5.

through revealing the distinction between numbers and things numbered. For instance, one share in the distribution might consist of many sheep or chaplets; or a cup containing several coins would be in one respect one, and in another a plurality. These are precisely the philosophical problems mentioned in the *Republic* as arising in the study of elementary arithmetic (524d-525b).

Next the child proceeds to problems involved in measuring lines, surfaces, volumes, sounds, and motions (819d; 747a). This would mean an introduction to the elements of plane and solid geometry, acoustics, and kinetics. Here we are evidently at the secondary level of instruction; and at this point the student is introduced to the problem of incommensurable magnitudes, an innovation to which Plato attaches peculiar importance. The widespread belief that all magnitudes are somehow commensurable he regards as absurd and a disgrace to the Greeks. "My dear Cleinias, I must say that when I was informed quite recently of our ignorance in this regard, I was surprised; such a state seemed to me more appropriate to hog-like creatures than to men, and I was ashamed, not merely for myself alone, but for all the Greeks."[171] To believe that all magnitudes are somehow commensurable with one another is natural to us. To see that this belief is in fact false would be to rise above one's human nature; it would be an instance of that power of mathematics which the Athenian says constitutes its greatest benefit. In truth there is no more striking introduction to the force of mathematical necessity than the demonstration that the side and diagonal of a square are incommensurable, despite the ability of imagination to suggest a limitless series of ever smaller units as divisors.[172] This and similar

[171] 819d. Like Taylor (206n.), I find it difficult to believe that Plato has only lately learned of the existence of incommensurables, which is the usual interpretation. Incommensurables are referred to frequently in the dialogues from the early period onward. But I find it almost equally incredible to interpret him as saying that he has only lately learned of the widespread ignorance of the subject among the Greeks. I can only think either (a) that the Athenian Stranger here has to be taken as not simply a spokesman for Plato, but as a fellow countryman who is pictured as having recently seen the light; or (b) that this is a polite way of emphasizing the lamentable lack of mathematical knowledge among the Dorians. Cleinias had shortly before (818e) referred to the neglect of mathematical studies among his countrymen, and it is implied frequently in the later discussion. Perhaps a combination of the two suggestions affords the best solution to our problem.

[172] The demonstration mentioned by Aristotle (*Anal. Pr.* 41a 26-27)—a reductio ad absurdum showing that the assumption of commensurability implies that the same number is both odd and even—was doubtless the one used by the Pythagoreans and would be well known to Plato. For the demonstration see Heath, *op.cit.* I, 91.

facts concerning incommensurables must be learned by the young; and the Athenian suggests that the older men would find the study of the theory of incommensurables an even more absorbing pastime than the game of draughts (820cd).[173] Such studies are not hard, and when pursued as a game they will do no damage to our state, but instead will be of great advantage to it. Yet—as if recalling that this is perhaps too intellectual an innovation to be accepted by a Cretan colony—the Athenian ends by laying down these proposals as provisional only, subject to revocation if they prove unacceptable to the legislators or to the people for whom the legislation is intended (820e).

Finally, the young students are to be introduced to certain problems in astronomy, in order to correct another "intolerable" error current among the Hellenes (820e). The error is twofold, being compounded of a prejudice against inquiries into the nature of the heavenly bodies—the μετεωρολογία of which Socrates was accused in Aristophanes' *Clouds*—and an impious acquiescence in ignorance about the actual nature and motions of these heavenly bodies. If the sun and moon are really divine beings, as popular opinion holds, then the study (μάθημα) of astronomy can only be right and beneficial to the state and dear to the gods. It would make it possible to address these "heavenly gods" correctly in prayer and sacrifices, and avoid the blasphemy of speaking falsely about their motions (821a-d). But the fact is that most Hellenes believe the sun, moon, and other stars are "wanderers" (πλανῆται), following not one fixed path but many paths and irregularly. This error should be replaced by what Plato thinks is the true view of their paths in the heavens. This simplification of the mathematical picture of the motions of these heavenly bodies is something which seems to have been worked out in the Academy under Plato's guidance.[174] Whether Plato conceived the earth or the sun to be the center of these circular motions, and if the earth, whether he regarded it as stationary or in revolution, he does not tell us in this brief résumé of his views. Nor can we pause to ex-

---

[173] Πεττεία is mentioned as a science and closely associated with mathematics in *Polit.* 299e; and with mathematics and letters in *Phaedr.* 274d.

[174] The Athenian refers to the truth in this matter as something which he learned late in life. There seems to be no difficulty here, as there was in 819d, in taking the Athenian Stranger as a spokesman for Plato himself. On the divinity of the heavenly bodies and the study of astronomy in the Academy, see Chapter VIII, The Gods and their Worship.

amine the question, which has sharply divided the commentators.[175] All that Plato insists on is the superior accuracy, or truthfulness, of the scientific account as compared with the traditional beliefs based on sense perception. Hence this study, though indispensable for a proper ritual of worship, seems to be important primarily because of its capacity to emancipate the student from his instinctive sense-bound beliefs and thus, like the study of incommensurables, raise him above his human nature.

The importance of Plato's innovation in this part of his curriculum can hardly be overestimated. It lies not in the fact that he included mathematics in his program of study—that, as we have seen, was an accepted fact in his times; nor merely in that he attached less importance to the practical advantages of this study than to its effects upon the student's mind. Isocrates also had commended such studies because they sharpen a boy's wits and train him to fix his attention.[176] But what Plato had in mind was a purpose far profounder than Isocrates could comprehend. These studies are a means of introducing all young citizens to the realm of scientific necessity upon which law and policy must be based, and of preparing some of them to undertake that higher study of this realm which would equip them for responsible leadership in the state. Isocrates, who could only look upon such studies as unfitting a man for giving practical counsel to his fellows,[177] seems to have won out over Plato among their contemporaries and immediate successors; but the long future belonged to Plato. For it is he who formulated both the specific program and the ideal purpose of what we in modern times have conceived to be secondary education.[178]

The higher studies that Plato has in mind for a "certain few" (818a) are here dismissed with some remarks about the problem of organizing them properly. After enumerating the elementary mathematical knowledge he intends to require of the young, the Athenian proceeds as follows: "It is the height of folly to suppose that all these [i.e. the

[175] For the ancient testimony regarding Plato's final astronomical views, see Plut. *Numa* 11 and *Quaest. Plat.* VIII. For modern interpretations see Heath, *Aristarchus of Samos*, Oxford, 1913, 174-189; Taylor, *Commentary on Plato's Timaeus*, Oxford, 1928, 226-239; Burnet, *Greek Philosophy*, London, 1920, 225-227; Ritter, *Kommentar*, 228-250.

[176] Isoc. XV, 262-267.   [177] Isoc. XII, 28-29, XV, 268-269.

[178] Cf. Marrou 116: "On ne saurait trop insister sur l'immense portée historique de cette doctrine, qui marque une date capitale dans l'histoire de la pédagogie: Platon n'introduit ici rien moins que la notion idéale et le programme spécifique de ce qu'il faut bien appeler un enseignement secondaire."

elementary] studies are not necessary for a man who is going to comprehend anything at all of the highest sciences. What these [i.e. the higher] branches of study are like, how many there are, and when they should be taken up for study—what parts should be studied together and what may be studied independently of the rest, and the various ways of combining them—all this we must comprehend rightly if anyone, having mastered the first subjects, is to proceed under their guidance to the others. . . . But it is too early to make a precise legal enactment on this point. Later, if you are willing, we can determine it more precisely" (818de). In spite of the ambiguity of the pronouns in this text, it seems clear that Plato is here speaking of the organization of the higher studies, not of the elementary disciplines which are the main theme in this part of his work. And likewise it is to these higher studies that he refers in a cryptic sentence a few lines later. When Cleinias accuses the Athenian of hesitating to speak out because he is embarrassed at the neglect of mathematical studies among the Dorians, the Athenian replies that this indeed is one reason for his hesitation; but a more important one is that he is alarmed by his observation of students who have taken them up in the wrong way. "Complete ignorance of these subjects is not so terrible or extreme an evil; far more harmful is proficiency and experience in them when combined with a bad bringing up" (πολυπειρία καὶ πολυμαθία μετὰ κακῆς ἀγωγῆς, 819a). This is not, as has been thought by some commentators,[179] a suggestion that complete ignorance of mathematics is no great evil. That interpretation would falsify all that we have just found in Plato's description of this part of his curriculum. Rather it is that the higher mathematical studies may well be omitted for those who are not prepared to pursue them properly. Taken in this way the passage is the parallel to the proposals in the *Republic* for restricting dialectic to those students who are qualified, and deferring it even in their case until they are mature. The sentiment in both works is no doubt inspired by Plato's observation of the practice of the Sophists, who thought that the higher culture could be given to anyone (τῷ τυχόντι) and of the unfortunate consequences of this procedure, both for the student and for philosophy.[180]

[179] Including the writer in an earlier article, "Plato's Conception of Persuasion," PR LXII, 1953, 247.

[180] Cf. *Rep.* 539d; 535c, 536b. "Il faut à la fois éprouver et préparer les candidats philosophes," remarks Marrou (117).

The promise to deal more precisely later with this program of higher studies is not fulfilled. In the account of the Nocturnal Council at the end of the *Laws* we are told that the higher knowledge which the guardians must possess presupposes these necessary preliminary sciences, together with a knowledge of musical theory and its connection with moral rules and institutions, and a steadfast conviction of the primacy of soul and of reason as the orderers of all things (965ff.). But again the difficulty is stressed of prescribing a fixed program for the study of these higher matters (968de). The work ends with the Athenian Stranger's exhortation to Cleinias to proceed with the establishment of his state, and his offer to help him by expounding his views on the education and training of the guardians (969a).[181] This has sometimes been taken as an anticipation of the *Epinomis* by those who regard that as Plato's work; and it was undoubtedly the motive for its composition if it is the work of some one else. But another interpretation is open to us, on the whole a more plausible one. Since this higher education has already been discussed at length in the *Republic*, the Athenian's closing remark may be simply a way of avoiding a recapitulation of Plato's well-known views, while suggesting that he himself, or any student acquainted with his doctrine, would be able to give the advice required.

There is little in his proposals for instruction in letters and mathematics that Plato could have borrowed from Sparta. The Spartans seem to have made it a point of honor, as a recent historian has put it, to remain in a state of semiliteracy.[182] This is attested both by statements of their contemporaries and by the anarchic condition of the orthography in their inscriptions. Isocrates remarks that the Spartans do not study letters, and that if any one of them ever comes to know what he has written in the *Panathenaicus* it will be because somebody has read it to him.[183] They were even less interested, if possible, in mathematics. When Hippias is asked, in Plato's dialogue, whether he had taught geometry to the Lacedaemonians, "Hardly," he replies: "many of them don't even know how to count."[184] Plato

---

181 For more on what Plato says about this higher education, see Chapter IX.

182 Marrou 40, 473 n. 1.

183 Isoc. XII, 208-209, 250-251. Cf. Plut. *Lyc.* 16, 6; *Apophth. Lac.* 221B; and the statement in *Dissoi Logoi*, the work of a Doric-writing Sophist of about 400, that the Lacedaemonians think it noble not to learn music and letters, whereas the Ionians consider it a disgrace; Diels-Kranz II, 408 (10).

184 *Hipp. Mj.* 285c.

follows here the tradition of his native city and of the Ionians generally under the cultural leadership of Athens.

In music and gymnastics, however, Plato's proposals come much nearer to Lacedaemonian practice. The arts of choristry at Sparta were the living expression of an ancient tradition, somewhat more conservative of the older canons than suited Athenian taste, but for that reason all the more approved, apparently, by Plato. In gymnastics he adopts wholeheartedly the Spartan principle (which was also the older Athenian conception) that the purpose of physical training is to prepare the citizen for the defense of his fatherland, rejecting both the technical developments and the spirit of professional athletics. Like the Spartans, he insists on physical training for women as well as men, going even beyond the Spartans in regarding the purpose of this training as military, not merely the production of sturdy offspring. Like the Spartans he discourages contests in boxing, ground wrestling, and the pancratium which are of little use in war, but substitutes for them other events of his own devising which were looked upon with little favor at Sparta, such as armed contests of hoplites, peltasts, and cavalry.[185]

These departures from Spartan practice indicate only a more logical adoption of their fundamental conception of physical training. But there are other divergences which cannot be so interpreted, and these upon examination are striking and significant. Some of the most characteristic features of the Spartan agoge are absent from Plato's proposals. There is no hint that his youth are to be organized into bands under the leadership of older boys, a feature of central importance in the Spartan system, as is attested by both Xenophon and Plutarch.[186] Indeed Plato's only reference to this Spartan institution seems to be a stern reproof (666e). Nor is there any encouragement to the systematized pugnacity between these bands by which the Spartans conceived they were developing the fighting qualities of their young.[187] The Spartan youth seem to have lived together in these bands, away from their homes; but in Plato's state the children are apparently to sleep in their parents' homes, going at dawn to their teachers, as was customary at Athens (808cd). The practice of theft, even as a game, is explicitly forbidden in Plato's state (823e); whereas this was an important part of the Spartan training of the

[185] See the next section of this chapter, ad fin.
[186] Xen. *Const. Lac.* 11, 11; Plut. *Lyc.* 16, 4.
[187] On this "systematized pugnaciousness" see Freeman, *op.cit.* 27f., and Note 313.

youth in resourcefulness and daring.[188] Nor is there any hint in Plato's text of such contests in endurance of pain as the flogging of the youth at the temple of Artemis Orthia, which became such a notorious feature of Spartan life that in later times a special theatre was erected within sight of the temple altar to accommodate the spectators.[189] The omission of these matters from Plato's proposals is the more striking in that most of them are mentioned by Megillus at the beginning of the dialogue as characteristic parts of Spartan training (633bc). Aristotle remarks that the Spartan method of instilling courage into the young turned them into savages, and we can only assume that Plato, as Plutarch suggests, shared this opinion.[190] Clearly Plato has adopted the Spartan agoge only in part; he has actually discarded what later generations considered its most picturesque and characteristic features.

FESTIVALS

Regular religious festivals (ἑορταί) were a universal feature of Greek civic life. Each local community had its recurrent days of merrymaking or solemn rites about the local sanctuary; and the larger cities had their more elaborate calendars of feast days, each with its prescribed sacrifices, games, and dances. Festivals seem to have been more numerous at Athens than elsewhere, to judge from the comments of ancient writers;[191] but Sparta, though notoriously less hospitable to visitors and therefore less well known, cannot have been far behind Athens in this respect.[192] The greater Athenian festivals, such as the Dionysia and the Panathenaea, attracted crowds of visitors from abroad; but high also was the renown of the Lacedaemonian Hyacinthia and Carnea, both feasts of Apollo, and the festival of Artemis Orthia. These were primarily and originally religious festivals, but because of the close connection between re-

---

[188] Freeman, *op.cit.* 22-24; Plut. *Lyc.* 17-18; Xen. *Const. Lac.* II, 6-8.

[189] Plut. *Lyc.* 18; Paus. III, xvi, 10-11; Xen. *Const. Lac.* II, 9; Lucian *Anacharsis* 38; schol. to *Laws* 633b. The fourth-century rite was probably less brutal than the ceremony which attracted the crowds of foreigners in later times. See Jeanmaire, *Couroi et Courètes*, 513-518, and R. M. Dawkins, ed. *The Sanctuary of Artemis Orthia*, London, 1929, 289, 405.

[190] *Pol.* 1338b 11ff.; Plut. *Lyc.* 28.

[191] Note Pericles' boast in Thuc. II, 38; Ps. Xen. *Const. Ath.* III, 2 (cf. III, 8); Plato *Alc. II*, 148e; the comments of the fourth-century traveler quoted by Frazer, *Pausanias* I, xliii; and of Maximus of Tyre by Ludwig Deubner, *Attische Feste*, Berlin, 1932, 5. It is generally believed that no less than seventy days of the year were set aside at Athens for festivals of various sorts (E. A. Gardner, in Whibley, *Companion to Greek Studies*, 4th edn., Cambridge, 1931, 406).

[192] See the impressive list of Spartan festivals in Ziehen, RE s.v. Sparta, 1508-1520.

ligion and the state in Greek life they were civic festivals as well; they were presided over and controlled by public officials and were regarded as a regular part of the life of the city. They were civic also in a deeper sense, as powerful agencies in promoting unity of feeling among citizens and in fostering the sentiments of loyalty and devotion to their native land.

Plato shows that he is well aware of the important moral and political functions performed by these civic festivals. He sees that the sentiments and habits acquired in youth are likely to become weaker as a man grows older, and may even be completely lost, unless there are means of periodically refreshing and confirming them. The religious festivals fulfill this purpose. They are divinely ordained, he says, not merely as respite from toil, but as opportunities for the citizens to "correct their ways" (ἵν᾽ ἐπανορθῶνται τὰς τροφάς) by associating with one another and with the gods in song and dance (653cd).[193] How many festivals there are to be is hard to determine exactly. There will be an official sacrifice on each day of the year to some god or daemon on behalf of the city (828b); but of the formal festivals with games and processions the number will be considerably less, though more than was usual in Greek cities, since "there is no city that can compare with ours in leisure and command of the necessary means" (828d). Of the twelve gods after whom the tribes are named each is to have two annual festivals, one in the city

---

[193] 653d; ἀναπαύλας τε αὐτοῖς τῶν πόνων ἐτάξαντο τὰς τῶν ἑορτῶν ἀμοιβὰς τοῖς θεοῖς, καὶ Μούσας Ἀπόλλωνά τε μουσηγέτην καὶ Διόνυσον συνεορταστὰς ἔδοσαν, ἵν᾽ ἐπανορθῶνται τάς τε τροφὰς . . . γενομένας ἐν ταῖς ἑορταῖς μετὰ θεῶν. For the correct interpretation of this important but difficult and apparently corrupt passage, it seems to me essential (despite England) to reject Burnet's comma after ἐπανορθῶνται. That punctuation requires us, as England sees, to take the Muses, Apollo, and Dionysus as the subject of the verb, and as its object τὰς ἑορτάς understood. But surely the early part of the sentence indicates that it is not the festivals that are to be set right, but the results of early education and training, which the cares of adult life tend to alter and obliterate; τροφάς is the object of the verb required by the sense of the whole passage. Bury appears to have rendered the thought correctly: "that they may at least set right again their modes of discipline by associating in their feasts with the gods." So also Apelt, Jowett and Cassarà.

To explain the awkward τε in τάς τε τροφάς (which Bury changes to γε, following Hermann) I would follow Post (TAPA LXI, 1930, 36) and assume that a few words have dropped out of the text before γενομένας, such as καὶ τὰς παιδείας ὀρθάς.

With England, however, I would interpret ἀμοιβάς (d3) as "change," or "variety," taking τῶν ἑορτῶν as a genitive of definition (i.e. the gods gave men festivals as a relief), not as "cycle" (Taylor: "the cycle of their festivals"). On this passage see also Boyancé, op.cit. (in Note 36), 171; and Reverdin, 69-70. Pericles (Thuc. II, 38) also describes the feasts as ἀνάπαυλαι τῶν πόνων, and Aristotle as ἀναπαύσεις (Nic. Eth. 1160a 24-25).

and one in the country, so distributed as to make a series of monthly sacrifices (771d; cf. 828c).[194] Once each month the entire city is to engage in military exercises in the field for a period of a day or more, with sacrifices, music, and games, and there are to be other such field days for the separate tribes (829bc). Festivals for women also are mentioned, some reserved for women only,[195] others to which men are admitted (828c). From these indications it is safe to infer that the citizen would devote at least a sixth of the days of the year, in whole or in part, to these religious and civic ceremonies. They are even asserted to be one of his chief occupations (835e). "A man must pass his life in these kinds of play—in sacrificing, singing, and dancing—in order to win the favor of the gods and be able to repel the enemy in battle" (803e).

But these festivals must be carefully supervised if they are to have the educative function that Plato desires. The legislation governing this matter is given only tentatively and in outline, the details being left to be filled in by the guardians and the religious officials (828b; cf. 804a). First a list of the festivals is to be drawn up, showing the days of the year on which they are to be held and the gods or divinities to be honored at each. Next there are to be ordinances prescribing what hymn is to be sung at each festival and with what dances each is to be accompanied. When this calendar and its liturgy have been completed, the whole is to be consecrated by a public sacrifice to the Moerae and all the other gods, and each hymn dedicated to its appropriate god (799ab). Thereafter anyone who introduces at the worship of any god a hymn or dance other than those prescribed shall be punished and expelled from the festival, and made liable to a public suit for impiety if he refuses to obey (799b, 800a). The selection of these official hymns and dances is entrusted to a group of examiners (δοκιμασταί), consisting of men not less than fifty years of age, who have liberty to select for the liturgy any of the older songs and dances that they think appropriate (and there are many

---

[194] Plato's text probably does not mean that there are to be monthly feasts to *each* god, though Bury takes it thus (in 828c). There are to be monthly festivals (ἔμμηνα ἱερά) but each month is apparently to be sacred to a different one of the twelve gods. Plato is here following implicitly a common Greek practice. Both in the Attic calendar and in those of other cities most months carried names designating the feast to be celebrated during its duration, or recalling the god in whose honor the feast was established.

[195] Like the Haloa, the Skira, and the Thesmophoria at Athens, and certain Spartan festivals of Demeter. See Paus. VII, xxvii, 10; IV, xvii, 1; Aristoph. *Eccles.* 18, 59; and Nilsson, *Griechische Feste*, Leipzig, 1906.

fine compositions of the "ancients," the Athenian says admiringly), or to reject or revise them as they think fit (802ab). Poets and musicians are to be consulted for their technical knowledge, but their tastes and preferences are to be followed with caution. The primary standard the examiners are to use in making this selection is that of "auspicious speech" (εὐφημία)—a criterion broad enough to exclude as "abusive speech" (βλασφημία) not merely irreverent words or gestures in the presence of the gods, but also dolorous strains and dances out of accord with the serenity appropriate to a religious feast (800d). The law will also forbid the utterance of prayers for things regarded as good but really of doubtful value, such as wealth, and more generally all expression of sentiments contrary to the laws and customs of the state (801a-c). In this fashion our songs (nomes, νόμοι) will really become laws, says Plato, playing once more upon the double meaning of the word νόμος (799e).[196]

This procedure suggests a canon of authorized songs and dances to be preserved without change for all future time (816c). The Athenian mentions with favor the hieratic art of the Egyptians which, he says, has preserved the canons of painting, sculpture, and music for literally ten thousand years (656de; cf. 799a). It is possible that Plato here speaks from personal observation. If he visited Egypt during the years of his travels he could hardly fail to be impressed by the archaizing spirit of the art of the Saïtic revival, deliberately imitating the masterpieces of the Memphite kingdom.[197] But Plato's text, when carefully examined, is far from suggesting an endless reproduction of identical copies. "If you examine them," says the Athenian, referring to the works of Egyptian art, "you will find that the paintings and sculptures made there ten thousand years ago . . . are no whit better or worse than the productions of today, but executed with the same art" (656e). Elsewhere he asserts that variety within the fundamental forms is necessary if the singers' zest for singing is to remain fresh and unsated (665c). Furthermore, the tribe of poets must be reckoned with, and there will inevitably be new compositions pressing for a hearing (801cd). It seems, then, that what Plato is proposing is the consecration of the traditional forms, or

[196] See Note 48.

[197] See Schuhl, *Platon et l'art de son temps*, Paris, 1952, 18-20. But the statement in Plato's text is far from accurate. The models imitated by Saïtic art were at most twenty-five hundred years old, and the Egyptian art of Plato's time represented a revival, not the continued existence of the older forms.

canons, of composition. This will give them power to resist changes in popular taste (no one can laugh them off as being old-fashioned, 657b), but would not preclude variations within the forms themselves.[198] The change in music to which the decline of the Athenian constitution is elsewhere attributed (700f.) was the violation of canons, not merely the introduction of new songs. It is clear that Plato is chiefly concerned with supporting the older types of choral composition as against the anarchic innovations of the newer styles; and that his preference for the older style stems from his conviction of its accord with the ancestral morality, as one can appropriately call it, which he wishes these festivals to impress upon his citizens. As for the pleasure of the auditors and participants, we need only reflect that a man likes what he has been accustomed to hear; and if our citizens have been habituated from youth to hearing only music that is sober and regulated they will not even enjoy the "honeyed strains" of the moderns, but will call them vulgar (802cd).

But even the proposal to consecrate the older styles presents difficulties of which Plato, as an artist, is well aware. He expresses severe criticism elsewhere of subjecting art to written rules; if investigation and innovation were prohibited, the arts would utterly perish.[199] So in the Laws it seems that modification of the forms and canons themselves is to be permitted, at least so long as the legislators have not yet reached the standard of correctness (657b). The conflict in Plato's thought here between the demands of regulation and the need for novelty in the musical arts is but an aspect of the larger problem of reconciling stability and change in the social order; and we can only assume that his decision on the larger problem would also apply to the regulation of music. Since there are provisions for amending the laws, we cannot assume that Plato intended his canons of music to be immune to improvement with the passage of time; although in this part of his legislation we might expect the authority of tradition and the dangers of frequent or sudden alterations to be more emphasized than elsewhere.

But if a tradition in music or in any other art is to be preserved as a living influence, not merely as a dead object of veneration, it must be through the authority and the taste of persons actually engaged in the art. It is at this point that the chorus of elders, which we

[198] In *Rep.* 424bc it is not the "new song" (νέον ᾆσμα) but the "new way of song" (τρόπος ᾠδῆς νέος) that unsettles political and social customs.
[199] *Polit.* 299de.

discussed earlier, plays its important part. The commission of examiners to select the hymns and dances for the public festivals appears to be the legal equivalent of the chorus of Dionysus. Plato seems to have thought that in their convivial assemblies, where persons of mature taste and character, themselves amateurs and past proficients in the arts of χορεία, discuss and rehearse with the experts the older compositions and compare them with the newer products of the musician's and poet's art, the older traditions would retain their vitality and any innovations adopted would be the result of sober judgment and trained taste. Whether this commission of examiners is identical with the guardians or with the Nocturnal Council we can only speculate; but it is safe to say that some, at least, of this elderly chorus would be members of one or both the other bodies. Their function, in any case, is to formulate the standards, and in some cases the details, of the musical presentations at the public festivals. The correction of offenders against the canons they have laid down lies not with them, but with the priests and priestesses presiding at the festival and with the guardians—the representatives respectively, Plato seems to say, of religious and secular law (799b).

The poets, therefore, are expected to conform to these canons of music, and before any new work of theirs can be performed it must be officially approved by the educational officers and by the guardians.[200] This is another implication that the official liturgy permits of variation at certain points, after the analogy of the later Greek and Roman churches. In Plato's state such variations would have to be licensed in advance. But there is one occasion on which the requirement of advance approval is waived. In some of the festivals there will be songs or poems in praise of distinguished citizens—e.g. a victor in a contest or someone whose general character and achievements merit eulogy. There will also be opportunities for denunciation and condemnation. Not everyone is to be permitted to sing such songs of praise or blame, but only a man of mature age (fifty years or older) who has himself won honor in the city for his character and

[200] 801cd. Literally "by the designated judges (ἀποδεδειγμένοις κριταῖς) and the guardians." The educator is mentioned two lines later as one of the officials meant. The text implies that it has already been made clear who these other persons are who will be the νομοθέται for music; but unless this is a reference to the chorus of Dionysus, it can only be taken as referring to the ἄρχοντες μουσικῆς of 764c. The mention of the ἐπιμελητής τῆς παιδείας supports this supposition, for his election is described in the same context, 765de. But the difficulty is that the ἄρχοντες of 764c are not judges; κριταί are referred to in 765d, but nothing is said as to who they are or how they are to be selected. See Note 277.

deeds. He alone is to have "freedom of song" (παρρησία ἐν Μού-σαις), i.e. the privilege of singing without advance approval of his composition; and this privilege is explicitly granted in each case by the educator and the guardians (829cd).

But χορεία includes dancing (ὄρχησις) as well as singing; and here also the legislator is called on to formulate canons of what is permissible. It must be recalled once more that the term ὄρχησις covered a much wider range of rhythmic movements and actions than the modern word "dancing," including much that we would call simply ceremonial or processional, and involving a much richer use of costumes and expressive gestures than we can easily imagine today.[201] Its importance in a Greek festival would be taken for granted. We have seen that the liturgy of the public sacrifices contains not only prescriptions of songs to be sung, but also of dances that are to accompany them (802a, 803e). The processions in honor of the gods are described as dances (796c), and even the monthly field day, with its military exercises and contests, is called a χορεία (831b). There are also to be choral dances of marriageable youths and maidens at the rural festivals, to give them an opportunity to see each other's physical charms (772a). Remembering that all dancing is an imitation of character and action, we can see that regulation is necessary here to preserve the standards of sentiment and conduct that the law presupposes.

The Greek genius was as prolifically creative in the dance as in the other arts, and a legislator of Plato's time would have an almost limitless variety of material from which to make his choice, ranging over the whole gamut from the restrained and stately choruses of maidens (παρθένεια) or the manly war dances (ἐνόπλια παίγνια) to the buffoonery and vulgarity of the κόρδαξ and the σίκιννις.[202] Plato divides this rich material into two main classes: one kind of dancing that is serious (σπουδαῖον) and majestic (σεμνόν), being an imitation of the movements of beautiful bodies and expressing the

---

[201] On the other hand, Greek ὄρχησις did not include what seems to be most characteristic of modern social dancing, the pairing of partners of different sex.

[202] For this richness as seen by the ancients, see Lucian *The Dance*, Athen. 628-631, and Poll. IV, 99-105. Scaliger, the first scholar after the revival of learning to deal with the subject, listed almost two hundred different dances mentioned and sometimes described by the ancient authors. For more recent treatments, see Emmanuel, *op.cit.* (in Note 22); Kurt Latte, *De Saltationibus Graecorum*, Giessen, 1913; Séchan, *op.cit.* (in Note 134); and Fritz Weege, *Der Tanz in der Antike*, Halle, 1926.

sentiments of noble minds; and another that is common or trivial (φαῦλον). Each of these is in turn divided into two species (814e, 816d). Of the serious dancing the two main kinds are the warlike or "pyrrhic" dance (πυρρίχη, 815ab), and the pacific dances, called by Plato and the Greeks generally ἐμμέλειαι (816b), the latter again being divided into two subspecies (815de). Of the common dances, one species is the dance of comedy (816d); what the other is we shall have to guess later. Plato's classification of dances, while apparently determined by his moral and political interests, nevertheless follows closely the natural divisions of his material.[203] We find echoes of it, or parallels to it, in Athenaeus' sources; and Séchan takes it as the basis for his own admirable treatment. But this classification provides only the outline of legislation, the Athenian says. It is the responsibility of the educator, with the help of the elderly choristers, to select the particular dances that correspond to the types described and assign them, with appropriate music, to the various feasts (816c; cf. 799a, 802a).

The pyrrhic dance, in which Plato clearly shows a very special interest, was one of a variety of armed dances widely current in Greece and of great antiquity. Such armed dances are found very often among primitive peoples; they may originally have had a magical or apotropaic function among the Greeks, as elsewhere. But very early they became associated with religious festivals, and in the fifth century were regarded as an important instrument of education. The pyrrhic was taught to Spartan youth from the age of five onward,[204] and the Cretans seem to have been equally devoted to it.[205] Crete may have played an important part in the genesis and diffusion of this dance; so at least the ancients believed, though their widely varying accounts of its origin and of the derivation of its name show that they had no reliable knowledge on the subject.[206] The name which became attached to it, however, is definitely Doric.[207] Whether Plato

---

[203] Plato seems to say that he is himself following the traditional classification as well as nomenclature (816bc).

[204] *Athen.* 631a.

[205] Strabo x, iv, 16.

[206] Aristotle attributes it to Achilles, who danced it around the funeral pyre of Patroclus; hence its name παρὰ τὴν πύραν (Fr. 519, Rose). Others derived it from Neoptolemus of Pyrrhus, the son of Achilles (Lucian *The Dance* 9; Paus. III, xxv, 2); and still others from a mythical Pyrrhichus, evidently invented for this very purpose (Aristoxenus, in Athen. 630e; cf. Strabo x, iii, 8; and Paus. *loc.cit.*

[207] As Latte has shown (*op.cit.* 28f.), πύρριχος is a Doric diminutive of πυρρός, meaning "red." The dance probably acquired its name from the red garments worn

would concede a Doric origin for the dance may well be doubted. For him it was characteristic of the worship of Athena, and though in one passage he associates the armed dances of Athena with the "armed sports" of the Curetes in Crete and the dances of the Dioscuri at Sparta (796b), yet clearly Athena retains her independence in the group, and elsewhere he explains her epithet "Pallas" as derived from the armed dances in which she delights.[208] Evidently Plato looked on these dances as a common Greek inheritance transcending the distinction felt in classical times between Ionian and Dorian.

The pyrrhic dance was regarded in the fifth century as an important means of developing bodily agility and preparing the youth for actual combat.[209] It could be danced by a single man against an imaginary antagonist, or by one or more pairs of antagonists in a single choral ensemble, accompanied by chants and by music from the lyre or flute. The dancers are represented in the reliefs and vase paintings as wearing helmets and carrying shields and spears.[210] The fullest literary evidence of the character of this dance is contained in Plato's own text. "It imitates the eluding of blows and missiles of all sorts, by head movements and swervings and jumpings up and crouchings; and also motions of an opposite sort connected with attack, such motions as imitate the shooting of bows, the hurling of javelins, and the delivering of all kinds of blows."[211] When danced

---

by warriors in primitive times (Arist. Fr. 542; Xen. *Const. Lac.* XI, 3; Dion. Hal. VII, 72; Plut. *Arist.* 21; Poll. IV, 116). Plato's reference later (815a) to the appropriateness of this name implies that it denotes a characteristic of the dance rather than the identity of its inventor. Like Aristotle (see above, Note 206), Plato probably thought of its connection with fire ($\pi\hat{\upsilon}\rho$) or fiery red ($\pi\upsilon\rho\rho\acute{o}s$).

[208] *Crat.* 406e. Epicharmus apparently claimed that it was Athena who gave the ἐνόπλιον to the Dioscuri (Athen. 184f; cf. Dion. Hal. VII, 72; and Lucian *Dialogues of the Gods* 8).

[209] Athen. 628f quotes a verse of Socrates: "They who honor the gods best with dances (χοροῖς) are best in war." The connection between dancing and warfare was sometimes very close indeed. Lucian (*The Dance* 14) says that in Thessaly the front-rank men in battle were called προορχηστῆς, "front-dancers"; and reports a monument to one of their dead warriors that carried the inscription: "He danced the battle well."

[210] For the archaeological evidence see Séchan, *op.cit.* 96ff., and for the literary evidence W. E. D. Downes, "The Offensive Weapon in the Pyrrhic," *Class. Rev.* XVIII, 1904, 101ff.; and Latte, *op.cit.* 35-36.

[211] 815a. There is a surprising change of construction in the latter part of this passage as transmitted to us in the MS. where we have ἐπιχειρούσας modifying ἐναντίας, when we should have expected ἐπιχειροῦσαν modifying πυρρίχην; but I fail to detect the "mira quaedam confusio" charged by Stallbaum, whom most later commentators have echoed. "Imitations of motions that imitate offensive action" is as intelligible as "imitations of motions of offensive action." I agree with England that the "confusio," if it is that, is preferable to the suggested emendations.

in groups, the pyrrhic became "the natural ornament of civic festivals."[212] It was danced at the feast of the Dioscuri at Sparta, and was at least a preliminary part of the festival of the Gymnopaediae.[213] Even the main dances at this festival seem to have been a gymnastic presentation, without arms, of the pyrrhic steps. It was held in equal honor at Athens, being an ancient feature of the Panathenaic and Dionysiac festivals.[214] Every Attic tribe appears to have presented a team of contestants for these dances, and the expense of equipping and training a chorus was an important liturgy devolving on the wealthier members of the tribe. The spectacle of these choruses, equipped in varying degrees of magnificence according to the wealth or generosity of the choregoi, and executing their intricate and exacting movements to the sound of the flute and to the chant of special songs composed for the occasion, must have made a deep impression upon all observers; for the pyrrhic is the dance most often referred to by ancient authors. This in itself, apart from the educational and military value of the exercises, would account for the special attention Plato pays to it.

But Plato adds to his description of this dance a critical comment whose precise significance is not easy to determine. "Such movements attain vigor and correctness when they represent good bodies and souls, the limbs of the body being extended straight for the most part" (815ab). It is clear that Plato is not merely invoking a standard of physical culture here. But what precisely is the moral or aesthetic standard hinted at? I suggest that this passage must be read in the light of the evidence we have that the pyrrhic dance, like the older musical canons by which Plato set such store, was in process of degeneration in the fourth century.[215] The evidence is clear that in later times its warlike significance had been forgotten, except at Sparta, and it had become mixed with Dionysiac and Bacchic elements. The dancers carried thyrsoi instead of spears and danced incidents from the legend of Dionysus.[216] Athenaeus' source seems to think this an improvement, and praises the high quality of the lyrics that accompany the dance. But it was nevertheless a fundamental change of style, and one of which Plato would not approve. This change seems to have set in as early as the fifth century, for among

---

[212] Séchan, *op.cit.* 97.   [213] Athen. 631c.
[214] Latte, *op.cit.* 32f.; Lys. XXI, 4; Isaeus v, 36.
[215] For the details of this degeneration, see Latte, *op.cit.* 40ff.
[216] Athen. 631ab.

the reliefs of this period are occasional representations of satyrs armed with shields, or carrying fawnskins and phallic-shaped spears.[217] This points to a mingling of the pyrrhic with the satyr dance, a mixture easily understood because both dances were characterized by speed.[218] And if some elements of the populace showed a taste for this mixture, there were certainly poets and musicians who would not be above catering to them.[219] It is safe to say that Plato, like Aristophanes, took a dim view of such innovations. If the purpose of Plato's remark in the passage just quoted is to protect the pyrrhic dance from corruption by satyric or Bacchic elements, then we can understand the prescription that the movements of the limbs must for the most part be in a straight line. A comparison of the surviving representations of the pyrrhic dance with the reliefs and vase paintings portraying dances of satyrs, Bacchae, maenads, and the like, shows the surprising aptness of Plato's technical criterion.[220]

Of the nonwarlike (εἰρηνική) but serious dances there are many particular forms; and in each case, Plato says, we must ask whether the dance presents the grace of bodily movement and the nobility of sentiment that is appropriate to law-abiding men (815b). But before proceeding further he says it is necessary to draw a line between dancing that is questionable in nature (ἀμφισβητουμένη) and that which is above criticism. "All Bacchic dances, and those of a similar nature, in which, while celebrating certain rites of purification, the dancers 'imitate,' as the phrase is, drunken persons, calling them Nymphs, Pans, Sileni, and Satyrs—this kind of dancing is, as a whole, neither peaceful nor warlike, and it is hard to determine what its purpose is."[221] The interpretation of Plato's meaning and intention

---

[217] Latte, op.cit. 56ff.   [218] Athen. 630d.

[219] Such as Cinesias, one of these innovators whose reputation was none too savory among his contemporaries, to judge from the opinion of Aristophanes (*Frogs* 153), of Lysias (XXI, 20; cf. Athen. 551de), of Pherecrates (cited in Plut. *De Mus.* 30), and of Plato himself (*Gorg.* 501e).

[220] Compare, for example, the chorus of pyrrhic dancers on the Acropolis relief (Séchan, op.cit. Pl. IV, No. 2) and another similar chorus from a relief in the Vatican Museum (*ibid.* No. 3), with the Satyr and Bacchante from the Villa Albani (*ibid.* Fig. 34), the chorus of Bacchantes from a cup in the Berlin Museum (*ibid.* Fig. 32) and the Maenad and Silenus from a cup in the Wurzburg Museum (*ibid.* Fig. 41).

[221] 815c: ὅση μὲν βακχεία τ'ἐστὶν καὶ τῶν ταύταις ἑπομένων, ἃς Νύμφας τε καὶ Πᾶνας καὶ Σειληνοὺς καὶ Σατύρους ἐπονομάζοντες, ὥς φασιν, μιμοῦνται κατῳνωμένους, περὶ καθαρμούς τε καὶ τελετάς τινας ἀποτελούντων. . . . The antecedent of ταύταις (c2) is ὀρχήσεις, the plural implied in ὅση (sc. ὄρχησις). England's emendation αἷς (c3) is easier syntactically than the ἃς of the manuscripts, but the

here presents no little difficulty. "Bacchic dancing" must apparently be taken as including all dances associated with the worship of Dionysus, for Bacchus was his Lydian name and was used by the Greeks of Plato's time almost interchangeably with Dionysus. But the figures most intimately associated with Dionysus in his worship were the maenads, the frenzied women of his thiasoi, and it is to be noted that they are not mentioned in Plato's description. Whether this omission has any significance is a point that will concern us later. But along with the maneads in the vase paintings of Dionysiac rites there often occur representations of sileni and satyrs—creatures of the woodland, expressive of Dionysus' connection, as god of trees and vegetation, with the fructifying forces in nature—usually accompanied by a cup, or crater, or some other symbol of the intoxicating gift of Dionysus. We must conclude that it is especially the dances characteristic of these creatures that Plato regards as objectionable.

The typical satyr dance was the σίκιννις. The figures and movements of this dance, as portrayed on the vases, have been carefully studied by Festa;[222] and it included some features that would be offensive to modern taste. There is clear evidence that they were looked upon by the ancients also with some misgiving and distaste. The attitude of classical times can best be described as a mixture of disgust and religious respect, such as we find in Heraclitus. "If it were not to Dionysus that they made the procession and sang the phallic song, it would be a most disgraceful thing to do."[223] The phallos is one of the

---

latter yields the same sense, being taken as a cognate accusative after μιμοῦνται. Τῶν ταύταις ἐπομένων is more naturally taken as I have rendered it than as referring to practitioners of this dance; ἕπομαι is often used in Plato in the sense of "follow suit" or "resemble" (e.g. *Phaedr.* 239d, 240d, *Rep.* 406d; *Laws* 632c).

Τελεταί does not imply that Plato is thinking of secret or mystery cults; the term means simply "rites" and "may be used of any kind of religious ceremony, though it is applied mostly to rites in which the prime purpose is not to worship the gods, but to procure peace for the soul of the participant" (I. M. Linforth, *The Arts of Orpheus*, University of California Press, 1941, 68).

[222] Vincenzo Festa, *Sikinnis: Storia di un' antica danza*, in *Memorie della Reale Accademia di Archeologia, Lettere e Belle Arti di Napoli*, III, 1918, 2nd part, 35-74.

[223] Fr. 127, Bywater. Cf. Arist. *Nic. Eth.* 1128a 18ff. and *Poet.* 1449a 11ff. There is also the evidence of linguistic usage; αἰδοῖα often seems to be used as a euphemism for φάλλος, and this substitute word is itself packed with ambivalence. The source of this part of Dionysiac worship is still a riddle. There is no trace of phallic worship in Minoan-Mycenaean religion. But evidences of it are rather abundant in the cult of Artemis in the Peloponnesus, hence it can hardly be explained entirely as an importation from Asia Minor, though it was re-enforced later by the cult of Priapus, whose origin seems to have been northwestern Asia Minor. See Nilsson I, 560.

oldest symbols connected with Dionysus, and phallic processions formed a part of almost every Dionysiac festival in Attica, not only of the rural Dionysia, but also of the city festivals, the Lenaea and the Greater Dionysia.[224] Phallic dances were a feature of festivals elsewhere in Greece, particularly those associated with the worship of Artemis in the Peloponnesus.[225] There is no evidence that these were called Bacchic, but their spirit was similar, and Plato's language seems intended to include them.

Clearly the dances described here cannot be fitted into Plato's classification. Being concerned with rites of purification, they can hardly be relegated to the class of common and trivial dances. But they do not belong in either of the species of serious dancing; they are not war dances, nor can they be classed as ἐμμέλειαι, because they lack the grace and self-restraint that are characteristic of these dances, which Plato describes immediately afterwards. Why then does Plato not consider them a third species of serious dancing? His reason cannot be merely reluctance to disturb the traditional classification that he is following; but what it is we can only guess. "Probably the best thing we can do is to say that this kind of dancing is οὐ πολιτικόν and let it be" (ἐάσαντας κεῖσθαι, 815d). This is a cryptic statement, and it is tempting to interpret οὐ πολιτικόν as meaning "not fitted for our city (or our citizens), i.e. uncivilized."[226] In this case these dances should be excluded. But Plato does not exclude them; instead we are to let them be, and proceed to matters that especially concern us, viz. the two recognized species of serious dances. Again, it would be rather odd if Plato's intention is to prohibit all Bacchic dances, for we have seen that he defends Dionysus' gift of wine to men as an act of beneficence, not vengeance, and even gives his name to the chorus of elders who are to be the arbiters of musical and moral taste in the community. An interpretation alternative to the usual one is suggested by the use of πολιτικόν in writers of the fifth and fourth centuries to distinguish what belongs to the province of the statesman, as distinct from private and religious matters.[227] The statement would then mean that the regulation of such dancing is not within our responsibilities as legislators.[228] It is obvious that,

---

[224] Nilsson I, 557ff.　　　　　[225] Nilsson I, 150.
[226] As do Jowett, Taylor, England, Diès and Robin.
[227] See LSJ s.v. πολιτικός III and IV. The distinction between ὅσιον and πολιτικόν is sometimes emphasized by Plato (e.g. 697c).
[228] For this interpretation, see also Linforth, op.cit. (Note 106), 161n.

despite the questionable character of these dances, Plato hesitates to legislate against them; and this hesitation may be due to a reluctance to lay hands upon long-established religious practices. We shall see in the next chapter that in the sphere of religious observance the statesman has to follow ancient traditions as interpreted by religious officers whose authority is independent of his. Both Plato and Aristotle recognize that many things are permitted in connection with Dionysiac worship that would not ordinarily be regarded as proper, and they appear to acquiesce.

It may even be that the passage we are considering means to define as questionable only pseudo-Bacchic—i.e. satyr—dances.[229] The kind of dancing that historians of Greek religion regard as essential in the worship of Dionysus was the ecstatic and frenzied dancing of the maenads, whose effect was to produce a release of the personality from conventional restraints, and its identification, for a short time at least, with divinity itself. Such Bacchic dancing is represented on dozens of vases showing maenads, with thyrsoi and fawnskins, with torches and cult symbols, in varying degrees of excitement or intoxication, sometimes falling completely exhausted into the arms of their companions.[230] The omission of maenads from Plato's description may indicate that he has no intention of questioning this kind of religious dancing. In the *Phaedrus* (244e, 265b) "telestic madness" inspired by Dionysus is proclaimed as a divine gift that brings blessings to those who have experienced it. This must be taken seriously, for there is other evidence that Plato, like Aristotle, recognizes the value of such orgiastic dances and music, both as effecting cures of certain emotional disorders and as providing an intrinsically satisfying religious experience.[231] Yet even if such dances are not socially or morally objectionable, they would still fall outside Plato's classificatory scheme.

For the second species of "noble dancing" ($\kappa\alpha\lambda\grave{\eta}$ $\check{o}\rho\chi\eta\sigma\iota\varsigma$) Plato

[229] The passage is quoted in Note 221. "$O\sigma\eta$ $\beta\alpha\kappa\chi\epsilon\acute{\iota}\alpha$ may be intended to be restricted by the following phrase $\kappa\alpha\grave{\iota}$ $\tau\hat{\omega}\nu$ $\kappa\tau\lambda$.

[230] For the evidence, see Lillian B. Lawler, *The Maenads: A Contribution to the Study of the Dance in Ancient Greece*; in *Memoirs of the American Academy in Rome* VI, 1927, 69-110. The wild beauty and mystic fervor of this part of the religion of Dionysus has been presented in imperishable fashion in Euripides' *Bacchae*. For the religious background of this play see the Introduction and Commentary in the edition of E. R. Dodds, Oxford, 1944.

[231] Dodds, *The Greeks and the Irrational*, 75ff.; Linforth, "Corybantic Rites in Plato," and "Telestic Madness in Plato," in *Univ. of Cal. Publ. in Class. Phil.* XIII, 1944-1950, 121-172.

adopts with enthusiasm a traditional term, ἐμμέλεια, that he thinks particularly apt.²³² The adjective ἐμμελής occurs frequently in Plato's later dialogues. Its root meaning is "harmonious," or "graceful"; but in Plato's usage it seems always to carry an additional connotation of intellectual grace and moral elegance. The aptness of the traditional designation is made clear in the immediately preceding part of Plato's text. These are primarily religious dances ("dances in which men do honor to the gods"); they are dances of peace and expressive of a state of well-being, sometimes the lively sense of well-being that is experienced when men have just escaped from serious dangers or toils, and sometimes merely the more sober sense of existent blessings and desire for their continuance and increase. These dances will therefore differ in liveliness, and such variety Plato regards as natural. But there is also the quality of the soul to be considered. A man whose character is "exercised in courage" (πρὸς ἀνδρείαν γεγυμνασμένον) will express his feelings less violently than the undisciplined man (ἀγύμναστος). It is essential, therefore, that the dance be in harmony (ἐμμελής) with the emotions that a good man would feel. In dances of the livelier sort, restraint is especially called for, lest the dancer express the coward's rather than the brave man's character, or lapse into unseemliness and vulgarity. The canons of the traditional ἐμμέλειαι seemed to Plato to embody this principle of harmony, and to have consecrated it through long-established usage. They are dances of rejoicing, expressive of external prosperity (ὀρχήσεις τῶν εὖ πραττόντων); but they are restrained, as befits men who practice moderation in their enjoyments (ὄντων μετρίων πρὸς τὰς ἡδονάς, 816b).

Plato does not name any particular dances here, but we can infer what he has in mind from other passages and from what we know of the rich development of this type of dancing among the Greeks. Hymns to the gods form a part of every sacrifice in Plato's state (799ab), and it is clear that these sacrificial hymns are intended to be accompanied by dancing of some sort, even if only expressive gestures or a solemn march.²³³ The dance thus becomes a form of corporeal prayer, as Séchan puts it,²³⁴ whereby the sentiments of the

---

²³² 816b. England translates: "How correctly and how like a true musician he gave the name, whoever he was, and how philosophically he assigns to the whole class the name ἐμμέλειαι." England also calls attention to the association of ἐμμέλεια with musical taste and philosophic insight in *Soph.* 259e. Cf. 757a.

²³³ "Hymns are sometimes danced, sometimes not," says Athenaeus (631d).

²³⁴ Séchan, *op.cit.* 118.

songs and music are translated into postures and movements of the body, and the whole man, body as well as soul, becomes permeated with religious feeling. Of the religious hymns in Plato's Greece the paean easily held first place. It was originally addressed to Apollo, the Healer, grave and stately in rhythm, yet joyous.[235] There was a tradition, as we have seen, that the paean was introduced into Sparta by Thaletas of Crete.[236] Sung in the Dorian mode and dedicated to the god especially honored among the Dorians, the paean was particularly cultivated at Sparta,[237] but became a feature of practically all feasts of Apollo throughout Greece. So great was the popularity of this form that the paean came to be regarded as appropriate for other gods as well, and was sung to Zeus the Savior, to Artemis, to Poseidon, and even to Dionysus.[238] Plato's admiration for the paean is evident from references in other dialogues.[239] One of the three choruses in the *Laws* is called the chorus of Apollo, and there is a reference to Apollo Παιάν in the brief description of its performances (664c). The paean certainly would be classed by Plato among the ἐμμέλειαι.

We can be equally sure of the dithyramb. This was originally a hymn to Dionysus. First developed at Corinth and cultivated especially among the Dorians, it was brought to Athens in the sixth century, where it reached the height of its development and attained a popularity that outlasted the changes of taste at the end of the fifth century.[240] Competitions of dithyrambic choruses were a part of the Dionysiac festivals, and some of the greatest fifth-century poets, such as Simonides, Pindar, and Bacchylides, took part in these competitions. Similar dithyrambic contests were held at the Thargelian festival of Apollo, and at the Lesser Panathenaea, the Prometheia, and

---

[235] Reinach in ds s.v. Paean, 266f.; Nilsson 1, 147, 512; *Iliad* 1, 472-474.

[236] The connection with Crete is emphasized also in the Homeric *Hymn to Pythian Apollo* 516ff.

[237] It was chanted at the Gymnopaediae (Athen. 678c) and marked the climax of the Hyacinthia (Xen. *Hell.* iv, v, 11; *Ages.* ii, 17).

[238] Reinach, *loc.cit.* Among the Athenians the paean was sung to Asclepius, who had taken Apollo's place as the god of healing; August Mommsen, *Feste der Stadt Athen im Altertum*, Leipzig, 1898, 435. Paeans were sometimes sung to outstanding men, such as the paean addressed by the Samians to Lysander after the battle of Aegospotami. The Athenians had more reverence for the original usage; Aristotle was indicted for impiety in 323 for having written, it was alleged, a paean to Hermeias of Atarneus (Athen. 696a-e).

[239] In *Ion* 534d Socrates praises the paean of Tynnichus of Chalcis: "it is about the finest of our songs." Cf. also *Crit.* 108c.

[240] Pickard-Cambridge, *Dithyramb, Tragedy and Comedy*; Castets in ds s.v. Dithyrambus. Plato refers to its connection with Dionysus in 700b.

the Hephaestia. Its chants were of a passionate character, sung in the Phrygian mode, and they depicted incidents from the story of Dionysus, not dramatically, but "in the words of the poet himself," as Plato puts it in the *Republic*. Socrates approves of this form of artistic representation, and the Phrygian mode is one of the two which he retains for his city.[241] In the *Laws* the dithyramb is mentioned as one of the classical forms cultivated in its purity in the older days at Athens before degeneration had set in (700b).

Another type of song and dance mentioned in Plato's account of the festivals is ἐγκώμια, songs in praise of the gods and of famous men (801e). This is clearly a reference to metrical compositions of the type of which Pindar's odes are an outstanding example. But it may be that Plato has in mind not particularly the odes of Pindar or Bacchylides, but such songs as those of the maidens of Delos, so beautifully described in the Homeric *Hymn to Delian Apollo*, for something like their singing is prescribed as part of the funeral rites for a dead euthynos.[242] Similar encomia will be sung to "heroes," i.e. great men of the past whose memory is honored by sanctuaries and periodic rites (801e); and even to living citizens, men and women who have achieved special distinction (829c; cf. 802a).

There is more doubt about the lament (θρῆνος), another recognized form of poetic art (cf. 700b). The threnos was of ancient origin, and it is probable that compositions written in this form in Plato's day did not differ essentially from those of Homeric times. One or more persons, generally close relatives of the dead, were the "leaders of the laments" (θρήνων ἔξαρχοι); they sang lamentations in turn, the rest of those present joining in at intervals in a refrain of woe.[243] Such lugubrious performances are definitely forbidden at funerals in Plato's state (947b, 960a); and at a public sacrifice it is nothing less than blasphemy to have a chorus rack the souls of the listeners with dolorous words and melodies (800d). If compositions of this sort must be heard on occasion (and Plato seems to think they must), it should not be on festival days, but on "days of ill omen" (ἡμέραι

---

[241] *Rep.* 394c, 399a.

[242] After the body has been laid out in a public place, two choruses of fifteen members each—a chorus of maidens on one side of the bier and a chorus of young men on the other—shall alternate in singing hymns of praise, "blessing him with their songs the whole day long" (947c). Cf. the *Hymn to Delian Apollo*, 156-161.

[243] Lécrivain in DS s. v. Funus, 1369, 1373. For the Homeric θρῆνος, see *Iliad* XXII, 408ff.; XXIV, 719ff.

ἀποφράδες)—such as those set apart for the rites of Pluto[244]—and would better be performed, not by citizens, but by hired foreign choirs (800e). Many of the choral odes in Greek tragedy are θρῆνοι and obviously would be excluded from ἐμμέλειαι, as Plato understood the term. Whether they would be forbidden depends on the treatment of tragedy, to which we shall come later.

Women as well as men play a part in the religious dancing at these festivals, as indeed was the custom generally in Greece. But the legislator, Plato declares, must be careful to assign his songs and dances appropriately, i.e. in accordance with the natural differences between the two sexes. The women's dances must be in harmony with the feminine type, which inclines to modesty and sedateness (802de). These words suggest the partheneia, or dances of maidens, another of those creations of ancient choral art at Sparta under the leadership of Alcman and his colleagues. These dances were especially associated with Dorian lands, but the art seems to have spread throughout Greece during the sixth and fifth centuries. Its remains at Athens are particularly impressive, for the partheneia had a strong and understandable attraction for the ancient artists. Some of the representations of them in the surviving reliefs and vase paintings are among the most delightful and deeply moving examples we have of Hellenic dignity and grace.[245] Another type that Plato might well have included is the dance of the Caryatides, the young women at the Spartan feast of Artemis Caryatis.[246] This dance—performed, so we are told, by young girls of the best families—was a very lively one, with short steps and pirouettes, and executed on the tips of the toes. Its gaiety and grace were such as to make it popular elsewhere in Greece and likewise a favorite subject for the artist. This would indeed be an appropriate dance for the rural festivals with their choruses of young men and young women (772a).[247]

[244] Plato emphasizes the joyous aspect of religion and shows a marked distaste for the chthonic elements of worship; see Chapter VIII, The Gods and their Worship.

[245] For example, the Athenian reliefs reproduced in Séchan, *op.cit.* Pl. vi. Nos. 1 and 2; and the painting on an Athenian crater now at the Villa Giulia (*ibid.* No. 3).

[246] Séchan, *op.cit.* 134ff.

[247] Plato does not mention the hyporcheme, another of those contributions to Spartan culture attributed to the Cretan Thaletas, though Delos has perhaps a better claim to be its birthplace (Reinach in ds s.v. 352ff.; Lucian *The Dance* 16; cf. the Homeric *Hymn to Delian Apollo* 156). In the hyporcheme only a part of the chorus danced, while the others chanted a lively and joyful ode. From Crete and Delos it spread to continental Greece—to Delphi, Thebes, and especially Lacedaemon. It fell

These dances we can assume, with more or less certainty, to be included in Plato's class of ἐμμέλειαι. But according to Pickard-Cambridge the term covered a much wider variety of dances, "ranging from the fine serenity of the Colonus ode to the raging of the Furies and the ecstatic devotions of the Bakchai, adapting itself to every kind and degree of emotion, and presenting every form of lyric beauty."[248] If Pickard-Cambridge is right in this interpretation, Plato's use of the term is much stricter than was customary in his day. For we have seen that he is inclined to exclude the threnos, and definitely puts the dances of the Bacchae outside his classificatory scheme. Ἐμμέλεια means for him not merely harmony between character and the expressive words and movements of the choric performance, but especially harmony between a noble character and the words and gestures used to express it. This form of dance is described, in summary, as the χορεία of "fair bodies and noble souls" (816d).

Contrasted with this serious dancing is that which represents "unseemliness of body and mind," more particularly that kind "which aims at the ridiculous and the comic."[249] In an earlier passage, it will be recalled, Plato has said that there are two subspecies of the "common" (φαῦλον) kind of dancing; but when its turn comes to be discussed only comic dancing is mentioned, without any explicit distinction of types within it. It appears that the formal division announced in 814e is not carried out. The only way to retain it is to regard the satyr dance discussed above as the other subspecies of common dancing. This is not too implausible, for the satyr dance described in 815c is that associated with religious rites, and its use on other occasions—for example, in the satyr play that usually concluded a tragic trilogy at the great dramatic festivals—would put it definitely in the sphere of the legislator's competence. If this is Plato's intention he could properly assume that his readers would take comic dances as referring both to satyr plays and to comedies in the narrower sense of the word, thus supplying the two subspecies he has announced.

---

into decadence at the end of the fifth century, though it continued to be cultivated at Sparta. *Ion* 534c shows that Plato was well acquainted, as we should expect, with its distinctness as a form of choral composition.

[248] Pickard-Cambridge, *The Dramatic Festivals of Athens*, 259.

[249] 816d: τὰ τῶν αἰσχρῶν σωμάτων καὶ διανοημάτων καὶ τῶν ἐπὶ τὰ τοῦ γέλωτος κωμῳδήματα τετραμμένων. If we take comic dancing to be the second of the two species of disreputable dancing, the phrase καὶ τῶν ἐπὶ κτλ gives its specific differentia within the genus τὰ τῶν αἰσχρῶν which precedes.

The ancient authorities are unanimous in asserting that the dance peculiarly characteristic of comedy was the κόρδαξ.[250] It was a solo dance, vulgar and even obscene in character. The ancient writers describe it as φορτικός, αἰσχρός, ἀσχήμων.[251] Theophrastus says that to dance it when not drunk was the mark of a man who had lost all sense of decency.[252] It was too vulgar for Aristophanes, who prides himself that he has not introduced it into the *Clouds*.[253] This dance, with others similar to it (the μόθων, the καλλαβίς, and the καρυδᾶν), apparently had its origin in the Peloponnesus as a part of the magical fertility rites practised by the pre-Dorian peoples. The Dorian invaders at first adopted it, but later, as its religious significance disappeared, abandoned it to the lower strata of the population. In the meantime it had contributed to the birth of comic drama at Corinth and at Megara, and it continued to be an important constituent of comedy until its use was restricted by Aristophanes. As a "dance for porters and sailors," and for drunken revelries in private life, it maintained itself through all the classical period.[254] It may also have been practised by the country folk at the rural festivals of Dionysus in Attica and elsewhere, and probably was a part of the "jests from the wagons" at the Dionysiac feasts at Athens. That Plato had such spectacles in mind we know from an earlier reference by Megillus to the shameful excesses he had witnessed at Athens and at Tarentum at the feast of Dionysus.[255]

But it is not merely these riotous accompaniments of Dionysiac festivals that Plato has in mind here, and not only the indecent dances that formed an incidental feature of comic performances. The word "comedy" seems to serve as a stimulus to enlarge the range of his

[250] Poll. IV, 99; Aristox. in FHG II, 283-284; schol. to Aristoph. *Clouds* 540; Lucian *The Dance* 26; Athen. 630e.

[251] Athen. 631d; schol. to Aristoph. *Clouds* 540; Dem. II, 18. For the history of this dance and a reconstruction of its σχήματα, see Heinz Schnabel, *Kordax: Archäologische Studien zur Geschichte eines Antiken Tanzes und zum Ursprung der Griechischen Komödie*, Munich, 1910.

[252] *Char.* VI, 3.

[253] Line 540. The scholiast, however, points out that he did bring it into the *Wasps*, probably referring to the drunken dance of Philocleon at the end (1474ff.).

[254] Schnabel, *op.cit.* esp. 62ff.

[255] 637ab. The sacred marriage of Dionysus with the wife of the king was celebrated on the second day of the Anthesteria. A cart carrying the god led the procession and was followed by wagons whose riders engaged in revelry and shouted scurrilous and insulting jokes at one another and the crowd. Similar σκώμματα ἐκ τῶν ἁμαξῶν occurred at the Lenaean festival.

consideration to embrace the whole of comic representations—"all mimicry, whether by words, song, or dance, presented in comic fashion."[256] One of the characteristic features of comedy, in ancient as in modern times, is its addiction to personal ridicule and invective. This was especially marked in fifth-century Athenian comedy, with its unrestrained satire of public figures and public policies. The glorious days of the Old Comedy were past when Plato wrote the *Laws*; even Aristophanes in the later part of his career was forced, by law or public opinion, to limit the range of his satire. But personal invective—sometimes veiled, sometimes open (ὀνομαστί)—was still the fashion, though directed less toward public officials than to persons prominent in private life. The philosophers were a favorite target of fourth-century comedy, and Plato and the Academy received special attention.[257] The comedy that we know of elsewhere in Greece was similarly inclined. The Spartans had an ancient type of comic sport, Sosibius reports, in which ridicule of selected individuals played an important part.[258] The farces known as φλύακες in southern Italy, a more developed form of comedy than the Spartan, were travesties of heroic legends, probably interspersed with ridicule of contemporary figures.[259] Now ridicule, even in jest, Plato says later, is a form of abuse; and when prompted by malice it not only arouses enmity and hatred in its object, but degrades the man who indulges in it (934e-935b). We must therefore curb the "readiness of comic writers to ridicule their fellow men" (935d), if we wish to preserve friendship and gentlemanliness among our citizens.[260] Aristotle in the *Ethics* echoes Plato's thought: "The mark of him who jests well is the fact that his jests are appropriate to a free man, a man of culture." Aristotle further remarks, again echoing Plato, that the jest is a form of abuse; the law has forbidden certain kinds of abuse, and perhaps it should also forbid certain kinds of jests.[261]

[256] 816d: κατὰ λέξιν τε καὶ ᾠδὴν καὶ κατὰ ὄρχησιν καὶ κατὰ τὰ τούτων πάντων μιμήματα κεκωμῳδημένα. I follow England in taking τούτων πάντων as a subjective genitive.

[257] A long fragment of Epicrates (Athen. 59d-f) ridicules the practice of "divisions" in the Academy; Aristophon wrote a comedy entitled Πλάτων (Athen. 552e), and the *Shipwrecked* of Ephippus also made fun of Plato and his disciples (Athen. 509bc). These are obvious examples of what the schol. to Aristoph. *Acharn.* 67 calls ὀνομαστὶ κωμῳδεῖν.

[258] Athen. 621de. These comic actors, or mummers, were called δεικηλισταί. Plutarch (*Ages.* 21) shows that the term was not a complimentary one.

[259] W. Christ, *Gesch. der Griech. Litteratur*, Nördlingen, 1889, 411f.; F. Susemihl, *Gesch. der Griech. Litteratur in der Alexandrinerzeit*, Leipzig, 1891, I, 235-243.

[260] Cf. *Rep.* 390a.   [261] *Nic. Eth.* 1128a 20-31.

Nevertheless comedy is not excluded from Plato's state; in fact it is a necessary part of the citizen's education.[262] "For it is impossible to know serious things without becoming acquainted with the ridiculous, or to know any one of two contraries without knowing the other."[263] But it is equally impossible for a man to imitate both the serious and the comic (or vulgar) life. Hence Plato prescribes that comic representations, though allowed, shall always be performed by slaves or foreign professionals; no citizen is to take them seriously (except as representations of conduct to be avoided) or spend time learning to do them. Presumably the same requirement holds for satyr dances and satyr plays. Furthermore, there must always be some element of novelty in the production—probably, as Bury comments, "lest the public taste should be debased by the repeated exhibition of any one piece of vulgarity."[264] In this prescription Plato seems to be following, whether wittingly or not, the practice of the Spartans, among whom the κόρδαξ and the μόθων were dances of the Helots and other subject elements of the population; and it may have been, as Plutarch reports, a deliberate policy of the Spartans to use the drunken dances of the Helots as a deterring example to their young men.[265] Plato's law here implies a more sophisticated doctrine of imitation than he had expressed in the *Republic*. There the witnessing of unseemly dramatic imitations is forbidden, as well as participation in them; but here it is implied that the spectators of such performances, when they have a strong sense of their superiority to the performers, are more likely to despise than to imitate.[266] As for the

[262] 816d: ἀνάγκη μὲν θεάσασθαι καὶ γνωρίζειν (sc. τὰ κωμῳδήματα). Bury, Taylor, and Robin have missed the sense of this passage, interpreting it as meaning only that the legislator must know these comic imitations. The following γὰρ clause indicates that what is necessary is that the citizens should come to know the comic if they are to understand serious matters. Apelt and Jowett have the correct rendering.

[263] "The science of contraries is one" was an ἔνδοξον accepted by both Plato and Aristotle. Cf. Arist. *Top.* 104a 15.

[264] II, 97n.

[265] *Lyc.* 28; it was a Spartan custom to make their Helots drunk, then bring them into the eating halls and have them dance and sing indecently, in order to show the young men what drunkenness leads to.

[266] Yet the *Republic* contains intimations of the later doctrine; e.g. 396a. Aristotle would have handled this problem differently, to judge from his provisional statement of principles in *Pol.* 1336b 2ff.: indecent pictures and speeches should be completely banished from the stage, and the young should not be allowed to be spectators of comedy until they have reached the age at which their education will have armed them against its evil influences.

element of ridicule in comic performances, Plato prescribes that the
composer of a comedy, or a lampoon, or any other form of song,
shall be strictly forbidden to ridicule a citizen upon pain of being
banished from the state (935e).[267] Citizens, however, are allowed to
make fun of one another, and may even be given permission to deliver lampoons at the public festivals, but only if it is done in jest,
without malice (936ab; cf. 829cd). The educator has the responsibility of deciding, in each case, whether this condition has been met.

Nor does Plato exclude the "jests from the wagons," which so
shocked Megillus at the Athenian Dionysia (637ab). "Such practices
are to be approved (ἐπαινετά)," the Athenian replies, "when done
with restraint (ὅπου τινὲς ἔνεισι καρτερήσεις); otherwise they are
rather stupid (βλακικώτερα)." Concerning the motives for Plato's
approval we can only speculate. Perhaps it was respect for long-established customs connected with certain festivals. Aristotle, whose
canons of censorship seem to have been even sterner than Plato's,
makes an exception for "those gods at whose festivals the law permits even ribaldry."[268] Or perhaps it was a recognition of the human
need for occasional release from the bonds of convention and of the
benefit which such release confers.[269] Or even more probably (and
this is the suggestion that comes from the immediate context of
the passage) Plato looks upon these revels as presenting opportunities, like those afforded by the use of wine at symposia, for the
practice of self-control. In any case, the citizens must have the moral
fiber to witness and participate in them with restraint.

After comedy Plato turns his attention to tragedy, which in our
eyes was the crowning glory of the great festivals at Athens. Tragedy
is permitted in Plato's state, but grudgingly, as it were, and under
strict control. Plato frankly recognizes its power to mold public
opinion and manners (658d; 838c). Unlike the comedians, the tragic
poets are serious (σπουδαῖοι) and inspired (θεῖοι);[270] and Plato the
lawgiver pays them the high compliment of regarding them as his

[267] Here it is obviously assumed that the comic poet, as well as the performers,
will be slaves or foreign professionals. One of the items of the indictment that Cleon
brought against Aristophanes was that he had ridiculed the Athenians before foreigners, i.e. in a play performed at the Greater Dionysia, when numerous visitors
were present in the city to enjoy the festival (schol. to Aristoph. *Acharn.* 378). How
much worse would it have seemed if their ridicule had proceeded from the mouths
of foreign troupers! Plato's provision here is decidedly an expression of current
Hellenic feeling. Cf. Isoc. VIII, 14.
[268] *Pol.* 1336b 16f.   [269] Cf. *Phaedr.* 265a.
[270] 817a. On the meaning of θεῖος, here and elsewhere, see Chapter VIII, Note 33.

rivals. "We ourselves are the authors of a tragedy of the fairest and noblest sort we can conceive; that is, our constitution has been set up as an imitation of the fairest and noblest life, and this, we assert in all earnestness, is the truest tragedy" (817b). A serious legislator therefore cannot lightly allow his rivals to set up their tents in the market place and seduce the populace (δημηγορεῖν . . . πρὸς τὸν ὄχλον) with their dulcet tones and voices louder than his.[271] Since their themes are the same, viz. the duties of citizens and the institutions of the state, he must at least be assured that their teaching will not contradict his own, as the tragic dramas so often do. The tragic poet must therefore first exhibit his chants (ᾠδαί, which here obviously carries Plato's familiar implication of "enchantments") before the officials. If they find that his teaching is the same as that of the law, or even better, he will be granted a chorus; otherwise not (817d).

Despite this appearance of drastic censorship, the procedure Plato proposes is—formally, at least—quite similar to that followed at Athens. To produce a tragedy the author first had to be granted a chorus—by the archon eponymous for the Dionysia, by the king for the Lenaea. Who are the officials who will perform the corresponding function in Plato's state? The term ἄρχοντες, when used without further qualification, can usually be taken as referring to the guardians, who as we saw discharge many of the duties assigned to the archons at Athens. But Plato's language indicates that the decision is to rest not with a single official, but with the board of guardians— or perhaps with that part of the board, including the educator, referred to as the chorus of Dionysus. The use of the familiar phrase "granting a chorus" suggests that in Plato's state, as at Athens, the chorus and actors would be citizens; and if this is so, it implies that tragedy of the proper sort is not unworthy of study by the citizen. It is even suggested, it will be noted, that a tragic poet might actually present a conception of life loftier than that embodied in the legislator's drama. So far has Plato retreated from the position he took in the *Republic*.[272]

[271] 817c. A reference to the tragedians' appeal to the emotions, which are always more vociferous than law and reason (cf. *Rep.* 604b-605b).

[272] The graphic language (817a) in which Plato describes the tragic poets as inquiring whether they will be permitted to enter the city with their poetry would, if taken literally, imply that tragedies, like comedies, are to be written and performed by foreigners. It is tempting to interpret it thus. Athens was the chief source of dramatic art in the fourth century, and it would be Athenian tragedians who would

To understand Plato's assertion that the teaching of the tragic dramatists is "for the most part" utterly contradictory to his own (817c) we need only refer to his criticism of the poets in the *Republic*, substituting references to the dramatists for his citations of Homer. We have already noted that he has no place for the threnos, or song of lamentation; but such threnodies by the chorus, and passages of lamentation in the actors' speeches, are a striking feature of Attic tragedy. In the *Republic* Plato had sternly condemned this misrepresentation of the heroic nature (387ff.); and many a modern reader has had the same sense of unreality when reading, for example, the *Ajax* or the *Trachinian Women*. Are these really the great Ajax and Heracles, these men who trouble deaf heaven with their bootless cries? Something is seriously lacking here of the usual Hellenic restraint. For Plato this is more than a lapse of aesthetic taste; it is a misrepresentation of the heroic nature and a definite violation of one of his canons of literary criticism, viz. that the artist should present his subject truly. Greek tragedy not only gives an imperfect imitation of the tragic hero; it often fails equally to present truly the nature of the gods, according to the canons of theology laid down in the *Republic*.[273] The shady conduct of Apollo in Euripides' *Ion*, the wrathful and deceptive vengeance of Artemis in *Hippolytus*, the savagery and jealousy of Zeus in the *Prometheus* of Aeschylus—these and other episodes in the great tragedies must have seemed merely travesties of the divine nature as Plato conceived it, made all the more inappropriate because these representations were part of a religious festival. Again, it is safe to say that few of the extant tragedies would satisfy Plato's criterion that the just life should be portrayed as leading to happiness.[274] Not many modern critics would agree with Plato that dramatic art should be subjected to such a restriction; but it helps us further to understand Plato's curious reluctance to applaud what is for us one of the greatest achievements of the Greek genius. Finally, we must remember that our knowledge of ancient tragedy is comparatively limited, for the little more than a score of plays that have been preserved are but a small fraction of the evidence on which Plato formed his judgment. It is beyond question that this

be requesting permission to enter Plato's Cretan colony. But in the light of the other details in the text it is more plausible to take this as merely a dramatic touch, paralleling the very similar passage in *Rep.* 398ab.

[273] 380a, 381d, and 383b make specific references to passages in lost dramas of Aeschylus in which Plato thought such misrepresentation occurred.

[274] 660e; cf. *Rep.* 392b.

evidence included many crude and highly objectionable pieces that have been lost to us.[275]

No Greek festival would have been regarded as complete without its contests, more or less elaborately organized according to the importance of the occasion and the wealth and skill of the participants. The Greek passion for competition, in which the individual had an opportunity to demonstrate his superiority in some area of mental or bodily excellence, was a heritage of the heroic age which persisted through all classical times.[276] Thus in Plato's state there are to be contests, both in music and gymnastics (796d, 829b-834d), with prizes for the winners. The importance of this aspect of the festivals is such that a special section in Plato's constitution (764c-765d) is concerned with the method of selecting the officers who supervise such contests.

There are to be two ἀθλοθέται in music, one for solo contests, the other for competitions of choruses. The former is to be not less than thirty years of age, the latter not less than forty, and each is to hold office for a year. They are to be selected by a combination of voting and the lot, in an assembly composed of "all those citizens who are amateurs of such matters" (765a). The guardians are to decide who comes under this designation and to impose fines for absence; but it appears that any persons who wish may attend and take part in the election. Ten persons are first chosen by show of hands from among the recognized experts (ἔμπειροι) in music. From this number, one is selected by lot, and when he has passed the scrutiny and his status as an ἔμπειρος has been established, he is to be the supervisor of choral contests for the ensuing year. The supervisor of solo performances is chosen in the same way.[277] It appears that these ath-

---

[275] We hear, for example, of various tragedies dealing with the theme of paederasty, which Plato—at least in his old age—regarded with unqualified disfavor. See J. A. Symonds, *A Problem in Greek Ethics*, London, 1901, 27ff. For Plato's attitude, see Ronald B. Levinson, *In Defense of Plato*, Harvard University Press, 1953, 81ff.

[276] Cf. *Iliad* VI, 208, where Glaucon recalls his father's parting injunction: "Always be first and show your superiority to others." The classical description of *der agonale Mensch* is Jakob Burckhardt's in *Griechische Kulturgeschichte*, Berlin, 1898-1902, IV, 86ff.

[277] 765bc: ὃς δ' ἂν εἰς ἐκ προχειροτονηθέντων δέκα λάχῃ, δοκιμασθείς, τὸν ἐνιαυτὸν τῶν χορῶν ἀρχέτω κατὰ νόμον. κατὰ ταὐτὰ δὲ τούτοις καὶ ταύτῃ ὁ λαχὼν τὸν ἐνιαυτὸν ἐκεῖνον τῶν ἀφικομένων εἰς κρίσιν μονῳδιῶν τε καὶ συναυλιῶν ἀρχέτω, εἰς τοὺς κριτὰς ἀποδιδοὺς ὁ λαχὼν τὴν κρίσιν. The interpretation of these lines has been a subject of controversy, for the details of which see England's notes. What is the pur-

lothetai are not judges; their responsibility is to select the contestants, to make arrangements for the competitions, and to preside over them on the appointed day. The decision among the contestants is the function of κριταί (765b) about whom nothing further is said.[278]

No doubt the details that Plato presupposes here could be supplied by his readers from their experience of Athenian life. We have little information about the procedure at Athens for selecting judges in such contests,[279] but it was probably similar to the method of select-

---

pose of the scrutiny? England supposes that it is to select the *best* of the ten persons elected by show of hands (the προχειροτονηθέντων δέκα), the only purpose of the lot being to determine the order in which they appear before the board of scrutiny. But this flagrantly contradicts Plato's previous statement (b2) that at the δοκιμασία the only point to be raised is whether the person examined is ἔμπειρος or ἄπειρος. Furthermore, the procedure Plato describes here is that which has already been prescribed for the selection of the council (756e), the astynomoi (763de), the agoranomoi (763e), and will shortly be prescribed for the other ἀθλοθέται (765c). In these other cases the lot selects a man to fill the office and the scrutiny confirms (or rejects) him by showing that he has (or has not) the necessary qualifications; that is obviously Plato's intention here also.

Another point in dispute is whether τῶν ἀφικομένων εἰς κρίσιν (b6) is dependent on the preceding ὁ λαχών, or object of ἀρχέτω in the following line. If we take it in the former way, since the total phrase of which it becomes a part is the parallel to ὃς δ' ἂν . . . λάχῃ (b3-4), it must mean "of those coming up for the judgment [of the lot]." It is unusual to have κλήρωσις imply κρίσις; and even if we allow it to do so in this case, κλήρωσις is not δοκιμασία. The ἀφικόμενοι, therefore, cannot be candidates for the scrutiny, but must be competitors in the contest; the meaning is that he on whom the lot has fallen (i.e. ὁ λαχών) presides for the coming year over those coming up in the solo competitions, as the previously elected officer does over choral contests.

Finally, how must we interpret εἰς τοὺς κριτὰς ἀποδιδοὺς ὁ λαχὼν τὴν κρίσιν (c1)? Taking κρίσις here in the same sense as in b7, it must mean "the decision [between the contestants]," and the phrase as a whole means that the designated athlothetes (ὁ λαχών, which looks suspiciously like an interpolation in the text here) does not himself determine the winner, but turns that function over to "the judges" (for this use of κριταί, see 949a). If it is taken as referring to the δοκιμασία which the λαχών must undergo, it not only introduces a different meaning of κρίσις (a meaning which it admittedly has in d1, but that is eight lines later), but also repeats unnecessarily what has already been said. England sees the tautology but refuses to accept the other interpretation, which he thinks would "stultify the whole description of these elections," for "the one most important function of these Presidents is undoubtedly to *judge* at the contests." But τὴν διάκρισιν ἱκανῶς ἀποδιδοὺς (765a 3-4), to which he refers, may simply denote the competence of the athlothetes to determine who shall be admitted to the competition, and I have interpreted it thus in my exposition. The only alternative is to follow Wagner and Schanz in rejecting εἰς τοὺς . . . τὴν κρίσιν; but such an extreme measure is justified only when demonstrably necessary, and I see no necessity for it here.

[278] The supervisory function is evident from ἄρχοντας and ἄρχων (764e 6), εἰσαγωγεύς (765a 2), ἄρχοντα καὶ διαθετῆρα (a4), and ἀρχέτω (b5, b7). For evidence that this supervision does not include the judging of contests, see the preceding note.

[279] In the singing contests at Sparta mentioned in Athen. 630f the prize was awarded by the commander of the troops concerned. Cf. Lyc. 1, 107.

ing judges for the dramatic contests of which Pickard-Cambridge has recently provided a plausible account.[280] After the choruses had been granted and the choregoi appointed, the council drew up a list of names, an equal number from each of the ten tribes. These names, separated according to tribes, were then placed in ten urns, which were sealed by the prytanies and the choregoi and deposited on the Acropolis. At the beginning of the contest these urns were placed in the theatre, the archon drew one name from each, and the ten persons designated took oath to give an impartial verdict. At the end of the contest each wrote his ranking of the contestants on a tablet. These were placed in an urn, from which the archon drew five at random, and by these five tablets the issue of the contest was decided. If Plato is presupposing some such procedure in his state, the athlothetai would doubtless perform the functions of the archon in the above account. When we recall Plato's concern for the maintenance of proper standards in music, it is at first surprising that he makes no provision to assure that the judges shall be persons of special competence. But the regulations discussed earlier in this section for the control of musical performances would certainly apply to these contests; hence the judges would be expected only to appraise the skill with which the various contestants execute these officially approved compositions. Plato's special concern shows itself here only in his insistence that the supervisors of musical contests be persons of recognized experience in these arts.

One passage toward the end of the *Laws* (949cd) appears to assume the familiar Athenian institution of the choregia, whereby the distinction (and the burden) of training and equipping the choruses required for the various festivals was assigned to the wealthier citizens. This is surprising, for it was only the great disparities of wealth at Athens which made this institution appropriate and tolerable, and one would have assumed that Plato intended to prevent such degrees of inequality in his own state. The choregia (and other liturgies) assumed by the wealthier citizens at Athens gave rise to considerable litigation; but there is no mention in Plato's law of the σκῆψις or ἀντίδοσις of Attic law by which a citizen could contest a liturgy placed upon him.[281] Except for the single passage referred to above, we could safely infer that it was Plato's intention to have the city treasury bear the expense of these contests. This policy was

---

[280] Pickard-Cambridge, *The Dramatic Festivals of Athens*, 96-100.
[281] Lipsius 588ff.

in fact introduced at Athens a half century after Plato's death under Demetrius of Phalerum.[282]

The selection of athlothetai for gymnastic contests is markedly different. These officials are chosen from the members of the second and third property classes, and all citizens belonging to the first three classes are required to attend the electing assembly, the members of the fourth class being excused. Twenty candidates are selected by the raising of hands, and from these three are chosen by lot and subjected to the scrutiny (765cd), which in this case can only be for the purpose of establishing that a candidate is in fact a citizen in good standing and a member of one of the two property classes mentioned. No technical qualifications seem to be necessary; probably any Greek with enough force of personality to be chosen by his fellow citizens could stage such a contest and preside over it effectively.[283] The reason for a property qualification is fairly obvious: the arranging of such contests is likely to involve a great deal of time and perhaps some expense, and the poorest class should not be asked to make this sacrifice. And Plato omits the first property class probably in order to equalize the burdens of public office. The first timema has just been made responsible for filling the offices of astynomos and temple treasurer (759e, 763d), and jointly responsible with the second class for the office of agoranomos (763e).

At Athens the responsibility for all the events occurring at any festival, whether musical or athletic, was borne by the official or officials in charge of the festival in question. The Dionysia and the Thargelia were under the archon, the Lenaea under the king, the funeral games under the polemarch, the quadrennial festivals (with the exception of the Panathenaea) under the ἱεροποιοί, and the Panathenaea were supervised by officials bearing the same title as Plato's. All these officers were chosen by lot at Athens, and all except the last held office for one year only, the athlothetai from one Panathenaic festival to the next.[284] The differences in the powers and responsibilities of these various officials were the result of historical circumstances. Plato's law (except insofar as it provides separate officials for musical contests) represents a decided simplification of Athenian

[282] Busolt-Swoboda 930.
[283] Cf. the account in Xenophon of the games arranged by the Ten Thousand when they reached Trebizond after their long and hazardous passage of the mountains (*Anab.* IV, viii, 25ff.).
[284] For these details, see Arist. *Const. Ath.* LIV, 6-7; LVI, 5; LVII, 1; LVIII, 1; LX, 1.

procedure. Demetrius of Phalerum went a step further in simplification by creating a single officer, the ἀγωνοθέτης, to be responsible for all the festivals and their contests.[285]

The program of athletic contests prescribed for Plato's festivals is of considerable interest, both for what it omits from the conventional schedule of Olympic and other Panhellenic games, and for what it adds.[286] We have already noted his contempt for the professional athlete and his conviction that gymnastic exercises should serve primarily the purpose of military training. Hence the prescription that only those contests are to be instituted that afford preparation for war. These are of two main sorts, contests of swiftness and contests of strength.[287] Running (δρόμος) was the oldest of all the familiar contests at Olympia and appears in Plato's program in an even greater variety of forms than was known in his time. The fundamental event is the στάδιον, a race from one end of the stadium to the other—a distance at Olympia of about 625 feet, at Delphi of about 580 feet. Second comes the δίαυλος, double the length of the stadium, the runners returning to their starting point. Third is the ἐφίππιος,[288] double the length of the δίαυλος; and fourth the δόλιχος, or "long race," a distance of probably twelve stadia, or six times the length of the stadium and back.[289] Lastly, Plato mentions two cross-country events, one a race between armed hoplites over a course of one hundred twenty stadia ("sixty stadia to a temple of Ares and back"), and the other between bowmen with their equipment running a distance of two hundred stadia ("one hundred stadia to a

[285] Busolt-Swoboda 930.

[286] Plato's program of athletic contests is presented most fully at 832d-834d; but cf. also 794c, 796a, 804c, 813de, 829bc and 830de. On the contests at Olympia and elsewhere, see Gardiner, *op.cit.* (Note 111); Schröder, *op.cit.* (Note 119); and J. H. Krause, *Die Gymnastik und Agonistik der Hellenen*, 2 vols., Leipzig, 1841, which is still very valuable, both for its documentation and for its interpretations.

[287] This distinction in athletic theory between δρόμος and ἰσχύς was a common one. Cf. Xen. *Const. Lac.* I, 1, 4; Arist. *Nic. Eth.* 1101b 16.

[288] Called also ἱππικός by the ancients. Both names derived from the fact that it was a length favored for horse races (cf. Paus. VI, xvi, 4, and Gardiner, *op.cit.* 270, 452); but there is no reference to horse racing at this part of Plato's text. The ἐφίππιος apparently was not on the Olympic program.

[289] The length of the δόλιχος is variously given by ancient authorities; for a good discussion of the evidence, see Krause, *op.cit.* 348. Its length was obviously some multiple of the length of the stadium (or of the hippodrome, which was twice the length of the stadium). It may have varied from place to place; but the adoption by the mathematicians of twelve stadia as the length of the δόλιχος (cf. Heron, *Geom.* IV, 13) seems to me decisive as to the most common usage.

temple of Apollo and Artemis and back"), over varied and mountainous country.[290] I think it likely that both of these are Plato's inventions. Running over open country does not seem to have been practised as a sport in Plato's time; it was used only for the speedy transmission of news or military orders.[291] There was a race known as the "hoplite," but it was a δίαυλος and took place in the stadium. In setting up these new races it seems that Plato appropriates this familiar name for one of them (ὁπλίτην ἐπονομάζοντες) and assigns a new name, the "bowman" (τοξότης), to its companion event.

The contestants in all these races, not merely the last two mentioned, are to run with arms; "no contest shall be set up for unarmed competitors" (834c). Races in armor were introduced into Greece about the middle of the sixth century.[292] In the early days the runners were fully armed, with helmet, shield, and greaves; in later times with shield and helmet only. Plato's text does not enable us to decide whether he intends to follow the older or the later style. The armed race at Olympia and at Athens was a δίαυλος;[293] Plato's extension of it to all contests in running is evidence of his serious concern with the development of military hardiness. The same intention is evident in his provision for three divisions of these races—one for boys (παῖδες), one for "beardless youth" (ἀγένειοι) and a third for men (ἄνδρες). This threefold division was found at the Isthmian and Nemean games, but at Olympia there were only two classes, boys and men.[294] For the ἀγένειοι Plato prescribes that the course in each event is to be two thirds the length set for the men, and for the boys one half—"whether they are racing as hoplites or as bowmen" (833c), a phrase which indicates a further distinction in the armed races between hoplites and light-armed runners.

Women as well as men are to take part in these contests. The στά-διον, δίαυλος, ἐφίππιος and δόλιχος are explicitly prescribed for

---

[290] The text of 833b is notoriously difficult; see England's note on b3. I follow Burnet's punctuation but reject Taylor's and Robin's supposition that Plato is describing a race between a hoplite and a bowman, the greater distance and the rougher terrain the latter has to cover balancing the heavier weight of the hoplite's armor. This seems to me an incredible kind of race. These must be two events, not one.

[291] Schröder, *op.cit.* 105; Herod. VI, 105; IX, 12. Cf. Plato, *Prot.* 335e and *Laws* 625d.

[292] Gardiner, *op.cit.* 285ff.; Schröder, *op.cit.* 107.

[293] Gardiner, *op.cit.* 287; Schröder, *op.cit.* 107. Elsewhere it may have been different.

[294] Gardiner, *op.cit.* 271-272.

them, but only two age divisions are indicated: girls below the age of puberty, and those between thirteen and twenty or the time of their marriage (833cd).[295] The younger ones are to run naked (γυμναί), the older ones "clad in decent apparel" (πρεπούσῃ στολῇ), probably a short chiton extending half way to the knees, like that in some of the representations of Spartan maidens racing, or perhaps the tight-fitting diaperlike garment portrayed on certain bronzes and vase paintings from the Peloponnesus.[296] Here Plato is obviously following the example of Sparta, which ran counter to the common Greek custom. The attention paid in the Lycurgan legislation to the athletic development of women and the scanty costume worn by Spartan maidens in these contests are well known.[297] It seems that Plato even out-Spartans the Spartans in requiring that these maidens run in armor; his motive in prescribing exercises for women was to produce not merely healthy mothers, but able defenders of the state.

Turning to the second sort of gymnastics, that which aims at developing strength (τὰ κατ' ἰσχύν), we find that Plato omits from his contests all the heavy events that figured in the Olympic program: viz. wrestling (πάλη), boxing (πυγμή), and the pancratium.[298] All of these were very ancient parts of the Olympic games and highly popular.[299] They were especially cultivated at Athens, which produced many victors in boxing and the pancratium, and was the home of some of the most celebrated masters of wrestling.[300] The importance of πάλη in Greek athletics is evident from the very word παλαίστρα. It was the final, and some think the most decisive, event in the pentathlon;[301] and there were also at Olympia separate contests in wrestling. The Spartans, who specialized in running and wrestling (apparently disdaining to contend in boxing and the pancratium), were highly proficient in these events. The first vic-

[295] In the races for girls at the Olympic Heraea the contestants were divided into three age groups (Paus. v, xvi, 2).

[296] There is a good discussion of this topic in Schröder, *op.cit.* 163ff.

[297] See Plut. *Lyc.* 14-15; Xen. *Const. Lac.* i, i, 4.

[298] Wrestling is explicitly rejected in 833d (ἀντὶ μὲν πάλης) and the others implicitly (καὶ τῶν τοιούτων τὰ νῦν ὅσα βαρέα). The pancratium is explicitly rejected in 834a, and boxing with ἱμάντες in 796a (see Note 307 below).

[299] Greek tradition, which seems reliable, placed the introduction of wrestling at Olympia in the 18th Olympiad (708), of boxing in the 23rd (688) and of the pancratium in the 33rd (648). Gardiner, *op.cit.* 435.

[300] For the evidence see Krause, *op.cit.* 76 and 766. Cf. Plato, *Meno,* 94cd; Pind. *Nem.* v, 49.

[301] Gardiner would disagree; *op.cit.* 365ff. For the most recent discussion of this moot question, see George E. Bean, "Victory in the Pentathlon," *Am. Journal of Archaeology* lx, 1956, 361-368.

tor in wrestling after the contest was introduced at Olympia was a Spartan, and the Spartans continued to carry off most of the prizes until they ceased contending about the middle of the sixth century.[302] Plato was himself well acquainted with the stand-up wrestling which we have seen he urgently prescribes as gymnastic exercise for youth.[303] This ὀρθὴ πάλη was the only sort allowed in the pentathlon and in the separate wrestling competitions at Olympia, victory in the match being gained by winning three falls. Since Plato says that the skills gained in this exercise are "useful for all purposes" (796a) it is difficult at first to see why no wrestling contest is prescribed, for contests usually served as an incentive to mastery and a test of skill, and are so used elsewhere in Plato's program. One answer seems to be that the very development of this art, with its elaborate prescriptions regarding diet and regimen, rendered the trained wrestler physically unfit for a military campaign, and particularly exposed him to the evils of professionalism, with its temptation to aim at individual glory at all costs.[304] The Spartans seem to have disdained the technical developments of the art, and this may be the reason why they ceased to enter the contest at Olympia.[305] Plato's omission of the contest shows his community of mind with them, but he had the wit not merely to eliminate it but to substitute for it something that he thought better, as we shall see.

Boxing was another ancient and popular sport, richly represented in the vase paintings and in literature.[306] Plato's text itself contains one of the best representations we have of the fourth-century boxer preparing himself for a match, donning the heavy σφαῖραι[307] instead

---

[302] Krause, *op.cit.* 668f. For the decline in Spartan interest in the games, see Gardiner, *op.cit.* 56-59.

[303] Plato is said to have learned gymnastics under the Argive wrestler Ariston (Diog. III, 4). On his description of wrestling (796a) as consisting in "the disentangling of neck and hands and sides" Gardiner comments (*op.cit.* 380): "A masterly definition, showing a true understanding of wrestling, for the wrestler's art is shown more perhaps in his ability to escape from or break a grip than in his skill in fixing one. The vases show that the omission of legholds in Plato's definition is no accident."

[304] Note the φιλονεικίας ἀχρήστου of 796a.

[305] Plut. *Apoph. Lac.* 233E; *Anthologia Palatina*, XVI, I.

[306] *Iliad* XXIII, 664ff.; *Odyss.* XVIII, 32ff.; Schröder, *op.cit.* 149ff.; Gardiner, *op.cit.* 402ff. The Delphians sacrificed to Apollo πύκτης. Heracles, Tydeus, and Polydeuces were all famous boxers. The invention of boxing is ascribed to Theseus, but it is of course much older; the archaeological evidence shows that boxing was a popular sport in Crete in Minoan times.

[307] The ἱμάντες are "soft gloves" (μαλακώτεροι or μείλιχοι) in contrast to the much more elaborate and formidable σφαῖραι. Plato's text shows that a boxer

of the leather thongs (ἱμάντες) used in contests, and when he can find no sparring partner to practise with, exercising himself by punching a dummy (830b). This sport in its simple form was highly prized by the Spartans as a preparation for war. Xenophon says that whenever the young Spartans came together they boxed with each other; if the combat became too heated, a bystander was authorized to separate them.[308] This of course was boxing with bare fists, in the Homeric fashion; the later "art" involved the wrapping of the hands in leather thongs and the observance of a number of technical rules. It is apparently this development that Plato forbids even as exercise for the young, since it is completely useless in war.[309] It is this art that the Spartans disdained; no Spartan is listed as victor in the πυγμή at Olympia, though many Athenian contestants are known to have gained glory in this and in the pancratium.[310]

The pancratium is sometimes described as a combination of boxing and wrestling; but it was a separate and distinct art, with its own rules, and highly prized as "the most glorious of the Olympic contests."[311] It is perhaps better to characterize it, as Gardiner does, as a "development of the primitive rough and tumble," disciplined and reduced to a competitive sport by rules of the game.[312] These rules seem to us particularly lax; no holds or blows were barred, except biting and gouging with the fingers in the eyes or mouth. The rules permitted wrestling of all sorts (here occurred the wrestling on the ground to which Plato objects), hitting, kicking, and even strangling. The contest continued until one of the contestants acknowledged that he was beaten.[313] The Greeks must have found it exciting to watch, and in its best days it was no doubt, as Gardiner declares, a contest no less of skill than of strength; but judged by modern standards of sportsmanship it was savage and far from gentlemanly. Undoubtedly Plato's chief reason for rejecting boxing and the more savage pan-

---

training for a contest subjected himself to more difficult conditions and to heavier punishment than he was likely to encounter in the contest itself.

[308] *Const. Lac.* IV, 6.

[309] 796a. On Amycus, Antaeus, and Epeius see Note 130 above.

[310] For the Spartans, see Krause, *op.cit.* 54; and for the Athenians, 766-767.

[311] Philostratus *Imag.* II, 6.

[312] Gardiner, *op.cit.* 435ff.

[313] It was apparently an unregulated form of this sport practised by the Spartan boys of later days in the celebrated contest at the place called Plane-Tree Grove (Paus. III, xi, 2; xiv, 8-10; Lucian *Anacharsis* 38). The two bands of contestants entered the area by separate bridges and the contest apparently lasted until one of them was driven off the island. "They fight with their hands, they kick with their feet, they bite and gouge out one another's eyes," reports Pausanias.

cratium is that, being contests without arms, they do not serve his conception of preparation for war. But another reason that one may plausibly attribute to him was the danger of overdeveloping the θυμός, the spirited element in human nature. The best professors of the art were aware of the danger of letting anger distort skill, a danger particularly acute in such body-to-body encounters.[314]

For wrestling Plato proposes to substitute the "armed combat" (τὴν ἐν τοῖς ὅπλοις μάχην). No further details of this art are given, but we may assume it is the same as the ὁπλομαχία whose educational value is discussed by Nicias and Laches in the dialogue *Laches*. It evidently had its practitioners and experts,[315] but there is no evidence that it was ever used in athletic games. Plato's text indeed shows that it was not, for it will be necessary, he says, to summon the experts to draw up a set of rules for determining the victor in this contest, analogous to the rules governing wrestling matches. The discussion between the two generals in the *Laches* shows that this art was not highly regarded at Sparta, but that much could be said in praise of it as an exercise befitting a freeman and as contributing to proficiency "in that contest [i.e. war] in which we are the athletes" (182a). It will apparently provide a variety of contests in Plato's state, contests between single competitors and between teams of various sizes, from two to ten members. Women as well as men are to take part in these contests, but whether in separate divisions, or with or against the men, Plato does not say.[316]

Likewise for the pancratium Plato has a substitute, a general peltastic contest (πελταστική), i.e. a mimic battle between light-armed troops, with bows and arrows, darts, javelins, stones, and slings (834a; 830e). This contest also seems to be an invention of Plato's, for laws governing it will have to be formulated, as for the hoplomachy just mentioned. It is fair to assume that it will consist of a variety of contests between individuals and teams of various sizes and variously armed, forming thus for the light-armed services a parallel to the hoplomachy for the heavy-armed.

Last in Plato's list comes the contest of horses (ἵππων ἀγών), which in Plato's day included chariot races (ἅρματα) as well as races on

---

[314] Seneca (*On Anger*, II, xiv, 3) cites the trainer Pyrrhus on this point.

[315] Note the reference to the ἄκροι περὶ ὁπλομαχίαν in 833e, and to Stesilaus and other professors of the art in *Laches*, e.g. 183c. Democritus is said to have written a ῾Οπλομαχικόν; Diog. IX, 48.

[316] Schröder (*op.cit.* 163ff.) refers to several representations of wrestling matches between women and men, one of which is reproduced in his text. See also Athen. 566e.

riding horses (μόνιπποι). Both Athens and Sparta were distinguished by the success of their citizens in winning prizes in these events.[317] But chariot races are omitted from Plato's program, and that for obvious reasons. Their military importance was negligible; they were but an aristocratic imitation of the warfare of Homeric chieftains. Furthermore, the expensive equipment required for the contest limited it to the very rich, and there will be no such class in Plato's state.[318] But there will be races on horseback of the sort familiar in his time, carefully graded into sections according to the age of the horses—one for colts, another for half-grown, and a third for full-grown animals (834c). Besides these Plato mentions, almost as if it were an afterthought, contests—not necessarily races—between mounted archers and javelin throwers. This is mentioned as a sport to which the Cretans might be especially attracted. Cretan bowmen were a familiar feature in the wars of the time, but we do not hear of their being mounted. We do know, however, that javelin throwing from horseback was practised by the aristocratic youth in the Athenian cavalry.[319] Perhaps we have here an abortive sketch of a third contest under simulated battle conditions; like the hoplomachy for the heavy-armed troops and the peltastic contest for the light-armed, this one to be a contest for the third branch of the service, the cavalry, in which Plato throughout the *Laws* exhibits a marked interest.

In general the horse plays a much more important part in Plato's state than it did in Crete or could naturally be expected to play in a Cretan city.[320] Plato makes the cavalry (the ἱππεῖς) one of the three divisions of his armed forces (755e), riding (ἱππική) is prescribed

[317] Krause, *op.cit.* 670ff. (for Sparta), 767ff. (for Athens). On the craze for horses at Athens in the fifth century, see Aristoph. *Clouds* 15-35, 74, 243. Cimon, a particular enthusiast, had his favorite horses buried in a tomb outside the Melite gate opposite his own family tomb. Herod. vi, 103; Judeich, *Topographie von Athen*, 409. Miltiades, Callias, and Alcibiades were other noted Athenian contestants in the chariot races.

[318] On one occasion Alcibiades entered seven teams and chariots in the races at Olympia and carried off first, second and fourth prizes (Thuc. vi, 16); but Alcibiades was the perfect example of that ruthless and self-centered individualism which Plato decried. King Agesilaus of Sparta induced his sister to enter a team of her horses in the races; her victory showed, as he intended it should, that the contest was no test of manly strength, but only of wealth (Xen. *Ages.* ix, 6).

[319] Gardiner, *op.cit.* 356f.; Schröder, *op.cit.* 140. Cf. *Meno* 93d. Xenophon recommends the practice of this sport for cavalrymen (*Hipparch.* i, 6; *Horsemanship*, viii, 10).

[320] The unimportance of the horse in Crete is mentioned both in 625d and in the present passage (834b) dealing with horse races. On Plato's fondness for horses, see *Diog.* vi, 7.

as an exercise and a study for the youth from the very earliest age (794c, 813e), hunting on horseback is a favored sport (824a), and mounted parades are a feature of the great festivals (796c). It is as if Plato, in spite of obstacles in Cretan custom and topography, proposed to establish in his model state something of the splendor of military training as he remembers it in the Athens of his youth, when he was serving in the cavalry and perhaps participating on occasion in the great Panathenaic procession. But there is more than an Athenian's preference involved. The Spartans also had cavalry in their armed forces,[321] and took delight in the parade of boys on horseback at their Hyacinthia.[322]

It is evident that Plato has set up a panel of sports in frank rivalry with the classic Olympic contests. Instead of the familiar foot races, there are to be races in light and heavy armor; hoplomachy replaces wrestling, and the peltastic contest replaces the pancratium; chariot racing disappears and we have, perhaps as its substitute, a contest between cavalry teams. Discus throwing and jumping, the other two traditional contests, are not even mentioned in Plato's account. The guiding purpose of this program, evident both in what is left out and in the novel competitive elements it contains, is to fit the citizen for effective service in war. In this conception he is at one with the Spartans, going even beyond them in the consistency with which he applies the principle. One might well ask if he has forgotten his indictment of the Spartan agoge as a one-sided training in military virtues to the neglect of temperance and justice. The answer is that gymnastics is only one part of education, and there can be no objection to its doing its own part well, provided that it is supplemented by music and letters. Moreover, we have Plato's constant insistence that these exercises are games, serious indeed, but enjoyable withal, and worth pursuing on their own account. He recognizes that this program may be derided; for "such choristry and contests hardly exist anywhere at present" (831b). The reason is not the ignorance of legislators, he asserts, but the lust for wealth, which leaves citizens little leisure for them, and the spirit of faction, which discourages the development of excellence in any but the ruling class. When these causes have been removed, as Plato thinks he has removed them from his state, the legislator can establish, and the citizens will

[321] Herod. i, 67; Plut. *Lyc.* 23; Thuc. iv, 55. Xenophon (*Hell.* vi, iv, 10-11) shows that it was not always the best trained.
[322] Athen. 139e.

heartily welcome, this natural and logical combination of sport with military training (831b-832d).

COMMON MEALS

"As to common meals (συσσίτια)," says Aristotle, "there is general agreement that they are advantageous to a well-ordered state."[323] This is one feature of Cretan and Spartan life that Plato seems to take for granted, as something so firmly established in the practice of his Dorian colonists that it hardly needs explicit legislation.[324] Common meals are also prescribed for the guardians in the *Republic* and they are pictured for the warriors in the imaginary account of ancient Athens in the *Critias*.[325] Neither Plato nor Aristotle gives explicit reasons for including this institution in his ideal state. Aristotle's promise to give such reasons is not fulfilled in the uncompleted sketch of his ideal polity. Plato's reasons, however, can be clearly seen in the preface to his longest treatment of the subject, where he points out the necessity of regulating the private as well as the public life of the citizens if public order is to be secure (780a). The common meals, therefore, are a part of that life-long education to which the citizen is to be subjected, and by which the law imprints its principles upon his manners and sentiments.

Common meals are mentioned in all the ancient accounts of Spartan and Cretan life as something distinguishing them in the fourth century not only from Ionian cities, but also from most of their own Dorian colonies. We are not fully informed as to the details of their organization.[326] At Sparta it seems that all full-fledged Spartans, the

---

[323] *Pol.* 1330a 3.

[324] 842bc. Although common meals are frequently mentioned as one of the distinctive Spartan and Cretan institutions (625e, 633a, 780b,e), and their presence in the new colony is presupposed (780-782, 806e, 839c), yet nowhere is there explicit legislation establishing them. The absence of such legislation is implied in 783b, for its preliminaries (τὰ ἐπίπροσθεν αὐτῶν sc. τῶν συσσιτίων) are said to have not yet been laid down; and the following clause says that we shall come closer to the subject later (προσμείξαντες αὐτοῖς ἐγγύθεν). In 842b, however, we find that they have been established (b1). In the specific context it might be taken, at first sight, to mean only their establishment in Crete and Sparta. But Plato proceeds at once to a question involved (ἀκόλουθον) in the institution of συσσίτια, viz. the organization of the food supply, and "how to make this fit in with the meals," as Bury translates (taking αὐτοῖς in 842c 2 as referring to the συσσίτια; see England's note). This makes it certain that κατεσκευάσθαι and κατεσκευασμένα in 842b refer to Plato's state as well as to Crete and Sparta. The promise in 783c of a more precise treatment of the organization of these meals is not fulfilled.

[325] *Rep.* 416e, 458c, 547d; *Crit.* 112c.

[326] For Sparta our literary sources are primarily Plut. *Lyc.* 10, 12 and schol. to

"peers" (ὅμοιοι), were members of eating clubs (φιδίτια), each consisting of approximately fifteen members.[327] Each club had its house, also called φιδίτιον,[328] in which the members, when not on active duty with the armed forces, not only took their meals but also slept, at least until the age of thirty. The young Spartan became eligible for admission to a φιδίτιον upon completing the agoge at the age of twenty. Membership was by election on secret ballot, and one adverse vote was sufficient to debar an applicant. Attendance at these meals was strictly compulsory, even for the kings and other officials; only a family sacrifice or delay in returning from a hunt were acceptable excuses for absence. Each member contributed monthly a prescribed quantity of flour, dates or figs, cheese, and wine. This diet was often supplemented by game contributed by members who had been lucky in the chase, but it had the reputation of being at best a frugal and unappetizing fare.[329] The meals seem to have been under the general supervision of the polemarchs, and we may infer that each club had its own presiding officers, whether selected on the basis of age or otherwise we cannot say. So much, and little more, do we know about the common meals at Sparta. We know even less about the details of the institution at Crete. As at Sparta, a Cretan was required to belong to a club (called ἑταιρία), which had its president (ἀρχός), but not its separate house, only a table in the common "men's house" (ἀνδρεῖον) where all the clubs of a city took their meals together. It seems that the Cretan boys regularly—instead of occasionally, as at Sparta—attended these common meals, taking their food on the floor, and waiting upon their elders at table.

Xenophon attributes the Spartan institution to Lycurgus, and so does Plutarch later, though with the addition that Lycurgus was in-

Laws 633a; for Crete Strabo x, iv, 16, 18, 20; Arist. Pol. 1271a 28ff., 1272a 12ff.; and Dosiades apud Athen. 143ab. For the interpretation of these sources, see Busolt-Swoboda 698ff., 746, 754ff.; Nilsson, "Grundlagen des Spartanischen Lebens," in Klio XII, 1912, 315ff.; Willetts, Aristocratic Society in Ancient Crete, 18ff.; and Jeanmaire, Couroi et Courètes, 422ff., 483ff. The inscriptions give little additional information for Sparta; but it is possible that the Cretan inscriptions, which have as yet been imperfectly examined from this point of view, will be more revealing.

[327] Miss Chrimes (Ancient Sparta, 244-245) has plausibly suggested that Plutarch's source is in error here, and that these messes had a much larger membership and a more distinct connection with family groups than Plutarch indicates. If she is right, some of the incompatibility pointed out below between this institution and the household is removed.

[328] Plut. Lyc. 26, 4.

[329] See the apothegm in Plut. Lyc. 12: "You have to bathe in the Eurotas [i.e. be a Spartan] before you can relish the Spartan broth."

fluenced by Crete in his legislation.[330] Both Aristotle and Ephorus say that the Cretan institution is the earlier one from which the Spartan was derived.[331] Aristotle looks even beyond Crete, finding the earliest origin of the institution among the ancient Oenotrians in southern Italy. But he adds that this and many other institutions must have been invented independently many times over, as their necessity became evident. The Homeric poems give evidence of something like common meals in Achaean society, at least for the warriors and nobles;[332] and there are sufficient parallels in other Greek states of historical times, and enough survivals in all of them, to indicate that the institution was once much more widely spread.[333] The organization of men into clubs, eating and living together and sometimes practising secret rites, is now known to be a common characteristic of primitive societies; and classical scholars acquainted with the results of modern anthropology have found it enlightening to characterize the Spartan and Cretan institution as a survival of such primitive social organization.[334] But why did these institutions survive into historical times in Sparta and Crete but shrivel away elsewhere? The Spartans and Cretans were certainly not primitive peoples in the fifth and fourth centuries. The special factor that influenced them was obviously the peculiar military needs of their societies. Both were conquering peoples who did not assimilate, but continued to hold in subjection, the peoples whom they had conquered; hence their retention, for a longer time than the other Greeks, of a social organization more akin to that of an army which must be ready at any time for instant battle.[335]

[330] Xen. *Const. Lac.* v, 2; Plut. *Lyc.* 10; cf. 4.

[331] *Pol.* 1272a 1ff.; 1329b 5ff.; Strabo x, iv, 18. Both Aristotle and Ephorus remark that the Cretans still use the old word ἀνδρεῖα, replaced at Sparta by φιδίτια.

[332] *Iliad* iv, 257ff.; xvii, 248ff.; xxii, 492ff.; *Odyss.* iv, 621ff.; xi, 184ff.

[333] For parallels at Miletus, Thebes, and Thurii, see *Laws* 636b; and for Megara, Theog. 309. Survivals are the common meals for magistrates, which are found in most Greek states, and are especially attested for Athens. "Diese auch dem heutigen südlichen Leben nicht fernliegende Sitte des Zusammenlebens der Männer, für Sparta allbekannt, findet sich nicht nur bei den Doriern, sondern auch bei den ionischen Kolonisten in Kleinasien und war bis zu einem gewissen Grade wohl allgemein hellenischer Brauch." Helmut Berve, *Griech. Gesch.* Freiburg, 1931, 1, 69.

[334] Nilsson, *op.cit.* (Note 326).

[335] Xenophon (*Const. Lac.* v, 2) designates the common meals at Sparta by the word συσκήνια, which even more definitely suggests army life. He knew Sparta well, and it may be that this particular term was a "Laconian expression" (Busolt-Swoboda 698; Willetts, *op.cit.* 21-22). The usual Spartan designation seems to have been φιδίτια or φιλίτια. The latter, but not the former, also occurs frequently in Xenophon. This confusion in pronunciation (for such it must have been) and the

Plato refers on several occasions to the military origin of the common meals, but regards them as serving in Spartan and Cretan life other purposes than military readiness. "After you had had experience of these common meals, which you had been obliged to adopt because of war or some other emergency, you came to see that they contributed immensely to your security" (780b; cf. 625e, 633a). Plato's contemporaries also saw something more in the institution than a means of keeping the fighting forces in readiness for action. At the common tables all citizens, rich and poor alike, had the same fare. This leads Aristotle to look upon them as a device for making property common,[336] and Ephorus for permitting the poor to share equally with the rich.[337] Xenophon attributes to Lycurgus the intention of preventing self-indulgence and assuring the more ready observance of his prescriptions.[338] Plutarch has an even broader interpretation: he describes the institution not only as a blow at luxury and the desire for wealth, but also as a kind of school of citizenship and good manners, to which the children were sometimes admitted in order to profit by the discourse of their elders. "Here they were instructed in state affairs by listening to experienced statesmen; here they learned to converse with pleasantry, to make jests without scurrility, and take them without ill humor."[339] Plutarch evidently regards these meals as an important part of the Lycurgan discipline which, as he says later, continued into adult life, accustoming the citizen not even to wish to live by himself or for himself, but to become one with the interests of the state and to live for it alone.[340]

Plutarch's interpretation points the way toward understanding Plato's admiration of common meals. They are a part of the education and discipline of adult life, designed to make the citizen accept more fully the ideal which the laws expound and which constitutes the essential purpose of the state (780ab,d). There is probably no better way of confirming a man's convictions than having him break bread regularly with persons of the same beliefs. Such was the practice of the early Christians and, as we now see from the recently discovered Dead Sea Scrolls, also of the Essene communities in first-century

---

variations in the spelling of both terms that are found in the inscriptions and the manuscripts, are a reflection of that semiliteracy mentioned above in which the Spartans seemed to take a certain pride. See LSJ s.v. φιδίτιον.

[336] *Pol.* 1263b 41.   [337] Strabo x, iv, 16.

[338] *Const. Lac.* V, 2.
[339] *Lyc.* 10 and 12. For a similar description of the talk in the Cretan ἀνδρεῖα, see Dosiades, in Athen. 143d.

[340] *Lyc.* 24-25.

Palestine. The monastic refectories of the Middle Ages, the halls in Oxford and Cambridge colleges, even the luncheon clubs of twentieth-century America and the dining rooms in college fraternities are testimony both to the attractiveness and to the influence of such common meals among persons of like mind. When these groups are small, as they were in Crete and Sparta, and when the exchanges that take place at table are protected by a tradition of secrecy, as we are told they were at Sparta, they provide unique opportunities for learning the character of one's fellows and being influenced by them.

Groups of this sort had a peculiar attraction for the Greeks. In classical times cultural life depended, far more than it does today, on meetings of men with men—from the informal groups at the gymnasia or the palastrae described in Plato's dialogues, or the symposia arranged by rich and convivial citizens, to the more permanently constituted clubs, or ἑταιρίαι, and the philosophical and religious θίασοι.[341] When formally organized, these assemblies and organizations had something of an aristocratic character. Plato's and Aristotle's proposals imply the extension of this practice to include all the citizens in the state, thus making common what was hitherto, except in Crete and Sparta, the privilege and obligation of the few. The inclusion of all citizens in the institution, and its transformation into a compulsory and semipermanent organization are the points, we may properly assume, which would make its establishment difficult in any states except Sparta and Crete (839cd, 842b; cf. 780c, 783b). It is not the desirability but the practicability that Plato thinks most persons would question.

Since there is no precise legislation regarding the common meals, we must rely on a number of scattered references to determine Plato's intentions. The longest of such references contends that there should be common meals for women as well as men (780e-781d). This was contrary to all historical precedent—Aristotle indeed lists it as something peculiar (ἴδιον) to Plato[342]—and Plato is well aware of the protest and ridicule it will evoke. But the issue is an important one,

[341] Marrou, op.cit. 75: "Le cadre de la vie culturelle archaïque, c'est le club d'hommes, l'ἀνδρεῖον crétois, l'ἑταιρία athénienne; c'est la causerie, λέσχη, le 'banquet,' συμπόσιον, c'est-à-dire la beuverie qui suit le repas du soir, avec ces règles formelles et sa stricte étiquette." See also Newman, The Politics of Aristotle I, 335. That invaluable treasury of ancient lore, Athenaeus' Deipnosophists, is a monumental testimony to the cultural tradition of the banquet among the Greeks.
[342] Pol. 1274b 11. Aristotle also records that Lycurgus, according to tradition, tried "to bring the women under the laws," but they resisted him and he gave up. Pol. 1270a 6.

he thinks; for if the common meals are a valuable means of education and discipline, the legislator who does not extend them to
women as well as men is neglecting half his task—indeed more than
half, "inasmuch as the nature of women is inferior to that of man
in virtue" (781ab). At the end of this passage the Athenian asserts
that the merits of his proposal will be more readily seen when the
laws regarding common meals have been formulated (783bc). Unfortunately the promise implicit here is never fulfilled in Plato's text.

There will be common meals for magistrates during their terms of
office. They are explicitly required for the agronomoi, and there are
stringent regulations against the absence of any officer or man without authorization (762cd). We can assume also common meals for
the prytanies of the council (758b-d), as was customary at Athens,[343]
and for other boards of officials, such as the astynomoi and the agoranomoi, whose duties require that they be readily available at all
times. The "residences of officials" (οἰκήσεις ἀρχόντων) mentioned
in 778c are obviously not their family homes, but the places where
they live and perform their functions during their terms of office.
Of these the houses of the astynomoi and the agoranomoi are specifically mentioned elsewhere (917e, 918a).[344] Plato also mentions houses,
like the φιδίτια at Sparta, for the other eating clubs required for
the citizenry.[345] Where they are to be located in the city and the villages is not said; we know only that the eating places for men and
"those for their households, including the girls and their mothers,"
are to be separate but not far apart (806e).[346] This passage shows us
that the girls would take their meals with their mothers' clubs; as
for the boys, we can infer that the very youngest would eat with their

[343] Arist. Const. Ath. XLIII, 3; for the archons and ἀθλοθέται see LXII, 2. In his
sketch of an ideal state Aristotle speaks of συσσίτια for officials (1331a 25), for
priests (1331b 5), and for the multitude of the citizenry (1331a 19).

[344] How a citizen's membership in his regular eating club would be affected by
his becoming an official and participating for his term of office in a different mess,
we can only speculate. The practice of Sparta would be available as a precedent.
Plutarch (Cleom. 8) refers to the συσσίτιον of the ephors. Since the ephors held
office for one year only, each of them at the expiration of his term must either have
returned to the φιδίτιον to which he previously belonged or obtained admission to
a new one. The οἴκημα mentioned in this passage in which their meals took place
must have been an official building occupied by successive boards of ephors.

[345] The συσσίτια of 762c must certainly be understood as referring to permanent
houses in which the meals are taken. The Spartan word φιδίτιον and the Cretan
ἀνδρεῖον had a similar double meaning. Likewise the συσσίτια of 780b and 806e
must refer to houses as well as meals. For this use of the word, see Crit. 112c.

[346] The φιδίτια at Sparta seem to have been located on the street called Hya-
cinthus. Busolt-Swoboda 698 n. 3.

mothers, but those six years of age and older would be separated from the girls, as they were in their lessons, and would eat with their fathers. This passage also shows that each of these clubs is to have its ἄρχων (or ἄρχουσα, for the women) to supervise the conduct of the members, preside over the libations, and dismiss the assemblies (cf. 640a-e). It suggests further that Plato thought of these clubs as merely eating places, the members retiring to their homes after the evening meal; but it is possible that this detail applies only to the older men, and that Plato would follow the Spartan custom of requiring men below the age of thirty to live as well as eat together. The regulations regarding the use of wine suggest a differentiation between clubs for younger and for older men (666ab). Finally, what we have learned previously about the chorus of Dionysus must be put into the framework of the common meals. It seems clear that the convivial assemblies of this chorus, to which Plato attaches such importance, are merely a specially important case of the variety of συσσίτια which he seems to envisage.

How are the common meals to be supported in Plato's state? Aristotle distinguishes sharply between the Cretan and the Spartan methods of supporting the tables: at Sparta a contribution was required from each member, whereas at Crete they were supported from the public revenues, i.e. from the produce and livestock raised on the public land and from the taxes paid by the perioikoi, "so that all persons, men, women, and children, were fed at public cost."[347] There is only one passage in the *Laws* that mentions the subject. In 955e it is said that one way of determining a citizen's taxes is to ascertain what his income is, "apart from his contributions to the syssitia." This apparently takes for granted that the meals will be supported by contributions from individual citizens, as at Sparta. The earlier law regarding the distribution of the annual produce (847e-848c) confirms this interpretation. This law provides that all products from the land are to be divided annually into three parts, not necessarily equal, but κατὰ λόγον—one for the citizens (here called "freemen"), one for their slaves, and a third for the foreign residents and visitors. This third portion must be put up for sale to the noncitizen households; over the other two parts the citizen lot holder retains the right of disposal and may make distributions from them to the slave and free members of his household as he thinks fit. Since this law provides for the distribution of all the annual product, and since there is no

[347] *Pol.* 1272a 12-21.

provision for the common meals, it implies that if there are to be common meals they will be supported by contributions from that portion of a citizen's produce over which he has free disposal.

There is indeed another inference that one can draw from this passage, viz. that Plato has temporarily lost sight of the common meals.[348] This is unlikely, since these words follow by only a few pages his declaration that we may now consider the common meals as having been established (842b). But this earlier passage itself is most puzzling and reveals the indecision of Plato's thought. "We have now come to the point in our discussion where we can consider that common meals have been established . . . but as to the manner in which they are to be set up, whether as they are here in Crete, or as in Lacedaemon, or in some other third fashion different from and better than both of these—this does not seem to me a difficult matter to decide, nor one which, if decided, would afford us any great advantage, since they are quite satisfactory as actually established" (842b). This appears to be merely a reassertion that common meals in some form are to exist in Plato's state, coupled with a refusal to determine the specific form they are to have. Dramatically it might do, as expressing a concession by the Athenian to his two companions, for each of whom the common meals, as established by his own state, doubtless appeared to be satisfactory. But to Plato's readers it looks more like the abdication of the legislator in the face of a problem too difficult for him to solve. What precisely are the difficulties that prevent Plato from carrying out his intention and setting up common meals for all the citizens of his state?

One of them certainly is the incompatibility of this institution with an agrarian economy of small proprietors; and such an economy, analogous to that of early Athens, seems to be Plato's most usual conception of his state.[349] The common meals, as an institution for all citizens, are best suited to an aristocratic minority supported in idleness by the labor of slaves and serfs. There is indeed one passage in the *Laws* in which Plato describes his citizens as devoting all their time to the conduct of public affairs and the practice of virtue, the necessities of life being provided for them by the labors of a subject class who turn over to the citizens a proportion of their produce, as under the Spartan system (806de). But in general he conceives of his citizens as engaged in economic activity, many of them living

---

[348] As Gernet (xcix) suggests.
[349] Gernet c.

scattered in villages on the land. Even so, common meals might be established; but they would be obviously quite different from the syssitia at Sparta or the andreia in Crete, where all citizens came together for meals in common. Another and perhaps graver difficulty arises from the incompatibility between a society organized according to syssitia and one organized around the family, as we have seen Plato's to be. "The συσσίτιον and the family are incompatible institutions," says Nilsson.[350] In the state described in the *Republic*, where the family is abolished, this difficulty does not arise;[351] but having reinstated the family, Plato must have found it increasingly difficult, as he proceeded in his legislation, to set up these other groups in a way that would not undermine the position of the household.

Some other traces of Plato's perplexity should be pointed out. There is his silence regarding any connection between the common meals and the training of the young, which was a prominent feature of Spartan and Cretan life; the absence of any reference to common sleeping quarters (except for the agronomoi) which was a part of the system at Sparta for the younger men; and most striking of all, the vacillation in his prescriptions regarding marriage. At Sparta every young man upon completing the agoge at the age of twenty was required to marry, though he continued until his thirtieth year to sleep and eat in his φιδίτιον, seeing his wife only by stealth at night. But Plato regards the first ten years of marriage as the most important (783e-784b). The man who marries must take his bride away from both his and her fathers' houses, "as if they were going to a colony," and set up a new establishment to be the nursery of their young (776ab). On the other hand it is prescribed that married people shall "make their δίαιτα" in the συσσίτια neither more nor less after marriage than they did before (780ab). In one passage the age of marriage is said to be from twenty-five to thirty-five (772d); in others from thirty to thirty-five (721b, 785b). The latter prescription would be compatible with the Spartan custom, permitting the young man to live with his comrades in his συσσίτιον until the age of thirty; the former would be incompatible with it.

These inconsistencies are part of the evidence usually adduced for the unfinished character of the *Laws,* and that they are. But it is

---

[350] Nilsson, *op.cit.* (Note 326), 331.

[351] Although there is another inconsistency, that of retaining the συσσίτια in a state in which all men are to be equally dear to one another, as Aristotle points out (*Pol.* 1264a 6ff.). Plato notes in 636b that they are conducive to faction.

important to see that the unfinished character of this part of Plato's legislation has a deeper reason than the approach of death. It lies in the difficulty of reconciling two types of social organization, one essentially Dorian, and another which, as we have seen, is copied from his native Athens.

CHAPTER VIII

RELIGION

IT IS DIFFICULT for readers whose ideas of religion have been molded by influences of an Asiatic origin to find in the Greek gods the basis, and in Greek worship the expression, of those feelings that we regard as most truly religious. We can understand why Plato, from personal conviction and from conformity with the feelings of his countrymen, should regard the ceremonies of public worship as an essential part of a well-ordered state.[1] But he adopts so faithfully the details of historical Greek religion that we are inclined, at first sight, to regard him here as a pure opportunist, willing, at any sacrifice of personal feeling and philosophical integrity, to make use of familiar religious practices to support his political order. But if we examine the details of this part of the *Laws* with the careful and sympathetic interest that is required to bring out Plato's intentions—something that has seldom been done—we are likely to be surprised by the extent to which he transforms the spirit, while adhering to the form, of the worship that he finds among his countrymen.[2]

We have already noted the function of the festivals in bringing the citizens into joyous fellowship with one another and with the gods who are their companions in these festivities, and have seen how the educator will supervise the accompanying songs and dances so that they will confirm the teaching of the law. But the purpose of the law is not merely to promote freedom, wisdom, and friendliness among the citizens but also to make them just and happy. Now the justice which produces happiness is that which has its pattern in the nature of God. "Not man, as they say, but God is the measure of all things" (716c). It follows—and Plato explicitly draws the inference—that true fellowship between men and gods, and the lasting favor of the gods, can be attained only in so far as men are like God (716d). He quotes the ancient saying that "like is dear to like," but amends it by

---

[1] For the close connection in Greek life between religion and the state see Friedrich Solmsen, *Plato's Theology*, Cornell Univ. Press, 1942, 3-13; Busolt 514ff.; and Nilsson I, 670ff., 681ff. On piety as a civic duty, see Schmidt, *Die Ethik der Alten Griechen*, II, 48. For the Greek the state was a religious as well as a political community; Georg Jellinek, *Allgemeine Staatslehre*, 3rd. edn., Berlin, 1920, 311.

[2] Plato's theology has often been examined, Plato's religion less often, and the religion of Plato's state almost not at all. In this area the recent book of Reverdin is almost a pioneer. See also George N. Belknap, *Religion in Plato's States*, University of Oregon Publications, 1935.

adding "when it is measured (μέτριον); for unmeasured things (ἄμετρα) can be friendly neither to themselves nor to what is measured."[3]

This brief passage contains a profound reinterpretation of familiar practices. Worship is appropriate and beneficial only to good men: "in vain is all the labor that the unholy (ἀνόσιοι) spend upon the gods" (717a). It is not an exchange of services between men and gods (the *do ut des* of primitive ritualism), but a means of assimilating oneself to the gods one worships by adopting the orderliness that characterizes the divine nature. Likewise the favor that religious worship procures from the gods is the approbation of the worshipper's character, not an external reward for the correct performance of a ritual. And finally, the consequences of divine favor will be primarily the "divine goods"—wisdom, temperance, justice, and courage—and only secondarily the human goods of health, beauty, and wealth (631b-d). Thus "for a good man to engage continually in sacrifice and communion with the gods, by prayers and dedications and all kinds of worship, is an exceedingly good and glorious thing and most conducive to a happy life" (716d).

But to find in the divine nature that pattern of orderliness and measure that Plato embodies in his law involves a further transformation of his countrymen's beliefs. It is not the gods of Homer and the dramatists, with their all-too-human frailties, still less the gods of the soothsayers and the vendors of magical charms, that can provide the standard he requires. The divine nature as he conceives it is the eternal source of order and wisdom, the artisan and the guardian of the good in the world, exempt from vacillation and change, free of deceit and jealousy, and incorruptible.[4] Such a conception of God is the construction of philosophic reason, not of the poets. Yet there are in the poets enough intimations of this divine nature, and in common law and custom enough tacit reliance upon some such source of law and justice, to lead Plato not to reject the familiar gods of his countrymen, but to attempt to maintain and enhance their

[3] This conception of law and the moral ideal of the μέτριον are treated more fully below, in Chapters X and XI. For their relation to Plato's general philosophy see Culbert G. Rutenber, *The Doctrine of the Imitation of God in Plato*, New York, 1946.

[4] This statement of Plato's beliefs will stand, I think, whether or not we regard his God as the Good, the Ideas, the "best soul," or the cosmic Nous. The philosophical interpretation of Plato's theology is not strictly relevant here, and I intend to avoid it as much as possible in what follows.

status as beings worthy of veneration. It is not a new religion that Plato proposes for his state, but the old religion, purified of its unwitting errors, and illuminated by a more penetrating conception of the meaning of religious worship.

The fact that Plato deliberately pours his new wine into old bottles by proposing a system of religious observances comparable, in most external respects, to the familiar religion of his countrymen, is capable of various interpretations, all probably containing a measure of truth. Undoubtedly Plato, as a political demiurge, thought that there was much to be gained by adding the support of familiar religious ideas and practices to the other institutions of his state. Again Plato, the poet and myth-maker, was well aware that there is a child in all of us that may be indifferent to the appeal of philosophic reason, but responsive to concrete and sensuous images. Reason and demonstration there will certainly be; the proofs of the gods' existence will be one of the concerns of the Nocturnal Council (966c); indeed no one is really eligible to the office of guardian who has not labored at such studies (966cd), and rational persuasion will be employed on any others who may require it (885de). But most men "learn" their beliefs about the gods not from scientific instruction but through habituation—from listening in infancy to the stories told them by their nurses and mothers, from hearing the prayers at the public sacrifices and eagerly watching the spectacles that follow them, and from seeing how earnest their parents are in prayers and supplications on behalf of themselves and their children. These religious prayers and practices are so many forms of enchantment whereby the minds of the young are formed and those of their elders confirmed. The Athenian Stranger expresses a certain indignation at the unbelievers upon whom these solemn experiences have not produced the expected effect, and who must be argued out of their scepticism (887cd). It may be that Plato is here recalling his own experiences, and expressing the delight he takes in the ceremonies of public and private worship and in the forms of art that accompany them. This suggests a third, perhaps more important, reason for the care with which Plato fosters the traditional ceremonies of religion in his state. Such ceremonies are for him not merely useful supports to public law and order, nor merely a concession to the child in us, but intrinsically desirable forms of that "serious play" in which men should pass their lives, "sacrificing, singing, and dancing, and thus winning the favor of the gods" (803e).

APOLLO AND THE SACRED LAW

In deliberating what shrines ought to be established and after what gods or daemons they should be named, whether in founding a new city or restoring an old one that has been destroyed, no man with any sense will attempt to alter the injunctions that have come from Delphi or Dodona or Ammon, or from ancient traditions (παλαιοὶ λόγοι). However these traditions may have worked their persuasion, whether by visions of the gods (φασμάτων θεῶν) or an alleged inspiration (ἐπιπνοίας λεχθείσης), under their influence the men of old time established sacrifices and rites, sometimes of local origin and sometimes imported from Tyrrhenia or Cyprus or from other parts, and by means of such traditions have sanctified oracles and statues and altars and temples and marked off for each of them its sacred area. None of these ought the legislator to change in the slightest degree. 738bc

The religion of a Greek city was never the simple and systematic whole that the word suggests; it was always a complex of beliefs and practices only loosely related to one another and of diverse provenance—some local in origin, some imported from elsewhere under the influence of war, trade, or political alliances. The gods honored in these practices were equally diverse in their origin, history, and divine status. Some, such as Zeus and Apollo, were widely worshipped throughout the Greek world and even beyond, though the identity of the god's name often concealed a real diversity of practices and beliefs in the various areas in which he was worshipped, honored in one place (or at one time of the year) under one of his numerous cult titles, at other places and times under others. Each city had its patron deities whom it especially revered, as Athena was honored at Athens and Hera at Argos; but these goddesses were also worshipped elsewhere, just as their protégés at Athens and Argos recognized and honored other divinities as well. Within the city each tribe and clan had its own special deity or hero, with its separate rites and ceremonies of worship; and there were other gods whose worship was still more localized, being limited sometimes to a single sanctuary about a sacred spring or cave. The Greek mind was as fertile in religion as in other areas, peopling the woods with nymphs, the waters with naiads and river gods, and investing each aspect of family or community life with its divine patron. And it was equally receptive. The cults and sanctuaries which were the deposit of this fertile fancy were never thought of as precluding the establishment of rites and practices in honor of other divinities as occasion suggested. In fact the religious history of Greece is to a great extent the history of the diffusion of local cults which spread beyond the area of their origin and were accepted elsewhere, either alongside the worship already established or as a new element incorporated into it.

The religion of the state for which Plato is legislating will be a similar mixture of cults of varying provenance. His city occupies the site of one long since destroyed, and it is assumed that if there are any local deities or shrines of ancient gods whose memories are still preserved, their worship will continue as before (848d). This was common Hellenic tradition and practice. Even the casual traveller, still more the permanent settler in a new land, would exercise the elementary precaution of making his peace with the gods of the land he had entered.[5] Thucydides tells us that even in warfare the conqueror of enemy territory was expected to see that the customary rites at any temple that might have fallen into his hands should be carried on as before, so far as possible.[6] Much of the complexity of Greek religion is to be explained by the fact that successive waves of invaders from the north respected the religion of the conquered peoples, whose rites and beliefs remained as a clearly distinguishable element underlying or incorporated into their own practices. Plato's colonists also will bring with them the patron deities of their own native cities, and their ancestral deities and heroes of clan and tribe. Since they come from different parts of Crete and the Peloponnesus, these imported cults will themselves be diverse. Plato is content with this, for each is regarded as of divine origin. Evidently he feels it is supremely important, as England remarks,[7] to preserve "every available feeling of veneration in his citizens, no matter whence obtained."

Plato regards all these traditional practices as having the authority of the oracles and ancient traditions. The oracles, especially Delphi, had an immense influence in the archaic and the classical periods in regulating religious worship, in establishing new cults and modifying old ones, in transferring the bones of heroes, in adjusting the boundaries of sacred areas and protecting them from encroachment.[8]

[5] See Guthrie, *The Greeks and their Gods*, 28f., who calls attention to the scholium on Apoll. Rhod. II, 1271ff.: "Jason's offerings are in accordance with ancient custom, which is that those who have arrived in a strange land make offering to the gods of the locality (τοῖς ἐγχωρίοις θεοῖς)."

[6] Thuc. IV, 98, 2.   [7] On 738b 4.

[8] Most of our evidence on this point comes from legend and tradition, the παλαιοὶ λόγοι to which Plato refers. Such materials cannot be relied on for historical details, but they provide massive evidence of what the Greeks believed about their oracles

The oracle was the spokesman of the gods; it could reveal the grounds of their displeasure, whether manifested in a plague, a military defeat, a failure of the harvests, or a natural portent, and suggest ways of removing it. When Xenophon desired to build a sanctuary to Artemis Ephesia, he consulted the oracle as to where it should be located. The Spartans were repeatedly defeated by the Tegeans; they asked the oracle what god they should conciliate in order to gain the upper hand, and the oracle advised them to bring back the bones of Orestes to Sparta. The tyrant Cleisthenes of Sicyon asked the oracle whether he would be justified in removing the bones of the Argive hero Adrastus and abolishing his heroön, and when the answer was unfavorable he desisted from his purpose, but with Theban permission contrived to bring to Sicyon another hero, Adrastus' deadly enemy Melanippus—this time without consulting the oracle —and transferred the rites of Adrastus to Melanippus. Another Cleisthenes, the Athenian one, instituted the eponymous heroes of his ten new tribes by asking the Pythian oracle to select them from a previously chosen list of one hundred.[9] These are but a few instances that illustrate the authority ascribed to Delphi in religious matters, an authority that could be flouted only with circumspection. Our evidence shows that the prestige of Delphi in such matters was still great in Plato's time. When the Athenians in 352 desired to put under cultivation the ἱερὰ ὀργάς of Demeter and Persephone on the borders of Megara, they took elaborate precautions to ascertain truly Apollo's will in the matter.[10]

We hear less about the authority of Dodona and Ammon, but they also enjoyed great prestige as centers for ascertaining the will of the gods. Croesus consulted them both, as well as Delphi and other oracles, before undertaking his fateful expedition against the Persians.[11] Dodona, lying at the foot of Mount Tmarus in Epirus, was believed to be the oldest of the oracles.[12] Homer and Hesiod recog-

---

and what they expected from them. The literary and epigraphical evidence confirms the attitude revealed by the legends. See Nilsson 1, 595-598; H. W. Parke, *History of the Delphic Oracle*, Oxford, 1939, 325ff.; and for the regulation of the cult of Dionysus, Nilsson 1, 540ff., and Parke, *op.cit.*, 335ff. For the incidents mentioned in the text the authorities are Xen. *Anab.* v, iii, 7; Herod. 1, 67; v, 67.

[9] Arist. *Const. Ath.* xxi, 6; cf. Paus. x, x, 1.

[10] *Syll.* No. 204; Nilsson 1, 71.

[11] Herod. 1, 46. The three oracles of Plato's text appear together in Aristoph. *Birds* 716; cf. also Cic. *De Divin.* 1, 3 and 95.

[12] Plato, *Phaedr.* 275b; Plut. *Pyr.* 1.

nize it as a sacred spot where "Pelasgian Zeus" enounces his will,[13] and it continued to be consulted throughout classical times, usually in conjunction with Delphi.[14] The oracle of Ammon was located in the oasis of Siwa in western Egypt; it had first become known to the Greeks with the settlement of Cyrene in the seventh century, and was especially popular in Sparta, Elis, and Boeotia.[15] Ammon came to be identified with Zeus, Apollo at Delphi gave him support, and the priests at Dodona were willing to recognize his oracle as of equal antiquity with their own.[16] It was consulted by Cimon during his campaign in Cyprus, and by the Athenians before the Sicilian expedition; and in the next century they had a state trireme to convey sacred embassies to the coast of Cyrene on their way to the oracle of Ammon.[17] Lysander tried to bribe it, good evidence that it was important; but he was no more successful here than he had been in a previous attempt to buy the support of Delphi.[18] And a generation after Plato, Alexander made a long and hazardous march across the desert sands in order to consult it.[19]

Of these three oracles, Apollo is evidently to be the chief interpreter of the will of the gods in Plato's state, for Dodona and Ammon are nowhere else referred to in his text,[20] whereas Delphi appears on numerous occasions in connection with details of religious law. This supremacy given to Apollo is not merely an expression of Plato's personal preference, or a result of the influence of Socrates or the Pythagoreans.[21] The sanctuary at Delphi had from the sixth century onward been pre-eminent over all the other sanctuaries in Greece. It was believed to be the geographical center of Greece and of the

---

[13] *Iliad*, XVI, 233ff.; *Odyss.* XIV, 327f., XIX, 296f.; Hesiod, Loeb Classical Library edn. 214. Cf. Aesch. *Prom.* 830ff.; Soph. *Trach.* 1166ff.

[14] Xen. *Ways and Means* VI, 2; Dem. XXI, 51-53; Plut. *Phoc.* 28; Paus. VIII, xi, 12.

[15] Paus. III, xviii, 3 (Sparta); V, xv, 11 (Elis); IX, xvi, 1 (Thebes); Cook, *Zeus* I, 351ff.

[16] Herod. II, 55f., Plut. *Alex.* 3.

[17] Plut. *Cimon* 18; *Nic.* 13; Plato, *Alc. II* 148e. In *Polit.* 257b Theodorus, of Cyrene, swears "by our god, Ammon." For Athenian connection with the oracles of Ammon and Dodona, see Sterling Dow, *Harv. Theol. Rev.* XXX, 1937, 184f.; Sandys, *Aristotle's Constitution of Athens*, 2nd edn. 245.

[18] Plut. *Lys.* 20, 25.

[19] Plut. *Alex.* 26-27.

[20] Though other oracles are implied in 772d, πάσας θεῶν μαντείας.

[21] But there is probably also a personal preference involved. Plato created within the Academy a Μουσεῖον, or shrine of the Muses (Diog. IV, 1; Olympiodorus, *Vita Plat.* 6). Apollo was the favorite god of the Pythagoreans, with whom Plato had much in common. One should recall the Apollo theme in the *Phaedo* (60d, 85a) and Speusippus' eulogy of Plato as "the son of Apollo."

world. It was certainly a religious center to which the most widely dispersed cults and holy places were attached and from which they drew their authority. It was the seat of the Delphic Amphictyony, an organization composed of the leading Greek cities and capable on occasion of exercising considerable political influence. As a magnet for thinkers and artists, whose maxims and monuments enriched its holy precinct, the sanctuary of Delphi might well be regarded as the capital of Greek culture.[22] How this ascendancy was attained—whether as a result of the favorable geographical situation of Delphi, or of its awe-inspiring physical setting, or of its celebrated Panhellenic games, or of the special character of Apollo (the most Hellenic of all the gods), or of the religious and moral teaching that emanated from the oracle, assisted by persistent and astute propaganda (as Defradas has recently maintained)—the fact of this ascendancy is indisputable. The row of treasuries along the Sacred Way in the holy precinct, and the multitude of rich monuments and trophies erected by private persons and states, are evidence of the truly international character of this god and the profound reverence felt for him.

Moreover, Apollo seems to have had particularly intimate relations with both Sparta and Athens. Of the two seats on the Amphictyonic Council reserved for the Ionians, one was permanently set aside for Athens; and of the two reserved for the Dorians, Sparta held one. The Lacedaemonians claimed to have got sanction from Delphi for their Lycurgan laws; during the Peloponnesian War the oracle seems to have been openly favorable to them, promising them victory if they conducted the war vigorously, and on many occasions giving them special encouragement and assistance.[23] It is not so generally recognized to what extent the worship of the Delphic god was rooted at Athens, and what great importance Athenian statesmen attached to it as a matter of public policy. At a very early period the cult of Pythian Apollo was assimilated to the worship of Apollo Patroös, the ancestral god of the Athenians, and the legends of Pythian Apollo's northern origin were modified to emphasize his connection with Delos, the sacred Ionian isle under the protection of Athens.[24] He had a sanctuary among the ancient structures on the

[22] Defradas, *Les Thèmes de la propagande delphique*, 10.
[23] Thuc. I, 118, 3; Parke, *op.cit.* 99ff.
[24] G. Colin, *Le Culte d'Apollon Pythien à Athènes*, Paris, 1905, 1-13, 92ff., 176ff.; Defradas, *op.cit.* 193 n. 7, 198ff. Athena is supposed to have assisted at Apollo's

south side of the Acropolis, whose origin dates from at least the time of Pisistratus; another on Mount Poikilos, on the road to Eleusis, the present site of the monastery of Daphne; and most important of all in classical times, a temple on the west side of the agora between the Stoa Basileios and the Metroön.[25] Solon consulted the oracle before he drew up his famous laws, and his "constitution" provided that the archons on entering office should take an oath to abide by these laws and dedicate a life-size golden statue at Delphi if they departed from them.[26] It was the Athenian Alcmaeonidae who rebuilt the temple of Apollo at Delphi, largely at their own expense, after it had been destroyed by fire in the sixth century; and their fellow citizens continued to adorn the sacred area with monuments and offerings. Every four years a sacred embassy was sent from Athens for ceremonies and games. All this indicates not only a desire to win the support of the oracle for Athenian policy, but also the veneration accorded to Apollo's cult by at least the more substantial elements of the Athenian population. In return, the Pythian oracle is said to have declared Athens the happiest of cities and the most beloved of the gods, and to have warned Lysander, after the victory of the Spartans at the end of the Peloponnesian War, not to destroy this "common hearth" of the Hellenes.[27]

In distinguishing the sacred law from the other laws of the city, and in placing it under an authority to a large extent independent of state officials, Plato is following a precedent of long standing at Athens and in Greece generally. Religious law—the law concerning τὰ ἱερά or τὰ θεῖα—was the part of the ancestral law (τὰ πάτρια) which longest resisted inclusion in, or subordination to, the law of the polis as it was progressively formulated by Solon, Cleisthenes, and the later legislative commissions of the Athenian demos. At the revision of the laws which occurred at Athens in the last decade of

---

birth, and according to a later tradition she led him to Delphi and helped him to gain possession of his sanctuary there. In Euripides' *Ion* he is pictured as the father of Ion and the ancestor of the Athenian people.

[25] The sixth-century temple was destroyed by the Persians and the site lay vacant in Plato's day; but shortly after his death another temple of Apollo Patroös was erected, and its foundations are a conspicuous feature of the west side of the Agora as it appears today.

[26] Arist. *Const. Ath.* VII, 1; Plato, *Phaedr.* 235d and scholia; Plut. *Solon* 14 and 25. Solon appears to have influenced the Amphictyony to intervene in favor of Delphi in the First Sacred War; Plut. *Solon* 11; Georges Daux, "Athènes et Delphes," *Harv. Stud. in Class. Phil. Suppl.* I, 1940, 41-42.

[27] Dem. *Epist.* IV, 3; Aelian *Var. Hist.* IV, 6; Athen. 187d.

the fifth century the religious law (i.e. the laws regarding the annual, biennial, and quadrennial sacrifices and festivals) was carefully distinguished from the rest and set forth in a different part of the code.[28] The source of religious law was the utterances of the god, in part preserved in the details of particular cults and the traditions regarding their establishment, partly in unwritten proverbial wisdom and pious observance, and partly in the writings of Homer and Hesiod, Musaeus and Orpheus. Besides these traditions there was a living source of religious law, the responses of the oracle to contemporary consultants; for whenever the recognized authorities did not give sufficient light the advice of the oracle could always be invoked. So it was at Athens, and so it will be in Plato's state. It is explicitly prescribed occasionally (856e, 914a, 947d), and other references (cf. τοῦ θεοῦ in 871d) show that it is a recourse always in reserve.[29]

Plato's recognition of this religious law is not simply a concession to his countrymen's sentiments, nor is it to be taken as a mark of his old age; it merely reaffirms a doctrine he had expressed much earlier in the *Republic*. After Socrates has outlined the structure of his state and has described the nature of the guardian class and the manner of their education, Glaucon asks what part of "our legislation" is still to be enacted.

"For us nothing," I replied, "but for the Apollo of Delphi the chief, the fairest, and the first of enactments."

"And what are these?" he asked.

"Sacrifices, and the founding of temples, and other services of worship to gods, daemons, and heroes. . . . For we who are founding the city know nothing of such matters, nor if we are wise shall we use any other interpreter than our ancestral one. For this God who delivers his interpretation from his seat in the middle and at the very navel of the earth is surely the ancestral interpreter in religious matters for all mankind." 427bc[30]

It is but a reassertion of this fundamental principle when in the *Laws* the Athenian Stranger declares simply: "We must bring from Delphi laws about all matters of religion and appoint interpreters of them" (759c). There is irony and pathos in the fact that when

---

[28] For the fragments of this revised code that have been discovered in the Athenian Agora, see Oliver, *Hesperia* IV, 1935, 5-32; and Dow, *ibid*. X, 1941, 31-37.

[29] As it is in the *Republic*: e.g. 461c, 540c.

[30] For Apollo as the ἐξηγητής of Zeus, see Aesch. *Eumen.* 595, 622ff; IG I² 78; and Nilsson I, 596.

Plato was writing this, Delphi was passing through a time of trial and humiliation. The temple had been destroyed in 373 (probably by an earthquake) and had not yet been rebuilt. The Third Sacred War was raging; the Phocians had taken possession of the sanctuary and were melting down the offerings and the contents of the treasury for their military expenses; and the service of the oracle had been almost completely suspended.[31] There is no hint of this in the *Laws*, which shows that Plato thought the eclipse was temporary. The temple did in fact rise again, and the oracle continued to give its advice to earnest inquirers for many centuries after Plato's death.

It may seem somewhat puzzling to find that Plato recognizes a higher authority than the philosophical legislator, and we wonder why. It does not help us much to ask whether Plato believes the Pythia to be inspired. In some sense of the term he would undoubtedly attribute the utterances of the oracle to inspiration. But inspired also are the poets and the "godlike men" (θεῖοι) who arise from time to time and find the good for themselves and their cities without benefit of philosophical discourse and demonstration.[32] Of such sort is the unnamed legislator (whom we have identified with the Lycurgus of tradition) who established the gerousia at Sparta and laid the basis of the eunomia for which Sparta was so famous (691e). Likewise the philosopher and the philosophical legislator are θεῖοι in their own fashion (704d; cf. 969b).[33] But the special task of the philosopher seems to be to criticize the alleged inspiration of these other leaders of the people and to determine, by reason, which of their utterances are "right opinion" and which are false. The part played in human history by θεία μοῖρα is frequently asserted in Plato's writings; and his exposition in the *Timaeus* of the demiurgic ordering of the world implies that divine providence is at work. But there are other events and circumstances that are merely the work of Necessity or Chance.[34] So the religious belief in divine providence actually sets the problem for the philosopher, viz. to disentangle the results of divine guidance from the accidents of circumstance and human perversity. We are thus left with our original question: why,

[31] Parke, *op.cit.* 237ff.

[32] 682a; *Meno* 99cd; *Ion* 534cd; *Rep.* 331e; *Phil.* 18b.

[33] Plato's use of θεῖος in these passages follows popular usage and involves no philosophical or theological theory of inspiration. See J. Van Camp and P. Canart, *Le sens du mot θεῖος chez Platon*, Louvain, 1956, 414 and passim.

[34] See the author's "Necessity and Persuasion in Plato's *Timaeus*," PR LIX, 1950, 147-163.

in this segment of Plato's laws, does the philosopher seem to abdicate his function to the Pythian oracle?

Part of the answer is certainly that in the region of "the sacred" (τὰ θεῖα) the authority of tradition and long-established observance is especially important if a legislator wishes to make use of religion at all as an ordering factor in his state. Here the legislator must build on the habitual forms of reverence that he finds in his citizens, and the decision to do so is itself an act of philosophical reflection. Nor was it an abdication of his function for a philosophical legislator of Plato's time to designate Delphi as the final authority in matters of observance. Undoubtedly Plato saw in Delphi, as Dodds has well said, "a great conservative force which could be harnessed to the task of stabilizing the Greek religious tradition and checking both the spread of materialism and the growth of aberrant tendencies within the tradition itself."[35] Above all, we must not forget that the religion of Delphi was a distinctly moralizing and civilizing agent in Greek life.[36] The Apolline spirit breathed moderation and respect for law; Apollo was himself the patron of legislation.[37] In his temple at Delphi were engraved those sayings of the Seven Sages—such as "Know thyself," "Nothing in excess"—that so impressed Socrates, Plato, and their countrymen.[38] The oracle itself was sometimes asked to say who was the wisest of men, or the happiest, or the most pious; and the answers, as preserved in later traditions, show a consistent tendency to rebuke the proud and self-righteous and honor the humble and unassuming. The response to the question of Chaerephon, whether anyone at Athens was wiser than Socrates, is an example of Apollo's penchant for finding peculiar excellence in those who laid

[35] Dodds, *The Greeks and the Irrational*, 223.

[36] An early response preserved by Herodotus (vi, 86) contains an uncompromising rebuke to an inquirer who asked whether he would be justified in forswearing himself in order to retain possession of a large sum of money entrusted to him by a friend. Cf. also Herodotus' story of Cleobis and Biton (i, 31).

[37] See Nilsson i, 607ff.

[38] Plato's references to these sayings are numerous: *Charm.* 164d, *Prot.* 343b, *Phaedr.* 229e, *Phil.* 48c, *Laws* 923a, *Alc. I* 124a, 129a, 132c. The tradition of the Seven Sages is itself connected with Delphi, though it is difficult to reconstruct the details of its origin; the first list of seven is found in Plato (*Prot.* 343a), but Herodotus seems to have known of it, without anywhere mentioning the seven members of the group. See Defradas, *op.cit.* 268, 274ff. "En les adoptant [i.e. the maxims of the Seven Sages] le clergé d'Apollon avait revendiqué pour son dieu le rôle d'un dieu de sagesse. Les maximes devenaient l'expression de la sagesse apollonienne, et, indépendamment de leur contenu, elles marquent, par leur seule présence, que le temple de Delphe n'est pas un temple comme les autres, que la religion d'Apollon met au premier plan les préoccupations morales" (*ibid.* 276).

least claim to it.[39] Delphi even taught that ritual was less important than the inner disposition of the wrongdoer; and the law of purification for homicide contained an awareness that differences of motive and intent imply different degrees of impurity to be cleansed.[40] "Writers of histories take it for granted," says Ephorus, "that Apollo, with Themis, established the oracle because he wished to help our race; and that . . . he summoned men to gentleness and self-control."[41]

The adaptability of the oracle to Plato's purposes was furthered by two conspicuous features of Delphic policy. Its pronouncements, though delivered as the voice of the god, could not be more than solemn advice; the sanctions of this advice were the consequences experienced from following or disregarding it, and the oracle attained only the credit resulting from giving wise counsel. In the second place, its advice regarding the cult was ordinarily restricted to the externals of observance. Delphi was therefore not an oppressive force; there was always the possibility of interpreting its utterances so as to give a deeper meaning to the practices it enjoined. For Plato, with his belief in the importance of ritual and observance in the molding of habits and sentiments, the advice of the oracle, hallowed by so many centuries of reverence, would constitute a priceless asset to the forces making for moral training in his state, particularly since, by a judicious choice of the songs to be sung and the dances to be performed at the religious ceremonies, the legislator could introduce into these traditional rites the desired content of moral and religious beliefs.

RELIGIOUS OFFICIALS

In every Greek city the temples, with the sacred areas surrounding them, were the local residences of the gods and the places to which worshippers would come for sacrifices and prayers around the altars. In Plato's state the first step in the division of the land is to mark off a ἱερόν for Hestia, Zeus, and Athena, to be known as the acropolis, and surround it with a wall (745b). Near this will be an agora, with other temples around it (778c). There are to be similar sacred areas in each village (848d) and others scattered over the countryside, dedicated perhaps to local divinities whose worship the legislator

[39] *Apol.* 21a; Xen. *Apol.* 14.
[40] See the schol. to *Laws* 865b; Parke, *op.cit.*, 386ff., 432; Defradas, *op.cit.* 118.
[41] Strabo IX, iii, 11.

must leave undisturbed, or to the special gods to whom these tribal and local divisions have been assigned (745d; cf. 761c). Most of these sacred precincts will possess temples or shrines of the gods to whom they belong and altars for sacrifice.[42] Some of these sacred areas will also contain buildings for the lodging of the priests and for the entertainment of foreign visitors (953a). Some will be extensive enough to include cultivable land, whose products become, like the land and the temple, the property of the god (759e); and sometimes they will include lakes or streams, the "sacred waters" of 824c.[43]

The temples with their treasures deposited by worshippers, the other buildings in the sacred precincts, the cultivated land with its products, the revenues from these and other sources, are property that has to be maintained and protected and whose use has to be supervised. Such duties in Plato's time were usually assigned to one or more officers, nonpriestly in character, but belonging to the general category of religious as distinct from secular officials.[44] In Plato's state the protection of the temples, and their restoration when they

[42] The term ἱερόν, most frequently employed by Plato, may denote either sacred area or temple; τέμενος, which is often used (738c, 758e, 759e, 761c, 945e, 946d), clearly denotes the precinct. But the reference to altars (βωμοί) and temples (ναοί) in 738c, and the inclusion of ἱερά among the tasks of οἰκοδομική that have to be taken care of in the new city (778b) show that ἱερά in Plato's text often means temples, as it did in current usage (see below, Note 44). Some structure would clearly be necessary, in Plato's state as in the real cities of his time, to safeguard the votive offerings and other treasures that belonged to the god. Cf. the law against the robbing of temples (ἱεροσυλία) in 853d-854e (cf. 885a), and the prescription that certain fines shall be payable to the temples (774b,d).

In 955e there is an apparent prohibition against consecrating land because it is already sacred to the gods. This passage is often cited by Hellenistic writers, and sometimes is interpreted as forbidding the building of temples, which is obviously not Plato's meaning. In its context it is most naturally interpreted as forbidding the dedication by a citizen of a part of his lot; thus interpreted it supplements the law against unauthorized private shrines (909d). On the use of this passage by ancient authors see des Places, REG, LXIII, 1955, 182.

[43] All of this is a reflection of current Greek usage; cf. the regulations regarding the τεμένη ἐξῃρημένα in the Athenian decree for the establishment of the colony at Brea in 445 (Tod I, No. 44). The framers of this decree seem concerned to set a limit to the extension of the sacred domain. On sacred waters see Stengel, 20, nn. 3 and 4; on fines payable to temples, *ibid.* 21, nn. 5 and 6.

[44] Arist. *Pol.* 1322b 17ff. Aristotle mentions as illustrations of such officers ἱεροποιοί, ναοφύλακες and ταμίαι. These ἱεροποιοί are not to be confused with the officers called by this name at Athens, who were concerned with the conduct of festivals and sacrifices, not with the oversight of property (Arist. *Const. Ath.* LIV, 6-7). At Athens the repair of the temples was the responsibility of ten ἱερῶν ἐπισκευασταί, selected annually by lot (*Const. Ath.* L, 1). There was also an ἀρχιτέκτων ἐπὶ τὰ ἱερά (Stengel 51). We have evidence of still other designations for such officers, such as νεωποιοί, ἱεροφύλακες, and φρουροί (Stengel 51).

have been damaged, seem to be a part of the responsibilities of secular officials—of the agoranomoi and the astynomoi in the city, and of the agronomoi in the country.[45] The only special officers that Plato designates for the sacred property are "treasurers" (ταμίαι). They are to be responsible for the sacred funds (ἱερὰ χρήματα) in the temples to which they are appointed, and for the disposal of the harvests of sacred lands and the leasing of temple properties (759e).[46] Such officers, even for the smaller temples, are almost always found in the Greek cities of Plato's day.[47] In earlier times it seems the handling of temple funds was left to the priests of the gods concerned; but as these funds increased and as the state often found it necessary to borrow from them, they were brought under officials elected by the state; the sacred funds, however, were always regarded as distinct from the city treasury and were administered by special officers.[48] Plato prescribes that there shall be three treasurers for the larger temples, for the smaller ones two, and for the smallest, one. Each of these is to hold office for one year only. They are to be elected, like the astynomoi, from the highest property classes, and doubtless for the same reason, i.e. they must have both the ability and the necessary leisure to look after public property (759e-760a).[49] Their election takes place in the manner prescribed for generals, by a majority vote in the full assembly from a list of nominees presented by the guardians (755cd). In historical states such officers were subject to an accounting at the end of their terms, and the same would certainly be true in Plato's state.

The more strictly religious officers attached to the various temples are the priests and priestesses (ἱερῆς, ἱέρειαι, 759a). Of priesthoods Plato recognizes both hereditary (πάτριαι ἱερόσυναι) and annual. A hereditary priesthood in Plato's day was one which belonged by tradition in a certain family and when it fell vacant through the death of the incumbent was filled within the family according to the particular rules of succession that governed it. Such priesthoods usually traced their authorities back to some oracle or other sign of divine favor that had established them; they belong, therefore, to that area

---

[45] See above, Chapter V, The Magistrates.

[46] For the meaning of μισθώσεις in 759e see Stengel 19; Arist. *Const. Ath.* XLVII, 4; Dem. LVII, 63.

[47] Arist. *Pol. loc.cit.* Stengel 52.

[48] Busolt-Swoboda 501ff.

[49] It was a law of Solon, still in effect in Aristotle's day, that the treasurers of Athena should be selected from the "five-hundred-bushel" class. Arist. *Const. Ath.* XLVII, I.

of traditional observance that the legislator must not touch.⁵⁰ Plato
prescribes that hereditary priesthoods are to be left undisturbed
(759a);⁵¹ but he evidently thinks there are likely to be few such establishments in the area of the new colony (759b) and he gives the
matter no further attention. We must assume, of course, that any new
hereditary priesthood established at the command of Delphi would
be recognized.

Annual priesthoods are to be filled by lot (759c). The use of the
lot, rare in Plato's law, is justified here on the ground that it enables
"the god himself" to do what pleases him through "divine chance"
($\theta\epsilon i\alpha$ $\tau \acute{v}\chi\eta$). The lot was the most common method of filling such
offices in Plato's time, and it is fair to suppose that he is following
common Greek opinion in justifying it as he does.⁵² Plato nowhere
states explicitly the duties of priests; but it is implied that they maintain order ($\kappa \acute{o}\sigma\mu o\varsigma$) in and about the temples and sacred areas
(759ab), and elsewhere there are references to their performing
sacrifices (909d), and entertaining certain types of foreign visitors
(953a).⁵³ The holder of a priesthood must be sixty years of age or
older (759d); he must be physically perfect ($\acute{o}\lambda\acute{o}\kappa\lambda\eta\rho o\varsigma$, i.e. un-
mutilated), legitimate ($\gamma\nu\acute{\eta}\sigma\iota o\varsigma$), free of the pollution of bloodshed and of other similar offences against religion, and of father and
mother equally pure (759c). These requirements parallel for the

⁵⁰ The most famous of such priests at Athens was the Hierophant, the head of
the Eleusinian cult of Demeter, who was chosen for life from the family of the
Eumolpidae, and whose chief duties were to preside over the Eleusinian mysteries.
At Sparta the important priesthoods of Artemis Orthia, of Apollo Carneios, and of
the Dioscuri were hereditary. For other examples of hereditary priesthoods at Athens
and elsewhere, see Stengel 44; Nilsson 1, 671f.; and Busolt-Swoboda 498 n. 3. Since
priesthoods carried certain emoluments, sometimes considerable ones, they were frequently a matter of litigation. Cf. Arist. *Const. Ath.* XLII, 5; LVII, 2.
⁵¹ This was the policy also of Solon and Cleisthenes; Feaver, *Yale Classical Studies*
xv, 1957, 132, 133.
⁵² So Stengel (45) assumes. Feaver (*op.cit.* 146, 148) asserts that Plato makes the
selection for annual priesthoods a $\kappa\lambda\acute{\eta}\rho\omega\sigma\iota\varsigma$ $\acute{\epsilon}\kappa$ $\pi\rho o\kappa\rho\acute{\iota}\tau\omega\nu$; but he cites no references, and his opinion may be merely an inference from the fact that this method
is frequently used in the selection of other public officials.
⁵³ Feaver (*op.cit.* 123, 148) seems clearly mistaken in saying that their fundamental
function is that of public officials administering sacred property. Likewise Reverdin
(62) is in error in assuming that they have charge of the registers of property
deposited in the temples (741c). This passage says that these registers are to be
guarded by specially competent officers ($\acute{a}\rho\chi\acute{\eta}$), obviously an anticipation of the
guardians, to whom this responsibility is explicitly assigned in 754d.
For other references in Plato to the functions of priests, see *Rep.* 461a and *Symp.*
202e. In the latter passage the $\tau\acute{\epsilon}\chi\nu\eta$ of priests includes prophecy ($\mu\alpha\nu\tau\epsilon\acute{\iota}\alpha$) and
witchcraft ($\gamma o\eta\tau\epsilon\acute{\iota}\alpha$). For $\mu\alpha\nu\tau\epsilon\acute{\iota}\alpha$ and $\gamma o\eta\tau\epsilon\acute{\iota}\alpha$ (forbidden in the *Laws*) see the
Index.

most part those of positive Greek law. The test of legitimacy will insure that the offices are held by citizens; for Plato this would be an obvious requisite, as it was in the Athens of his day.[54] Likewise freedom from bodily blemish or mutilation was a familiar requirement to Plato's contemporaries.[55] Plato's age requirement is more restrictive than that at Athens; most priests and priestesses in his day seem to have been grown men and women, though youths and maidens sometimes filled these offices, particularly when virginity was a requirement.[56] Aristotle also prescribes for his ideal state that the priesthoods shall be filled by the older men, who can appropriately spend their retirement from other duties in service to the gods.[57] Unlike Aristotle, Plato follows the familiar Greek custom of admitting women to the priesthood.[58] But in his requirement of purity there is a suggestion of something deeper than conventional ideas. In insisting that a priest must be free of the pollution of bloodshed, and in extending this requirement to the father and mother of the candidate, he is only expressing common Greek sentiment, if not Greek law; but he prefaces this requirement with the statement that a candidate and his family must be "as pure as possible." We read elsewhere that what defiles a man is wickedness; only the good man is pure ($\kappa\alpha\theta\alpha\rho\acute{o}s$), and he only may properly offer gifts to the gods (716e). It may be that the words just quoted are intended to suggest that more than ceremonial purity is desired for the performance of this important office.[59]

The caretakers ($\nu\epsilon\omega\kappa\acute{o}\rho\omega$) mentioned in 759a are obviously subordinate attendants in the various sanctuaries, as they were in the Greece of Plato's day. No procedure is mentioned for their selection, and it is possible that they are to be appointed by the priests or priestesses whom they assist, as was occasionally done in fourth-century

[54] In Dem. LVII, 46 Euxitheos adduces as special evidence of his Athenian citizenship that he was approved ($\pi\rho\omicron\epsilon\kappa\rho\acute{\iota}\theta\eta$) as a candidate for a priesthood of Heracles.
[55] Stengel 38. Anaxandrides (Athen. 300a) contrasts Greek and Egyptian sentiments on this point. Cf. Herod. II, 37.
[56] Stengel 37; Busolt-Swoboda 498 and n. 2.
[57] *Pol.* 1329a 30ff.
[58] Note the recurring formula: $\iota\epsilon\rho\hat{\eta}s$ $\kappa\alpha\grave{\iota}$ $\iota\acute{\epsilon}\rho\epsilon\iota\alpha\iota$: 741c, 759a, 799b, 800b, 909d, 947d.
[59] Bloodshed was the chief source of ceremonial uncleanness in Plato's day. Another source was contact with a corpse; Plato elsewhere shows that his priests are ordinarily debarred from approaching tombs (947d). There is definitely more than ritual impurity meant in 910e—$o\grave{\upsilon}$ $\kappa\alpha\theta\alpha\rho\grave{o}s$ $\mathring{\omega}\nu$ $\theta\acute{\upsilon}\omega\nu$—for the offender in this case is a disbeliever. The distinction between ceremonial and moral purity is not peculiar to Plato. See Dodds, *op.cit.* 55 n. 47.

Greece. Their title literally means temple sweepers: they were certainly concerned with the housekeeping of the buildings in the sacred enclosure, and they perhaps assisted in performing the sacrifices and in enforcing the rules regarding admission to the sanctuary.[60] Such helpers would not be needed in the smaller sanctuaries, and doubtless it is these that Plato has in mind when he speaks of the priests and priestesses as themselves νεωκόροι to the gods (759b).

Plato's text implies that political officials as well as priests will perform sacrifices on behalf of the city; the number of our festivals must be such, he says, that on every day of the year there will be at least one officer (μία γέ τις ἀρχή) sacrificing to some god or daemon on behalf of the city, its people, and its property (828b). This is again in accord with common Greek usage. In ancient times the king as head of the people was their intercessor with the gods in the sacrifices; and these religious functions of the ancient king were preserved not merely at Sparta,[61] where kingship itself persisted into Plato's time, but also at Athens, where the ancient title was still carried by one of the nine archons. The functions specifically assigned to the king at Athens were primarily connected with religious observances and religious law: he directed the "ancestral sacrifices" (πάτριοι θυσίαι), he heard all charges of homicide, pronounced against suspected persons the prohibition of exclusion from sacred areas and rites, and introduced these cases to their respective courts for trial. He also superintended the mysteries and certain other sacred festivals and contests.[62] The archon and the polemarch also had certain religious functions, including not merely the oversight of festivals but also the performance of sacrifices.[63] The inscriptions show that sacrifices were also offered by generals and by prytanes.[64] So it seems to be understood, though Plato hardly thinks it necessary

---

[60] Stengel (51) gives the epigraphical and literary evidence for such attendants and their duties in classical times. Ion, in Euripides' drama, seems to have been a νεωκόρος. When the play opens he is chiefly concerned with sweeping the temple, sprinkling the entrance in preparation for the sacrifice, and keeping the birds from soiling the building and its monuments (102-183; cf. 794-795). Later he is shown enforcing a rule regarding admission to the sanctuary (221ff.).

In later times, particularly in Asia, the office of νεωκόρος was of considerable dignity. Despite their title, such officials had nothing to do with the menial tasks about the sanctuary.

[61] Xen. *Const. Lac.* XIII, 2; XV, 2.

[62] Arist. *Const. Ath.* LVII; *Pol.* 1285b 17, 1322b 27ff.; Ps. Lysias VI, 4; Plato *Polit.* 290de.

[63] Arist. *Const. Ath.* LVI and LVIII.

[64] Stengel 34; cf. Theoph. *Char.* XXI, 11.

to say so, that certain public sacrifices and prayers will be performed by his secular archons officiating in something like a priestly role. It is probable that when the ceremony takes place at one of the sanctuaries (as distinct from the "common hearth" of the city) the priest of the sanctuary would have to be present and take part in the rites. But the line of demarcation between the functions of political officials and those of priests in the strict sense is not clearly drawn in Plato's text, any more than it seems to have been in Greek law and custom.

This recognition that the functions of political officials are sometimes religious in character receives striking expression in the provision that the euthynoi shall be designated priests of Helios and Apollo. That this is not an empty phrase is clear from the circumstances surrounding their election and the special honors they enjoy during their lifetime.[65] These honors and prerogatives—the wearing of garlands of olive and laurel, front seats at the festivals, residence in the sacred precincts—have their parallels in the distinctions accorded at Athens and in the Greek world generally to the holders of the most important priesthoods.[66] But we have no evidence, I believe, that political officials ever bore the title of priest in Plato's time, in spite of their functioning quite often in a priestly capacity in the public sacrifices. Plato also provides that one of the euthynoi is to be selected annually as "high priest" ($\dot{a}\rho\chi\iota\dot{\epsilon}\rho\epsilon\omega s$), and the year is to carry his name in the official chronology. Eponymous priests (or priestesses) seem to have been rare, although not unknown, in Plato's time; but they are abundantly attested for the following and later centuries.[67] Again, although the title of "high priest" must have been known to readers of Herodotus' account of Egypt, it is not attested for any Greek city until after the middle of the third century.[68] After this time it becomes very common; in the Athens of Roman days the high priest seems to have ranked above the exegetes of Apollo and just below the two Eleusinian exegetes.[69] Since the euthynoi are one

---

[65] 947a. See Chapter V, The Scrutiny and the Audit.

[66] Stengel 39, 47; on $\pi\rho o\epsilon\delta\rho\dot{\iota}a\iota$ in the Theatre of Dionysus at Athens, see Aristoph. *Frogs* 297; and for later times, Oliver, *The Athenian Expounders of the Sacred and Ancestral Law*, Baltimore, 1950, 41ff.

[67] Busolt-Swoboda 499-500; Stengel 39, 46-47; Reverdin 61 n. 12.

[68] Stengel 47. See Herodotus II, 37.

[69] Oliver, *op.cit.* 41, 100-101. Plato's use of the Ionic form ($\dot{a}\rho\chi\iota\dot{\epsilon}\rho\epsilon\omega s$) found in Herodotus (II, 37) may be taken as confirmation of the other evidence that this is a novel suggestion. The Attic form $\dot{a}\rho\chi\iota\epsilon\rho\epsilon\dot{u}s$ was commonly used in the Hellenistic period. For the reading of Plato's text, see Bekker, *Anecdota* I, 449.

of the most important boards of officers in his state, its members holding office until death or retirement at the age of seventy-five, this union of political and religious honors in their persons may have a special significance. No duties of an expressly religious sort are assigned to them, though we may assume that like other officials they often preside at public sacrifices. Plato's thought may have been that in the very work of their office they will be performing an essentially religious function, through encouraging in the state's officials that imitation of the divine orderliness which it is the function of all religious ceremonies to induce in the citzens. Whatever Plato's reasons, the *Laws* anticipates the future and may have been an important influence upon Athenian practices in Hellenistic times.

It is clear that every priest is attached to a certain sanctuary, in the service of the deity to whom it is dedicated. There are to be no priests in general in Plato's state, any more than there were in his native city. The priests of a Greek city were not even connected in any formal fashion with one another, not even the priests who served the same god in different sanctuaries.[70] The short tenure of their office, the lack of any ecclesiastical organization, and the fact that the priests had no monopoly in the exercise of sacrificial functions, made the rise of such a class impossible. These are the conditions assumed in Plato's state. His "high priest" has only an honorific title; he is not the head of a religious hierarchy; what authority he exercises he has as euthynos, not as priest, and it is not specifically authority over other priests, but generally over all other officials of the state. Nor is there any provision in Plato's law for the training of priests other than the educational program prescribed for all citizens of the state.

But the performance of sacrifices and prayers according to the accepted ritual requires both knowledge and skill, and one wonders how they were to be acquired. No doubt attendance upon religious ceremonies would give all citizens a general familiarity with the way things were done, and devotion to a certain sanctuary and frequent attendance at its rites would give a man special knowledge of its particular ritual. It is possible that only those who had a more than ordinary interest in the worship in a given sanctuary would present themselves as candidates for its priesthood. But there is no hint in

[70] Stengel 33.

Plato's law, nor in the evidence we have about common Greek practice, that such considerations were taken into account in the selection of priests.[71] This may be regarded as another indication of the general level of competence among its citizens that the Greek city-state everywhere presupposed, and such general competence would no doubt suffice for ordinary purposes. But on unusual occasions, whether a personal or family crisis, or an emergency facing the whole community, or any occasion of dispute as to the way in which a ceremony should be conducted, there would be need of something like professional advice in placating the gods and averting their displeasure. The expedient of consulting Delphi or some other oracle was always available; but such a proceeding was time-consuming and costly, and would not after all dispense with the need of expert guidance in interpreting the response.

Such expert guidance is presumably to be provided in Plato's state by another group of religious officers, the exegetes, or "interpreters." "We must bring from Delphi laws about all matters of religion and appoint interpreters (ἐξηγηταί) of them."[72] The description of their election which follows immediately is cryptic and has given rise to widely varying interpretations, but it may most plausibly, I think, be rendered as follows:[73]

The exegetes shall be three. Three times shall four tribes select four from their own members, of whom three—those receiving the most votes—shall be subjected to the scrutiny and the nine [names resulting] shall be sent to Delphi [for the oracle] to select one from each group of three. The scrutiny, and the age qualification, shall be [the same] as for the priests. These shall be exegetes for life; and when one dies, the four tribes in which the vacancy occurred shall make the preliminary selection. 759de

[71] "Anyone can be a priest," says Isocrates (II, 6). This is not an expression of contempt for the office, as Stengel points out (*op.cit.* 33 n. 6), but only an assertion that it requires no special qualification. In some sanctuaries there were inscriptions containing instructions for the conduct of the rites, or a book for the guidance of the priest. A. W. Persson, *Die Exegeten und Delphi* (in *Acta Universitatis Lundensis*, 1918), 9; Jules Martha, *Les Sacerdoces athéniens*, Paris, 1882, 29. Cf. Paus. IV, xxvii, 5; Dem. XVIII, 259.

[72] 759c: ἐκ Δελφῶν δὲ χρὴ νόμους περὶ τὰ θεῖα πάντα κομισαμένους καὶ καταστήσαντας ἐπ' αὐτοῖς ἐξηγητὰς τούτοις χρῆσθαι. The last two words are not translated above. Whether the antecedent of τούτοις is ἐξηγητάς or νόμους is not clear. It makes little difference to the sense which alternative we choose; but if the former was intended by Plato, he is emphasizing the official status of these exegetes, as compared with unofficial advisors, and the emphasis may spring from his consciousness of the recent establishment of this office at Athens.

[73] See Excursus E, below.

These are quite clearly religious officers of peculiar importance and dignity, since they hold office for life. The manner of their election is most unusual. No reason is given for the division of the twelve tribes into three groups, nor any explanation of the way in which these groups are to be made up; and the details of the further procedure of election are so scanty as to make it impossible to determine precisely what is intended. All this indicates that Plato is taking over something that is already familiar to his readers and does not require explanation. The only points that are emphasized are (1) that the choice of three candidates from each group is to be effected by election (οἷς ἂν πλείστη γένηται ψῆφος), not by the lot, and (2) that the final selection of one from each group of three is to be made by the oracle at Delphi.

We have both literary and epigraphical evidence that one or more persons with this title existed at Athens in the fourth century; but whether such officers (if officers they were) existed in earlier days, or were a product of the legislative reorganization at the end of the Peloponnesian War, has recently been a matter of acute controversy.[74] In any case, the need for expert declaration and interpretation of religious law must have existed long before the fourth century. In early times this function of ἐξήγησις was probably exercised by the Eupatridae, the heads of the ancient γένη, who were the repositories of the ancestral law (τὰ πάτρια) of the Athenians; and just as the declaration and interpretation of secular law was gradually taken from their hands—with the introduction of written laws, elected magistrates, and courts of justice—so it is likely that something analogous was felt to be necessary in the area of religious law. But at what date the city assumed the responsibility of designating an official exegete, or exegetes, cannot be determined.[75] Besides the exegetes of Athenian ancestral law there were also exegetes of the sacred law of Eleusis, who must have been, as they were in later

[74] The former alternative is the one traditionally accepted; see Jacoby, *Atthis*, 20-21, 248-249, and FGH IIIb, Suppl. II, 534f. The traditional view has been challenged by Oliver, *op.cit.* 24-32. For the controversy, see Herbert Bloch, AJP LXXIV, 1953, 407-418, and *Harv. Stud. in Class. Phil.* LXII, 1957, 37-49; Oliver, AJP LXXIII, 1952, 406-413, and LXXV, 1954, 160-174. For another recent statement of the traditional view, and a survey of the controversy, see Defradas, *op.cit.* 199, 205-207.

[75] The evidence that has been alleged for official exegetes even in the fifth century is a doubtful, and disputed, restoration of the Prytaneum Decree (IG I² 77). For the controversy regarding this decree, see Bloch and Oliver (preceding note), and Martin Ostwald, AJP LXXII, 1951, 24-46. Defradas (*op.cit.* 200-201) has argued that certain passages in Aeschylus' *Choephorae* and *Eumenides* constitute "le premier témoignage historique sur les exégètes athéniens." But such evidence is not conclusive as to their official status.

times, selected from the Eumolpidae, the Eleusinian clan that had ancestral jurisdiction over the celebration of the mysteries.[76] The recognition given by the Athenian state to the exegesis of the Eumolpidae is irrelevant to the problem we are discussing, except that the existence of this other body of exegetes complicates the interpretation of the scanty evidence available about exegetes at Athens. The earliest reference to Athenian exegetes in anything like an official sense is found in Plato's *Euthyphro* (4c, 9a), whose dramatic date is 399 and which was probably written early in the fourth century. But not even the *Euthyphro* enables us to determine how many exegetes there were at this time (the singular is used in 4c, the plural in 9a), nor how they were selected, nor what their precise official status was. Nor does the other fourth-century evidence throw any light on these points.[77] From the evidence of Hellenistic times one may form hypotheses as to the number and status of exegetes in the fourth century, as Oliver has done;[78] but since the earliest of this later evidence is separated by more than two centuries from Plato's *Laws*, such suppositions are by no means assured conclusions.

Because of the scantiness of other evidence Plato's text has become peculiarly important for the interpretation of the fourth-century institution. But it has to be used with the utmost circumspection, since Plato is legislating for an imaginary city, and we can by no means assume that he is simply recording current Athenian practice. The lack of any explanation of the unusual method of election indeed shows that he is incorporating familiar practices into his law; and its apparently archaic features suggest that these practices are ancient ones. But beyond this we cannot go with any confidence. Jacoby's supposition that Plato is simply copying a law of Solon's time—overlooking the fact that his state consists of twelve tribes, not four, as was the case in Solonian Athens—not only attributes an unlikely error to Plato, but also contradicts the closing passage of Plato's law itself.[79] A more promising suggestion is Oliver's that the

[76] Exegesis by the Eumolpidae in the fifth century is attested by IG I² 76 (= Tod I, No. 74) if the commonly accepted restoration is correct, and by Ps. Lysias VI, 10. On these texts see Oliver (*Expounders* 18-21), who, however, contends that the right of exegesis belonged to the clan, and that there was no "college of exegetes of the Eumolpidae" until later.

[77] The only other fourth-century evidence is Isaeus (VIII, 39), Ps. Demosthenes (XLVII, 68), Theophrastus (*Char.* XVI, 6), and one inscription (see Note 90).

[78] *Op.cit.* 34ff.

[79] Jacoby, *loc.cit.* The closing sentence of Plato's text provides for the filling of a vacancy in the board of exegetes "by the four tribes in which the vacancy has occurred." This would be a meaningless provision if there were only four tribes in the state.

twelve tribes in Plato's state reflect the twelve old Attic trittyes of the pre-Cleisthenean constitution. Recent evidence indicates that these old Attic trittyes persisted in the religious law of fourth-century Athens; and it may be, as Oliver maintains, that they customarily met in three big local assemblies for nominations and certain other business.[80] Plato's provision for this election would then be simply an adoption of this ancient practice, so familiar as not to need further clarification for Athenian readers. But until we have other evidence about these old Attic trittyes in the fourth century, we can only regard Oliver's suggestion as a promising lead for further inquiry.

Thus the scantiness of our evidence regarding the number and mode of selection of Athenian exegetes in the fourth century makes it impossible to compare Plato's law on these points with that of contemporary Athens. One thing nevertheless may be confidently asserted. In Plato's state all three exegetes will be selected by Apollo. This is contrary to the practice of Hellenistic times, according to the evidence so ably marshaled by Oliver, when only one of the two Athenian exegetes was named by the oracle.[81] If we assume, as Oliver does, that this is evidence of what was done in Plato's day, then Plato's law is a deliberate protest against it. A similar protest might be read in the *Republic* (427bc): "We will have no other exegete than our ancestral one (οὐδὲ χρησόμεθα ἐξηγητῇ ἀλλ' ἢ τῷ πατρίῳ). For this god who delivers his interpretation (ἐξηγεῖται) from his seat in the middle and at the very navel of the earth is surely the ancestral interpreter (πάτριος ἐξηγητής) of religious matters for all mankind." But this may also be interpreted as a protest against consulting any unofficial interpreter, such as the chresmologoi or manteis, of whose pretensions to be the spokesmen of the gods we hear so much in earlier days.[82] This suggests another interpretation of the evidence, one which I believe has not hitherto been enter-

[80] *Op.cit.* 54, 64ff., and AJP LXXIII, 1952, 412. For recent evidence of old Attic trittyes in the fourth century, see Oliver and Ferguson, as cited in Chapter IV, Note 91. But Oliver's suggestion implies that the exegetes, like the method by which they were elected, were far older than the fourth century—which appears to be contrary to the main thesis of his book.

[81] Apollo's designate was ὁ πυθόχρηστος, the other was ὁ ὑπὸ τοῦ δήμου καθεστα-μένος. Oliver, *Expounders*, 36ff., 142ff.

[82] In fifth-century Athens advice was often provided by persons known as χρησμολόγοι, who claimed to possess something like professional knowledge of the oracles, but who were certainly not officials. For their importance on the eve of Salamis, see Herod. VII, 142-143; for a comic picture of their pretensions see Aristoph. *Birds* 959-991, and *Peace* 1046-1126; and for the public indignation against them after the Sicilian disaster, Thuc. VIII, 1. Μάντεις are treated more fully below.

tained, viz. that not even in the fourth century did Athens have an official exegete or board of exegetes comparable to those proposed in Plato's law. The restatement of the law that took place at the end of the fifth century may have been limited, so far as religious law was concerned, to the inclusion of certain hitherto unwritten rules regarding sacrifices and festivals. These are matters of such public importance that it may have been thought necessary to relieve them of the need of exegesis, while other matters of religious law could be left to the familiar but unofficial (Eupatrid?) exegetes. It may then have been Plato who first felt the necessity of bringing all religious law under official exegesis, while preserving its relative independence by making Apollo the sole source of its authority. This interpretation is, I think, compatible with the fourth-century evidence,[83] and explains the absence of all mention of such officials by Aristotle. If it is the correct interpretation—and to support it properly would involve a more thorough inquiry than can be undertaken here—then Plato's *Laws* certainly influenced the form that the institution of exegetes took in later times, and helped to establish the supremacy of Apollo in the religious life of Hellenistic Athens.

There was an institution analogous to the Athenian exegetes in the four Πύθιοι at Sparta. Unfortunately we know very little about their functions. Each of the two kings had the right to name two "Pythians," who became his tent companions and took their meals with him. Their name indicates their connection with Delphi, and Herodotus says they were θεοπρόποι εἰς Δελφούς, i.e. official messengers sent to inquire of the oracle.[84] Thus they were at least reporters of the Delphic responses, and perhaps also expounders, by virtue of their high official position in association with the kings and the experience acquired through long tenure of office. One important function of the Spartan kings was to preside at all public sacrifices and interpret the omens at the beginning of a military expedition.[85] It is logical to connect the Pythians with these religious functions of the kings; but further than this it is hazardous to speculate.

There is no general statement in Plato's text as to the duties of the exegetes, except that they are to be interpreters of the sacred law. Their competence would therefore extend to all the areas included in that law. If we take the passage in the *Republic* as a guide, we see

[83] See Notes 77 and 90.
[84] Herod. VI, 57; Xen. *Const. Lac.* xv, 5; cf. Cic. *De Divin.* I, 95.
[85] Xen. *Const. Lac.* XIII, 2-5; xv, 2; Herod. VI, 57.

that religious law covered the founding of temples, sacrifices, and all other "services" (θεραπεῖαι) to gods, daemons, and heroes, as well as the burial of the dead and rites to the gods of the underworld. Of all these matters Apollo is to be the interpreter. We get further information, however, from references in the *Laws* to occasions on which the judgment and advice of the exegetes will be required.

The largest number of these references concern purifications (καθαρμοί) for various occasions. This is appropriate, for the rites of purification as practised in Greece traced their origin almost universally to Apollo (cf. 865b). Most forms of homicide, even those that involved no legal penalty, were thought to bring pollution on the shedder of blood and his family, and upon the state as a whole, a pollution that could only be removed by ceremonial purification.[86] Such purifications are mentioned as necessary in all the forms of homicide distinguished in Platonic law—homicide done in madness (864e), accidental killing in games or military exercises (865a), all other forms of accidental killing (865c-866c), homicide committed in passion (867c-869d), and deliberate murder (871a-c). In one instance the exegetes are said to have authority over these rites of purification (865c), so that we may assume they are always implied, even when not explicitly mentioned. A suicide must also be purified before being buried, and here again the exegetes are explicitly mentioned, together with the "laws concerning such matters," obviously the religious laws that lie within their competence (873d). A household into which a slave guilty of homicide has been brought must be purified "according to the law of the exegetes" (916c). Even the house of a murderer who dies childless requires purification "according to law" before it can be assigned to another family (877e); and the previous examples show that the law referred to here is that of the exegetes. Finally, we have a reference to the function of the exegetes in purifying a spring or cistern that has been polluted by drugs or sorcery (845e).[87]

---

[86] Bonner and Smith I, 53ff.; Treston, *Poine*, passim.

[87] The φαρμακεῖαι referred to here must be interpreted in the light of the distinction between two types of φαρμακεία at 932e—i.e. that which works by means of drugs, and that which uses sorcery and spells. Sorcery is a delusion, Plato says, but human nature is such that it can be easily deceived and imposed on by the sorcerer's claims. One obvious way to counteract its effects is by religious rites. Since the effects of poison are equally mysterious to the common mind, there is good reason for connecting these two kinds of φαρμακεία here. In any case, one suspects that the purification of the springs or cisterns is more than ceremonial.

Closely connected with these functions of purification is the supervision of the exegetes over funeral rites. Contact with the dead is one source of pollution recognized in Greek law and accepted also by Plato (947d). But death is also an occasion calling for certain rites "both to the gods above and to those below"; and it is the exegetes who are recognized as the proper authority to decide what these rites shall be and to what gods they shall be performed (873d, 958d). But secular law limits the authority of the exegetes here by prescribing that burial shall be on the third day, to avoid an elaborate period of mourning; that no cultivable land shall be used for tombs; and that no tomb or memorial monument shall exceed a certain size (958e-959a).[88]

Marriage is another solemn occasion calling for special ceremonies, and here again the exegetes prescribe what sacrifices or prayers are to precede, accompany, and follow the marriage (775a). To secular law, however, belongs the responsibility of prescribing the age for marriage (721b, 772d, 785b), the conditions of betrothal (774e), and the regulations concerning dowries (774c).

Finally, there is a reference to the exegetes in the law concerning the calendar of festivals. The Delphic oracles ($\mu\alpha\nu\tau\epsilon\hat{\iota}\alpha\iota$, i.e. oracular responses) are to be invoked to determine what sacrifices there shall be and to what gods they shall be offered; but the times and number of the festivals are for the legislator to determine (828a). The calendar is to be drawn up by the exegetes, priests, priestesses, and soothsayers ($\mu\acute{\alpha}\nu\tau\epsilon\iota\varsigma$), together with the guardians (828b)—an assembly containing representatives of both sacred and secular law.[89]

How closely these provisions parallel in detail the law and custom at Athens we cannot say. Epigraphical data for comparison are almost totally lacking.[90] What evidence we have shows the exegetes

[88] This last mentioned prescription may be the source of the edict of Demetrius of Phalerum putting an end to the production of the grave steles which were so popular in the fourth century and which are among the most moving products of ancient sculpture. So at least Wilamowitz believes (*Platon* I, 702), though Ferguson traces Demetrius' reforms to Theophrastus (*Hellenistic Athens*, 42). Besides the matters mentioned in the text, it is the legislator who prescribes the details for the funeral of a euthynos, which is to be quite different from that of ordinary citizens (947b-e). See below, Note 218.

[89] It was precisely this part of the religious law, it seems, that was included in the codification of the civic law at Athens at the end of the fifth century. On the influence of the exegetes on the organization of the festivals at Athens, see Persson, *op.cit.* 31.

[90] The material is conveniently collected in Oliver, *Expounders*, 139ff.: a late fifth-century inscription from Eleusis records an Athenian decree prescribing that the first fruits delivered to Eleusis be used for sacrifice "according to the exegesis of

occupied with the practice of the cults and the preservation of religious objects, matters which are implied, as we have seen, in Plato's conception of the office. The literary evidence, though sparse, is somewhat more revealing. Theophrastus' "superstitious man" (δεισιδαί-μων) finds that a mouse has gnawed a hole in his meal sack and, obviously thinking it a portent, consults the exegete as to what he shall do.[91] A client of Isaeus consults the exegete regarding his rights to his grandfather's estate, of which he thinks he is being defrauded, and receives very shrewd advice concerning additional funeral rites that he may appropriately perform on his grandfather's grave to nullify the previous actions of the other claimants.[92] Two other literary sources show the exegetes being consulted in cases of homicide.[93] All these cases easily fall into categories corresponding to responsibilities assigned to the exegetes in Plato's state; and the last three are instances in which religious and secular law come together in a peculiarly intimate fashion, and in which the exposition of the former could hardly be separated from consideration of the latter.[94]

There must have been many cases in Athens in which religious and secular law were, if not actually in conflict, so intimately involved that it required nice handling to adjust their respective demands. Plato is well aware of this delicate relationship between the two. "It is easy enough for the legislator to declare that such proceedings must be accompanied by invocations and sacrifices to the gods whose concern it is to prevent the occurrence of murders in states; but who these gods are, and what method of introducing suits in such cases would be in most correct accord with religion—this is

the Eumolpidae" (καθότι ἂν Εὐμολπίδαι ἐξηγῶνται); another from Eleusis belonging to the second half of the fourth century refers to payment made to "the exegetes of the Eumolpidae" for two yokes of oxen used in the mysteries; and another badly mutilated inscription of the same period from Athens mentions "the exegete" in a decree concerning the restoration of a statue of Athena Nike. Only the last (*Syll.* No. 264) can possibly refer to an "Athenian" exegete. Unfortunately the context is too fragmentary to be intelligible, though ἐπειδὴ ὁ ἐξηγητὴς κελεύει can be read. This however does not imply that "the exegete" is an official of the state; in fact it suggests the opposite.

[91] *Char.* xvi, 6. The exegete tells him, according to Theophrastus, to take the sack to a leather shop and have it mended. If this is drawn from life, it indicates that the exegetes discharged their functions with humor and common sense.

[92] Isaeus VIII, 39. Athen. 409f quotes from a work called Ἐξηγητικός by a certain Anticleides (or Cleidemos) concerning certain rites (ἐναγισμοί) to the dead, and from another writer named Dorotheos who gives details of the Eupatrid ritual for the cleansing of suppliants.

[93] Plato *Euthyp.* 4c, 9a; Ps. Dem. XLVII, 68-70.

[94] For a good discussion of these cases, see Kurt von Fritz, in TAPA LXXI, 1940, 96-102.

something for the guardians to enact into law in consultation with the exegetes and the soothsayers (μάντεις) and the God" (871cd). Examples of matters lying peculiarly on the borderline between religious and secular law would be the nature of the πρόρρησις (the warning of exclusion from sacred areas), who should pronounce it, and who is competent to prosecute a shedder of blood. Some of Plato's procedural law respecting homicide is hardly consistent with the more strict older law that only a kinsman is competent to prosecute for murder;[95] and there are gaps in this law which later legislation would have to fill.[96] It is significant that Plato recommends that such gaps be filled by secular and religious officials jointly.

Finally, there is an important reference to the exegetes towards the end of the *Laws* which puts their activities in the larger setting of Plato's purposes. The exegetes are classed with teachers and lawgivers as persons who should be specially competent to set forth the distinction between virtue and vice to those who need to be enlightened (964bc). In Plato's commonwealth the interpretation of religious law functions, like teaching and lawgiving, as a distinct but co-operating agency in fulfilling the fundamental purpose of the state, the education of its citizens. Apollo, the interpreter of sacred law, here reveals his identity with Apollo the legislator, and with the Apollo who, as giver of dance and song, is the author of education.

In the passage last quoted (871cd), there appears another group of religious persons, μάντεις—i.e. seers, soothsayers, or prophets—who take part in the deliberations concerning the ritual requirements of the law of homicide. They are mentioned elsewhere (828b) as being consulted by the guardians, together with the exegetes and priests and priestesses, in the establishment of a calendar of religious festivals. These μάντεις are not listed among the officials, and no procedure for their selection is prescribed; yet on the occasions referred to they play something like an official role. How are we to understand them and their functions?

The mantis is a type that we encounter at the very beginning of Greek history. The belief that the gods give intimations to men as to what they should or should not do was widespread among the Greeks at all times. Such intimations were believed to be given by

---

[95] For example, the law in 872a regarding the murder of an alien; see the author's article cited in Chapter IV, Note 154.
[96] *Plato's Law of Slavery*, 51ff.

means of omens, dreams, natural portents, by the flight of birds, or the appearance of the entrails of sacrificial victims. Sometimes these signs were so clear that no help was needed to interpret them; but in most cases it was felt necessary to call in the aid of men who had become expert in such matters through experience, or to whom the gods had given a special ability to read their meaning or otherwise interpret the future. Calchas in Homer and Tiresias in the Theban cycle are the first representatives of a type that we meet in all later Greek history. So far as we know, these were always self-appointed experts, but they carried the title of their "profession," their title being recognized, if not by law, at least by public opinion.[97] Manteis read the signs at certain public sacrifices at Athens in Aristotle's day;[98] and Plutarch mentions a mantis who was a member of Plato's Academy.[99] Such persons were not priests attached to a sanctuary; they seem never to have had any official position, though they sometimes participated with officials in public functions; but the art (μαντική) they professed sometimes gave them great prestige and influence, as is shown by the careers of Lampon and Diopeithes.[100] The art itself seems to have become more intricate and complicated with the passage of time.[101] The absurd pretensions of μαντική, and the hold its proficients had over large segments of the population in both the Greek and the Roman world, underlie the elaborate

[97] Solon mentions the μάντις, along with the merchant, the farmer, the artisan, the minstrel, as gaining his livelihood by a special craft, to which Apollo has appointed him (Fr. 13, Edmonds, 53-56). A certain "Telenikos, mantis" is mentioned in a casualty list of the tribe Erechtheis from the middle of the fifth century (IG I² 929+ = Tod I, No. 26, lines 128-129). Nicias had a mantis in his household whom he consulted continually on public and private matters, and he took an experienced mantis with him on the ill-fated Sicilian expedition (Plut. *Nic.* 4 and 23). The pious Xenophon makes frequent mention of manteis who were with the Ten Thousand or whom they encountered along the way and whose advice they made use of. *Anab.* I, vii, 18 and passim.

[98] *Const. Ath.* LIV, 6; cf. Cic. *De Divin.* I, 95.

[99] *Dion* 22.

[100] Lampon was a friend and adviser of Pericles; he played a prominent part in the founding of Thurii and headed the list of Athenian signers of the Peace of Nicias in 421, and also of the treaty of alliance with Sparta signed the same year. Plut. *Per.* 6; Thuc. v, 19, 2 and 24, 1; schol. to Aristoph. *Birds* 521 and 988 and *Peace* 1084; and IG I² 76 (= Tod I, No. 74) lines 47ff. Diopeithes was the author of the decree under which Anaxagoras was condemned for impiety. Plut. *Per.* 32 and schol. to Aristoph. *Birds* 988.

[101] Books were written expounding it. A certain Antiphon (for his identity see Dodds, *op.cit.* 132 n. 100), a contemporary of Socrates, composed rules for the interpretation of dreams; Cic. *De Divin.* I, 39 and 116. Isoc. XIX, 5-6 mentions a mantis named Thrasyllus who had been able to set himself up in the profession through a legacy of books from the mantis Polemaenetus. The Attidographer Philochorus, a generation after Plato, wrote a book on μαντική; Clem. Alex. *Strom.* i, 21, 134, 4.

polemic that Cicero three centuries later directed against the practice of it.

This art and its professors are frequently mentioned in Plato's other dialogues. They are "thought to be" the interpreters of the gods to men;[102] they claim to know the future by reading signs, particularly the flight of birds;[103] and they are experts in religious law and in rituals of expiation and purgation.[104] They are often impostors, making gain from the gullibility of individuals and states;[105] but sometimes θεῖοι, declaring the divine will not by their fancied art, but rather by a kind of madness, or divine inspiration.[106] Socrates declares himself to be a mantis of sorts in the *Phaedrus*, when his δαιμόνιον prevents him, after his first speech about Eros, from leaving the scene before he has purified himself (242c).

It is obvious that Plato's attitude toward these diviners cannot be clearly stated without drawing a distinction between technique and inspiration. Plato thinks as little of their professed art of reading signs to foretell the future as does Cicero later;[107] but there is another sort of divination, what in Cicero's dialogue is called natural as distinct from artificial divination, that comes from the direct communication of the soul with the divine.[108] Toward this class of diviners Plato exhibits much more sympathy; he describes them as being possessed (ἐνθουσιάζοντες) and uttering many wise and true things of which they can give no rational account (ὧν οὐδὲν ἴσασι), for God has taken their wits (νοῦς) away.[109] How much of this is ironical is hard to say; yet Socrates with his daimonion must have seemed to Plato a genuine example of this kind of divination. The divine leading that Socrates claimed to have had shows that these communications from the gods give individual guidance, and this seems also to have been an article of Plato's faith. Even the future is sometimes revealed, in glimpses at least, in the dreams of a good man who

---

[102] *Polit.* 290c; cf. *Ion* 534cd, *Tim.* 71e ff.

[103] *Charm.* 174a, *Theaet.* 179a, *Lach.* 195e, *Phil.* 67b, *Ion* 538e ff.; cf. *Laws* 933e.

[104] *Euthyp.* 3e, *Rep.* 364bc.

[105] Such as Hierocles in Aristophanes' *Peace* and Eurycles in the *Wasps*; cf. *Rep.* 364b-e, *Laws* 908d.

[106] *Phaedr.* 244a-d, *Phil.* 44c, *Tim.* 71e.

[107] The honorific τῇ καλλίστῃ τέχνῃ of *Phaedr.* 244c is offset by the dialectic of *Lach.* 198d and the humor of *Phil.* 67b.

[108] Cic. *De Divin.* 1, 12, 34 and passim. Ziehen (in RE s.v. μάντις) shows that this distinction goes back to the earliest times. Cf. also Stengel 55.

[109] Such are the θεομάντεις (and χρησμῳδοί) of *Apol.* 22c and *Meno* 99c, and the μάντεις of *Ion* 534c. See also the passages cited in Note 106 above.

has lain down to sleep with his soul in order.[110] For sleep is like death in its partial emancipation of the soul from the body; and for a similar reason the approach of death gives a man prophetic power.[111] These ideas are too close to the heart of Plato's conception of the soul to be regarded as merely a record of Socratic traits. For Plato, as for Socrates, μαντικὸν γέ τι καὶ ἡ ψυχή, the soul has at least some prophetic power.[112]

Thus the appearance of manteis in Plato's state is not merely a concession to the strength of popular belief.[113] But there is certainly some concession, for the practice of divining, in the sense in which Plato rejects it, seems to be presupposed; the legislator does not banish the mantis, but only attempts to prevent his using his art (or his pretensions) to injure his fellow men or the state. Like that other recipient of "inspiration," the poet, he must be controlled and made a servant of the legislator's end. The two abuses of the diviner's power to which Plato's legislation pays particular attention are the establishment of private cults and the practice of magic. The unscrupulous diviner can inveigle men into thinking that he has the power to persuade the gods by special prayers, sacrifices, and incantations not recognized by the state (908d, 909b,e), and induce them to set up shrines in their own homes before which these secret rites can be celebrated (910bc). Plato's law forbids such private worship, because it lacks the authority of Delphi and may involve the whole state in impiety.[114] The diviners who encourage the establishment of private rites are like wild beasts (θηριώδεις), not only inciting the superstition of their fellows (909ab), but also compounding their offense with duplicity and cupidity. Plato suggests also that such persons may have secret political ambitions that would

---

[110] *Rep.* 572a; cf. Socrates' dreams in *Crito* 44ab and *Phaedo* 60e. This also seems to have been an article of Aristotle's faith, at least in his early years; cf. the fragment from his lost Περὶ φιλοσοφίας (Fr. 10, Rose). His attitude in *De Divin. per Somnum* is more cautious.

[111] *Apol.* 39c.

[112] *Phaedr.* 242c. On Socrates' (and Plato's) attitude toward μαντική see E. Derenne, *Les Procès d'impiété intentés aux philosophes à Athènes*, Liège 1930, 107-110; Dodds, *op.cit.* 157 n. 3; Stengel 56-57.

[113] Cicero, who thought that the superstition of divination ought to be torn up by the roots from the minds of thinking men (*De Divin.* II, 148), nevertheless admitted that it should be cultivated out of respect for the opinions of the *vulgus* and in order to have a state religion (II, 28 and 70); and in his *De Re Publica* provided for a college of augurs.

[114] 909d-910b. This does not mean that Plato's law forbids all private or family worship, as we shall see later.

threaten the established polity (908d). A man convicted of such practices shall be imprisoned for life, and at his death his body shall be cast beyond the border without burial (909bc). Plato's law (933a) is even more severe on the mantis who practises magic, who "persuades those who are emboldened to injure their fellow men that they can do so by certain sorceries (μαγγανείαις) and spells (ἐπῳδαῖς) and "bindings" (καταδέσεσι), and convinces others that they are actually being injured by persons able to work these spells (δυναμένων γοητεύειν)." In this case, if the agent is a mantis, the penalty is death, whatever the degree of the injury he has brought about (933e).

These parts of Plato's legislation are directed at two "regressive" aspects of popular religion in the fourth century. The predilection for secret rites of purification or initiation, particularly of a foreign or exotic character, seems to have set in at Athens during the stresses of the Peloponnesian War. It was at this time that the worship of the Thracian goddess Bendis was introduced; and in the following century we hear of other similar cults, such as those of the Phrygian Sabazius, the Thracian Cotys, and the Asiatic Attis and Adonis.[115] In an earlier age these new gods and goddesses might have been incorporated into the older worship, as Dionysus had been. But the official religion had lost its power of assimilation, and these new cults remained in the hands of self-appointed priests and prophets, frowned upon, it would seem, by the upper strata of the population, but a source of comfort and excitement to many of the common folk. With this tendency toward mystic and exotic rites is coupled a marked growth in superstition and magic in the fourth century.[116] Evidence of curses, spells, and charms intended to injure an enemy and his household has been found in great quantity by excavators in the Mediterranean area. If you wished to injure a man—cause his death, or make him impotent to carry out his purposes—you inscribed his name with the proper formula on some durable medium, such as a piece of lead or a potsherd, and placed it—usually in a grave—where the gods of the underworld could see it. These are the καταδέσεις,

---

[115] Nilsson 1, 782ff.; Dodds, *op.cit.* 193-194, and *Harv. Theol. Rev.* xxxiii, 1940, 171ff.; see also Ferguson in *Harv. Theol. Rev.* xxxvii, 1944, 89f.

[116] On the practice of magic in the fourth century see Nilsson 1, 752ff.; Guthrie, *op.cit.* (Note 5), 270ff.; Dodds, *The Greeks and the Irrational*, 194f.; Jane Harrison, *Prolegomena to the Study of Greek Religion*, Cambridge, 1903, 138ff.; and on the καταδεσμοί in particular, Nilsson 1, 757 n. 2.

or "bindings," referred to in Plato's text.[117] They have been found in great numbers in the Mediterranean area, and the oldest of them seem to have come from Greece. Another method of attack was to make a wax image of your enemy, distort or mutilate it, and place it at the entrance to his house, or at some spot where an agent of the under-world would come across it. This is an old method of aggressive magic, and Plato's text shows that it was practised in the Greece of his day (933b). It cannot be altogether an accident that evidences of magical practices are relatively rare for the fifth century but suddenly become very numerous in the fourth. Plato's law against magic does not seem to be new,[118] but the practice clearly had become more preva-lent in his time, and it may be that Athenian law was forced to take greater cognizance of it and attempt to suppress it.[119]

It is obvious that Plato could not have believed there was any efficacy in such magical practices without himself being guilty of one of the forms of impiety that he attacks so vigorously in the tenth book. The practice of magic rests on the belief that the gods can be won over by bribes, or seduced by prayers and incantations to do a wicked man's bidding; and Plato argues the falsity of this belief with great fervor (905d-907b).[120] What disturbs him apparently is the wide-

---

[117] And the καταδεσμοί in the parallel passage in the *Republic* (364c).

[118] *Meno* 80b implies that a magician (γόης) elsewhere than in Athens could be apprehended and confined (ἀπάγω in the legal sense means to lead off to death or to prison). A fifth-century inscription from Teos is evidence that magic was feared as a public danger. See Harrison, *op.cit.* 142f.

[119] Dem. xxv, 79ff. mentions a φαρμακίς named Theoris (a ἱέρεια, according to Plut. *Dem.* 14) who was put to death, with her entire family, for the practice of sorcery. Harpocration says (s.v. θεωρίς), on the authority of Philochorus, that the formal charge was ἀσέβεια; see Dodds, *op.cit.* 205 n. 98.

[120] At the same time there is a curious suspension of judgment in 933a: "About all such matters it is not easy to know what is really the truth, nor if a man could know would it be easy to persuade others." I agree with Dodds (*op.cit.* 205 n. 97) that the second part of this sentence hints at a greater degree of scepticism than Plato chooses to express. But why should he here profess to have an open mind on a question to which a vigorous answer has already been given in the preceding book? A related puzzle is presented by the sentence immediately following, which is particularly difficult to construe (see England's note on 933a 7ff.). If we take the key phrase—μὴ σαφὲς ἔχουσι δόγμα περὶ αὐτῶν—as a dative following οὐκ ἄξιον (ἐστί), Plato is implying that his spokesman, the Athenian, has no fixed opinion on the subject (i.e. the efficacy of magic). Even if, following England's preference, we take it with διακελεύεσθαι and understand it as saying "it is not ap-propriate to exhort them (i.e. the suspicious and timorous multitude) because they hold no sure opinion on the subject," this expression of reluctance to exhort appears strange after the vigorous demonstration already given. Plato elsewhere insists on the legislator's duty to dissuade men from error; but here such dissuasion appears as a difficult task which ought not to be imposed on the legislator (μηδ᾽ αὖ τὸν νομοθέ-την . . . ἀναγκάζειν ἐξιᾶσθαι, 933c). Despite the difficulty of interpreting this pas-

spread belief that these are efficacious ways of doing harm, and the mutual suspicion that such practices create among men who hold this belief. The users of these spells and incantations frighten the multitude, like a gang of children (933c). The legislator's ultimate aim, it is clear, is to cure them of such fears (ἐξιᾶσθαι τῶν ἀνθρώπων τοὺς τοιούτους φόβους). But it is futile for him to approach men "whose minds are filled with dark suspicion of one another (ταῖς ψυχαῖς δυσωπουμένους πρὸς ἀλλήλους)" and try to persuade them to make light of it when they see wax images at their doorways, or at places where three ways meet, or on the tomb of an ancestor (933ab). What he can do immediately is to try to remove the causes of their fears by forbidding the resort to such practices and imposing severe penalties upon the violators of the law. This law is a vivid expression of the state of popular opinion in Plato's time and amply confirms the other evidence we have about the spread of magic in the fourth century.

Why does not Plato eliminate entirely from his state a class of persons of such questionable pretensions and of such doubtful services as the manteis? From Calchas and the sacrifice of Iphigenia, to Diopeithes and the prosecutions of Anaxagoras and Socrates, they had been a source of mischief and cruelty; and in the fourth century they were undoubtedly contributing much to swell the rising tide of superstition that threatened to engulf the Greek world. Perhaps it should be credited to Plato that he almost leaves them out; they are brought in nearly as an afterthought, and their functions are much reduced from those they enjoyed in his time. Their profession becomes an exceedingly hazardous one, since it is subject to the drastic penalties just considered. There is no suggestion that manteis are to participate in the big public sacrifices, read the omens, or advise the leaders of the state in a crisis. They are put at the service of the state only on occasions when religious law is to be formulated, i.e. with respect to the formalities of prosecution for bloodshed and the arrangement of the calendar of festivals. These examples perhaps give us a clue to Plato's reason for retaining them. We have seen that he believes there are some genuinely inspired prophets, speaking the divine will to men. Like the oracles, these genuine manteis are a living source of religious law, and for that reason their services should not be dis-

_____

sage, the principle established in the argument of Book X must be taken as Plato's opinion, especially since it is supported by the tone of 909b and the parallel passage in the *Republic* (364c-e).

pensed with. But even here they are under control. Plato takes from them their ancient prerogative of interpreting the oracles and sets up a board of exegetes for the authoritative exposition of religious law; and when their services are invoked it is only in consultation with these official expositors and the guardians. Their claims to inspiration (claims that in some cases are well founded, Plato thinks) give them only the right to help in the formulation of religious law.

THE GODS AND THEIR WORSHIP

The gods worshipped in Plato's state are likely to appear at first a strangely varied and unordered assemblage; but on closer examination they are found to constitute a clearly graded hierarchy of divine and semidivine beings, of varying majesty and power, but all qualifying as objects of reverence and devotion.[121] At the summit of the hierarchy are the Olympians—Zeus, Hera, and the other gods whom Homer pictures as having their dwelling on Mount Olympus, an appropriate seat for these beings of the upper air and bright sky.[122] Below them are the gods of the underworld, the Chthonioi ($\chi\theta\delta\nu\iota o\iota$), of whom Pluto (or Hades) is the chief representative. Next come daemons ($\delta\alpha\iota\mu o\nu\epsilon\varsigma$), heroes ($\eta\rho\omega\epsilon\varsigma$), ancestors ($\pi\rho\delta\gamma o\nu o\iota$), and lastly, the living parents ($\gamma o\nu\epsilon\hat{\iota}\varsigma$) in the household. The system that Plato uses here is not arbitrarily imposed; it reflects throughout the distinctions recognized by his countrymen and merely makes explicit the ranking implied in their opinions and in their practices of worship. We can best understand this graded world of Plato's gods, and the worship that he thinks appropriate at each level, by proceeding systematically from the summit to the base of the hierarchy.

The Olympian gods were frequently referred to in classical times as "the Twelve."[123] The phrase appears in Plato's text (745d, 828c),

[121] This hierarchy is most fully seen in 717ab; but it appears also in 727a, 738d, 771d, 801e, 818c, 828c, 910a.

[122] In one passage they are called "heavenly gods" ($o\dot{v}\rho\dot{a}\nu\iota o\iota\ \theta\epsilon o\iota$), in contrast with the $\chi\theta\delta\nu\iota o\iota$ (828c). There is another use of this phrase in Plato's text, to denote the sun, moon and planets. Their place in Plato's state we will consider later.

[123] Cf. the oath "by the Twelve!" in Aristoph. *Knights* 235. There was an altar to the twelve gods in the Agora at Athens (Herod. II, 7; VI, 108), now identified by the recent excavations, and this altar was believed to have been erected by Pisistratus the Younger (Thuc. VI, 54,6). There were altars to them also at Olympia (Pindar *Ol.* x, 49ff.). The Olympians named, or otherwise referred to in Plato's text, are thirteen in number. Even if we leave out Dionysus, who seems not to have been included in the Athenian twelve (though he is one of the twelve in the frieze of the Parthenon, Hestia being absent), we still have difficulties; for Plato prescribes

and the number is appropriate; for each of his twelve tribes is to bear the name of one of these twelve gods. This use of the Olympians as eponyms for his tribes is a notable innovation. The ten tribes at Athens in Plato's time bore the names of heroes, and the four earlier tribes which they had replaced had names whose origin it is difficult for us to interpret, but they seem not to have been the names of gods, and certainly not the names of Olympians. Nor do we find anywhere else in Greece a precedent for Plato's proposal. Its import is to place the primary organization of the state under the direct patronage of the highest gods—and gods, moreover, who are not merely local in their significance but worshipped by the entire state. This is both to make more sacred and inviolable the tribal divisions, and at the same time to take away some of the divisiveness that might accompany them. Thus the Olympian gods become a part of the fundamental structure of Plato's state and are peculiarly entitled to the familiar designation that Plato gives them, "the gods that hold the city."[124]

Individual members of the Twelve are referred to often in Plato's text; and almost every one of the Olympians is connected—as protector, patron, or divine exemplar—with some particular aspect of the city's life. In this allotment of functions to individual gods Plato is faithful, in the main, to the traditions he follows. Three of them—Hestia, Zeus, and Athena—are to have a sacred area at the heart of the city, the acropolis, and other temples at the center of each of the surrounding villages (745b, 848d).[125] Hestia is mentioned first in both these passages, despite her shadowy and only half-personified nature, and the absence of any mythology concerning her and of any peculiar

that the twelfth month is to be sacred to Pluto (828d), and it is a natural inference that he intends him to be one of the eponymous gods. Plato does not tell us who the other eleven are. But this is not surprising, for it seems that the "Twelve Gods" could vary from place to place, in accordance with local preferences and the special attachment of certain gods to certain areas. See Guthrie, *op.cit.* (Note 5), 111-112.

[124] 717a: Ὀλυμπίους τε καὶ τοὺς τὴν πόλιν ἔχοντας θεούς. This is grammatically an ambiguous phrase. The τε καὶ could be taken as implying two distinct classes of divinities. But this is clearly impossible. Some of the Olympians are explicitly called πολιοῦχοι in Plato's text, and it is quite likely that he thought of all of them as city-holding gods. This would be in accord with Greek tradition. Nor is there any hint that he conceives it possible, as England suggests, that any other god not included in the list of Olympians would become the patron of the city he is establishing.
It is possible that τοῖς τὴν ἀγορὰν ἔχουσι θεοῖς (917d) is another reference to the Olympians, or at least to Zeus, Athena, and Hestia.

[125] For the inclusion of Athena with Zeus and Hestia in this group I can find no explanation in Plato's text. It may be that Plato is unconsciously representing his native city, where Athena had the place of honor on the Acropolis.

festivals in her honor. But in naming her first, Plato is following a familiar convention in Greek ritual, loyally respecting the priority assigned her, according to tradition, by Zeus himself.[126] This priority expresses the importance of the family hearth in ancient society. The goddess of the hearth was naturally the center of all worship and sacrifice performed in the family, and the king's hearth, in particular, became a symbol of the people's corporate life. In later times when monarchy had disappeared almost everywhere, the tradition of a "common hearth" was still maintained, located now in the prytaneum, or magistrates' hall, where in some cities—at Athens, for example—a fire was kept perpetually burning.[127] We may well doubt, therefore, whether Plato thinks of Hestia as having a temple on his acropolis, for temples to her were almost nonexistent in Greece.[128] He doubtless has in mind some public building where there would be a hearth, and possibly also a statue of Hestia, as there was in the prytaneum at Athens.[129] It is on the altar of Hestia in Plato's state that the evidence taken at the trial for a capital offense is to be deposited, and in Hestia's name all the judges of the court take oath before giving a judgment that may mean the death of one of the citizens (856a).

But the Olympian most frequently mentioned in Plato's text is Zeus, whose supremacy in the divine family as "the father of gods and men" was a familiar article of Greek faith. Zeus had many functions in Greek religion and was worshipped under a great variety of cult titles. He was the god of the bright sky, the god of clouds, lightning, and fruitful showers, and of the human activities dependent on his control of these forces of nature. But Plato's thought passes quickly from his primacy in the cosmos to his function as guardian of the moral and social order.

God who, as the ancient tradition (παλαιὸς λόγος) tells us, holds the beginning, the end, and the middle of all things, completes his circuit without deviation according to his nature. In his train follows Justice (Δίκη), the avenger of those who fall short of the divine law; and she in turn is fol-

[126] "There is nothing better attested in Greek religious literature than this ritual priority of Hestia in certain private and public cult acts of the Hellenic household and state." Farnell, *Cults of the Greek States*, Oxford, 1896-1909, v, 346. For the origin of her ritual priority, see the Homeric *Hymn to Aphrodite* 21-32. Cf. Plato, *Crat.* 401d: τὸ πρὸ πάντων θεῶν τῇ Ἑστίᾳ πρώτῃ προθύειν. Whence the proverb, ἀφ' Ἑστίας ἄρχου; Nilsson I, 135.
[127] Cf. Pind. *Nem.* xi, 1-2; Poll. I, 7; Arist. *Pol.* 1322b 28.
[128] Farnell, *op.cit.* v, 362.
[129] Paus. I, xviii, 3.

lowed, in humility and orderliness, by every mortal who would be happy.
715e-716a

It is certain that Plato is citing an Orphic doctrine in this passage,[130]
but the Orphics had simply exploited a vein of thought that lay in
the Greek conception of Zeus from very early times.[131] Justice presented itself to the Greeks as embodied not only in written law, but
also in the unwritten principles of right and justice that both support
and extend the written law of the city; and it is the latter with which
Zeus was usually identified.[132] Thus in Plato's legislation he is the
god of strangers, Ζεὺς ξένιος (730a, 843a, 879e; cf. 718a), the protector of those persons who, without kinsmen in the city, are peculiarly subject to exploitation. The stranger in need of protection
usually appears as a suppliant; though Ζεὺς ἱκέσιος is not explicitly
named in Plato's text, his function as protector of suppliants is implied
(730a). Again he is the god of boundaries, Ζεὺς ὅριος (842e), extending his protection not only to citizens, but also to foreigners on
the frontier whose holdings may be threatened by the shifting of a
boundary stone. He enforces contracts entered into with artisans, a
class of persons who would not be citizens in Plato's state and there-

---

[130] The name of Zeus does not actually appear in Plato's text here, but the scholiast
explains the παλαιὸς λόγος by citing the Orphic λόγος: Ζεὺς ἀρχή, Ζεὺς μέσσα,
Διὸς δ' ἐκ πάντα τέτυκται, Ζεὺς πυθμὴν γαιής τε καὶ οὐρανοῦ ἀστερόεντος. Cf. Dem.
XXV, 11: τὴν ἀπαραίτητον καὶ σεμνὴν Δίκην, ἣν ὁ τὰς ἁγιωτάτας ἡμῖν τελετὰς κατα-
δείξας Ὀρφεὺς παρὰ τὸν τοῦ Διὸς θρόνου φησὶ καθημένην. By calling this doctrine
"Orphic" we can only mean—and perhaps the ancient authorities just cited only
meant—that it belonged to a collection of religious poems which, for some reason
we cannot now explain, were attached to the name of Orpheus. There are grave
doubts whether we can properly speak of an Orphic sect, of which these poems were
the sacred writings, or even of a consistent body of teaching expounded in them.
But they were alike in that they were concerned with the myths of the mysteries,
and contained speculations as to the implications of these mysteries for the nature
of the cosmos and the destiny of the human soul. See Linforth, *The Arts of Orpheus*;
Guthrie, *Orpheus and Greek Religion*, London, 1935, and *The Greeks and Their
Gods*, 307-332.

[131] Homer *Iliad* xvi, 385ff.; Hesiod *Theog.* 902. On the exaltation of Justice in
Greek religion, see Farnell, *Higher Aspects of Greek Religion*, 108; cf. Eur. fr. 490
Nauck, and Arist. *Nic. Eth.* 1129b 28. Dodds (*op.cit.* 28ff., 52 n. 18) maintains
that the tendency to transform Zeus into an agent of justice is not Homeric, but
a characteristic of the archaic age. I find it hard to accept this view. The Homeric
Zeus is of course not concerned with "justice as such"—that would involve a level
of abstraction attained only much later—but with concrete rights and wrongs. Of
these he clearly seems the protector and the avenger: cf. e.g. *Iliad* IV, 160ff.; XIII,
622ff.; *Odyss.* XXIV, 351ff.

[132] His role as the source of Cretan law is properly recognized by Plato in the
early books of the *Laws* (624a, 632d, 636d; cf. 633a, 662c). But elsewhere than in
Crete the Greeks apparently did not think of him as a lawgiver except through
Apollo, his spokesman.

fore less able to take advantage of the rights the law accords them (921c). Heralds and ambassadors are under his special oversight (941a). He is the patron of the oath, that primitive guarantee of truth and fair dealing between men (936e). In his paternal aspect he is the god of kinship and parentage—Ζεὺς ὁμόγνιος καὶ πατρῷος (881d), Ζεὺς ὁμόφυλος (843a)—and thus the protector of the family and tribal organization at the basis of the state. As such he is peculiarly "city-holding Zeus," Ζεὺς πολιοῦχος (921c); and sacred embassies are to be sent to his Panhellenic festival at Olympia (950e).

Athena does not often appear openly in Plato's legislation, although she is one of the three gods with temples on the acropolis—probably a reflection of Plato's native city. Her connection with Athens is referred to by Cleinias on one occasion (626d), and the Athenian speaks of her in true Athenian fashion as ἡ θεός (844d) and again as "our virgin lady and mistress," ἡ παρ' ἡμῖν κόρη καὶ δέσποινα (796b). She is the warrior goddess, delighting in the armed dances of the young men, and with Ares is the patron of the "craftsmen of war" (920e), which in turn is but a phase of the larger function she has, with Hephaestus, as patron of the whole class of craftsmen "who have helped to furnish our life with the arts" (920d). This latter is the attribute of Athena which is praised elsewhere in Plato's dialogues; and nothing is more characteristic of Greek religious feeling than this association of the gods with the development of the arts and sciences.[133] Hellenic also is the practical corollary: failure to pay a craftsman the wages agreed upon is a dishonor to her as well as an offense punishable by law (921c).

Apollo is second only to Zeus, whose interpreter he is, and thereby the guardian both of the religious and of the secular law of the city. His position as the lawgiver of Lacedaemon is emphasized at the beginning of the dialogue (624a, 632d; cf. 686a), and we have seen that Plato's own legislation is at many points contingent upon the approval of Delphi. He is the author of dance and song and hence of all education; and as companion in the festivals he graces and heightens these occasions of merrymaking and good fellowship which Plato regards as so important for the "straightening of character." In these last two functions he is called Apollo Μουσηγέτης (653d) and

---

[133] *Crit.* 109c; *Polit.* 274c; *Prot.* 321d. Cf. the Homeric *Hymn to Hephaestus.* See the statement of Farnell cited in Chapter IV, Note 148.

Apollo Παιάν (664c).[134] The important office of educator is to be filled by an election held at his temple (766b), and again it is at the "temple of Apollo and Helios" that the citizens meet to elect the euthynoi, the powerful board that examines the conduct and accounts of all officers (945e). The euthynoi are themselves to be priests of Apollo and Helios. It is the word of Apollo, of course, that is sought whenever the exegetes, his spokesmen, are called upon to interpret the sacred law; and consultation of his oracle is always possible, and sometimes expressly enjoined, when the official interpreters can give no answer. Plato prescribes that his city shall follow the custom of all Greek states where Apollo's cult was established, and send embassies to Delphi for participation in the sacrifices and games in his honor (950e).

Hera appears, quite naturally, only in Plato's law concerning marriage; for the protection of marriage and of the wife's rights seems to have been her chief function in Greek religion.[135] Despite the amours and infidelities attributed to the Zeus of mythology, he and Hera were regarded not merely as patrons but also as divine exemplars of marriage.[136] In Plato's law the treasurer of her temple collects the fine imposed for failing to marry by the prescribed age, and the fine for excessive dowries (774ab,d).[137] Plato will have certain women appointed as inspectors to keep an eye on newly married couples to see that they perform their duties to the state (784a). These inspectors hold daily meetings at the temple of Eileithyia, the goddess of childbirth—which may be intended as a reference to Hera, for she sometimes explicitly bore this designation.[138] For Plato, as for the Greeks generally, marriage was not the satisfaction of personal inclination, but the performance of a duty; and in the choice of a mate a man should not be guided by romantic considerations—this the Greeks would have considered selfish and irresponsible—but by the interests of his family and the state. Hence it was natural that such a duty should be presented in a strong religious light. Since the holder

[134] It may be that these titles point to an original differentiation of cults, but there is no reason for doubting that in Plato's time they were all connected with the god of Delphi. See Reverdin 104n.

[135] Nilsson I, 401ff.

[136] Farnell, *op.cit.* 37.

[137] Fines for such delinquency are not attested for Athens; but for Sparta, see Plut. *Lyc.* 15 and Poll. VIII, 40. In Crete also there was an obligation to marry at a certain age; Strabo x, iv, 20.

[138] Nilsson I, 405.

of a lot in Plato's state is responsible for the worship and tendance of the gods of the household,[139] it is essential that he assure a successor to himself. Marriage, says Plato in language reminiscent of the *Symposium*, is "the way in which the human race by its nature participates in immortality. . . . A man must lay hold on eternal nature by leaving children and children's children behind him to act as servants of God in his stead" (721b; 773e).[140]

Ares has a temple (833b) and he is coupled with Athena as a patron of the military officers, the "artisans of defense" (920e; cf. 671e). Temples to Ares were rare in northern and central Greece (actually the only one we know of is that in the Athenian Agora), though more common in the Peloponnesus.[141] Artemis shares a temple with her brother Apollo, located apparently in the wilder and rougher sections of the country (833b). We have noted that Hephaestus is mentioned with Athena as a patron of craftsmen and their beneficial arts, but there is no mention of a temple. Remembering the Hephaesteum overlooking the Agora at Athens, we can hardly regard this omission as more than an oversight. Hermes appears with Zeus as the patron of heralds and ambassadors, and faithlessness in this office is indictable on the ground of impiety to both gods (941a). Hermes had various other characters in Greek religion—as the god of boundaries, as protector of the wayfarer on country roads or city streets, as the guide of souls to the other world, as the patron of deception and theft—but he appears to have none of these in Plato's state. In fact against the last-mentioned conception of this god Plato enters a strong protest: "No son of Zeus makes a practice of theft by fraud or violence. Let no one therefore be misled by the poets, or any other tellers of mistaken myths, into believing that when he steals by craft or violence he is doing nothing shameful, but only what the gods themselves do" (941b). There is no mention of a temple, but this accords with Greek usage; the worship of Hermes was connected rather with the stone heaps scattered over the countryside to mark boundaries, paths, and graves, and with the rough images of him set up in the streets and before the doors of houses to keep away the spooks.

Demeter—with her daughter Kore, and the youth Triptolemus—is mentioned as patron of agriculture (782b); this suggests the fa-

---

139 As we shall see later in this section.
140 On the moral beauty of this conception, see Farnell, *op.cit.* 36.
141 Nilsson I, 487.

miliar agrarian cult of Demeter and Persephone, which Plato takes for granted in his state, as we shall see later. Aphrodite is mentioned by name in only one passage referring to masculine love, the "so-called lawless Aphrodite," against which Plato pronounces a vigorous condemnation (840e);[142] elsewhere she appears only in the adjective ἀφροδίσιος in the prescriptions regulating sexual relations (836c, 839e, 841a,e), and no cult in her honor is suggested.[143] The name of Poseidon does not appear in Plato's text, but he is implied in the mention of sacred embassies that are to be sent to the Isthmian games (950e), which we know were celebrated in his honor. This carries the further implication that he is to have a temple and cult, though these are not elsewhere referred to, and there is no discernible function that he performs in the social order. Why then the sacred embassies to his festivals? Perhaps because his worship was widespread in the Peloponnesus,[144] from which a large part of Plato's colonists will come; perhaps it is because of his traditional connection with the breeding and use of horses, for which Plato shows a special fondness; but it is possible that this festival is mentioned merely as one of the famous four Panhellenic gatherings, all of which are named in this passage. Plato will have his colony maintain good relations with the larger Hellenic community.[145]

Finally, Dionysus is regarded as joint author with Apollo of rhythm and melody (672d), like him also a companion in the festivals (653d), and thus a patron of education. It is the authentic Dionysus of fourth-century Athens that Plato is thinking of—the god of wine (672b, 775b, 643a), the patron and protector of the grape harvest (844de), the author of "Bacchic dances and frenzied choruses" (672b). Plato tolerates even the more popular and rowdy aspects of his worship; for when Megillus comments on the unseemly revels in which his Athenian worshippers often indulge at his festivals,

[142] Cf. the criticism in *Ep. VII* 335b of the use of Aphrodite's name to denote this "slavish and graceless pleasure"; and the protest implied in *Phil.* 12b.

[143] But again this may be an unintentional omission. At Athens there was a temple of Aphrodite ἐν κήποις outside the walls to the southeast, a shrine to Aphrodite Pandemus near the Hephaesteum, and one to Aphrodite Ourania directly under the Acropolis at the southwest corner. Judeich, *Topographie von Athen*, 285, 368, 424.

[144] Diod. xv, 49 says that the Peloponnesus was peculiarly sacred to him and that its cities honored him most of all the immortals. The evidence of his popularity in this area is in fact impressive. Cf. Farnell, *Cults* iv, 75ff.; Nilsson i, 419. But it must be remembered that he also had a seat on the Acropolis at Athens.

[145] In contrast, the *Critias* presents Poseidon as the chief deity of the mythical kingdom of Atlantis; he is not only the ancestor of the people, but the author of their laws (113c, 117b, 119cd).

the Athenian replies that such indulgences are to be approved, as long as the participants retain their self-control (ὅπου τινὲς ἔνεισι καρτερήσεις, 637b). Elsewhere he implies that the law against drunkenness may properly be relaxed at the "feasts of the wine god" (775b); and we have seen in the preceding chapter that he seems reluctant to legislate concerning Bacchic dances, implying that they are not in the province of the statesman. It would be a mistake to suppose that Plato's tolerance of these aspects of Dionysiac worship is merely evidence of his respect for long-established religious practices. The gifts of Dionysus, the Athenian says, are not really baneful, as some persons think, but beneficial when properly used (672b,d). Wine is a valuable means of training the young in resistance to pleasure;[146] and Bacchic dancing has a curative effect in overcoming frenzy and restoring the mind to sanity (791a).[147] Even more striking is the role of Dionysus in the chorus of elders. These arbiters of taste and morals in song and dance meet in convivial assemblies under the patronage of Dionysus, who relieves the crabbedness of age and gives them ability to sing and lead the choruses in the state.[148]

But all these Dionysiac practices must be regulated—by law or by the citizens' self-control—if they are to produce their beneficial effect. The symposia just mentioned, like those in which the younger citizens are trained in temperance, are to be carefully supervised (671d, 640a-e). The use of wine is not to be regarded as mere amusement to be enjoyed by anyone, with anyone, in any way they please; it must be associated with law and directed to the end of temperance. In this way it becomes something of serious value to the state.[149] If, however, the lawless Bacchus is the only one the people can recognize, the alternative Plato suggests is to go beyond even the Cretan and Spartan law in restricting the use of wine (674a-c).[150] But Plato evidently

[146] See the elaborate argument and exposition, 643b-650b; and Boyancé, *Le Culte des Muses*, 91. No doubt the Dionysiac revels mentioned in 637b are ἐπαινετά precisely because they provide an opportunity for the exercise of self-control.

[147] "The mechanistic explanation of the catharsis produced by the Corybantic rites is called Democritean by Delatte and Croissant, Pythagorean by Boyancé, but may quite possibly be Plato's own." Dodds, *op.cit.* 231 n. 59.

[148] 665b ff., 670a ff.; see Chapter VII, Music and the Dance.

[149] 673e: οὔσης σπουδῆς obviously requires μέθης (d10) to complete it; and similarly μέθη must be understood with ὡς παιδιᾷ in e8.

[150] Some interpreters have erroneously taken the series of prohibitions at the end of Book II (674a-c) as Plato's prescriptions for his model colony (e.g. Gomperz, *Plat. Aufsätze*, III, 29; Vanhoutte, *La Philosophie politique de Platon dans les Lois*, 26). But the context shows that they represent an alternative and second-best policy. His own prescriptions are put forward briefly in 666ab: complete abstinence for

hopes that his citizens will have sufficient strength of character (the καρτερήσεις of 637b) to enjoy with restraint the gift of Dionysus and the other pleasures associated with his worship.

These references show that Plato is following common Greek precedent in regarding the gods as patrons and protectors of the civic order; and if we add details not given, but which he assumes his readers will know from current beliefs and practices, it is evident that in every affair of the city, in every act or event of the citizen's life, the gods will be present, as examples for imitation and as beings whose favor and fellowship the good citizen will want to enjoy. What we have here is no invention of Plato's; it is the religion of his people, "a religion unique," as Farnell has well said, "for its almost naïvely intimate association with the whole political and social life of the people."[151]

But this veneration of the Olympians does not mean that Plato approves of and adopts all the current mythology associated with them, much of which he had already severely condemned in the *Republic.* Zeus' mutilation of his father Kronos—"a wrong, even if it was a punishment"; the amours of Ares and Aphrodite and the trick of Hephaestus that fettered them in their embraces for all the gods to laugh at; the deceptive disguises assumed by Hera, Athena, and even by Zeus himself in their relations with mortals; the bickerings and jealousies among the gods, their partiality to undeserving favorites, their susceptibility to bribes and flattery, their indiscriminate assigning of good and evil lots to men, their lust, their passionate anger and grief, their jealousy of fortunate mortals, their ridicule of the unfortunate—such primitive and cruel details are out of place in stories about the gods.[152] God can be represented truly only if he is represented as good and the author of good alone. The *Laws* gives additional examples of myths that Plato repudiates; Hermes was not a thief, no matter what the poets say (941b); the story of Zeus' infatuation for Ganymede is a fiction of the Cretans to justify their

---

persons under eighteen; wine in moderation for young men under the age of thirty, with complete abstention from intoxication (μέθη) and heavy drinking (πολυοινία); for persons above that age there seems to be no law, but drunkenness is always unseemly (except at Dionysiac festivals) and particularly so at marriage feasts, when it especially behooves the bride and bridegroom to be sober (775bc). Thus there is no contradiction, as Vanhoutte alleges, with the doctrine of Book I that symposia are a valuable means of educating youth.

[151] Farnell, *Higher Aspects,* 69.
[152] *Rep.* 377e-390e. See also *Euthyp.* 6a.

own lawless passions (636cd); and as for the story that Hera made Dionysus mad, and that his gift of wine and Bacchic dancing was an act of vengeance, let them tell it who think it safe to do so; for the Athenian Stranger it is obviously an affront to both divinities (672bc). To suppose that there is inconsistency or insincerity in proposing the Olympian gods for worship and repudiating the mythology which is all that most moderns know about them is to misunderstand Greek religion. Mythology was not religion; it was a poetic embroidery on the cults, and though it often influenced them, it was not essential to worship. Plato was as sincere as Pindar, or Aeschylus, who were only two of his forerunners in the attempt to purge the luxuriant license of poetic imagination and make it conform to the higher morality of their age.

So much one can readily understand. As a legislator drawing up a constitution for a fourth-century Greek city, Plato must necessarily, if his city is to have any religion at all, use the religion which his future citizens already practise, and his attention will be directed only to purging it of irregular additions contrary to what he conceives to be its essential purpose. But did Plato, as a philosopher, accept as gods these creations of Greek fancy, even when shorn of the poetic embroidery that often conceals from us their true nature as felt by a Greek worshipper? The question must be asked, but it is very difficult to answer. Plato himself nowhere answers it for us. In the *Timaeus* (40d-41a) he accepts, with a certain irony, the story of the traditional gods in the early theogonies; "for those who gave us these accounts were, as they say, descendants of the gods; and surely they must have known who their ancestors were. We cannot doubt the word of the children of the gods." This certainly indicates scepticism, especially since these traditions are said to be without any probable or necessary proof, so that they fall not only outside the realm of science, but also outside the "myth" or "probable tale" that Plato himself gives us in the *Timaeus*. Again there is Socrates' forthright statement in the *Phaedrus* (246cd): "We have never seen or adequately conceived God ($\theta\epsilon\acute{o}\nu$), but we imagine ($\pi\lambda\acute{a}\tau\tau o\mu\epsilon\nu$) him as a kind of immortal creature ($\dot{a}\theta\acute{a}\nu\alpha\tau\acute{o}\nu\ \tau\iota\ \zeta\hat{\omega}o\nu$) possessing both a soul and a body combined in a unity which is to last forever." Yet in the splendid myth that follows, Zeus, Hera, and the other Olympians play an essential part. "Of the gods we know nothing," says Socrates in the *Cratylus* (400d). Yet both Socrates, as Plato portrays him, and Plato himself continually speak not only of God, but of the traditional gods, with genuine religious feeling. It is hard for us to share this feeling, detached as we are from the religious world in which Socrates and Plato lived; but we cannot legitimately expect them to share our detachment. If Plato participated in public worship, of which we can have no doubt, it would be in prayers and sacrifices to the gods of his people, "the gods established by law" (904a). As a philosopher he could not fail to regard them as pictorial representations of the divine nature which can be truly apprehended only by nonsensuous thought. Yet he could discern more in these objects of veneration, and in the practices of the cult, than his nonphilosophical fellow worshippers felt; and he could well acquiesce in the traditions as containing intimations—or "images"—of the divine, of whose reality he had no philosophical doubt.

There is another order of heavenly beings—the sun, the moon and the planets—who rank as gods in Plato's state. In the *Timaeus* (41a) these are distinguished from the traditional gods in that they traverse the heavens openly (περιπολοῦσι φανερῶς), whereas the gods of mythology reveal themselves only "when they will" (καθ' ὅσον ἂν ἐθέλωσιν). To worship the latter men set up images to assist them (931a); but the images of the former are a part of the order of nature, as set forth in the myth of the *Timaeus*.[153] The worship as well as the recognition of these heavenly gods is taken for granted in Plato's text. In the educational program such worship is assumed as a justification for the study of astronomy, the science that studies these gods in the heavens (θεῶν τῶν κατ' οὐρανόν) and enables us to speak truly and piously about them when we are sacrificing and praying (821d). We have seen also that the election of the euthynoi takes place in a temple of Apollo and Helios, and the persons elected to this high office become priests of these two divinities (947a). This is the only part of Plato's text that gives any details of the astral worship that is implied; such details would obviously fall under the sacred law and be dictated by Apollo and his interpreters. But the importance of such worship is indicated by the theological argument in the tenth book, in which the divinity of the heavenly bodies, or

---

[153] *Tim.* 41a. In *Laws* 930e-931a Plato recalls this distinction between the gods who are visible and those who are worshipped through lifeless images, though he uses it for a special purpose, viz. to argue that living parents and grandparents are more venerable than any images.

rather of the souls that move them, is established by demonstration (899b); and in the *Epinomis*, which can at least claim to be the earliest exposition (either by Plato or by one of his disciples) of the theology presupposed by the *Laws*, the divinity of the heavenly bodies is the central theme.

To what extent does this part of Plato's law represent an innovation on the customs of his people? The sun was certainly regarded as a divinity by the Greeks from earliest times. Agamemnon invokes Helios, together with Zeus, as witnesses of the agreement between the Achaeans and the Trojans for the settlement of the war by single combat.[154] The chorus in Sophocles' *Oedipus Tyrannus* addresses Helios as "the chief of all the gods." Anaxagoras was indicted for impiety for implying that the sun was not a god. Socrates argues in the *Apology* that it would be absurd to think he does not believe that the sun and moon are gods, as the rest of mankind do. The *Symposium* describes him as offering a prayer to the sun after his day and night of meditation at Potidaea.[155] But public worship of Helios and Selene was regarded as more typical of barbarians than of Greeks, who preferred to worship gods more personal in character and more accessible to human prayers. Nevertheless it was a common practice to invoke Helios in ceremonies of oath taking; and "prostrations and devotions at the risings and settings of the sun and moon" must have been, as 887e says, common phenomena among Greeks and barbarians alike. The deified heroes, the Dioscuri, had found their place among the stars as the "heavenly twins."[156] This order of thought was so widespread that Plato's acceptance of the divinity of the heavenly bodies would be regarded as natural. It is to be noticed that it arouses no sign of protest or dissent in Cleinias and Megillus when the Athenian Stranger mentions it. The innovation lies in the proposal to establish a public cult of these gods;[157] no

---

[154] *Iliad* III, 277 and XIX, 259. Cf. also Hesiod *Works and Days* 338ff.; the episode of the "cattle of the sun," *Odyss.* XII 322ff., and the "country of Helios," in the Homeric *Hymn to Pythian Apollo* 410ff.

[155] *Oed. Tyr.* 660; *Apol.* 26d; *Symp.* 220d. Cf. also the famous oath of Prometheus in Aesch. *Prom.* 88ff.; Aristoph. *Peace* 406ff. and *Plutus* 771. In *Crat.* 397d Socrates advances the view that primitive men believed only in those gods—sun, moon, earth, stars, sky—which many barbarians still believe in. Cf. Arist. *Met.* 1074b 1 and Plato *Rep.* 508a.

[156] Eur. *Or.* 1629ff. gives Helen also an immortal place in the stars alongside Castor and Polydeuces; and Aristoph. *Peace* 828ff. makes play with the belief that the souls of dead men become stars.

[157] As Dodds points out, *op.cit.* 220.

such cult existed, so far as we know, in Sparta, Athens, or Crete. But there is no absolute novelty even here, for the cult of Helios was not unknown elsewhere.[158] It is clearly misguided, however, to suppose[159] that Plato hoped to replace the traditional worship of the Olympians by a rational worship of the stars. This is precluded by what we have just seen of the importance of the Olympians in Plato's state, and by Plato's deference to the guidance of Apollo in religious matters. What should be said is that Plato hoped to enlarge or enrich current religion by directing attention to other manifestations of the divine than those usually recognized in worship. Apollo is not repudiated; he is associated with Helios in a common cult.

In this union of Apollo and Helios we have a hint of the future. The identification of Apollo with the sun-god was a commonplace in Hellenistic times, and is still widely prevalent in popular expositions of Greek religion. But there is no consciousness of such identity or association in Homer, in Hesiod, or in the Homeric hymns. A fragment of Euripides, however, declares that those who know the "secret names" of the gods rightly call Apollo Helios, which shows that the designation was speculative, though perhaps not uncommon.[160] The association of these two divinities might have been suggested by Apollo's ancient epithet "Phoebus"—"the pure and radiant one"; or by the analogy between the arrows of Apollo and the rays of the sun; or more generally by Apollo's character of lordly detachment; a god of clear-eyed cognition, he maintains his distance and works from afar.[161] In any case, this identification was a commonplace among the Stoics, and is found in the Orphic hymns. Whether Plato was influenced by Euripides, or by contemporary Orphics, or was an independent contributor to this current of speculation, we cannot pause to inquire.[162] But his motive can easily be made out. The identification of Apollo with the brightest of the astral gods provides a

[158] There was a cult of Helios on the island of Rhodes, and temples of Helios at Hermione and Cos; Farnell, *Cults* v, 418f.

[159] As many commentators have done, including the author in an earlier article (PR LXII, 1953, 247); see also A.-J. Festugière, *La Révélation d'Hermès Trismégisthe*, Paris, 1949, II, 100.

[160] Eur. Fr. 781, Nauck. For criticism of the Hellenistic interpretation see Farnell, *op.cit.* IV, 136ff.

[161] On this aspect of Apollo see W. F. Otto, *The Homeric Gods*, New York, 1954, 77ff.

[162] There is no hint of this identification in *Crat.* 405ab, where Apollo is described in the conventional way as the god of music, prophecy, medicine, and archery. Cf. also *Symp.* 197a.

natural bridge between the common man's ideas and those of the intellectuals,[163] and was undoubtedly used by Plato as the easiest way to suggest that enrichment of current worship which he has in mind. This part of the *Laws*, with the *Epinomis*, was undoubtedly an important influence in setting the pattern of Hellenistic thought.

The inclusion of the astral gods in worship is not only quite intelligible from the standpoint of the theology of the tenth book, but is also founded on the traditional religion which Plato presupposes. Apollo and the Olympians for whom he stands were worshipped as sponsors of the moral and social order, as supporters of the oath, of marriage and kinship obligations, of the rights of strangers and suppliants. The cosmological divinities—Helios and other nature-gods—are religious expressions of the same divine power acting on a larger stage. Such nature-gods had been more prominent in the older mythology than in the worship of the classical period, but they had not been forgotten. Thus for Plato and for the Greeks generally the "city-holding gods"—the "younger gods" of mythology—were far from representing fully the divine nature. If we would see that divine nature and worship it in its fullness we must go beyond the personalities and functions of the Olympians, and for Plato this would mean apprehending the Nous that orders the whole of nature. Now the sun, moon, and stars, moving in orderly and unceasing procession through the heavens, are the most visible evidence of that ordering Nous, and the sun, the leader of this chorus, its most resplendent image. In thus extending his hierarchy of gods to beings above the Olympians, Plato is following the direction in which his own philosophy points, and at the same time reviving for his contemporaries an older and deeper motive present in their ancestral religion.[164]

[163] See Dodds, *op.cit.* 221. This may be, however, not a "desperate" attempt to save the unity of Greek belief, but rather the confident assertion of its unrealized wealth.

[164] Much attention has been given recently to the possibility of Chaldean influences on Plato's thought during the last ten years of his life. The evidence is well marshaled by Jaeger, *Aristoteles*, 1923, 133ff.; see also des Places, "Platon et l'astrologie chaldéenne," in *Mélanges Cumont*, 1936, 129-142; Joseph Bidez, *Eos ou Platon et l'Orient*, Brussels, 1945; and Festugière, "Platon et l'Orient," in *Rev. de Philol.* xxi, 1947, 5-45. It is quite likely that the observational data and calculations of the Chaldean astronomers were used by Eudoxus in establishing the proof, to which Plato refers (821e), of the real regularity of the motions of the heavenly bodies, apparently so irregular, and thus in confirming his hypothesis of their divinity. But belief in the divinity of the heavenly bodies is much older, in fact was an old Greek view, as the evidence above has shown. And before one accepts the further inference that Plato adopted from these Chaldean sources the Iranian dualism between the

With the Chthonioi (717a, 828c) we come to another phase of
Greek religion, one which was formerly almost ignored because of
the greater splendor of the Olympians, but whose importance is
coming to be more and more recognized. Greek worship was not
always cheerful and gay, a happy fellowship with the gods in feasting and dancing and games. It had also its Erinnyes, its Hekate, its
Gorgons and Keres, and above all the dread custodian of the dead
in the underworld, Hades. In contrast with the Olympians, the
Chthonioi were divinities who had their residence and their sphere
of operation in the earth.[165] They had a double function: they en-
sured the fertility of the land, and they guarded or presided over the
souls of the dead that had been committed to the earth. These functions seem to be equally primitive, and the gods who were thought
of as exercising them belong to the earliest and lowest stratum of
Greek religion. The sharp contrast between the Olympians and
the Chthonioi—"the one fundamental cleavage in Greek religion,"
Guthrie says[166]—has usually been explained as a result of the mixture
of cultures, that of the earlier inhabitants, chiefly Mediterranean in
stock, still persisting beneath the practices and beliefs of the northern invaders. This history explains also why the cleavage was not
absolute. On the one hand, there were aspects and functions of the
Olympians that seem clearly derived from chthonic beliefs. The Zeus
of mythology is a thinly disguised mixture; he is both the god of the
bright sky whose dwelling is above the clouds, and also the Zeus of
Crete, born in a cave, and worshipped with mystic dancing and
ecstasy. A similar mixture of cultures is discernible in Hermes, in
Demeter, in Dionysus, and even in Apollo. On the other hand, the
chief chthonic deities seem often to have been thought of as the
Olympians in another guise; such at least we may infer from the
cult-names, or euphemisms, by which they were sometimes designated—such as Ζεὺς καταχθόνιος for Hades.[167] Nevertheless these
two orders of divinities were clearly distinguished in Greek religion
by the sharply different rites used in their worship. The worship appropriate to the Olympians was burnt sacrifice and prayer, conducted

---

good and evil forces in nature, one would first have to show that there is such a
dualism in Plato's latest thought. To me this is by no means evident. Nor is it to
Festugière, *Révélation* II, 127 n. 2; nor to des Places, REG LXVIII, 1955, 179.

[165] For the distinction between these two kinds of gods, see Guthrie, *The Greeks
and Their Gods*, 209ff., and E. Rohde, *Psyche*, 4th edn. Tübingen, 1907, I, 204ff.

[166] *Op.cit.* 220.

[167] And the Ζεὺς ἄλλος who sits to judge the dead, according to Aesch. *Suppl.* 231.

in broad daylight around an altar before a temple, and followed usually by games, feasting, and all the other aspects of festival. The atmosphere of chthonic worship, on the other hand, was one of fear and gloom. Its rites were usually performed at night, in a cave or around a hole in the ground; and if a sacrifice was involved it was a holocaust, the worshippers not partaking of it. The former rites invite the gods' presence; the latter are designed to keep them away, or invoke them only to enlist their aid against kindred evils. The distinction between these two sorts of ritual was linguistically marked: to worship the Olympians was θύειν; to worship the Chthonioi was ἐναγίζειν.[168]

Both the cheerful and the somber phases of Greek religion will have a place in Plato's state; but it does not follow that he regards them with equal favor. "We will most truly hit the mark of piety if we assign to the gods of the underworld the even, the secondary, and the left, and the opposites of these to the Olympians" (717ab). This seems to have been a Pythagorean precept.[169] In the Pythagorean table of opposites the odd belonged in the right-hand column, the column of the good, the limit, and the one; while the even was placed in the column with the unlimited and plurality.[170] The import of this passage is then to assign the superior honors to the Olympians, the inferior to the gods of the underworld. But it probably also hints at ritual distinctions analogous to those we have noted. The opposi-

---

[168] Herod. II, 44; Isoc. x, 63. For other differences between these two kinds of rites, see Guthrie, op.cit. 221f.; Harrison, op.cit. (Note 116), 7ff.; and Stengel 125, 141ff., 151. The theoretical distinction that Plato accepts here has its parallels in statements of his contemporaries. Isoc. v, 117 refers to two classes of divinities: "those called Olympians, who are the causes of good things to us, and those with more unpleasing designations that preside over calamities and punishments." There is something similar in the Hippocratic De Somniis, 89, ad fin. It remains true, however, that this theoretical distinction is more rigid than Greek practice, as A. D. Nock has shown (Harv. Theol. Rev. xxxvii, 1944, 164). In fact it is too rigid to apply accurately even to Plato's state, as we shall see.

[169] Porph. Vita Pythag. 38: τοῖς μὲν οὐρανίοις θεοῖς περιττὰ θύειν, τοῖς δὲ χθονίοις ἄρτια. It is to be noted that in Plato's other reference to this distinction (828c), the Olympians of 717a are called οὐράνιοι.

[170] Porph. loc.cit. and Aristotle Met. 986a 23ff. Plato often uses this Pythagorean symbolism. Thus in the myth of Er the souls that are condemned descend into the earth through the opening to the left, the just souls go upward through the opening in the heavens on the right (Rep. 614c). Likewise in the same myth the motion of the outer—and nobler—circle of the heavenly bodies is to the right, that of the inner circles to the left (617c), just as in the Timaeus the circle of the Same in the world-soul moves to the right, the circle of the Other to the left (36c). In the Phaedrus the application of division to the concept of Eros leads us to a "left-handed and evil love" (266a).

tion between light and darkness figured in the Pythagorean table of opposites; and it is perhaps not without significance that the worship of the Olympians took place by day, that of the chthonic deities by night, and that the favored sacrificial victims in the former case were white, in the latter dark.[171] Whatever these ritual implications are, Plato does not dwell on them, but it is clear that he takes them for granted. There is a reference to them in his advice to the man who is obsessed by a criminal desire to betake himself to the "rites of guilt-averting" (ἐπὶ τὰς ἀποδιοπομπήσεις) at the sacred places of the "deities that turn away evil" (θεῶν ἀποτροπαίων, 854b). Both phrases used here are technical terms in Greek ritual.[172] Again we hear of "days of ill omen" (ἡμέραι ἀποφράδες), to which doleful songs are appropriate, and costumes of mourning (800de). At Athens certain days of the great festivals were designated ἀποφράδες, such as the first and third days of the Anthesteria, at which the souls of the dead, it seems, were evoked. But these passages show that Plato does not like to dwell on such details; the emphasis of his religion is to be joy and fellowship with the gods. It is in sacrifice and prayer to the Olympians that the good man most happily and fittingly engages, he says.[173] Hence he not only proposes to segregate the chthonic rites from the worship of the Olympians and put them in a special month apart—the month sacred to Pluto (828cd)—but also endeavors to shift the emphasis of these rites themselves from gloom to confident hope.

The proposal to segregate the chthonic rites in a special month sacred to Pluto is indeed an innovation. Festugière has claimed that the idea of divine patrons for the twelve months is of Babylonian origin, transmitted to the Academy through Eudoxus.[174] This view does not seem plausible, for after all there was an Attic month named for Poseidon, many of the others got their names from the festivals celebrated in them, and it would be but a step further to think of

[171] Stengel 125ff., 149ff. Cf. 956a: white offerings are most appropriate to the gods. Athenaeus (410a) quotes from Anticleides' book on ἐναγισμοί: "Dig a trench to the west of the tomb, etc." Plato would regard this as to the left of the tomb (cf. 760d).

[172] Cf. also the prescription for the purification of a hapless and impious house in 877e: καθήρασθαι καὶ ἀποδιοπομπήσασθαι τὸν οἶκον; and the metaphor of 900b: ἀποδιοπομπήσασθαι λόγοις, i.e. to avert the pollution of atheism by arguments.

[173] 716d. That this is the implication of the passage is clear from the terms θύειν and θεραπεία used of this worship. On θύειν see above, and on θεραπεία, Harrison, *op.cit.* 3-4.

[174] *Rev. de Philol.* xxi, 1947, 29.

these months as sacred to the gods honored in the corresponding festivals.[175] Plato's real innovation is to name a month for Pluto and
by implication to admit him to the circle of "the Twelve." Although
Pluto—or Hades—was a son of Kronos, like Zeus and Poseidon, he
seems never to have been accorded a seat with the Olympians, and
under the name of Hades was only rarely an object of worship among
the Greeks.[176] He was the lord of the underworld, the grim door-
keeper (πυλάρτης) of that region from which no one returns. Plato's
reason for elevating him to the Olympian circle is evidently a desire
to counteract the unwholesome dread with which the underworld
and the afterlife were contemplated by his countrymen. In the *Republic* Socrates insists that the poets shall be required not to dispraise
(μὴ λοιδορεῖν) the underworld, but rather to praise it; "what they
now tell us about it is neither true nor useful to men who are to be
warriors" (386bc).[177] This judgment is generalized in the *Laws*
(727d): "Again, when a man counts it good to live at all costs, that
also is dishonor to the soul; 'tis surrender to that within him which
accounts the unseen world (τὰ ἐν Ἅιδου) merely evil, whereas a man
should make head against his fancy with cogent proof that he knows
not even whether our chiefest good may not be in the gift of the gods
of that land."[178] For one who believes, as Plato does, that death is
not necessarily an evil, but may be the entrance to a richer life for
the immortal soul, the truth about the afterlife is quite different from
the pictures of popular imagination.

Hence for the purposes of religious worship Plato seizes upon that

[175] Thuc. v, 54 says the month Καρνεῖος was sacred to the Dorians, and Karneios
was an epithet of Apollo. The names of Artemis, Apollo, and Poseidon occur frequently in the calendars of other Greek cities; see Ruelle in DS. s.v. Calendrier,
and Bischoff in RE s.v. Kalender. Herod. II, 82 reports something similar for Egypt.

[176] Paus. VI, xxv. 2 mentions a temple of Hades at Elis and says that the Eleans
are "the only men we know of" who worship him.

[177] The only examples given by Socrates of the kind of poetry he disapproves of
are taken from Homer, though the faults involved are attributed to "Homer and
the other poets" (387b). Aristophanes' picture of the underworld in the *Frogs* goes
beyond Homer in frightfulness. Its terrors are burlesques, it is true, but they must
have been burlesques of popular conceptions; Nilsson I, 769. Other evidence is afforded by Cephalus' remarks in the opening scene of the *Republic* (330de), and by
a fragment of Democritus (Diels-Kranz II, Fr. 297). Polygnotus' famous painting
of the underworld in the λέσχη of the Cnidians at Delphi, so fully described in
Paus. x, xxviii-xxxi, contained some gruesome details of judgment and punishment
after death.

[178] Taylor's translation. There is another implied protest against current views in
Crat. 403a-404a: the fear of being with Hades after death is absurd; the power of
this god to hold those committed to his care is due to the benefits he confers upon
them, benefits that he cannot give to men who are still bound to the body.

more cheerful aspect of Hades shown in the popular agrarian cult of Demeter and Persephone. The traditional origin of this cult was familiar to Plato's countrymen from the Homeric *Hymn to Demeter*, recounting the rape of Persephone to the underworld by Aidoneus (another name for Hades), the mourning of her mother Demeter, the death of all vegetation, the intervention of Zeus, and the final agreement whereby Persephone was released, but on condition that she return to the underworld for a third part of every year thereafter. The myth reflects the contrast, so mysterious and so important for tillers of the soil, between the growing period of the year and the months when vegetation appears to die or to sleep. As an agent in this beneficent cycle of death and rebirth, Hades appears in the worship of Demeter and Persephone, but under his cult name of Pluto. This name—derived from πλοῦτος, wealth—means that Pluto is the "giver of wealth" to men; so Plato interprets it in the *Cratylus*, and so it was interpreted by his countrymen.[179] That Plato had this myth in mind is evident not only from his use of the name of Pluto, but also from his choice of the month to be named after him. Plato's year begins, as did the Attic year, with the summer solstice (767c); hence his twelfth month, which is to be sacred to Pluto, would correspond to the Attic month Skirophorion, so called from the festival which was celebrated during it. This festival was analogous to the Thesmophoria, celebrated in the early autumn in the month Pyanepsion; both were connected with the mysteries of Eleusis and the story of the rape of Persephone by Pluto.[180] It is possible that one or both of the months of these festivals were popularly regarded as sacred to Pluto, even though his name does not appear in the calendar.[181]

[179] *Crat.* 403a. Pluto is often represented in vase paintings as an old man holding a cornucopia. Nilsson 1, 442 and n. 4.

[180] On the Skira as a festival of Demeter and Kore, see Deubner, *Attische Feste*, 45ff.; on the Thesmophoria, 50ff. See Deubner also (40ff.) for the text and exegesis of the scholium to Lucian, which is of capital importance for the understanding of these festivals; also Harrison, *op.cit.* 121ff.

[181] If Nilsson's plausible interpretation (1, 442f.) of the story of Persephone is correct, the period between these two festivals would correspond rather accurately to the period between Persephone's κάθοδος to the underworld at the beginning of summer, when vegetation begins to die, and her ἄνοδος just before the autumn rains begin. Thus the period of her absence corresponds not to the winter season, as northern interpreters have instinctively thought, but to the four months of summer when, as every visitor to Greece will remember, the earth lies bare and parched. In Greece the growing season for grain—and the cult of Demeter was certainly a cult of grains, not of vegetation in general—begins in the autumn and continues almost without a pause through the winter and spring.

Closely connected with the worship of Demeter at Athens were the Eleusinian mysteries, in whose practices and symbols the contrasting roles of Pluto as lord of the dead and as giver of wealth were impressively combined and reconciled. In them the story of Persephone and the cycle of vegetation which it dramatically symbolized—the planting of the dead seed in the earth and its rebirth to new and glorious life—offered through many centuries an assurance of a kind of immortality which appears to have been indescribably precious to the initiated.[182] What Plato's attitude towards these mysteries was is itself something of a mystery.[183] They were presided over by priests chosen from the family of the Eumolpidae by laws of the clan which the Athenian state did not try to control, though it gave public recognition to their office. Whether there would be an offshoot of this Eleusinian cult in Plato's model colony (we know there were offshoots elsewhere in Greece) would depend on the accidents of emigration and the utterances of the oracle. But the possibility of such a development, and perhaps the hope of it, may have been in Plato's mind. In any case he could take for granted in his readers a knowledge of the brighter aspect of this cult of Demeter and Persephone and Pluto, and could argue, in support of his introduction of Pluto into the Olympian circle, that warrior men should not cherish repugnance for such a god (828d). He could also add an expression of personal belief, in which his Academic friends would find a reminder of the

---

[182] The symbolism lived on in the Christian tradition; cf. *The Gospel According to John* xii, 24; and Paul's *First Epistle to the Corinthians* xv, 36-37.

[183] There is no explicit mention of the Eleusinian mysteries in any of the dialogues. But Boyancé (*op.cit.* 14-31) thinks that they are included in the condemnation of Orphic books and practices in *Rep.* 363c, 364b-365a. Reverdin (227) is impressed by Boyancé's arguments and points out the close parallel in thought and diction between the *Republic* passage and *Laws* 908a-e and 909ab. But Dodds (*op.cit.* 234 n. 82) cannot believe Plato means to suggest in the *Laws* that the Eleusinian priesthood are guilty of an offense which he regards as worse than atheism (cf. 907b). Again Nilsson (*Harv. Theol. Rev.* xxviii, 1935, 208) interprets the *Republic* passage itself not as a condemnation of "Orphism as such," but of the "vile jugglers" and "hangers-on" of the Orphic movement. Certainly there are other references to Orphic teachings in the dialogues which are the reverse of critical (see 715e, and Note 130); and there are others in which Plato appears to employ aspects or stages of Eleusinian initiation as an aid in the exposition of his own thought. Both *Gorg.* 497c and *Symp.* 209e refer to "lesser and greater mysteries"; *Phaedo* 69c seems to treat the Eleusinian doctrine as a riddling anticipation of Plato's own view of the future life; and the final vision attained by the ascending soul (*Phaedr.* 250bc, *Symp.* 210f.) looks like a philosophical counterpart to the epoptic stage of the ceremonies at Eleusis. Was Plato himself an Eleusinian initiate? If the passages just mentioned are references to the Eleusinian mysteries, they appear to reflect the attitude, not of an outside observer, but of one who had himself experienced them.

myths of the *Phaedo*, the *Phaedrus*, and the *Republic*. "Union of soul and body, as I would assure you in all earnest, is no way better than dissolution."[184] This conviction is expressed more fully in the solemn words of prelude to the law governing the burial of the dead: the soul is the real man, his body merely an attendant image; and when he dies his likeness remains behind, but the man himself, i.e. his immortal soul, departs to the presence of "other gods" to fulfill his destiny (959ab).[185]

It is puzzling to find that Plato seems to forget these canons of criticism when he turns on his own account to a portrayal of what awaits the unjust soul in the other world. The tales of judgment after death and retribution exacted through cycles of reincarnation, which are given with such vivid detail in the *Gorgias*, *Phaedo* and *Republic*, are usually regarded as having their basis in the teaching of the Orphics;[186] in any case they may conveniently be referred to as his "Orphic tales." Their substance recurs in the *Laws*, particularly in the section dealing with homicide. In the prelude to the law covering murder, Plato refers to the λόγος told in mystic rites that vengeance for such acts is exacted in Hades, and that those who upon reincarnation live again on earth are destined to suffer from others the identical wrong they have inflicted upon their victims in their previous life (870d).[187] The same "myth or story" (μῦθος ἢ λόγος) is referred to in the special law governing the murder of kindred; here it is said to be derived "from the priests of old time" (ἐκ παλαιῶν ἱερέων, 872e).[188] To understand Plato's motives for insisting on such tales we must remember that these underworld avengers (οἱ ὑπὸ γῆς τιμωροί) are thought of as instruments of Justice (881a); they are the Nemesis described in an earlier passage as the messenger of that Dike who follows in the train of Zeus (717d).[189] These stories are admitted to have little effect upon some persons (881a); their purpose therefore

[184] 828d, Taylor's translation. Cf. 727d and *Phaedo* 63b.
[185] These "other gods" are the χθόνιοι θεοί, as *Phaedo* 63b makes clear.
[186] Albrecht Dieterich, *Nekyia*, Leipzig, 1893, 113-124; Nilsson 1, 649-652; and above, Note 130. For a dissenting opinion see E. R. Dodds, *Plato: Gorgias*, Oxford, 1959, 372-376.
[187] This was dramatically illustrated in Polygnotus' painting in the λέσχη of the Cnidians at Delphi; Paus. x, xxviii, 4. Cf. also Plato's reference in 959c to the soul that departs from this life unpunished: τελευτήσας ἀτιμώρητος κακῶν ἁμαρτημάτων.
[188] Cf. *Ep. VII* 335a: "We must always firmly believe those ancient and holy words declaring to us that the soul is immortal and when it has separated from the body will go before the judges and pay the utmost penalties." On these ἱεροὶ λόγοι see *Meno* 81a-c, *Phaedo* 70c.
[189] Cf. Aesch. Fr. 266, Wecklein.

is not merely deterrence, but rather reassurance as to the supremacy of the all-seeing and incorruptible Providence, or order of destiny, which allots each soul eventually to the place in the cosmos for which its character fits it (904c-e). Thus the accounting which, according to the "ancestral law," every soul has to render at death before these "other gods" is a prospect that may be faced with courage by the good, but with utmost dread by the wicked (959b).

The strength of the Greek feeling for justice, and the close connection between Zeus and Dike in Greek tradition, have already been noted. It was from this feeling that the Orphic doctrine derived much of its inspiration and its influence on thoughtful minds.[190] The old principle that the sins of the fathers are punished in their sons was repugnant to the growing individualism of the sixth and later centuries, of which Orphism was one expression. This led to the demand that since guilt is personal, its punishment must be visited upon the doer himself. The doctrines of immortality and reincarnation were admirably fitted to satisfy this demand; they showed how in the divine ordering of the world every wrong could eventually find its just retribution, despite the prosperity of the wicked in this life. This motive was clearly present in Plato's adoption and use of the Orphic tales.[191] His criticism of the poets arises from his conviction that their pictures were too simple and undiscriminating, taking no account of the difference between the fate of the just and that of the unjust; for all alike the abode of the dead was pictured as a realm of gloom, without light and without hope.[192] But this would hardly be a fair criticism; though true perhaps of Homer, it does little justice to the popular opinions of Plato's time. Aristophanes' portrayal in the *Frogs* of Hades' realm contains one of his loveliest choruses, the song of the initiated pursuing in the next life their happy festivals, in sharp contrast to the horrors of the slime and the daemons visiting punishment on the wicked. Polygnotus' painting at Delphi had its happy as well as its somber details. The truth seems to be that Plato is both unfair to "the poets," and is himself the victim of the

---

[190] Nilsson 1, 652ff.; and Note 130.

[191] It is particularly evident in one striking development he gives to these tales. In the myth of the *Gorgias* the familiar trio of judges—Minos, Rhadamanthys, and Aeacus (cf. *Apol.* 41a; Dem. XVIII, 127)—are so ranked as to provide two stages of procedure: Rhadamanthys and Aeacus to give preliminary judgment on all cases, and Minos to make the final decision if either of the others is in doubt (524a). For Plato's use of judicial review in his system of justice, see Chapter VI, The Courts.

[192] Cf. *Rep.* 386b: we must beg the poets μὴ λοιδορεῖν ἁπλῶς.

same divided mind so characteristic of his contemporaries. He would have the atmosphere of his religion cheerful and bright; but his sense of justice requires him to dwell with relentless intensity upon the punishment of the wicked. "The sense of justice," as Nilsson aptly remarks, "can lead one to pitiless severity; and this severity is no more absent in the idealist Plato than it was in Greek penal law. The following ages drew dangerous inspiration from it."[193]

Next to the high gods just mentioned, Plato's law provides for the worship of daemons (δαίμονες) and heroes (ἥρωες). The spiritual agencies known as daemons played a large part in the religion of Plato's countrymen, though it is difficult to say what conception of the nature and status of these beings underlay their worship. The concept of δαίμων seems to include the very gods from whom δαίμονες are distinguished; the former is but an old word for divinity, and is used in Homer sometimes to denote an individual god, sometimes in the abstract sense of the divine power manifested in the world and in the destinies of men.[194] On the other hand, the line between daemons and heroes is equally indistinct, for heroes are also superhuman in their powers, as in their origin, and can lay claim in worship to the title of daemons.[195] It is seldom possible to view the object of worship in clear conceptual outlines; in any case cult practices are more fundamental than theory in such matters. Plato is not writing theology but laying down religious law, following in the main the long-hallowed practices of his countrymen; so we should not expect him to reduce to conceptual system what remained for the Greeks only vaguely organized sentiments of reverence and fear. The most he does is to insist on the hierarchy of gods, daemons, and heroes. This itself represents perhaps too rigid a fixation of categories that in practice remained fluid; nevertheless the distinctions involved were not invented by Plato, and we shall see that in the *Laws* he is in the main merely reflecting what he found in Greek religion.[196]

---

[193] Nilsson I, 774.

[194] Farnell, *Greek Hero Cults*, Oxford, 1921, 76ff.; Nilsson I, 201ff.

[195] Cf. Hesiod *Works and Days* 122ff.; *Theog.* 989-990. Cf. Plato *Rep.* 468e-469a.

[196] There are suggestions of theory in other dialogues. Δαίμονες are either gods or sons of gods, argues Socrates in *Apol.* 27cd. In *Symp.* 202de Diotima asserts that daemons are neither gods nor men, but beings intermediate between the two, transporting prayers and sacrifices from men to the gods, and commands and requitals from gods to men. In *Crat.* 397e-398a, after asserting that the word δαίμονες is Hesiod's term for δαήμονες, "knowing ones," Socrates declares that every man who is good—and therefore wise—is daemonic (δαιμόνιος) and may rightly

The religious calendar prescribes a sacrifice every day "to some god or daemon" (828b),[197] and some of the temples or sacred areas in the state will be dedicated to daemons (738b). The wise man will perform rites in their honor (ὀργιάζοιτ' ἄν) with prayers and hymns of praise as to the gods (717b, 801e). Each division of the land is to be assigned to some god or daemon or hero as its protector (738d, 771d). Since the tribal divisions have been identified with the Olympians, it must be the subdivisions of the tribes (771b) that are to bear the names of daemons or heroes. These daemons are clearly lesser divinities (713bc).[198] Some of them are attached to special areas, not merely as eponymous patrons, nor through immemorial tradition (848d), but through divine allotment (747e).[199] Some function as guardian deities to individuals and to groups (729e, 732c, 877a). Others have still more specific functions, like the "goddess of the way-side" (ἐνοδία δαίμων) who looks after property that a traveler has left behind (914b). They are generally spoken of as attached to the train of one of the gods, like the stranger's guardian daemons who "follow in the train of Zeus Xenios" (τῷ ξενίῳ συνεπόμενοι Διί, 730a).[200] Similarly Dike, with Nemesis and the avenging deities,

be called a daemon. In *Tim.* 90a the intelligent part of man's soul is said to be a daemon, the gift of God that enables man to retain his connection with his "kindred in heaven" (τὴν ἐν οὐρανῷ συγγένειαν). But despite Reverdin (131ff.) these suggestions do not add up to a "daemonology"—certainly not to a consistent one. The view that daemons are intermediaries between gods and men came to be common after Plato's time, and Plutarch considers it a great clarification (*De Def. Orac.* 10). A more elaborate view is set forth in *Epin.* 984b-985b, positing three orders of daemons—corresponding to the three elements of ether, air, and water intermediate between the divine region of fire and the earthly region of man—all of them serving as messengers and intermediaries. Some such view may underlie the prescriptions in the *Laws*, but it is nowhere expressed. On the development of the concept of δαίμων from Plato onwards, see Dieterich, *op.cit.* 59ff.

[197] Cf. 807a, which implies that every day is to be sacred to one of the gods. Θεοῖς here must include δαίμοσι, and perhaps also ἥρωσι, since there would not be enough gods, in the strict sense of the term, to fill a month, still less a year.

[198] This passage recounts briefly the myth of the Age of Kronos in the *Politicus*, when all the tribes of animals were in the charge of δαίμονες, οἷον νομῆς θείοι (271d).

[199] I cannot agree with England that δαιμόνων λήξεις of 747e refers back to the provisions of 738d and 745d, for the point here is that certain districts are especially favored by having a θεία ἐπίπνοια and being under the care of daemons. Since each district in Plato's state would have its patron deity, this passage points to a further differentiation.

[200] Ἑπόμενοι, often used in connection with daemons, must be taken in this vivid sense. Thus the cryptic τῶν τούτοις ἑπομένων of 828c is clarified by the τῶν ἑπομένων θεοῖς δαιμόνων of 848d, and the τῷ ξενίῳ συνεπόμενοι Διί of 730a. Cf. 727a for another expression of the same idea. All these passages recall the picture in the *Phaedrus* of the procession of the gods led by Zeus, who is followed by an army of

attends on Zeus (716a); and the Moerae also belong in his train.[201]
The Muses and the Graces attend on Apollo (653d, 664c, 672d, 796e);
Kore and Triptolemus on Demeter (782b); and Eileithyia perhaps
on Hera (784a). It is thus, apparently, that they qualify as objects
of worship, because they serve the higher gods and assist them in
their care of things here below. Socrates' beautiful prayer to Pan at
the close of the *Phaedrus* is an example of the religious sentiment
that such beings could inspire. "The gods and daemons are our allies," says Plato toward the end, "and we are their possessions"
(906a).

Much closer to the human level were the heroes, i.e. noteworthy
men and women of the past who were thought of as still having
power to affect human affairs for good or ill, and to whom divine
honors were accorded.[202] The cult of heroes was of great antiquity.
Because of the special circumstances of the hero's birth and human
career, his worship was usually local in character, centered about his
tomb (or what was thought to be his tomb), and his worshippers
were the descendants of the persons with whom he had been most
associated in life and in whose welfare he was presumably still most
interested. An all-Greek hero—such as Achilles, or Ajax. or Dio-
medes, or Heracles—would be so well known from poetry and legend
that his worship would transcend the particular locality with which
he was associated during life, and legends would be constantly arising to explain his connection with new areas in which his cult was
established, or to justify a city's claim to be the real possessor of his
remains. But the very growth of these legends testifies to the fact
that the worship of a hero was something that satisfied local needs;
the hero was thought to be connected with his worshippers in a particularly intimate way, and his worship bound them together. The
need for some such tie was so strongly felt that when a clan, or a
community, or a group of artisans had no authentic historical hero
available, they usually invented one for their purposes.

---

gods and daemons (τῷ δ' ἕπεται στρατιὰ θεῶν τε καὶ δαιμόνων) arranged in eleven
bands, each led by one of the Olympians (246e).

[201] 799b; cf. 960c. Hesiod *Theog.* 903ff. makes them the daughters of Zeus and
Themis.

[202] All general statements in this area are subject to exceptions and qualifications,
since the concept of hero was no more sharply defined than the concept of δαίμων
in Greek religion. The classic treatment in English is Farnell's *Greek Hero Cults*,
Oxford, 1921. See also Nilsson 1, 170ff.; Rohde, *op.cit.* 1, 146ff.; Guthrie, *op.cit.*
(Note 5), 223ff.

Like the daemons, heroes will serve as eponyms or patron deities for local subdivisions,[203] and the names of the more important heroes will probably find places in the religious calendar. But Plato always ranks them below the daemons in his hierarchy. The reason for this is obvious: they are not gods, but sons of gods.[204] Furthermore, the rites used in the worship of heroes were basically chthonic in character, for having passed through the gates of death they belonged to the underworld. Sometimes, however, regular athletic games formed a part of their worship.[205] Plato ignores the chthonic side and suggests that their worship, like that of the gods, will consist of prayers and festival songs and dances (801e), another evidence of his emphasis on the festive side of Greek religion. How seriously Plato took the heroes' claims to divine ancestry it is difficult for us to judge.[206] But he was jealous of their reputation, and in the *Republic* had criticized the poets severely for misrepresenting them (377e, 388ab, 390a,e, 391a-d, 408b). They were obviously important in his world, as they were in his countrymen's imagination. The legends of their virtues and exploits had entered so deeply into his own thought that he instinctively turns for illustration or emphasis to some detail of the traditions about them. More than forty different heroes are thus referred to, some of them several times, in the course of his dialogues. It was near the precincts of such a local hero in the suburbs of Athens that his Academy was set up, and from Academus it took the name by which it and all its successors in the western world have been known.

These details of Plato's law concerning daemons and heroes, scanty as they are, clearly reflect the religious life of Plato's Attica and of the Hellenic world. Besides the great gods of the city, every tribe, phratry, deme, and village seems to have had its own divinity, wor-

---

[203] Cleisthenes' ten new Attic tribes were named after ten heroes selected from a list of one hundred sent to Delphi (Arist. *Const. Ath.* XXI, 6). The statues of these ten eponymous heroes occupied a prominent place in the Athenian Agora near the Council House.

848d suggests that the ἀρχηγός of each of the tribes will have his shrine. This indicates some confusion in Plato's mind here, for the tribes arise only after the settlement (745bc).

[204] 853c; cf. *Rep.* 391d. Most of the heroes in Greek legends have one divine and one human parent. In *Crat.* 398cd the word ἥρως is said to come from ἔρως: "They were all born because a god fell in love with a mortal woman, or a mortal man with a goddess" (398cd).

[205] See Herod. I, 167.

[206] It gives us pause to think that Plato's first biographer, his nephew Speusippus, asserted that Plato was the son of Apollo. Diog. III, 2.

shipped with special rites often hallowed by great antiquity, each tracing its original establishment or its later confirmation to the words of some oracle. And there were other divine agencies, less restricted locally, but specialized in their functions, to whom a devout man could turn in a moment of need. All of them were vaguely thought of as lesser gods, but still as allies and agents of the high gods, and especially of Zeus, "the father of gods and men." Thus all things are full of gods, according to the saying of Thales which Plato's Athenian Stranger quotes on one occasion (899b). But Plato is not merely expressing the conditions of his own time; he is reflecting a need that manifests itself in every religion, even the most advanced—the need of an intermediary, or intermediaries, between the divine power in all its dread majesty and the particular wants and aspirations of the common man. Just as many a pious Christian of today instinctively feels that the saints are more approachable and more sensitive to his particular needs than the Almighty could possibly be, so the average Greek of Plato's time was much more likely to turn in his hour of need or thankfulness to one of these lesser deities than to the distant gods of Olympus.

A fiction of ancestry was often invoked to explain an important hero cult; but ancestor worship in the stricter sense was found in Greece from the earliest times alongside the worship of heroes. It was commonly believed that the forefathers of the living, though resting in their graves, still take an interest in the fortunes of their descendants and possess some vague power to bless or harm.[207] They are beings whose aid it is often important to enlist and whose ill will it is always important not to arouse. These sentiments of mixed reverence and fear were expressed in annual rites (ἐναγίσματα) at the tombs of the dead, and also in family shrines, in which the dead members, through their images, were honored participants in the family sacrifices. Such a cult of ancestors (προγόνων θεραπεία, 723e) is found also in Plato's state. This is both loyalty to established usages supported by Apollo, and a consequence of Plato's insistence on maintaining the integrity and continuity of the 5,040 households. The holder of a lot is the temporary head and servant of a larger group consisting of all members of the family (γένος), those living, those dead, and those yet to be born (923a). He is not only the holder of

[207] Arist. *Nic. Eth.* 1100a 29, 1101a 22ff.

a lot (ἑστιοῦχος) but the minister (θεραπευτής) of holy and sacred things (878a), i.e. "the minister to the gods of his γένος and the city, of the dead members as well as the living."[208] Naturally, therefore, there will be private shrines of ancestral deities (ἱδρύματα ἴδια πατρῴων θεῶν) with their legally authorized rites (κατὰ νόμον ὀργιαζόμενα.[209] "By doing honor and reverence (τιμῶν καὶ σεβόμενος) to his kindred and the whole fellowship of those who have the same blood and worship the family gods, a man will make the gods of birth (γενέθλιοι θεοί) correspondingly more propitious toward his own begetting of children."[210]

But what does Plato mean by the θεραπεία of ancestors? The Greek term when used of religious ceremonies implied sacrifices, prayers, and votive offerings (cf. 716d). It had also, of course, a quite secular sense of "service" or "attendance"—a sense which Socrates exploits in his discussion with Euthyphro concerning the nature of piety—and when applied to ancestors it might mean only the service involved in looking after their tombs and keeping their memories green. But ὀργιαζόμενα in 717b certainly means more than this. The term ὄργια was most often applied to ceremonies of a secret character, such as Orphic and Bacchic rites, or the rites of initiation into the mysteries of Eleusis, or those performed by members of the private religious brotherhoods (ὀργεῶνες) that became common at Athens from the late fifth century onward. Plato regards such private

[208] 740bc: θεραπευτὴν θεῶν καὶ γένους καὶ πόλεως. I follow England in taking γένους and πόλεως as genitives dependent upon θεῶν, rather than making all three coordinate and dependent upon θεραπευτήν. This is more in accord with Plato's other declarations on the continuity of the family and the religious cult that symbolizes it. The following clause—τῶν τε ζώντων κτλ—is in apposition to γένους and πόλεως, emphasizing individual members of clan and city.

[209] 717b; cf. 729c, 785a. Ἱδρύματα suggests statues as well as shrines, as England points out. When emphasizing the honors due to aged parents, Plato later calls them living ἱδρύματα, much more κύρια (potent? or authentic?) than any lifeless image that one could possess (931a,de). The erecting of images (εἰκόνες) in memory of the loved and honored dead was common in this century. Cf. the terms of Aristotle's will (Diog. v, 15), and Note 217 below. These shrines might also contain images (ἀγάλματα) of Apollo Patroös and Zeus Herkeios, who were regarded as πατρῷοι by the Athenians (Arist. Const. Ath. LV, 3). A vivid glimpse of this family cult is given in the opening scene in the Republic, where Socrates finds the aged Cephalus seated with a wreath on his head resting from the sacrifices he has just performed in the courtyard (328c); later he returns to complete them (331d).

[210] 729c. For this interpretation, see England's note with its reference to Poll. III, 5: θεῶν ὁμογνίων κοινοὶ καὶ τῆς αὐτῆς ἑστίας μέτοχοι. There seems to be a reference here to a custom, said to have been peculiar to the Athenians, of sacrificing and praying to the τριτοπάτορες (i.e. the Forefathers) in order to secure fertility in marriage. For this explanation of the term see Rohde, op.cit. I, 247 n. 4; Harrison, op.cit. 179 n. 2; Farnell, Greek Hero Cults, 355.

cults as a danger to the state and his law explicitly forbids them (909e-910c). The practices presupposed in 717b might seem to be excluded by the law later laid down, and if so, Plato's legislation on this point is inconsistent. But it is perhaps better to interpret the earlier passage as anticipating the later in the provision that such family rites must be duly authorized (κατὰ νόμον). They will be ὄργια, as ceremonies in which only the members of the family group participate; but the law will forbid their conversion into associations for purification and initiation, under the instigation of impious manteis.[211]

But what kind of rites would be lawful? The ritual of the cult of ancestors, like that of the hero cults, was identical in the main with the worship of the underworld gods discussed above.[212] To cut the throat of the sacrificial victim so that the blood could flow down into the earth, sometimes through carefully prepared channels, and thus nourish the dead man below, was a primitive action based on the belief of his continued existence under ground;[213] and such chthonic ceremonies at the tomb were a part of what was thought to be appropriate in Plato's day.[214] But for Plato—with his conception of the soul as the real man and the corpse as merely the attendant image which the dead man has left behind—such practices would clearly not seem appropriate. It is fitting, of course, that as the soul departs on its journey rites should be celebrated to the underworld gods; what these should be will be determined by custom and the instructions of the exegetes (958d); but there shall be no prolonged period of mourning, nor extravagant expenditure upon the tomb,[215] which is but "a soulless altar of the dead" (ἄψυχος χθονίων βωμός, 959d)[216]

[211] See below, The Law Against Impiety.

[212] Farnell, op.cit. 343ff.; Rohde, op.cit. I, 240.

[213] On the importance of blood in giving consciousness and thought to the shades in the underworld, see Odyss. XI, 34ff.

[214] Isaeus' orations are particularly instructive regarding what was thought proper (τὰ νομιζόμενα) in this area of piety, viz, libations and chthonic sacrifices (ἐναγίσματα) at the tomb. See II, 10, 46; VI, 51, 65; VII, 30; IX, 7.

[215] Such attempts to curb extravagance at funerals were very old; they go back at least to the time of Solon (Plut. Solon 21), Lycurgus (Plut. Lyc. 27), Gelon (Diod. XI, 38) and perhaps Charondas (Stob. XLIV, 40), and they seem to have been constantly renewed in later centuries. See Nilsson I, 676; and Reverdin 110ff. This reform was probably an expression of the democratic insurgence against the older aristocracy, as well as an effort to prevent the waste of resources needed by the living, as is suggested in Plato's law, and perhaps also an expression of good taste. The restrictions were drawn even tighter after Plato's time by the edicts of Demetrius of Phalerum: Cic. De Leg. II, 66. See Note 88 above.

[216] This I believe to be the meaning of this cryptic phrase, despite my inability

—a cryptic way of denying the popular belief that the dead man lives on in his tomb. Nor is there any hint of chthonic ceremonies in the mention of the annual honors paid to the dead. "In the same fashion [i.e. modestly], he should bestow every year becoming attention (ἐπιμελείας τὰς κόσμον φερούσας) upon the dead. Above all he should honor them by never failing to keep their memory alive, and by spending upon them a due proportion of the means with which fortune has provided him" (717e-718a). This passage is remarkable for what it fails to say, if by the annual attentions (ἐπιμέλειαι) Plato means the customary chthonic rites at the tomb of the dead. The word is noncommittal and could apply as well to other sorts of attention, such as decorating the tomb, or celebrating the birthdays of deceased parents, or erecting images of them in the household or at some center of public worship. These other methods of commemoration were widely practised in certain higher circles, and give us a better indication, no doubt, of the sort of expenditure that Plato thought piety required.[217]

It is only at the funeral of a euthynos that Plato's law enjoins any pomp or ceremony. These high officers—these "archons of archons" (945c)—are to have funeral ceremonies different from those of other citizens (947b-e). The ceremonies shall extend over two days. Only white garments shall be worn by the participants, and there are to be no dirges or lamentations. On the first day a choir of girls and an-

---

to find any contemporary parallel to this usage of χθόνιοι; but this meaning lies so close to its attested usages that it would be a natural association to express. In any case, Plato is using familiar ritual terms in an unusual way, and the phrase, rather lifeless in its English dress, would probably be a striking one to his readers. Βωμός would seem inappropriate to the word that precedes it, for the worship of chthonic gods took place not before an altar, but around an open pit, an ἐσχάρα. The first of the three words would add its own element of strangeness. Ἄψυχος would ordinarily be taken as meaning "lifeless." But the literal application of this adjective to an altar would be puzzling, for it is a privative term which, as Aristotle says, implies the absence of something that is normally present. The puzzled reader would be likely to think at once of the soul of the dead man, which was ordinarily thought to be present in the tomb. To assert that the tomb is ἄψυχον would then be equivalent to denying this popular belief; the tomb is something "around which no spirit hovers," as Taylor translates it.

[217] Epicurus made provision in his will for annual ἐναγίσματα to his parents and for the annual celebration of his own birthday, both presumably being ways of honoring the dead (Diog. x, 18). Aristotle's will provides for the dedication of an image of his mother to Demeter at Nemea (Diog. v, 16). Theophrastus seems to have had an image of Aristotle erected in the ἱερόν of the Lyceum, and his will suggests a like memorial to himself (Diog. v, 51, 54). For a similar provision in the will of Lyco, see Diog. v, 71. Plato's will does not contain any provision of this sort, but *Ep. XIII* (if it is genuine) shows his concern to give his mother a proper burial and monument (361e).

other of boys shall stand around the bier, and alternate in chanting hymns of praise to the honored dead. The next day the bier shall be escorted to the tomb by a selected group of one hundred schoolboys singing the national anthem (τὸ πάτριον μέλος), preceded by a parade of all the military forces with their appropriate arms and uniforms, and followed by choruses of girls and women, priests and priestesses. The dead man is to be laid to rest beside his predecessors in a large underground vault of stone, fitted with stone couches side by side; and the mound over the vault is to be surrounded by a grove of trees. Every year there are to be contests of music, gymnastics, and horse racing in his honor. There is no hint in this of any chthonic rites. In fact they seem to be definitely excluded; this tomb is pure (ὡς καθαρεύοντι τῷ τάφῳ, 947d), as is shown by the white garments of the participants and the presence of the priests and priestesses. For this exception to the usual practice, Plato evidently thinks the approval of the Pythian oracle must be obtained.[218]

This graphic and detailed picture of the ceremonies that Plato thinks appropriate at the close of a good man's life shows that he had no liking for chthonic rites. Yet these rites were encouraged by Delphi, and Plato apparently shared some of the beliefs on which they rested, particularly the belief that the dead have some influence over the fortunes of the living. One of the passages from which I have quoted concludes with the assurance that a man who performs such acts of piety as have been enjoined will receive his reward from the gods and "whatever beings are higher (κρείττονες) than ourselves" (718a). The dead were sometimes called κρείττονες,[219] and Plato's language may be taken as a pious reminder of this common belief in the influence of the dead, if not as an expression of Plato's own conviction. Again in the law regarding the care of orphans,

---

[218] For a fuller discussion of the funeral and entombment of a euthynos, see Reverdin 251-258. Reverdin regards these provisions of Plato's law, when taken in connection with *Rep.* 469a, 540bc, and *Crat.* 398ab, as showing that Plato would have the dead euthynoi (and possibly other honored dead) venerated as daemons rather than as heroes (127ff.). He adduces the posthumous honors accorded to Plato by the disciples whose minds he had formed as lending support to this interpretation. May this not, however, be giving too much weight to a distinction which was certainly not a clear-cut one to Plato's contemporaries, and seems to have been equally imprecise to him? It seems enough, I think, merely to point out the non-chthonic character of the rites that Plato prescribes for the glorious dead, leaving the "theology" in the background, where Plato left it (see Note 196 above). On the evidences of posthumous honors accorded to Plato and the difficulties in interpreting them, see Boyancé, *op.cit.* (Note 146), 249ff.

[219] Cf. Arist. Fr. 44, Rose.

Plato solemnly enjoins the guardians to fear not only the gods above, who are sensible of the loneliness of orphans, but also the souls of the dead parents, "whose nature it is to be especially concerned for their offspring, and who will be kindly disposed towards those who honor them and hostile to those who dishonor them" (927ab). This belief is supported by a reference to ancient sayings ($\phi\hat{\eta}\mu\alpha\iota$) which, Plato says, must be accepted as true. Finally, his homicide law contains a reminder of the ancient "myth"—that the soul of a man who has died by violence, even though the fatal act was accidental and without malice, is wroth with his slayer, and when he sees him going about his business as the dead man used to do, haunts and disturbs him in all his actions (865de), and turns his wrath also against a kinsman who has been remiss in prosecuting (866b).[220] This is the belief that underlay the complicated and archaic procedures at Athens for the punishment of homicide, graphic evidence of the lively feeling that the dead man was still a factor to be reckoned with. The dead man's wrath was thought to be effective only in the regions which he frequented during life; hence the requirement of the law that the involuntary or accidental slayer shall absent himself from his victim's country for a year, in order to allow his wrath to abate. When the slaying has been deliberate, Plato invokes also the Orphic doctrine of reincarnation and exact retribution in a future life (870d, 872e), which would seem to supersede the archaic myth that underlay Attic law. Yet the Attic law of homicide, and the elaborate rites of purification that accompanied the legal procedures, were an area of law and custom peculiarly under the protection of Apollo; and Plato could well give to this and the other beliefs in the influence of the dead a deeper meaning than they had for the more superstitious of his contemporaries. The dead man has the slayer's conscience ($\mu\nu\dot{\eta}\mu\eta$) as his ally, Plato says (865e); it is this that gives the guilty man no peace until he has done penance for his wrong.

The sense of interdependence between the living and the dead members of a family has its obverse side, the belief in inherited guilt, in the suffering of the children for the sins of their fathers. This ancient belief still lingered on in the fourth century; the orators appeal to the slowness of divine vengeance—in exacting retribution not from

---

[220] 866b: $\tau o \hat{v} \pi \alpha \theta \acute{o} \nu \tau o \varsigma \pi \rho o \sigma \tau \rho \epsilon \pi o \mu \acute{\epsilon} \nu o v$. See Rohde's note on this passage, *op.cit.* 1, 264 n. 2: "Die zürnende Seele wird zum $\pi \rho o \sigma \tau \rho \acute{o} \pi \alpha \iota o \varsigma$. $\Pi \rho o \sigma \tau \rho \acute{o} \pi \alpha \iota o \varsigma$ heisst wohl nur abgeleiteter Weise ein des Todten sich annehmender $\delta \alpha \acute{\iota} \mu \omega \nu$ (im Besonderen $Z \grave{\epsilon} \grave{v} \varsigma \pi \rho o \sigma \tau \rho \acute{o} \pi \alpha \iota o \varsigma$): eigentlich ist dies die Bezeichnung der Rache heischenden Seele selbst." Ant. *Tetral.* I, γ, 10; IV, δ, 10; Aesch. *Choëph.* 287.

the evil doer himself but from his children or grandchildren—as a pious commonplace that would be generally accepted.[221] This was one of the beliefs exploited for their profit by the fraudulent sooth-sayers and magicians whom Plato excoriates in the *Republic*. It was contrary to his sense of divine justice; but there are nevertheless some traces of it in his own law. As a general rule, he says, punishment and disgrace inflicted upon a father shall not descend to his children; but when a family has had three successive generations of men judged guilty of capital offenses, the descendants shall be required to emigrate to the country from which the family came, taking their property with them (856cd). Again a man who is obsessed by the temptation to rob a temple or shrine is warned that this impulse in him may arise from some unexpiated wrong in the distant past, and he is advised to take refuge in apotropaic rites, and furthermore to seek the company of good men and avoid evil companions (854bc). It is difficult to believe that Plato thought the first half of this advice would be efficacious without the other. Finally, if a man is to be eligible for a priesthood, his ancestry as well as his own personal life must be pure—that is, free of the taint of murder and of other offenses against religious law (759c). In these details the dark region of chthonic powers seeps into the bright religious world from which in general Plato excludes it.

Finally, from the cult of ancestors we come to the primary and most intimate stage of worship in Plato's state, the paying of honors (τιμαί) and respect (εὐφημία) to living parents and grandparents (717b-d; cf. 724a). These "honors" include, of course, the generally recognized duties of supporting and caring for them in their old age, and of refraining from doing them any physical injury, even in self-defense against what seems to be unprovoked assault (869bc). Attic law was clear and strict with respect to these duties; Plato's law is equally clear and even more strict.[222] These obligations are not merely

---

[221] Lys. vi, 20; Dem. lvii, 27; cf. Plato *Theat.* 173d, *Rep.* 613a.

[222] In Attic law the public suit (γραφή) for mistreatment of parents κακώσεως γονέων) could be brought by any citizen, and without liability to penalty for failing to make a case; Arist. *Const. Ath.* lvi, 6. It covered all the forms of neglect and physical injury mentioned above; Lipsius 343f. Penalty for conviction was loss of civic rights, among others the right to hold office or to address the assembly. For the Greek conception of the moral obligation underlying Attic law, see Xen. *Mem.* ii, ii. Plato's law provides that prosecution may be initiated by one of the three eldest guardians upon information supplied by the parent or by any person, slave or free (932a-d). For neglect the punishment is stripes, fines, or imprisonment; for physical assault the penalties range from banishment to death. See also 877b, 878e, 880e-881d.

a debt of gratitude owed to one's earliest and greatest benefactors; they are also a religious obligation, requiring reverent speech and demeanor toward those who are one's natural superiors (690a, 917a) and whose rights are jealously protected by the gods (717d, 931d). We all believe, Plato says, in the efficacy of a father's curse.[223] By parity of reasoning—and this is the positive side of Plato's admonition —the gods will be correspondingly well disposed to those who honor their parents. And parents are themselves living images of the divine, as worthy of θεραπεία as the lifeless images of ancestors. "If anyone then has such treasure in his house as a father or mother laid up with age, or one of their fathers or mothers, let him not think that, while he has such a figure as this at his hearth, any other image could be more potent—if, that is, its owner worships it duly and rightly" (931a).

Thus the spirit of worship in Plato's state covers the whole gamut —from sacrifices and prayers to the Olympians, to the affectionate tendance of the honored elders of the household, those persons in whom the young child gets his first glimpse of divinity. Spreading out from the household in ever-widening circles of family rites, local festivals, and tribal ceremonies, to the great occasions on which with all his fellows he gathers to invoke and do honor to the city-holding gods, the religion of the citizen in Plato's state puts his life everywhere in contact with divine agencies—some near and intimate, others more remote, majestic and inscrutable—who summon him to the observance of his duties and reward him with the satisfaction of their fellowship. Religion is not something apart from other areas of life; it penetrates them all. It gives authority to the magistrates and the laws they enforce; it sanctifies family ties; it is the patron of the arts and crafts; it safeguards contracts and oaths, and the rights of strangers and suppliants; it is the partner in all recreation, dance, and song. This religious atmosphere in which all life is lived is of tremendous importance, Plato obviously thinks, for the molding of character and the training of the sentiments by which the virtues are made secure. Its importance lies both in the ideas it is constantly presenting of higher forms of being invested with divine authority, and in the sentiments it fosters of devotion to these ideas through the constant repetition of acts of worship in which this devotion is expressed. This area of tradition and reverence is what Plato calls

[223] Farnell, *Higher Aspects*, 50-53; and Schmidt, *Die Ethik der Alten Griechen*, I, 91.

the divine sanctions to the performance of our duties. There is another more human level of sanctions, the level of prudential reason, which leads us, from a consideration of the nature of pleasure and pain as they are associated with the different kinds of life, to the rational insight that the choice of temperance, courage, and wisdom is best (732e-734d). The teaching of religion, then, is in full accord with the judgment of practical wisdom; but religion has an immense advantage in being able to produce its effects, as Plato asserts in the *Republic* and reiterates in the *Laws*, during the time of life when reason is still immature.

The religion of Plato's state is the religion of his people, as seen through the eyes of a philosopher capable of penetrating below its attendant mythology, and its sometimes archaic rites and customs, to the profound and beneficent sentiments that supported it.[224] In its formal aspects it is but little modified for the needs of his state. The supremacy of Delphi in sacred law would prevent Plato from introducing any external changes. But into this time-honored ritual he intends to infuse a deeper conception of the meaning of worship, not as an exchange of services between gods and men, but as fellowship in which the human worshipper models himself after the divinity he worships. In becoming like God the worshipper is rendering his greatest homage. Compared to this, votive offerings (ἀναθήματα) are of little importance. Plato condemns this kind of religious ostentation; a reasonable man will present offerings of moderate value.[225] But not only is the citizen in becoming like God rendering his greatest homage, he is also enjoying the greatest benefit the gods can confer.[226] There are other more concrete blessings with which the gods reward their worshippers, as Plato recognizes. In times of misfortune one can cherish the hope that God will lighten one's miseries

[224] "Profound and beneficent sentiments." On this point see Farnell, *op.cit.* passim.

[225] 955e. This is followed by detailed prescriptions concerning the kinds of offerings appropriate, the materials of which they may be made—i.e. wood, stone, or cloth; not ivory, gold, silver, iron, or bronze—and the maximum labor that may be expended on a single offering. There seem to be no historical precedents for some of these restrictions (Reverdin 67).

[226] It is interesting to note that this communion with God and becoming like him is something that Plato conceives as resulting from the worship of the Olympians. There has been a recent tendency to try to interpret the Greek effort to overcome the traditional gulf between men and gods as resulting from the resurgence of the chthonic stratum in Greek religion, in alliance with Orphism and Pythagoreanism. See the works of Rohde, Jane Harrison, and Guthrie cited above. But the chthonic element is definitely not the basis of Plato's ὁμοίωσις θεῷ.

by gifts within his power to bestow, or change present evils into goods; and in times of prosperity one can hope for an even greater share of blessing, with the help of good fortune (732cd). There is more than a hint here of material benefits; but the real goods and evils, Plato insists, are the goods and evils of the soul. These it is which affect the destiny of men, both in this life and after death, and these the worshipper can most appropriately expect from his gods.

Included in this deeper conception of worship there is a loftier idea of the divine nature. Not in the Apollo who seduced Creusa and concealed his escapade; not in the Zeus engaged in secret amours, the patron of boy love; not in the Hermes who stole his brother's cattle—it is not here that Plato finds his idea of divinity. He would agree with Euripides' protest: "If they do wrong, they are not gods."[227] Such tales are not a part of religion, but only the product of irresponsible poetic fancy; and it is one purpose of his law to suppress them, and of his chorus of Dionysus to set a better standard of singing and dancing. Plato's God, with his attendant gods and daemons, is the unchanging source of all that is good; this is the God who is worshipped in the ceremonies and to whom the worshipper endeavors to liken himself.

It is convenient, and often necessary, to distinguish between Plato's religion and the religion of Plato's state; and it is the latter we have been describing in the preceding pages. But as we come to the end of the account we realize that these two things can be distinguished, but not separated, still less contrasted. If one asks whether Plato believed in the gods whose worship he prescribes for his state, one might well answer by quoting the pious argument cited by Sextus Empiricus: "Of course the gods exist; else how could one worship them?"[228]

THE LAW AGAINST IMPIETY

If participation in religious worship was a citizen's duty in order to help retain the favor of the "city-holding gods," then neglect of this worship would be an offense, and if deliberate and flagrant, or if occurring at a time of strain for the city, a serious offense. Yet we hear of little legislation at Athens intended to define and punish it, and the reason is clear. The requirements of piety fell in the main

[227] Eur. Fr. 294, Nauck.
[228] *Adv. Dogm.* III, 123.

under the sacred law, the law concerning τὰ θεῖα; and this law was contained not in written ordinances of the state, but in familiar religious customs (τὰ πάτρια), ancestral observances (πάτριοι νόμοι), or unwritten laws (ἄγραφοι νόμοι). When a question arose as to whether there had been a violation of religious law, the opinion of specially competent interpreters would be sought, or the advice of the oracles, especially Delphi.[229] The phrase used to describe the religious obligation of a citizen—νομίζειν τοὺς θεοὺς οὓς ἡ πόλις νομίζει, "acknowledging the gods whom the city acknowledges"— indeed usually meant to pious and patriotic Athenians something more than conformity to established custom in worship;[230] it implied a belief in, or devotion to, the gods honored in the customary rites. But to formulate a legal definition of piety in this subjective sense, and to specify the kinds of action that a court could regard as evidence of its absence, was something which the Athenians in general wisely refrained from trying to do, leaving it to the dicasteries to formulate, for each case coming before them, their own criteria for judgment.

The long list of trials for ἀσέβεια at Athens during the fifth and fourth centuries shows that the Athenians regarded impiety as an indictable offense, and a serious one.[231] Aeschylus was charged with ἀσέβεια for revealing secrets of the mysteries—the first case of which we have knowledge; Alcibiades and his companions for mutilating the Hermae and for parodying the mysteries; Anaxagoras for having declared the sun to be a red-hot mass of stone; Protagoras for beginning his book *On the Gods* by saying that he knew not whether or not they existed, or what form they had; Diagoras of Melos for ridiculing the mysteries of Eleusis; Socrates for not acknowledging the gods of the city and introducing new divinities, and for corrupting the youth by this teaching. We hear of other prosecutions of philosophers in the fourth century—of Stilpo of Megara because of a ribald joke about Athena; of Theodorus of Cyrene, whose notorious beliefs won him in antiquity the title of "atheist" (ὁ ἄθεος); of Aristotle for his alleged paean to Hermeias; and of Theophrastus on some ground unknown. A certain Archias, hierophant at the time, was

---

[229] Lys. VI, 10 recalls an occasion on which Pericles advised the people in judging cases of impiety to use not only the written law, but also the ἄγραφοι νόμοι, καθ' οὓς Εὐμολπίδαι ἐξηγοῦνται.

[230] On the meaning of the formula see Derenne, *op.cit.* (Note 112), 217-222.

[231] For supporting references on the cases mentioned below, and for other cases not mentioned, see Lipsius, 359ff.; and Derenne, *op.cit.* passim.

charged with impiety and punished, perhaps with death, for conducting a religious sacrifice παρὰ τὰ πάτρια, contrary to traditional rites. Andocides was charged with impiety for having entered sacred places and participated in the mysteries when he was not entitled to. A priestess named Ninus, and another named Theoris, were put to death (the latter being prosecuted by Demosthenes himself) for celebrating unauthorized rites. Association with a man burdened with bloodguilt counted as impiety; so did an assault upon the choregus at a festival of Dionysus, and cutting down a sacred olive tree.

This list of cases shows that ἀσέβεια in the Attic courts was a label broad enough to cover any act or word that was thought to be a danger or an insult to the established religion—whether departure from the ritual of established cults, or profanation of a sacred area or object, or mimicry of a religious rite, or indignity offered to a religious official during a public ceremony, or words casting discredit upon any of the gods and their worship. To this variety of offenses that could be classed as impiety there was a corresponding diversity of procedures open to persons desiring to prosecute.[232] An ambitious citizen could institute a γραφή, as Meletus, Anytus, and Lycon did in the case of Socrates; or if he did not wish to risk the fine for unsuccessful prosecution, he could proceed in one of at least three other ways, by ἔνδειξις, φάσις, or ἀπαγωγή.[233] If the impiety concerned the mysteries, he could bring his accusation before the Eumolpidae; and it is likely that the older procedure of εἰσαγγελία, used against Anaxagoras and against the profaners of the mysteries in 415, was still available in the fourth century if the case was thought to be important enough. This indicates that the reputation of the Athenians in antiquity for being especially serious about religion and "the most pious of men," was probably well deserved.[234] They considered it an obligation of citizens and officials to protect religion and regarded an attack upon it as a threat to the state. The orators argued that failure to punish ἀσέβεια would expose the city to the anger of the gods;

[232] Lipsius 366f.; Derenne, *op.cit.* 236ff.

[233] For ἔνδειξις and φάσις see Chapter VI, Note 81. Ἀπαγωγή, like ἔνδειξις, was a summary procedure of taking a malefactor directly before the magistrates, who were authorized to confine him immediately if he could not furnish bail. In the γραφή a formal summons (πρόσκλησις) was issued to the defendant, and no steps were taken to secure his person before the trial.

[234] Lyc. I, 15; Lys. xxx, 17ff.; Eupolis, Fr. 307, Kock; for later times, *Acts of the Apostles* xvii, 22-23; Paus. I, xxiv, 3. Cf. Paul Decharme, *Critique des croyances religieuses chez les Grecs*, Paris, 1904, 178: "Ce que les Athéniens ne tolérèrent jamais, ce furent les manifestations de l'athéisme."

and statesmen, however sceptical, agreed with the rest that religion was a necessary aid to morality and public order.[235]

How, then, are we to explain the undeniably real freedom of thought and expression at Athens? The well-known license of the comic poets on political and religious matters was a special prerogative of merrymaking enjoyed by the participants in a festival of Dionysus, so that this very freedom had its religious sanction. The freedom enjoyed by the philosophers was, however, due to other factors —the interest in new ideas so characteristic of the Athenians, and perhaps a natural disposition towards tolerance; but most important of all, the special character of the Athenian legal system. Since there was no public prosecutor, any action against an offender—whether a violator of religious or secular law—had to be privately initiated. The fine that was imposed for an egregiously unsuccessful prosecution, and the labor and worry attendant upon any prosecution, even if successful, made it necessary that some strong personal motive should be at work if a man was to undertake the task of "defending the laws." This motive might be personal enmity, or political rivalry, or a genuine concern for the public welfare. However strong his personal interest in the case might be, the prosecutor usually tried to convince the court that the public interest was uppermost in his mind. Some of the prosecutions of philosophers at Athens for impiety seem in fact to have been politically motivated, and it is likely that most of them were.[236] The prosecution of Anaxagoras was instigated by the political enemies of Pericles; Socrates appears to have been indicted because of his association with the leaders of the hated oligarchs; and in the following century the prosecution of Aristotle, the friend of Alexander, was set afoot by the leaders of the anti-Macedonian party. But a philosopher who had no political enemies would not be likely to be prosecuted, especially if he had many friends.[237] Hippo of Rhegium, a contemporary of Anaxagoras and a notorious atheist, was never prosecuted; nor was Aristodemus, Socrates' friend, "who neither sacrificed nor used μαντική" and laughed at those who did. Aristodemus' views must have been well known, for Xenophon pictures Socrates as arguing with him and en-

---

[235] Lys. vi, 13, 33; Ps. Dem. lix, 109; Critias, in Diels-Kranz ii, 386-389.
[236] Schmidt, *op.cit.* ii, 25-26.
[237] Diog. v, 37 tells us that Theophrastus had so many friends at Athens that his prosecutor barely escaped having to pay the fine—that is, he got little more than one fifth of the votes of the judges.

deavoring to convert him from his impiety.[238] For these reasons the intellectual atmosphere of Athens did not ordinarily seem oppressive.[239] Nevertheless this is the only Greek city we know of in which prosecutions of the sort mentioned were possible. The philosophers convicted of impiety at Athens seem to have had no difficulty in taking up residence in other cities, and they were sometimes received with great honor. States like Sparta that entirely excluded foreign teachers of philosophy and rhetoric were of course less liberal than Athens, even though no prosecutions for impiety are reported of them.

It should be noted that there are other offenses in Platonic law besides unbelief which are subject to prosecution as impiety. Most of these are matters of religious law, and here Plato follows the spirit, if not always the letter, of contemporary Athenian law. For example, anyone who in a moment of anger has killed his or her child, or his or her spouse, after undergoing the prescribed punishment (purification and exile for three years), is forbidden to engage in family worship, or even to sit at table with the surviving members of the family; whoever disobeys this law is liable to a δίκη ἀσεβείας (868de).[240] This has its analogue in Attic law, as Gernet points out.[241] The same provision applies to one who has killed a brother or sister. Again a child who in anger inflicts a fatal wound on his parent and has not been pardoned before the death of the victim shall be liable not only to prosecution for assault, but also for impiety (869ab). All deliberate and unjustifiable homicide involves impiety; the offender is to be put to death and refused burial in the land of his victim (871d). No doubt also the charge of impiety would lie, as we know it did in Attic law, against a man guilty of bloodshed who ignores the warning against entering sacred places, for this warning (πρόρρησις) is universally presupposed in Plato's law. The charge of impiety that may be brought against a man who refuses to obey the orders of an

[238] Xen. *Mem.* I, iv.

[239] Although stories current in later days indicate that a wise man was often cautious in expressing his opinions. Diog. II, 116-117.

[240] Though Plato is aware of the distinction between γραφή and δίκη in Attic law (see *Euthyp.* 2a) and quite often emphasizes it in his own legislation, he uniformly refers to prosecution for impiety as a δίκη, ignoring completely the γραφὴ ἀσεβείας of Attic law. Plato's legal terminology is generally so accurate that we must take this usage as deliberate. It appears to confirm the thesis of Derenne (*op.cit.* 239f.) that prosecutions for violation of religious law, such as those brought before the Eumolpidae, were δίκαι, not γραφαί. To the γραφὴ ἀσεβείας of Attic law Plato provides an alternative procedure, as we shall see below, analogous to the εἰσαγγελία.

[241] cxciii n. 1.

official in a religious ceremony (799b) is analogous to the ἀσέβεια of which Meidias was accused because of his attack upon Demosthenes when Demosthenes was acting as choregus at a festival of Dionysus.[242] The prosecution for violation of prescribed ritual that could occur at Athens does not appear in Platonic law, but we have seen how insistent Plato is on the careful observance of religious tradition, and it is safe to assume that this kind of offense would be punishable also in his state.[243] Peculiar to Plato, perhaps, is the liability to prosecution for ἀσέβεια that is prescribed for a man who gives burial to the body of a person convicted of the gravest form of impiety under Plato's famous law (909c). Temple robbing is a major offense against religion in Plato's as in Attic law; but Plato deals with it separately, as Attic law did, by prosecution for ἱεροσυλία, rather than for ἀσέβεια.[244] Finally, it is possible that Plato makes an ambassador or herald who is guilty of faithlessness (παραπρεσβεία) liable to indictment for impiety (941a).[245]

In these details Plato is following a familiar pattern, as he also is in assuming that the state may properly take cognizance of expressions of opinion detrimental to the established worship. We have seen that Athenian courts were often concerned with this form of impiety, though they were without any clear guiding principle for passing judgment. The only "law" that we know of at Athens is the famous Decree of Diopeithes, enacted about the year 430, which authorized prosecution of persons "who do not acknowledge (or respect) divine matters (τοὺς τὰ θεῖα μὴ νομίζοντας) or teach theories (λόγους) about the heavenly bodies."[246] This was used to bring about the condemnation of Anaxagoras, the friend of Pericles—which was its in-

---

[242] Dem. XXI, 51.

[243] It is certainly implied in 910e: ὡς οὐ καθαρὸς ὢν θύων θανάτῳ ζημιούσθω.

[244] Gernet, *Platon, Lois, Livre IX*, 66: "Le délit d'impiété et le délit de sacrilège sont parfaitement distingués. . . . En cela Plato se rapproche encore de la législation Athénienne qui parait avoir établi entre les deux notions une distinction plus radicale que les autres cités."

[245] Attic law, however, provided a γραφὴ παραπρεσβείας for such accusations, and it may be that Plato's language—γραφαὶ κατὰ τούτων [i.e. false ambassadors or heralds] ἔστων ἀσεβησάντων—should be regarded as hortatory, rather than legal, in intent. There is no doubt that Demosthenes, in his speech prosecuting Aeschines for παραπρεσβεία, regards him as guilty not only of accepting bribes from Philip and of deceiving the Athenians, but also of impiety against the gods.

[246] Plut. *Per.* 32. On this Diopeithes and his decree, see Derenne, *op.cit.* 19-24. Reverdin's assumption (213) that this decree was modified in 399 or replaced by a different law may be correct, but there is no evidence for it except the known prosecutions, and these can be well enough explained without it.

tention, according to Plutarch—and was undoubtedly invoked in later instances of prosecution against philosophers for impious opinions. Plato must have regarded this as a particularly clumsy and perverse piece of legislation. It was motivated by partisanship, not zeal for religion, and in attempting to make more precise the meaning of "not acknowledging divine matters" it stigmatized as impious the very astronomical inquiries that he regards as especially valuable because they dispel blasphemous notions about the heavenly gods (821cd). He would agree with his countrymen that impiety can be shown in words as well as in deeds; but as a legislator believing in the rule of law, he would insist that the offenses which are punishable should be clearly and precisely set forth in the law, together with the penalties attached to them.

The law of impiety (ἀσεβείας πέρι νόμος, 907d) enunciated in his tenth book may then be properly regarded as an attempt to fill what Plato regarded as a noticeable gap in Attic law. The hand of a systematic legislator is evident from the context in which the law is introduced. Plato brings it up as a new chapter in the criminal law, with which he has been occupied in the preceding book. He has already dealt with offenses against the state (temple robbing, treason, and sedition), and with homicide, and assault; and he has carefully distinguished the different species of offense under each of the last two heads. The Athenian now turns to "offenses committed against the gods, whether by word or deed, in discourse or in action" (ὅσα δὲ λόγῳ καὶ ὅσα ἔργῳ περὶ θεοὺς ὑβρίζει τις λέγων ἢ πράττων, 885b). The Greek of this passage shows that the offenses mentioned here are thought of as ὕβρις against the gods. Hybris in Greek law and morals is a concept difficult to clarify; but when applied to a legally punishable offense it implies a kind of presumptuous act that involves not only injury but also insult to another, such as an injury to a person's reputation, dignity, or authority. Its religious associations make this term peculiarly apt as a designation of offenses against the gods. But Plato does not leave it with its usual religious vagueness. Such actions are the result of erroneous beliefs about the gods, and he immediately proceeds to distinguish three kinds of such errors of opinion.

No one who believes that there are gods as prescribed by law (θεοὺς εἶναι κατὰ νόμους) has ever knowingly done an impious act or uttered an unlawful word. But one of three things is true: either he denies that there are gods, or though he admits their existence he thinks that they give no attention to human affairs, or thirdly, he thinks that they are easy to persuade and can be won over by sacrifices and prayers. 885b

Apparently we have three species of hybris against the gods, like the species of homicide so carefully distinguished in the previous book, and the corresponding species of assault. It is hybris against the gods to say that they do not exist, or to say that they have no care for men, or to say that they can be turned aside from justice. Now one or more of these varieties of disbelief were implied in the prosecution of the cases mentioned above that came before the Athenian courts. The first or the second, or both of them, must have been charged against the philosophers accused of impiety.[247] The third species borders on the domain of magic, which was sometimes regarded as ἀσέβεια in fourth-century Athens and heavily punished;[248] and it includes, as we shall see, the introduction of new mystery-cults and the practice of private rites of initiation and purification, which responsible Athenians generally viewed with distrust. Plato's law, then, can be regarded as an attempt to formulate distinctions present, but confused, in Athenian practice.

In conformity with his principles that the legislator should not be content with commands and prohibitions, but must attempt to persuade his citizens, Plato introduces his law against impiety with a prelude intended to persuade offenders of the error of their impious beliefs. It is the longest of all such preludes in the *Laws*,[249] and it differs markedly from all the others in professing to demonstrate as well as persuade. There are hortatory passages in it, but its main part is concerned with the establishment of premises, in the dialectical manner familiar from the other Platonic dialogues, and with the drawing of conclusions from them by logical inference. Despite the pretense that this is a prelude to a legal enactment, it is probably not seriously intended that these arguments refuting the various forms of atheism and establishing what has been called Plato's three articles of theology shall be published in the unresponsive language of a legal document (891a); or if this is his intention, Plato cannot have thought that publication is the best way of making these arguments

[247] Diagoras of Melos was remembered in antiquity both as an atheist and as one who denied the providence of the gods. Derenne, *op.cit.* 64-65.

[248] See Note 119 above, and Reverdin 215-216.

[249] It is longer even than the initial discourse which precedes the work of legislation (715e to 734e), if we do not count the long digression (718c to 723e) justifying the use of such preludes.

effective. Dialectical discussions such as these cannot be reduced to the lifeless statement of a proof. To produce their effect, Plato elsewhere maintains, they have to be developed through questions and answers between a teacher and a student; for only thus will they lay hold of the learner's real self and appear as conclusions to which he is irresistibly led in consequence of premises he wholly accepts. We must assume that these arguments represent in part that higher education which is a prerequisite for holding office as a guardian, and which presumably takes place in the Nocturnal Council (966d-968a).[250] They are an example of the kind of discourse that the members of this body would hold with the impious man who has been confined for correction (908e-909a), or more generally, that any teacher or official might carry on with a younger man who has honest doubts.[251] For the reader, of course, they serve as preludes in the literal sense, and are intended to show that the law condemning impiety is an expression of that Nous which is the source of all authority in Plato's state.

To omit the examination of this prelude and proceed at once to the law would be contrary to all precedent in Platonic studies; and indeed the precedent should be followed, for in no other way can we appreciate the depth of religious feeling and philosophical conviction that underlie Plato's law. The Athenian Stranger implies that the three forms of disbelief mentioned are widespread. They are caused, he says, not primarily by incontinence, as Cleinias suggests, but by writings—some ancient, some more recent—which have persuaded the young that the old beliefs are without basis in reason (886b-e). The earliest of these writings are the so-called theogonies of the poets (such as Hesiod and Pherecydes, no doubt) which relate how the primary nature ($\pi\rho\acute{\omega}\tau\eta$ $\phi\acute{\upsilon}\sigma\iota\varsigma$) of heaven and all else came into being and then how the gods were born and lived with one another. Because of the antiquity of these accounts and their other merits, Plato is reluctant to criticize them; but he is sure they are of little use in promoting the honor and tendance due to parents,[252] and he is also sure that they are fundamentally false. But his chief concern is

---

[250] See below, Chapter IX.

[251] It is the young men that Plato has chiefly in mind here; note the reference to them at the very beginning (884) and later at 888a, 890a, 900c, 903b, 904e; and a reference seems to be implied in 886d and in 905c.

[252] This is obviously a repetition of the criticism (*Rep.* 377e-378a) of Hesiod's tales of what Kronos did to his father Ouranos and what Zeus in turn did to his father Kronos. Cf. *Euthyp.* 6a; Aristoph. *Clouds* 903ff.

the writings of the "modern wise men" (τῶν νέων καὶ σοφῶν, 886d), which he regards as the cause of the wrong opinions he deplores. In a sense it is the whole of previous physical science, from Thales to Democritus, that he criticizes here,[253] but it is the application of these principles of natural science to questions of morals, politics, and religion that he has chiefly in mind; and this application was not explicitly made nor the consequences of it fully drawn until the fifth century, in the ferment of free-ranging speculation that characterized the Periclean age. Plato sees the development of these ideas from the perspective of a later time and can evaluate their effects upon his generation, particularly upon his younger contemporaries. And he thinks he can point to the fallacy which has misled all these students of nature into presenting as the highest wisdom (μεγίστη φρόνησις, 886b) what is really only senseless opinion (ἀνόητος δόξα, 891c) and grievous ignorance (ἀμαθία χαλεπή, 886b).

All the thinkers Plato has in mind here were inquirers into "nature" (φύσις), not "nature" taken as the environment in which human life is lived, but as what is permanent, primary, and elemental in this environment and what, if known, would enable us to understand the origin and behavior of the cosmos and all its parts. This is the more precise meaning of that search for the physis of things to which the Greek thinkers, with a sure philosophical instinct, devoted their attention from the very first. Their answers were various; but whether they conceived this physis as water, or air, or all four kinds of body, or a boundless and indeterminate stuff, or infinitely varied seeds, or homogeneous indivisible atoms—in every case this physis was considered as primary and elemental, more truly Being than the familiar things and events of ordinary sense perception. It was this contrast between the real nature of things as revealed by scientific inquiry and the conventional beliefs of common life which, when applied to questions of law and morals, produced the most dramatic and far-reaching issue in fifth-century thought. The whole of morality and law was asserted to belong to the secondary and variable order of things, not to the primary and enduring order of nature.[254] Or alternatively, a distinction was made within the moral order between those precepts which are natural (φύσει) and those that are

---

[253] The view of J. Tate (CQ, xxx, 1936, 48-54) that certain fourth-century contemporaries are the object of Plato's refutation here seems implausible; see Gregory Vlastos, Class. Phil. XLII, 1947, 176 n. 177.

[254] See the fragments of Archelaus, Democritus, and Antiphon in Diels-Kranz II, 45-46, 139, 346ff.

merely matters of convention (νόμῳ); and the latter included most of what was ordinarily called morality, while the morality of nature prescribed only the principles of self-preservation and self-aggrandizement by any means within one's power.[255] Some thinkers indeed tried to rescue the principles of right and justice by regarding them as divine commands, in contrast to the enactments of human legislators, the latter being judged by their agreement or disagreement with these eternal and unwritten divine laws.[256] But the answer to this was that the gods themselves are matters of convention, explicitly invented to give authority to laws of human enactment.[257]

It is this culmination of the thought of the physiologers that Plato sets forth in his presentation of the views of the "modern wise men." All things come into being, they say, partly by nature, partly by art, and partly by chance. Fire, water, air, and earth exist by nature and chance; so also do the earth, sun, moon, stars, and the whole of the heavens, as well as all animals and plants. These are structures and combinations that come about not by art, but by the unregulated (i.e. chance) interplay of the primary elements, acting in accordance with their special powers.[258] Art appears later as the product of these more elemental forces, and its own products are mainly trivial playthings. The arts that produce anything serious—medicine, agriculture, gymnastics—do so by joining their powers with nature. Politics does this to a small extent, though it is mainly art (i.e. artifice); and legislation is entirely so, its assumptions regarding the existence of the gods and of the nature of honor and justice being simply conventions that vary according to time and place. There is something naturally noble (καλόν)—i.e. living as nature prescribes, getting what one can and ruling over others wherever it is possible; but there is no natural justice, since all laws are constantly being changed, and what authority they have when men adopt them is simply the authority of convention (888e-890a).

Now Plato had been engaged in combating this body of ideas since the very beginning of his philosophical career and he had already formulated a decisive refutation of it. If we are looking for what is

---

[255] As maintained by Callicles in Plato's *Gorgias* (482e-484c) and by the Athenian envoys in the dialogue with the Melians (Thuc. v, 86-111).

[256] Soph. *Oed. Tyr.* 865-870.

[257] This view had been espoused by Plato's cousin Critias; see Diels-Kranz II, 386ff. Cf. also Eur. *Hec.* 799f.

[258] For my interpretation of chance (τύχη) here and in the *Timaeus* see the article cited above, Note 34. Cf. also W. C. Greene, *Moira*, Harvard University Press, 1948, 299f.

truly real, in contrast to the variable world of sensation, opinion, and convention, we can only find it in the Ideas, the unchanging and intelligible entities that alone enable us to understand the flux of existence, and of which the sensible world can best be regarded as an imperfect imitation. The Ideas, he had said on numerous occasions, are what is truly real (ὄντως ὄντα); they are what exists by nature (φύσει ὄντα). One of these Ideas is the Idea of Justice; "justice itself" (αὐτὸ τὸ δίκαιον) is the "natural justice" (φύσει δίκαιον) whose existence these thinkers denied. Thus assuming, as they did, that nature is primary and provides an authoritative standard of judgment, he had not only turned their doctrine upside down, but also provided a basis for a genuine science of politics and legislation.[259] Plato says nothing of this doctrine of Ideas in the present passage, but we should keep it in mind if we hope to understand why he regards belief in God as a necessary foundation of the state. To deny the existence of God (or the gods), or their concern for justice, is for Plato equivalent to denying the reality of any transcendental source of law; and this he believes would make impossible not only any political science, but also any art or practice of statesmanship.

In the present context Plato presents an argument that endeavors to meet the physiologers on their own ground, the sphere of physical occurrences. If soul can be shown to be primary in all motion and change, then not only will soul be prior to body, but also the things that are akin to soul—such as opinion, foresight, thought, art, law —will be prior to body and to such bodily qualities as hot, cold, moist, dry, on which the physiologers relied (892ab). The argument is a more elaborate version of the doctrine of the *Phaedrus* (245e) that soul is the source of change (ἀρχὴ κινήσεως), since soul is that which can move itself as well as impart motion to other things.[260] The primary realities of the physiologers—water, air, and the other elements —are capable of motion only when acted upon by something else, hence are obviously secondary to the self-moving soul. Since without soul there would be no motion nor change, hence no nature in the current sense of the word, soul is obviously a primary factor in na-

[259] For a fuller account of the φύσις - νόμος controversy and the steps by which Plato resolves the antithesis, see my "Plato and the Law of Nature," in *Essays in Political Theory Presented to George H. Sabine*, eds. Konvitz and Murphy, 1948, 17-44. See also Greene, *op.cit.* 281ff.; and J. P. Maguire, "Plato's Theory of Natural Law," *Yale Classical Studies*, x, 1947, 151-178.

[260] J. B. Skemp, *The Theory of Motion in Plato's Later Dialogues*, Cambridge, 1942, 3-10, 96ff.

ture; and law and art, which are products of soul, will exist "by nature or by something not less than nature" (φύσει ἤ φύσεως οὐχ
ἥττονι, 890d). What this cryptically designated other factor is we
shall see later.

The application of this doctrine to the heavens, that is to the whole
of visible nature, implies that the motions of the heavenly bodies have
their source and origin in a soul or souls. But the qualities of soul are
various: a soul may be the seat of true or false opinion, of fear, pain,
hatred, as well as of joy, confidence, and love. It may take reason as
its helper and move all things rightly and happily, or it may associate
with unreason and produce effects of the opposite sort. What kind of
soul are we to assume as directing the heavenly motions? Now the
development of mathematics and astronomy in Plato's time had led
to a momentous hypothesis—first advanced, so far as we know, by
Eudoxus of Cnidos, one of Plato's colleagues in the Academy—which
permitted an explanation of the apparently erratic movements of the
"wanderers," i.e. the sun, moon, and planets, in terms of regular
uniform circular paths, the movement of each of these heavenly
bodies being analyzable as a complex result of two or more simple
circular motions. The development of this hypothesis was one of the
most decisive events in the history of the Academy. It presupposes the
solution of certain problems of geometry and mechanics that originated in the school of Archytas of Tarentum,[261] and it may be that
Plato became acquainted with this line of investigation on his visit
to southern Italy during his *Wanderjahre* and introduced it into the
Academy. There is a tradition that he set for his students the problem of finding a set of regular uniform motions that would con-
jointly explain the apparently complex and erratic motions of the
heavenly bodies, and it may be that Eudoxus was set to this task after
coming to Athens.[262] But Eudoxus also was a pupil of Archytas, and
it is more likely that his school at Cyzicus had already been working
in this direction. In any case these various investigations bore memorable fruit in the environment of the Academy, under Plato's interested oversight and perhaps with his personal participation in them.

The solution of this problem provides the answer to the question
whether the soul that moves the heavens is rational or irrational.
Since these motions are shown to be complex but perfectly intelli-

---

[261] Festugière, "Platon et l'Orient," *Rev. de Philol.* XXI, 1947, 15; Erich Frank,
Platon und die Sogenannten Pythagoreer, Halle, 1923, 205.
[262] Simplicius on Arist. *De Caelo*, 488, lines 21-24, Heiberg.

gible mathematical curves, Plato was presented, as it were, with a visible embodiment of that intelligible world which he had long regarded as a divine order of genuine being. The ordering cause of these motions is manifestly reason, not unreason. But these mathematical curves involved are difficult to grasp and they would be beyond the powers of the Athenian's two companions. Hence in presenting the case to Cleinias and Megillus, the Athenian Stranger does not expound, but merely hints at, the complex mathematical considerations. To ask them to look at Eudoxus' or Archytas' theorems would be to blind them, as if they were asked to look directly at the sun; instead Plato gives them an "image" of rational motion. That motion which combines in itself stability with never-ending variety, such as the motion of a wheel about its center or of a sphere on its axis (898ab)[263]—this is the motion which reason most resembles, and this is the motion visibly evident in the heavens. By contrast, the image of unreason is motion that has uniformity neither in itself nor in relation to other motions, and is without any order or system or rule. Confronted with these alternatives, Cleinias asserts that it would be impious to say anything other than that the circle of heaven is moved by a supremely good soul or souls (898c). And these souls can only be declared to be gods (899b).

For Plato's theology it is important to note that the distinction between the heavenly bodies and the souls that move them is immediately insisted upon, and the question is left open as to the way in which the soul in the star can be thought of as moving its body. The body is of course visible; but the soul, the truly divine being in the heavens, remains imperceptible to sense and accessible by reason alone.[264] Furthermore, these invisible powers are divine only when allied with reason. It is therefore not soul *tout court* that characterizes the divine being, for soul is the source of all motion, whether good or bad, reasonable or unreasonable.[265] Nous, or Reason, is the prime

---

[263] Plato uses this image elsewhere as a symbol of the unity in variety and the self-containedness that characterize a perfect object of thought; *Tim.* 33b, 34a, 37de.

[264] It is not strictly correct, therefore, to call these heavenly bodies "visible gods," as Plato seems to do in *Tim.* 41a, and as the author of the *Epinomis* certainly does (985d). This must be taken in the Platonic texts as an elliptical expression for the visible embodiment of invisible gods.

[265] This throws light, I think, on the cosmology of the *Timaeus.* The distinction there made between the rational cause and the wandering cause, between Reason and Necessity, between real and auxiliary causes, can be interpreted in the light of the *Laws* as a distinction between a soul or souls completely under the guidance of reason, and souls in whose actions unreason plays a part. But being souls, these

factor in the ordering of the world—so Plato declares both in the *Timaeus* and in the *Laws* (966e)—and this is in the highest sense the divine. On the other hand, Nous can only function as a cause operating in the world when in alliance with a soul.[266] Whether Plato's God, then, is to be thought of as impersonal Reason, or as a soul in which reason operates with a supremacy impossible to any created soul, is a question that we cannot answer with certainty.

Having thus disposed of the first form of disbelief, the Athenian Stranger turns to the second, the belief that the gods do not concern themselves with human affairs. To deny the providence of the gods while affirming their existence may seem too strange a combination of piety and scepticism to be real. Nevertheless it was a reality in Plato's day; in fact it must have been far more common than simple atheism. Dogmatic atheists were extremely rare in antiquity; but doubts whether the gods really punish wrongdoers and reward the righteous, as tradition has it, are likely to arise in any man confronted by a spectacle of outrageous and triumphant injustice. Examples can be found in all epochs of Greek literature from the *Iliad* to the *Trojan Women*. An important part of Aeschylus' dramatic purpose was to answer such doubts and provide a kind of theodicy. In most men such doubts are temporary phases of opinion and are readily removed by a sudden turn of fortune; but in more reflective persons they can easily solidify into permanent disbelief. This combination of piety and scepticism was given philosophical standing in the doctrines of Epicurus a half-century after Plato, and the early popularity of Epicureanism shows that the ground was well prepared for it. This was therefore a large class in Plato's day, and an influential one. But why should Plato regard this opinion as a threat to the foundation of the state? This kind of sceptic has a certain kinship to the divine, or as Plato points out, he would never have recognized the existence of gods. Epicurus, for instance, despite his opposition to religion, was much admired, even by his Stoic opponents, for his godlike character. The higher nature of such a sceptic would restrain him from the forms of lawless self-aggrandizement which the first form of unbelief seems to justify as "natural." On the other hand,

---

irrational causes are subject to "persuasion," the means employed by the Demiurge to produce his desired effects. I have attempted to develop this interpretation in the article cited above, Note 34.

[266] Both *Phil.* 30c and *Tim.* 30b say that νοῦς implies ψυχή. Cf. also *Soph.* 249a: if the Real (τὸ παντελῶς ὄν) possesses νοῦς, it must also possess life and soul.

THE LAW AGAINST IMPIETY

THE LAW AGAINST IMPIETY

the effects upon other men of his denial of divine justice might be indistinguishable from those of simple atheism. The real danger in this doctrine is its denial of a quality Plato regarded as essential to the divine nature—that supervising justice which was the first attribute of Zeus, according to tradition, and which the Orphics made the central theme of their eschatology. For Plato it is therefore as serious an error as simple atheism and must be refuted.

The actual refutation is very simple and brief (900d-903a). First of all, on what grounds could one explain this alleged indifference of the gods to human affairs? Certainly not because they lacked the power, nor because they lacked the courage and concern, nor again because they lacked the knowledge to deal with the details of human fortune. Weakness, indolence, indifference, and ignorance are characteristics of men, not of gods. Reverting to his favorite metaphor, Plato argues that God cannot be regarded as inferior to a competent human craftsman, who knows that in order to turn out a good piece of work he has to execute each detail with nice artistry. But why then are the details of God's work often so poorly executed? The answer here is to deny that this allegation can be made good. The excellence of any detail can be judged only by the quality and purpose of the whole of which it is a part, and no indictment of divine artistry can claim to be so well established. But this *ignoramus* does not always satisfy, and Plato adds a section of admonition and persuasion by means of enchantments (ἐπῳδαί) and myths (μῦθοι), a section sharply distinguished from the preceding argument and obviously intended to be a statement of faith rather than a dialectically established result (903b-905d). First the doubter is admonished to try to see that what in his case is best for the All (τῷ παντί) is also best for him, a doctrine that later became the chief inspiration for the Stoic attitude of world-loyalty. "Whatsoever thou wishest, O Universe, that wish I also." But neither Plato nor the Stoics after him interpreted this as a counsel of resignation. The parts in this Universe are immortal souls, and the supervision of the gods follows the simple principle of assigning each soul to that place and that company for which it is best suited, the good souls to the superior region and the worse souls to an inferior one. As a soul then in its successive incarnations becomes better or worse, it is shifted upward or downward according to the law that like attracts like. This is the verdict (δίκη, 904e) from which no one can escape, and a man's ultimate destiny is what he makes it. So Plato invokes his Orphic tales again to provide that vivid apprehension, which dialectic cannot give, of the Justice that governs all things. The exhortation culminates in the same lesson as that presented in the myth of Er in the *Republic* (617e): αἰτία ἐλομένου · θεὸς ἀναίτιος—"he who chooses is to blame; God is not responsible."

The third form of disbelief that Plato attacks was apparently the most widespread of all in his day and the most dangerous (907b). The perplexed young man is pictured as saying at the very beginning of this book (885cd): "Before threatening us with harsh penalties, you must first try to persuade us; show us, by adequate evidence, that there are gods and that they are too good to be turned aside from justice by wheedling gifts. At present this, and other things like it, is what we hear from our most highly reputed poets, orators, sooth-sayers, priests, and from countless others; the result is that most of us, instead of being turned away from doing injustice, do wrong and then try to make amends." It is the same complaint as that advanced by Adeimantus in the *Republic* (365de): "If there are gods and they pay heed to our affairs, we know of them in no other way than from what we hear in the stories about them and in the works of the poets who describe their ancestry; but these same persons tell us that they are such as to be persuaded and won over by sacrifices and dedications and placating litanies."

This disease—of indulgences, of ritual atonements, of penances measured and prescribed—is one that grows out of the very heart of piety itself. Springing from the belief that the gods are merciful as well as just, and will forgive when there is visible evidence of penitence for wrong done, it ends by taking the external act as equivalent to the penitential heart, and giving an unholy authority to the holy men who claim the right to prescribe the penances. The Greeks were happily free from the evils of an organized priestly class; but they had, as we have seen, a class of self-appointed holy men—the soothsayers and manteis and purveyors of secret rites of atonement and purification—a class that gained increasing influence with the growth of superstition in the fourth century. To Plato this form of impiety was not only an affront to the gods, making their mercy depend upon material gifts (906cd); it was also a travesty of worship, and it opened the way to new forms of knavery and deception that could bring disaster not only to individuals but to whole states (909b). There is little need for formal refutation; the doctrine itself is too absurd. It assumes that the gods are like sheep dogs who can be bribed by wolves to relax their guard in return for a piece of mutton. Plato's indignation is evident in the unprecedented warmth of this part of the argument, for which he offers a kind of apology at the conclusion (907c).

Thus Plato has established the error of the various forms of impiety; and, by his positive demonstration of the existence of God and the moral government of the world from the known facts of the visible order, he has laid the foundation, as Taylor remarks, of all subsequent natural theology. This portion of the *Laws* has therefore been amply studied. For our purpose it is relevant only to point out that Plato's argument exhibits a remarkable *ignoratio elenchi*. Natural theology, as it is exemplified here, was distinguished by the ancients from two other kinds of theology—mythical, and political.[267] Natural theology is concerned with the gods of the philosophers, mythical theology with the gods of the poets, and political theology with the gods recognized by law. Now what the Athenian Stranger professes to do at the outset is to convince the young sceptics of the existence of the gods "established by law" (885b)—i.e. of Zeus, Apollo, and the other Olympians recognized in both Greek and Platonic law; but what the argument establishes is the existence of divine beings, or a single divine being, of a different sort, of the sort that can be apprehended only by philosophical reflection. If the Athenian's argument is to have its intended force in Plato's state it has to be supplemented by considerations that Plato does not make explicit but which we may, I think, venture to supply. The recognition of the divine and providential ordering of the cosmos lends authority to the lesser divinities, since they are themselves pictured as guardians and administrators of the order brought about by the cosmic Nous. Though creations of fancy, they contain intimations of the divine principle apprehended by philosophical reason. The philosopher can therefore build on this fundamentally correct intuition that underlies positive religion and, by controlling the expressions of religious and poetic fancy, can make that religion, for worshippers at any level of philosophic insight, the means of genuine worship. The situation here is analogous to what we shall find later in the area of

---

[267] For this distinction, see Varro (apud Augustine *De Civ. Dei* VI, 5) and Scaevola (also cited by Augustine, *op.cit.* IV, 27); cf. also Aetius, *Placita* I, 6, 9 (in Diels, *Doxographi Graeci*, Berlin, 1879, 295).

law. Only "right law," the expression of Nous, is entitled to authority in a state; but in so far as positive law is an imitation of that right law it participates, like all imitations, in the authority that its model and archetype enjoys.[268]

We are now ready for the statement of Plato's law.

> If any man commits impiety in word or deed, he who encounters it must come to the aid of the laws by giving information (σημαίνων) to the magistrates; and the first magistrates who learn of it shall bring the offender before the court appointed by law to judge such cases; and if any magistrate upon hearing of such an offense fails to take action, he shall himself be liable to a charge of impiety brought by anyone who wishes to defend the laws. And if a man is convicted, the court shall impose one penalty for each of the separate kinds of impiety. 907de

The method prescribed here for initiating prosecution suggests the denunciation (εἰσαγγελία) of Attic law.[269] This procedure was available at Athens if anyone thought that a fellow citizen by his action was "injuring the people"—a phrase that would aptly apply to Plato's conception of impiety. Whether the "magistrates" (ἄρχοντες) of Plato's law are the council or the guardians is not clear. Perhaps Plato intended to leave both avenues open; this is suggested by "the first magistrates who learn of it." Like the council under Attic law, Plato's officials have little discretion, for they are themselves liable if they do not bring the accused before the proper court, although the particular sanction Plato imposes—liability to a suit for impiety—is foreign to Attic law. What court such cases would be referred to Plato does not say, though his language implies that it has already been indicated. We can infer that the court for capital offenses would be the final tribunal, at least in the judgment of cases for which the death penalty is provided; but Plato may intend that all cases should be referred in the first instance to the court of the demos.[270]

In this ominous passage Plato becomes the first political thinker to propose that errors of opinion be made crimes punishable by law. The three species of hybris that he has distinguished are three kinds of opinions about the gods; impiety then becomes a *délit d'opinion*,

---

[268] See Chapter XI.
[269] This suggestion is supported by the εἰσαγγελλέτω (910c) in Plato's supplementary law covering private cults.
[270] For these courts, see Chapter VI, The Courts.

as Gernet puts it. This conclusion is not altered by the fact that Plato sometimes presents these three species of wrong belief as the three *causes* of impiety (885b, 908ab), which might tempt us to deny that the opinions themselves are regarded as delicts.[271] The question is settled unambiguously by the distinction Plato draws immediately between two kinds of offenders, those in whom disbelief is accompanied by honorable character, and those whose impiety is rooted in lawless desires perhaps garbed in the cloak of piety. A person of the first class may have a "naturally just character," he may "hate injustice and feel no inclination towards it whatever," yet he is punishable because he may destroy the faith of others, not all of whom can be presumed to have his own high standards of conduct (908bc). Thus the application of Plato's intellectual powers to the clarification of the practices of Athenian law had fateful consequences in western history, for henceforth the punishment of errors of opinion could claim the sanction of one of the highest authorities. But one must be just to Plato and the Athenians whose practice his law reflects. It is the *expression* of opinion "by word or deed" that is punishable. So far as Plato's law is concerned, a man is free to hold any belief, provided that he keeps it to himself or in his expression of it does not offend his fellow citizens so grossly as to cause one of them to lodge information against him with the magistrates. This is indeed a dubious kind of freedom, but it indicates the absence from Plato's state of anything like an Inquisition into opinions, a later invention which made the prosecution of disbelief so cruel and oppressive in the late Middle Ages. There are no officials in Plato's city entrusted with the task of ferreting out impiety, any more than there were at Athens.[272]

[271] As apparently do Derenne (*op.cit.* 251) and Reverdin (220, 240).
[272] "In the institution of the Nocturnal Council, secretly watching over religion and morals, with powers of life and death, Plato has been said to have anticipated the Inquisition. The likeness here is more than superficial." So F. M. Cornford, *The Unwritten Philosophy*, Cambridge, 1950, 66. The following chapter will show, I think, that this description of the powers of the Nocturnal Council has little foundation in Plato's text. Taylor also seems to have gone beyond the evidence in regarding Plato as proposing "to erect an inquisition to suppress 'heretical pravity'" (li). Quite similar is Renan's indignant misunderstanding of Athens (*Les Apôtres*, 314): "Il ne faut pas l'oublier, Athènes avait bel et bien l'inquisition. L'inquisiteur, c'était l'archonte-roi, le Saint Office, c'était le Portique Royale ou ressortissaient les actions d'impiété" (quoted by Derenne, *op.cit.* 247). To anyone who realizes that the king was an ordinary citizen, chosen for one year, whose responsibility was only to give a preliminary hearing to a γραφὴ ἀσεβείας brought before him and pass it on, if it was legally in order, to the heliastic courts, Renan's outburst appears eminently silly.

Plato's law then proceeds to state the penalties to be imposed by the courts. Offenders under each of the three forms of impiety we have examined will fall into two subclasses. Disbelief in the existence of the gods, for example, when held by a man of honorable and upright character is far less productive of evil, and deserves a much milder penalty, than atheism accompanied by lawless desires and keen wits intent on gratifying them (908b-e). A similar distinction should be made within each of the other two classes of offenders. This gives us six varieties of impious persons whose punishments should differ in kind and amount (908b). But in fact Plato's law mentions only two distinct penalties.[273] For the honorable atheist who hates injustice, shuns evil-doers, and seeks the company of good men, the punishment prescribed is confinement for a minimum of five years in the "house of correction" ($\sigma\omega\phi\rho\sigma\nu\iota\sigma\tau\eta\rho\iota\sigma\nu$), where he will be shut off from communication with any of his fellow citizens except the members of the Nocturnal Council, who will visit and admonish him "for the saving of his soul." At the end of his term he is released, if he seems to be restored to his right mind ($\dot{\epsilon}\dot{\alpha}\nu$ $\delta o\kappa\hat{\eta}$ $\sigma\omega\phi\rho\sigma\nu\epsilon\hat{\iota}\nu$), to resume his life among his "sober" ($\sigma\dot{\omega}\phi\rho\sigma\nu\epsilon s$) fellow citizens. But if he is brought to trial and convicted a second time for the same offense, the penalty shall be death (909a). The contrasted type of offender is he who, besides denying the existence of the gods, or believing in their indifference to human affairs or their venalty, exploits the piety of his fellowmen to his own profit. In claiming to bring back souls from the dead and to work magically upon the gods through sacrifices, prayers, and incantations, he can bring ruin not only to individuals but also to whole families and cities. Such a man deserves death many times over. But the law does not in fact prescribe the death penalty; the guilty man is to be condemned to solitary confinement for life, in a prison located in the wildest and most unfrequented part of the land (908a), where no free citizen at all can visit him; and when he dies his body is to be cast beyond the border without burial. Any citizen who assists in burying him in disregard of this verdict shall himself be liable to a charge of impiety (909bc).

These are obviously the two extremes of penalty to be imposed; the punishments appropriate to the other four classes of offenders will lie

---

[273] For a fuller exposition of the text see Egil A. Wyller, "Platons Gesetz gegen die Gottesleugner," in *Hermes* LXXXV, 1957, 292-314.

between these limits, and are left presumably for later legislators to formulate. These two are enough to illustrate how the punishments for different types of offenses will differ both in severity and in kind, according to the principle laid down in 908b—οὐκ ἴσης οὐδ᾽ ὁμοίας δίκης δεόμενα. How the other four kinds of offense would be ranked in gravity Plato does not say, and it is perhaps unprofitable to speculate.

Attic law permitted a variety of penalties for impiety, from fines and atimia to exile and death. Plato's prescriptions exhibit both simplification and innovation. Imprisonment was rarely used in Attic law, except as a means of holding an accused person for trial, or a condemned man for execution; these obvious functions are served in Plato's state by a prison located near the market place (908a). His innovation consists in distinguishing sharply two other purposes—reform and retribution—which imprisonment may serve, and in proposing additional and separate establishments for these two purposes. The proposal of a prison for correction appears to be without precedent in Plato's time;[274] it is a practical application of his firm conviction that punishment should have for its purpose either to reform the offender or to exhibit him as a deterrent example to others.[275] One may well doubt whether instruction and admonition under these circumstances can really have any educational effect; but our doubts are based upon experience which Plato did not have, and on experience in trying to do something like what he proposes. What is most likely to offend us is Plato's intention to reform not the man's character—for in the case supposed this is above reproach—but his beliefs; and we are today all too well aware of the barbarities of "brain washing" to which such efforts lead, when carried out by inhumane and fanatical authorities. Considering the fallibility of human beings when given such authority over others, we may well suppose that the lonely citizen in Plato's "house of correction" would often be subjected to severe inquisitorial pressure.[276] The law prescribes that if at the expiration of his term the prisoner "seems to be in his right mind" (ἐὰν δοκῇ σωφρονεῖν) he is to be released.

[274] Reverdin 223.

[275] Gorgias 525b; see Chapter XI, Notes 15 and 16.

[276] To "die Massregeln einer strengen Inquisition" (Wyller, op.cit. 298n.). It should be noted that Inquisition here does not mean the institution (see Note 272 above) but the procedure of inquisitorial examination (the βάσανος) which Plato regards as desirable in any judicial process. See Chapter VI, Procedure, and Index, βάσανος.

This may suggest that the officials have discretion to end or prolong his confinement; but it is hard to see how they could be expected to distinguish between a clever dissembler and a person genuinely convinced of the error of his previous beliefs, except by his future conduct. This is evidently what Plato intends. "If not," he says, "and if he is convicted again for the same offense, he shall be condemned to death."

The denial of burial on native soil prescribed for the graver class of offenders is not Plato's invention, but a familiar sanction of Attic law. To refuse burial to a dead man was a serious matter, for it meant that the soul, according to traditional belief, could not enter Hades; and gloomy as that realm was, to be refused admission to it was even worse. In Attic law the body of such an offender was usually cast over the border, as prescribed in Plato's law. The significance of this penalty is that it was a solemn way of cutting the offender off from all connection with his state; it was a kind of posthumous exile. There are several other instances of this penalty in Platonic law, all of them with their Attic parallels.[277]

As a supplement to the law we have just been considering Plato proposes another designed to remove one of the chief causes, he thinks, of the forms of impiety just mentioned, viz. the possession of private shrines and the practice of unauthorized rites. This supplementary law, as it is eventually formulated,[278] reads as follows:

Let there be no rites (ἱερά) to the gods in private houses. If anyone is shown to have a shrine or to be celebrating rites other than those that are publicly established, he who learns of it shall give information to the

---

[277] The Platonic code also refuses burial on native soil (1) to robbers of temples, (2) to traitors and conspirators against the constitution, and (3) to murderers of father, mother, child, brother, or sister. The general principle is stated in 854e-855a, 856e-857a; for details see 856b, 873ab. In the third of the three cases mentioned above the body of the offender is to be publicly stoned before being cast across the borders (873b). Cf. the ἄταφοι πράξεις, 960b. For the penalty of nonburial in Attic law see Thuc. I, 126, 138; Xen. *Hell.* I, vii, 22; Lyc. I, 113, 115; Diod. xvi, 25; Plut. *Phoc.* 37; *Syll.* No. 147, lines 61-63.

In Plato's law a murderer is refused burial "in the country of his victim" (871d); the animal that has killed a man is to be put to death and cast across the border (873e), and likewise any inanimate object that has brought about the death of a human being (874a).

[278] Plato apparently begins the statement of the law in 909d, but interrupts it to give the reasons that underlie the law, then starts afresh in 910b. Ἐπὶ τούτοις πᾶσιν in 909d is generally taken to mean "all the above-mentioned forms of impiety"; but it is hard to see how this law would serve as a preventive of—or even be relevant to—the first and second types of unbelief. Therefore I take τούτοις to refer to the manifestations of the third form of impiety, of which, as Plato's description shows, there are many varieties.

guardians; and if the possessor of these rites, whether man or woman, has done no great or impious wrong, they shall order him to transfer his private worship to the public shrines; and if he is reluctant they shall fine him until he moves them. But whoever is shown to have committed not the thoughtless impiety of a child, but the grave impiety of an unholy man, whether in a privately established shrine or in a public sacrifice to gods of his own choosing, shall be put to death for sacrificing in a state of impurity. The guardians shall decide whether or not it is a childish act and bring such offenders before the court for the punishment of their impiety.[279]

We have already noted that this law, if taken literally, would abolish the family and tribal shrines that are taken for granted elsewhere in the *Laws*. If there is not a strange inconsistency in Plato's thought we must interpret the law just quoted in a special sense. The reasons advanced for it (909e-910a) give us the clue. There is a natural tendency, Plato says, for a man or woman in peril or distress, or at a time of specially good fortune, or when under the influence of a terrifying dream or hallucination, to make an impromptu dedication and to vow a sacrifice or establish a shrine to some god, daemon, or hero. Now the right establishment of shrines and worship is not a light matter and requires much thought; such irresponsible foundations are therefore not to be encouraged, especially since there are traders in superstition ready to exploit this weakness of human nature. Thus we are brought back to the same class of impostors we met at the conclusion of the previous law, the greedy mystery mongers and sellers of purifications who had aroused Plato's indignation from his earliest reflections on religious matters. It is therefore not the private cults of family and phratry and tribe that Plato has in mind here; none of these is the result of a private whim, but an expression of group worship sanctioned by long tradition. Plato's idea in this law is, as Gernet says,[280] that the only cult valid in the state is the cult established in the city's sanctuaries and in the family and tribal subdivisions which are themselves an essential part of the city's structure.

This law is a clear expression of the tendency manifested in the Athens of classical times to connect the cults more and more closely

---

[279] 910cd. Ἱερά carries the double sense of "shrine" and "rites." The latter sense is evident in ὀργιάζοντα (c1) and θύσας ἱερὰ θεοῖς (c8); but rites always take place around a shrine, hence this sense also is implied throughout.

[280] Gernet cxcv.

with the organization of the state.[281] The reverse side of this tendency was the suspicion of cults of foreign origin that was felt in the late fifth and the fourth centuries, and the reluctance manifested by the more responsible leaders of the city to give them legal tolerance. It is not certain that there was ever a law at Athens proscribing the practice of foreign cults;[282] if there was one, it was not applied with any consistency and vigor, because of the inclination among the mass of the population toward these exotic rites.[283] But we can understand how a responsible statesman who looked upon the city's religion as an important buttress to patriotic feeling and civic unity could be alarmed at the effects of these private cults, especially if they were of foreign origin, as tending to weaken the unity of the city by destroying the common fellowship in the worship of the city's gods.

From the material we have reviewed in this section it is clear that in his law against impiety Plato builds on the law of his native city. He endeavors to introduce system and precision into the miscellany of ill-defined beliefs punishable as impiety under Attic law; he provides for the correction, rather than the punishment, of certain types of offenders; and we may assume, from the care with which he constructs his judicial system, that he intends charges of ἀσέβεια to be more judiciously handled in his state than they were at Athens. But he holds even more strongly than the Athenians that belief in a transcendental source of law and justice is necessary for the health of a city, and he sees no impropriety in supporting this belief, or punishing departures from it, by the force of law. No doubt in the state which he plans there would be a great deal of the freedom that existed at Athens through the lack of organs of inquisition and the reluctance of citizens to prosecute. But if so it would not be through his conscious intention. For he is aware of this trait in the Athenian character, and if moral exhortation has its intended effect this weakness will be little evident in his state. He frequently insists upon the citizen's duty to aid the magistrates in the enforcement of the laws by laying information before them, or bringing suit against offenders (730d, 856c); and this duty is mentioned specifically in connection with the present law (907de). The condemnation of Socrates was a

[281] Nilsson I, 670ff.
[282] As Schmidt (op.cit. II, 49ff.) and Paul Foucart (Associations religieuses chez les Grecs, Paris, 1873, 127ff.) affirmed and Derenne has recently argued (op.cit. 224ff.).
[283] Gernet cxcv n. I.

miscarriage of justice, he certainly thought, but it came about not because of a wrong policy of suppressing impiety, but through the unintelligent application to Socrates of a judgment "which he of all men least deserved."[284] Plato's conception of piety is far more profound than that of the usual prosecutors or judges in the Athenian courts, and his conception of the way to deal with impiety embodies a humane distinction between the correction of curable offenders and the punishment of the incurable. But he does not take issue with the fundamental policy expressed in the Athenian law; he would only make this policy more clear-sighted, vigorous, and consistent.

The law against impiety also shows that in providing for religion in his state Plato is not merely actuated by a belief that the fourth-century Greek could not live without it; his religious law is not a concession to circumstances which the legislator has no option but to accept. If that were the case, we should probably see him willing to let these unnecessary and uncongenial religious practices alone, hoping they would eventually die of their own accord; we should certainly not find him strengthening them by a law which, so far as we know, had its positive parallel in few Greek states, perhaps only in Athens. Plato could see all too well that the Greeks of his time were beginning to live without that kind of religion that strengthens the mind and character. It is to provide a corrective to this degeneration in the religious life of his time that Plato insists on the state's protecting it—and not only protecting it, but controlling it, so far as that is consistent with the authority of Delphi, in order to safeguard those elements that promote the "imitation of God."

There is another more common misinterpretation of Plato's motives against which this material should put us on our guard—the view, namely, that he proceeds in the spirit of a realistic (and perhaps cynical) legislator who avails himself of religious sanctions because of their immediate practical utility in maintaining the supremacy of the laws.[285] This realism is certainly a factor in Plato's thinking. The conception of the gods as unseen magistrates observing violations of the laws and marking offenders for punishment is unquestionably a

---

[284] *Ep. VII* 325b. There is a distinct implication in this passage that Socrates' condemnation was an act of political reprisal.

[285] The adoption of this interpretation is a fundamental defect in the otherwise careful summary of Belknap, *op.cit.* (Note 2). "The positive value of religion in Plato's ideal and second-best cities consists principally in the protecting, conservative power of sanctity which it places at the disposal of the state at points of social stress and weakness" (1).

powerful sanction in some minds, perhaps in all minds at some times. Plato's law against impiety is certainly directed in part against those who would weaken the belief in the existence or the integrity of these unseen guardians of the laws. But the order that Plato wishes to establish in his state is not one based primarily on the fear of punishment. We have seen in the previous chapter how the chthonic and fearful aspects of religion are deliberately subordinated to the joyous and festive. For him the gods give sanction to the laws not so much by punishing violators, as by presenting themselves and the standards they uphold as objects of veneration and respect, as patterns which the citizen can delight in imitating. Worship becomes a festival, an intrinsically desirable form of that serious play in which men should pass their lives, sacrificing, singing, and dancing, and thus winning the favor of the gods (803e).[286] If it is the citizen's happiness to become as much like these divine objects of veneration as he can, therein also lies the salvation of the state.

EXCURSUS E. THE ELECTION
OF THE EXEGETES

The highly compressed passage (759d 5 - 759e 3) in which Plato describes the selection of these officials is extremely difficult. In Burnet's text it is given as follows: τοὺς δὲ ἐξηγητὰς τρὶς φερέτωσαν μὲν αἱ τέτταρες φυλαὶ τέτταρας, ἕκαστον ἐξ αὐτῶν, τρεῖς δέ, οἷς ἂν πλείστη γένηται ψῆφος, δοκιμάσαντας, ἐννέα πέμπειν εἰς Δελφοὺς ἀνελεῖν ἐξ ἑκάστης τριάδος ἕνα· τὴν δὲ δοκιμασίαν αὐτῶν καὶ τοῦ χρόνου τὴν ἡλικίαν εἶναι καθάπερ τῶν ἱερέων. οὗτοι δὲ ἔστων ἐξηγηταὶ διὰ βίου. τὸν δέ γε λιπόντα προαιρείσθωσαν αἱ τέτταρες φυλαὶ ὅθεν ἂν ἐκλίπῃ. Its interpretation has been the subject of violent and somewhat inconclusive controversy. For varying interpretations see Ritter, *Kommentar*, 1896, 163-165; Philipp Ehrmann, *De juris sacri interpretibus Atticis*, Giessen, 1908, 365; Persson, *Die Exegeten und Delphi*, 10; Wade-Gery, cq xxv, 1931, 85-89; Reverdin, 96f.; Oliver, *Athenian Expounders*, 55-63; Jacoby, *Atthis*, 249; and Hammond, cq xlvi, 1952, 4-12.

All commentators are agreed that Plato's intention is to have three exegetes appointed by Delphi, one from each of three groups of

---

286 It is worth recalling again how Athenian this view is. See Schmidt, *op.cit.* ii, 28f.

candidates selected each by a group of four tribes. The issue in controversy is whether Plato also intends to have three other exegetes
elected by the state. In Roman times, and perhaps also in the fourth
century, Athenian law provided for an exegete selected by the demos
from the Eupatridae, as well as an exegete selected by the oracle at
Delphi. The prevailing opinion until recently, it is fair to say, was
that this feature of later Athenian law is anticipated in Plato's legislation. This is the interpretation of Ehrmann, Persson, England,
Apelt, Bury, Cassarà, des Places, and Robin among recent translators and commentators; and it goes back through Stallbaum to Bekker and even to Ficinus. It is probable that Timaeus the Lexicographer in late antiquity interpreted Plato's text in this way (see
Oliver, *op.cit.* 58-61). But this interpretation has had its vigorous
challengers—such as Ast in earlier times, and more recently Ritter,
Wade-Gery, Reverdin, Jacoby, Oliver, and Hammond.

According to this earlier but now challenged interpretation, Plato's
text proposes the appointment of six exegetes, three by the demos and
three by Delphi. Each group of four tribes elects four candidates. From
each of these groups the demos takes the candidate who has received
the most votes, subjects him to the dokimasia, and confirms his election. The names of the remaining nine are sent to Delphi for Apollo's
choice of three, one from each of the three groups. It is fairly ob-
jected against this interpretation that it makes the dokimasia apply
only to the candidates who are elected by the demos, not to those
whose names are sent to Delphi (Wade-Gery, *op.cit.* 87). Wade-
Gery also argues that the description of the procedure for filling a
vacancy seems to exclude the idea of two methods of election and
that the particular procedure described ($\pi\rho o\alpha\iota\rho\epsilon\acute{\iota}\sigma\theta\omega\sigma\alpha\nu$) suggests
the preliminary selection by the tribes of a list to be sent to Delphi,
not the election ($\alpha\acute{\iota}\rho\epsilon\sigma\iota\varsigma$) which would be called for to fill a vacancy
among the three exegetes appointed by the demos. Reverdin points
out that $\tau\grave{o}\nu$ $\lambda\iota\pi\acute{o}\nu\tau\alpha$ in the same clause is better understood if we
admit that each group of four tribes has only one representative
(96n.).

The other interpretation finds only three exegetes in the text, viz.
the three appointed by Apollo. But its supporters have had difficulty
in explaining why each of the tribal groups elects four persons when
the names of only three of these four are to be sent to Delphi. Wade-
Gery thinks it is in order to have a representative from each tribe

on the preliminary list; but he admits that ἕκαστον ἐξ αὐτῶν will not bear the meaning he thinks Plato intends. Oliver supposes that the προαίρεσις by the tribal groups is followed by a αἵρεσις by the demos. Hammond points out that the verb φέρειν sometimes means "nominate" in Plato's electoral prescriptions, and he interprets the sentence as meaning that each member of a four-tribe assembly nominates four persons; the three whose names occur most often on these nominating ballots are the three who are subjected to the scrutiny. Thus each of the tribal groups elects three, not four, candidates, and from three such elections there will result nine names to be scrutinized and sent to Delphi. Oliver (AJP LXXIII, 1952, 412) objects to this that it strains the text to make αἱ τέτταρες φυλαί mean "each member of the four tribes"; it is more natural to take it as meaning that the four-tribe assembly nominates four, three of whom are to be chosen by election in a full assembly of all the tribes.

Between Oliver's and Hammond's interpretations it is difficult to choose. The latter gives the better explanation of the number four in the preliminary elections in the tribal groups. The screening of a list of nominees by the application of the majority principle is a method used elsewhere in Plato's electoral laws (e.g. 753cd, 756c-e, 946a). In this case four is the minimum number of nominations required from each individual to *ensure* enough candidates for the application of the majority principle, though the normal result of such nominating procedure would be to present many more than four names for the final election. On Oliver's view apparently only four names would be presented at the later election in the assembly; this would only enable the demos, as Oliver says, "to eliminate one unpopular man"—which would hardly seem enough to justify a separate election. Yet the designation of the election in the tribal group as a προαίρεσις (e3) suggests a αἵρεσις by the demos; and this consideration, plus the difficulty of taking αἱ τέτταρες φυλαί as meaning "each individual in the group of four tribes" gives the greater weight of probability to Oliver's view. Perhaps Plato means that each tribal group should present *at least* four candidates for the election by the demos.

Despite the difficulty of ascertaining precisely what Plato's intentions are on this point, this uncertainty does not affect the essence of the interpretation supported in common by Wade-Gery, Jacoby, Oliver, Hammond and the other adherents to the newer view. Plato will have only three exegetes, all appointed eventually by Apollo. The objections against the older interpretation seem conclusive.

Hammond also argues for the restoration of τρεῖς in d5 in place of τρίς which is preferred in all the standard texts. Τρεῖς is the reading of A and O, the manuscripts that have the greatest authority in determining the text of the *Laws*, and it is also (as Hammond points out) the reading of the manuscripts of Stobaeus that contain this passage. The only authority for τρίς is its presence in the margin of A, and an ι written over τρεῖς in O. If τρεῖς is retained it should be taken not as the object of φερέτωσαν, but with τοὺς ἐξηγητάς as an accusative with infinitive (εἶναι) understood. There are a half-dozen examples of this infinitive construction in the present passage, from ἱερέας . . . μὴ κινεῖν (759a 8) to αἵρεσιν . . . γίγνεσθαι (760a 3). On the other hand, the reasons of sense that have led to the retention of τρίς cannot be ignored. The procedure described beginning with φερέτωσαν must occur thrice, i.e. in three assemblies of tribal groups, and this ought to be in the text somewhere. Furthermore, the later scrutiny is also concerned with thrice three candidates. Τρίς, placed at the beginning of the description and thus modifying both φερέτωσαν and δοκιμάσαντας, seems required to express Plato's intention. My guess is that the text, as Plato wrote it, was as follows: τοὺς δὲ ἐξηγητὰς τρεῖς (sc. εἶναι)· τρὶς φερέτωσαν κτλ. It would be only too easy for one of these two similar adjacent words to get lost, particularly as ει and ι became assimilated in pronunciation.

CHAPTER IX

THE NOCTURNAL COUNCIL

No PART of Plato's scheme is more familiar than the institution of the Nocturnal Council, but perhaps none is more difficult to interpret. Plato introduces it only in the closing books of the *Laws*, and indeed leaves the explicit discussion of its purpose and functioning to the end of the twelfth book, when his legislation is practically (σχεδόν) finished (960b). Its introduction thus late in the exposition has led some commentators to regard it as something of an appendage, if not an afterthought, tacked on—by Plato himself or by Philippus of Opus[1]—to a constitution and system of laws already complete. This interpretation is not impossible, but it should be accepted only as a last resort. On the other hand, if we respect the integrity of the *Laws* as it has been transmitted to us and regard the Nocturnal Council as a considered part of Plato's legislation, we may think its inclusion necessitates the denial, or at least the reconstruction, of much that has gone before.[2] Let us see whether this inference is justified.

At this point (960b) the legislation for the Cretan city is, in a sense, complete—with its assembly, council, guardians, and all the minor magistrates; its courts of justice and laws, covering at least the most important of the citizens' activities, which the magistrates and the courts will apply and enforce; its provisions for a form of education that will supplement the law through the development of character and intelligence, and for religious institutions to give the laws ideal guidance and sanction. What then is still needed to make our legislation actually complete? "We are never at the end of a task," says

---

[1] For Philippus of Opus, see Excursus F, below.

[2] Edward Zeller, *Plato and the Older Academy*, trans. by Alleyn and Goodwin, London, 1888, 539-540: "As the rest of the government is in no way based upon this council of the wise, and as the council itself is not incorporated into the organism of the state by any definite official sphere of action, there is a certain ambiguity and uncertainty about the whole scheme." George H. Sabine, *History of Political Theory*, New York, 1937, 85: the Nocturnal Council "not only fails to articulate in any way with the other institutions of the state but also contradicts the purpose of planning a state in which the law is supreme." Barker 349: the Nocturnal Council is to control, "in ways that are never explained, a system of political machinery into which [it is] never fitted." Ronald B. Levinson, *In Defense of Plato*, Harvard University Press, 1953, 517 n. 38, thinks that this institution "introduced at the end of the *Laws*" engenders a contradiction in the entire fabric of Plato's state. Gerhard Müller, *Studien zu den Platonischen Nomoi*, Munich, 1951, 169-170: "Der nächtliche Rat fügt sich . . . in die anderen Institutionen, die historischer Herkunft sind, nicht ein."

the Athenian, "when we have merely made something, or acquired it, or brought it into being; in the present case we shall not have done all that we should have done, and our work will be incomplete, if we have not found some device that will assure the preservation, in its perfection and through all time, of what we have brought into being." Of the three Fates, he recalls, Atropos is the "third and savior," because, as her name implies, she gives the quality of irreversibility[3] to the dooms assigned and ratified by her sisters (960cd). The clear implication is that in our state we have assigned and ratified the institutions and laws; what we now need is some means of assuring their "salvation" (σωτηρία).[4]

Now the salvation of the laws implies something more than the preservation of a code rigidly and unthinkingly adhered to. Any legislator who has founded a city hopes that those who come after him will understand his purposes and interpret his provisions with the same insight that he has used in constructing them; otherwise his legislation, even though retaining its form, will have changed its spirit. Plato above all would have cause to be concerned lest his successors not be equipped to understand his law, for its foundations are based on a philosophical conception of the good, individual and political; it is the expression of a reason that transcends ordinary experience, and those who are to interpret it, or apply it, cannot do so properly unless they are equipped to understand the Reason (Nous) it contains. This conception is the ripe fruit of the Socratic doctrine that virtue is knowledge; and in expounding it to his Dorian companions the Athenian Stranger makes use of the familiar Socratic analogies. If legislation and statesmanship are arts, as we think they are, analogous to the arts of medicine, navigation, and generalship, and if it is characteristic of a good craftsman to have a clear conception of his end and of the means of attaining it, then any state that expects even to retain the wisdom of its founder must have some organ within it to keep alive the knowledge of the purpose of its laws and their dependence upon cosmic Reason, and to examine the way in which they are accomplishing or failing to accomplish this ideal purpose (961e-962c).

Even more will it need such an organ if it hopes to improve upon its founder. In this context we see the full meaning of a long passage

---

[3] I.e. ἀτροπία; though Plato here uses a synonym, ἡ ἀμετάστροφος δύναμις.

[4] This interpretation of σχεδὸν . . . τέλος ἂν ἔχοι (960b) is confirmed by the context of the parallel passage in 962b: εἴπερ μέλλει τέλος . . . ἕξειν. Cf. Rep. 620e.

in the sixth book (769a-771a). The Athenian Stranger there compares himself to a painter who seems never to tire of embellishing and improving what he has done and who, if he could, would leave behind him a successor with similar skill to keep watch over his picture, repair any damage to it, and even introduce improvements or correct defects in the original craftsmanship. So the legislator realizes that his own workmanship cannot reach the perfection that he wishes to attain and would like to leave successors behind him to correct his mistakes, in order that the constitution of his state may not deteriorate but always grow better (ἵνα μηδαμῇ χείρων, βελτίω δὲ ἡ πολιτεία . . . ἀεὶ γίγνηται). "If anyone knew of a device to this end and could teach anyone else, by words or deeds, to understand in some degree how the laws are to be guarded and corrected, do you think he would leave off talking about it until he had brought it into being?" (769de). The means that Plato eventually adopts are not fully described in the sequel to this passage. The Athenian Stranger merely declares that we must entrust this function to the guardians, who are to become "νομοθέται as well as νομοφύλακες" (770a; cf. 770c); and he addresses to them a general statement of the ends to which legislation is directed, enjoining them to keep these aims in mind, censuring the laws that are found from experience not to serve the purpose announced, and heartily accepting and enforcing those that do. Likewise we see the meaning of a still earlier passage in which the Athenian, after surveying the areas of life which a scientific legislator must try to regulate and the ends to which his laws should be directed, adds that "for all these laws he will appoint guardians, some guided by knowledge (φρόνησις), others by right opinion, in order that reason (νοῦς), binding the whole together, may exhibit them as in conformity with temperance and justice" (632c).

Throughout the *Laws*, then, Plato sees that the state he is constructing will require that some of its officials be equipped with philosophical and juristic intelligence to preserve, expound, and apply the principles on which the laws are based. It is the same requirement that is laid down in the *Republic*. If a good state, and the philosophical spirit that designed it, are to escape degeneration, says Socrates, "there must always be resident in it some element having the same conception (λόγος) of the constitution that you the legislator had in making your laws" (497cd). The Nocturnal Council is the means designed to satisfy this requirement in Plato's Cretan city. Hence these closing pages are as integral a part of the *Laws* as are Books VI and VII of the *Republic*. The Nocturnal Council will be the "head" of the state (961d)—to use the metaphor that recurs so constantly here—the head in the sense that it is the intelligence which apprehends the reason in the law and the source of this reason in the ordered cosmos. Let us see how Plato proposes to provide such a head for his state.

The constitution of the Nocturnal Council[5] is dealt with in two separate passages (951de, 961ab) which have some discrepancies, though on the main points they are in accord.[6] The Council is to consist of (1) the ten eldest guardians of the laws; (2) the "priests who have been awarded ἀριστεῖα," which obviously includes the euthynoi (946b) and possibly others;[7] (3) the educator and all his predecessors in the office;[8] (4) certain citizens who have traveled

[5] It is called νυκτερινὸς σύλλογος at 909a, 968a (cf. 908a); and once it is called the σύλλογος τῶν περὶ νόμους ἐποπτευόντων (951d), a cryptic formula whose meaning is discussed in Note 17. Σύλλογος is more correctly rendered "assembly"; but "Nocturnal Council" has been so generally used to designate this body that to avoid confusion I have retained it.

The requirement of daily meetings at dawn (951d) sounds rather grim; but then Plato was not one to make things easy for his chosen ones. The early hour probably would not seem so strange to Plato's readers as to us. The activities of the day began early in Greece: see Chapter VII, Note 104.

The phrase συλλεγόμενος ἀπ' ὄρθρου μέχριπερ ἂν ἥλιος ἀνάσχῃ (951d) is puzzling if it is taken as prescribing the duration of their sessions. It probably should be taken as indicating the time at which they are to assemble.

[6] Bruns and Krieg (see Excursus F) regard the σύλλογος described at 961ff. as the creation of Philippus of Opus; the genuine Platonic σύλλογος is the one mentioned in Book X (908a, 909a) and described in 951de, which is concerned only with practical knowledge about the laws, not the higher philosophical knowledge cultivated by the one described later (Bruns, *op.cit.* 204; Krieg, *op.cit.* 38). Again, according to these critics, the Platonic Council has only an advisory function and therefore is compatible with the functions of the magistrates already described; the Council of Philippus, however, has executive and judicial powers, and thus in effect supplants the nomophylakes, just as it takes over their name (cf. οἱ ὄντως φύλακες τῶν νόμων, 966b). But it was evidently Philippus' intention, on this hypothesis, to make the two councils appear identical (cf. 962c, 961ab). Why then did he not make the constitution of his council identical with that of the one Plato describes? Or, if the slight differences that he introduces are significant for his purpose, why did he not revise Plato's account so as to bring it into accord with his own? Furthermore, the claim that this Council supplants the nomophylakes cannot be established, as I think my exposition shows.

[7] On ἀριστεῖα see Chapter VI, Note 65.

[8] These are included in the earlier passage but omitted from the second; but the office is such an important one that it is not likely that Plato has changed his mind and decided to leave them out. Furthermore, election to this office seems to be the

abroad and who on their return have been examined by the Council and adjudged worthy of membership;[9] and (5) perhaps other citizens who have received awards of merit.[10] Each member of this body is to associate with himself a younger citizen between the ages of thirty and forty, who if approved by the other members shall attend the meetings of the Council and engage in its discussions. These younger citizens are apparently not regarded as members in the same sense as their elders are. A younger man's association might cease with the death or retirement of his sponsor, and in any case would come to an end when he himself reaches the age of forty. This provision seems strange, but its meaning will be evident in the sequel.

The sessions of this body are first described in connection with the regulations regarding foreign travel. No city can be civilized, Plato says, if it is unacquainted with other men, both good and bad; nor can it preserve its own laws if it holds them only by habit and not by understanding as well (951b). Hence in addition to the embassies and contestants sent to the Panhellenic festivals at Delphi, Olympia, and the Isthmus, the city should also send out other qualified observers to make a more leisurely examination of foreign customs and carry on more extended conversations with the wise men of other lands. "There are always among the mass of men a few, not many, inspired ones ($\theta\epsilon\hat{\iota}o\acute{\iota}$ $\tau\iota\nu\epsilon\varsigma$) whose conversation is above price. They spring up indifferently in good and in badly ordered states. These men we must track down, if we live in a well ordered state, searching them out by sea and land . . . in order to confirm those parts of our legislation that are well established and correct anything that is amiss. Without such observation ($\theta\epsilon\omega\rho\acute{\iota}a$) and inquiry ($\zeta\acute{\eta}\tau\eta\sigma\iota\varsigma$) no city can ever remain in a state of perfection, nor can it if this inquiry is conducted badly" (951bc). These observers, or envoys—their designation $\theta\epsilon\omega\rho o\acute{\iota}$ carries both meanings—must be between fifty and sixty years of age; they must be chosen as good ambassadors of their country's laws, and as persons not liable to corruption by what

equivalent of an award of merit (cf. 766a). The statement in 961b is said to be a repetition of what was said earlier, so that Plato is not conscious of any change of intention.

[9] The provision for the inclusion of these $\theta\epsilon\omega\rho o\acute{\iota}$ is explicit in the second passage and implied in the sequel (952bc) to the earlier one.

[10] Theodor Bergk (*Fünf Abhandlungen*, Leipzig, 1883, 94) thinks that 961a should be emended, after the analogy of 951d ($\tau\hat{\omega}\nu$ $\dot{\iota}\epsilon\rho\acute{\epsilon}\omega\nu$ $\tau\hat{\omega}\nu$ $\tau\grave{a}$ $\dot{a}\rho\iota\sigma\tau\epsilon\hat{\iota}a$ $\epsilon\dot{\iota}\lambda\eta\phi\acute{o}\tau\omega\nu$), to read $\tauo\grave{\upsilon}\varsigma$ $\delta\epsilon$ $\langle\dot{\iota}\epsilon\rho\acute{\epsilon}a\varsigma$ $\tauo\grave{\upsilon}\varsigma\rangle$ $\tau\acute{a}\rho\iota\sigma\tau\epsilon\hat{\iota}a$ $\epsilon\dot{\iota}\lambda\eta\phi\acute{o}\tau a\varsigma$. If this emendation is accepted, there is no need to add the fifth category mentioned in my text; but though plausible it is by no means necessary, and I prefer to adhere to the received text.

they see abroad. They may apparently go where they please and remain as long as they like within the ten years permitted them.[11] When one of them returns he is to go at once to the Nocturnal Council and report to them any wise saying (φήμη) he has heard about legislation or education, and any new ideas of his own that have come from his experiences (951d, 952b). At this point we have a brief statement—almost by way of digression—concerning the meetings of this Council. "Their conferences (συνουσία) and discussions (λόγοι) shall always be about laws—both the laws of their own city and any different laws that they may learn of elsewhere; and especially about any branches of learning (μαθήματα) which may seem to aid them in this inquiry by shedding light upon matters of law (τὰ περὶ νόμους)" (951e-952a).

From this passage it appears that the purpose of the Nocturnal Council is to help selected officers and distinguished citizens attain a deeper understanding of their laws, sharpened by comparison with the laws of other states, and enriched by insight into the nature of law in general. Further, it is evident that for the understanding of these matters other studies are necessary. We are not here told what these μαθήματα are that will assist the Councillors in gaining a clearer insight into law; but when the Nocturnal Council is taken up again ten pages later we have an account of the kind of inquiries with which this body will be concerned. The Athenian points out that if this Council is to be an adequate "head"—i.e. guiding intelligence—of the state, it must be able to apprehend clearly the political mark (σκοπός) to be aimed at in all legislation and must know also how this end may be attained and what laws and what men may best assist (συμβουλεύειν) in attaining it (962b). Now the end to which all laws should be directed is virtue (963a). But the knowledge of virtue is no simple matter, the Athenian shows. Moral goodness manifests itself traditionally in four main forms: courage, temperance, wisdom, and justice; yet these are somehow one (963c-e). To grasp the single principle that pervades them all, while not destroying their differences; to understand their various powers and effects, their relationship to one another, and to the Nous which stands above them; and to be able to expound them to the earnest inquirer—this requires that expertness in dialectic, in seeing the One in the Many, in "giving

---

[11] This seems an echo of Plato's visit to the Pythagoreans in Italy and to other lands during his years of travel after the death of Socrates.

and receiving λόγους," which had long been the heart of Plato's philosophical method.[12] Furthermore, those who are to guard our laws must in the same fashion apprehend the truth on all matters of earnest inquiry (περὶ πάντων τῶν σπουδαίων), of which the most important are the nature of the soul, the movements of the heavenly bodies, and the existence of the gods (966b-e). Finally there is at the end a reference to certain preliminary sciences (τὰ πρὸ τούτων ἀναγκαῖα μαθήματα, 967e), obviously mathematics and harmonics, which are necessary for the proper understanding of the high matters just mentioned. Thus Plato outlines for his Council a program of studies, beginning with the preliminary sciences last mentioned, and proceeding (we cannot determine precisely in what order) through moral philosophy and dialectic to cosmology and theology.[13]

Are these the studies that will assist the inquirer in attaining a clearer understanding of law? We are not told this explicitly, nor can we see clearly how they could serve this function. But we can see how Plato thought they could, and this is enough to reveal his intention. Law, as we learn in the *Philebus*, results from the application of the Limit (πέρας) to an indefinitely varying qualitative continuum (ἄπειρον), and the Limit is conceived of as analogous to mathematical order.[14] The most striking illustration of its use is the production of harmony in a musical instrument through the imposing of mathematical ratios upon the indefinite possibilities of tension in its various strings. Moral order in the soul, and justice in the state, were both thought of in Platonic circles as analogous modes of attunement through the introduction of the required ratios and proportions.[15] The use of mathematics in the latest period of Plato's thought was evidently much more extensive than anything revealed to us in the dialogues; we know from ancient testimony that his famous lectures on the Good were disconcertingly mathematical in content.[16] And the discovery of the precise mathematical character

---

[12] The familiar marks of Plato's dialectic are numerous in this passage. Besides the problem of the one and the many (πρὸς μίαν ἰδέαν ἐκ τῶν πολλῶν καὶ ἀνομοίων, 965c; cf. 963c-964c), note ὄνομα καὶ λόγος, 964a; τὴν ἔνδειξιν . . . ἐνδείκνυσθαι, 966b; λόγῳ ἑρμηνεύειν, 966b; δοῦναι τὸν λόγον, 967e.

[13] For the most part this course of higher studies parallels that laid down for the guardians in *Rep.* vii. The astronomy, the theology, and the doctrine of the soul are additions.

[14] *Phil.* 23c-26b; see also below, Chapter XI.

[15] Recall Aristotle's mathematical discussion of the Mean in *Nic. Eth.* Bk. ii and of Justice in Bk. v.

[16] Aristoxenus, *Harm. El.* ii, 30.16-31.3. Aristotle's testimony in the *Metaphysics*

of the apparently confused motions of the heavenly bodies was for Plato an unexpected revelation of orderliness in the heavens, which then became for him a visible image of that orderliness that he had always known to exist in the intelligible world. There may be a reference to the illuminating effect of such studies in the striking designation of the Council as the σύλλογος τῶν περὶ νόμους ἐποπτευόντων.[17] There is no reason to doubt, then, that the studies described in the later passage are those that Plato prescribes in the earlier one as helpful in assisting the Councillors to attain insight into the nature of law.

The implication is that whatever else the Council may be, it is first of all an institution for the higher education of its members. This is confirmed later (968ab) when the Athenian formally proposes that this Council, "having gone through all the education we have described" (παιδείας ὁπόσης διεληλύθαμεν κοινωνὸν γενόμενον), shall be legally established as the guardian and savior of the state. (The participial clause, as England sees, contains the most important point in the Athenian's pronouncement.) In again another passage (965b) the studies pursued in the Council are attached to the account of education given in the seventh book. At the end of the prescriptions regarding the study of mathematics there is mention of a "certain few" who are to pursue these studies with greater thoroughness and exactness (σύμπαντα ὡς ἀκριβείας ἐχόμενα διαπονεῖν 818a); the studies of the Nocturnal Council are here said to be a "more exact education" (ἀκριβεστέρα παιδεία) than that described earlier; these "certain few," then, are obviously the members of the Council. But the promise made in that earlier passage to deal with the program of studies in detail is not fulfilled; the order in which these inquiries are

---

to the later mathematical stage of the theory of Ideas certainly applies, in part at least, to Plato. On the contents of the famous lecture (or lectures) on the Good see the interpretation of Paul Wilpert, *Zwei Aristotelische Frühschriften über die Ideenlehre*, Regensburg, 1949, 121-221.

[17] 951d. The verb ἐποπτεύω is poetic, and its meaning here is not easy to fix precisely; it can mean "supervise," "meditate upon," or "contemplate." It is used in one of the most eloquent passages in the *Phaedrus* (250c) to describe the relation of the soul to the shining visions of the invisible world (cf. τὰ δὲ τέλεα καὶ ἐποπτικά, *Symp.* 210a). An ἐπόπτης in the mysteries was one who had been initiated into the highest grade. We may perhaps take this word as indicating Plato's belief that the kind of study here proposed would result, not merely in enlightenment, but also in illumination (cf. the designation θεῖος σύλλογος, 969b).

The *Epinomis* describes at some length the higher studies of the Nocturnal Council (cf. 992d). This is probably not Plato's work, but at least it shows what Philippus thought he intended.

to be taken up and the time to be devoted to each will vary with individuals, the Athenian Stranger here says, and can best be left to the Council itself after it has been established;[18] though he adds that he will be willing to help, and can also find other helpers if they are needed, in setting up such an institution in the new colony (968b). This remark at the end of the *Laws* is Plato's signature to the work he has completed, and the "other helpers" are his colleagues in the Academy.

It is now clear why the Council includes junior as well as senior members. One of its purposes evidently is to provide this higher education to the more promising of the younger citizens, to those who are likely in time to become officers themselves. These junior members are presumably the persons mentioned in 968d as "fitted by age, intellectual powers, and moral character and conduct for becoming guardians." Their admission to association with the Council is carefully controlled. A candidate must first be proposed by one of the Councillors as a man who, by nature and training ($\phi \acute{v}\sigma\epsilon\iota$ $\kappa\alpha\grave{\iota}$ $\tau\rho\sigma\phi\tilde{\eta}$, 961b), is worthy of this junior membership, and this proposal must receive the assent of the other members. (Plato adds that if a man is rejected, no word of it must get out, least of all to the man himself; and furthermore, that if after being accepted a man proves to be unworthy, his sponsor shall receive the rebuke of the Council.) These junior members are to study diligently whatever matters their seniors deem appropriate (952a), and the other citizens are to watch them carefully and honor them if they acquit themselves well. The Nocturnal Council cannot of itself assure their later election to office, though it might facilitate it through the exercise of the scrutiny, which comes directly or indirectly under the authority of the guardians; but membership in the Council would of itself bring considerable prestige to a gifted young citizen. Here also we see the meaning of the curious provision limiting a junior's membership to the period before his fortieth year. At this age public duties will no doubt claim him, and his retirement from the Council will make room for another young citizen to profit from association in its studies; later if he becomes a guardian or a euthynos, or receives an award of merit, he may re-enter as a senior member. These provisions of the *Laws* recall the program laid down in the *Republic* whereby a period of higher

18 This at least is my interpretation of the $\tau\tilde{\omega}\nu$ $\tau\sigma\iota\sigma\acute{v}\tau\omega\nu$ in 968c 3. On this difficult text see below, Note 22.

study is followed by service in administrative posts, and this again followed by alternate periods of study and public office.

There is another more picturesque reason why this Council may best be a "mixture of young and old" (951d). Its purpose is not merely the study of law and justice in the abstract, but the observation, protection, and improvement of the particular laws under which they all live (962b). Since the Council is to be the head of the state (to revert to the metaphor that is in the background of Plato's thought throughout), and since a head requires keen sense organs as well as memory and intelligence if it is to be an adequate "savior," we need younger men in the Council to serve as its eyes and ears, and to report to the older men what they see around them in the state. Together they will then take counsel as to the meaning of these reports and the means necessary for protecting the state (961d, 964e).

There is no parallel to this Council in the government of any historical Greek city that we know of.[19] But the actual institution from which Plato's imaginary Council is derived is not hard to find. Its studies bear an unmistakable resemblance to those cultivated in Plato's Academy, and the purpose they are intended to serve is identical with one important end to which the Academy was dedicated—perhaps its most important end in Plato's eyes—viz. to apply philosophy to the saving of the city-state. Like the Academy, it will have wise men from abroad associated with it from time to time; for Plato prescribes that when a theoros comes from another land, interested "like our own theoroi" in observing and learning, he shall be received by the educator or by someone else who has been awarded aristeia; and associating with men of this sort (συνὼν τούτων τισίν) he shall be both a teacher and a learner, apparently for as long a time as he sees fit (953cd). Among the courtesies extended to such a distinguished visitor would undoubtedly be admission to the morning meetings of the Council. Plato's Nocturnal Council will differ from his Academy in that its members will be primarily important officers of government, an indication, no doubt, that at Athens Plato would have liked

---

[19] Gernet (cvi) points out the existence of a νυκτερινὸς σύλλογος in Cyme in Aeolia that exercised jurisdiction over the "kings" (Plut. *Questiones Graecae* 2), but adds that the expression may be the choice of Plutarch the Platonist. Rivaud (*Hist. de la phil.* 1, 209) says that this body appears in the *Critias*, and suggests that it is an institution taken from the Cretans; but no references are given in support of either statement, and I can find no substantiation for them. All the aristocratic councils that we know of lacked what is essential in the Platonic institution, viz. its preoccupation with the theory or science of law.

to see a closer connection between the wise men in his group and the statesmen who held power. His Council also provides for the inclusion of the nonpolitical theoros, the man who, like Plato himself, had traveled widely and had much to contribute to public counsels. We have seen that a theoros who has observed foreign laws and customs may be able to correct something amiss in the laws of his own country. Thus Plato in constructing his model state makes provision for the establishment of something like the Academy to which he has devoted the greater part of his life, in a form which he thought would most effectively assure its influence upon public affairs.

No procedure is mentioned whereby the Nocturnal Council is to make its insight and intelligence effective in the affairs of the state. Yet it is clearly intended to exert influence, both in criticizing and making amendments and supplements to the laws, and in evaluating the persons who are to exercise authority (962b). In an earlier passage (952bc) it is empowered to hear and judge the reports of theoroi who return from foreign travel, to commend them, and to decree special honors for them if they have brought back something of value to the state. On the other hand, if a theoros appears to have been corrupted by his experiences abroad they may require him to retire to private life (ἰδιώτης ζήτω), making no pretence to teach his fellowmen (μηδενὶ συγγιγνέσθω ... προσποιούμενος εἶναι σοφός). This judgment is obviously a command which the returned theoros must obey or be subject to prosecution. In a still earlier passage (909a) the Councillors are appointed to instruct and admonish a person who has been imprisoned for atheism, and they will presumably have authority to judge whether or not he is to be released at the end of his five-year sentence. These are the only explicit responsibilities assigned to the Council, and they are obviously of minor importance. This absence of legal powers commensurate with the functions which the Council is designed to accomplish is indeed puzzling and is the basis of the criticism frequently made that it is a useless appendage to Plato's construction.[20]

Yet a little reflection will show us that there are many ways whereby the Council could influence public policy in an interpretative and advisory capacity. We have already seen how it could assist promising young men to become leaders in the state by selecting them for associate membership. Since its members will include all the

[20] See the criticisms cited in Note 2 above.

euthynoi and the ten senior guardians, its influence upon both these bodies would surely be considerable, even though neither of them should be legally bound to follow its lead. Any formal proposals for revision of the laws—such proposals would be submitted by the guardians, we have assumed, to the council and assembly—would be influenced both in form and substance by the studies of the Nocturnal Council. Its influence would likewise be great in the day-by-day administrative interpretation and expansion of the law. No statute can ever prescribe for all conceivable contingencies, as Plato recognizes in the *Politicus*, and an officer might well need guidance in the exercise of the discretion left to him; or a guardian or a euthynos might be in doubt whether to proceed against an inferior officer for abuse of his discretion. In such cases the Nocturnal Council, with its daily meetings, could readily be consulted.

Furthermore it is hardly correct to regard the Nocturnal Council as a superfluous appendage when we realize that its function, as we have examined it in detail in the preceding pages, appears to be quite distinct from that assigned to any of the boards of officers. Its function is not adjudication, nor administration, nor deliberation and decision on matters of public policy, but education and inquiry; and the distinctness of this function remains, even though most of its members will themselves be administrators or judges, and even though the ultimate purpose of their studies is the wise conduct of public affairs. Thus the Council provides for something additional to what has been set up, an addition clearly necessary if one believes, as Plato does—and as most civilized societies after him have done—that there should be provision for advanced studies in law and government. Nor is it correct to say that the Council does not articulate with Plato's other institutions; one might better say that it articulates all too well. The chief criticism that one could make is that it would be difficult for it to carry on disinterested inquiry when most of its members have important political responsibilities, and when the ultimate purpose of such inquiry is so clearly defined by the moral interests of the society. It would be better to have less of this kind of articulation. From the perspective of today it appears probable that Plato's Academy, poorly articulated as it was with the government of Athens, served its city far better in the long run than an institution of this sort could have done.

If we keep the distinctness of this function in mind we shall be able to deal better with another criticism often advanced. Some interpreters have understood the absence of any legal determination of the powers of the Nocturnal Council as implying a grant of omnicompetence. If this is true, then the Council is above the law, and its introduction here at the end contradicts Plato's purpose of establishing a state in which law is sovereign. There is indeed a passage on the very last page that suggests this extreme interpretation. "If, my dear friends, our divine Council really should come into being, we must put the city in its hands (παραδοτέον τούτῳ τὴν πόλιν). None of our legislators of the present, I think I can say, would dispute this. We shall have brought into living reality what a short time ago in our discussion we apprehended only as a dream ... if we have chosen these men with care, instructed them appropriately, and when instructed have established them in the acropolis of our land, to become finished guardians of our safety, such as we have never seen the like of before" (969bc). Here we are back at the *Republic*, one is inclined to say, the philosopher-guardians installed in the acropolis, the city completely in their hands. In terms of the usual interpretation of the *Republic* as advocating the rule of a select few, untrammeled by laws or customs or traditions,[21] this would indeed be a complete repudiation of the substance of what Plato has been laboring to establish in all the previous work. Rather than hang such a momentous and inherently implausible conclusion upon a single passage, it would be better to see if another interpretation is possible.

This passage is a kind of peroration, and one should recognize that a peroration does not always contain the most precise statement of a speaker's or writer's thought. Παραδοτέον τούτῳ τὴν πόλιν is obviously too vague to support an inference as to the legal powers of the Nocturnal Council; it may simply express Plato's conviction of the importance of philosophical inquiry and insight, and of this Council as the body designed to provide the wisdom needed to prevent his state from deteriorating. I have already shown how it could provide such wisdom and philosophical guidance without being invested with legal sovereignty, and the παραδοτέον passage is quite compatible with the assumption that the Council is not intended to upset the rule of law. Except for this passage there is nothing in the *Laws* to warrant the contrary interpretation, nor any evidence that Plato intends to give it power to override the law. Its members, most of

---

[21] An interpretation which is examined and rejected in Chapter XII.

them officeholders, are always subject to the numerous checks that Plato's law provides. It has no power to impose penalties. For example, the theoros whom it thinks to have been corrupted by his experience abroad is to live without penalty, provided that he does not meddle with education and legislation; if he does his case is to come before the courts for judgment by the regular processes of justice (952cd). This prescription looks as if it were definitely intended to forestall a possible misinterpretation of the Council's powers. Again, if the atheist whom the Council has been appointed to admonish has not been reformed but offends against the law after being released, he has to be convicted again in court (ἐὰν . . . ὀφείλῃ αὖθις τὴν τοιαύτην δίκην, 909a) before being punished. These details indicate that it is Plato's intention to have the Council act within the laws already laid down, or those to be established regarding it (968c).[22] Is it possible that on the very last page Plato completely reverses himself, and repudiates not only what he has just said, but also the fundamental principles he has insisted upon in three hundred and forty-five previous pages of text? To assume this is to violate all sound criteria of interpretation.

Far from being inconsistent with the rule of law, the Nocturnal Council seems to be essential for the maintenance of that principle. Every society in which the sovereignty of law is affirmed has to pro-

---

[22] 968c is certainly cryptic and possibly corrupt: οὐκέτι νόμους . . . περὶ τῶν τοιούτων δυνατόν ἐστιν νομοθετεῖν, πρὶν ἂν κοσμηθῇ—τότε δὲ κυρίους ὢν αὐτοὺς δεῖ γίγνεσθαι νομοθετεῖν—ἀλλὰ κτλ. Τῶν τοιούτων refers, I am sure, to the organization of the higher studies of the Council, the matter on which the Athenian himself has just offered to give assistance and of which he says he has had much experience (968b). It obviously refers to the same thing as τὰ τοιαῦτα two lines later, where it is said that to arrange such matters properly would involve διδαχὴ μετὰ συνουσίας πολλῆς, i.e. just that joint study and inquiry which the Council itself, after it has been established, is to pursue. In other words, the Council must already have been engaged in these studies before any rules can be laid down concerning the order in which they are to pursue them—a paradoxical condition that is well reflected in the puzzling syntax of the passage. For a similar interpretation, see Harold Cherniss, *Gnomon*, xxv, 1953, 373-374.

But most translators and commentators have strangely taken τῶν τοιούτων as referring to the general powers of the Council. Some, i.e. Ritter (*Kommentar*, 364) and Bury, think the Council itself is to determine what authority it is to have, evidently taking κυρίους ὢν αὐτοὺς κτλ as the subject of the following νομοθετεῖν; while Jowett, Apelt, England, Diès and Robin—either taking νομοθετεῖν as an indirect imperative, or supposing ἡμᾶς to be understood as its subject—read only that further legislation will be necessary as to the powers the Council is to have.

Whatever its precise meaning, this passage, with its use of νόμους and its repetition of νομοθετεῖν, indicates that Plato was to the last concerned with the rule of law.

vide some method for interpreting and expanding its inherited rules. Instead of the ad hoc legislative commissions set up at Athens whenever the need of revision was felt, and as an alternative to the jurisdiction of the popular courts over administrative interpretation, Plato would set up a standing body of experienced and learned persons to act as a permanent agency for the study of the laws.[23] The Athenian practices are a tribute to the versatility of the average citizen at Athens; but, as Sir Henry Maine remarked, "no durable system of jurisprudence could be developed in this way."[24] In setting up his Nocturnal Council and in giving it something of the character of a learned body, Plato is providing a remedy for what modern students generally recognize as a glaring defect in Greek law. If Plato's intentions are realized, the members of the Nocturnal Council will be not mere empiricists, but scientific and philosophical students of the law. Something like the function he here assigns to them was discharged in later antiquity by the jurisconsults under the Roman emperors. We might plausibly argue that Plato's *Laws*, through its influence upon the Stoics and Cicero, was an important factor in the rise of this class of professional jurists at Rome.

This institution is one of Plato's most striking inventions. In the combination it proposes to bring about between philosophical insight and legal concepts and practices, nothing that we know of can be compared with it in Greek law and politics. It springs not only from Plato's conviction of the importance of philosophy as the guide of life, but also from a perception—which has not often been credited to him—that philosophical reason must be employed not in the void, but upon the concepts and principles of the law, which are matters of historical experience, not a priori inventions.[25] This is the way Plato himself proceeds in his own legislation, and it is the way he wishes his successors to follow. Just as Plato's Academy has been the prototype of countless later institutions of higher learning, so his Nocturnal Council can be regarded as the first of the long series of learned bodies of jurists, commissions of experts, and law councils that have been set up since his time to act as guides to legislators. "If you frame your state aright," says the Athenian Stranger after having demonstrated the need for such a Council, "you will achieve high

[23] Cf. Henry Sidgwick's proposal for a Law Council; *Elements of Politics*, 2nd edn. London, 1897, 482.
[24] *Ancient Law*, 44 (Everyman's Library edn.).
[25] See the penetrating remarks of Gernet, ccv-ccvi.

renown, or at least will gain the reputation of being the boldest of your successors."[26]

EXCURSUS F. PHILIPPUS
OF OPUS

The question of the changes made in the text of the *Laws* after Plato's death is peculiarly relevant when we are considering the Nocturnal Council. According to Diogenes Laertius, our earliest source of information on this point, some persons in his day said that Philippus of Opus τοὺς Νόμους μετέγραψεν, ὄντας ἐν κηρῷ (III, 37). This Philippus is apparently the same as the philosopher referred to in Suidas (s.v. φιλόσοφος) who divided the *Laws* into twelve books (adding a thirteenth, i.e. the *Epinomis*, said to be his own composition) and is probably also identical with the Philippus from Medma mentioned by Stephanus of Byzantium (s.v. Μέδμη), and also with Φίλιππος ὁ Μενδαῖος (or Μεδναῖος) described by Proclus (*Com. on Euclid*, 67f., Friedlein) as a mathematician and a pupil of Plato's. (For these identifications see von Fritz in RE s.v. Philippus, 2351ff.) He has also been identified with the ἀστρολόγος mentioned in the *Academicorum Index Herculaneum* (ed. Mekler, 13) as having been Plato's pupil and secretary at the end of Plato's life.

If these identifications are accepted, Philippus is revealed as the author of numerous works, ranging from mathematics and natural science to ethics and theology. But the nature and extent of the editorial work he did on the *Laws* is left uncertain. The μετέγραψεν in the Diogenes Laertius passage may mean either "copied" or "revised." Likewise the significance of ἐν κηρῷ ("in wax") is not clear. Is that a metaphorical way of saying that the work was in process of composition, or that it was essentially finished, like the wax-covered model in a studio ready to be cast in bronze, as suggested by Bergk (*op.cit.* infra, 44)? Olympiodorus (*Prol. in Plat.* 25) quotes Proclus as saying that Plato did not have time to correct (διορθώσασθαι) the *Laws* before his death; and in the previous chapter Olympiodorus says that Plato left the *Laws* ἀδιορθώτους καὶ συγκεχυμένους, i.e. not only uncorrected (which might mean lacking only the final touches) but confused (which implies something different). "If the work now seems properly organized, that is due not to Plato, but

---

[26] 969ab. Bury's translation.

to a certain Philippus of Opus, who later became head (διάδοχος) of Plato's school." One suspects that Olympiodorus, apart from his misinformation about Philippus (he was never διάδοχος of the Academy), merely gives an embellishment of what he found in Proclus. (See Vanhoutte, *La Philosophie politique de Platon dans les Lois*, 3-4.) From this evidence we cannot say whether Philippus simply prepared a corrected edition—which is what διόρθωσις would mean, and which corresponds to what Cicero (*Att.* XIII, 21, 5) says was the custom with regard to the publication of Plato's dialogues—or whether his work involved revision and reorganization.

The latter alternative was once widely accepted by Platonic scholars, probably as a result of Zeller's attitude toward the *Laws*. Though in later life Zeller retracted his early judgment that the *Laws* was spurious, he continued to regard it as puzzlingly different in style and content from the rest of the dialogues, and treated it as a sort of appendage to Plato's philosophy. The acceptance of the revisionist hypothesis invited further speculation regarding the nature and extent of the modifications introduced by Philippus. Ivor Bruns (*Plato's Gesetze vor und nach ihrer Herausgabe durch Philippos von Opus*, 1880) supposed that Philippus found, in addition to the almost completed work dealing with the Cretan colony, fragments of another more "idealistic" treatment of a similar theme by Plato, and that the similarity of the material tempted him to make them into one work. The account of the Cretan colony, according to Bruns, embraced what we now have from the beginning of Book III to 960b in Book XII; the fragments of the earlier idealistic work are to be found in Book I (from the beginning to 632d) and in Book XII (960b to the end); whereas the remainder of Book I and all of Book II consist of Philippus' own work, with extensive use of material that was originally connected with the account of education in Book VII. Three years after Bruns' work, and admittedly stimulated by it, Theodor Bergk put forward an even more extravagant hypothesis (in *Fünf Abhandlungen zur Geschichte der griechischen Philosophie und Astronomie*, Leipzig, 1883, 41-116). From 739a-e, where Plato declares his intention to describe the constitution not only of a second-best but also of a third-best state, Bergk supposed that this intention was in fact carried out, but that the account of the second-best constitution, the one nearest the ideal, was almost completely destroyed through some "unfortunate accident," and that what we have is in the main the second part of Plato's project; Philippus, not knowing Plato's larger intention, took the second part as the whole and fitted into it and around it the surviving fragments of the lost earlier part. Ernest Praetorius (*De Legibus Platonicis a Philippo Opuntio Retractatis*, Bonn, 1883) attributed to Philippus a complete revision and alteration of Plato's work, such that "almost every page betrays the hand of Philippus" and "nowhere will we find the words of Plato himself." Max Krieg (*Die Überarbeitung der Platonischen Gesetze durch Philipp von Opus*, Freiburg, 1896) took issue with Praetorius and reasserted the more modest hypothesis of Bruns, which he followed with minor reservations.

These speculations, particularly those of Bruns and Bergk, were subjected to a thorough examination by Theodor Gomperz (*Platonische Aufsätze*, III, Vienna, 1902), who showed so clearly the lack of evidence to support the special hypotheses they require, and the questionable character of the critical principles relied upon by their authors, that no attempt has since been made to revive them. At the same time Gomperz adduced impressive evidence of the unity of the *Laws*, in the multitude of its cross references from one part to another (all of them, with minor exceptions, accurate) and in the occasional passages of retrospect and anticipation which reveal that the author had his whole plan firmly in view. It is incredible that such a pervasive and deep-seated unity could have been produced by an editor. Evidence that Philippus respected the integrity of Plato's text as he found it is that he retained certain contradictions (such as that between the legal marriage age as stated in 772d and that given in 721b and 785b) which could hardly have escaped his notice and would have been very easy to remove. I have shown above (Excursus D) another instance, his retention of two versions of the election of the guardians. There are numerous other minor incoherencies in the *Laws*, many of which are mentioned in these pages, which would have been easy to remove; they suggest rather that the work lacked final revision by its author than that it was mutilated by a later editor.

The prevailing view at present among those who have studied the *Laws* with care is that the work as we have it comes from Plato. This is admitted by the severest of its recent critics, Gerhard Müller (*Studien zu den Platonischen Nomoi*, 1951), who regards as an interpolation only a short section (732d 8 to 734e 2) which contains a theory of the relation of virtue to pleasure that he cannot regard as genuinely Platonic. But to exclude altogether the hand of Philippus is probably an opposite extreme of error. Ancient literary conventions would have required that an editor fill up any lacunae as best he could, and add sentences of transition between separate parts if Plato had not already supplied them; and there are occasional signs of such editorial touches (e.g. in the sentence introducing Book III, and in the sentence commented on in Excursus D). Nevertheless the "axiom that every word comes from Plato" (as von Fritz puts it, *op.cit.* 2359) is an excellent heuristic principle, forcing us to try to explain any obscurities we may find through a more penetrating understanding of Plato's intentions, rather than by hastily blaming Plato's posthumous editor.

PART THREE

PLATO'S PRINCIPLES

CHAPTER X

THE MIXED CONSTITUTION

ALTHOUGH Plato has been regarded from antiquity as one of the first expounders, if not the originator, of the theory of the mixed constitution,[1] this term—πολιτεία μεικτή or μεμειγμένη—occurs nowhere in the *Laws*. The concept that serves as guide to the Athenian legislator in the designing of his constitution is the mean—the μέτριον, or μετριότης—and it is upon this that the theory of the mixed constitution depends.

Of constitutions there are, so to speak, two mother forms from which we can rightly say that the others have been derived. One of these we may properly call monarchy, the other democracy; and of these the Persians represent the extreme of the one, and we [Athenians] the extreme of the other; while almost all the rest, as I said, are variously blended of these two. A constitution must necessarily partake of them both, if there is to be freedom and friendship, together with wisdom. . . . Now the Persians have cultivated the monarchical element alone, and we the element of freedom, more than is proper; neither of us has preserved the mean between them (τὰ μέτρια τούτων), but your states, the Lacedaemonian and the Cretan, have done so more. 693de

The Athenian adds that the Persian and Athenian states were at one time more moderate, and goes on to describe at some length the change in the Persian empire from the relative freedom it enjoyed under Cyrus to the despotism of later days, and the opposite decline of Athens from the moderate constitution of the time before the Persian Wars to the extreme of freedom that now characterizes it. Thus when the Athenians and the Persians followed the mean (μετριότης) between despotism (τοῦ δεσπόζειν) and freedom (τοῦ ἐλευθεριάσαι) they prospered, but the deviation toward an extreme (ἐπὶ τὸ ἄκρον) was profitable in neither case (701e). This passage, occurring at the end of the third book and concluding the preliminary discussion of principles, may properly be taken as supplying the clue to the legislation for Cleinias' Cretan colony which begins with the following book. The legislator must attain the mean between des-

---

[1] Arist. *Pol.* 1265b 26-35; Barker, 340; Sabine, *History of Political Theory*, 77, and *Cicero on the Commonwealth*, Ohio State University Press, 1929, 32; Gomperz, *Griechische Denker*, Leipzig, 1896-1909, II, 502-503; Kurt von Fritz, *The Theory of the Mixed Constitution in Antiquity*, Columbia University Press, 1954, 78ff.

potism and freedom if he would bring about wisdom, freedom, and friendship in his state.

There was nothing new—nor would Plato claim there was—in this idea of a middle way. It is but the political application of one of the oldest and most widely accepted canons of Greek life and thought. That the good for man is to be found in the avoidance of excess, that to be happy he must respect the limit—this principle had long been the recurrent theme of sages and poets, and every worshipper at Delphi would be reminded of it in the solemn warning μηδὲν ἄγαν inscribed in the temple. It had already found political expression, notably in Aeschylus' admonition in the *Eumenides* to follow the middle way between despotism and anarchy, and in the idealized portrait of Athens that Euripides puts into the mouth of Theseus in the *Suppliants*.[2] When Solon sought advice from the oracle at Delphi before making his reforms, he is said to have been told to "sit in the middle of the boat"—which he took as an injunction to follow the middle way,[3] and this is what he claims to have done. In the strife between the demos and "those who possessed power and wealth" he says that he refused to accept in full the claims of either side, but was content to alleviate the plight of the one party and diminish the privileges of the other, thus giving all a share—though not an equal share—in the state, and restoring the community that was in danger of being broken apart.[4] This Solonian moderation seems to have been explicitly invoked by the group of conservatives led by Theramenes during the closing years of the fifth century.[5] At this time the positions of the two parties were reversed; it was the few who were now in revolt against the excessive claims of the demos, and the intent of the moderates, in appealing to the ancestral constitution of Solon, was to reinstate the Solonian balance. Theramenes' defense before the boule, as recorded by Xenophon, bears a striking resemblance to Solon's defense of himself in his poems. In answer to Critias' charge that he had been a "trimmer," willing to accommodate his views to all occasions, Theramenes asserted that he had pleased neither the democrats nor the oligarchs, but had opposed both—the former in their contention that true (καλή) democracy could only be established when "the slaves and the poor who would sell the state

---

[2] Aesch. *Eumen.* 529ff.; Eur. *Suppl.* 238-245.
[3] Plut. *Solon* 14.
[4] See the fragment of the poem quoted by Aristotle (*Const. Ath.* xii, 1).
[5] On the fifth-century controversy regarding Solon's "constitution" and Plato's interest in it, see Chapter III.

for a drachma" take part in the government, and the latter in their belief that true oligarchy means the subjection of the city to the tyranny of the few.[6]

Theramenes and his followers played a part in both the oligarchic revolutions at Athens, and on both occasions the policies of the extremists with whom he was collaborating forced him eventually into opposition. In the second of these revolutions, the one that led to the establishment of the Thirty, the extremists found it necessary to remove him before they could proceed with their plans, and he was condemned to death by the "lovely Critias."[7] His apparent willingness to compromise, up to a point, with the oligarchic extremists, and his lack of foresight as to the consequences of his collaboration, have made him rather a sorry figure in the eyes of most historians; but he had substantial admirers in antiquity. Thucydides praises the constitution of Theramenes that was voted in 411. It is the first time in my experience, he says, that the Athenians have been well governed; and he characterizes this constitution as a "measured fusion" (μετρία ξύγκρασις) of the interests of the many and the interests of the few.[8] Aristotle, three-quarters of a century later, lists him with Nicias and Thucydides (the son of Melesias) as one of the three best politicians of Athens' later days, though he admits that not everybody would put Theramenes in such company.[9] It is quite likely that Plato shared this admiration, and that Theramenes' presence in the group of revolutionaries was one of the circumstances that led him to expect something good to follow from the overthrow of the democracy. The revulsion of feeling he experienced when he saw to what extremes events were tending was therefore similar to that shown by Theramenes himself; and the death of this leader in defense of his moderate principles must have impressed them more firmly on the memory of Plato and others to whom they were already congenial.

But to conceive of this middle way as resulting from a mixture of the two extremes involves a further step in theory and suggests that some philosophical influence, probably of a Pythagorean sort, had been at work upon the older common-sense doctrine. In the Pythagorean theory of continued proportion the nature of the middle

[6] Xen. *Hell.* II, iii, 48.　　　[7] Xen. *Hell.* II, iii, 56.
[8] Thuc. VIII, 97; cf. Fuks, *The Ancestral Constitution*, 8.
[9] *Const. Ath.* XXVIII, 5. The "one man" referred to in *Pol.* 1296a 38 is usually taken to be Theramenes. For a modern attempt to brighten his reputation, see Perrin in *Am. Hist. Rev.* IX, 1904, 649-669.

or mean term is constituted by its relation to the two extremes. In arithmetic proportion it falls short of the one extreme and exceeds the other by the same absolute amount; in geometric proportion the one extreme bears to the mean the same ratio as the mean bears to the other extreme; and in harmonic proportion the mean is determined by the application of an identical fraction to the two extremes, in the one case to diminish and in the other case to augment it.[10] These mathematical formulas not only give precision to the popular concept of the mean, but they also suggest that the mean carries in itself proportionate elements of the two extremes. All these types of proportion and their formulas were known in the fourth century, and the first two certainly (and probably also the other) in the fifth century.

Plato's interest in the mathematical theory of proportion is well known. "Geometrical equality has a mighty power among both gods and men," he declares, for example, in the *Gorgias* (508a); and in

[10] More clearly in algebraic language:

Arithmetic proportion: $a-b = b-c$; i.e. $\dfrac{a-b}{b-c} = \dfrac{a}{a}$; e.g. 3, 2, 1.

Geometric proportion: $\dfrac{a}{b} = \dfrac{b}{c}$; i.e. $\dfrac{a-b}{b-c} = \dfrac{a}{b}$; e.g. 8, 4, 2.

Harmonic proportion: $a - \dfrac{a}{n} = b = c + \dfrac{c}{n}$; i.e. $\dfrac{a-b}{b-c} = \dfrac{a}{c}$; e.g. 6, 4, 3.

It will be noted that in arithmetic proportion the ratio $\dfrac{a}{b}$ (when a, b, c are in order of decreasing magnitude) is less than the ratio $\dfrac{b}{c}$; in harmonic proportion $\dfrac{a}{b}$ is greater than $\dfrac{b}{c}$; whereas in geometric proportion these ratios are equal. The later Pythagoreans gave a political interpretation to these characteristics of the equations. The geometric proportion is democratic, for it represents equality of ratios; the arithmetic is oligarchic, for it symbolizes the greater power enjoyed by the less important parts of the state, the rich; and the harmonic is aristocratic, for here the more important members—the wise—enjoy the greater power. This interpretation goes back to Archytas, if the fragments attributed to him are genuine (Stob. *Flor.* XLIII, 133—i.e. II, 137, Meineke; for an exposition and commentary on this passage, see Armand Delatte, *Essai sur la politique pythagoricienne*, Paris, 1922, 95ff.). There is no hint of this in Plato; the only proportion he uses in an ethical or political context is the geometric (*Gorg.* 465bc). Equality of ratios is for him the only true equality (cf. 757bc, 744bc); and it is this, I suggest, that is meant in the cryptic tradition (Diog. III, 23) reporting that Plato declined to legislate for the Megalopolitans when he heard that they were unwilling to accept "equality." On Plato's knowledge of mathematical proportion, see Paul Tannery, "L'education platonicienne," *Revue Philosophique* XI, 1881, 290-292, 294n.

the *Timaeus* he uses it to explain the relation of the four primary bodies and to construct the world soul (31b-36d). It is almost certain that this mathematical conception of the mean is present in Plato's thought of the political mean, and it may be the source of the idea that the mean in politics is a mixture of its two extremes. But it is possible that this theory is earlier than Plato.[11] It is suggested by Thucydides' characterization of Theramenes' constitution as a "measured fusion" of the many and the few. If this passage reflects Theramenes' (not merely Thucydides') idea of this constitution, it would indicate that Theramenes had come under some philosophical influence of the sort just discussed. Diodorus tells us that he had studied philosophy with Socrates,[12] which sounds plausible; and if the historical Socrates was intrigued by Pythagorean ideas, as the Socrates of Plato's dialogues certainly is, then Theramenes could have got this conception of the political mean from Socrates. But these assumptions are too uncertain to permit any sure inference from them. All we can safely say is that, however the idea of mixture came to be associated with the mean, this association would be strongly reenforced by Pythagorean mathematics in the minds of those who were acquainted with it, as Plato was.

The extreme terms in Plato's political proportion—the two "mother forms" of constitution of which every rightly ordered state must have a share—are said to be monarchy and democracy. They are mentioned later in an incidental reaffirmation of the general principle: "Our constitution must always keep the middle path between the monarchical and the democratic constitutions" (756e; cf. 759b). But is this what Plato really means? Aristotle, who quotes this formula, objects that there seems to be no monarchical element at all in Plato's state; its features seem rather to be taken from oligarchy and democracy; and in another passage he actually describes Plato's state as intended to be a μέση between oligarchy and democracy.[13] Aris-

---

[11] Later writers were certainly inclined to find it earlier. Plutarch (*Per.* 3) calls the constitution of Cleisthenes a πολιτεία ἄριστα κεκραμένη πρὸς ὁμόνοιαν καὶ σωτηρίαν; and Isocrates regards the ancient Athenian constitution as a δημοκρατία . . . ἀριστοκρατίᾳ μεμιγμένη (XII, 153). Fuks (*op.cit.* 12-13) suggests that the tradition of Cleisthenes' mixed or aristocratic constitution stems from one or more of the conservative Attidographers.

[12] Diod. XIV, 5, 1-3. See Chapter II, Note 2.

[13] *Pol.* 1265b 28ff., 1266a 2ff. In the second of these passages Aristotle actually writes "tyranny" for the "monarchy" of Plato's text, but corrects himself in the sentence immediately following. In the *Politicus* (291e) Plato regards monarchy as taking two forms, kingship and tyranny. Since tyranny is the more extreme form,

totle is literally correct; there is no provision for kings in Plato's constitution, not even for a king as emasculated of his ancient powers as was the Athenian βασιλεύς. But it is an error to take monarchy in such a literal sense. There was no monarchy in the Roman government in Polybius' time, yet Polybius regards it as a mixture of aristocracy, democracy, and monarchy, the monarchical element being found in the power of the consuls.[14] Nor is there any hint that Plato thinks the constitution of ancient Athens, which he praises, owed its virtue to the presence of monarchy in any literal sense (cf. 698b). Kingship had disappeared from Athens long before the constitution of which he is speaking.

Obviously we have to find Plato's monarchical element in some more general feature of political constitutions. As a first approximation we can say that what Plato means is some recognized center or source of authority in the state, an ἀρχή or ἀρχαί, relatively independent of the changeable and often conflicting wishes of the demos. In a sense this condition is satisfied in any government at all with officers possessing stated powers; but in Plato's sense it would not be satisfied by the annually selected officers in the Athenian democracy, strictly limited in competence and indistinguishable in personal qualities from the other citizens over whom they exercised authority. Our officers must be like the warp in the social fabric, he says elsewhere, able to give strength and structure to the softer and more pliable woof (734e-735a). The source of authority in the state should be, Plato obviously thinks, one or more officers (whether they are called kings is unimportant)[15] more carefully selected and possessing much greater authority than the annually elected officers in a Greek democracy. This condition is certainly fulfilled in the constitution he outlines later. The guardians of the laws are a board possessing powers without parallel in the democracies of Plato's time; the board of

it correctly expresses Plato's idea of what is to be avoided, though not so well his idea of what is to be included in the mean. The other objection that Aristotle raises in 1266a 4 is more puzzling. Tyranny and democracy could hardly be called constitutions at all, he says, or if so they are the worst. But this is precisely what one would expect of extremes, as Aristotle himself clearly recognizes in his doctrine of the mean. Cf. *Pol.* 1294b 13ff., and his own account of μίξις in *De Gen. et Corr.* 328a 32ff.

[14] Polyb. VI, v, 11-12.

[15] The constitution Plato proposes for the faction-ridden city of Syracuse, which has many features similar to those of the *Laws*, actually provides for three kings (*Ep. VIII* 355e-356b), but this reflects the peculiar circumstances of the situation in Syracuse.

euthynoi is almost equally important; and the court of select judges is invested with a legal supremacy before which these other officers, powerful as they are, can be called to account. There was a similar trio of powerful officers in the Spartan constitution—the kings, the elders, and the ephors. Such officers, by virtue of their inherent quality, their long tenure of office, and the experience which this brings (in this respect the Spartan ephors, being annually elected, are an exception), and the wide range of their competence, should be able not merely to govern a society, but also to set its tone and determine its character. Such is the role that has frequently been played in history by powerful monarchs, and Plato is well aware of this aspect of the government that a king or tyrant can give his people. In one passage of the *Laws* he asserts his earlier doctrine expressed in the *Republic* that the easiest and quickest way of changing the laws of a city is through the leadership of a wise and powerful tyrant (711bc).

But it is essential that this monarchical element be prudent (σώ-φρον) and moderate (μέτριον), otherwise the other two aims of the legislator—freedom and friendship—are jeopardized. Ruthless and stupid exercise of power destroys both. This is the lesson the Athenian draws from the experience of the Persians. Under Cyrus the subjects had a measure of freedom and equality with their king; if any one among them was wise and able to give good advice, the king showed no jealousy, but permitted freedom of speech and rewarded those who advised well. Soldiers were friendly with their generals and eagerly exposed themselves to dangers. Thus wisdom was placed at the disposal of the common interest, and all things prospered because of their freedom and friendship and community of mind (694ab). But the despotism of the later Persian kings destroyed this friendship and community; and when this has been destroyed, the deliberation of the ruler is no longer directed to the good of his subjects but to the preservation and extension of his power; and when it is necessary for him to call upon his people to fight, there is no common interest to make them willing to risk danger; and although the Great King has countless subjects, he is so poor in real defenders of the state that he has to employ mercenaries from abroad (697c-e). This is probably, like Xenophon's, an idealized portrait of Cyrus,[16] but it reflects the real weakness of the Persian

[16] Though 694c shows that Plato thought Cyrus' excellence as a general and a ruler were due to nature rather than education—"ein Seitenhieb auf den Kyros des Xenophon," as Wilamowitz (*Platon* I, 666n.) points out.

empire in the fourth century as it was revealed, again by Xenophon, in his memorable account of the expedition of the Ten Thousand. Thus it is essential in Plato's opinion that this monarchical element be moderate. Its rule must be a rule over willing subjects, whose obedience does not have to be exacted by force (690c, 832c). This is one criterion that he uses in the *Politicus* for distinguishing between kingship and tyranny (291e), and it is the "willing obedience" of the ancient Athenians that he emphasizes as the character of their moderate constitution (698b, 700a, 701b). "We must not have great and unmixed (ἄμεικτοι) offices, for we want our city to be free and wise and friendly to itself" (693b).

The problem of constructing a genuine executive in the state, wise and powerful enough to give direction to the people's life and serve their long-term interests effectively, without becoming so powerful as to be able to destroy itself and them through ignorance and self-interest—this is a problem of political craftsmanship whose importance and whose delicacy Plato seems to have been the first thinker to realize. The executive must be an effective sovereign power, yet it is a sovereignty that is de jure limited; for the real sovereign in Plato's state is to be the law, or the Nous of which the laws are the expression (713a, 714a). We shall examine later Plato's highly original contribution to the solution of this problem. For the moment we should note that the plurality of offices that embody the monarchical element is an obvious expedient for moderating its power. This is what gives Plato's monarchical element the appearance of oligarchy that Aristotle notes; and the mean he aims at could well be described, in terms of contemporary political thought, as a middle way between oligarchy and democracy. For in Plato's times it was oligarchy which, in the main, claimed to stand for the principle of authority in the state, and democracy that insisted upon the primacy of freedom. Hence from a first look at Plato's institutions one would be inclined to say, as Aristotle does, that most of them seem to be taken from oligarchy and democracy, and that his middle way is a compromise, combination, or mixture of these two extremes. Let us see how far Aristotle's interpretation will take us.

In the previous chapters we have noted elements in Plato's law that his contemporaries would regard as oligarchical and others that they would label as democratic. His conception of citizenship is democratic, as judged by the criterion Aristotle puts forward; there is no property qualification for attending the assembly, for sitting on courts of law, or for holding any of the offices, except a few minor ones, and in these exceptional cases the motive seems to be more a desire to lighten the burdens of citizenship for the poor than to exclude them from honor and office. "In democracies all citizens participate in all the functions of government," says Aristotle.[17] On the other hand we must recognize that any Greek state with a large slave and metic population would seem to us oligarchic, whether or not it called itself a democracy, because of the restriction of full rights in the community to its citizen members. In our sense Athens, as well as Plato's state, would be looked upon as something like an oligarchy. But democratic in our sense is the provision that officers are to be elected by the full citizen body, though Plato's contemporaries would regard this rather as aristocratic, or oligarchical; and his general refusal to use the lot, except to effect a decision among candidates previously elected by voting, would have been regarded as undemocratic. Yet the combination of election and the lot is a device certainly suggested to Plato by procedures in democratic Athens. Plato does not provide pay for attendance at the assembly, for holding office, or for serving on the dicasteries or in the armed forces—definitely a departure from the policy of Athens; and the fine he imposes for nonperformance of public duties is, as Aristotle says, an oligarchical trait. Again Aristotle says that Plato's method of electing the council is oligarchical, but we have had reason to question Aristotle's judgment here, and to recognize in Plato's scheme not a conventional oligarchical proposal, but a novel device—which Aristotle himself elsewhere commends—for obtaining equal representation of different economic classes in the deliberative body and thus improving the quality of its deliberations. Oligarchical clearly is the greater administrative and judicial authority that Plato gives the magistrates in his state, whereas the denial of judicial sovereignty to the popular courts is a marked departure from democratic traditions. But Plato's judicial system as a whole, with its provision for popular participation, repeated consideration, and final decision in difficult cases by especially selected officials, is a compromise in which the democratic and the oligarchical principles are both employed—in this case a

---

[17] *Pol.* 1328b 33; for Aristotle's definition of citizenship, see 1275a 22 and 1275b 6. The confirming evidence for the statements in this and the next few paragraphs will be found in the relevant portions of the previous chapters.

compromise whose originality and judicious character show Plato the political craftsman at his best.

But the most important of Plato's institutions seem to be neither oligarchical nor democratic in the ancient meaning of these terms. The guardians of the laws are a body of officials whose like we find nowhere else in Plato's time, though Aristotle's and Xenophon's references indicate that if such officials existed at all they were to be found in "aristocracies." Their prototype seems to be the Athenian Areopagus, invested with even more dignity and authority than this aristocratic council enjoyed in earlier Athens in the days of the "ancestral democracy." Plato's board of euthynoi is another institution that has no parallel in his time. The purpose it serves—i.e. to assure that every officer should be subject to an equitable accounting at the end of his term—was one which was recognized as legitimate and necessary by Greek states generally, democracies as well as oligarchies; but no state that we know of had a body of such continuing and authoritative character to accomplish this purpose. Finally, Plato's Nocturnal Council is a proposal for introducing into the heart of the political system something of the educational value of the studies in law and government and the relevant higher sciences carried on in the Academy—truly a *proles sine matre* in the political world of Plato's time. These parts of Plato's state are such free creations that they might be claimed by adherents of either oligarchy or democracy if they had a passion for good government; and their importance in the state is so great as to make irrelevant Aristotle's somewhat pedantic inquiry whether Plato's institutions lean more toward oligarchy or democracy.[18] Plato's political imagination rises to heights which Aristotle apparently did not appreciate.

We must therefore look beyond a simple mixture of these familiar

[18] Equally irrelevant is Aristotle's pedantic discussion of the ways in which a blending of these two forms can be accomplished (*Pol.* 1294a 35). He points out that one way is to adopt the institutions of both; for example, to fine the rich for refusing jury service, as in the oligarchies, and at the same time to pay the poor for serving, as was done in Athenian democracy. Another is to follow a middle course between the regulations of each; e.g. if oligarchies insist on a large property qualification for admission to the assembly and democracies on none at all, the middle way is to impose a moderate qualification. Finally, the legislator may adopt one feature from one form and another from the other; for example, the oligarchic practice of filling offices by election, and the democratic absence of property qualifications for office. It is likely that one source of Aristotle's analysis is Plato's procedure in the *Laws*; but the most important of Plato's proposals fall completely outside Aristotle's little logical net.

political devices for an understanding of Plato's doctrine of the "middle way." The antithesis between oligarchy and democracy in Plato's time was itself something more than a controversy over political forms; it was a conflict between social classes, the rich and the poor. This was the fundamental source of faction in Greek political life, as both Plato and Aristotle realize. Plato's solution is to prevent the rise of the problem in his state by making impossible the extremes of wealth and poverty that produce it. Equal and unalienable lots for all citizen families, restriction on ownership of movable property to a maximum of four times the value of the lot—by these measures every citizen is assured of a competence and no citizen can become excessively wealthy. Luxury and poverty are both eliminated by this fundamental law; its aim is to assure a sufficient but modest level of comfort for all citizens—such a competence as suffices for persons who are themselves moderate in their desires—and at the same time to permit some variation as a recognition of differences in industry, skill, or luck. Within these variations the claims of the more prosperous to superior power and position are recognized, but only in minor matters; in fundamental political privileges all citizens are equal. Thus are recognized both the democratic principle of arithmetic equality and the oligarchic equality proportioned to property. The aristocratic idea of equality proportioned to merit is no doubt what Plato aims at; but this mixture of aristocratic and democratic equality is apparently the best that he thinks he can do toward realizing it. Again Plato's law of property sets up a middle way between an economy that permits free sale or disposal of all kinds of property, and a regime that denies altogether the legitimacy of private ownership. Land is to be privately owned, though unalienable and subject to special controls by the state; upon alienation of movable property, above what is necessary as equipment for the lot, there is no restriction. But mortgaging of property of any kind, as well as other transactions characteristic of a capitalist state, are forbidden. The citizens will derive most of their wealth from the soil, a condition that ipso facto makes for moderation, for the sources of greatest gain—trading and money lending—are closed to them.

Despite the recognition of slavery and of a slave population in his state, it seems not to be Plato's intention that his citizens shall be exempt from the care of their property and from personal labor on their land. The "agricultural laws" of 842e seem clearly intended for citi-

zens, not for a noncitizen class of slaves or serfs. There is no glorification of physical labor in Plato; it seems to be regarded as a dis-
agreeable necessity; but the moderation of desires for material goods
that should follow from his legislation means that such labor need
not be excessive. The citizens will have leisure, some more, and some
less, but all of them enough for performing the necessary tasks that
the state imposes and for engaging in the festivals and other acts of
worship and fellowship. The life of Plato's citizens is to be generally
more like a festival than a corvée, a life filled with play, but play
limited by the seriousness with which they must prepare for the
defense of their land and safeguard the laws by which they live.

In education it is more difficult to see the middle way that Plato
extols. In making it compulsory and uniform for all his citizens he
tips the balance definitely toward authority rather than freedom.
This is at least the way it appears to us, and doubtless also it so appeared to many of Plato's contemporaries. Yet within this authoritarian system there are moderating features. It is to be a mixture of
music and gymnastics, as in the *Republic*, in order to prevent an
overdevelopment either of the warlike or of the gentle and philosophic element in human nature. Though compulsory, it is to be
made as much like play as possible, and the tasks assigned must never
be too much for the powers of the young who are to do them. And
though it is uniform for all, there is provision for higher education
for the minority who have an aptitude for it. This minority is the
group on which Plato pins his hopes for the proper filling of the
offices and the wise direction of the state.

In religion there is a clearly discernible middle way, as judged by
the concepts and practices of his time. The encouragement and protection of religion was generally recognized as a function of the state.
But the control and protection usually given was sporadic and un-
calculated. Greek religion had strong centrifugal tendencies, because
of the multiplicity of cults and rites recognized even within a single
state. The great stabilizing influence was the prestige of Apollo's
oracle at Delphi, and Plato puts religion in his state under this authority. He recognizes the distinctness of the sacred law and refrains
—on some occasions clearly in conflict with his personal inclinations—
from legislating contrary to it. All ancient practices and cults that
have the support of the oracle are tolerated, and even new ones, if
sponsored by Apollo or his exegetes, will have to be admitted. In

these respects Plato may be said to have provided for an extreme of religious freedom—one might even say religious anarchy—in his state. On the other hand, private cults that have no oracular support are strictly forbidden; and Plato's law against impiety, though formally only a restatement of the Athenian law, would in effect have seriously limited freedom of discussion on religious matters. His middle way consists in the toleration of all forms of religion sponsored by tradition or the oracle, coupled with repression of all open denial of fundamental religious beliefs. But something has to be added. The very conception of religion that Plato proposes is a middle way: it accepts the old forms, but endeavors to infuse into them the higher morality—and science—of his age, thus effecting an alliance of religion, ethics, and philosophy that persisted through all later antiquity and the Middle Ages that followed.

Finally, we should note another pronounced type of mixture in Plato's state, the mixture of Dorian and Ionian. This is suggested in the very structure of the dialogue, with the Athenian Stranger discoursing upon and correcting the practices of his two Dorian companions. So far as we can see with our present knowledge of Cretan institutions, it is chiefly Spartan and Athenian customs that Plato takes account of; hence we can best get an idea of the nature of his mixture by considering the elements that he takes from these two cities. From Sparta certainly comes the idea of self-containedness, the abstention of the city from commercial and naval enterprise, the rigid discipline of the citizens' activities, and the relatively simple life that he proposes, with its emphasis upon physical training, choral singing and dancing, and the preservation of the old-fashioned canons in music and conduct. Spartan also is the division of the land into equal lots, and the restriction of citizenship to the members of landowning families. But the unalienability of the land, and in general the agrarian aristocracy which is based upon it, have their sources as much in ancient Attica as in Sparta. The idea of compulsory common education again seems to have been suggested by the Spartan agoge; but the purpose and the content of Plato's common education is decidedly different from the Spartan. In purpose it is broadly moral instead of narrowly military; and in content it regards as essential a study of letters and mathematics that the Spartans never encouraged. From Sparta also Plato takes over the idea that women as well as men should be provided for in the program of education, but again enlarges the purpose of this innovation to include the preparation of women for the tasks of citizenship, including the defense of their native land in war. The common meals, which Plato takes for granted, are another borrowing from the Dorian tradition; but here the older Athenian tradition of the family prevails and prevents his working them into his state in any definitive fashion.

But when we come to the political structure of Plato's state the influence of Sparta almost completely disappears. It has no kings, no ephors; its basic structure—with its assembly, council, prytanies, and annually elected officers, is thoroughly Athenian. The only offices that are non-Athenian are Plato's own inventions, and all of them (except the agronomoi, where the influence of the Spartan krypteia may possibly be detected) are inventions suggested by Athenian traditions or by the intellectual life of Athens. Plato's judicial system is a strikingly new creation, but the elements of which it is constructed seem to be Athenian rather than Spartan or Cretan; and the procedure prescribed for trials in his courts is based in general and in detail upon Attic law, whose technical terms and devices Plato follows even in his innovations. For example, his novel remedy for judicial tyranny—a suit in the common courts against the judge involved—is typically Attic in spirit, as is the γραφὴ κακοδικίας against a citizen for excessive litigation. Finally, Plato's Nocturnal Council, devoted as it is to the cultivation of the higher sciences and their application to law and government, is an institution that could only be suggested by an Athenian, or by some quite atypical Dorian, such as Archytas of Tarentum. It is in fact so incongruous in the Cretan setting Plato proposes for it that it threatens to introduce a dramatic inconsistency into Plato's dialogue; and this may be the reason—and not any felt inconsistency with previous legislation—that accounts for the emphasis at the end of the Laws upon the difficulty of establishing it.

Is there a middle way discernible here? I think there is, but it can best be expressed in terms of the extremes that Plato seeks to avoid. The Spartans' preoccupation with military hardness, their indifference to letters and the cultivation of the higher sciences, their emphasis upon courage to the neglect of other parts of virtue—these are clearly defects to be avoided; so also is the cult of freedom at Athens, leading to variability and fondness for meaningless innovations, to a versatility sometimes aimless, and to the rejection of all authority over individual tastes and ambitions. But Spartan sturdiness and sense of community coupled with Athenian enterprise and intellectual curiosity; Spartan loyalty to law plus Athenian ingenuity in exploring its foundations and applications; Spartan gravity mingled with Athenian festivity—these, plus the common Greek ambition for excellence and the recognition that it is to be found in the μέτριον, are some of the components of Plato's mixture. And this mixture, like the others we have considered, exemplifies the general aim of finding a proper combination of authority and freedom, a middle way between monarchy and democracy.

These are the chief mixtures in Plato's constitution; but one whose attention has been called to the topic will find in the details of the *Laws* many other instances of what Plato regards as effective mingling. Thus law operates by a mixture of persuasion and compulsion (722bc, 921e); a proper marriage involves a mixture of families with contrasting qualities (773a); justice is a mixture of prudence, temperance, and courage (631c); the Nocturnal Council is a mixture of old and young (951d), and it is this mixture of experienced intelligence with keen perceptions that makes it a trusty guardian of the state's welfare (961d). There is even a mixed love, i.e. manly attachment without sensuous gratification (837b,d). In short, "the state must be well mixed, like a crater of wine" (773d). Even more numerous are the references to the mean (the μέτριον), which is the aim of such mixtures. The moderate man is μέτριος with respect to pleasures (816b), with respect to gains in transactions with other men (920c); he will make modest offerings to the gods (955e), and give a modest burial to a loved one (719cd); only μέτριοι can be friendly, for the "unmeasured" (ἄμετρα) can be friendly neither to those who are like nor to those who are unlike themselves (716c); and the essence of religion is to liken oneself to God, who is the "measure" of all things. Thus the state, in all its parts and in all its citizens, should exemplify that measure which is the result of a proper mixture of differing qualities.

This idea of mixture as the secret of excellence and stability is not peculiar to the *Laws*, but plays a large part also in other dialogues of Plato's later period. In the *Philebus* the good life for man appears not as pure pleasure, nor even as pure knowledge (that is appropriate only for the gods), but as a mixture of the two. The exercises in classification and division so prominent in the *Sophist* and *Politicus* are attempts to trace the mixtures involved in the various kinds of entities, natural and social, that come into being in the world of change; and the statesman's art, in particular, is described as analogous to the art of weaving in its effort to intertwine threads of different characters into a sturdy fabric. In the *Timaeus* the cosmos itself is described as a mixture of necessity and persuasion; the world soul is a mixture of divisible and indivisible being, sameness and otherness; and similarly all concrete kinds of things owe their being to the judicious mixture of simpler qualities and entities. Evidently we have in the doctrine of the mixed constitution not something peculiar to Plato's political theory, but the application of a much more general principle, one which is clearly connected with the increased interest in the sense world that is found in his later thought. For a general exposition of this philosophic principle we must turn to the *Philebus*. Here we learn that it is the application of the Limit (πέρας) to the indefinitely varying continuum of more-and-less (the ἄπειρον) that brings about "the generation into being" (γένεσις εἰς οὐσίαν) of determinate qualities and structures.[19] This limit in any given case is the μέτριον, for it determines what constitutes too much or too little of the fundamental more-and-less to constitute the quality under consideration. Similarly the *Politicus* asserts that the true art of measurement (μετρητική) involves not merely the comparison of qualities with one another, but their comparison with a standard, the μέτριον; and to ignore the μέτριον is to destroy all the arts and their products.[20] Where several qualitative continua are involved in the structure of a thing the Limit is more complicated; it expresses the symmetry (συμμετρία) which must be attained if the mixture is to have stable and enduring being.[21] It follows that mixture in itself is not necessarily a good;[22] it must be such as to attain the μέ-

---

[19] *Phil.* 23b-26d. This is the abstract statement of a principle that is clearly employed in certain parts of the *Timaeus*. The mathematical development of Plato's later dialectic seems to have been linked with an increasing interest in the explanation of the sense world. This phase of Plato's philosophy can only be mentioned here; in fact we are not yet able to interpret it with any assurance. But it forms the theme of some of the most exciting of recent Platonic studies. See Julius Stenzel, *Studien zur Entwicklung der Platonischen Dialektik*, 1917; 2nd edn. Leipzig, 1931 (English translation by D. J. Allan, *Plato's Method of Dialectic*, Oxford, 1940); *Zahl und Gestalt bei Platon und Aristoteles*, Leipzig, 1924; 2nd edn. 1933; and Paul Wilpert, *Zwei Aristotelische Frühschriften über die Ideenlehre*, Regensburg, 1949.

[20] *Polit.* 283c-285b.

[21] *Phil.* 64d.

[22] Some mixtures are bad; e.g. the mixture of chthonic and Olympian rites (828c), of foreign customs in a well-ordered state (949e), of Greeks and barbarians

τριον, or the συμμετρία, that gives permanence to its combination of elements. Thus the good life for man is not merely a mixture of pleasure and knowledge, but a determinate kind of mixture, with its elements carefully selected and the whole characterized by symmetry and beauty.[23]

Applying this doctrine to the construction of a constitution, we can see that the political μέτριον for Plato is such a συμμετρία of the constituent parts of the polis as will give it stability and security. The primary constituents of the polis are obviously rulers and subjects; hence the chief concern of a genuine political craftsman is to establish such a balance between authority and freedom as will ensure the unity and friendship of these constituents through the willing obedience of the subjects and the wisdom and self-restraint of the rulers. Essential to this unity and friendship is the realization by both parties that the μέτριον is something distinct from their personal wishes and interests, except as these are included in the common good. The laws of such a polis will express the conditions of this common good, and these laws, or the Nous from which they are derived, will be the real sovereign. The subjects then will be obeying not the rulers, but the laws they guard and administer; and the rulers will not be executing their personal wishes, but guarding and administering laws sovereign over themselves as well as over their subjects. These are the conditions of the wisdom, freedom, and friendship that the Athenian asserts to be the end of legislation.

(693a). There are parallels in the *Republic*; e.g. the mixture of bronze and gold, of silver and iron, in the imperfect states (547a); the mixture of wealth, poverty, disease, and health, in the lots from which the immortal soul chooses (618b); impure pleasures, i.e. mixed with pains (586b; cf. *Phil.* 46a). In the myth of the *Phaedrus* the teams of the gods are well matched, but those of mortals are "mixed" (246a). In his earlier dialogues Plato seems to be less tolerant of mixture, as implying the contamination of an original purity; whereas in his later period he recognizes that the constituents of sense objects are inevitably imperfect, and relies on mixture as a device for the mutual correction of imperfections. The later doctrine, however, seems to be not something new, but only a greater emphasis upon a feature latent, but undeveloped, in his earlier thought. At the end of the *Republic*, for example, there is the suggestion of a science of proper mixtures which should be cultivated (618bc).

[23] Paul Kucharski (*Les Chemins du savoir dans les derniers dialogues de Platon*, Paris, 1949, 141-142) finds an important antecedent of Plato's theory in the Hippocratic doctrine of humors and foods as mixtures of bodies or simple qualities, each of which has its proper nature and its specific action; as long as the mixture is perfect, these elements neutralize each other, but if one of them gets separated and acts alone, sickness or suffering results. See Hippocrates, *Ancient Medicine*, 14.

Thus far we have been examining Plato's general doctrine of the mixed constitution. Coupled with it—and frequently confused with it—is another doctrine of mixture which is designed as an answer to the peculiarly difficult and delicate problem mentioned earlier, that of establishing an executive power in the state that can provide effective control and give to the community the guidance it needs, without making it so powerful as to threaten the freedom of the subjects and endanger the sovereignty of the very laws it administers.

Plato's reflections on the history of the Spartan kingdom suggested a solution to this problem. Spartan law obviously fell short of the Nous that he looked upon as the final source of right and justice; nevertheless, for what it was, it had maintained itself through many generations, he believed, and this very fact was a political phenomenon of extraordinary importance. In Sparta, as everywhere else, authority was exercised by human beings, not gods; and human nature is peculiarly liable to corruption through the possession of power. It is natural for every man to desire that all things, so far as possible, should happen in accordance with his own wishes; and if these wishes are unwise, his very power to influence events brings about his own destruction and with it the power that he has (687c-688c). Kings are peculiarly liable to this infirmity, for the possession of supreme power brings about a special blindness in its possessors (619cd). Against these dangers the Spartan kingship has been providentially protected, as Plato sees it. In the words of the Athenian Stranger,

Some god who foresaw the future and was concerned for your welfare caused twin families to grow out of your single royal house and reduced it to more moderate dimensions (εἰς τὸ μέτριον μᾶλλον συνέστειλε). Furthermore, some time afterwards a man in whose nature there was a mixture of divine power saw that your royal office was still inflamed, and tempered (μείγνυσι) the self-willed force of royal birth with the wisdom that comes of age by setting up the eight-and-twenty elders with a power equal to that of the kings on important matters. And your "third savior," seeing that authority with you was still swollen and violent, placed as it were a bridle upon it in the power of the ephors, introducing something like the function of the lot. This is the reason why your kingship, having been compounded (σύμμεικτος γενομένη) of the elements it needed and thus attaining moderation (μέτρον ἔχουσι), has by its own survival become a source of salvation to others. 691d-692a.

By the mixture which the Athenian here describes, the Spartan kingship became one of three powerful components in the executive part of the state, each of them having something like an equal weight with the others. The mixture, therefore, was not a mixture involving the state as a whole, nor, strictly speaking, a mixture within the monarchy, unless that term be taken broadly to denote the executive as a whole; it was a mixture within the executive, in which each of the components found its power limited by that of the others. Its value in Plato's eyes is that it substituted for the weak compulsion of the oath, or for hazardous reliance upon the ruler's wisdom and conscience, an automatic check by other agents each interested in maintaining and exercising its power. The insufficiency of the oath taken at the founding of the three Dorian states is frequently mentioned in this account (691a, 692b; cf. 683d, 684a); and here and elsewhere in the *Laws* Plato expresses his doubt whether any man in supreme power can avoid misusing it through ignorance or self-interest (691c, 714a). On the other hand, he is equally convinced of the tendency of any power to seek its own extension (697d, 714c ff., 715a). This fact indicates both the danger against which a legislator must take precautions, and the means by which it can be met: he must set up offices to balance one another, in the expectation that each, in maintaining its own powers, will automatically serve as a check on the powers of the others. Thus he will be able to "moderate the offices" ($\mu\epsilon\tau\rho\iota\acute{a}\sigma\alpha\iota$ $\tau\grave{a}\varsigma$ $\mathring{a}\rho\chi\acute{a}\varsigma$) by making "one out of three" ($\mu\acute{\iota}\alpha\nu$ $\mathring{\epsilon}\kappa$ $\tau\rho\iota\mathring{\omega}\nu$), i.e. a single executive with three components (692c). Offices not so checked are called "unmixed" ($\mathring{a}\mu\epsilon\iota\kappa\tau o\iota$), and these the legislator must avoid setting up if he hopes to preserve the mean between despotism and freedom (693b).[24]

This is clearly a doctrine of political checks and balances, and it is the first formulation of that doctrine of which we have any knowledge. Polybius, who expounds the same doctrine a century or more later, does not acknowledge any indebtedness to Plato, but it is more than likely that the sources upon which he drew had got it from Plato, especially since it is associated with praise of the Spartans for having first embodied this expedient in their constitution.[25] From

[24] The facts seem to show that the checks in the Spartan constitution did not always work as effectively as Plato seemed to think. But this is irrelevant to the theory they suggested to him; just as Montesquieu's misinterpretation of the English constitution is no refutation of the theory of separation of powers that he thought he found there.

[25] Polyb. vi, xi, 11-12 is a clear echo of *Laws* 712d, as Gomperz (*Griechische Denker*, ii, 610) has pointed out.

Polybius, as is well known, the tradition of this doctrine comes down through the Middle Ages to Montesquieu and the theorists of modern times. But it should be remembered that in Montesquieu it is associated with a new doctrine, that of the separation of the executive, legislative, and judicial powers; and it is the balancing of these against one another that for Montesquieu is the safeguard of liberty. The "separation of powers" in this later sense does not appear in Plato.

It hardly needs to be pointed out that this special theory of mixture within the executive power is not the same as the general doctrine of the mixed constitution that we discussed earlier. This special theory is an ingenious suggestion for assuring the supremacy of law in that part of the state which is peculiarly likely to bring about its subversion. The μέτριον of course has to be produced in other parts of the state as well, so that this theory is only a subordinate part of Plato's general theory of the mixed constitution. But the peculiar importance of the political balance of powers in maintaining the stability of a state, and the originality of the special theory itself, meant that later thinkers came to be preoccupied with it and even to confuse it with the general doctrine. The doctrine that the "best constitution" is a mixture of monarchy, aristocracy, and democracy, or (according to one version) a mixture of all the pure forms, seems to have had its origin in this Platonic passage and to represent the very confusion I have just mentioned. It is very likely that this later doctrine arose in discussions that took place in the Academy during Plato's lifetime. It is clear, I think, that the mixture involved in this doctrine does not represent the starting point of Plato's thought; but let us see how Plato's text could have given rise to it.

There is at least a suggestion of it in the three components of the executive power that Plato recognizes at Sparta. Of the kings, the elders, and the ephors, the first seems to be a monarchical factor; and the third, which is said to represent something like "the function of the lot," would suggest democracy. These two being given, a reader might be tempted to find in the gerousia an aristocratic element, especially since its members were supposed to be chosen for their virtue. But this is not Plato's thought; the elders, he says, are the wisdom of age which was added to temper the self-willed force of royal birth. It is clear that in writing this passage Plato is not thinking of the three forms of government that later became canonical elements in the mixed constitution, but rather of the claims (ἀξιώματα) to power that had been enumerated two pages earlier (690a-c). These claims are (1) that of the father over his children, (2) that of the nobly born over the base, (3) that of elders over younger persons, (4) that of the master over his slaves, (5) that of the strong over the weak, (6) that of the wise over the ignorant, and (7) that of those chosen by lot over those not so favored. All these claims apparently have some justification, even Pindar's "natural right" of the strong, and all of them are supported by powerful human sentiments. But they conflict with one another and are a perennial source of faction. The problem of the legislator is to cure the faction while utilizing these principles—the only ones available—for his purpose. Three of them —the claims of royal birth, of age, and of the lot—Plato finds in the complex executive that held power at Sparta. Of the others, the first and the fourth are primarily relevant to the management of households, not states, and are properly ignored here; the fifth is recognized by implication in the governmental authority given to the components of the Spartan mixture; and the sixth, the claim of wisdom, which is the most important, is associated with the claim of age. But it is really a function not of age, but of education; and we shall see that Plato's legislator eventually stakes all his chances upon his educational program; if it is even partially effective in accomplishing its aim, all the officers of government will embody some wisdom as well as the other qualifications for exercising power. Plato's description of the Spartan executive may have been the point of departure for his own or later speculation about the mixed constitution, but it was evidently not written to expound that later theory.

There is another passage which, when conjoined with the one we have just examined, would give further encouragement to the formation of the later theory. When Megillus is asked which of the recognized forms of constitution is exemplified in the Spartan state, he replies that it is difficult to answer; in the power of the ephors it resembles a tyranny, yet in some respects it seems to be the most democratic of states; it would be foolish not to regard it as an aristocracy, and its ancient tradition of life-long kingship makes men universally call it a monarchy (712de). This passage—or the thought it expresses, which Plato may have expounded orally in the Academy—is undoubtedly the source of Aristotle's principle that the criterion of a well-mixed constitution is the uncertainty as to what it should be called.²⁶ For he proceeds to cite the Spartan constitution as an illustration of his principle. But Aristotle's text, while it shows that there was general acceptance among his colleagues of the mixed character of the Spartan constitution, also indicates that there were varying opinions as to the components of the mixture.²⁷ Some accepted the four elements in Megillus' statement—monarchy, oligarchy, democracy, tyranny—while others apparently followed the suggestion of the earlier passage in the *Laws* and regarded it as a mixture of monarchy, oligarchy, and democracy. Again, they differed in their identification of the democratic element; some found it in the office of the ephors, which is suggested by the mention of the lot in the earlier of Plato's two passages, while others found it in the common education provided for all classes and in the simplicity and uniformity of Spartan dress and manners; and for this suggestions are found both in Megillus' statement and in other passages of the *Laws*. These details show that Plato's analysis of the Spartan constitution and his speculations about the secret of its stability were basic to the later developments.

Which, if any, of these later versions received Plato's adherence it is impossible to say; but we can hardly doubt that he was familiar with them. Nor is it improbable that in his own thinking he played with such ideas, despite his general indifference to this popular classification, and despite his characterization of each of these types as faction states. A craftsman has to use imperfect materials, and his general doctrine of mixture shows that he recognized the possibility of a mixed whole whose parts served to correct each other's imperfections. He seems to have used some such doctrine to describe the ancestral constitution of Athens in the *Menexenus*, how seriously it is impossible to say. Furthermore, we found it plausible to suppose that he, or his fellows in the Academy, are the source of Aristotle's description of the Solonian legislation as effecting a proper mixture of aristocracy, oligarchy, and democracy. This supposition becomes even more plausible now that we have examined Plato's exposition of the mixed constitution; for what this unnamed admirer of Solon seems to have said is that he put an end to the oligarchy, which was "too unmixed" (λίαν ἄκρατον)—an obscure phrase whose meaning becomes clear in the light of the passages we have examined in the *Laws*.

²⁶ *Pol.* 1294b 14.   ²⁷ Cf. 1265b 33ff.

That this was not the sole interpretation of early Athens, even among advocates of a mixed constitution, is evident from Isocrates, who thinks of the constitution of Solon and Cleisthenes as a mixture of two, not three, elements—aristocracy and democracy. But the three-element version triumphed in political theory. This is the version we find in Polybius and the Stoics, for whom the best constitution was a combination of kingship, aristocracy, and democracy;[28] and this is the version of the "best constitution" that Dicaearchus, a pupil of Aristotle, expounded in his *Tripolitikos*, taking Sparta as the historical realization of his ideal.[29] To judge from the scanty evidence we have, Dicaearchus evidently considered himself the author of this canonical doctrine of the mixed constitution; for he modestly called this fourth type, arising from a mixture of the three familiar forms, the "Dicaearchic form." Yet Aristotle clearly refers to such a theory in the early part of the *Politics*,[30] and on chronological grounds it is improbable, if not impossible, that he should be referring to Dicaearchus here. But it is unlikely that Dicaearchus would have attached his name to a doctrine if it had already been publicly expounded by someone of eminence; so we can best conclude that Aristotle is referring to opinions that originated in discussions in the Platonic-Aristotelian circle. If this is so, Plato may be regarded as indirectly the author of the theory, for he was the guiding spirit in this circle. Moreover, as I have shown, his analysis of the Spartan constitution contained elements that would suggest such a theory. The fact that Dicaearchus attacks Plato is no argument against this view, for Plato's "best constitution" was really different from Dicaearchus'. Besides, Dicaearchus' attack is in accord with one of the most familiar maxims of academic controversy: establish your claim to an idea by criticizing the man from whom you got it.

[28] Polyb. vi, 3; Diog. vii, 131.
[29] Wehrli, *Die Schule des Aristoteles* i, 28-29; 65; Photius, *Bibl.* 37.
[30] 1265b 33.

CHAPTER XI

THE RULE OF LAW

A state in which the law is subject and without authority I consider ripe for destruction; but when the law is despot (δεσπότης) over the rulers, and the rulers are slaves (δοῦλοι) of the law—then, as I see it, the state will have security (σωτηρία) and all the other good things that the gods bestow. 715d.

THIS passage states in peculiarly vivid fashion one of the most characteristic elements of Plato's political theory. His reasons for adopting this principle are stated with equal vigor. Its alternative is to entrust the sovereignty to men—either a single man or a group—and this is a responsibility and a burden that human nature is too weak to bear; for when a man is entrusted with supreme and irresponsible power he inevitably loses his wisdom and integrity (691cd, 713c, 875ab). This judgment is directed not only at the tyrannies and despotisms generally viewed with horror by the Greeks, but also at many of the familiar and accepted forms of government, in which—as Thrasymachus describes it in the *Republic*—the law is determined by the group in power to serve its own interests. These familiar forms— monarchy, oligarchy, democracy—get their names from the class or faction in power; they are not genuine states, but στασιωτεῖαι, strife-ridden communities in which one faction is always endeavoring to entrench itself at the expense of its rivals (715ab, 832c). None of these names, says the Athenian, is appropriate to our state; it should be called after that god who is the sovereign of all wise men, viz. Law, which is the ordinance of Reason (713a, 714a). For it is Law that is of divine origin, not the persons who rule. The very title we have given our rulers—guardians of the laws—indicates that they are ministers and servants of a sovereignty that they do not themselves possess; and we have called them this, not for the sake of novelty, but for the safety of the state (715cd).[1]

The Athenian admits that a government thus limited by law may not be ideally the best; if a man could be found without the limitations of human ignorance and self-interest, it would be wrong to

---

[1] Aristotle makes the same proposal (*Pol.* 1287a 21): if it is better that certain persons should rule, they should be made guardians (νομοφύλακες) or servants (ὑπηρέται) of the laws.

subject him to law, for no law has higher authority than knowledge.[2] But the possibility of finding such a ruler is not great; he is to be found, if at all, only in the proverbial age of Kronos, when men are said to have been ruled by semidivine beings higher than themselves (713de). Hence we must exclude the sovereignty of men from our city; the best we can do in the present age is to imitate the ordered life of that legendary era and make law our sovereign.

But the rule of law is very difficult to make effective in any political system. For law is an impersonal thing, whereas power in any society is always exercised by persons or groups of persons. Again, law is general and abstract; its interpretation and its application to specific circumstances have to be entrusted to human agents, with their special interests, their personal sentiments and springs of action, their limited insight and intelligence. How is it possible to make law sovereign when it depends so inescapably upon these imperfect instruments, not only for its effective authority in a society, but even for the very interpretation of that authority it is supposed to exercise? In the face of these difficulties the realist is tempted to evade the problem by declaring that law and justice are simply the declared will, or interest, of the ruling power ($\tau\grave{o}$ $\tau o\hat{v}$ $\kappa\rho\epsilon\acute{\iota}\tau\tau o\nu os$ $\sigma\nu\mu\phi\acute{\epsilon}\rho o\nu$, 714c), and that this ruling power is itself sovereign—a specious solution, containing internal contradictions, and seldom accepted wholeheartedly by its professed proponents, as Plato shows in the *Gorgias* and the *Republic*. But Plato also is a realist in his own way; and the doctrine of the rule of law, as it is presented in the institutions he devises, takes full account of the complexity of the problem. In fact it is his awareness of the difficulties involved, and his demiurgic attempt to meet and overcome them, that are responsible for some of the most striking features of the *Laws*.

What is this law which Plato declares to be sovereign? The question must be answered eventually in Plato's terms, but for the present it is enough to take his principle at the lower level of popular understanding. "A people should fight for its laws more than for its walls," says Heraclitus. The laws of a people were the rules by which it lived —some of immemorial antiquity, some the work of historical legislators; some set forth in written statutes, learned in the schools, sung at banquets and festivals; others unwritten customs of family and community life. All of this came under the capacious word $\nu\acute{o}\mu o\iota$ as

[2] 875cd. "Such a man is himself the law," as Aristotle puts it (*Pol.* 1284a 13).

it was understood in Plato's time. These laws of a people were something that it could willingly obey, the Greeks thought, as compared with the commands of a tyrant, which compelled obedience. Thus the rule of law involved a doctrine of consent, never explicitly formulated, but certainly implied in the current equation between the rule of law and rule over willing subjects (ἀρχὴ ἑκόντων), and the parallel equation between unlawful rule and rule over unwilling subjects (ἀρχὴ ἀκόντων).[3] The precise meaning of "willing" in this phrase is not clear, nor were any criteria worked out for deciding when consent had been obtained, other than familiarity, or ease of enforcement. But it was taken for granted that an Athenian or a Spartan obeying his city's law was subjecting himself not to an alien authority, but rather to something intimately connected with himself; and furthermore, that in obeying the law a man was not yielding merely to the wish of another man, but to a higher authority, however vaguely conceived. These were the components of the popular and instinctive support of the rule of law, so characteristic of the Greeks that they themselves often thought of it as the chief distinction between themselves and the barbarians around them.

There are certain basic conditions presupposed in a regime of law which the Greeks, and particularly the Athenians, had already brought about in their political history; and Plato takes these over without question. In the first place, if the laws of a people are to afford them any protection against arbitrary power they must be clearly formulated and declared, so that a citizen will know what is expected of him, and will have an objective criterion to appeal to in a case of what seems to him a violation of justice or an abuse of authority. This was something firmly established in the practices of the Athenians. More than two centuries before Plato, in the time of Draco, the Athenians had broken the monopoly of the Eupatrid families as the traditional repositories and interpreters of the law, and obtained written statements of procedures and penalties in at least a part of their customary law. Draco was followed by Solon and Cleisthenes and the leaders of fifth-century democracy. In the course of time the law declared in this fashion had become so voluminous and so confused, possibly through the lack of a proper system of archives,[4] that at the end of the fifth century it was thought necessary

---

[3] Arist. *Pol.* 1285a 27-28; Plato, *Polit.* 291e, 293a,c.
[4] On the possible lack of central archives before 401, see Kahrstedt, in *Klio* xxxi,

to appoint a commission to make a systematic codification of the laws; and when this commission completed its work in 401 after the restoration of the democracy, the principle of written law was again affirmed explicitly in a provision that henceforth no appeal should be made to any law not included in the written code.[5]

This primary condition for the rule of law is everywhere presupposed in Plato's state. Plato recognizes the importance of written law in his account of the development of political society (680a-681d), and the very purpose of the *Laws* is to provide such a known and standing law for the citizens of his state. He would go even farther than was thought necessary at Athens and have the legislator reduce to writing—not in the form of laws, but as admonition and advice —as much as possible of the "unwritten customs" or moral rules that he expects his citizens to observe. These "unwritten laws" are not strictly laws; nevertheless they are the bonds of the social structure and if they are not firm or well-fitted the whole will come to ruin.[6] The formulation of these unwritten observances will be particularly important in his state, for each group among his colonists will arrive with somewhat different ancestral customs, and they must be harmonized and consciously designed to support the structure that is built upon them.

Again, the rule of law requires an adequate system of courts to which a citizen with a grievance can have ready access, and before which, if he is accused, he can expect to receive an equitable hearing. "A city is not a city," says Plato, "unless it has courts properly established" (766d). It is in this respect, he seems to think, that the rule of law in his native city was particularly defective; and his system of courts, though following Athenian precedents, is ingeniously devised to prevent the miscarriages of justice that he thought were too likely to occur under the supremacy of the popular dicasteries. He makes generous provisions for appeal from a lower court to a higher one, and modifies Athenian procedure in important respects so as to assure leisurely consideration of every case, and an opportunity at

---

1938, 28ff.; A. R. W. Harrison, in JHS LXXV, 1955, 28f., and von Fritz, TAPA LXXI, 1940, 115-124.

[5] Andoc. 1, 89; cf. Dem. XXIV, 42.

[6] 793ab; cf. 730b, 788b, 822d-823a, 838ab, 841b. Examples of these ἄγραφα νόμιμα or ἄγραφοι νόμοι, are precepts on hunting, on sexual relations, on the early care of children. In one passage Plato identifies these with what are called πάτριοι νόμοι, "ancestral customs." Isocrates held a similar view of their importance, VII, 39ff. On this part of Plato's doctrine, see Cairns, *Legal Philosophy from Plato to Hegel*, 46.

some stage for an inquisitorial examination into charges and evidence.[7]

Finally, there must be devices to prevent abuse by magistrates of the executive and judicial powers with which they are entrusted. Like the Athenians, Plato often considers his law as consisting of instructions to magistrates, prescribing the rules they are to administer and the procedures they are to follow.[8] The Greeks in general (and particularly the Athenians) were well aware of the need for legal control over their officials and had developed some very efficient means of keeping them within the bounds of their authority, many of which Plato incorporates as a matter of course into his state. He adopts the Athenian device of the dokimasia of newly designated officers before they take office, and the euthyna required of officers at the end of their terms. At Athens both these functions were discharged by the popular courts, but Plato would evidently entrust them to smaller and more competent bodies; dokimasia seems to be a function of the guardians, while for the euthyna he creates a new body of officials, of exceptional quality and dignity.[9] Athenian law also provided that at any sovereign meeting of the assembly—that is, ten times a year—a vote ($\dot{\epsilon}\pi\iota\chi\epsilon\iota\rho\sigma\tau\sigma\nu\dot{\iota}\alpha$) could be taken on the conduct of any official, and if the vote was adverse the official concerned was suspended from office and committed for trial before a dicastery. This remedy does not appear in Plato's law, but he provides a more apt alternative: any citizen who considers that he has been wronged by a magistrate's action or decision may bring suit for damages against the magistrate or judge concerned.[10] Finally, Plato adds another group of officers, the nomophylakes, whose responsibilities include supervising the lower magistrates and prosecuting them for misuse or neglect of their powers. This was a function ostensibly discharged by the council at Athens, and undoubtedly Plato's council is also intended to function similarly. But he obviously thinks it necessary for the proper exercise of this supervision to have a smaller body

[7] See Chapter VI, The Courts.
[8] See Chapter V, The Guardians of the Laws.
[9] See Chapter V, The Scrutiny and the Audit.
[10] Both the general principle (that no judge or official is to be irresponsible, i.e. $\dot{\alpha}\nu\upsilon\pi\epsilon\dot{\upsilon}\theta\upsilon\nu\sigma\varsigma$) and the remedy (a suit for damages in the "common courts") are stated in 762ab, and again in 846b. For a fuller discussion, see Chapter VI, Justice before the Magistrates. The most striking feature of this proposal is its making judges liable for misuse of their judicial powers. There is, as far as I know, no historical counterpart in the procedure of any Greek state, certainly not at Athens, where the judicial power was exercised anonymously by the dicasts in the popular courts.

of more experienced senior magistrates with a longer tenure of office, analogous to the ancient Areopagus at Athens.

But how are these guardians, and the other higher officers, to be prevented from misusing their powers? "The most difficult questions as to the structure of the Judiciary," says Sidgwick, "are connected with its function of maintaining legal order against the guardians of that order themselves."[11] In discussing the functions of the guardians we have seen that Plato's law seems generally to assume, and usually explicitly prescribes, that in the exercise of their powers they will make use of the courts, i.e. they will see that the machinery of the law is set in motion and operates for its ordained purpose, and it is seldom their privilege to give final judgment in any process of litigation. So much for the intent of Plato's law; what are the mechanisms by which the accomplishment of this intent can be reasonably assured? In the first place, these high magistrates, like the lower ones, are subject to euthyna at the end of their terms of office, and to the continuing inspection which the euthynoi are empowered to exercise over all officials; furthermore, they are subject, like the lower magistrates, to prosecution by a citizen for negligence or willful injustice in the conduct of their office (928b). The law here cited refers specifically to a guardian's faithlessness in a wardship of orphans, and we may safely infer that the action would lie for malfeasance in other spheres of their duty. Such an action is brought before the select judges, apparently without going through the lower courts, a recognition of its peculiar gravity and importance. Thus both the euthynoi and the select judges have a check upon the guardians' powers.

But the select judges and the euthynoi are in turn responsible. The members of both groups are subject individually to the euthyna, like all other officials. In addition, the select judges are subject to prosecution if anyone thinks that one of them has deliberately given an unjust verdict (767e); in this case the trial takes place before the guardians of the laws sitting as a court. Likewise an official who thinks he has been unjustly condemned by the euthynoi may appeal his case to the select judges, subject to a double penalty if he loses; but if he succeeds in vindicating himself he may bring legal action against the euthynos who has judged him falsely (946de). Furthermore, a euthynos is subject to prosecution by any citizen who thinks him unworthy of his office and its dignities and cares to institute a

---

[11] Sidgwick, *Elements of Politics*, 487.

γραφή against him (947e). The trial in the latter case, and perhaps also in the former, takes place before a special court consisting of the guardians, the select judges, and the other euthynoi.

Evidently the intent of these provisions is to confer on each of these bodies a check upon the activity of the others. These are the three most powerful bodies of officials, and this reciprocal check seems to be the equivalent in Plato's state of the automatic self-control that he found in the tripartite executive at Sparta. But his three boards of magistrates bear little resemblance, either in nature or in function, to the kings, gerousia and ephors of the Spartan constitution, nor are the mutual checks precisely analogous. The Spartan ephors conducted the euthyna of all officers, even of their own predecessors; but the kings and elders, holding office for life, were exempt from this form of control. The ephors, moreover, seem to have been competent to hear (perhaps also to initiate) charges against any officer, including a king; and their judgment, even if formally it required the assent of the people, was likely to be final, through their privilege of summoning the assembly (the apella) and laying proposals before it which it could only accept or reject. We have no evidence, I believe, of any action against a member of the gerousia, but this can only be an accident. On the other hand, the kings, who seem to have originally appointed the ephors, retained some trace of this ancient authority even after the ephors came to be selected independently, and sometimes made use of it to depose them and appoint others in their stead. The truth is, our evidence of Spartan constitutional law consists only of reports by the historians of actions taken by the Lacedaemonians or their various officials; and Spartan practice was so much a matter of custom, not written law, and hence depended so much upon extralegal combinations of forces, that we can hardly reduce it to anything like judicial precision.[12] But Plato thinks as a jurist. For him it is not power, but authority, that counts; and the final authority is the responsible judge or court, acting in the name of the law. The ingenious system he proposes—without parallel, so far as we know, in any constitution of his time—is clearly an expression of his determination that every official shall be subject to accounting before a body that is legally competent to judge him. There is even something like a separation of the judicial from the

---

[12] But for an impressive attempt to do so, see Kahrstedt, *Sparta und seine Symmachie*. On the points mentioned above, see 150ff., 223ff., 237ff.

other powers in the state. For neither the select judges nor the euthynoi are executive officials; their function is only to hear and judge. And the mutual check that they exercise upon each other is a safeguard against the tyranny of the judiciary, a danger that is often too little appreciated by exponents of the rule of law.[13]

The presence of a known and standing law, the responsibility of all officers of government for their official acts, the provision of legal remedies for assessing and redressing abuses of official power, and the absence of any personal sovereignty with authority to override the law—these features of Plato's state are now taken for granted in the western world as necessary conditions of the rule of law. Plato even anticipates a principle dear to Anglo-Saxon jurists, viz. that officials shall be called to account before the ordinary courts, not before special tribunals.[14] Most of these elements of Plato's constructions are based upon Athenian precedents, but Plato goes much further in

---

[13] Plato's proposals, however, lead to complications that can only be partially resolved from his text. We can clearly distinguish, I think, between a legal action that is in effect an appeal from a previous judicial decision, and one that constitutes an indictment of the official who rendered that decision. Thus when a magistrate who thinks he has been condemned unjustly by a euthynos takes his case to the select judges, this hearing becomes in effect a review which may result in setting aside the previous verdict. This is the clear import of ἐὰν ἀποφύγῃ τὰς εὐθύνας of 946d 8. The suit in question is not against the euthynos; that will lie later if the plaintiff magistrate chooses to take further action after having been cleared of the euthynoi's charges. The fact that the euthynoi would have to appear in court at the appeal to justify the action under review explains the words εἰσαγέτω τοὺς εὐθύνους. On the other hand, neither the euthynoi nor the guardians seem to have the right to reverse a decision of the select judges. The guardians may entertain a suit against one of them for injustice, but the judgment in this case, being damages to the injured plaintiff if he wins, implies that the original judgment stands—as is reasonable, since the original case was presumably a civil suit, on which the select judges are a final court of appeal. And the euthynoi may of course find against a select judge at his euthyna; but this, no more than the previous action, would seem to involve a reversal of judicial decisions already taken.

A further complication is not so easily resolved. If a guardian is condemned by the select judges, could he then bring suit against one or more members of the court that condemned him? If so, by the same reasoning a select judge who loses this suit could later bring action against one or more of the guardians. This would open the way to endless litigation. Plato evidently sees the need for providing some court competent to say the last word on any matter in dispute. It seems likely, therefore, that he considers the select judges, when judging a charge against a guardian, as competent to put an end to this particular issue, and similarly for the guardians when judging a charge against a select judge. Every member of both boards would later have to defend himself at his euthyna, where accusations of illegality could be brought; and the liability to this accounting would undoubtedly serve as a check on malice or caprice in rendering judgment.

[14] Such as the special courts provided by the *droit administratif* of France, for example, and by the procedure of other countries under the influence of Roman law. This alternative was, however, known to the Greeks; cf. Arist. *Pol.* 1300b 21-22.

the direction which these precedents established, sagaciously avoiding some of the pitfalls concealed in Athenian procedure, and providing remedies for evils which the Athenians, however much they deplored them, were not able to overcome. Those who cherish the rule of law as a protection against arbitrary power would do well to remember that Plato was the first western thinker to work out its implications in a systematic way, and to see clearly the legal institutions that are necessary if it is to be realized.

But for Plato the doctrine of the rule of law faces in two directions —against tyranny, on the one hand, and against anarchy, self-will, and caprice on the other. Its purpose is not only to protect the citizen against arbitrary power, but also to bring about his obedience to duly constituted authority. One aspect of Spartan and Cretan eunomia that especially impressed Plato was the supremacy of the law in the mind and habits of the ordinary citizen; this is what he calls "the natural rule of law, without force, over willing subjects" (690c), and it can be realized only through moral instruction and the persuasive molding of character. Physical force must indeed be used on occasion, as it is in the fines, imprisonment, atimia, and death penalty of Plato's penal law. But the purpose of these penalties is either to cure the offender, or if that is impossible, to deter others from similar offenses.[15] This explains why the penalties imposed upon "incurable" offenders are, to modern ways of thinking, extraordinarily severe; they are designed to direct the attention of others to the fearful consequences of disobedience. But law that is obeyed only because of the fear of punishment cannot be said to be willingly obeyed; and a more fundamental task of the legislator is to make the application of penalties so far as possible unnecessary. Laws are laid down, Plato says, for the purpose of instructing good men as well as deterring wicked ones (880de), and for him the former function is primary.[16]

Now a legislator who thinks of law in this fashion must recognize that his task is more than to formulate rules and prescribe penalties; he must also inform the citizens of the reasons for the rules laid

---

[15] 862de: The noblest work of law is to change the character of the offender. See Gernet, *Platon, Lois, Livre IX*, 79.

[16] Cf. *Gorg.* 464b, where legislation (νομοθετική) bears the same relation to justice in the courts (δικαιοσύνη) as gymnastics has to its corrective supplement, medicine.

down and dispose them to accept their authority.[17] Unlike the slave physician, who merely gives his prescription for the sick man's illness and then departs, the competent legislator will resemble the free practitioner who treats his equals. Such a physician will enter into conversation with the sick man and his family, both to learn more about his patient and to instruct him about his illness; and he will not prescribe a treatment until he has prepared him to follow instructions faithfully (720cd). This was a novel conception of the legislator's function, and Plato anticipates criticism. It will be said: "Whoever treats of laws in the way we are doing is schooling the citizens, rather than legislating" (857de). But such criticisms, he implies, will come only from routine practitioners rather than from philosophic experts, and he proceeds to formulate the consequences that follow for his legislation.

The most important of these consequences is a provision, almost unique in political philosophy, that the laws as a whole, and each individual law, should be prefaced by preambles (προοίμια) or exhortations (παραμύθια), so that those who are expected to obey will not only understand the purpose of the law concerned, but will also become more disposed to recognize its authority.[18] Thus every law will consist of two parts—the statement of the rule or prohibition with the penalties involved for violating it, and the introductory preamble stating the good, individual or social, which the law is intended to secure and the reasons why the citizen should conform to it. This procedure is followed by Plato himself in his legislation and forms one of the most characteristic features of the *Laws*. An elaborate preamble precedes the legislation as a whole, in the form of an address to the citizens of the new colony. This address covers the whole duty of man—to the gods, to his fellowmen and to himself—setting forth in proper order the objects one should admire and value, with the reasons that Plato draws from his long experience of life for this ordering of them (715e-718a, 726e-734e). In the detailed legislation that follows there are many formal preludes to specific laws: on the ownership of land (741a-c); on marriage (772e-773e); on hunting (823d-824c); on temple robbery (854bc); on murder (870a-d); on trading (916de); on bequests (923a-c); on honoring parents

[17] The Athenian emphasizes this point at the beginning of his legislation (718cd) and reverts to it on numerous occasions thereafter.
[18] This proposal is discussed and defended in two important passages, first at the very beginning of the legislation (718b-723d), and again at 857c-859b.

(930e-932a). At other points the substance of a preamble precedes the law, though not in formal fashion—e.g. on military discipline (942a-943a); on intercourse with foreign lands (949e-950d); on burial of the dead (959a-c). And on other occasions the preamble takes the form of a dialogue, eliciting through questions and answers the distinctions and values that underlie the law to follow—as in the discussion of motive that precedes the law of homicide (857e-864c), and in the refutation of atheism that introduces the law against impiety (887a-907d).[19] Plato obviously does not intend that the two lengthy discussions just mentioned shall be prefixed to the statutes that follow them; for the law of impiety the briefer statement in 885b is evidently the formal preamble. These discourses, however, show the kind of defense that he thinks a legislator should be able to give for his prescriptions and that he expects the officials in the new state to be able to give if required. Moreover, they are not to be stored away in the archives and known only to officials, for they are the pattern of prose literature that may be safely put into the hands of school children and citizens (811c-e).

Something like Plato's procedure has become a familiar feature of English and American legislation, where preambles are often prefixed to enactments to set forth the ends they serve and the mischiefs they are designed to remedy.[20] Modern jurists differ as to whether the preamble is to be regarded as an integral part of the statute; but the prevailing opinion is that it is an important guide to construction when the language of the enactment is general or not clear.[21] Plato probably would not have thought it strange or undesirable that the language of the preamble should affect the interpretation of the law that follows, if it should need interpretation. But the distinctness of the preamble from the enactment is as carefully preserved in Plato's texts as in modern statutes, and is deliberately emphasized; what needs to be said by way of prelude, declares the Athenian, cannot be put in the form of a law (718b). The command or prohibition, he evidently thinks, is the law proper (νόμος ἄκρατος, 723a); and these parts of Plato's texts are usually marked by the most meticulous preci-

[19] That the former of these two passages is intended to be the substance of a prooemion is shown by the fact that the value of such preambles in legislation is here reasserted and re-established; the second is explicitly called a prooimion after it has been brought to its conclusion.
[20] As to the desirability of preambles opinions differ. See Cairns, op.cit. 51-52.
[21] See Craies on Statute Law, 4th edn., London, 1936, 182-188.

sion. The preambles, on the contrary, are discursive and explanatory; their language is not imperative, but informative and persuasive.

But Plato's preambles differ strikingly from those of most later legislators in that they appeal to ultimate goods rather than to immediate and particular ends. Bentham, although he was apparently unaware of the fact, is Plato's authentic successor in this respect, and perhaps his only one; for he believed strongly that a code of laws should be accompanied, in general and in its special parts, with a Rationale, or "body of reasons," which would establish the connection of the law with the ultimate end, the "greatest happiness of the greatest number."[22] Such a statement of reasons will serve, he thinks, "as an instrument of interpretation, as a source of satisfaction, and as a code of instruction, moral and intellectual together."[23] The parallel, however, is not complete, for Plato would include, as we shall see, a greater variety of nonrational persuasive material than Bentham, living in the Age of Reason, evidently thought was necessary.

It is of more relevance, however, to consider what Plato's contemporaries would have thought of his proposal. Aristotle makes no comment upon it, and it does not appear in his list of the things peculiar ($ἴδια$) to Plato's legislation.[24] But the pains which the Athenian takes to establish his point, his dissatisfaction with previous legislators (857c), and his declaration that no one before him has used this device (722e), show that his proposal is a novel one and needs explanation and defense. There is indeed a tradition that both Zaleucus and Charondas attached preambles of this sort to certain of their laws, and some alleged fragments of these preambles have been preserved.[25] But it is more than likely that the writings from which Diodorus and Stobaeus drew their excerpts are a later composition fictitiously ascribed to these early legislators, analogous to the political writings attributed to Archytas, and perhaps a product of the same Pythagorean circles.[26] It is more probable that Plato influenced the

[22] "No mass of the matter of law is what it might be, and therefore ought to be, otherwise than in so far as, throughout the whole extent of it, it is furnished with a correspondent body of reasons for its accompaniment and support." *Works*, Bowring's edn. IV, 492.

[23] *Ibid.* IV, 538. Like Plato, Bentham believes that this quality of "justifiedness, or manifest usefulness" has "never yet been numbered by any person among the properties desirable in, or properly appertaining to, any such work" (IV, 480).

[24] *Pol.* 1274b 9-15.

[25] Stob. *Flor.* XLIV, 20, 40; Diod. XII, 20; cf. Cic. *De Leg.* II, 14.

[26] Armand Delatte (*Études sur la littérature pythagoricienne*, Paris, 1915, 182ff.) believes them to be the work of fifth-century Pythagoreans. But Mühl (*Klio* XXII,

later tradition about Zaleucus and Charondas than that they influenced him. In any case he could not be drawing upon Athenian tradition. The Attic laws that have been preserved are without preambles, and are addressed to the magistrates who are to enforce them, not to the general public. "The philosophic notion of law as an instrument of instruction for a virtuous and well-ordered life found little if any expression in the legislation of Athens."[27] Nor could Plato have been influenced here by Sparta. Persuasion, "even understood in a wider sense as the generally accepted form which determined the relation between rulers and those ruled, would not be typical of Sparta."[28] In the absence of better evidence than we have for the genuineness of the fragments of Zaleucus and Charondas, we must conclude that this doctrine is original with Plato.

Its origin in Plato's thought lay in the conviction that legislation can be made a science, and that a legislator who has formulated his laws scientifically will be able to give the rational grounds on which they rest. The meaning of this doctrine and its implication for the work of the legislator we will consider later. For the moment we should note that to justify the proposal of preludes it has to be coupled with another doctrine, viz. that the citizens for whom the legislation is intended can in some way be moved to accept the rational principles implied, at least in the form of "right opinions" ($\dot{\alpha}\lambda\eta\theta\epsilon\hat{\iota}\varsigma$ $\delta\acute{o}\xi\alpha\iota$). It would be false to say that Plato thinks of the subjects of the law as rational beings, without qualification. He is too well aware of the nonrational elements in this "mortal nature" ($\theta\nu\eta\tau\grave{\eta}$ $\phi\acute{v}\sigma\iota\varsigma$, 875b). On one occasion, in fact, the Athenian is reproached for having such a mean opinion of the human race.[29] Plato's view is expressed most graphically in his comparison of man to a puppet ($\theta\alpha\hat{v}\mu\alpha$) whose movements are controlled by strings. Some of these strings are tough and "iron-like," such as the tugs of fear or pain or pleasure, and they pull the little creature, sometimes irresistibly, in this or that direction. But one of these leading strings is the "sacred

---

1928, 118) finds that the preamble ascribed to Zaleucus by Diodorus (XII, 20) contains too many evidences of Stoic ideas to be genuine. That quoted by Stobaeus (XLIV, 20) includes not only ideas but even phrases characteristic of the *Laws*.

[27] J. W. Jones, *The Law and Legal Theory of the Greeks*, Oxford, 1956, 15.

[28] Ehrenberg, *Aspects of the Ancient World*, 78, on *Laws* 718ff.

[29] 804b. Cf. 766a: Man, we say, is a tame animal ($\H{\eta}\mu\epsilon\rho\rho\nu$ $\zeta\hat{\omega}o\nu$); it would be better to say that with a good disposition ($\phi\acute{v}\sigma\iota\varsigma$) and a proper education he becomes the most godlike and gentle of animals; but if he has had insufficient or improper training he is the most savage of all earth's creatures.

and golden cord" of reasoning (λογισμός), which Plato identifies
with the "common law" (κοινὸς νόμος) of the city. Since this sacred
cord is golden, it lacks the tensile strength of the forces it must resist
and therefore needs servants (ὑπηρέται) in order to hold its own
against them (644d-645b; cf. 803c). In this graphic image Plato
plainly indicates that more than reasoning is required to bring human
nature under the control of the law; hence in his preambles, as in all
the other institutions of his state, he often employs nonrational means
of persuasion.

These nonrational servants of the golden cord are of the utmost
variety. The preambles contain not only rational statements of the
good which the law serves, but also persuasive encomia of this good,
with appeals to the sentiments of honor and self-respect, of love for
the fatherland, of concern for the preservation of the family, or of
awe before the larger cosmos in which the individual man plays such
a feeble part. Sometimes the "ancient tales" of punishment after
death and of the anger of avenging spirits are invoked to moderate
the force of passion. Sometimes the legislator indulges in something
close to beneficent deception.[30] And above all there is the spell exercised by noble words, whose power Plato knows well and is determined to employ in his state, and by which even the poets are to
be persuaded to write in the vein approved by the laws. The word
Plato frequently employs for this type of persuasion is "enchantment"; but in using this term he is not implying that it is a form of
magic,[31] nor that it makes no appeal to reason. These preambles are

[30] In 663d-664a the legislator must teach that the just life is also the happiest,
and ought to teach it even if it were not true; the story of the dragon's teeth shows
that men can be led to believe anything. Again in 951a the returning theoros will
tell the young that the laws of other states are "second-rate" as compared with their
own—which is patriotic, but might not be his honest opinion; this he must reserve
for the Nocturnal Council. One thinks of the myth of the three "races" in the
Republic (414b-415c) and of the deception to be practised by the guardians in the
distribution of the marriage lots (459c-460a). But this aspect of Plato's method
seems to have been exaggerated out of due proportion by his critics, partly because
of Plato's own terminology. A myth is hardly a lie, though Plato does call it a ψεῦδος.
The two instances from the *Laws*—the only two I have been able to find—are
hardly examples of gross deception. The Athenian is himself sure that justice leads
to happiness—"I am as sure of this as I am that Crete is an island," he declares
(662b); and to sound the praises of one's own country (even if one has secret reservations) is a venial fault, particularly if one expresses his ideas for amendment
to the persons competent to do something about them. The charge that Plato advocates indiscriminate lying and deception rests more on suspicion than on Plato's
text.

[31] As Boyancé believes: see Chapter VII, Note 44 and the relevant text.

intelligently persuasive; they are persuasion at the high level of rational insight suffused with emotion.

It is not, however, in the preambles, presumably addressed to the older citizens, but in the regulations for the training of the young that the scope of these nonrational methods of persuasion is most fully evident. The purpose of education is, as we have seen, to mold the character of the young citizen so that he will habitually like what the law commands and dislike what it forbids. To produce this effect the educator must not only inculcate right opinions, but also the sentiments that accord with them; and the training of the sentiments must come first, for they operate before reason has been awakened. Hence Plato's concern for the proper forms of music and dancing, the media through which the emotions, he thinks, are most naturally expressed and through which they can most easily become engrained. Hence also his concern to regulate the poets and musicians, that they may present for imitation by the young only representations of the good in character and conduct. These are so many forms of enchantment whereby through constant repetition and imitation the character is formed and the springs of action properly set. And in later life the common meals and public festivals, with their prescribed singing and dancing, carry on the process of enchantment and confirm the imprint of the law upon the older citizen's character. There must be eunomia in the souls of the citizens, Plato says, if there is to be any security for the laws (960d).

To a reader nourished on the liberal traditions of later thought there is undoubtedly something appalling in the role that Plato here assigns to the legislator, coupled as it is with his very evident faith in the power of philosophical rhetoric to lead and mold the souls of men.[32] Philosophical rhetoric—that is, rhetoric that is not a mere knack, but a technique based upon a scientific knowledge of the souls of the hearers and of the proper means for producing the effects it desires—is the art of leading souls (ψυχαγωγία), and education (ἀγωγή) is but an application of it.[33] A legislator who knew human

---

[32] This conception of philosophical rhetoric is formulated in the *Phaedrus* (270b-272b) and reiterated in the *Politicus* (303e, 304de), where it is described as persuading men to do justice and assisting in guiding the helm of the state. These passages furnish the background for the proper understanding of the many references to persuasion in the *Laws*. See my "Plato's Conception of Persuasion," PR LXII, 1953, 234-250.

[33] On παιδεία as ἀγωγή see 659d, and Chapter VII, Note 14.

nature as thoroughly as does Plato's genuine rhetorician would have a truly divine or diabolical power to do with human beings as he wished. Of course the legislator equipped with such perfect knowledge is not likely to appear, and if he should appear, checks would have to be provided to prevent misuse of his power. All this Plato undoubtedly sees, and we shall ask later what checks are provided in his state against this particular abuse of authority. There is obviously no place for the check that operates in most modern societies through the existence of a variety of educational institutions and of freedom for expressing dissenting opinions. The forces of persuasion in Plato's state are to be centrally directed, and the influences that would counteract its effects are to be sternly controlled or repressed.

Yet these forces of persuasion are used for instruction, i.e. for inculcating true beliefs regarding the health of the soul, about the ends a man should seek, the permanent sources of satisfaction, and the delusory character of many apparently satisfying ends. These beliefs are not merely what seemed true to Plato, but what moral teachers have generally taught and men have usually acknowledged. Not many of us would really doubt the validity of the principles that Plato wishes his citizens to accept and live by; most of this doctrine is completely obvious. Furthermore, the methods he advocates for moral instruction—the training of the feelings, the discipline of the passions, the formation of habits to supplement the teaching of principles—are precisely those used in all ages by teachers who take seriously the training of character. They try to enchant the soul so that it will instinctively love what intelligent judgment pronounces best.[34] Perhaps when we use these techniques of persuasion we are unconsciously relying either upon the correcting effect of other influences (which we however usually deplore), or upon the knowledge that our scientific skill is far from adequate for anything like the creation of character (which again we are often grieved to have to admit). If we were completely consistent in our procedure, and thoroughly confident of the ends we set ourselves, it seems we should welcome wholeheartedly the scientific persuasion Plato proposes for the control of human behavior. This extension of the role of science in human affairs has become almost a commonplace among recent scientists

[34] It is clearly unjustified, therefore, to accuse Plato of a lack of moral integrity, or of advocating "foul means of persuasion," as does Popper, *The Open Society and its Enemies*, Chap. vii, n. 10.

and philosophers.[35] But most of us, however rational we consider ourselves, are reluctant to admit the rule of science in this thorough-
going sense, though why we should feel so is too much of a puzzle
to be solved here. Plato obviously felt no such reluctance.

Plato uses "law" to denote all the rules, whether moral or legal,
whereby the individual's life can be made orderly and comely (718a).
This usage reflects his countrymen's habits of thought; for νόμος was
generally considered as embracing not merely the formal laws publicly inscribed, but also the unwritten rules of conduct and behavior
generally recognized as binding. But Plato's conception also has a
firm foundation in his philosophy, as will be clear if we look again
at the *Philebus*. In its most general sense law corresponds to the second of the four factors mentioned in the analysis on which the argument of that dialogue is based (23b-d). It is the Limit (πέρας)
which, when imposed on the indeterminate more-and-less (the ἄπειρον) brings to birth whatever is stable or good or beautiful in nature
and in human life. "Our goddess," says Socrates, "observing the insolence and corruption of all things, since there is no inherent limit
in pleasures or satisfactions, appointed law and order (νόμος καὶ
τάξις) to provide that limit" (26b). This law that produces order
in the soul is formally identical with the Limit that produces health
in the bodily parts and humors; or music out of the indeterminate
range of high and low tones, fast and slow rhythms; or good weather
from the too-much and too-little of hot and cold; or beauty or
strength or any other good thing from the indefinitely varying con-

---

[35] For example, see the conclusion of C. D. Broad's *The Mind and its Place in Nature* (London, 1925, 665-666): "Human control over inorganic nature provides men
with means of destroying life and property on a vast scale; whilst the present emotional make-up of men, and their extraordinarily crude and inept forms of social
organization, make it only too likely that these means will be used. This danger,
so far as I can see, could be averted only by deliberately altering the emotional
constitution of mankind, and deliberately constructing more sensible forms of social
organization. And it is quite useless to attempt the latter without the former. In
order to do this a vast development of scientific psychology would be needed for two
different reasons. . . . It would obviously be needed in order to know how to alter
the emotional make-up of the individual. But . . . we might know how to do these
things, and yet it might be quite impossible to get people to submit to having these
things done to them. For this purpose we should need an enormous development
of what Kant calls 'the wholesome art of persuasion'; and this could arise only on
the basis of a profound theoretical knowledge of the factors which produce, modify,
and remove nonrational beliefs." A vivid picture of such a scientifically controlled
society is to be found in Aldous Huxley's *Brave New World*. Few readers of this
book find the prospect an attractive one.

stituents that go into their composition (25e-26b). The functions of the Limit that concern Plato in the *Laws* are obviously the orderliness that makes a good man out of the desires, feelings, and thoughts that belong to human nature, and the orderliness that makes a good city out of the varieties of individuals and institutions that are found together in a community.

Thus morality and law are two species of a common genus, and sometimes one and sometimes the other seems to be uppermost in Plato's thought. This explains why the end of law is stated in two apparently different ways in his text. Sometimes law is said to aim at the production of virtue in the individual citizens, especially at the greatest of the virtues, wisdom, ($\phi\rho\acute{o}\nu\eta\sigma\iota\varsigma$), and with it temperance ($\sigma\omega\phi\rho\sigma\sigma\acute{v}\nu\eta$), justice ($\delta\iota\kappa\alpha\iota\sigma\acute{v}\nu\eta$), and courage ($\dot{\alpha}\nu$-$\delta\rho\epsilon\acute{\iota}\alpha$).[36] The gravest fault the Athenian finds in Cretan and Spartan laws is that they aim at only a part of virtue, and that the lowest. In an early passage the Athenian suggests that this conception of law as aiming at the production of complete virtue provides a scheme for the systematic arrangement of the laws, each section of the code being designed to further a particular virtue or make secure certain goods (631b-632e; cf. 718ab); and he asks his companions to call him to task if he ever seems to be aiming at something other than virtue or a part of it in his legislation (705e).

But in other passages the emphasis is upon the function of law in ordering the city. The end of law is said to be the common good ($\tau\dot{o}$ $\kappa\sigma\iota\nu\hat{\eta}$ $\sigma\nu\mu\phi\acute{\epsilon}\rho\sigma\nu$), not the interests of a part of the state (714c-715d, 875a); and the best laws are those that succeed in making the state as unified as possible (739c-e). In this last passage Plato recalls the ideal of complete communism expressed in the *Republic* and declares that no other conception can surpass it in excellence; it is suited, however, only for "gods or sons of gods." In the state we are constructing the legislator must aim instead at wisdom, freedom, and friendship,[37] all obviously traits that promote unity or are characteristic of it. Wisdom—here thought of not as an individual virtue but as the character of a good society—is the quality of a state with

[36] 630a, 688ab, 705d, 707d, 708d, 770d; cf. *Gorg.* 504d, 506d, 508a.
[37] 701d, 693b. Plato's triad of ends forms an interesting contrast to the Liberty, Equality, and Fraternity of the French Revolution. Equality does not appear in Plato's "slogan," though there is a place for it in his state, i.e. for proportionate, not arithmetical, equality. Equality of proportion promotes friendship, whereas the undiscerning equality of number is a source of division (757a).

rulers capable of giving intelligent guidance without overstepping their authority (688e-692c). Good laws will provide for the production of such leaders and for their necessary restraint. Liberty receives rather scanty treatment in Plato's text, and it seems to have meant for him primarily the status of free men under a law which they can invoke for their protection. In this sense it is of course extremely important, being a constituent of the rule of law; without it there can be no concord, since "slaves and masters never can be friends" (757a). There is another meaning of freedom—i.e. political independence, freedom from external domination—which Plato likewise treats as a self-evident good, but this meaning is of minor relevance to the internal organization of a state.[38] Of more relevance to us is the freedom of speech and the resulting "community of mind" that characterized the ancient Persians before they fell into despotism (694b). But the control Plato provides over art, education, and daily life shows that he did not value the kind of liberty that has played such an important part in modern political philosophy. In fact he almost uses ἐλευθερία to denote one of the two political extremes to be avoided.[39] But the importance of friendship is repeatedly emphasized; it is the trait that best expresses the ideal unity of which our state is only a second-best imitation.[40]

These two functions of law—in regulating the individual and in regulating the state—though distinct, are not for Plato incompatible. For the city is simply the collection of its citizens,[41] and its welfare is their welfare. The common interest which law tries to further is not that the state should be great or rich or powerful, but that its citizens should be the best and happiest possible (742d; cf. 743c, 707d). Conversely, the virtue it aims at is the virtue of the citizen, not of the man without a country (643e). This reconciliation of the individual and the common good presupposes the argument of the *Republic* that happiness for man is possible only in a community, and that whatever differences of function and privilege are required to make a proper community are a part of the individual's good (cf. 875a); but its chief support in the *Laws* is the ancient doctrine that

---

[38] Cf. the praise of Athens in the *Menexenus* (239ff.) as the champion of liberty in this sense.

[39] Cf. ἐλευθεριάσαι, 701e.

[40] On the importance of φιλία see 627e-628a, 738de, 743c, 759b, 771d. "Friendship is more important than justice," says Aristotle (*Nic. Eth.* 1155a 22-24).

[41] Plato's city is οἱ Μάγνητες (see Chapter I, Note 59), just as Athens was οἱ Ἀθηναῖοι, Sparta οἱ Λακεδαιμόνιοι, in universal Greek usage.

the real goods are the goods of the soul—i.e. the virtues themselves
—whereas the goods of the body and external possessions are of secondary value.[42] Good citizens, therefore, will compete with one another in virtue, a form of competition that results in multiplying the
goods to be shared, so that all are the gainers. There is latent here the
question later discussed at some length by Aristotle, whether the
virtue of the good man and the virtue of the good citizen are one
and the same thing.[43] Aristotle answers it, in Platonic fashion, by
saying that they coincide in a good state, which is what Plato is
endeavoring to construct.

Besides this distinction between morality and law, there is another
that is always implied in Plato's text, the distinction between ideal
and positive law. In these various statements regarding the nature
and end of law Plato is obviously thinking of the ideal, not of the
written rules and customs that made up the laws of the cities that
he and his contemporaries knew. Some of these positive laws are
not even aimed at the virtue of the citizens or at the common good
—for example, those designed only with a view to the greatness,
wealth, or power of a city (742d), or enacted in the interests of the
ruling faction (714bc); and others, though rightly aimed, miss the
mark through want of skill on the part of the legislator. The Athenian's criticisms of Crete and Sparta and of his own city show that
many so-called laws, even in well-ordered states, do not meet the
criterion that he has formulated. Strictly speaking, such laws are not
really entitled to the name; and this conclusion is actually drawn
and defended by Socrates in the *Minos* (317bc). The *Laws* does not
make this inference; it insists rather on the concept of "right laws"
(ὀρθοὶ νόμοι) as the standard by which existing laws are to be judged,
and the "true legislator" (ὁ ὀρθῶς νομοθετῶν) as showing the way to
others. The passages referring to right laws and to rightness in legislation are numerous enough to show that this is the conception Plato
is working with.[44] But generally the term "law" is used without

---

[42] 631c, 697bc, 743e, 744a. Aristotle (*Nic. Eth.* 1098b 13-18) says that this ranking
of the three sorts of goods was ancient and agreed upon by the philosophers.

[43] *Pol.* 1276b 16 - 1277b 32; 1278a 40 - b 5.

[44] See 674b, 715b, ὀρθοὶ νόμοι; 705e, τίθεσθαι τὸν νόμον ὀρθῶς; 751b, τοῖς εὖ
κειμένοις νόμοις; 631b, ἔχουσιν γὰρ ὀρθῶς (sc. οἱ Κρητῶν νόμοι; 742d, τόν γε
ὀρθῶς νομοθετοῦντα; 739b, νόμοι ἄριστοι; cf. 632e, 657a, 659d, and *Hipp. Mj.* 284d.
This doctrine of "richtiges Recht" in Plato has been clearly seen and expounded by
Walther Eckstein, *Das Antike Naturrecht in Sozialphilosophischer Beleuchtung,*

qualification, even when it is clear that Plato means "right law"; and this use of the term, now to denote the ideal, and at other times as a designation for positive prescriptions, shows that in Plato's text it is already infected with the ambiguity that has ever since clung to it. But the careful reader can have no doubt of Plato's intention. In a passage that reproduces in brief the myth of the *Politicus* Plato describes the ideal as represented in the so-called "age of Kronos," when men lived under the rule of higher beings, with reverence (αἰδώς) and lawfulness (εὐνομία) in their souls, in peace, happiness, and justice with one another (713cd). This is the pattern of life that the legislator must imitate, "giving to Reason's ordering the name of law" (714a).

If we ask how this pattern of right legislation is to be discerned, Plato's answer is, by the use of Reason. Nous is presented in the *Philebus* as the cause of that mixture of the Limit and the Indefinite from which arise the determinate qualities and structures in the world of Becoming. Nous then, is the source of law; for law as it operates in human society is, we have seen, but a special case of the operation of the Limit. As a cosmic factor, Nous is the source of the orderliness of the heavenly bodies, those "visible gods" that Plato finds to be the most resplendent images of the divine in nature; and it is the working of this Nous upon the region of Necessity that is described in the *Timaeus*, under the metaphor of the demiurge, as bringing into being this ordered cosmos and all its parts. But nous is also a constituent of human nature. The wise legislator is frequently described as one who has nous (νοῦν ἔχων, 742d and elsewhere)—a popular designation for a man who, as we say, has his wits about him, but one which Plato obviously uses in a deeper sense. For nous is the highest of various manifestations of intelligence in man. There is calculation (λογισμός) of better and worse (645ab), which has the function of resisting the tug of pain and fear in this puppet nature which is man's; there is opinion (δόξα), which under proper instruction can be true opinion (632c); there is wisdom (φρόνησις), which seems to include both the knowledge (ἐπιστήμη) of the *Republic* as well as moral sanity (σωφροσύνη), an accord between knowledge and feeling (688b); but nous appears to be the

---

Vienna and Leipzig, 1926, 55-71. The same concept appears in the early Aristotle; see Frag. 13W of the *Protrepticus*: μόνου τῶν δημιουργῶν τοῦ φιλοσόφου καὶ νόμοι καὶ πράξεις εἰσὶν ὀρθαὶ καὶ καλαί.

highest expression of intelligence, whether as the most important constituent in phronesis, or above it, is hard to say (632c). It is the nous in the members of the Nocturnal Council that affords salvation to the state (961d). The wise legislator, then, by virtue of the nous in him which participates in the cosmic Nous, is able to apprehend and prescribe right laws for his city. Against those who assert that all law is positive law, that no law has any foundation in "nature," Plato argues vigorously that the primary moving force in nature is soul; hence law and art, which are products of soul, are at least as primary as nature. Thus he resolves the antithesis between φύσις and νόμος; law is "the offspring of Nous by right reason" (νοῦ γέννημα κατὰ λόγον ὀρθόν, 890d); it is the name we give to the "regulation of Nous" (τὴν τοῦ νοῦ διανομήν, 714a).

This is essentially the doctrine of the Law of Nature, as it was later formulated by the Stoics—the conception of a higher law of Reason which serves as a norm or pattern for positive law, and which man can apprehend by virtue of his participation in the world Logos. Plato, to be sure, nowhere uses the phrase "law of nature," but it was he who provided the philosophical foundation which permitted the conjunction of these two terms, previously regarded as antithetical. If the writings of the early Stoics had not come down to us in such a fragmentary state we should be able to see more clearly the influence of Plato's thought upon the formation of the Stoic doctrine. As it is we know that Panaetius was indebted to Plato, and Cicero was a devotee of both; and the Stoic formulas presuppose such a developed philosophy of man and the cosmos as only Plato's teaching, so far as we know, could have supplied.[45] Plato's contribution to the formulation of this Stoic doctrine has seldom been appreciated; but clearly the *Laws* should receive a large part of the credit for the beneficent influence which the stern idealism of the Stoic doctrine has had upon all later jurisprudence and legislation.

As an offspring or manifestation of Nous, law should be capable of rational formulation; and so it is that the competent legislator is thought of as possessing an art (τέχνη), analogous to the art of the

---

[45] See my article cited in Chapter VIII, Note 259. To the small group of students who have recognized Plato's contribution to the development of this doctrine should now be added Jerome Hall, "Plato's Legal Philosophy," *Indiana Law Journal* XXXI, 1956, 201-205.

pilot or the physician.[46] Like any other body of rational knowledge, legislation will be systematic, its various parts properly arranged into an intelligible whole. At the beginning of the dialogue Plato's Athenian seems to be preoccupied with the philosophical task of finding a system in the legislation of Minos and Lycurgus that would be clear to the skilled jurist (διάδηλα τῷ περὶ νόμων ἐμπείρῳ τέχνῃ, 632d), and himself gives a brief illustration of a systematic code arranged according to the table of virtues, in sharp contrast to the Athenian code drawn up at the end of the fifth century, in which the laws were arranged, it seems, merely according to the various officers whose duty it was to administer them.[47] Plato's legislation for his imaginary colony is a more elaborate example of legal system, with its sharp separation of constitutional law ("the establishment of offices") from the rest of his legislation, and the division of the latter into separate chapters dealing with marriage and the family, education, agriculture, offenses against the public, homicide, assault, hybris (including hybris against the gods), property, theft, contracts and sales, judicial procedure, and military duties.[48] Such a rational construction must be consistent. The legislator cannot say two contrary things about the same subject at different times; that is the privilege of the poet, Plato says ironically (719cd). Again, legislation must be definite, stating the punishable offenses clearly and differentiating them into as many kinds as justice requires;[49] examples of this are his distinctions between the kinds of homicide, assault, injury, and (a region where Attic law was most vague) impiety. In thus conceiving of legislation as the technique of introducing systematic unity, clarity, and consistency into a mass of separate prescriptions, Plato has apprehended an essential characteristic of juristic science, and his own legislation provides an example of it without precedent up to his time. This is one meaning of his doctrine that right law has its source in Nous.

[46] Cf. the kingly art (βασιλικὴ τέχνη) discussed and defined in the *Politicus*, an art which includes that of legislation (νομοθετική, 294a).

[47] See Kahrstedt, *Klio* xxxi, 1938, 11; and Chapter V, "Aristocracy with the Approval of the People."

[48] There is explicit recognition of these separate chapters in 842de. Gernet, ccv: "Ce qui est beaucoup plus visible dans le traitement de la matière juridique, c'est un souci d'ordonnance et de rigeur logique. On l'attendait bien: c'est la part du philosophe dans l'affaire que ce rationalisme constructif."

The contents of the last two books exhibit much less system than Books VI to X. Plato was evidently still at work on them when he died, and their present arrangement may be due to Philippus of Opus; see Excursus F.

[49] 769d, 865a, 874e, 885ab.

But the material content and purpose of the legal system is an even more important aspect of juristic science as Plato conceives it. The competent legislator will have a rational grasp of the end to which law, if it is to be right law, must be directed, and must know also the proper means of accomplishing this end through appropriate prescriptions (962b). The principle that right law aims at the virtue of the citizen and at freedom, wisdom, and friendship in the community, is obviously not a matter of scientific demonstration; but neither is it an arbitrarily selected principle, a postulate of no greater worth than any other that one might adopt as the foundation for a legislative code. It can itself be reached by rational methods, so Plato thinks, and rational inquiry will further clarify it and reveal its implications. This is the clear import of the passage describing the higher studies of the Nocturnal Council. Their meetings are described as occasions for pursuing the more abstruse aspects of mathematics, music, and astronomy, and carrying on the dialectic examination of the nature of virtue and its various parts. There is no hint that Plato thinks of intelligence at this stage as evaporating into mystic insight or ecstasy. There will be illumination and inspiration from such studies; but it will be the illumination that comes from the exercise of reason, and the inspiration that is implied in the student's possession of the nous connecting him with the reason in the cosmos. Juristic reason here becomes jurisprudence, for it has attained in some degree the wisdom by which the technique of legislation is to be guided.

To say that legislation is the work of reason does not mean, for Plato, that it will take no account of experience. It is well to emphasize this point, for Plato's rationalism has often been misconceived. The dramatic structure of the dialogue, in which the Athenian, the Cretan, and the Lacedaemonian pool their experiences, and the mass of empirical material in the legislation that results, which we have seen is almost always a reflection of positive law and customs, are indications of the way Plato thinks a competent legislator will use the facts of experience and the lessons of history. He is like a stone mason who, from the pile of rock brought to the site of his construction, chooses carefully the blocks that will fit into his wall, laying some aside and setting the others in positions for which they are best adapted (858b). Some of these materials will be laws devised by previous legislators; some will be long-established customs whose very survival through many generations shows that they have some merit; others will be accepted merely because there is no available alternative. Like the pilot, or the physician, or the general, the legislator shows his skill in knowing the structure of the end he wants to attain and finding the empirical means that are adapted to it (962b; cf. 709b). Thus the work of reason is not to deduce laws from a first principle, but to select from experience those principles and practices that conduce to the legislator's end and fit them into an articulated and mutually supporting whole.[50]

Plato's recognition of this empirical material as adaptable to the legislator's purpose implies that it already contains some traces of the ideal which is the legislator's goal; for if the Nous that is the source of right law is not already present to some degree in the customs and institutions of history there would be an intolerable contradiction between his doctrine and his practice. How is this presence of Nous to be explained? Solon and Lycurgus, and other great legislators who have left their mark upon their people's institutions, are to be credited, of course, with a share of this cosmic Nous. Besides them there are countless unrecorded wise men who have seen the good for their cities and persuaded their peoples to accept their counsel. And there is also a divine chance or providence ($\theta\epsilon\hat{\iota}\alpha$ $\mu o\hat{\iota}\rho\alpha$) which plays a part in human history; and many customs that appear to have sprung up spontaneously, or to have been determined by accident, are the result of some such divine leading. There are many references in Plato's thought to the presence and effects of this factor.[51] But it is everywhere entangled with the works of blind chance and circumstance, and it is the task of the philosophical legislator to screen it out, guided by his clear awareness of the nature of Nous and its demands.

Like the demiurge described in the *Timaeus*, the legislator has to

[50] Cf. the statement of Rudolf Stammler, a modern exponent of Natural Law: "Vernunft heisst nicht das Vermögen, rechtliche Einrichtungen und staatliche Bildungen neu zu erschaffen, sondern vielmehr das Vermögen des Menschen, den geschichtlich bedingten Stoff nach Prinzipien zu bearbeiten, d.h. unter zwei sich bietenden Möglichkeiten die richtige Wahl zu treffen." *Rechts- und Staatstheorien der Neuzeit*, 45. Gernet (ccv) characterizes Plato's procedure as a "rationalisme constructif," which proceeds "nullement à priori, et pour une raison très simple: on peut inventer, à la rigeur, un système sociale, on ne peut inventer des notions de droit, qui sont de l'ordre du technique. On peut seulement les déplacer, les limiter, les élargir—c'est un travail de réformateur; ou les réflechir, dégager l'intelligibilité de leur ensembles—c'est un travail de juriste. Les deux ne sont pas incompatibles; ils ne sont pas chez Platon."

[51] E.g. *Rep.* 493a, 499b; *Laws* 642c, 875c; *Ep. VII* 326b.

work with materials that are to some extent intractable, and under circumstances that are only partially subject to his control. The citizens for whom he is legislating are not the sons of gods, but human offspring (cf. 853c); and he is legislating in a world where the circumstances of war, or famine, or disease, or unlucky conjunctures of events often play the deciding part (709ab). The Athenian is tempted to declare that man never legislates; God and chance rule the affairs of men. But then he recalls that in any emergency—whether a severe illness, a storm at sea, or a military peril—the possession of skill (τέχνη) always contributes something to the averting of evils. Like the pilot, the physician, and the general, the legislator can never be sure of success, even when circumstances are most favorable; but his art is indispensable, and he must do the best he can.

If now we ask what is the law that is sovereign in Plato's state, we shall have to say that only "right law," strictly speaking, can be sovereign, for it alone is a full and unblemished expression of Nous. It may then seem that the ambiguity of the term "law" has led Plato into a self-contradiction. For it is positive law—the law of his proposed city—whose supremacy he takes such pains to assure through the devices we have discussed in this chapter, whereas it is ideal law that has an imprescriptible right to rule. Yet the contradiction is partially removed when we recall his conception of a pattern and its imitations. His law is an imitation of the ideal, and on this ground is entitled to the obedience of citizens and officials. So also would be the laws of any other state which aim at the moral perfection of the citizens, and their wisdom, freedom, and concord in community. Would Plato advocate the rule of law when the laws serve only the wealth, power, or security of a city, or are designed in the interests of a special class? The argument of the *Politicus* suggests that obedience to law is always preferable to subjection to the will of ignorant and self-interested officials; so that even in the worst-ordered cities there is at least some imitation of the ideal. There is no hint in any of the dialogues that Plato recognizes the right of civil disobedience. A citizen may try to persuade the laws that they are wrong, as Socrates puts it in the *Crito* (52a), but he may not disobey; and the abhorrence of political violence that Plato expresses on many occasions shows that the convictions of Socrates are his also.[52] His advocacy of

---

[52] See especially *Ep. VII* 331b-d.

the rule of law can therefore be taken in its full range, from the popular to the philosophical level; but it is the philosophical conception of law as the expression of reason that alone justifies the attitude of the multitude towards it.

If no human legislation, not even that which is being formulated in the *Laws*, can be more than an imitation of the ideal, it would seem that provision must be made for its amendment and improvement. An ideal system of law should be immutable (ἀκίνητα); and there are passages in which Plato suggests that his own laws should not be changed, at least after they have been brought to perfection.[53] But he is aware that his legislation will need to be supplemented at many points—judicial procedure (846bc, 855cd, 957ab) and the regulation of sacrifices, songs and dances (772a, 835ab) are the most conspicuous instances—and in one passage he implies that his work will not be complete until he has provided for a group of persons who will be competent to touch it up, remove its defects, and in general to see that it does not grow worse, but better, as time goes on (769de). Except for this passage, Plato seems to think that after a certain time (ten years is mentioned in one place) there will have been sufficient trial and experience to justify making the laws henceforth immutable. He seems to have no idea of indefinite progress; one cannot improve upon perfection, and like Bentham he is apparently so confident of his science of legislation as to think that perfection is not far distant. Nevertheless it is a fact that he contemplates the amending of his laws. Naturally he intends that the process of amendment, like the original lawmaking, shall be under the guidance of Nous and be aimed at making the existing law an even closer likeness of the ideal. The Nocturnal Council, with its carefully selected members, its daily conferences on law, and its concern with the higher sciences that prepare the mind for apprehending the source of law in the cosmic Nous, is obviously the organ intended for apprehending and declaring the higher principles on which law, if it is right law, must depend. And the injunction that the members of this Council shall study the working of their own laws and compare them with the laws of other lands, as learned from the reports of their own theoroi and of visiting theoroi from abroad, shows that in making proposals for revision they are expected to proceed as did

[53] 656de, 772c, 798ab, 816c, 846c, 957ab.

the original legislator, i.e. by taking account of the lessons of history and experience.

No general procedure is laid down for giving effect to the Nocturnal Council's proposals for amendment; but there is a suggestion of such a procedure in a passage referring to the amendment of the laws regarding choruses and dancing. In this case the proposals for change must be referred to "the people (δῆμος), the officers, and all the oracles" (772cd). It is very likely that Plato thought of this, or something like it, as the procedure that would naturally be employed in any proposal for amendment.[54] Some such public ratification or acceptance, sometimes even an oath of obedience, generally followed the work of a legislator, so far as we can determine. As to the part the Nocturnal Council would play in such a procedure, we have not even a suggestion; but it is probable, since no legal powers are explicitly conferred upon it, that the process of amendment would be initiated by the guardians, the Nocturnal Council serving rather as a learned body, like the legislative commissions of modern times, whose part it is to make studies and proposals for action by the legally constituted officers. This is a conjecture, but I think a plausible one; for it accords with the part which Plato's Academy seems to have played at Athens through the participation of some of its Athenian members in public life.

Thus the rule of law becomes in Plato's hands a doctrine of tremendous range and power. The instinctive respect for law among the Greeks is shown to have a philosophical justification, for the claims of law to be sovereign are eventually its claim to be the expression of reason—reason in its simplest manifestation as the good sense of honest men endeavoring to order their lives prudently, and of good statesmen trying to bring virtue and happiness to their cities; and in its higher forms this same human reason become aware through philosophic discipline of the cosmic Nous upon which it depends. But the genius of Plato lies not only in his providing a

---

[54] The language of 772cd could be interpreted as actually prescribing this procedure for all changes in the laws; but the context shows, I think, that it is the laws regarding the canons of dancing and choruses that Plato has in mind here. The additional provision that any objector to the change can veto it—τὸν κωλύοντα ἀεὶ κατὰ νόμον κρατεῖν—if taken as meaning any member of the assembly or officers, would make change practically impossible and this passage pointless. Plato would make change difficult, but at least possible. For this reason I think it means that if any of the three consulting bodies refuses to approve, the change shall not take effect.

philosophical justification for the rule of law. It is shown even more in his demiurgic skill in finding means to make this authority effective—through common education that produces eunomia in the souls of the citizens, through legal procedures to prevent the overthrow of law by official caprice or ignorance, and through provision for higher studies to make possible the orderly interpretation and amendment of the laws. Above all is his own example of a comprehensive code intended to express, both in its rational and systematic form, and in the consistent teleology of its content, the reason that gives it authority. In the *Laws* the philosopher, the spectator of all time and all existence, joins forces with the jurist, the student and critic of legal concepts and procedures. Plato would probably not have regarded these as two different sides of his genius; but we have usually tended to disjoin them and to think of him primarily as a philosopher. It is well for us to redress the balance of our appreciation and recognize that as a jurist also he is an intellectual creator, the daemonic first member of a long line of eminent successors.[55]

[55] On the "mentalité de juriste" that Plato exhibits in the *Laws*, see Gernet, *Le Droit grec ancien: Notions générales*, 46.

CHAPTER XII

THE RULE OF PHILOSOPHY

THE WORD φιλοσοφία does not appear in the *Laws*, and its cognates only rarely; and we hear little of the familiar doctrine of Ideas.[1] But the distinction between an ideal or "pattern" world, and the world of opinions and conventions that imitates it more or less faithfully, is fundamental, as we have seen, to the rule of law on which the state is based; and this affirmation of a higher and more intelligible order, whose apprehension not only gives understanding of our world but also provides the motive and guidance for its improvement is, I believe, the essential trait of Plato's conception of philosophy. The laws under which the citizens will live are the work of a philosopher; for the Athenian Stranger is a personage so like the author of the *Laws* that we are justified in regarding him, if not as a spokesman for Plato himself, at least as some like-minded member of the Academy familiar with the disciplines required for philosophical legislation. And the Athenian Stranger in formulating the laws to be accepted either employs (in the conversational passages) the dialectical methods made familiar to us in Plato's other dialogues, or relies upon the insights which these dialogues arrive at through philosophical inquiry.[2]

Finally, the "head" of the state is to be the Nocturnal Council, an institution designed to perpetuate the founder's apprehension of the law and its purposes; its members are "the true guardians of the laws" (966b). Few readers have failed to recognize in the Nocturnal Councillors of the *Laws* the philosopher-kings of the *Republic*. The programs of higher education in the two works are strikingly similar in content and purpose. As in the *Republic* the goal of these higher studies is unified insight based on knowledge of the Good, so in the *Laws* their purpose is synthesis—an apprehension of the one end of the state that includes all lesser ends (962de, 965cd), of the unity that pervades the variety of the virtues (963a-964a). Dialectic is an

---

[1] It is not indeed ignored; there are rather clear references to this doctrine in the closing pages (965bc). See Victor Brochard, *Études de philosophie ancienne et de philosophie moderne*, Paris, 1912, 154ff.; and Harold Cherniss, *Gnomon* xxv, 1953, 375-376.

[2] The persuasive preambles, by analogy with the discourses of the free physician to his patients, will use something close to philosophy in their arguments (τοῦ φιλοσοφεῖν ἐγγὺς χρώμενον τοῖς λόγοις, 857d).

essential method in both groups of studies—explicitly described in the *Republic*, illustrated in the *Laws* by a short and very elementary dialogue on the problem of the unity and plurality of the virtues (963d-967b). Mathematics, with harmonics and music, is necessary in both programs for the proper apprehension of ultimate truth (967de). It is at first sight surprising that these preliminary sciences, as well as the other elements of this higher education just mentioned, are treated so briefly in the *Laws* in comparison with the lengthy discussion of them in the *Republic*. But Plato's advanced age gave him no time for repeating himself here, even if that had been desirable; instead he gives attention to inquiries not mentioned in the *Republic*—cosmology and theology—and emphasizes certain doctrines that he had apparently seen clearly only after writing the earlier work, viz. the priority of the soul in the cosmos, the orderly movements of the heavenly bodies, and the cosmic theology to which they lead—doctrines which he has indeed treated quite fully in the tenth book of the *Laws*. This means that there is a stronger theological tinge in the philosophy of this later program; but the philosopher's God is the cosmic Nous which is the source of all right law, and therefore presupposes, though it may also go beyond, the Idea of the Good. In short, the studies mentioned in the *Laws* do not displace but rather supplement the ones described in the *Republic*, and like them are a preparation for philosophical guardianship.

It is obvious, however, that Plato has not provided, either in the *Republic* or in the *Laws*, the conditions that we think necessary for that free exercise of mind in criticising accepted opinions, in adopting alternative hypotheses and tracing out their implications, and arriving by dialectic at a clearer apprehension of first principles—conditions that we associate with the study of philosophy. The sessions of the Nocturnal Council will indeed give some opportunity for this kind of critical inquiry. So long as it is felt that the legislation is still imperfect, the Council will not merely be a forum for a closed system of doctrine. Plato's recognition that no principles can remain alive unless they are perpetually apprehended afresh, and his care to include within the Council's sessions an equal number of younger men who are to be the eyes and ears of the assembly, show that he intends it to be a medium for the enlivening of convictions and the attaining of fresh insights. But the restriction of critical inquiry to this highly selected body, and the stern indoctrination to which most of its members have been subjected in earlier years and continue to be exposed outside its precincts, make us doubt whether it could really maintain its position as an island of free inquiry in the midst of such an ocean of social pressures as Plato elsewhere provides. The assumption that the laws are very near perfection would inevitably narrow the range of inquiry. Whatever criticisms may properly be made of the *Laws* can be directed with equal force against the *Republic*, where the minds of the philosopher-guardians are molded with similar rigor, and their selection for high office is even stricter.[3] Plato never succeeded in reconciling his demand for the exercise of critical reason in human affairs with his concern for the moral and intellectual health, as he conceived it, of his fellowmen.

Yet it can hardly be denied that Plato intends the Nocturnal Council to be a means of bringing critical intelligence to bear upon the problems of law and social policy, and this would make it to some degree a forum for controversy. More clearly than some liberals of later times, he sees that differences of opinion are likely to be fruitful only against a background of tenets held in common. Where there is no common faith—social, moral, or religious—intellectual disputes are usually nothing but the thinly disguised clash of irreconcilable interests and temperaments. The common faith that Plato presupposes and would make secure among his citizens is certainly broad enough to accommodate many divergent growths within it. Furthermore, his Council provides a certain check upon the misuse of persuasion, a problem to which I called attention in the preceding chapter. Outside the Council there will be few influences to counteract the effects of official doctrine, if Plato's intent is realized; but there might be many such forces inside it to curb eccentric and arbitrary policy, and to moderate the official program of public instruction and persuasion. Its decisions and proposals, being the result of collaboration, would resemble the reports of a President's Commission or a Church Council—seldom advocating any revolutionary change, yet not altogether closed to new ideas if these ideas are "sound" and their advocates persuasive.[4]

[3] Note, for example, the postponement of dialectic until the thirtieth year (*Rep.* 537d), and the scorn expressed for the freedom of disputation enjoyed by the young men in some states (539b-d).

[4] One of the qualifications of the ἱκανὸς ἄρχων emphasized at the close of Plato's account of the Nocturnal Council (967e) is that he should be able to "give the reason" (δοῦναι τὸν λόγον) for whatever has reason behind it (ὅσα λόγον ἔχει). Dialectic is commonly described by Plato as the ability λόγον διδόναι καὶ δέξασθαι

Thus philosophy is to play a fundamental part in the life of Plato's Cretan city, not merely at its founding, but also in the later study, interpretation, and revision of its initial laws. But is it the ruling element? Plato asserts so often that law is to rule, he devotes so much attention to the formulation of written laws and the establishment of courts by whose judgments these laws are applied and enforced, and there are so many devices for holding officials responsible for acting within the law, that we must assume he means what he says. The Nocturnal Council should not be taken as a violation of this principle, if the arguments I have advanced in earlier chapters are cogent. It appears that Plato intends it to be a kind of institute of higher studies, with powers chiefly interpretative and advisory; and that whatever its recommendations might be, they are to become effective only through appropriate action by the officers and the courts. Its moral influence is undoubtedly intended to be very great, as it should be; for it will provide the reflective guidance to officials which is necessary if the authority of law is to be maintained. On this interpretation, the Nocturnal Council does not upset the rule of law, but rather makes it possible in a living society, where standing law is in continual need of interpretation, if not revision.

But if this philosophical body is subject to an authority other than itself, it would seem to follow that Plato has abandoned the rule of philosophy. The situation, however, is by no means so simple. What gives law its title to rule is, as we have seen, the Nous it contains; and it is the work of philosophy to apprehend this Nous and to embody it in legislation. The dialectical method of inquiry, which is sometimes what Plato means by philosophy, might indeed be regarded as a handmaid to law, an instrument for finding its proper form and content; but the doctrines and principles resulting from philosophical inquiry must surely be regarded as the authoritative substance in the law which embodies them. Looked at in this light, the authority of philosophy is not only compatible with the rule of law, but actually essential to it; and law becomes a kind of formal sovereign, a politically authoritative expression of the insights of philosophy, so far as they bear upon the ordering of states. At the same time law becomes essential to the effective authority of philosophy; for it is not abstract theoretical insights that govern the city,

(cf. *Prot.* 336bc, *Polit.* 286a, *Rep.* 531e, 534b). It is clearly his intent that the persuasion employed in the Council shall be at the high level of intelligent discussion.

but these insights formulated in legal terms and publicly declared as rules for the ordering of the state. There would thus be a kind of compound sovereignty[5]—of legal technique and scientific knowledge, neither of which is capable of accomplishing its political task without the other. Thus in the *Laws* the rule of law and the rule of philosophy are inseparably combined.

This interpretation of the *Laws* appears to be incompatible with the thesis of the *Politicus* that there is an antithesis between scientific rule and the rule of law, and with the *Republic*, in which, so it is usually said, the presence of law is regarded as a hindrance to the philosopher-kings in the exercise of their scientific rule. If my interpretation is correct, it implies not—as is usually believed—that the Plato of the *Laws* has abandoned the rule of philosophy for the rule of law,[6] but rather that he has reconciled the competing claims of these two rivals for the position of supreme authority. This is inherently a more plausible interpretation of Plato's philosophical development than the supposition that he completely reversed himself. There is reason to think, moreover, that the antithesis between philosophy and law was never so irreconcilable for Plato as it has been for his interpreters. There was development in Plato's thinking about the respective functions of law and philosophy in a properly constituted state, and about the institutions through which they can effectively exert their authority; the solution finally described in the *Laws*, however, does not involve a break with the earlier dialogues, but rather a development of what they imply. To see that this is indeed the case we must take a fresh look at these earlier dialogues in the light afforded by the union of law and philosophy that we find in the later work.

Let us begin with the *Republic*. This work is generally supposed

[5] The words "sovereign" and "sovereignty" are used here as meaning "supreme" and "supreme authority." In Plato's state there is obviously no sovereign in the sense that this term usually has in modern political philosophy, for there is no officer or board of officers whose power is supreme. Indeed it can be regarded as a merit of Plato's thought that he avoids the maze in which even the most acute of modern thinkers have found themselves in trying to locate the determinate person or body of persons who exercise sovereignty in a state that recognizes the rule of law.

[6] Zeller's interpretation has set the pattern for generations of students. "The *Republic* makes philosophy the groundwork of rational political life and, presupposing philosophical rulers, plans the state purely from the Idea; the *Laws* seeks to show how far, and through what means, the state may be adequate to its task without this presupposition." *Plato and the Older Academy*, 522.

to have been constructed upon the assumption that the presence of law would be a hindrance to the exercise of scientific rule. Socrates describes a society, so it is said, in which intelligence is completely sovereign—intelligence of the highest sort, of course, entirely beneficient in its aims, utilizing and directing the materials of human nature and society to bring about justice in the state and in the individuals that compose it. Such a sovereign must be free not merely from ignorance and self-interest, but also from tradition, precedent, and prescription; for without such freedom it cannot make the fullest application of its knowledge to the problems with which it has to deal.[7] This interpretation of the *Republic* has a long and respected history and may probably be taken as the orthodox view. But is law really absent from the *Republic*, as this interpretation asserts?

Whoever reads the *Republic* with this question in mind will be struck by the frequent references to laws (νόμοι) and legislation (νομοθεσία).[8] There are laws regulating poetry (380bc, 383c), laws regarding religion (427b) and festivals (459e), laws governing the practice of medicine (409e), laws prescribing community of wives and children (453d, 457c), laws forbidding private property for the guardians (417b), laws of war (471b), laws concerning military honors (468b), laws prescribing mathematics (525b, 530c) and dialectic (534de) in higher education. Plato emphasizes lawlessness (παρανομία) as the source of degeneration in the state (424d), and the necessity of inculcating lawfulness (εὐνομία) in the citizens from their earliest childhood (425a). Opinion in accord with law (δόξα ἔννομος) is one of the stabilizing factors in a city (433c). These numerous passages show that it cannot have been Plato's intention to exclude law entirely from the state which Socrates describes. There is a certain disdain expressed in two or three passages for the petty details of legislation, but the meaning of these passages has often been distorted. For example, Socrates is reluctant to legislate about business transactions and the niceties of procedure in litigation. The laws that are necessary here (ὅσα δεῖ νομοθετήσασθαι), he says, can be easily worked out by the citizens of our state, "provided they preserve the laws we have previously laid down" (425e). Thus this pas-

---

[7] For this interpretation of the *Republic* see Barker 180 and 205; Sabine, *History of Political Theory*, 63-68; Gomperz, *Griechische Denker* II, 415; and for an able dissent, Hall, "Plato's Legal Philosophy," *Indiana Law Journal* XXXI, 1956, 171-206, esp. 177-184.

[8] The texts are numerous. Besides the passages cited, see 403b, 445e, 456c, 458c, 462a, 484b.

sage does not say, as is sometimes supposed,[9] that no legislation will be necessary on these matters; in fact it says quite the opposite; it only emphasizes that without a faithful observance of more fundamental laws it will be of no use to tinker at minor details (427a).

But "law" is a tricky term; and what is sometimes meant by the exclusion of law from the *Republic* is the exclusion of customary or traditional law.[10] In this restricted sense of the term there is more justification for thinking that Socrates discounts the importance of law; for the laws in which he is most interested are products of free philosophical imagination; they often ignore or openly flout ancestral laws and customs. Yet it hardly seems legitimate to restrict the term "law" to customary law, and to refuse to apply it to other rules which have effective authority in a state, as Socrates assumes his will have. The Greeks, like us, were quite familiar with such exercises in rational lawmaking; the work of all their legislators involved considerable alteration or replacement of ancestral laws. Yet they did not refuse the name νόμος to these legislative inventions, and Plato's usage is quite normal in this respect. But what is more important, if for this reason we regard law as omitted from the *Republic*, we must ignore the respects in which Socrates does introduce traditional law into his state. Empirical legal material is to be found in the *Republic* as well as in the *Laws*, though it is so subordinated to the exposition and illustration of principles that it is easily overlooked. The program of early education, for example, is explicitly borrowed from the past;[11] and in the field of religious observance the philosopher completely refrains from altering established tradition (427b). No doubt Plato's respect for history and tradition steadily increased as he grew older; in the *Laws* what the philosophical legislator uses in the making of his state consists mainly of historically given materials, the customs and institutions of fourth-century Greece. But the recognition of the importance of custom, and true respect for certain elements of fourth-century customary law, are a part of Plato's attitude from the first. Socrates in the *Republic* evidently pins his hopes upon making his laws, however new they may be at the outset, into

[9] Barker, 278, corrected by Hall, *op.cit.* 180-181.

[10] When Sabine speaks of the "omission of law" it seems to be always this massive body of empirical matter that he has in mind. "Law belongs to the class of convention; it rises through use and wont; it is the product of experience growing slowly from precedent to precedent." *Op.cit.* 65.

[11] "It would be hard," says Socrates, "to find a better system than that which long time has discovered." *Rep.* 376e.

living traditions and inveterate customs, what the "laws of Solon"—also quite new and revolutionary when they were propounded—had become for the Athenians.

Thus in neither the broader nor the narrower sense of the term does it seem legitimate to say that law is excluded from the *Republic*. The situation in which Socrates stands is the familiar one of a legislator utilizing and modifying existing traditions, or inventing new institutions for his purpose, just like the Solon or the Lycurgus or the Charondas and Zaleucus of history. He is referred to as the νομοθέτης (458c, 497d), his task is νομοθεσία (427b, 502c), and there is constant use of the dramatic fiction that he is founding a city, as if he were the οἰκιστής of a colony.[12] The situation is comparable to that of the Athenian Stranger and his two companions in the *Laws*, except that it is less concrete and the scope for philosophical imagination is much greater. Both works are based upon the conception of a philosopher exercising the powers so frequently conferred upon the lawmakers and city founders of Greek experience.

Yet the dramatic way in which the idea of philosopher-kings is introduced in the *Republic* (473d) shows that the rule of the philosophers is a paradoxical proposal. Glaucon remarks at once that Socrates must expect to be attacked ruthlessly by many persons of importance. But not apparently because his proposal is taken to mean the omission or exclusion of law, for Socrates' defense does not touch this question at all. Instead he defends his thesis by showing who the genuine philosophers are, what their nature is, and why it belongs to them and to no others to rule. This would certainly be enough to make his proposal paradoxical; it would shock the democrats, who thought that the right to hold office, almost any office, was one of the prerogatives of citizenship; and it would shock the oligarchs and aristocrats, who saw in wealth and good ancestry the proper qualifications for office. No doubt also, as the defense shows, Plato is combating the opinion that philosophy, of all pursuits, was peculiarly likely to unfit a man for public responsibilities. Socrates had declared in the *Gorgias* that he was almost the only true statesman of his time (521d). To one who did not share Plato's admiration of Socrates, or did not understand the meaning of his claim, it would have seemed the height of paradox to advocate that persons of Socra-

[12] Note ᾠκίζομεν, 595a at the end of the legislation; for other examples see 403b, 420b, 421c, 427bc,e, 428c,e, 434e, 443b, 453b, 470e, 497c, 519c.

tes' type be placed in office. But for one who held that the true aim of statesmanship is to improve the citizens, as Socrates maintains in the *Gorgias*, then obviously the first step in political reform would be to put good and wise men in authority over them. Plato's chief concern in the *Republic* is to point out where such good and wise men are to be found, and how they are to be trained for their heavy responsibilities.

Here we come to the crux of the issue. What is to be the character of the rule of these good and wise men? Are they to rule in accordance with law, or are they to be exempt from such control? In trying to see clearly Plato's thought on this point it is necessary to distinguish between the situation at the founding of a city, which obviously confers special powers upon those in charge of events, and the state of affairs after the proposals have become an established polity. In the former case it is apparently presumed that the legislator will have a free hand; he is to devise a constitution and laws as near his ideal as possible, and has the right to use or discard, as he pleases, whatever previous law does or does not serve his purpose. This also is the situation that seems to be presupposed in the passage about the "philosophic dynasts" (φιλόσοφοι δυνάσται, 540d). Here Socrates assumes a city in which a clique of philosophers has come into power and discusses what steps they may most appropriately take to reorganize their city. The "speediest and easiest way," he says, of instituting the constitution that has been described would be to "send out into the fields" all persons above the age of ten and bring up the children under the laws and manners of the new polity, without the contagion of tradition and parental example. This is as ruthless as the exchange of populations between Greece and Turkey at the end of World War I, and like that famous example could only be justified by the greater good that would eventually result. But it does not follow, from the unrestricted prerogatives allowed at the founding of a state, that the rulers in it after it has been established will be free to ignore the law. Let us forget—as Socrates does, if his words are to be taken as a serious proposal—the psychological difficulty that when rulers have begun with such an act of unusual power it will not be easy for them later to accept a more restricted function. Socrates' primary purpose is to depict the working of an ideal state, and only secondarily to show that it could be established and by what means. Let us therefore concentrate our attention on the titles he gives these rulers, and on his description of their functions in the state once it has been established.

When Socrates refers to the rulers of his state by other than the colorless word ἄρχοντες, he calls them guardians (φύλακες). The full meaning of this concept of guardianship (φυλακή) is developed only gradually. At first the guardians are merely the watchdogs of the flock, the military defenders of the state, the artisans of its freedom, i.e. its independence of other states. Then as the philosophic element is seen to be necessary if they are to be true guardians, it appears that they must be guardians of themselves; they must be capable of preserving—against forgetfulness, persuasion, pains, and pleasures—the conviction that their first duty is the welfare of the state (412e). In particular, those who are selected for rule must be "guardians of the education they have received" (413e, 423e; cf. 458c). When they depart from the convictions instilled by their education, lawlessness (παρανομία) enters into the state (424d). Finally, Socrates calls them explicitly "guardians of the laws" (421a, 504c; cf. 484b), using a phrase that Plato later is to make into a title for the highest magistrates in the *Laws*. Thus the function of his guardians in the *Republic* is to maintain the integrity of the state and of the laws that give it the character it has. Socrates affirms that if they preserve the training and education which they have received, these guardians— even if they are only one in number—will not alter "any of the really important laws of the city."[13]

Thus in Socrates' state law is indeed sovereign in right. The rulers are bound by it, though they have helped to formulate it.[14] But the constraint upon them is moral, not legal. This conception of a sovereign who is bound *in foro interno* by the laws under which he rules was familiar to the Greeks; it was in fact their normal conception of a king. Of the five species of kingship mentioned by Aristotle in the *Politics*[15] each, except one (an unusual kind), is characterized as a βασιλεία κατὰ νόμον. In the *Critias* (120a) Plato pictures the kings of the legendary island of Atlantis as taking oath to abide by the laws of Poseidon inscribed on pillars in the center of their city; and

[13] 445e: οὐ . . . κινήσειεν ἂν τῶν ἀξίων λόγου νόμων τῆς πόλεως. See Adam's note on this passage, which refers, for the genitive, to *Gorg.* 514a, *Rep.* 485b.
[14] The guardians must themselves obey the laws. *Rep.* 458c: τὰ μὲν αὐτοὺς [sc. τοὺς ἄρχοντας] πειθομένους τοῖς νόμοις, τὰ δὲ καὶ μιμουμένους, ὅσα ἂν ἐκείνοις ἐπιτρέψωμεν.
[15] *Pol.* 1285a 2ff. Cf. Nilsson 1, 324: "Die griechische Auffassung des Königtums, nach der der König zwar Rechte hatte, aber durch das Recht gebunden ist. . . ."

it is certainly an Academic, if not a Platonic, tradition that is preserved in the Pseudo-Platonic *Definitions*, where a king (βασιλεύς) is defined as an ἄρχων κατὰ νόμους ἀνυπεύθυνος (415b).[16] In the *Republic* Plato sees that only persons with a philosophical nature and training can be trusted to exercise such power wisely and honestly; this explains the care with which in the ensuing discussion he delineates the nature of the genuine philosopher and the training he must have if he is to hold irresponsible power.

It is from this point—and not from a supposed absence of law—that we must measure the difference between the *Republic* and Plato's later work. Philosophers are only human, and pseudo-philosophers are sufficiently numerous to be a hazard, as Plato recognizes in the *Republic* (495f.). His experience at Syracuse, and in other cases in which he had been called upon for legislative advice, must have contributed to form his later view that no human being can be trusted with irresponsible power (691cd, 875ab). Whatever the precise reasons for this increased realism, one of the essential conditions of the state he describes in the *Laws* is that there must be ways of preventing the abuse of power and of eliminating from office those whose actions show that their conscience is not a sufficient safeguard. "No judge or officer is to be ἀνυπεύθυνος" (761e; cf. 946c), he declares; and he carefully sets up legal devices by which all officers in the state may be required to give an accounting of their actions and be held liable to penalty if charges against them are sustained. It is here, rather than in a belated recognition of the importance of law, that the difference between the *Laws* and the *Republic* is to be found.

To this should be added another refinement of Plato's later thought, though it is not worked out so emphatically as the point just mentioned. Any system of laws, however admirable, will inevitably require amendment from time to time. This is recognized even in the *Republic*; I have already quoted Socrates' statement that his guardians will not change any of the really important laws of the city. But this implies that they may make some changes; and since they are assumed to be genuine philosophers, he describes them as contemplating the "vivid pattern" of the ideal which they carry in their souls when they make regulations for their city,[17] just as the founding legislator did

---

[16] 415b: ἀνυπεύθυνος, i.e. not subject to the legal accounting (εὔθυνα) which was usually required of office holders.

[17] *Rep.* 484b-d. See also the passage quoted in Note 14.

when laying down the initial legislation. Plato's later refinement is to see that this task of revision and improvement, if it is to be secure against human ignorance and selfishness, requires a legally constituted body. In the *Laws* it is not the rulers in general who are entrusted with this function, but the elected nomophylakes, aided by the studies and advice of the Nocturnal Council; and their proposals must be accepted, or ratified, in some legally prescribed way before they can take effect (772cd).

Thus when Plato in his later work asserts the rule of law he is merely emphasizing a principle that he had never denied. But this emphasis is weighted with the results of intervening decades of experience and reflection. He had probably been disappointed in persons whom he had thought promising agents of political reform, and he had also become aware of theoretical difficulties in the relation between philosophy and law which were ignored, perhaps not even recognized, when he wrote the *Republic*. About the personal disappointments we can only speculate; but of the theoretical difficulties that he confronted we have evidence in the *Politicus*. This dialogue is generally recognized as forming a kind of bridge between the *Republic* and the *Laws*. It was certainly written during Plato's later period, probably during the early years of his work on the *Laws*; and with its twists and turns of argument and its apparent inconsistencies it gives us valuable evidence of what these theoretical difficulties were and how seriously Plato wrestled with them.

One of these difficulties, perhaps the crucial one, arises from the unavoidable generality of any law laid down for the guidance of citizens and officials. Law cannot take account of all the special conditions present in individual cases; it is, moreover, too rigid to adapt itself to changing circumstances. These defects are inherent in the nature of law; and to make law supreme is like putting ourselves under a stupid and stubborn master who is unwilling to allow exceptions to his orders and unable to adjust them to changed circumstances (294c). Such a principle, if applied to any other art, would mean its extinction (299e); and it is obviously incompatible with the art of ruling, the βασιλικὴ τέχνη. The rule of law, therefore, can only be a hindrance to the scientific ruler in the exercise of his knowledge, and the scientific ruler is, of course, the only true and authentic statesman.

But there is another side to the argument, and the Eleatic Stranger in the dialogue immediately brings it up. If the rule of law as just described is absurd, it would be even more absurd to allow an official who has no special knowledge to attempt its improvement, or an official without principles to disregard it for personal gain or to do a favor to a friend (300a). The rule of law does at least eliminate the rule of presumptuous ignorance and of personal or party interest; and from this point of view it is indispensable as a protection of the citizen against abuse of power (298a-e).

To the dilemma thus confronting the philosophical legislator a solution has been suggested in the myth (271-274) which contrasts the legendary golden age of Kronos, when men were ruled by the gods or their semidivine agents, and the present age, when rulers are "more like their subjects in nature and education" (275c); and the Eleatic Stranger adds the warning that we must not try to define the statesman of the present age in terms appropriate only to the rulers of that legendary time. Stripped of its mythical elements, this appears to mean that Plato renounces the belief (if he ever held it) that any human being could be found who possesses the qualities ascribed to that paragon of character and intelligence, the "genuine philosopher" described in the *Republic*. Since it is these qualities that justify entrusting him and his kind with irresponsible power, it follows that when these qualities are lacking, as they will be to some degree in any human being, it is right that we should hold our rulers responsible. This is that renunciation of irresponsible rule which is so prominent in the *Laws*.

But this does not solve all the difficulties; for we still have the problem of relating science (or philosophy) to law in the governments with which the practical legislator is concerned, the governments by fallible human rulers. Some readers seem to have interpreted this part of the *Politicus* as carrying the implication that in renouncing irresponsible rule Plato has also renounced the rule of philosophy, substituting for it the rule of law which he had previously denounced as stupid. If this is taken seriously it means that Plato thought science and philosophy had no important part to play in affairs of government here and now. That, I think, is inherently implausible, and is definitely shown to be wrong by the prolonged effort Plato makes during his later years to formulate a constitution and laws for his imaginary Cretan city. If, then, science is not thrown out when we reject irresponsible rule, we are left with the original problem, how to reconcile the rule of law with any effective authority of philosophy, or indeed with philosophy at all.

Here it is relevant to consider another argument which the Eleatic Stranger introduces for the necessity of law. He makes his point by means of some of Plato's favorite analogies, the physician and the physical trainer. The professional trainer who is preparing a class of athletes for a contest cannot order what is best for each person's special physique and temperament, even though his knowledge would enable him to do so. Likewise the lawgiver, however scientific he may be, must legislate for the majority and only roughly for individuals (294d-295b). Again let us suppose that the physician or gymnastic trainer is going away and expects to be absent a long time from his patients or pupils. If he wishes them to remember his instructions while he is gone he will have to write them down (295c). Similarly, we can infer, a legislator who wishes his work to continue after his death must make use of written laws. But the analogy carries us even further, as the Eleatic Stranger shows. Most of the citizens in any community, even when the scientific statesman is at the seat of government and actively at work, will in fact be separated from him, forced to make their own decisions on the various activities of daily life (295b). With the best desire in the world to follow his directions they will be unable to do so, unless there are rules promulgated for their guidance which they can know and follow on their own initiative.

This argument for the necessity of law is based upon the very nature of government, and applies at least as much to the scientific ruler as to his empirical and tradition-bound imitators; for law is in any case an indispensable instrument of rule. The Eleatic Stranger adds only that we can hardly expect the scientific ruler to set up laws as hindrances to his skill, and he should therefore remain free to make changes in them if his science shows that the welfare of his subjects requires it (295d). If we translate this into terms appropriate to responsible rulers, it means that any system of laws must have in it some provision for its own improvement, so that its original purpose can still be accomplished under changed conditions.

Obviously, then, it is not the intention of this dialogue to establish an absolute opposition between science and law. Some interpreters have, however, read it in this way; and one source of misunderstanding will be evident if we consider its context, the current discussions to which it is relevant. Many of Plato's contemporaries agreed with him that the only hope for improvement in the political life of the Greek cities was to put really competent persons in authority, instead of the officials of average ability and limited powers who governed most Greek cities. But against these advocates of the rule of a strong man, or a group of strong men, were pitted the advocates of the rule of law, as it was traditionally understood by Plato's countrymen. Is it better to have a government of men or a government of law? These were the simple terms in which the issue was stated,[18] and Plato's dialogue seems to have been written as a contribution to this discussion, and perhaps with the intention of showing that the issue was really not so simple. For Plato is critical of both parties. Against the partisans of the common law he supports the claims, not of the strong man, but of the scientific ruler; on the other hand, against the strong man, claiming the right to remake his people's life without benefit of philosophy, he supports the authority of traditional law. In this context the opposition between law and scientific rule tends to be accentuated by the ambiguity of the terms used in the discussion. For the law which the one party defended (and Plato defends it with them against presumptuous oligarchs or ambitious strong men) was traditional, or positive law; and between this and scientific rule there is an obvious tension and opposition. But between scientific rule and philosophically formulated law the tension is much less, and under optimum conditions tends to disappear altogether. What Plato clearly needs here is the distinction between positive law and "right law"— the distinction which underlies his legislation in the *Laws*.[19]

This distinction is not made explicit in the *Politicus*, but it seems to be present to Plato's thought. For we have seen that law is a necessary instrument of government even for the scientific statesman. The law which will assist this kind of ruler is obviously not the stupid and imperfect rules of tradition, but "right law" as seen by philosophical intelligence. This is the only sense of the term "law" that would enable the Eleatic Stranger to say at the very beginning of the discussion that the scientific ruler may govern with or without law, which clearly implies that law is compatible with the exercise of sci-

---

[18] We find it so stated by Aristotle (*Pol.* 1286a 8). It is interesting to see that his conclusion is much the same as Plato's: "the ruler must necessarily be a legislator" (1286a 22).
[19] See Chapter XI.

entific rule.[20] Furthermore, he says that lawmaking (νομοθετική) belongs, in a sense (τρόπον τινὰ), to the "royal science" (294a); and the qualification here seems to mean that it is only the making of right law that forms part of this royal science. Finally, the idea of imitation, which is fundamental to Plato's description of imperfect states, carries the same implication. Of these imperfect states those in which the law is sovereign are closer to the ideal (302e-303b); in fact we are told that an imitation state, if it wishes to be saved, must imitate the written laws (συγγράμματα) of the ideal polity (297de). These συγγράμματα can obviously only be the "right law" of the philosopher-statesman.[21]

But in view of what Plato has said earlier about the inherent defects in the nature of law, how can he entertain the conception of "right law"? Any law, whether positive or right law, is necessarily general and, however detailed, will be unable to take account of the variety of particular cases. This is a theoretical difficulty which I believe Plato never completely solved. It would in fact seem insoluble in his terms; there can be no perfect law, if by that we mean a law that never needs to be adjusted to particular cases, or supplemented or revised because of changed circumstances. Such a law would cease to be a law; it would evaporate into an endless series of particular prescriptions for each individual for each moment of time. But any legislator, even a philosophical one, has to accept the generality of law; he can only try to mitigate the inevitable injustice it involves by making provision for an understanding of the purposes it aims at, and for its interpretation, enforcement, and revision by men who understand these purposes. Plato goes further than most legislators in securing these conditions by insisting upon preambles to the various sections of his law, so that both citizens and rulers will have this necessary knowledge. For the practical legislator, therefore, right law can only mean that law which is best fitted to accomplish the ends of law, viz. the virtue of the citizen, and freedom, wisdom, and friendship in the community. As compared with

---

[20] *Polit.* 293c. It also implies that the absence of law is compatible with the rule of science—a proposition which conflicts with the later showing that law is necessary in any form of rule. Evidently this sentence assumes, and perhaps consciously exploits, the ambiguity in the term law. What the scientific ruler can do without is traditional law; this he will often have to revise or override.

[21] Συγγράμματα (and γράμματα) are used frequently in this discussion in the sense of written laws; e.g. 293a, 295a, 295c, 299a, 300a,c, and elsewhere. Cf. Arist. *Pol.* 1286a 15.

the unsystematic and ignorant prescriptions of much positive law, such right law takes on something of the character of an ideal, albeit an ideal capable of further improvement as it embodies more clearly the Nous which makes it right.

The philosophical basis of this conception of the nature and purpose of law, as it is laid down in the *Philebus*, was set forth in the preceding chapter. When we recall that for Plato law has its source in the cosmic Nous, it becomes even clearer that the *Politicus* cannot be interpreted as asserting an antithesis between the rule of intelligence and the rule of philosophically informed law. For law is necessary in any form of rule, and at its best it is a fair imitation of that order which the cosmic Nous brings about in the whole of nature. The antithesis, then, is not between philosophy and law *tout court*, but between philosophy and that inferior manifestation of the rule of law that sanctifies the legislation of an imperfect state and contains in it no philosophical element with authority to revise and improve. Both the Sparta and the Athens of Plato's day could be regarded, in their different ways, as examples of this misplaced devotion; but both, we should add, are in Plato's eyes immeasurably superior to an oligarchy or a tyranny that recognizes the authority of no law at all above party or personal interest. The *Politicus* implies what the *Laws* asserts, that what philosophy does in the exercise of its proper function is not to remove law from the state (that it cannot do), but to make it into a more accurate imitation of the ideal ordering principles discerned by philosophical reflection.[22]

The rule of philosophy is the most famous, as well as the most

---

[22] The most recent interpretation of the *Politicus* is that of Skemp (*Plato's Statesman*, London, 1952). I agree with Skemp in rejecting (52ff.) G. M. A. Grube's suggestion (*Plato's Thought*, London, 1935, 279) that Plato relegates the philosopher-king of the *Republic* to a mythical past; for the philosophic ruler is certainly assumed in the *Politicus*. But Skemp in turn, I think, is mistaken in conceiving of the philosophic ruler as "governing without limitations of law" (57). So also is Barker in regarding law as unnecessary and even prejudicial to the statesman's art (278); for Plato the philosophic ruler can and must make use of law. Again Taylor is correct, I think, in saying that Plato means to decide definitely for constitutionalism (*Plato: the Man and his Work*, 393, 403); but this term covers a wide range of imperfect states, and it is only constitutionalism based on philosophically formulated law—i.e. "right law"—that Plato would fully approve of. Most students of Plato's political thought regard the *Politicus* as a bridge between the *Republic* and the *Laws*; but only this conception of philosophically formulated law shows how it can be such a bridge. If this conception is ignored, one must regard the *Politicus* either as marking a break with the doctrine of the *Republic*, as Sabine does (*op.cit.* 68ff.), or as still separated from the later doctrine of the *Laws*, which Skemp apparently believes it to be (49, 51f. and passim).

fundamental, of Plato's political principles; but its precise implications cannot be seen unless we examine with care the institutions in which Plato thinks it exemplified. We are able to do this most clearly in the *Laws*, where these institutions are described in detail. But there is enough in the *Republic* to enable us to see that from the first he thought the rule of philosophy implied the presence of law, and of law sovereign at least over the conscience of the rulers. It is difficult indeed to suppose that he meant by it the rule of an intelligence that is free not merely from the limitations of current custom and opinion, but also free to disregard its own principles and insights. There is much in the history of philosophy and the practice of philosophers to suggest to us in this later age that the rule of philosophy would be erratic and unpredictable. Like every other science, philosophy constantly endeavors to refine its principles; and philosophers, more than workers in other fields, claim the right to disregard precedents in choosing their principles. The picture of philosophical dialectic in the *Republic*—as proceeding by continued questioning of hypotheses, as willing to follow the argument wherever it may for the moment lead—might suggest that the rule of philosophers would be the rule of a sovereign who is constantly changing the bases of public law or—even worse—disregarding all law, even his own, when he sees something that he considers better. No political life would be possible under such conditions, and Plato may certainly be credited with having seen as much. But dialectic is not identical with the assured results that he believed philosophy could attain, results that he regarded as having authority. How to put philosophy into service so that it would be the salvation, not the ruin, of the state it professes to serve, was a deep concern of Plato's in the *Republic* (497d); and the problem expressed in this concern found its solution in the union of philosophy with law, a solution that we see most clearly in his later work. Law is sovereign, but it is law formulated and controlled in its interpretation and revision by philosophy. Philosophy also is sovereign, but not by the sacrifice of law; for it is only through law that a political philosopher can make his knowledge effective.

RETROSPECT

AT THE BEGINNING of this study it was suggested that the Plato of the *Laws* might well be regarded as a political craftsman faced with a problem analogous to that of his demiurge in the *Timaeus*, the task of constructing, out of indifferent and sometimes recalcitrant materials, a city that would approach, as nearly as he could make it, the character of the ideal. Now that we have examined the main parts of his construction and the historical materials that enter into them, we can see that the terms in which his problem was stated require qualification. His craftsmanship has turned out to be less the art of working upon alien and recalcitrant elements to make them serve an end to which they are indifferent, than the art of divining within the historical materials the immanent purpose which they imperfectly serve, and devising means for the better realization of their inherent ends. Again and again we have seen Plato take in hand some familiar historical institution—for example, the popular courts, the music and gymnastics of Athenian education, the worship of the Olympians—or some deeply rooted tradition—such as respect for the rule of law, or the devotion of citizens to their polis—and, in the light of the larger end which it is adapted to serve, make it over into a form fitted for his model city. Outright invention plays almost no part at all in his work. Even where his political imagination is most apparent—as in his system of courts, or the construction of the Nocturnal Council—we have seen that his creations are developments of beliefs and practices already in existence. In almost every case when he takes over some social or political institution he recognizes the healthy and beneficent sentiments on which it rests, and the sound elements of character and political strength which it fosters. Plato is more like a gardener than a carpenter in the tenderness with which he treats his political material, and in the care with which he prunes and shapes it for more sturdy and luxuriant growth. For the elements with which he works are intimations—or "imitations," as he would say—of the ideal. The Nous whose ordering principles the philosopher follows as his guide is already embodied, for the eye of the philosopher, in the materials of human history.

The counterpart to this fact is that the ideal itself which serves as his guide is not an irrelevant creation of philosophical imagination, but an ideal rooted in the soil of Greek history. The picture Plato draws for us is that of an idealized Hellenic city, a city expressing, as nearly as human institutions can, the type of character and of social life that the native gifts and long established traditions of his people, as he saw them, point to as the goal of their aspirations. The idealization is of course Plato's; the historical facts have gone through the crucible of his daemonic genius, have been refined in the fire of his philosophic criticism, and have taken on some of the glory of that supersensible perfection whose vision was never absent from Plato's imagination, any more than it was absent from the mind of any other Greek master of creative thought. Yet it is still a recognizable Greek city, so rooted in its environment that it could never be transplanted elsewhere, but for that very reason capable of drawing from its native soil the nourishment needed to sustain it and to promote its fuller and more luxuriant life.

We can go even further, I believe. It is not a Hellenic city in general that Plato draws for us, but an idealized Athens. Despite the Cretan setting, and the Dorian influences represented by the Athenian's two companions, there is so much of Athenian tradition embodied in Plato's construction, and there are so many obvious references to the problems of his native city, that we can only conclude that it is Athens which is the object of his chief concern, and in some respects the historical model that he likes to follow. Not indeed the Athens of his own time, except in so far as she had retained traces of her former constitution and was still capable of finding herself by returning to the older traditions neglected during the preceding century; but the Athens of an older time, before she had lost the moderation that characterized her early days, and when she still retained in greater measure those Hellenic qualities most associated in Plato's time with the Dorians. It is the Athens of an earlier time, lifted from the past, but equipped with many of the inventions in law and politics that characterized the sophisticated century in which Plato wrote, that he makes into a model for the legislators—of Athens and other Greek cities—to follow.

The *Laws* then is clearly a message prepared for Plato's own age and for his own people, a message delivered too late to have the effect that Plato doubtless hoped it would have. The day of the Greek city-state was over. While Plato was writing, Philip of Macedon was already nibbling at the frontiers of the free Greek world and clearly indicating his intention to play the part of leader and autocrat; and

less than a decade after Plato had written his last words, Philip won
the victory at Chaeronea which has since been regarded as marking
the end of Greek history. Never again, after the victories of Philip
and Alexander, would the Greeks live in their tight little communities, with such an exhilarating sense of being able to control their
destinies. This means that as a pattern for the construction of a city
Plato's design was soon obsolete. Not that the *Laws* was without influence in the Hellenistic Age. The history of that influence is still
to be written; but I have shown in the preceding pages many respects
in which the particular details of the *Laws* passed into the life and
practice of later times, so that clearly its influence was by no means
negligible. On the larger stage of European history its direct influence is not so easy to discern, but its indirect influence, as a part of
that ancient heritage from which so many of the churchmen and
statesmen of later times have drawn inspiration, has certainly been
far greater than is usually realized. Because the Greeks were such
universal men, the ideal of a Greek city can never be merely a Greek
ideal. The political wisdom that gave its peculiar character to that
historically determined experiment in common living that we call the
Greek polis has authority wherever other men in other ages attempt
to organize their common life. The principles of moderation, of the
rule of law, and of the rule of philosophy—these are κτήματα ἐς αἰεί,
and it is Plato in the *Laws* who first set them forth in their full
range and potency.

INDICES
GENERAL INDEX
INDEX OF PASSAGES
INDEX OF MODERN AUTHORS CITED

of to the assembly and the guardians, 175-176, 229

Courage, 47, 561

Courts of justice, three grades of, 256; arbitrators, 152, 246, 256-257; tribal, 257-261; court of select judges, 261-264, 527; court of the demos, 265-267, 269-270, 488; court for capital offenses, 250, 251, 264 n. 44, 267-270, 281-282, 488; summary of, 271-273

Cresphontes, 64

Cretan archers, 26 and n. 43, 28

Crete, relative isolation of in fourth century, 17; former glories of remembered, 17-18; relations of with Hellenic world in fifth and fourth centuries, 25-26; marriage regulations in, 439 n. 137; political relations within, 30; Plato's knowledge of, 5, 6, 25-31; his high regard for, 19, 20-21; Aristotle's interest in, 20; laws of akin to Spartan, 32-35

Cretic rhythms, 18, 23 n. 27

Critias, 41-42, 523

Criticism, standards of in the arts, 314-315

Croesus, 40

Curetes, dances of, 18, 360

Currency, possession of foreign forbidden, 139, 277 n. 83; Hellenic, 139, 192; Spartan, 140; Attic, 140

Cydonia, 26

Cynosarges, 327

Cyrene, visited by Plato, 5; Plato asked to legislate for, 8

Cyrus the Great, 298, 521, 527

Cyrus the Younger, 115

Daedalus, 18

Daemons, concept of, 457; cult of, 458-459

Damages, suits for, 183, 243-244, 264 n. 44; against a magistrate or judge, 246-247, 548

Damon, 305

Dances, Plato's classification of, 358-359, 370; armed, 18, 32, 359-362; pacific, 359, 365-370; questionable, 362-365; comic, 370-371

Dancing, as imitative, 307; importance of in education, 336-337

Days of ill omen, 368-369, 451

Dead, honors to the, 462 n. 209, 464; influence of on the living, 465-467

Death penalty, 267-268, 291, 294, 467 n. 22, 490

Deception, beneficent, 557

Decorum, public, 185-186, 202

Degrading occupation, prosecution for, 276

Deliberative, Plato's conception of the, 176-177; Aristotle on the, 171, 176-177

Delius, 8

Delos, 369 n. 247, 406

Delphi, games at, 193, 320, 504

Delphi, oracle of, 402; pre-eminence of in Greece, 405-406; temple of Apollo at, 407-409; relations of with Athens, 404, 406-

407; relations of with Sparta, 406; the guide in religious law, 425; stabilizing and civilizing influence of, 410-411, 522, 532; influence of on law of homicide, 120, 411; Lycurgus' consultation of, 56 n. 47; appeals to, 105, 106, 419, 425, 465; exegetes to be selected by, 497; embassies to, 439. See Apollo

Demaratus, 49

Demes, in Plato's state, 124-126; in Attic law, 125

Demeter, 290, 414 n. 50, 464 n. 217; and Persephone, cult of, 404, 440-441; 452-454

Demetrius of Phalerum, 9; reforms of, 195 n. 99, 199 n. 107, 380, 381, 463 n. 215

Demiurge, cosmic, 10, 145, 591; in politics, see Plato

Democracy, ancestral, 163-164, 237; in fourth century, 153, 157-158; marks of in Plato's constitution, 230, 232, 272, 528-530

Democritus, 221, 297 n. 1, 386 n. 315

Demos, sovereignty of the, 85, 177, 199, 230

Demosthenes, 44, 88, 221, 475

Denunciation, in Attic law, 266-267, 472, 488; in Plato's law, 277, 488

Desertion, prosecution for, 270, 276

Diagoras, 471, 477 n. 247

Dialectic, in the Academy, 5; in the Nocturnal Council, 506, n. 12; 573-574, 575 n. 4

Dicaearchus, 543

Dicte, Mount, 27 and n. 45, 95

Dike, in the train of Zeus, 436-437, 458-459. See Justice

Dinarchus, 146

Diogenes the Cynic, 297 n. 1

Dion, 7

Dionysia, 312, 352, 361, 364, 371, 374 n. 267, 375, 380, 473

Dionysius, the Elder, 7; the Younger, 7-8

Dionysus, 361, 434 n. 123; worship of, 308, 311, 365, 367; erroneous myths about, 315, 444; a benefactor by his gift of wine, 315-316, 364, 442, 444; functions of in the state, 441-442

Dionysus, Chorus of, 313-318, 343, 375, 395

Dionysus, Theatre of, 417 n. 66

Diopeithes, Decree of, 428, 475

Dioscuri, 360, 361, 414 n. 50, 446

Disinheritance, 120, 270-271

Dithyrambs, 62, 63, 304, 311, 367-368; contests of at Athens, 311-312, 336 n. 134, 367-368

Divination, natural and artificial, 429. See Soothsayers

Divorce, 271

Dodona, oracle of, 402, 404-405

Dokimasia. See Scrutiny

Dorian federation in Crete, 30 n. 57; in the Peloponnesus, 66

Dorian kingdoms, early history of, 55-58, 64-71

Protagoras, 4, 471
Prytaneum, 79
Prytaneum Decree, 420 n. 75
Prytanies, 166, 172-173, 208, 394
Public office, payment for, at Athens, 191-192; not prescribed in Plato's state, 134, 138, 143, 191-192
Public registers of land, 105, 196; of movable property, 132, 196
Public revenue, 191-194; — works, 149, 193; — wrongs, prosecution of, 275-278, extent of, 265
Punishment, purpose of, 491, 552; of children, 328
Purification, rites of, 18, 424, 431
Purity, ceremonial and moral, 415
Pylos, 49
Pyrrhaeans, 8
Pyrrhic dance, 336-337, 360-361; among Cretans and Spartans, 23 n. 27, 359-360; origin of, 359; degeneration of, 361-362
Pythagoreans, 5, 62, 104, 344, 450, 555 n. 26
Pytho, 8

Questioning, of litigants and witnesses, 281-283

Races, foot, 335, 381-383; on horseback, 387
Reading and writing, 332
Religion, provides divine sanctions to the performance of our duties, 468-469; philosophical worth of positive, 487
Religious law, distinguished from the law of the polis, 407-408; to be brought from Delphi, 408
Religious officials, 411-434
Responsibility of officials, 246-247, 250-251, 548-551, 583
Rhadamanthys, 24, 38-39, 456 n. 191
Rhetoric, philosophical, 558
Rhetra, the Big, 33
Rhodes, 447 n. 158
Ridicule, 372, 374
Riding, 335
Right law, distinguished from positive law, 155, 563-564, 587-588; has its source in Nous, 155-156, 564-565; expresses the conditions of the common good, 537; the model for positive law, 488, 569; to be formulated by the philosopher-statesman, 588-589
Right opinion, 502, 556, 557
Roads, 187

Sacadas, 304
Sacred War, the Third, 409
Sacrifices. See Worship
Salamis, Battle of, 26, 29, 40, 97, 321
Satyr dances, 361-365
Schools, 182, 319-320, 326-327
Scrutiny, at Athens, 215-217; in Plato's law, 217-219
Scythians, 6

Sea power, corrupting influence of, 96-100; effects of on Athenian democracy, 99, 158
Secret police, at Sparta, 47, 151, 157, 189-190
Sedition, 268, 276
Select judges, court of, 261-263; scrutiny of, 215 n. 48, 217-218; responsibility of, 263-264, 549; functions of, 225-226, 248
Seven Sages, the, 46, 410, 522
Sicily, 5
Sicyon, 62, 304
Sileni, 362
Simonides, 49, 367
Slander, 183
Slaves, taken for granted in Plato's state, 148, 183; public and private, 148-149; occupations of, 149, 188, 373; agricultural, 149-152; sale of, 150; emancipation of, 150; education of, 323-324; testimony of, 284; estimated number of in Plato's state, 129 n. 105
Social War, the, 98, 194
Socrates, indictment and trial of, 4, 268, 278, 321, 471, 473, 494-495; loyalty of to Athens, 87, 91; admiration of for Spartan eunomia, 42-43; and Theramenes, 41 n. 2, 43 n. 8, 525; on playing the lyre, 340-341; on dancing, 306 n. 31; on the citizen's obligation to athletics, 333-334; on the sun and moon as gods, 446; as legislator and city founder in the Republic, 580
Solitary confinement, as punishment for impiety, 490
Solon, Plato's references to, 80, 102; his opinion of, 80-86; poet, 81, 340 n. 149; archon, 195; legislator, 79, 201, 546; author of the ancestral constitution, 78-79, 522, 542; originator of the popular courts, 79, 219, 241, and of the democratic council, 165-166; encouraged trade and handicraft, 114, 141, 146; land reforms of, 102 n. 14, 109, 136 n. 118; other reforms of, 110, 202, 278, 321, 414 n. 51, 463 n. 215; and Delphi, 407; and the legend of Atlantis, 18 n. 8; and Epimenides, 19; on soothsaying as a craft, 428 n. 97
Soothsayers, 422, 425, 427-434; Plato's opinion of, 429-430; 486; activities of limited in Plato's state, 433-434
Sophists, 297, 333, 344
Sophron, 63
Sorcery. See Magic
Sortition, use of at Athens, 161, 238; in Plato's state, 161, 163, 168, 181, 233, 377-378; characteristic of democracies, 162-163, 238; regarded as a method of receiving divine guidance, 163 n. 20, 414
Sosicrates, 21 n. 22
Soul, its primacy in nature, 481-482; rational and irrational, 482
Sovereignty, meaning of, 577 n. 5
Sparta, 40-63; early history of, 64-73, 98 n. 5; admiration of in antiquity, 41-44; criti-

Walls, city, 182
War dance. See Pyrrhic dance
Warriors, under the protection of Athena, 438, and Ares, 440
Water supply, 183, 187, 193
Wine, laws regulating use of among Cretans and Spartans, 29, 32, 48; in Plato's city, 442-443
Witnesses, 285-287
Women, status of, 121, 157, 168; counted as citizens, 113; equal education of, 329-331, 351; common meals of, 393-394; legal competence of, 121, 285 and n. 111; foot races of, 382-383; dances of, 369; festivals of, 354; Plato's opinion of, 330-331, 393-394; place of in Athens, 330; defects in Spartan education of, 330-331
Worship, 399-400, 416, 462-463, 469-470. See Festivals
Wrestling, Plato's expert knowledge of, 384 and n. 303
Written law, a necessary condition of the rule of law, 546-547

Xenocrates, 8
Xenocritus, 304
Xenodamus, 304
Xenophon, on Lycurgus, 298, 390-391, 392; on nomophylakes, 196, 209; on the Areopagus, 212; on common meals, 392; on Attic currency, 140; on agriculture, 115; impressed by Spartan education, 298; disillusioned with Sparta, 44; consults soothsayers, 428 n. 97; and the Delphic oracle, 404
Xerxes, 40, 69

Zaleucus, 19, 555-556
Zeno, 146
Zeus, 290, 402, 434, 435, 452; the Savior, 367; Herkeios, 216, 462 n. 209; guardian of the oath, 438, 446; guardian of justice and the unwritten law, 436-438, 456; the source of Cretan law, 437 n. 132; born in Crete, 18, 449; erroneous mythology about, 376, 443, 478 n. 252
Zeus, Cave of, 3, 27-28
Zeuxis, 146

B. Greek

ἀγέλαι, 53, 325-326, 351
ἄγραφα νόμιμα, ἄγραφοι νόμοι, 328, 471 n. 229, 547 n. 6
ἀγωγή, 301 n. 14
αἵρεσις, 233-257
ἀνυπεύθυνος, 583 n. 16
ἀπαγωγή, 432 n. 118, 472, n. 233
ἀπομνύναι, 285 n. 114
ἀριστεῖα, 271 n. 65
ἀρχιέρεως, 417 n. 69
ἄρχοντες, 127 n. 101, 242 n. 2, 582; as designation of νομοφύλακες, 207 n. 117
βάσανος, 224 n. 175, 266, 267, 285 n. 110, 491 n. 276
βασιλεύς, 583
γεωμόροι, 114 n. 57
γραφαί, 276 n. 79
δῆμος, 157 n. 4, 163 n. 21; — πληθύων, 252, 265 n. 45
διαιτηταί, 257 n. 29
δίκαι, 132 n. 114, 276 n. 79
δικασταί, 257 n. 29
δικαστήρια, 242, 251, 258 n. 30, 260 n. 38
δίκη ἀσεβείας, 277 n. 82, 474 n. 240
ἐλεύθερος, 112 n. 51, 323 n. 88
ἐμμέλειαι, 359, 365-370
ἐμφύλιος, 112 n. 51
ἔνδειξις, 277 n. 81
ἐπιχώριος, 112 n. 51
ἐποπτεύω, 507 n. 17
ἐπῳδαί, 309-311
ἑστία, 113, 116
εὐθυντής, 221

Ἡλιαία, 252 n. 22
θεῖος, 409 n. 33, 429
θύειν, 450
ἱδρύματα, 462 n. 209
ἱερά, 493 n. 279
ἱεροὶ λόγοι, 455 n. 188
ἱερόν, 412 n. 42
καθιστάναι ἀρχάς, κατάστασις ἀρχῶν, 206 n. 116
κλῆρος, 103, 104 n. 20
κλήρωσις, κλήρωσις ἐκ προκρίτων, 161, 164 n. 25, 168, 195 n. 98, 233-238, 414 n. 52
μαρτυρία, 285 n. 110
νεωκόροι, 415-416
νικητήρια, 271 n. 65
οἰκέτης, 112 n. 51, 151 n. 165
ὅπλα παρεχόμενοι, 178 n. 60
ὄργια, 462
παλαιοὶ λόγοι, 403 n. 8, 436
πέρας, 506, 536-537
πλῆθος, 157 n. 4, 265 n. 45
πρόκρισις, 161 n. 15, 168, 217, 233-238
πυρρίχη, 359 n. 206
σύλλογος, 157 n. 4, 173, 503 n. 5
συσκήνια, 391 n. 335
τελεταί, 363 n. 221
τίμημα, 131, n. 110
ὑπεύθυνος, 219, 220
φάσις, 132 n. 114, 249, 277 n. 81
φέρειν, 160 n. 11, 169, 498
φιδίτια, φιλίτια, 22 n. 26, 182, 390, 391 n. 335
φυλέται, 260 n. 38

INDEX OF PASSAGES

B. In Other Platonic Works

INDEX OF MODERN AUTHORS CITED